The Indonesian Supreme Court
A Study of Institutional Collapse

Cornell University

Sebastiaan Pompe

The Indonesian Supreme Court
A Study of Institutional Collapse

SOUTHEAST ASIA PROGRAM PUBLICATIONS
Southeast Asia Program
Cornell University
Ithaca, New York
2005

Editorial Board
   Benedict R. O'G. Anderson
   Tamara Loos
   Stanley J. O'Connor
   Keith Taylor
   Andrew C. Willford

Cornell Southeast Asia Program Publications
640 Stewart Avenue, Ithaca, NY 14850-3857

Studies on Southeast Asia No. 39

© 2005 Cornell Southeast Asia Program.

All rights reserved. Except for brief quotations in a review, no part of this book may be reproduced or utilized in any form or by any means, electronic or mechanical, including photocopying and recording, or by any information storage or retrieval system, without permission in writing from the Cornell Southeast Asia Program.

Printed in the United States of America

ISBN-13: 978-0-877277-39-2 hc / ISBN-10: 0-877277-39-7 hc
ISBN-13: 978-0-877277-38-5 pb / ISBN-10: 0-877277-38-9 pb

Cover Design: Phil Wilson Design. **Cover photographs:** The new Supreme Court building (reprinted with permission, *TEMPO*/Donny Metri, 1992); President Sukarno congratulating Satochid Kartanegara upon his appointment as Vice Chief Justice, Oct. 24, 1951 (reprinted with permission, personal collection); Supreme Court Chairman Sarwata sharing tea with President Suharto (reprinted with permission, *DR*/Rully Kesuma)

Introduction

SAMBUTAN KETUA MAHKAMAH AGUNG REPUBLIK INDONESIA

Dimasa-masa awal "reformasi," ada dua persoalan pokok yang muncul mengenai pengadilan yaitu "independensi," dan "korupsi, kolusi, dan nepotisme" (KKN). Yang disebut terakhir, tidak hanya persoalan pengadilan, tetapi mengenai seluruh aparat penyelenggara negara dan pemerintahan. Tetapi, setelah memulai langkah-langkah pembaharuan pengadilan, ternyata persoalan yang dihadapi tidak hanya terbatas pada independensi dan KKN. Persoalan-persoalan besar lain mencakup juga masalah-masalah trans-paransi, akses publik terhadap pengadilan, mutu putusan yang tidak memuaskan, tata kerja (administrasi peradilan) yang lamban, fasilitas pendukung yang sangat memperihatinkan, anggaran yang sangat kecil, gaji hakim yang rendah, integritas sebagian hakim dan pegawai pengadilan yang dalam berbagai hal merugikan pencari keadilan. Semua persoalan tersebut telah merendahkan citra pengadilan, bahkan dalam semangat kekecewaan yang begitu mendalam ada yang menyatakan "rakyat tidak lagi percaya pada pengadilan dan mendorong di bentuk pengadilan rakyat."

Rasa tidak puas terhadap pengadilan bukan semata-mata dari luar melainkan juga dari dalam pengadilan. Berbagai usaha dilakukan tetapi kurang bahkan tidak berhasil. Lingkungan dan keadaan, tidak cukup memberi dukungan berbagai keinginan atau usaha pembaharuan. Sampai beberapa waktu reformasi berjalan, keadaan tetap tidak berubah. Pembaharuan pengadilan masih sekedar wacana yang dibicarakan dalam seminar, diskusi, dan komentar dalam wujud keluhan-keluhan. Momentum terjadi, pada saat Pemerintah dan DPR—atas dorongan kekuatan-kekuatan dalam masyarakat—sepakat "menyuntikkan," sejumlah ahli hukum bukan hakim menjadi Hakim Agung. Kehadiran mereka yang lazim disebut "hakim non karir," diharapkan menjadi "penyumbang darah segar" menunjang semangat pembaharuan yang sudah bersemi lama di Mahkamah Agung. Pacuan dipercepat dengan pengangkatan hakim non karir menjadi Ketua Mahkamah Agung. Banyak keraguan mengenai ketua baru. Selain karena sama sekali belum pernah mengenal administrasi peradilan, juga benar-benar sebagai "orang asing" yang tidak diketahui latar belakang dan kemampuannya. Bahkan ada suatu majalah terkenal yang meramalkan dalam waktu tidak terlalu lama, ketua akan menjadi "makanan politik" dari berbagai kekuatan yang ada. Menghadapi kenyataan tersebut, ada beberapa tugas pertama yang mesti dilakukan ketua. **Pertama**: meyakinkan bahwa kehadiran ketua baru—demikian juga hakim-hakim non karir—semata-mata didasarkan pada etikad baik untuk secara bersama-sama membangun kembali citra pengadilan sebagai lembaga yang terhormat dan dihormati. **Kedua**: menemukan sahabat-sahabat pembaharuan di dalam Mahkamah Agung. **Ketiga**: mengidentifikasi secara lebih rinci persoalan-persoalan pengadilan. **Keempat**: menyusun program-program sementara sebagai dasar melakukan pembaharuan, yang kemudian dirumuskan dalam rapat kerja nasional di Yogyakarta (2001). Ternyata, empat hal diatas tidak begitu sulit dilaksanakan. Tidak begitu lama, warga pengadilan dapat diyakinkan mengenai etikad baik pimpinan baru. Kemudahan ini tidak lain karena telah tersedia pembaharu-pembaharu dari dalam, yang selama ini menunggu-nunggu kesempatan untuk mewujud-kan angan-angan dan harapan memulihkan kewibawaan dan meraih kembali secara penuh kepercayaan publik terhadap pengadilan.

Momentum lain yang juga sanga penting yaitu "turun gunungnya" sejumlah Lembaba Swadaya Masyarakat yang selama ini hanya melakukan tugas mengamati, mengkritik, dan mengeluh, menjadi "operator-operator" pembaharuan pengadilan. Salah satu rintisan pertama yang disepakati dengan Mahkamah Agung yaitu keharusan ada sebuah cetak biru yang berisi rincian masalah, rencana, dan program yang mesti dikerjakanan selama lima tahun. Selain LSM, tidak kalah penting kebijakan negara-negara sahabat dan lembaga-lembaga internasional yang memberi porsi pembaharuan pengadilan sebagai sesuatu yang penting dalam reformasi. Berbagai bantuan ditawarkan kepada Mahkamah Agung. Tawaran internasional tersebut berefek ganda. **Pertama**: membuka peluang yang lebih terbuka untuk melaksanakan berbagai program, seperti menyusun cetak biru, latihan hakim, merintis sistem informasi, dan lain-lain. Satu hal yang perlu diketahui, Mahkamah Agung menetapkan kebijakan, bantuan internasional tidak diterima dalam bentuk uang. Disini salah satu peran penting LSM sebagai operator pembaharuan. Bantuan internasional disalurkan melalui LSM yang bersangkutan. Mahkamah Agung hanya berkepentingan agar program dapat terlaksana dengan baik. Patut disyukuri, sampai hari ini, berbagai LSM yang membantu Mahkamah Agung telah bekerja dengan tulus dengan hasil-hasil yang sangat memuaskan. **Kedua**: bantuan-bantuan internasional telah menggugah Pemerintah dan DPR untuk meningkarkan dari tahun ketahun anggaran Mahkamah Agung. Hal ini dimungkinkan juga karena sejumlah anggota DPR ikut dengan gigih memperjuangkan kenaikan anggaran. Meskipun penambahan dapat disebut dua atau tiga kali lipat dari sebelum pembaharuan, tetapi keseluruhan jumlahnya masih jauh dari kebutuhan, karena kelipatan itu dimulai dari jumlah yang sangat kecil. Menghadapi anggaran yang terlalu kecil, sedangkan penampilan pengadilan-pengadilan yang memprihatinkan, maka tidak berlebihan kalau disebut, pengadilan bukan saja lama terlantar tetapi sekaligus diterlantarkan.

Selama tiga tahun, dengan bantuan pihak-pihak yang disebutkan diatas, berbagai upaya telah dan sedang dilakukan. Tetapi yang dihasilkan masih jauh dari yang dicita-citakan. Perjalanan masih jauh, karena itu tetap dituntut kerja keras dan dukungan dari berbagai pihak seperti disebut terdahulu.

Tanpa bermaksud menyanjung secara berlebihan, Saudara Sebastiaan Pompe sebagai penulis disertasi yang ada dihadapan sidang pembaca, merupakan salah seorang yang sangat gigih membantu dan ikut mengerjakan berbagai program pembaharuan pengadilan kita. Kegigihan Saudara Sebastiaan Pompe ikut dalam pembaharuan pengadilan tidak semata-mata sebagai sebuah pekerjaan, melainkan bagian dari sikap dan cita-cita. Saudara Sebastiaan Pompe sangat jatuh cinta pada negeri ini. Kadang-kadang dengan bergurau, dalam memperkenalkan Saudara Sebastiaan Pompe kepada seseorang, saya katakan inilah orang Indonesia yang kebetulan lahir di negeri Belanda. Sebagai cita-cita, nampak dari disertasi yang sekarang menjadi buku yang ada dihadapan sidang pembaca. Menggunakan pendekatan "socio legal," Saudara Sebastiaan Pompe meneliti dengan sangat mendalam perjalanan Mahkamah Agung dan lembaga peradilan di Indonesia, baik secara normatif maupun sociologis. Sebagai konsekuansi ungkapan sosiologis, temuan-temuan akan berwujud kenyataan-kenyataan. Ada kenyataan yang menyenangkan, ada yang tidak menyenangkan. Tergantung pada tempat dan kepentingan pembaca. Tetapi yang dijumpai dalam buku ini semata-mata konsekuansi kerja keilmuan, bukan suatu rumusan kebijakan apalagi pesanan. Untuk itu sudah semestinya, diterima dengan ukuran keilmuan juga, bukan soal senang dan tidak senang, melainkan obyektifitas yang diungkapkan.

Dalam suasana menjalankan pembaharuan pengadilan, selain dibutuhkan sikap obyektif dari diri kita sendiri, dibutuhkan juga berbagai informasi dan pandangan. Makin banyak informasi dan luas pandangan, maka akan tersedia kesempatan yang lebih baik dalam merumuskan kebijakan, menyusun rencana, dan program. Bagi saya, disertasi (buku) Saudara Sebastiaan Pompe, tidak sekedar bahan yang menambah ilmu, melainkan menjadi salah satu bahan yang sangat berguna dalam rangka pembaharuan pengadilan yang sedang dijalankan sekrang ini. Selamat membaca.

Bagir Manan, Ketua Mahkamah Agung

Mahkamah Agung, Republik Indonesia

Jakarta 20, Maret 2005

INTRODUCTION BY THE CHIEF JUSTICE OF THE SUPREME COURT OF INDONESIA

At the beginning of the Reformasi period, two major challenges for the courts appeared. One was "independence" and the other "corruption, collusion, and nepotism" (korupsi, kolusi, dan nepotisme, known by the Indonesian acronym KKN). The latter was not a problem that affected only the courts, but touched the entire state and governance apparatus. As we became engaged in the court reform process, however, it became obvious that the challenges we faced were not limited to matters of independence or corruption, collusion, and nepotism. Other significant problems included issues of transparency, public access to the courts, the unsatisfactory quality of court decisions, protracted internal procedures (court administration), very worrisome support facilities, very small budgets, the low salaries of judges, and the integrity of some judges and staff that, in various ways, damaged the interests of those seeking justice. All these problems undermined respect for the judiciary to an extent that led, in some sectors of society, to profound disillusionment, evident in such statements as "the people no longer believe in the courts and demand the establishment of people's tribunals."

This dissatisfaction with the judiciary existed not only outside the judiciary but also on the inside. Various reform initiatives were begun, but were unsatisfactory and failed. The institutional environment and conditions provided inadequate support for both the wish for and effort at reform. Even when *Reformasi* had been underway for some time, there was little change. Judicial reform was much discussed in seminars and discussion groups, generally taking the form of complaints. Momentum developed when the government and Parliament, prompted by social pressure, agreed to "inject" into the Supreme Court a number of legal experts from outside the judiciary. This group, generally referred to as the "non-career judges," was expected to infuse new enthusiasm into the reform effort, long since dormant in the Supreme Court. The initiative was enhanced by the appointment of a non-career judge as the new Chief Justice. There were many doubts about the new Chief Justice. Aside from the fact that he had no prior experience in court administration, he was also very much a "foreigner" to the judicial system, and his background and abilities were little known. In fact, a well-known journal predicted that in a short time the new Chief Justice would become "political fodder" for various existing forces. In the face of these realities, there were certain basic tasks that the Chief Justice had to address. First, it had to be made clear that the presence of the new Chief Justice—as was true for other non-career judges—was based on good faith with a common purpose of restoring the judiciary as a respectable and respected institution. Second, he had to seek support for reform within the Supreme Court. Third, he had to identify with greater specificity the problems of the courts. Fourth, he had to put together interim programs as a basis for reform (programs which subsequently were discussed at a national meeting in Yogyakarta [2001]). As it happened, these four tasks were not so difficult. It did not take long for the judicial community to become convinced of the good will of the new leadership. It was relatively easy largely because there were already reformers in the court who had long been waiting for an opportunity to realize their ambitions and aspirations to recover the prestige of the judiciary and restore public faith in the courts.

Another development that provided momentum to reform was that a number of non-governmental organizations (NGOs) "came down from the hills" where they had been watching, criticizing, and complaining, to engage as participants in the judicial reform process. One of the first activities agreed upon with the Supreme Court was the need for "blueprints" that would identify in detail the challenges, objectives, and activities needed over the next five years. No less important than the NGOs, foreign governments and international organizations also contributed to the judicial reform process, recognizing it as an integral part of *Reformasi*. Various kinds of aid were offered to the Supreme Court. This international assistance had a cumulative effect. First, it created wider opportunities for realizing various programs: for example, designing the "blueprints," training judges, developing information systems, and so on. It is important to note here that the Supreme Court set the policy that it would not accept foreign assistance in the form of cash. Here the NGOs play an important function as implementers of reform, as donor assistance from NGOs is channeled through relevant civil society organizations. The only interest of the Supreme Court is that the programs are properly implemented. We should be thankful that, to the present, various NGOs assisting the Supreme Court have worked hard with very satisfactory results. Second, international assistance also challenged the government and Parliament to increase steadily the budget for the judiciary from year to year. A number of members of Parliament supported this process by fighting hard for larger budgets. Still, while it can be said that the budget increased about two or three times compared to what it was before the reform process began, yet even so the total is far from meeting our needs, because we started with little support. In the face of inadequate budgetary support, when the physical condition of courts is a matter of such deep concern, it is no exaggeration to say that the courts have not only been long neglected—they really have been abandoned.

Over the past three years, with the help of the aforementioned parties, various initiatives at reform have been and are being undertaken. The results, however, are still far from satisfying our aspirations. The road is still long, which demands hard work and support from various groups such as those already mentioned.

Without wishing to praise him excessively, I will say that Sebastiaan Pompe, the author of this book now made available to readers, is one of those who have been most heavily involved and supportive of the judicial reform process. His contribution to our judicial reform effort was not offered simply in his capacity as a professional scholar, but rather, in large part, as a matter of engagement and idealism. Sebastiaan Pompe fell deeply in love with this country. Occasionally, and in jest, when introducing him to someone else, I say that here is an Indonesian who happened to be born in the Netherlands. His idealism shines through the dissertation that has now been transformed into the book before you. Using a "social-legal" approach, Sebastiaan Pompe researched with extraordinary depth the historical course of the Supreme Court and judiciary in Indonesia, from both normative and sociological perspectives. As elements in a sociological study, his findings relate to realities. Some of these realities are positive; others are not. It depends on the position and interests of the reader. What is to be found in this book, however, is the result of academic research, not the consequence of a policy objective, let alone other ulterior interests. It follows that his discussion should be accepted according to academic standards, not on the grounds of whether it pleases, but rather based on the objectivity that it reflects.

Given the conditions in which we pursue our judicial reform, apart from our own need for objectivity, we also need information and views from elsewhere. The more information we have and the wider our perspectives, the more promising will be our possibilities for formulating policies and developing plans and programs. For myself, Sebastiaan Pompe's book is not merely a study that enhances academic knowledge, but rather is a valuable source of material that is exceedingly useful in the reconstruction of our judiciary now underway. You too will learn from this book.

Chief Justice Bagir Manan

Supreme Court, Republic of Indonesia

Jakarta, 20 March 2005

TABLE OF CONTENTS

Introduction by the Chief Justice of the Supreme Court of Indonesia	v
Table of Contents	1
Foreword, by Daniel S. Lev	3
Acknowledgments	7
Chapter 1: Colonial History	11
The Supreme Court in the Separation of Powers Doctrine	12
Judicial Autonomy in the Colonial State Context	16
The Closed Recruitment System	24
The Diverse Colonial Judicial System	27
Conclusion	33
Chapter 2: Parliamentary System and Guided Democracy (1945–1965): The Political Mobilization of the Judiciary	35
Revolutionary Challenges (1945–1950)	36
Parliamentary Democracy (1950–1959)	43
Guided Democracy (1959–1965)	52
The Emergence of the Major Political Actors	66
Chapter 3: New Order (1965–1970): Power Struggle and Failure	77
1965–1968: Realizing Internal Cohesion and Shaping the Political Agenda	80
1968: The Political Turn-about	100
1968–1970: Slipping and Losing	105
Chapter 4: Entrenched New Order (Post–1970): Political Co-optation of the Judiciary	111
1970–1985: The Political Co-optation of the Judiciary	112
Law no.14/1985: Affirming the Political Status Quo	129
1985–1992: The Old Regime Continued	136
1992–1995: Purwoto Gandasubrata's Attempts at Reform	141
1995–1998: Into the Vortex—Soerjono and Sarwata	158
Conclusion	171
Chapter 5: The Supreme Court and Judicial Organization	175
Judicial Organization	175
The Impact of Unification on Judicial Structures and Society	186

2   Table of Contents

Chapter 6: The Judicial Function	207
The Organizational Strengthening of the Supreme Court's Judicial Function	208
The Cassation Mechanism	215
The Policy on Appeal Barriers	237
Conclusion	250
Chapter 7: The Supreme Court Functions of Regulation and Supervision	251
Regulation and Procedural Law	252
Supervision	255
Conclusion	274
Chapter 8: The Organization of the Supreme Court	277
The Transformation of the Supreme Court's Formal Structure	280
Case Management	310
Budget	317
Problems	319
Conclusion	341
Chapter 9: The Judges	343
Conditions of Office	343
The Anatomy of the Supreme Court	377
The Role of Supreme Court Chairmen	399
Changes in Professional Culture	404
Conclusion	421
Chapter 10: The Impact of Supreme Court Decisions (Jurisprudence)	425
Court Decisions in the Indonesian Civil Law Context (Jurisprudence)	428
Access to Court Decisions and the Problem of Lawmaking	435
The Role of Jurisprudence	456
Conclusion	468
Conclusion	471
Abbreviations and Acronyms	478
Appendix I Schematic Historical Overview	479
Appendix II Court Dockets in Indonesia, 1969–1993	480
Appendix III High-Profile Cases of the 1990s	481
Appendix IV Photographs	483
Subject and Name Index	491

FOREWORD

When President Suharto resigned his presidency under pressure in May of 1998, one of the loudest and most insistent demands that ensued was for legal reform, which meant, basically, guaranteeing honest, consistent, and predictable legal process. It was hardly new. Since the fall of the parliamentary system and the appearance of Guided Democracy in the years 1957-1960, followed by the New Order's coup of 1965, regrets over the decline of the *negara hukum*—the "law state," Indonesia's version of the continental *rechtsstaat*—and demands that it be restored were among the loudest static that Indonesia's political elite heard and essentially ignored.

For a brief time after Suharto retired, hopes for legal reform seemed optimistic, particularly among disgusted citizens but even among some lawyers, academics, intellectuals, and especially foreign donors. The latter came equipped with confident approaches to rendering legal officials, administrators, and private lawyers more honest and competent, reducing corruption, and attuning just about everyone to the law and its institutions. The anger of students on the streets, reformist NGOs, several of them oriented specifically to legal reform, and much attention by the press made fundamental reform seem, not easy by any means, but inevitable. Pressure was directed at the courts, prosecution, police, the legal profession, parliament, and the Ministry of Justice. New commercial courts were established with assistance from the IMF. A newly appointed National Law Commission (Komisi Hukum Nasional) staffed by prominent and capable lawyers began to address basic issues of reform.

Within a year or so, as President Habibie (Suharto's vice-president) was replaced by Abdurrahman Wahid, a committed reformer later forced from office and succeeded by Megawati Sukarnoputri, the optimism began to fade, and is still fading as of this writing in late 2003. It is not as if nothing useful has happened, but the snail-paced accumulation of pressures and change has yet to persuade anyone that a transformation will come about soon, if at all. The corrupt and incompetent judiciary has begun slowly, very slowly, to give way, beginning at the top in the Supreme Court, the subject of this study, and the public prosecution is at least feeling a squeeze, while the private legal profession too has begun, more quickly than the others but hardly impressively, to remake itself. Parliament (DPR, Dewan Perwakilan Rakyat) and the People's Consultative Assembly (MPR, Majelis Permusyawaratan Rakyat) have generated formal statutory and constitutional changes, always easier to promulgate than to enforce, but the products seldom satisfy even generous observers. The sketchy 1945 Constitution has been amended substantially, new basic statutes have been debated, negotiated, and passed, only to be followed often by promises of amendment as criticism rains down.

The backbone and future of legal reform consists largely of the specialist NGOs mentioned above, most of them formed soon after Suharto's resignation seemed to open a door for change. Loaded with capable and committed young lawyers, along with a few non-lawyers, they have produced respectable quantities of research, criticism, arguments, ideas, information, and pressure. Among them are the Center for the Study of Law and Policy (PSHK, Pusat Studi Hukum dan Kebijakan Indonesia), Indonesian Corruption Watch (ICW), Kontras (Komisi Orang Hilang dan Korban Tindak Kekerasan, Commission for Disappearances and Victims of Violence, which covers victims of violence, but much more), Judicial Watch, ICEL (Indonesian Center for Environmental Law, which began as an environmental organization, but has expanded), and others. Along with some staff members of the oldest reform NGO, the Legal Aid Bureau (LBH, Lembaga Bantuan Hukum) founded in 1970, and new legal aid organizations oriented to specific constituencies, these organizations provide the base not only for future legal reform, but also perhaps for a professional segment of a successor political elite. Although many young professionals remain reluctant to engage politically, coalitions of reform NGOs—for a new constitution, for example, and other projects—have begun to emerge that may soon develop political coherence.

The significance of this evolution of a reform vanguard is submerged, however, and sometimes altogether lost, in a cloud of pessimism that descends steadily, with good reason, from the extraordinary complexity and difficulty of achieving substantial change. Few expected the problem to be so intractable, in part, at least, because not many understood just how the legal system had turned so rotten. Much of the early post-revolutionary history of Indonesia had either disappeared from memory or been consciously distorted during the New Order period, when only the virtues of the Suharto government were taught and celebrated. Consequently, relatively few citizens were aware that during the parliamentary period, from 1950 through 1959, the courts, prosecution, police, and professional advocacy actually worked remarkably well, given post-revolutionary conditions, lack of resources, lack of trained personnel, and much else.

The parliamentary system came to an end in the years after 1957, as the army became an open competitor for political influence, while political parties descended increasingly into street politics during the Guided Democracy years. The cohesion of the civilian political elite disappeared, authority and power were concentrated in Jakarta, and narrower interests took precedence over parliamentary adhesion to legal process under the liberal provisional constitution of the 1950, which was undone in 1959 by a presidential decree restoring the strong presidential constitution of 1945. In these conditions, the integrity of the legal system quickly came apart, as prosecutors and police (not always enthusiastically) cashed in on their political usefulness, judges eventually followed suit, and corruption began to infuse legal process. Following the coup of late 1965, the army took full control of the state, promising a return to law, but under no compulsion adequate to force delivery. The consequence, during over three decades of the New Order, was nothing less than the destruction of the Indonesian state. This statement may seem overly dramatic, but not if one defines the modern state in terms of its basic administrative and legal institutions and their orientation, in some degree, to the needs and purposes of a governed society. In Indonesia, these institutions, from top to bottom, were not merely corrupted—indeed, corruption was increasingly conceived less as corruption than a perquisite, even a right, of office. Their very functions were essentially vitiated as government increasingly took shape as a kind of fortress surrounded by exploitable territory.

To understand why and how the post-revolutionary *negara hukum* collapsed, one needs first to recognize that legal norms sit on a political base. In no set of state institutions and responsibilities is this elementary point more obvious (and more often missed or misunderstood) than in judicial systems—particularly courts, prosecution, police, and the private legal profession. With the partial exception of the police, though even they in significant ways, all rely on authority more than power. This authority derives from a more or less willing concession by those with political power, who gain from it a share of legitimate authority and even a guarantee of personal safety. More than any other, judicial institutions tend to define for citizens, practically and symbolically, the quality of their state and its political system and leadership. Yet, how they work and interact and exercise effective controls, how they maintain their integrity, or not, how they actually fashion a system, and to what purpose, is seldom all that clear to citizens. When judicial institutions work well, they may enjoy a kind of enigmatic aura. When they fail, as utterly as they did in Indonesia, authority disappears (in favor of raw power to enforce), and they provoke disgust, anger, contempt, shoe or egg tossing, and worse. And serious questions arise about why exactly they failed and how to make the system work.

Sebastiaan Pompe's study of Indonesia's Mahkamah Agung, the Supreme Court, is actually more than that, for while it provides one of the most careful and detailed analyses of high courts anywhere, it also serves as a history of judicial and legal pathology in a very complex country. It goes a long way towards answering the most basic questions about the failure of a judiciary—not the Mahkamah Agung alone—and its consequences. The work may well become a classic or, in any case, essential reading for anyone interested in modern Indonesian history, the intricacies of institutional distortion and failure, and the comparative study of courts. It is at once an extraordinarily intimate history of the Court and a rather wider effort to search out the causes of its decline into corruption and dependency, inevitably taking the rest of the civil judiciary with it—and without much of a battle. In Pompe's analysis, moreover, one can begin to understand why legal reform has been so frustratingly hard since 1998, and even perhaps to notice some implications for sensible strategies of reform. Soon after the author's original dissertation was presented at the University of Leiden faculty of law and a few copies made their way to Indonesia, its revelations of the Court's misdoings caused something of an uproar in interested Jakarta circles. Now revised for publication, it is likely to set off rather deeper debates over issues of Indonesian legal and political history and some necessary discussion of how, and with what consequences, the Indonesian state was transformed over the last fifty years.

It is hard to imagine one better qualified with comparatist credentials to do this research than Sebastiaan Pompe. With a law degree from the University of Leiden, he did Indonesian and Malay studies at the School of Oriental and African Studies in London, and added an MA degree in law at Cambridge. Amply equipped with useful languages, including Indonesian, he is also well versed in the variations of Continental civil law and English derived common law and the subtleties of their evolution as they spread around the world through colonial imposition, imitation, and adaptation. His previously published work includes a long list of significant articles on distinct issues in Indonesian law and the most complete survey available of writings on Indonesian law. For several years, until the end of 2004, Dr. Pompe was engaged in a program of judicial reform in Jakarta.

Daniel S. Lev

The new Supreme Court building
(reprinted with permission, *TEMPO*/Donny Metri, 1992)

Acknowledgments

The court system of a developing country, even a big one such as Indonesia, was not an obvious research topic in the early 1990s, all the more so because the country, to all appearances, seemed stable and had near double-digit growth. The Suharto regime looked unassailable, the economy appeared robust, and political opposition was, if at all manifest, political rather than legal or institutional. Institutions and the law were marginal, may have been even dysfunctional, but, whatever their condition, they manifestly were widely regarded as things that did not matter much. Closer inspection might have revealed some cracks in the system even at the time, such as the increase in the number of high-profile political cases before the courts, an emerging correspondence between decreases in court filings and increases in low-level violence, or increasing economic strains caused by a weak institutional infrastructure and absent law enforcement. But, at the time, these passed pretty much unnoticed and their significance was not understood until later.

The marginality of the courts was reflected in the dearth of traditional legal research materials. The traditional formal tools of legal analysis, notably statute, case law, and handbooks, were so limited and inadequate that they could hardly explain what the court did and, more important perhaps, what it did not. What few formal legal tools there were, these often were inconsistent. Sociology and political science made their way into this book not because such was the premise, but because they were necessary to understand the place and role of the Supreme Court in modern Indonesia.

I had the good fortune of being able to draw on three special resources to realize this. The first was the Indonesia law library of the Van Vollenhoven Institute of Leiden Law School, which probably is the best library on old and modern Indonesian law in the world. It covered pretty much all of the formal bases. The second was the personal archives of professor Dan Lev and, notably, his interview notes ranging from the 1950s onwards, which together with his extraordinary historical insight on legal institutions and professions, gave me a much better understanding of how courts had evolved over time. The third was a group of Supreme Court and Appeal Court Justices who were prepared to tell me about their work and their lives. While their accounts often were troubling, they also generally imbued me with a deep respect for them and their profession. For this specific group combined many special qualities: all were great jurists, hard working, upright, and devastated by the condition of their profession. They were willing to talk because they were trying to salvage it.

When the study was presented in 1996, it obviously challenged the status quo. It assigned importance to what seemed unimportant, it presumed to identify problems when much seemed well, and it identified as culprits some who were in power or close to it. It was not taken lightly as a result and caused problems at the university and beyond. It was not published, at least in part, because the powers that be felt the edges "had to be smoothed" first.

Unpublished though it was, unauthorized copies soon found their way into the Indonesian judiciary and elsewhere, and at one point it was put on the agenda for a meeting between the Indonesian authorities and the Dutch Embassy. Little did anyone know at the time that the regime would come crashing down within the year. Courts suddenly were top of the bill. This was, in part, by popular demand. In part, it was because the massive private debt forced the Indonesian authorities, with support of the IMF, to strengthen the institutional framework for private debt restructuring. Courts took a prominent place. I was called in to assist and suddenly found myself in the middle of major institutional-political change.

If the study lay unpublished, this does not mean it rested idle. Copies of the manuscript circulated in Indonesian Supreme Court circles; the Indonesian media reported on the research, NGOs were perusing it, and it was quoted in parliament during the fit and proper test of new Supreme Court justices. I was encouraged to publish by Indonesians, including some Supreme Court justices. All this acquired momentum with the appointment of chief justice Bagir Manan in 2002. Bagir Manan was an outsider to the judiciary, with an open mind on both its problems and ways to tackle them. He started a judicial reform process that is unprecedented in Indonesian history and with which I was closely involved. It focused on the development of a set of comprehensive policy documents for institutional reform, called the Blueprints. It was the first time in Indonesian history that the Supreme Court engaged in a comprehensive reform effort, moreover, one enlisting significant civil society involvement. The Supreme Court Blueprints, of which there are five, appeared in Fall 2003. While obviously homegrown, they also drew on this study. Despite being unpublished (or perhaps because of it), this study therefore stood at the root of institutional reform efforts after *Reformasi*.

It has been quite a road, which I would not have been able to travel without the good company and advice of many friends and colleagues.

My gratitude goes in the first place to professor Hans Franken, my supervisor and dean of Leiden Law School at the time. It was because of him that the manuscript overcame internal university opposition and was accepted with acclaim. He managed to combine a hands-off style with strong support and easy access whenever the situation called for it. Also, with his lifelong interest in legal theory and sociology of law, he supported the shift from formal law to legal sociology, which saved the study.

I did most of the theoretical research at the Van Vollenhoven Institute, which was a great place for research. I must thank the staff of the institute, particularly Harold Munneke, with his outstanding analytical and legal mind, and Leon Buskens, for being there. Also, I am grateful to Cora de Waaij, Albert Dekker, and Sylvia Holverda who were of great assistance in the library research. Jan Michiel Otto proposed the topic, and Nel de Jong helped in later stages. Similarly, I thank the library staff of the KITLV (Royal Institute for Anthropology and Linguistics) for their assistance over the years. The KITLV representative in Indonesia, Jaap Erkelens, with his unrivalled knowledge of archives in Indonesia, has been very helpful.

In Indonesia, my gratitude extends to more people than possibly can be mentioned. I still think it is best not to name names. This book would never have come about without major support from a group of Indonesian judges. It is difficult to do justice fully to their role, which resides not just in having provided concrete and vital information, but also in demonstrating extraordinary courage. It is hard enough to convey problematic information about one's lifetime employer, as the judiciary is for most Indonesian judges, and all the more so to an outsider, but to do so while retaining personal dignity is quite magnificent. At a time such as now, when court-bashing of a sometimes rather simplistic and crude form has become generally accepted, it serves to remember that this book would not have come about unless a group of Indonesian judges had acted with a dignity, courage, intelligence, and integrity that is exemplary for judges anywhere. I also thank several parliamentarians and state officials for their support.

Some names, I think, can be safely mentioned. Former chief justice Pak Purwoto Gandasubrata has given me most valuable input on the dissertation. We may not have agreed on some of the specifics, but, by and large, I believe we agreed on the essentials. I am grateful for the various discussions we have had and the dignified, dedicated, and informed way in which he treated me. Through an ironic twist of history, the 1997 Economic Crisis made us colleagues; it was a very constructive rapport, and, if anything, it increased my respect for him. Pak Setiawan and Ibu Retnowulan Sutianto have also been critical to this research.

I notably want to thank professor Mardjono Reksodiputro and Greg Churchill, good friends for more than fifteen years of my work in this country and subtle observers of Indonesian law and legal development. I would not have been where I am now if it were not for them.

At Cornell University, the late George McT. Kahin graciously gave me access to his records and made me feel most welcome. Ben Abel was of enormous assistance in the library. Ruth McVey's incisive comments on the first chapters during dinner in a small town square in Tuscany added focus.

I thank Julie, Franceline, and Dieuwertje, who have all been important. My brother-in-law Elwin Hendrikse was a great help. I wrote part of the study in the hospitable house of my good friend Fred Kaaij, who is an extraordinary guy. I thank Anselmo Reyes and Mark Baillie for being there. Erik Hammerstein suddenly appeared at a junction in my life and has been good support. Octa Sakke has been of great assistance.

The manuscript would not have appeared if not for professor Dan Lev, who is both a great scholar and a great friend. Dan was important and continues to be so in ways hard to do justice here. This research follows very much in an academic course of fact-based research on courts that he set out in the 1950s. On the academic side, he was instrumental in shifting the focus from law to sociology and political science. He gave me access to his many interview notes and records and was the only one to comment on draft chapters continuously, promptly, on substance, and in detail. If I did not take some of his advice, it is, in part, because of the sheer joy in being able to continue discussions. At a personal level, his role invariably has been one of intense interest, support, and encouragement. He was and indeed continues to be a continuous source of inspiration and intellectual guidance for many, and his house in Seattle with Arlene has been a second home.

Dr. Audrey Kahin edited the manuscript and, with gentle insistence during a visit to Jakarta, forced me to complete it in the end. Her professional standards, enormous patience, and kindness have been critical in seeing this through. I owe her a lot. The last legs of the publication process proved the hardest. They were completed only because of the seemingly endless patience of Deborah Homsher and Michael Wakoff of SEAP (Cornell Southeast Asia Program). I am enormously grateful to them both for the final work and for putting up with me. I would also like to thank Ben Abel for his generous assistance as a researcher who helped confirm a number of citations throughout the text.

This book captures some experiences from my youth. As a child at the dinner table, my father would sometimes recount some of the cases and practices he was facing at the European Court of Justice, which instilled in me an interest in court business and institutional problems. Also, his childhood interest in Indonesia, though never clearly defined, made me end up on shores I barely knew existed even in senior high school. My mother's academic interests were equally conditioning. In completing this dissertation, I never thought I would find myself in a mild and enjoyable competition with her on who would finish first, as she was writing her book on renaissance architecture, before turning to Egyptology. Her academic interests and drive carried over to me.

Finally, my thanks go to my wife Hieronyma. She has been most closely and intensely exposed to the travails and turpitudes of writing this, the institutional pressures which it generated, and the stress of not publishing for long afterwards. This study is not just a side product of an intellectual interest or professional occupation, but increasingly also of a way of life. It has not always been easy. It is hard enough to live with someone who cannot stop talking about courts and whose friends principally are people used to wearing gowns. What is more, our family with small children moved back and forth several times between Europe and Indonesia, during which Hieronyma carried much of the social burden as her partner happily raced off to meet judges. It was not always a self-evident thing: there was a prolonged illness, recovery has been a struggle, safety concerns have been significant. To be willing to share and to support; such are the greatest gifts.

I dedicate this book to my father and mother and to Hieronyma and our three sons, Sylvain, Lucas, and Benjamin.

Sebastiaan Pompe
Jakarta
January 2004

CHAPTER ONE

COLONIAL HISTORY

Courts have never been at the forefront of change in Indonesian history. They have the onerous reputation of being singular examples of the ways in which old forms and traditions have persisted in the modern age, serving no other purpose except to confirm and legitimate the political status quo. The law and legal institutions adopted from colonial times have progressively lost their meaning, potential, and vitality in a process of initially linguistic, then political and conceptual, attrition. This process ended up making them brittle and hollow vestiges of a different world. Their final demise is delayed only by the engrained conservatisms of the legal professions, shored up by a reactionary political regime.[1]

Colonial law and institutions matter still because they originally set down the beacons for post-independence institutional development. They continue to provide the markers by which the modern Indonesian judiciary navigates, if such is the appropriate term for its erratic movements, and by which any change in standards is measured. Both as legitimation and in rejection, this colonial legacy cannot be ignored if the development of the role and place of the modern Supreme Court is to be properly understood.

Four key features of the Dutch colonial system have acted as fault lines in debates concerning the institution. Over the decades and up until the present day, these features have determined institutional development.

First, there is the civil law separation of powers doctrine. In line with nineteenth-century continental (or English, for that matter) political and legal thinking, the doctrine clearly established the judiciary as a separate and autonomous power of government, but at the same time restricted its political role. The issue is reflected notably in two features, those being the fact that the court administration (personnel management, finance, and infrastructure) is under the control of the Department of Justice, and that the court has limited power to review legislation. In modern Indonesia, the question of whether the judiciary should have control over its own administration, and whether it should have the power of constitutional review, were key elements in the debate on institutional reform over a period of nearly fifty years. *Reformasi* introduced major changes in this area, but the judiciary is far from resolving its consequences, and these issues continue to stand at the heart of the problematic of judicial reform to the present day.

Second, the colonial condition restricted the role of the judiciary in Indonesia even further. In comparison with the contemporary European condition, a wide

---

[1] Daniel S. Lev, "Colonial Law and the Genesis of the Indonesian State," *Indonesia* 40 (October 1985): 57; H. J. Benda, "The Pattern of Reforms in the Closing Years of Dutch Rule in Indonesia," *Journal of Asian Studies* 25 (1966): 589; H. Sutherland, *The Making of a Bureaucratic Elite: The Colonial Transformation of the Javanese Priyayi* (Singapore: Heinemann, 1979); Benedict R. O'G. Anderson, "Old State, New Society: Indonesia's New Order in Comparative Historical Perspective," *Journal of Asian Studies* 42 (1983): 477.

range of executive actions were discretionary and not liable for review before the courts—this was particularly true in cases relating to the Indonesian population. Though not in the same specific terms as the colonial constitution, the 1945 Constitution has retained broadly defined executive discretion in Indonesia. In modern Indonesia, and notably under the 1945 Constitution, executive accountability before the courts has emerged as a key issue of debate.

Third, the colonial civil law judiciary was patterned on a career system, which was perpetuated in the independent state. It has been argued that career judges tend to sympathize more with the government than with the private sector. This remains a somewhat ambiguous issue. More importantly, career systems, unlike bar-recruited judiciaries, do not rely on, or further, the existence of private professional organizations, such as bar organizations, the membership of which can then be used as recruitment pools. It is now increasingly evident that such private professional organizations are key societal counterweights that help moderate government, or judicial, power excesses. In modern Indonesia, both broadening the judicial recruitment base and establishing a unified bar are key elements on the institutional reform agenda.

Fourth, the diverse system of colonial courts restricted the impact of the colonial Supreme Court and state concepts of justice on the Indonesian community. Of necessity, sweeping concepts regarding the separation of powers and judicial autonomy struck only shallow roots in that community. During the colonial era, separate and autonomous courts were, by and large, far removed from the day-to-day life of most Indonesians; the Supreme Court being a wholly remote institution. In modern Indonesia, the place and role of the Supreme Court has been heavily influenced by the institutional and societal challenges of bringing state justice concepts and institutions to the local level.

1. THE SUPREME COURT IN THE SEPARATION OF POWERS DOCTRINE

The colonial Supreme Court by its very nature remains an important symbol, which in the modern Indonesian state has become unthinkable to eradicate. Above all, it is a symbol of the functional specialization of government powers, a system that is meant to insure that legislation, government, and adjudication are separated and exercised by different persons and institutions.[2]

The colonial origins of the Supreme Court were rooted in French revolutionary ideas concerning the structure of government, which became influential in the Netherlands, and indeed in the rest of continental Europe, at the end of the eighteenth century.[3] These ideas were then transferred to the colonies.[4] The French

---

[2] W. J. Witteveen, *Eevenwicht der machten* (Zwolle: Tjeenk Willink, 1991), p. 22.

[3] In fact, the French ideas had taken hold on the Netherlands after its own subsidiary revolution and subsequent occupation by the French. Simon Schama, *Patriots and Liberators: Revolution in the Netherlands, 1780–1813* (New York: Knopf, 1977). For a historical novel dealing with this process of political awareness and French influence on the thinking of the Dutch political elite, see H. S. Haasse, *Schaduwbeeld of het geheim van Appeltern. Kroniek van een leven* (Amsterdam: Querido, 1990).

[4] For the colony of the Netherlands-Indies, these ideas were most clearly expressed perhaps by D. van Hogendorp, *Berigt van den tegenwoordigen toestand der Bataafsche bezittingen in Oost-Indië en den Handel op dezelve* (Den Haaag, 1799). This publication is in almost total accord with the 1803 Report of the Nederburgh commission as regards the administration of justice (art.85-89), with which I will deal later. One of the cornerstones of the Van Hogendorp reform

doctrine envisages a highly rationalized state organization based on "an extreme form of division of labor, in which each unit did do and could do only one thing."[5] Government, Parliament, and the courts are each absolutely sovereign in their own spheres, thereby forming what is referred to as a *separation* of powers structure. There is no interdependence among the powers of government, so that they are pitted against each other, as in the *balance* of powers system, which prevails in the United States.

The separation of powers doctrine has a number of important conceptual consequences for the organization and powers of the courts. In organizational terms, the system distinguishes between the judicial and administrative functions within the judicial organization. The former relates to the proper function of the courts, settling disputes. The latter concerns all other matters, such as personnel, financial, and office management. As these are essentially administrative functions, "la logique du système," as the French might say, requires that they be handled by government, rather than by the courts.[6] As a result, France, as well as countries that to some extent have adopted its system, such as Holland or Indonesia, are marked by a division of functions even within the judiciary. Typically, the judiciary exerts authority and ultimate control over judicial functions, whereas administrative functions, such as court administration or personnel matters, are handled by a government department, usually the Department of Justice. The department functions as a sort of administrative support to the judiciary, acting upon "requests" (note: not instructions) from whomever is in charge there, which is usually the Supreme Court.

Another important aspect to this systemic logic relates to political accountability, notably of funding. From the French (and Dutch) perspective, accountability for public funds is a basic constitutional obligation. Engagement in securing funds (i.e., submitting policy proposals and securing their funding), and their allocation and disbursement, are viewed as prime political duties, and those who accept such duties owe full accountability to the democratic constituency. It is therefore required that political appointees are invested with this authority, and that they can be held to account by the legislature for their actions in this regard, if need be through dismissal. As judicial independence is difficult to reconcile with public accountability, sanctioned by dismissal, financial accountability required a separation of functions.

In terms of judicial powers, the separation of powers doctrine does not permit encroachment of any power of government on the other. This means that one power of government perforce may not exercise vital functions belonging to the terrain of the other. Traditionally, therefore, the judiciary lacks controlling authority over other powers of government. Notably in the field of statutory review by the courts, this leads to two significant restrictions when compared to the US balance of

---

program was that a judicial organization be established under the supervision of a Supreme Court and independent from the administration. J. Ball, *Indonesian Legal History 1602-1848* (Sydney: Oughtershaw Press, 1982), p. 82.

[5] Martin Shapiro, *Courts: A Comparative and Political Analysis* (Chicago, IL: The University of Chicago Press, 1981), p. 31.

[6] To ensure judicial independence, working routine requires that the department serve as an essentially administrative conduit for judicial requests. Nevertheless, doctrine does not allow the judiciary to instruct the department to realize administrative functions, but can only request it.

powers system. First, courts have a very restricted right of review and quite specifically may not void acts of Parliament, or "formal laws" as they are called in the continental system. Acts of Parliament are qualified as the supreme expression of the democratic will, and, as a result, the sole legitimate source through which political power can be expressed. Consequently, courts may not question Acts of Parliament, although they are allowed to review inferior regulations on grounds of their violating superior law.[7] Second, even if such violation in lower statute were to be found, courts may not void the relevant statute, but only declare it inapplicable in the case before the court. It is left to the relevant legislative body to review its own legislative instrument.[8] This, of course, contrasts with the US system, which allows for acts of Congress to be voided on grounds of violating the Constitution.

The separation of powers doctrine was not seriously questioned during the Indonesian independence struggle, and it was adopted and became integral to the modern Indonesian state. There was never any fundamental debate on the place of the Supreme Court, renamed the Mahkamah Agung. It is important to note that in the end the Court's position was determined not by default, but rather by deliberate choice.

During the preparatory debates on the 1945 Constitution, participants questioned whether the doctrine was to be retained. A prominent member of the preparatory committee on the Constitution, Mohammad Yamin, asked whether Indonesia should introduce the US practice of constitutional review, which would allow the Mahkamah Agung to review the constitutionality of Acts of Parliament.[9] This point cut to the heart of the separation of powers doctrine, and, if accepted, would effectively have meant opting for a balance of powers system.

Steeped as it was in the French-Dutch legal tradition, the preparatory committee rejected Yamin's proposal.[10] The chairman of the constitutional drafting committee, Supomo, initially argued, somewhat lamely, that Indonesians had insufficient experience with constitutional review, and he did not exclude the possibility that it might be introduced at some later date (". . . for our young nation, it is too early to work out this issue. . . "). Nevertheless, Supomo had more deep-seated conceptual objections.[11] He argued that full powers of constitutional review implied a state structure out of harmony with the ideological foundations of the

---

[7] In this study, reviewing Acts of Parliament against the Constitution has been defined as "constitutional review" and reviewing inferior statute as "judicial review."

[8] This necessarily is a rather skeletal description of the system, which moreover does not account for post-World War II developments. Thus, France instituted a *Cour Constitutionnel* with powers of judicial review, while in Holland courts are allowed to review Acts of Parliament against international treaties, albeit not against the Constitution. These developments are not altogether irrelevant in the Indonesian context, as the Indonesian government steadfastly defends itself against claims for judicial review, for instance, with ideological references to the outdated French prewar system.

[9] Yamin also called for review with respect to customary law (*adat*) and Islam. In the wording of his proposed amendment art.24(4): "The Supreme Court may review laws made by Parliament on the basis of conflict with the Constitution, as well as acknowledged *adat* or Islamic law." M. Yamin, *Naskah persiapan Undang-undang Dasar 1945* (Jakarta: Jajasan Prapantja, 1959), p. 341.

[10] The Yamin proposal was voted down by the preparatory committee. Yamin's was the only vote in favor. J. H. A. Logemann, *Enkele gegevens over het ontstaan van de Indonesische Grondwet van 1945* (Amsterdam: Noord-Hollandsche Uitgevers Maatschappij, 1962), p. 694.

[11] These became more important in later years; see below Chapter 3.

Indonesian state envisaged in the draft constitution,[12] under which the president, much like a traditional patrimonial father, was viewed as a family head, with the responsibility of leading and uniting the people. The president embodied the unity of the people and in that capacity was above all parties. Clearly, a powerful Supreme Court, as proposed by Yamin, with the authority to review the constitutionality of legislation, conflicted with this idea.[13] Supomo asserted:

> ... in my opinion, Mr. Chairman, this constitution is not based on a principal separation of three government powers, so that the judiciary should not be empowered to control the legislature [*kekuasaan membentuk undang-undang*].[14]

In contemporary Indonesia, the Yamin proposal and its rejection are broadly recognized as a pivotal event in Indonesian constitutional law.[15] The proposal is

---

[12] Yamin, *Naskah persiapan*, p. 341. There is a problem with the crucial sentence as reported by Yamin. After a passage referring to Western constitutional models, this sentence runs as follows: "*Akan tetapi dinegeri democratie perbedaan atau perpisahaan antara tiga djenis kekuasaan itu tidak ada.*" This statement is followed by an explanation of the system of the Supomo draft constitution. The translation runs as follows: "But in democratic countries, a distinction or separation between three types of power does not exist." The sentence does not make sense, because a separation of powers of government does exist in democratic countries. Since the statement begins with a negation suggesting contrast with the preceding passage, however, it should probably be read together with the passage following it, which deals with the ideas of democracy underlying the Supomo constitution. If this interpretation is correct, as I hold it to be, a word has been left out in the Yamin records, and the original must have run more or less as follows: "*Akan tetapi dinegeri ini, democratie perbedaan atau perpisahan antara tiga djenis kekuasaan itu tidak ada,*" which can be translated: "Nevertheless, in this country a democracy which makes a distinction between or separates three types of powers does not exist."

[13] Yamin, *Naskah persiapan*, pp. 232-36. It is interesting to note that in an article on the Federal State published two years later, Supomo expressed ideas very much along the lines proposed by Yamin. See *Mimbar Indonesia* 7 February 1948. In Supomo's words: "I believe that it may be necessary for Indonesia as well to have a constitutional provision that authorizes a court, such as the Federal Supreme Court, to review the constitutionality of all legislation, both from the federal authorities as well as from the member states." See also A. A. Schiller, *The Formation of Federal Indonesia 1945-1949* (The Hague/Bandung: Van Hoeve, 1955), p. 294. Note that this view does not necessarily conflict with earlier opinions expressed by Supomo. Unlike unitary states, federal structures require legislative review by the courts as an instrument to coordinate regulatory regimes of member states.

[14] Yamin, *Naskah persiapan*, pp. 341.

[15] A. B. Nasution, *The Aspiration for Constitutional Government in Indonesia* (Jakarta: Pustaka Sinar Harapan, 1992), p. 122; T. M. Mulya Lubis, *In Search of Human Rights* (Jakarta: Gramedia, 1993), p. 119; J. C. T. Simorangkir, *Hukum dan Konstitusi Indonesia*, vol. 2 (Jakarta: Gunung Agung, 1986), p. 37; Sri Soemantri, *Hak menguji material di Indonesia* (Bandung: Almuni, 1986), pp. 47-48. While the importance of the Yamin proposal is evident in political-constitutional terms, it may be that too much is made of its contemporary historical significance. There are indications that the protagonists did not recognize the issue to be of fundamental importance, and that judicial review was one of many hot-air balloons floating about during those debates. Supomo did not think the proposal serious enough to deal with it thoroughly; his answer is equivocal and sloppy. Neither did the rest of the preparatory committee seem to recognize this as a significant issue, which contrasts sharply with their attitude toward other matters, such as human rights. One could portray Yamin as the visionary in the desert, but then Yamin did not push the issue at all. Indeed, rather than a highly prescient and astute political thinker, Yamin instead perhaps was part of the problem. Equipped with an acute mind, Yamin also had the reputation of being overzealous, loquacious, and somewhat self-important. He

viewed as a serious initiative which would have been accepted but for the unimaginative and reactionary Supomo.[16] The underlying idea is that Indonesia might very well have turned into a different country if the proposal had been accepted. This argument is speculative, of course, but has obvious attraction. The failure of the Supreme Court and the judiciary to retain their autonomy from government interference after independence inevitably makes one wonder whether perhaps they might have fared better under a different constitutional system.[17] The historical reality remains, however, that at independence Indonesia adhered to the French-Dutch separation of powers doctrine. Particularly under the New Order, the struggle to change the Supreme Court and the judiciary became increasingly focused on this doctrine and some of its prominent features. If change is to come, then it is the separation of powers doctrine that will have to be adopted first.

2. JUDICIAL AUTONOMY IN THE COLONIAL STATE CONTEXT

It is important to remember that the introduction of separate and independent courts into the colony in the nineteenth century was based largely on European political developments and the pressures these exerted on the colony.[18] Particularly in the nineteenth century, colonial society only selectively supported

---

tired out some of the members of the committee with his endless speeches and numerous interjections. This undermined his credibility, not in the least because his countless comments and suggestions went in all directions and at times lacked internal cohesion and focus. His treatment of judicial review was a case in point. Finally, though the authenticity of this part of the debates is not doubted, it is useful to remember that we only have Yamin's account of what went on, and it has been suggested recently that his records may not be altogether reliable, but may have been edited to inflate Yamin's own role therein. See M. Simandjuntak, *Pandangan negara integralistik* (Jakarta: Grafiti, 1994), pp. 17-21, 67-68, 255-57, and *Suara Pembaruan*, 19 June 1993, quoted therein.

[16] As a born and bred jurist, a member of the traditional Javanese elite, and part and parcel of the Europeanized bureaucratic elite in the colony, Supomo never was a person to advocate radical change. His personal and professional inclinations favored incremental, orderly, and rational, rather than radical and impressionistic, reforms. Yamin's proposal is remarkable because he in many ways belonged to the same group as Supomo. Nevertheless, he was the odd man out. His later career as failed putchist, poet, and patriarchal politician during an era in which the courts were radically marginalized revealed Yamin to be a character of much greater complexity than the talented but rather dull Supomo.

[17] Tempting though this argument may be, blaming constitutional systems for political developments puts the cart before the horse. In Indonesia, it was the political-economic environment heavily conditioned by colonialism, rather than the constitutional system, that undermined the place and role of the courts. It is not at all evident that a stronger court would have stopped this development.

[18] Colonies generally dispensed with the potent political mix created by a competing government and Parliament, a mix that is often instrumental in raising and sustaining judicial independence as a political issue. S. Shetreet, *Judges on Trial: A Study of the Appointment and Accountability of the English Judiciary* (Amsterdam: North Holland, 1976), p. 3. More important perhaps, by its very nature colonial society does not generate the forces nor, for that matter and with a few exceptions, the necessary intellectual resources that might attract political backing for stronger courts. For a discussion of the effects of the poor intellectual climate on the position of the judiciary, see M. C. Piepers, "Iets over de rechterlijke macht in het algemeen, hare verhouding tot de andere staatsmachten en tot de maatschappij," *Indisch Weekblad van het Recht* 777 (1878): 77-78.

separate and independent courts. Indeed, any support was strongly marked by the Western colonial elite's desire to protect its own interests. It was not at all evident that this protection should also extend to the Indonesian population. In line with developments in Europe, the colonial elite might have desired stronger courts for itself, but it looked to strong government rather than strong courts to ensure its position vis-à-vis the subjected nation. Within the context of the separation of powers doctrine, therefore, colonial society even further restricted the role of courts, with the government retaining extensive discretionary powers.

Functional specialization and separation of powers only slowly permeated colonial political structures. These doctrines, though embodied in the Constitution at the beginning of the nineteenth century, only became political fixtures for the large judicial organization from 1854 onwards. In this slow process the colonial Supreme Court took the leading position, and it was essentially through reform from the top that the separation of powers doctrine (and through it, judicial autonomy from executive interference) was introduced in the colony.

Prior to the nineteenth century, there was no basic state conception of judicial and other government functions being separated. There was little functional specialization, as indeed judges were also members of the co-governing *Raad van Indië* and, as a result, were prone to identify closely with executive interests.[19] Direct executive interference in the affairs of the judiciary was rampant, as the Governor-General would routinely instruct colonial judges how to decide a case, "which decision would then be read and pronounced with embarrassed faces [*beschaamde tronies*]."[20]

---

[19] This provision was relaxed in the course of the eighteenth century. J. La Bree, *De rechterlijek organisatie en rechtsbedeling te Batavia in de XVIIe eeuw* (Rotterdam: Nijgh and Van Ditmar, 1951), citing F. Valentijn, *Beschrijving van Groot Djawa*, pt. 4, p. 353. The 1803 Nederburgh Report shows little respect for colonial officers who combine administrative and judicial functions: "They frequently avail themselves of their combined political and judicial authority to give free rein to their particular impulses, which gives rise to grievous maltreatment. Very often one finds among them persons with only the barest knowledge of the administration of justice, with the result that procedures in cases of great importance are so thoroughly corrupted that it is impossible to set things right in appeal, even for the most skilled judge." P. Mijer, *Verzameling van Instructiën, Ordonanciën en Reglementen voor de Regering van Nederlandsch Indië enz.* (Batavia: Lands-Drukkerij, 1848), pp. 201-202. F. W. Stapel, "Uit de wordingsgeschiedenis van het Charter van 1804," *Bijdragen tot de Taal, Land en Volkenkunde van Nederlandsch-Indië* 90 (1933): 430 passim. F. W. Stapel (p. 433) cites a secret memorandum attached to the Nederburgh Report suggesting that the judges of the colonial Supreme Court at that moment were so excessively ignorant and had generated so little confidence that all reforms would come to naught unless the court were newly constituted in its entirety: ". . . with regret we must state that we have found no reason whatsoever which makes it desirable, much less necessary, to maintain any of the present members or ministers of the Supreme Court of Justice in Batavia in employment in a new *Hooggerechtshof*: the deep ignorance and engrained aversion of this group for all superior power in the Indies, the frequent and irritating conflicts in which this has resulted for so many years to the detriment of public authority, as well as of the authority and respect for Justice, so that it has altogether disappeared, have brought us to consider all improvements to the administration of justice as hopeless, though it may be unavoidable that this unhappy spirit of ignorance and of silly ambition and arrogance, whereby the named court has created an unbridgeable gap with the general public, will attach itself to the new court . . . ."

[20] P. A. van der Lith, *Nederlandsch Oost-Indië* (Leiden: Brill, 1893), pp. 530-31 on administrative interference and p. 530 for the quote. See also C. W. Margadant, *Het Regeeringsreglement van Nederlandsch-Indië*, vol. 3 (Batavia: Kolff, 1897), pp. 164-65. Note that general instructions to the effect that there shall be no administrative interference in the

As French revolutionary ideas permeated Europe, they inevitably influenced colonial government structures.[21] The first major official policy statement reflecting these new ideas was the famous Nederburgh Report of 1803.[22] It is a remarkably modern report. The principles which it seeks to realize and the practical approaches it recommends are nearly identical to many goals that the judiciary would seek to secure under *Reformasi* two hundred years later. It described the separation of judicial and administrative functions as "an excellent maxim of state," advising its implementation in the colony. Such implementation included

---

administration of justice exist as early as 1650. We note a portion of Missive 26 April 1650, which stated that the administration shall be under the obligation to effect decisions of the Batavia *Raad van Justitie*, that it may not pardon convicted persons (unless in the case of the death penalty), and may not frustrate the commencing of court proceedings by the prosecutor (*fiscael*). Nevertheless, twenty years later the courts were instructed to "motivate and give account" to the colonial administration. See Missives Heren XVII dated 25 August 1670 and 12 May 1671. These instructions arose from the first case in which the 1650 Missive affirming the court's independence was put to the test. In this 1669 case, the court tried to stave off administrative interference with reference to the 1650 instruction referred to above. The case was brought before the Heren XVII for advice, who did not manage to make up their minds concerning whether the colonial administration or their own instructions should prevail. In the end they severely qualified their own 1650 instruction. See N. P. van den Berg, *Uit de dagen der Compagnie* (Haarlem: Tjeenk Willink, 1904), p. 216 and for a more detailed analysis of the missives, see F. W. Stapel, "Bijdragen tot de geschiedenis der rechtspraak bij de Vereenigde Oostindische Compagnie," *Bijdragen tot de Taal-, Land- en Volkenkunde van Nederlandsch-Indië* 89 (1932): 60, 63.

[21] In fact, the Nederburgh Report was preceded by at least one missive, which, though very limited in scope, breathes the revolutionary spirit in this field of the administration of justice. By Missive dated 9 February 1798, the colony was instructed that henceforth judicial and administrative functions should be strictly separated. In fact, the result of this missive was that practically everybody holding dual employment opted for the administration. Already by October 1798, the judiciary was understaffed to the point that the Batavia *Hoge Raad van Justitie* had only two members qualified in law. In the lower judicial instances, the missive could not be effected at all for lack of personnel. J. A. van der Chijs, *Nederlandsch-Indisch Plakaatboek 1602-1811*, vol. 12 (1894): 766, 887, 893. Later, the Nederburgh Report was criticized on the basis of that experience: according to some contemporary authors of distinction such as Herman Warner Muntinghe, the circumstances in the colony, such as lack of skilled personnel, would not allow for such an ambitious and idealistic program of reform to be implemented. The separation of functions could not be realized in personnel terms. J. Hageman, "Geschiedenis van het Hollandsch Gouvernement op Java," *Tijdschrift voor Indische Taal-, Land- en Volkenkunde* 5 (1856): 164-284.

[22] Rapport der Commissie tot de Oost-Indische Zaken, 31 Augustus 1803, in P. Mijer, *Verzameling van Instructiën*, p. 119. The commission was constituted in 1802, its report was completed in 1803, but officially accepted only in 1804 (Decision Staatsbewind 27 September 1804 no.19a), and publications refer to the commission and the report with all three dates. The report consists of an introductory text, which serves essentially as an elucidation of the five draft regulations following it. The major draft regulation is the Charter, which constitutes the constitutional mandate and specifications concerning colonial government (*Charter tot vestiging van de Regeering en het Bestuur der Asiatische Bezittingen van de Bataafsche Republiek, tot betere Administratie der Justitie in dezelve, en tot het drijven van den Handel op en in Oost-Indiën*). A draft regulation on a Supreme Court is also included (*Instructie voor het Hoge Gerechtshof van Bataafsch Indiën*). The chairman of the commission was J. Meerman, but its two most prominent members were the more conservative S. C. Nederburgh and liberal D. van Hogendorp. There is some debate as to which of the two prevailed, but since Nederburgh is generally regarded as the winner, the commission is often referred to with reference to his name. See for instance H. A. Idema, "Overzicht van de Indische rechts- en staatkundige geschiedenis 1600-1854," *Koloniale Studiën* 12,2 (1928): 308 and passim.

the establishment of a separate judicial apparatus, independent of government interference. The draft Charter attached to the Nederburgh Report stated that "all interference of any political authority in the course of justice, not allowed by any provision of this Charter, is prohibited" (art.74).[23] It also recommended that the judges should have adequate legal training (art.59),[24] that a neutral system of appointments be installed (art.58), that judges be properly remunerated,[25] and that

---

[23] Some lack of clarity exists on the drafting history of the Report. With respect to the agrarian policy (art.56, 95, 99), the Charter is said to go Nederburgh's way, but as regards the administration of justice (art.85-89), it almost fully accords with the liberal ideas of Van Hogendorp published earlier. See D. van Hogendorp, *Berigt van den tegenwoordigen toestand*. Briefly summarized, these were that judges be properly remunerated, that a judicial hierarchy be established under a Supreme Court but independent from the administration, that officials administering justice be held accountable by holding session in public, and that the courts be staffed by professional judges. Ball, *Indonesian Legal History*, p. 82. This suggests that the Nederburgh Report was a compromise, as indicated by Van Hogendorp himself ("Nous avons amalgamé les opinions diverses en sacrifiant chacun quelque chose") and supported by F. de Haan, *Priangan: De Preanger-Regentschappen onder het Nederlandsch Bestuur tot 1811* (Batavia: Kolff, 1912), pt. 4, p. 766. In actual fact, Van Hogendorp seems to have done very little work on the section in the Report pertaining to the position of the Supreme Court. The Report says that two members were specifically delegated to work on this subject (P. Mijer, *Verzameling van Instructiën*, p. 202), and Stapel reveals that these were Nederburgh and W. Six. Stapel says that while Van Hogendorp presented a memorandum on the subject as well, the Nederburgh-Six draft was accepted "almost without changes," as stated by the Report. Stapel, "Uit de wordingsgeschiedenis," p. 428.

[24] As pointed out by La Bree, *De rechterlijke organisatie*, p. 56, legal training is mentioned as a criterion for judges as early as 1650. By 1656, most judges were graduates in law, but the standards gradually declined, and at the end of the eighteenth century judges are reported to have bought their degrees and to be fully ignorant on the law. The fact that some VOC employees ex officio were members of the court—such as the head of the VOC factory in Deshima (Japan)—cannot have improved the quality of the administration of justice.

[25] This understandably is a recommendation in the Report (P. Mijer, *Verzameling van Instructiën*, p. 204), not a provision in the Charter. The Charter does, however, specify that judges be remunerated sufficiently to eliminate any necessity of engaging in commerce (art.60), and the two are evidently closely connected. In the words of the commission: "If our recommendations are accepted, the salaries from these functions shall be sufficient to satisfy the reasonable expectations of the chairman and the members [of the Supreme Court], and they can in fairness be obliged to desist from any other functions or sources of income. This will be advantageous in two respects: first, the judiciary shall thus attract knowledgeable and dignified persons; second, Supreme Court judges shall never have anything to expect or to fear from the High Political Power in the Indies, and thus the road is blocked, by which the government, contrary to its best intentions might exercise undue influence on the judiciary." Mijer, *Verzameling van Instructiën*, p. 206. Stapel, *Uit de wordingsgeschiedenis*, p. 430, refers to a secret memorandum attached to the Nederburgh Report and of which Mijer was not aware, which suggests, amongst other things, that the Supreme Court members be awarded salaries ranging from 12.000 to 20.000 *rijksdaalders*. Apparently this information was kept secret because public opinion would have been inflamed if it became known that fellow citizens received such high rewards for state service.

dismissal be allowed only for misconduct (art.63).[26] Administrative interference was only permitted in specific cases[27] and following special procedures.[28]

It was for reasons of both principle and practicality that the Nederburgh Report focused on the Supreme Court. Guided by the revolutionary principle of separating government functions, and restricted by the lack of skilled personnel, which made it impossible for the commission to realize its ambitious plans in their entirety,[29] the commission chose to concentrate on the central organs of state. In the central government that they envisioned, the Supreme Court would serve as a "Palladium of Justice," the benefits of which would percolate through to the lower regions of government.

The Report was approved with a few minor changes in 1804. Its provision for a colonial Supreme Court established the institutional framework for separating government powers in the colony. Still, it would take until 1854 for the recommendations of the Nederburgh Report to be effected in full measure.[30] Admittedly, the subsequent colonial constitutions (*Regeringsreglement*) of 1806, 1815, and 1818, as well as subsequent legislation,[31] recognized the colonial Supreme Court as a highly significant, if not independent, institution of the administration.[32] The various constitutions politely reiterated some of the guarantees for judicial autonomy suggested by the Nederburgh commission. These included a general prohibition on administrative intervention in the affairs of the judiciary, notably regarding appointment and dismissal. It also restricted the right of government to grant pardons. Nevertheless, the efforts required to restore Dutch

---

[26] Charter art.63 provides that the colonial Supreme Court must itself decide whether behavior of one of its members is to be regarded as misconduct, after which the Prosecutor General may commence an investigation. The results of this investigation are to be submitted to the Supreme Court in the Netherlands, which after proper investigation of the dossier may advise the Governor-General to dismiss the judge. Awaiting the decision of the Dutch Supreme Court, the Governor-General may suspend the judge.

[27] Such as the Governor-General's right of pardon in the case of capital punishment (art.73).

[28] Art.71 provides that the Governor-General may suspend criminal procedures before the Court on "good and important" grounds, but only after the Court has been notified to that effect and has presented its opinion on the matter. If such a decision is taken, a copy of the dossier of the case must be transferred to the governing body of the colonies in the Netherlands (art.72).

[29] In the words of the commission: "If we were here only to serve justice, we would have to recommend the establishment of as many new courts, staffed by skilled judges and ministers, as there are territories of the state in the East. But even if the state were able to pay the high costs for such a large group of skilled civil servants, still the proposal would be frustrated for lack of sufficient numbers of skilled personnel." [The commission then goes on to point out that even in Holland none of the lower judges are trained jurists.] "The utmost that one can achieve is to constitute a Supreme Court for the Indies in such a way that it shall command the greatest respect and boundless faith of all state residents and that it can serve as a certain and safe harbor for their legitimate interests, even if they find themselves burdened by decisions of lower courts, in a word, that the Supreme Court serve as a Palladium of Justice in that part of the world." Mijer, *Verzameling van Instructiën*, pp. 202-203.

[30] *Reglement op het beleid van de Regeering en het Justitiewezen in de Aziatische Bezittingen van de Bataafsche Republiek en van den Handel op en in dezelve Bezittingen*. The title changed slightly in the 1815, 1818, and 1827 versions of this constitutional document for the colony, but from 1830 onward (1836, 1854, 1925), the authors settled on *Reglement op het beleid van de Regeering in Nederlandsch-Indië*, commonly abbreviated as *Regeringsreglement* or RR.

[31] Regulation on the administration of justice no.6/1819.

[32] M. C. Piepers, "Iets over de rechterlijke macht," p. 81.

administrative control and end the Java War conspired to render these legislative provisions inoperative. Although Governor-General Daendels took steps to improve the position of a Supreme Court and its judges, providing proper remuneration and forbidding them from partaking in commerce,[33] that was as far as he was prepared to go in implementing the reforms proposed by "a bunch of blind chatterers," as he called the Nederburgh commission.[34] The colonial Supreme Court remained firmly subject to his authority. In fact, he at one point summarily dismissed the Court chairman and one judge "for excessive attachment to the old regime."[35] In H. A. Idema's words, Nederburgh projected the top of the judicial pyramid, but Daendels and Governor-General Raffles only provided for the bottom and situated themselves at the top.[36] This, to be certain, applies to all Governors-General until the middle of the nineteenth century. When the Cultivation System was introduced, even their intent was lost, as the prime objective now became "money at the expense of all political and commercial considerations." It was indicative of the low regard in which the separation of powers doctrine was held

---

[33] F. De Haan, *Priangan*, p. 819. As noted by De Haan, this idea accorded with the suggestions of the Nederburgh commission and the patriotic movement's general conception that civil servants should be properly remunerated and forbidden from obtaining their livelihood from their official trade.

[34] J. D. Mijer, "Bijdrage tot de geschiedenis der codifcatie in Nederlandsch-Indië," *Tijdschrift voor Nederlandsch-Indië* 1 (1839): 258.

[35] The incident arose out of a case in which Governor-General Daendels, no stickler for rules and principles except those that would help clear out the mess of the old regime, had a number of Europeans who had been accused of corruption removed from prison and hanged, even while their cases were still under review before the colonial Supreme Court. When the Court protested, Daendels, living up to his reputation as the Thundering Big Lord ("Toean Besar Goentoer"), summarily dismissed chairman P. S. Maurisse and one of the judges. Maurisse was replaced by the famous Muntinghe. Daendels apparently had issues with Maurisse, which may help explain his expedited retirement. The only colonial newspaper of the day, the *Vendu Nieuws*, reports on 3 June 1809 that the wife of chairman Maurisse expressed herself in public to the effect that a number of ladies of the colonial elite were furthering their husbands' careers via Daendels's bedroom. She was officially admonished and informed that a repetition of such statements would lead to her expulsion from the colony. P. van 't Veer, *Daendels, Maarschalk van Holland* (Zeist: W. de Haan, 1963), pp. 133, 154; *Encyclopaedie van Nederlandsch-Indië* (The Hague: M. Nijhoff, 1919), pt. 3, p. 561.

[36] H. A. Idema, "Overzicht van de Indische rechts- en staatkundige geschiedenis 1600-1854," p. 320. He added that "... the connecting lines are drawn by the jurists (Elout, Muntinghe)." In his marvelous vitriolic pamphlet, C. P. K. Winckel put it as follows: "C'est par le bas qu'il faut, à Java, cimenter le temple de Thémis" (the temple of Themis needs to be rebuilt from the ground up). Winckel argued that the reform of the Supreme Court was a necessity in view of the poor quality of first instance courts. C. P. K. Winckel, *Essai sur les principes régissant l'administration de la justice aux Indes Orientales Hollandaises surtout dans les îles de Java et de Madoura et leur application* (Amsterdam: Van Dorp, 1880), p. 247. Daendels devised other methods of thwarting the judiciary, namely by circumventing it. As De Haan argues, Daendels liked to rule by administrative decree. De Haan, *Priangan*, p. 848. The colonial executive's total control over the administration of justice under the English administration is confirmed in the Lord Minto Proclamation of 11 September 1811: "The Lieutenant Governor will have the power of remitting, moderating, or confirming, all penalties . . . ." See also the Raffles Proclamation dated 11 February 1814, art.119, 121, 125, 169. Raffles's proclamation establishing the Supreme Court during his tenure (Proclamation no.33 dated 21 January 1812) explicitly refers to the Minto Proclamation above. In the Daendels regulation, the Court may inform the King of its objections to a contrary decision of the Governor-General, but it remains under the obligation to effect that decision (art.44).

that from 1830 onward, on repeated occasions and as late as 1846, the chairman of the Supreme Court sat as a member of the co-governing *Raad van Indië*.[37] Despite the Nederburgh Report's recommendations and the institutional framework of the Supreme Court, therefore, for the first half of the nineteenth century colonial realities dictated that the administration continued to hold supremacy over the Court in practice.

Substantial steps in the direction of more effective separation of powers and judicial autonomy in the colony only materialized when constitutional changes in the Netherlands established parliamentary control over the colony (through the 1848 Constitution),[38] which led to the creation of the 1854 Colonial Constitution.[39] With the enactment of these instruments, the separation of judicial and administrative powers was both formally acknowledged and practically effected—though never completely so. This separation was rooted in four principles: the functional specialization of an administration of justice effected by special officers; the prohibition of executive interference in the affairs of justice; the public character of the administration of justice; and the fact that decisions must be motivated.[40] The formal acknowledgement of security of tenure for Supreme Court judges was of particular importance in realizing a judicial apparatus that was not just separate, but also autonomous and independent (art.94-95). In 1869, a colonial Department of Justice was established which, in accordance with prevailing ideas on separation of powers at the time, took over administration of the judiciary from the colonial Supreme Court.[41]

The position of the colonial Supreme Court was further boosted by the enactment in 1848 of the Napoleonic codes in the colony. As a court of cassation, the Court had to ensure their uniform application. Indeed, partly as a result of this new legislation, and in part also because the separation of powers doctrine was implemented from the top down, the Supreme Court's workload increased rapidly, to the point that by the end of the nineteenth century the Court was barely able to manage its bloated docket.[42] As was the case with the Mahkamah Agung in later years, the colonial Supreme Court to some extent fell victim to its own success.

---

[37] The colonial constitutions of 1827, 1830, and 1836 are described as mere "instructions for the Governor General." These regulations, while still paying lip service to the independence of the Supreme Court, at the same time gave the Governor General dictatorial powers. Thus, when the *Raad van Indië* refused to give Governor-General Van den Bosch its whole-hearted support to realize the Cultivation System, RR 1830 was amended to reduce it to a mere advisory body. J. de Louter, *Handboek van het Staatsrecht en Administratief recht van Nederlandsch Indië* (The Hague: M. Nijhoff, 1914), p. 79.

[38] Ibid., p. 80.

[39] A preparatory step was taken by the 1847 Regulation on the Judicial Organization. *Reglement op de rechterlijke organisatie en het beleid der Justitie in Nederlandsch-Indië* S.1847: 23.

[40] J. de Louter, *Handboek van het Staatsrecht*, pp. 479-480.

[41] Een Rechterlijk Ambtenaar, *De magistratuur van Nederlandsch-Indië, eene studie over 't geen de rechterlijke macht in Nederlandsch-Indië is en wat zij zijn moest* (Semarang: De Groot, Kolff & Co., 1878), p. 31. (The phrase naming the author—"een rechterlijk ambtenaar"—means a member of the judiciary and is a pseudonym.)

[42] As far as cassation was concerned, the colonial Supreme Court could do very little until 1848, because there simply was no unified legislation to uphold. Reflecting the added weight after 1848, the number of criminal revision cases between 1850 and 1867 tripled from 2,900 to 7,281. A. J. Immink, *De regterlijke organisatie van Nederlandsch-Indië* (The Hague: Stemberg,

Thus, from the second half of the nineteenth century, the colonial Supreme Court progressively evolved into the "respected" power of government it would become in later years.[43] In the twentieth century, at least during the colonial years, its august position and autonomy were unquestioned.

But, despite the undisputed status the Court progressively enjoyed, the colonial context qualified its powers to an extent that exceeded the traditional restrictions associated with the separation of powers doctrine. The dominant needs of security and protection of colonial interests against the subjected nation came to be translated into considerable executive prerogatives. The Governor-General had the authority to act on his own in a broad variety of cases and circumstances, without recourse to the courts. His authority embraced administrative remedies, amnesty, and judicial proceedings against certain members of the Indonesian elite or senior colonial officers.[44] But some of these discretionary executive powers were very widely defined, notably with regard to the extraordinary powers (*exorbitante rechten*).[45] On the basis of these powers, the Governor-General could issue an order banning anyone who in his executive opinion constituted a danger to colonial public order. Such a person could be excluded from the whole or part of the colonial territory, or confined to a single place within that territory. Pending removal to that place, the person could be detained. Deciding whether the person in question was in fact a danger to public order was ultimately a matter of administrative discretion. These rights could be exercised without judicial intervention, and they superseded judicial action, so that, even if the persons concerned had committed criminal acts, prosecution was suspended. The *exorbitante rechten* hence developed at times into a substitute for judicial action. Even in cases where court action was under way against suspects, or where they had been freed by judicial decision for lack of evidence, these executive rights enabled the government to detain the suspects.[46]

These broadly defined executive powers may not have affected the separation of powers doctrine as such, but they quite clearly did restrict the role of the judiciary in the exercise of its functions. They characterize a typical regime that "systematically withdraws from the legally defined competence of the judiciary all matters of political interest to themselves."[47] The most important impact of executive supremacy was, therefore, to keep the Court out of the political domain. Both the doctrinal restriction and the colonial emphasis on executive prerogatives were geared toward keeping the Supreme Court from developing into an institution

---

1882), p. 389. By 1880, the number of criminal cases exceeded ten thousand, backlogs had crept up to two thousand cases, and members of the Court were physically exhausted, as six judges fell ill at the same time, leaving only three to do the job. A. J. Immink, *Iets over de tegenwoordige afhankelijkheid van de Nederlandsch Indische rechterlijke ambtenaren* (Amsterdam: De Bussy, 1880), pp. 24-25; *Indisch Weekblad van het Recht* 847 (1879); *Indisch Weekblad van het Recht* 886 (1879).

[43] Daniel S. Lev, "The Supreme Court of Indonesia: Comments on Evolution, Procedure, and Influence" (unpublished, 1967), p. 2.

[44] See for instance art.42, 140, 155 *Indische Staatsregeling* (Colonial Constitution 1925). Ph. Kleintjes, *Staatsinstellingen van Nederlandsch-Indië* (Amsterdam: De Bussy, 1933), pt. 2, p. 228.

[45] Art.35-37 *Indische Staatsregeling* (Colonial Constitution 1925).

[46] Ph. Kleintjes, *Staatsinstellingen*, p. 133.

[47] M. Shapiro, *Courts*, p. 32. Shapiro uses this description to define the executive-judicial relationship in contemporary Great Britain.

that might compete for political power with the colonial government. These restrictions limited the Court's activities to technical legal issues and helped shape the professional outlook of its judges and their political self-image. In the continental legal tradition, colonial Supreme Court judges saw themselves as excellent administrators, above and separate from the political mud-fights, and reluctant to engage in political controversies.

By the beginning of the twentieth century, the *exorbitante rechten* came under increasing criticism and became harder to legitimize. These powers were never repealed, however. On the contrary, the colonial government found them increasingly useful as instruments to suppress the emerging independence movement. One particular advantage was that these powers allowed the executive to bypass the colonial judiciary, which the government found to be too lenient in political cases. This general portrait confirms the autonomy of the colonial courts, and also suggests that the judiciary was creeping towards political power and, given time, might break out of its political constraints, as it was doing in the Netherlands.[48]

3. THE CLOSED RECRUITMENT SYSTEM

This self-image of judges as nonpolitical operators and elite administrators was enhanced by the system of closed recruitment characteristic of the civil law system prevailing in the colony. We will examine this issue in greater detail later (Chapter 9), but suffice it to point out here that the closed recruitment system is based on the idea of the judiciary as a career service. In the ideal type, the judiciary is a closed organization, patterned on government bureaucracies, with an elaborate personnel hierarchy, supervisory structures, control of transfers, promotions, supervision, and so on.

The system applicable in the colony may be best defined as a qualified career service,[49] in that its basic organization was purely careerist. Junior judges were recruited by the Minister of the Colonies,[50] and placed in inferior courts from where they had to claw their way up through the judicial hierarchy.[51] Subject to such stipulations as mandatory good behavior and the like, judicial advancement to all but the more senior functions was intimately linked to seniority, in accord with a ranking list primarily determined by the date of recruitment.[52] With respect to the senior judicial functions, however, advancement no longer automatically rewarded

---

[48] In 1928, Dutch courts dismissed criminal actions brought against Indonesian revolutionary leaders, including the later Indonesian Vice President Hatta.

[49] See generally V. van Huuksloot Kuilenburg, "Het promotiebeleid der rechterlijke macht in Nederlands-Indië ten aanzien van gegradueerde rechterlijke ambtenaren in de periode kort voor WO 2" (student paper, Van Vollenhoven Institute, 30 March 1994).

[50] *Bijzondere voorwaarden van benoembaarheid tot, en uitzending uit Nederland voor personeel met betrekkingen bij de rechterlijke macht in Nederlandsch-Indië* (S.1921:800).

[51] *Regeling der bezoldiging van de gegradueerde rechterlijke ambtenaren* (S.1920:508).

[52] *Het reglement op de rechterlijke organisatie en het beleid der justitie in Nederlandsch-Indië* (S.1847:23), art.19. What happened was that the Minister of the Colonies rated the new recruits based on a mixture of ability and seniority, and they were added to the existing list in the order he had determined.

graying hairs, but was determined by selection.[53] This effectively meant that such senior functions could be filled by outside appointment, although there was a statute and strong custom that, all other things being equal, the ranking list would prevail and such senior functions would also be filled from a pool of career judges.

In fact, while outside appointments did occur, notably to the Supreme Court, the judiciary vehemently resisted them. An example is I. A. Nederburgh's 1914 appointment to the Supreme Court. Nederburgh was not a career judge, but had previously served as colonial Director of Justice—a function comparable to that performed by the Minister of Justice. Dubbed an "outsider" even in contemporary reports, his appointment to the Court caused an uproar, which suggests that such outside appointments were unusual. In fact, resistance within the Court was particularly strong: the judges fully lived up to their reputation as a quarrelsome bunch.[54] Two Supreme Court judges (including the vice-chairman) resigned in protest, and one other refused to serve on the same bench with Mr. Nederburgh, which led to all sorts of organizational problems.[55]

It is argued in the literature that career judiciaries also reflect on the professional self-image of judges. As they spend their entire professional life in a working environment comparable to that found in state bureaucracies, judges have a close affinity with ordinary civil servants. Legal scholars have argued that, as a result, judges are inclined to identify more closely with state than with the private sector or societal interests.[56] Consequently, the closed recruitment system is not perceived as particularly conducive to creating assertive, independent-minded judges, as career judges tend to hold back from making controversial and potentially political choices. In the wording of the noted legal comparativist, Mauro Cappelletti:

> Career judges have less personality and, ultimately, are more inclined toward a bureaucratic mentality than judges selected from a group of talented advocates or even elected. They don't particularly mind handling thousands of

---

[53] These functions included all judges on the colonial Supreme Court, the chairmen and junior chairmen of all *Raden van Justitie*, and the chairmen of the *Landraden* of Batavia (Jakarta), Bandung, Surabaya, and Semarang. S.1848:23 art.16(2).

[54] Rows between colonial Supreme Court judges apparently were so frequent that the expression "the gentlemen are fighting" (*tuan tuan berkelahi*) became standard. "Bisbilles in den boezem van het Hooggerechtshof," *De Indische Gids* 1 (1915): 695.

[55] It may be that other factors contributed to this fierce judicial reaction. The early twentieth-century colonial Supreme Court consisted of politically conservative judges, who made it known to the liberal Governor-General Idenburg that they declined promotion under his administration. This forced the hand of the executive in selecting a new Supreme Court chairman. It must be added that the Minister of the Colonies, Th. B. Pleyte, was primarily responsible for this appointment and that he didn't get along with Governor-General Alexander W. F. Idenburg. We cannot delve too deeply into this, but the appointment of Nederburgh may also have had something to do with a power struggle between Pleyte and Idenburgh. E. A. A. van Eekeren, "De benoeming van Mr. G. André de la Porte tot Procureur Generaal en van Mr. I. A. Nederburgh tot President van het Hooggerechtshof van Ned.Ind.," *De Indische Gids* 2 (1914): 973-77.

[56] J. H. Merryman, *The Civil Law Tradition* (Stanford: Stanford University Press, 1985), p. 37.

little "routine" cases, rather than take the responsibility for selecting and deciding cases of greater impact.[57]

In this sense we find that the system of recruitment may very well have colored the perceptions and inclinations of judges in realizing their functions. We will see later that broad sections of both government and the general public in modern Indonesia agree with this view and believe that there must be a connection between the political reticence of the Supreme Court and the system of closed recruitment that it inherited.

Recent developments in other parts of the world suggest, however, that the image of career judiciaries promoting state rather than societal loyalties may require some qualification. The "careerist" Italian judiciary in the 1990s has been able and willing to make significant inroads against political corruption and mafia activities. Similarly, in France the judiciary in the past decade has been extremely pro-active in fighting political corruption networks. The rediscovered assertiveness of these judiciaries is directly linked to a breakdown of political interference in their affairs at the hands of the government. This suggests that political interference, rather than career structures, has suppressed assertive activity by judiciaries. The traditional reluctance and political inability of the Dutch government to interfere in the affairs of the judiciary helps explain the political assertiveness of Dutch courts. They have a track record of highly controversial political decisions, and have even begun to develop a *contra legem* jurisprudence (i.e., explicitly deciding against legislative provisions). If compared with the political conservatism of courts in Great Britain, Malaysia, or in the US recently, perhaps the career judiciaries do not fare so badly.

Important structural differences remain, however, of which one deserves particular mention. This is that career judiciaries do not rely on private professional organizations for their recruitment. They do not, therefore, require or stimulate the establishment and development of societal groups that can serve as important, articulate, and powerful counterweights to state authority. Arguably, the most significant contribution of the English judicial system to other countries is that it relies upon a self-governing bar association. In its close interaction with the bench, a powerful bar creates institutional and political space, which allows judges to assert greater distance from state institutions or interests.

In countries with career judiciaries, by way of contrast, the need to establish a bar association is less evident to lawyers. Lawyers may share common professional interests and loyalties, but the need and incentive to spend time organizing is not so clear. Bar associations, as a result, traditionally are often more loosely structured. They often most significantly lack self-policing authority or the critical license monopoly. This loose structure opens opportunities for state interference, as has happened in Indonesia, which destroys lawyers' potential to form a cohesive, national non-state organization. Also, and because the nation's corps of lawyers is not a natural recruiting ground for the judiciary, lawyers and judges do not necessarily see each other as political allies. This does not deny that powerful

---

[57] Quoted in André Tunc, "'Synthese' (La cour supreme. Enquete comparative)," *Revue internationale de droit comparé* 30,1 (1978): 25. My own translation from the French.

lawyers in career judiciaries can also help judges create distance from state institutions.[58]

4. THE DIVERSE COLONIAL JUDICIAL SYSTEM

A final feature that heavily influenced the place and role of the colonial Supreme Court is to be found in the diverse nature of the colonial court system. As we have already seen, the essence of that diversity, whatever its official justifications, resided in the blunt reality that courts primarily served dominant colonial interests. While in the early twentieth century this picture became more complex, the Indonesian community remained clearly subordinate to the Dutch, with separate bureaucracies serving the needs of each community.[59] As these needs were defined as different, not to say unequal, the bureaucracies also differed. The bureaucracy serving the European community reflected European ideas, restricted though they may have been by colonial realities, but these evidently did not extend to the Indonesian community. As a result, the European community was served by a much more complex, advanced, and (in contemporary terms) legally adequate apparatus than was the Indonesian.[60] This duality, and the European branch of government that ensured the administration's ultimate control, were particularly apparent in the complex court system, which consisted of two distinct parts, one serving the European community, and the other the Indonesian. Moreover, as shall become apparent, the Indonesian branch of the judiciary was ultimately subject to European control, both judicial and administrative.[61]

---

[58] Though the loose structure of bar associations is a widely shared feature in many civil law countries, it specifically does not apply to the Netherlands, which does have a single, self-policing bar association with a license monopoly. This principally is a post-World War II feature, however, and did not strike deep roots in the colony. But it does suggest that powerful bar associations can emerge even if there is not a (exclusive) bar-based judicial recruitment system. Without the judicial recruitment prod and incentive, however, the establishment of an effective bar depends on the willingness of lawyers to recognize a shared interest and organize themselves accordingly, rather like trade unionists. As with trade unions, it also requires some degree of state support. This makes it a much more complicated process.

[59] This refers primarily to the distinction between the European administration (the so-called *Binnenlands Bestuur*) and the Indonesian administration (the so-called *Inlands Bestuur*). This duality was pierced in certain instances, so that the two domains intercepted, as in the small claims courts in urban areas (*landgerechten*) and the city councils established in the early twentieth century (*gemeente*). Nevertheless, the dual administration was in essence retained until World War II.

[60] D. S. Lev, "Colonial Law and the Genesis of the Indonesian State," p. 57.

[61] See generally J. H. Carpentier Alting, *Grondslagen der rechtsbedeeling in Nederlandsch-Indië* (The Hague: M. Nijhoff, 1926); Ph. Kleintjes, *Staatsinstellingen van Nederlandsch-Indië*, pt. 2, ch. 23; G. André de la Porte, *Recht en rechtsbedeling in Nederlandsch-Indië* (The Hague: Belinfante, 1933); Supomo, *Sistem hukum di Indonesia sebelum Perang Dunia II* (Jakarta: Pradnya Paramita, 1982). Aside from the court reviewed here, it may be added that the colonial judicial organization was further complicated by a number of specialized jurisdictions. Thus, a separate military court system had been instituted, with its own supreme judicial appeals tribunal (*Hoog Militair Gerechtshof*) (S.1922:163 jo. S.1932:75). In actual fact, this highest military court overlapped to a certain extent with the Supreme Court. Supreme Court judges served conjunctly on the highest military appeals tribunal, and the tribunal used the same courtrooms (S.1933:5). Nevertheless, by law, it was regarded as a separate institution. The court was composed of high military officers, in addition to the civil judges, while both its substantive and procedural law differed from the law applied by the colonial Supreme Court. In

In terms of judicial organization, a fundamental distinction existed in the colony between the courts which served the European community (European courts) and courts serving Indonesians (indigenous courts). The European judicial hierarchy was made up of three courts: the small claims and misdemeanors resident's courts (*Residentiegerechten*) at the bottom; the major first instance council of justice courts (*Raden van Justitie*) at mid-level; and the colonial Supreme Court (*Hooggerechtshof*) at the top. These courts had their own law of civil and criminal procedure, which closely followed the corresponding codes in the Netherlands.[62]

The Indonesian (indigenous) judicial hierarchy was diverse, but can be essentially divided into government and indigenous courts. The former were under the authority of the colonial government, as in fact every court decision had the heading "In the name of the King" (*In naam des Konings*). The lowest rungs of the hierarchy of government courts for Indonesians consisted of a variety of small-claims and misdemeanors courts (*Regentschapsgerechten, Districtsgerechten*, for example). The *landraad* was the central judicial institution, subject to a different law of procedure, previously the Herziene Indonesisch Reglement, a loosely structured code which applied in both civil and criminal proceedings.[63] The indigenous courts existed in territories which retained some form of autonomy in their administration of justice.[64] Thus, the autonomous royal districts of Yogyakarta and Surakarta on Java had retained their own administration of justice.[65] Rooted in the local communities, these courts were known under a variety of names, such as *madjelis* in Menado, *kerapatan* on Kalimantan (Borneo), and strikingly enough, *mahkamat* in the Riau districts.

Even during the colonial period, the diverse judicial organization was the subject of intense debate, which concentrated essentially on the racial distinctions underlying the dualist structure of government courts. At the beginning of the twentieth century, under the impact of the Ethical Policy, some efforts were made to abandon this system altogether and replace it with a single unified law for the colony and, by the same token, a unified court system. The strong opposition to these initiatives was generated in part by a desire to protect European vested interests, but was also unexpectedly reinforced by the "ethical" argument that indigenous

---

addition, separate courts had been instituted to hear cases on Islamic law (*Priesterraden* S.1882:152). The 1882 regulation was supposed to be supplanted by a new one in 1941, whereby the *Priesterraden* were to be renamed the *Penghoeloegerechten*, but this regulation was never effected. A separate regulation existed for Kalimantan (S.1937:638), which falls outside the scope of this brief review. At least for the islands of Java and Madura, these cases were heard in final appeal by a separate appeals institute (S.1882:152 art.7(c) jo. S.1937:116).

[62] Civil procedure: *Reglement op de Burgerlijke Rechtsvordering* (S.1847:52 as frequently amended) for the islands of Java and Madura, and *Reglement tot regeling van het rechtswezen in de gewesten buiten Java en Madoera (Rechtsreglement Buitengewesten)* (S.1927:227 as frequently amended). Criminal Procedure: *Reglement op de Strafvordering* (S.1847:40 as frequently amended).

[63] *Inlandsch Reglement* (S.1848:16). After a profound revision in 1941 (S.1941:44), it was known as the *Herzien Inlandsch Reglement*. It was renamed the *Herzien Indonesisch Reglement* after the war.

[64] Ph. Kleintjes, *Staatsinstellingen*, pp. 225-26.

[65] In fact, the Indonesian courts in the territory of the minor Yogyakarta princely house of Pakualam had been abolished at the request of the ruler in 1908.

legal systems (*adat*), norms, and values should be respected.[66] The proposal to abolish the plural legal system and judicial organization was consequently replaced by a more equivocal approach, in which the dualist system of courts was ultimately retained.[67] Thus, on the one hand a first instance petty crimes court was instituted for all population groups in 1914, the so-called *landgerecht* (S.1914:317), and a unified criminal code was enacted for all inhabitants (S.1915:732). On the other hand, drafts for a unified civil code and code of criminal procedure were struck down, and steps to unify law and judicial organization in the late colonial period were frequently counterbalanced by measures fostering plurality. Thus, after the 1920s, Indonesian courts[68] and Indonesian indigenous law (*adat*)[69] were generally strengthened.

The dualism of the court system was immediately reflected in the role of the colonial Supreme Court. With a few exceptions,[70] it served essentially as the highest appeals tribunal for Europeans, while decisions from the Indonesian courts were largely excluded from review.[71] The most notable exclusion concerned *landraad* court decisions, in which unwritten and uncodified Indonesian indigenous law (*adat*) applied. The *landraad* was the principal first instance court in Indonesian cases, with the possibility of appeal before the *Raad van Justitie*. Since there already was an appellate court, these cases were only liable for review before the Supreme Court by means of cassation. As review in cassation was limited to statute, this broad category of *landraad* decisions was for reasons of doctrine excluded from review.[72] Cassation and *adat* were regarded as "mutually exclusive."[73] Nevertheless, there was another, no less important reason for the selective jurisdiction of the colonial Supreme Court. This was the political reality

---

[66] For a brief overview of the initiatives for unification and their frustration, see P. Burns, "The Netherlands East Indies: Colonial Legal Policy and the Definitions of Law," in *Laws of South-East Asia*, vol. II, *European Laws in South-East Asia*, ed. M. B. Hooker (Singapore: Butterworth, 1988), p. 179.

[67] A. D. A. de Kat Angelino, *Staatkundig beleid en bestuurszorg in Nederlandsch-Indië*, pt. 2 (The Hague: M. Nijhoff, 1930), p. 184.

[68] D. S. Lev, "Judicial Unification in Post-colonial Indonesia," *Indonesia* 16 (October 1973): 4.

[69] Thus, judges were instructed as late as 1935 (S.1935:102) that, before deciding a case involving Indonesians, they should check whether the case had already been decided by the Indonesian village chief, and if this were not the case, refer the parties to such a chief. *Indisch Tijdschrift van het Recht* 142 (1935): 109; J. F. Holleman, "Volksrecht in Leiden," *Nieuwsbrief voor Nederlandse Rechtssociologen, Rechtsantropologen, en Rechtspsychologen* (hereafter NNR) 2 (1981): 22-23.

[70] Thus, cassation was limited in a number of ways, cf. art.126 R.O. jo. art.170 (2) R.O., as well as art.95 (3) R.O. jo. art.170 (2) R.O. (S.1837:23).

[71] Carpentier Alting, *Grondslagen der rechtsbedeeling*, p. 279.

[72] In fact, the colonial Supreme Court, acting as court of cassation, consistently refused to hear cases on uncodified *adat* law. See for instance, Hooggerechtshof (HGH, colonial Supreme Court) 21 October 1880, *Indisch Tijdschrift van het Recht* 35: 324; HGH 1 March 1883, *Indisch Weekblad van het Recht* 21,1032 (9 April 1883): 57-59; HGH 1 May 1884, *Indisch Tijdschrift van het Recht* 43: 111; HGH 7 April 1892, *Indisch Weekblad van het Recht* 30,1511 (13 June 1892): 95; HGH 18 December 1897, *Indisch Tijdschrift van het Recht* 70: 148; HGH 16 February 1899 *Indisch Weekblad van het Recht* 37,1865 (27 March 1899): 49; J. J. de Jongh, "Het nieuwe cassatie instituut van Indonesië bezien in zijn verband met de rechterlijke organisatie hier te lande," bound mimeo of dissertation, accepted in Jakarta, 1951, p. 18.

[73] Wording of the colonial Bar Association. *Handelingen der Nederlandsch-Indische Juristen Vereniging* pt. 3 (1885): 254; J. J. de Jongh, *Het nieuwe cassatie instituut*, p. 18.

of the racial diversity underlying the plural colonial court system. The general logic of the system determined that the colonial Supreme Court primarily served European rather than Indonesian interests.[74] This was perhaps most sharply apparent when, at the beginning of this century, all cases decided by the *landraden* were excluded from appeal to the colonial Supreme Court, even if they were based on statute (as criminal cases were).[75]

Inequality between the Indonesian and European courts was a pervasive feature of the colonial court structure. The material law on the European side was more complex and granted a defendant in a criminal case more rights and opportunities to defend himself than did the law applying in the Indonesian courts. The entire indigenous court structure was justified "for political reasons, or because the government lacked the budgetary means and qualified personnel to introduce government courts,"[76] which, as Daniel Lev puts it, is another way of saying that the government didn't think them important enough.[77] The indigenous courts were staffed by local officials, not by colonial staff, and thus constituted an economical construct in two ways: they siphoned off the bulk of small disputes without burdening the colonial state administration and without the colonial state having to pay for it. Moreover, the more serious cases were invariably dealt with by the government courts, the *landraden*. These remained essentially under European control until World War II,[78] while the loosely structured law applicable to

---

[74] The role of appeal from *landraad* courts was very limited by any standard. According to 1927 data, the *landraden* decided 34,000 criminal and 36,000 civil cases, as against the four hundred civil cases decided by the *Raden van Justitie*. B. Ter Haar, "De voorgenomen hervorming van het strafprocesrecht," *De Stuw* 1,19 (15 December 1930): 4. He does not provide data on criminal cases. Already the justices of the *Raden van Justitie* were apparently strained by this workload. If one includes the original jurisdiction in these *Raden van Justitie* figures (i.e., as a first instance court for Europeans), it must be concluded that, at least by the early twentieth century, barely a case from the *landraden* was appealed.

[75] S.1901:124. See also Advice Dutch colonial Bar Association 1885, *Handelingen der Nederlandsch-Indische Juristen Vereniging* pt. 3 (1885): 268. The racial tones underlying the selective jurisdiction of the colonial Supreme Court was further emphasized by the exclusion of another broad category of cases that intimately affected the Indonesian community. These were the decisions of the Islamic courts (*Priesterraden*). Decisions from these courts were subjected to a separate appeals tribunal, the *Mahkamah Islam Tinggi*, and from there directly to the Governor-General. There was no appeal to the colonial Supreme Court. Daniel S. Lev, *Islamic Courts in Indonesia* (Berkeley: University of California Press, 1972), p. 30.

[76] Kleintjes, *Staatsinstellingen*, pp. 225-26.

[77] D. S. Lev, "Colonial Law and the Genesis of the Indonesian State," p. 58.

[78] As pointed out by D. S. Lev, ibid., p. 60, note 4, Indonesians were in the minority as regards *landraad* court chairmen: 28 Indonesians as against 47 Dutchmen (1939 figures). Nevertheless, it is worth pointing out that Indonesians were in the majority if one includes all other judges in these courts: Indonesian 60, Dutchmen 56, and Chinese 2. See *Regeeringsalmanak voor Nederlandsch-Indië 1942* (Batavia: Landsdrukkerij, 1942). This indicates that the European-Indonesian dichotomy was of some complexity, as indeed a daughter of an eminent Indonesian colonial judge (herself prominent in the New Order administration) recounts that, to her recollection, the colonial judiciary was perhaps a special mix in which race barriers were more easily breached than in any other profession:

"The colonial judiciary was marked by a great esprit de corps, in which it stood in notable contrast to other government services or to the advocacy, for that matter. Indonesians were fully integrated in the organization, and I remember that as children we often spent the night at the houses of our friends, who were children of the Dutch colleagues of my father. One of the Dutch judges wanted to adopt a sister of mine because they were without children. Why, when I

Indonesians allowed for a much more expedient settlement of cases than in the European courts. Thus, the *landraad* courts easily settled 36,000 civil cases in 1927 (in addition to 34,000 criminal cases), whereas the Raden van Justitie barely managed four hundred civil cases that same year.[79] This difference was caused by the comparative legal complexity of the European cases and indicated systemic inequality.

Perhaps the strongest indication of this inequality was precisely in the sphere of separation of functions for the Indonesian courts, particularly the *landraden*. The difficulties in effecting the separation of powers in these courts revealed the very essence of the colonial condition of political and economic inequality, which relied on strong government, not strong courts. The principle of separation of powers, which resulted in an independent judiciary, was put into effect for the European community, but never extended to Indonesian courts in a general fashion. Indeed, for a long time, the colonial government took the view that if such a separation were applied to Indonesians, it would divide and hence weaken colonial authority. As a result, the 1803 Nederburgh Report was purposely limited in application to the European courts, while from Daendels onwards the district officer who oversaw Indonesians' affairs headed *all* functions of government, serving as local legislator, local executive, and local judge conjunctly,[80] keeping the *landraad* under the firm control of the colonial district officers. Through much of the nineteenth century, Indonesian courts were, therefore, under direct executive control.

This situation became particularly apparent when in 1839 a bill was presented to Parliament that proposed introducing functional specialization down the line, notably by transferring the judicial authority of colonial administrators in the *landraad* courts to professional judges. The colonial community reacted fiercely. The conservative Minister of the Colonies, J. Chr. Baud, voiced its position with his habitual directness. In his view, professional judges would inevitably manifest themselves as protectors of the "common man," and government authority would thereby be undermined. According to him, it was imperative to retain the prevailing system in which the colonial district officer conjunctly served as administrator-judge. Admittedly, his judicial decisions could be appealed to the colonial Supreme Court, but, in Baud's view, such a remote institution did not remind Indonesians of the "existence of a judicial power of government independent of the Governor-General and superior to the *resident*,"[81] to the same degree that separate and independent local *landraden* would be liable to do. Colonial policy relied on the mandatory cultivation of crops, argued Baud, and recourse to separate and independent courts would frustrate its implementation. In the utilitarian colonial perspective of the early nineteenth century, an independent administration of justice should only be extended to Indonesians insofar as the cultivation of lucrative crops such as coffee, sugar, and indigo permitted.[82]

---

came to study in Holland after independence, I stayed with my father's colleagues there." Personal communication, August 7, 1994.

[79] B. Ter Haar, "De voorgenomen hervorming van het strafprocesrecht," p. 4.

[80] M. C. Piepers, *Macht tegen recht. De vervolging der Justitie in Nederlandsch-Indië* (Batavia: Van Dorp, 1884), p. 353. H. W. van den Doel, *De stille macht. Het Europese Binnenlands Bestuur op Java en Madoera 1808-1942* (Amsterdam: Bert Bakker, 1994), pp. 72-73.

[81] de Kat Angelino, *Staatkundig beleid en bestuurszorg*, Tweede deel, p. 150.

[82] M. C. Piepers, "Iets over de rechterlijke macht in het algemeen," p. 81.

His views prevailed, and even the 1847 and 1854 legislation envisaged true separation of functions only for the judiciary in the European domain: the colonial Supreme Court, the *Raden van Justitie*, and the circuit courts (which would soon be suspended). The administration of justice for Indonesians remained unaffected and continued to be managed by the colonial administration. Administrative officers were little concerned with their judicial functions, and, at least in the eyes of the colony's judicial elite, judging often had little to do with justice—a view probably shared by Indonesian litigants. "The guilty go free, and the innocent are punished," the Attorney General recorded, speaking about conditions in the *landraden* in 1864.[83] Even members of the colonial Supreme Court felt that the administration of justice for Indonesians was in such a poor condition that the Court publicly exposed decisions where it felt colonial administrative officers violated basic legal principles.[84]

Separation of functions for Indonesian courts, therefore, was never realized with the same natural completeness as had happened with the European courts. Only gradually did a series of incidental regulations transfer judicial functions from European or Indonesian administrative officers to the judiciary. In 1869, the first and most important step was taken, aimed at replacing the administrative district officers at the *landraad* courts with professional judges. It was followed by a smattering of regulations with comparable aim or effect. Thus, in 1910 the Indonesian administrative elite, the *regenten*, were no longer allowed to decide cases without prior legislative mandate, and in 1914 the adjudication of small claims and misdeameanors was transferred from the administration to the judiciary.[85]

Separation of administrative and judicial functions for the Indonesian courts was indeed a problematic affair. The 1869 law had been decided by the liberal Minister of the Colonies E. De Waal in the face of ardent opposition from both the colonial administration and society, and it remained wildly unpopular amongst colonial administrative officers. To them, appointment of professional judges was little less than an outright attack on their own power and prerogatives. Their attitude was not merely a matter of professional jealousy at having lost their erstwhile power. Rather, the appointment of independent judges for Indonesians challenged the very basis of the colonial administration that had existed since VOC (Vereenigde Oost-Indische Compagnie, Dutch East Indies Company) times, namely the monopoly of civil authority. Particularly with regard to the administration of justice over Indonesians, the corps of colonial administrators was deeply imbued with the idea that they were the ones who held ultimate responsibility for all aspects of government in their districts, that *landraden* were rightfully theirs to control, and that the establishment of separate and independent judges formally weakened colonial authority as a whole. As they could not reverse the situation imposed by the Dutch motherland, the colonial

---

[83] H. W. van den Doel, *De stille macht*, p. 73.

[84] The colonial Supreme Court did this by Circular Letter, on which see below, Chapter 7. See for instance, Circular Letters colonial Supreme Court no.2 dated 10 December 1861; no.1 dated 18 February 1863; no.1 dated 27 February 1861, in *Het Regt in Nederlandsch-Indië* part XXI, p. 76, and part XIX, p. 155.

[85] C. van Vollenhoven, "Scheiding van macht in het regeeren overzee," *Koloniaal Tijdschrift* 18 (1929).

administrators turned upon the judges, often with tacit approval of their superiors, sometimes including even the Governor-General. Friction between them and the *landraad* judges as a result became endemic and continued well into the twentieth century.[86]

It must be noted, moreover, that the separation of functions was never completed for the Indonesian courts. There were numerous gaps in the skeletal legislative framework through which the colonial administration could still exert its influence. For a start, the progressive devolution of judicial power from the administration to the judiciary envisioned in the 1869 law was never fully realized. Even if the judicial function of administrative officers was finally abolished in the colonial heartland of Java in 1901 (S.1901:15), it persisted in the Outer Islands, where until the Second World War a number of *landraad* courts continued to be chaired by administrative officers rather than professional judges. Furthermore, the colonial legislature curtailed some of the aims of the 1869 law by providing in the 1901 regulation that, even on Java, administrative officers might serve on courts "if no judicial personnel can be found." In addition, administrative officers retained almost total control of the small claims and misdemeanors courts (*residentie-gerechten*) throughout the Outer Islands. Finally, none of the legislative provisions concerning functional specialization mentioned above applied to those judicial functions which continued to be handled by Indonesians (*inheemse rechtspraak*). Indigenous courts as a result remained under the complete control of the administration throughout the colonial period.

5. CONCLUSION

This chapter gives an insight into the colonial courts that set the course for the postindependence Supreme Court. We have found that the Indonesian Republic inherited a Court that operated within a number of parameters that determined and indeed often restricted its place and role. The first parameter is that the constitutional system, transplanted from the European continent, called for separation of powers rather than a balance of government powers. This imposed dogmatic restrictions on the political role of the Supreme Court, most clearly apparent perhaps in the absence of any right of judicial (constitutional) review. The second is that while the colonial Supreme Court became a respected and autonomous third branch of government, particularly during the twentieth century, the colonial state by its very nature was inclined to permit the executive to retain extensive prerogatives beyond judicial control. The third parameter is that the civil law system brought with it a system of closed judicial recruitment, which arguably led to a judiciary that tended to sympathize with the state rather than society. The fourth parameter is that the colonial Supreme Court served essentially as an appeals court to the European community. Although it exercised supervisory powers over courts for Indonesians, it had hardly any appellate functions in that domain, with the result that its roots within the Indonesian

---

[86] A. J. Immink, *De regterlijke organisatie van Nederlandsch-Indië*; M. C. Piepers, *Macht tegen recht*; C. Bosscher, "Iets over de tegenwoordige afhankelijkheid van de Nederlandsch-Indische rechterlijke ambtenaren," *De Indische Gids* 2,2B (1880): 1039; van Vollenhoven, "Scheiding van macht," p. 229.

community were weak. Moreover, until independence many Indonesians remained subject to courts that were still partly under direct administrative control.

Given this situation, it becomes clear that separate and independent courts were a specifically Western colonial fixture essentially reserved for the European elite. They were far removed from Indonesian society, as indeed the colonial Supreme Court did not serve that community at all and from the Indonesian perspective might as well have been on a different planet. In addition, we have seen that, for all its separateness and autonomy, the colonial judiciary, including the Supreme Court, operated in an environment in which, for reasons having to do with constitutional doctrine, colonial interest, and judicial outlook favored executive over and above judicial power.

The old Supreme Court building dating back to colonial times
(reprinted with permission, *TEMPO*/Robin Ong, 1998)

CHAPTER TWO

PARLIAMENTARY SYSTEM AND GUIDED DEMOCRACY (1945–1965): THE POLITICAL MOBILIZATION OF THE JUDICIARY

In the late colonial state, the place and role of courts was respected and secure, however restricted it may have been in political terms, but after independence this role began to be eroded. As the political scene became more unstable, courts, with the Supreme Court (Mahkamah Agung) as their symbol, were increasingly challenged, and their separate and independent position became subject to attack. Supreme Court history, as a result, is principally the history of a political struggle to retain (and increasingly to regain) the Court's autonomy from political interference. This struggle continues to the present day.

It is a brutal historical fact that, within twenty years of Indonesian independence, the nation's judiciary officially ceased to exist as a separate and independent function of government. In retrospect, it is tempting to view this as a historical inevitability. In reality, it was a complex affair. A number of factors contributed to the decline of the judiciary and its lasting influence on Indonesian political structure. Yet throughout this process, alternative options were always available. In Indonesia, the judiciary was destroyed not in a fit of absent-mindedness, but through a deliberate process in which the judiciary played its own part. Several phases can be distinguished in these first twenty years.

The first phase, the revolutionary period (1945-1949), was important for the judiciary in two respects. First, prominent judges during those years revealed themselves to be lukewarm to the revolution; many of them defected to the Dutch. Their stance diminished their political stock after the transfer of sovereignty and placed them at a disadvantage in the ensuing political struggle. In addition, during the revolutionary period judges came to be exposed to considerable pressures in exercising their functions. In the turmoil of the revolution, the generally poorly disciplined armed forces of the fledgling Republic found it hard to resist interfering in the administration of justice. They felt that to ensure the survival of the Republic, everything had to be their business, including the courts. In addition, the government itself exerted pressure on the Supreme Court in the few cases that were brought before the court during the revolution. It was a clear early warning sign for the judiciary that its place and role might be subject to change.

The second phase runs from the transfer of sovereignty until the end of Parliamentary Democracy (1949-1959). During this period, the judiciary, and the Supreme Court in particular, came to be exposed to a variety of public humiliations at the hands of Indonesian state authorities. Initially these were the results of innocent oversights, but they soon intensified, as the state became engaged in a deliberate and systematic erosion of judicial status, with the aim of lowering public regard for judicial office. The comparative salary ranking of judges became the focal point of this struggle concerning status.

This struggle accelerated the erosion of the status of the judiciary during the third phase, Guided Democracy (1959-1965). This diminishment in status was an important factor that permitted more direct interference in the substance of court operations. In this period of revolutionary politics, judges lost not merely their status, but also their power and autonomy from executive interference. This loss shaped their political agenda, and the judicial agenda has been preoccupied with fundamental issues of status, power, and autonomy ever since.

The emerging political struggle transformed the Indonesian judiciary from an essentially apolitical, unorganized group of professionals into an organized group with a clear political platform. At the outset, the Indonesian judiciary was poorly equipped to deal with political challenges. Indonesian judges had been conditioned by the civil law system to remain out of politics, so at independence they were neither inclined nor oriented by training or professional background to become politically engaged. Moreover, they were disorganized. The status struggles in the 1950s changed this situation, welding the atomized district and appeal court judges into a Judges' Association (IKAHI, Ikatan Hakim Indonesia) with a clear political focus. The Association gave the judges a political agenda and political momentum that proved important for the future. In addition, the struggle shaped the political scene and defined the principal political actors and their roles. As shall become apparent, the Supreme Court did not join the Judges' Association, but remained an independent actor, whereas the Department of Justice came to identify ever more closely with government interests. Finally, we will find that some parties were excluded from the debates.

1. REVOLUTIONARY CHALLENGES (1945-1950)

Even before independence was fully secured, it had become clear that the courts' relationship with the political leadership of the country would be a turbulent one. The reason for this troubled relationship may have been partly rooted in historical tensions between them. In colonial times, Indonesian judges acted as dutiful servants of the colonial state and found themselves in outright opposition to the independence movement; indeed, in the courtroom judges and political activists literally confronted each other face to face.[1] As the political conflict deepened and became harsher in the 1930s and early 1940s,[2] not a single

---

[1] In 1942, Indonesian judges were in the majority in the *landraad* jurisdiction that tried Indonesian political cases in first instance (see previous chapter). Of the sixty Indonesian judges in 1942, twenty-three were university law graduates, the others being graduates of vernacular legal studies for Indonesians, the so-called *law-school* (*rechtsschool*). This gave them a solid education, but restricted their careers to the first instance *landraad* functions.

[2] Thus, when the Governor-General began to use his extraordinary executive prerogative, the controversial *exorbitante rechten*, to arrest and exile Indonesian political leaders without trial, no Indonesian judge protested, not even such senior judges as Kusumah Atmadja, who had objected to those rights in his 1922 dissertation. In that thesis, he suggested that the extraordinary rights of the Governor-General should be abolished on the grounds of their being unfettered and hence "despotic." Koesoemah Atmadja, *De Mohammedaansche vrome stichtingen in Indië* (The Hague: Adi Poestaka, 1922), thesis VI. In fact, Kusumah Atmadja's proposal was neither particularly innovative nor daring, as the colonial executive prerogative had already

Indonesian judge in the colonial judiciary resigned. And while there may have been occasional attempts at compromise, these were feeble and never fundamentally altered the political reality that the Indonesian judges were firmly in the colonial camp.[3] Their loyalty is most strikingly illustrated perhaps by the fact that the future Supreme Court chairman, Kusumah Atmadja, sent revolutionaries to prison for their support of future President Sukarno. These were "extreme nationalists," Kusumah Atmadja held, adding . . .

> . . . that it is very possible to bring about an "Indonesia Merdeka" in a legal manner which by itself does not imply disturbance of public order or an overthrow of governmental authority in the Netherlands and the Netherlands-Indies; that to bring about "Indonesia Merdeka" will admittedly be accompanied with changes of government, which need not however follow violent or illegal venues; that an independent "Indonesia" is very well imaginable with the same state organization as the English Dominions for example or even less independent legal communities in the Dutch Empire . . .[4]

Decisions such as these reflected the general attitude favoring compromise among Indonesian judges in the colonial judiciary, and quite obviously fueled the "strong antipathy" for the judiciary within the revolutionary movement, whose supporters were imprisoned by fellow Indonesians.[5]

The Japanese administration temporarily bridged this political gap by bringing both sides together.[6] In fact, during this period some judges did begin to

---

been challenged as indefensible eight years before. In 1917, forty Indonesian and Dutch associations in the colony issued a common declaration demanding that the rights be abolished. In 1919, two motions to the same effect were advanced in the Dutch Parliament but rejected, while in 1925 a similar amendment was rejected during the debates on the *Indische Staatsregeling*. In 1920, Hassan Djajadiningrat, as a member of the 1918 commission for constitutional reform (*Commissie tot Herziening van de Staatsinrichting van Nederlandsch-Indië*), issued a minority statement pleading, among other things, for the abolition of those rights. See generally for these developments, D. J. Jongeneel, "Verbanning en internering in Nederlandsch-Indië," *Koloniaal Tijdschrift* 20,2 (1931): 113-16. Against this background, Kusumah Atmadja seems to have been rather mild in his condemnation of the government prerogative.

[3] In one such case, a revolutionary was accused of declaring in public that "Queen Wilhelmina will be thrown out and cease to be Queen, but will cook my rice when I tell her and Juliana will become my concubine." The judge tried to avoid a conviction by questioning whether the statement had been made in private or public and citing extensive references to scholarly literature. His reasoning was not upheld, and the decision was overturned on appeal by the (Dutch-controlled) *Raad van Justitie*. See Landraad Indramajoe 5 June 1933, no.124/1933, *Indisch Tijdschrift van het Recht* 144 (1936): 616; and *Raad van Justitie* Batavia 17 June 1933, *Indisch Tijdschrift van het Recht* 144 (1936): 616.

[4] Landraad Batavia 21 Juli 1934, *Indisch Tijdschrift van het Recht* 144 (1936): 624.

[5] The wording is from Benedict Anderson's description of the relationship between the Indonesian political leaders and the traditional Javanese elite, which had been coopted by the colonial administration, the *pangreh pradja*. Benedict R. O'G. Anderson, *Java in a Time of Revolution* (Ithaca: Cornell University Press, 1972), p. 66. Note that almost all the senior Indonesian judges mentioned in the first footnote of this chapter belonged to this traditional elite: of the twenty-three judges who graduated from university, only two did not have the elite titles *Raden* or *Raden Mas*, namely Oerip Kartodirdjo and Zainal Abidin.

[6] With a few notable exceptions, such as Sjahrir, Amir Sjarifoedin, and Tan Malaka, the Indonesian political leadership were coopted by the Japanese, and barely any of the Indonesian

shift political ground,[7] but, as the revolution would later reveal, this by no means indicated a broad realignment of the judiciary or the political leadership.

The 1945 Constitution, enacted as Indonesian political leaders declared independence on August 17, 1945, was a loosely structured document. Although it provided for state institutions, their physical embodiment and roles remained to be fleshed out in practice.[8]

Inevitably, during the revolutionary struggle, the role of the law and of legal institutions was ambivalent. On the one hand, in the Republic's all-out physical struggle for survival, the law occupied only a marginal position. Thus, the first Supreme Court chairman was appointed at the time of the declaration of independence, but other Supreme Court judges were only appointed about a year later, as some sort of afterthought.[9] In fact, during the early years of intense political and military struggles, it is unclear what Supreme Court chairman Kusumah Atmadja actually did, or could do, other than serve on a number of committees.[10] On the other hand, the law and its institutions did strengthen the

---

judges resigned when the Japanese arrived. With only two exceptions, the entire Indonesian judicial elite of twenty-three law graduates was listed in a 1944 Japanese list of the Indonesian elite on Java. *Orang Indonesia jang terkemoeka di Djawa* (Jakarta: Gunseikanbu, 2604/1944]), p. 136. The two exceptions are judges Dzul Karnin and Achmed, who were not listed for the simple reason that they served on Sumatra and Celebes (Sulawesi). A 1946 Dutch record of internees from the judiciary lists Soumokil as sole Indonesian member (located in Bangkok in 1945), but he was a court clerk (*griffier*) to the Surabaya *Raad van Justitie* before the war, not a judge (Algemeen Rijksarchief [ARA]-II, The Hague, Algemene Secretarie no.4631).

[7] The clearest example of a person who experienced such a shift is Kusumah Atmadja. Although not listed as a participant in important Indonesian political committees at the beginning of the war, such as the Panitia Adat dan Tatanegara Dahulu or the Dewan Sanyo, his name suddenly crops up when things got serious in 1944–1945. There he appears alongside nationalist leaders such as Sukarno and Hatta and fellow reborn revolutionaries, such as Supomo in the BPKI (Badan Persiapan Kemerdekaan Indonesia) committee, which prepared for independence. Algemeen Rijksarchief [ARA]-II, The Hague, Algemene Secretarie no.4631, p. 20. The proceedings of this committee were largely kept secret, and his role is unclear. The BPKI was dissolved on June 1, 1945. Kusumah Atmadja's name also appears on a list of prominent Indonesians drawn up under the direction of Hatta, which included two thousand names and constituted the basis of the 1944 Japanese list of prominent Indonesian often referred to above. See *Orang Indonesia jang terkemoeka di Djawa*, p. 322. Anderson, *Java in a Time of Revolution*, pp. 10-11 and 18 on the history and the names of these committees. See also Algemeen Rijksarchief [ARA]-II, The Hague, Algemene Secretarie no.4631, p. 20. Finally, during the Japanese administration, together with Djoeanda and M. Enokh, Kusumah Atmadja created a political party in West Java supportive of the Republican cause: the Pagajoeban Pasoendan (Sundanese Association). It is not clear precisely when this party was established, but it seems to have been well under way after the war. Secret Police Report Batavia dated 30 December 1947 in P. J. Drooglever and M. J. B. Schouten, *Officiële bescheiden betreffende de Nederlands-Indonesische betrekkingen 1945-1950* (The Hague: M. Nijhoff, 1982) (1985), pt. XII, pp. 347-48 §181.

[8] For the judiciary, because of the armed conflict with the Dutch, there was little movement. The Supreme Court was established with the ephemeral Law no.7/1947, with rules of procedure being enacted the next year. Neither law could be properly effected because of the armed conflict. S. Mertokusumo, *Sedjarah peradilan dan perundang-undangan di Indonesia sedjak 1942 dan apakah kemanfaatnja bagi kita bangsa Indonesia* (Bandung: Kalimaju, 1971), p. 31.

[9] In late 1946, Noto Soebagio was appointed Supreme Court vice-chairman and Tirtaamidjaja Supreme Court judge. Government Decision no.9/S.D. (1946), *Berita Repoeblik Indonesia*, thn.II, no.15-16 dated 1 July 1946, pp. 145-46.

[10] In February 1946, prominent judges Kusumah Atmadja, Noto Soebagio, Satochid Kartanegara, Tirtaamadja, and Zainal Abidin were appointed to the commission for the drafting of new laws. Decision of the Minister of Justice dated 4 February 1946 no.T.73, *Berita*

fledgling Indonesian Republic's claims to legitimacy and independence. Indonesian political leaders were able to translate raw political power and action into institutions, however ephemeral, and this gave the struggle endurance and legitimacy to the outside world, in the end transforming the revolutionary movement into a Republic.[11] State institutions and the respect bestowed upon them were highly symbolic and no less real or important in political terms than the armed struggle because they embodied the legitimacy of Republican claims to authority.[12] Thus, while the law was under evident pressure, the more so as the war turned against the Indonesians, its symbolic importance still ensured that Republican authorities would try to strengthen it. As a result, the Indonesian judicial elite that had served under colonial rule was appointed to the senior judicial functions under the new Republic, as well as to a variety of pivotal legal and political committees.[13]

Nevertheless, as the conflict with the Dutch sharpened, the judges' political loyalty to the Republic began to waver. Its declining political fortunes and the

---

Repoeblik Indonesia, thn.II, no.7 dated 15 February 1946, pp. 58-59. Others soon to become prominent are listed as well, such as the later Minister of Justice Sahardjo. In April, Noto Soebagio was appointed as vice-chairman of the commission; see Decision of the Minister of Justice no.T 325 dated 2 April 1946, *Berita Repoeblik Indonesia,* thn.II, no.15-16 dated 1 July 1946, p. 147. In April 1946, Noto Soebagio is appointed to the distinctly political Republican advisory council for deliberations with the Dutch. *Berita Repoeblik Indonesia,* thn.II, no.25 dated 16 and 30 November 1946, p. 310.

[11] Much of the same logic underlies the one-sided composition of the PPKI (Panitia Persiapan Kemerdekaan Indonesia, Committee for the Preparation of Indonesian Independence) by the Japanese, as pointed out in B. Anderson, *Java in a Time of Revolution,* p. 65.

[12] Because of this, the 1946 theft of Kusumah Atmadja's car by Dutch troops evolved into a political incident. See Memorandum of Hatta to Brig. General King dated 8 October 1945, in *Officiële bescheiden betreffende de Nederlands-Indonesische betrekkingen 1945-1950,* pt. I, ed. S. L. van der Wal (The Hague: M. Nijhoff, 1971), p. 279, item 155. The fact that his child developed medical problems as a result of the economic blockade imposed by the Dutch was worthy of mention. See George McT. Kahin, *Nationalism and Revolution in Indonesia* (Ithaca: Cornell University Press, 1970), p. 253. This is the sole reference to Kusumah Atmadja in Kahin's authoritative account of the revolution, indicating the marginal importance of the judiciary in the revolutionary movement.

[13] By Presidential Decree dated 25 September 1945 all civil servants serving in the Japanese administration were coopted by the Republic. Koesnodiprodjo, *Himpunan Undang2, Peraturan2, Penetapan2 Pemerintah Republic Indonesia 1946-1949* (Semarang: Van Dorp, n.d.) (1951), p. 44. By way of example, Gondokoesoemo, Wirjono Koesoemo, and Soerjotjokro were appointed to the Semarang court of appeal, Koesnoen Tjitrowardhojo to the Surabaya court of appeal, Tirtaamidjaja and Zainal Abidin to the Jakarta court of appeal, and Tirtawinata to the Bogor first instance court. See for instance *Berita Repoeblik Indonesia,* thn.II, no.9 dated 15 March 1946, p. 90 and thn.II, no.17 dated 15 July 1946, p. 179.

pressures of the Dutch-imposed economic blockade[14] undermined the judges' resistance to overtures from the Netherlands' government.[15]

The judges' faltering commitment to the Republican cause was, ironically, fueled by Republican suspicions of their political loyalty. These suspicions translated into increasingly frequent political interference in the course of justice, when Republican authorities, and particularly the hard-to-control army of youngsters, the *Pemuda*, began to instruct judges on how cases should be decided and what punishment should be imposed. Judges were forced to free suspects on political grounds.[16] In the wording of one Indonesian judge, the entire judiciary was being "terrorized."[17]

Politically the most serious incident, and a bad omen for the future, occurred when the Supreme Court decided what was perhaps its first case, and one of great

---

[14] The Supreme Court chairman, Kusumah Atmadja, in 1949 was described as "dirt-poor" and surviving only "by selling off his own possessions." Kort Verslag De Regt dated 5 January 1949, ARA-II, Algemene Secretarie no.4659. The salary of the Supreme Court chairman started out at Rp.650 and was raised to Rp.700 in 1947 (with Rp.100 representation costs). Government Decree no.1/O.P., *Berita Repoeblik Indonesia,* thn.I, no.1 dated 17 November 1945; Peraturan Presiden no.1/1947 in Koesnodiprodjo, *Himpunan Undang2 1947* (Jakarta: S. K. Seno, 1951), pp. 307-308. Nevertheless, in 1945 rice cost Rp.10 a pound, but in July 1948 it was Rp.900. ARA-II, Algemene Secretarie no.2563.

[15] The Dutch were eager to re-enlist Indonesian judges for a number of reasons, not least the political symbolism that this invoked. They wanted to show the world that they had a working administration and were in control. Public relations were better served by establishing a functioning court system than by having an army running about. Enlisting Indonesian judges was also important for the Dutch simply because they lacked sufficient numbers of their own trained personnel. G. C. Zijlmans, *Eindstrijd en ondergang van de Indische bestuursdienst. Het corps Binnenlands Bestuur op Java 1945-1950* (Amsterdam: De Bataafsche Leeuw, 1985), pp. 41-42. In the Wizard-of-Id-wording of Military Commander for Java Schilling: "Will there be enough judges to adjudicate all suspects by Christian-human standards? Will not many persons escape the capital punishment they deserve?" van der Wal, ed., *Officiële bescheiden*, pt. 2, p. 164 §87. In addition, the changing political conditions made it more difficult for Dutch judges to decide Indonesian cases. In the courtroom, the ratio of Dutch judges facing Indonesian suspects could all too easily be translated as representing a political conflict in itself, as pointed out by the Indonesian top administrator on the Dutch side, Widjojoatmodjo: "To the outside observer, the newspaper reports of the *Raad van Justitie* session in Makassar in the Nadjamoeddin case, create the impression, however unintended, that an Indonesian is adjudicated by a Dutch court. Anti-Dutch groups use this to propagate the idea that colonialism still flourishes with glory in Makassar and that in fact the *Negara Indonesia Timoer* has given Indonesians nothing in terms of autonomy." He continued by strongly recommending the appointment of Indonesians to senior judicial functions. Letter of Widjojoatmodjo to Van Mook dated 23 October 1948, ARA-II, Algemene Secretarie no.3277. (Marginal notes to the letter, presumably from Van Mook, indicate approval of this suggestion.) Switching sides was also facilitated by a provision that would allow Indonesian judges to excuse themselves from deciding politically sensitive cases. Such cases would be decided by special circuit judges (*bijzondere rechters*). Voorlopig Rechtsreglement art.5 dated 19 July 1947, *Javase Courant* no.64, 15 August 1947. It was a measure directed at freeing the judges from fears of reprisal. In addition, it created the impression that switching sides was a mere formality, rather than the fundamental political choice it really was.

[16] Letter of Van Mook to Jonkman dated 14 August 1947, in Drooglever and Schouten, *Officiële bescheiden* (1982), p. 388, §262.

[17] ARA-II, Algemene Secretarie no.2803 letter of Van der Plas to Van Mook reporting a conversation he had with a thoroughly disaffected Oerip Kartodirdjo. Kartodirdjo may have had reason to make the situation out worse than it actually was, but later reports confirm the frequent harassment of judges by *Pemuda*.

political importance.[18] This was the so-called *Sudarsono case*, which arose out of an attempted coup d'état, the 1946 kidnapping of Prime Minister Sjahrir by disaffected army elements, supported by members of the political establishment (such as Mohammad Yamin). The attempt was foiled, and the leaders were brought to trial. Some of the defendants were closely linked to President Sukarno, and there were allegations that Sukarno brought pressure to bear on the Supreme Court to be lenient. In any event, Supreme Court chairman Kusumah Atmadja faced down the challenge, threatening to resign unless Sukarno backed off. At three points in the decision Kusumah Atmadja felt the need to emphasize forcefully that the Supreme Court was an independent institution that meant to remain free from executive interference.[19] Nevertheless, as Daniel Lev has pointed out, the incident could not fail to impress upon the judges that the Supreme Court's place in the new emerging state was not as secure as before. The incident did little to bolster the confidence of judges in the future course of events.[20]

As a result, in a movement that started as a trickle in 1946 and by the next year had become a flood, nearly all of the judiciary switched allegiance from the Republic to the Dutch.[21] The political fault lines ran right into the heart of the judicial establishment, as many of the most senior judges defected, including those who had served on important Republican political committees. Rubbing salt in the wound, the Dutch consistently appointed the Indonesian judges to senior positions in their own administration.[22] Thus, of the twenty-three senior Indonesian judges, only nine were still on the Republican side in 1948.[23] These nine were grouped around Kusumah Atmadja on the Supreme Court and constituted the hard core of resistance within the judiciary against Dutch pressures. By April 1949, however, some of these judges were so disillusioned with the Republic that there was talk they might shift their allegiance.[24] Even though Kusumah Atmadja was the one

---

[18] While it is generally regarded as the first case ever to have been decided by the Supreme Court, its registration number says 3, suggesting that two cases preceded it.

[19] *Sidang Mahkamah Tentara Agung dalam pemeriksaan Sudarsono c.s.* (stenographic account), p. 11 & p. 15 (twice); Daniel S. Lev archives, (hereafter *DSL*) 19 July 1967. (These are the personal interview notes of Daniel S. Lev; copies will be deposited in the University of Washington library [Seattle, WA], the Cornell University Kroch Collection [Ithaca, NY], and Pusat Studi Hukum dan Kebijakan [PSHK] in Jakarta.)

[20] D. S. Lev, "The Supreme Court in Indonesia: Comments on Evolution, Procedure and Influence," (typescript, 1967), p. 4.

[21] The secretary-general of the Department of Justice, Besar Mertokusumo, would relate later that, as a result of the economic blockade, living conditions had deteriorated to the point that he thought he could not stop the rush and forbid judges from looking after their families first. Interview, Daniel S. Lev, Fall 1992.

[22] Thus, in February 1947 Oerip Kartodirdjo was appointed to the colonial Supreme Court, and two years later was made chief public prosecutor. *Javase Courant*, no.14 Dinsdag 18 February 1947. Zainal Abidin ended up as a senior public prosecutor with the Dutch. ARA-II, Algemene Secretarie no.4643. Noto Soebagio and Koesnoen Tjitrowardhojo became judges on the colonial Supreme Court, Noto Soebagio having the doubtful distinction of being the only judge to have served on the Japanese, Indonesian, and Dutch Supreme Courts.

[23] Namely, Kusumah Atmadja, Wirjono Prodjodikoro, Wirjono Koesoemo, Soekardono, Satochid Kartanegara, Soerjotjokro, Tirtaamidjaja Gondokoesoemo, and Aroeman. Kort Verslag De Regt ARA-II, Algemene Secretarie no.4659 and Kan ARA-II, Algemene Secretarie no.3294.

[24] Supreme Court judge Soekardono reported to the Dutch that "after the completion of the political talks in Batavia, all judges will probably apply for duty again with the Dutch. . . ." Biegman to Chief Public Prosecutor dated 29 April 1949, ARA-II, Algemene Secretarie no.4659.

judge who seems to have come out of the revolution with his pro-Republican record unblemished, the reality may have been more complicated, as indeed there are indications that the *Pemuda* did not trust him. Dutch officials who interviewed him remarked on his apparent nervousness:

> . . . it may be noted that during my conversation with Mr. Kusumah Atmadja—and Mr. Vervloet told me the same later—that he never once sat quiet on his chair, but constantly peered outside as if he thought himself spied upon. He told me that every time we Dutchmen had come to visit him, *Pemuda* had dropped in to query him on the aim of our visit . . . [25]

Although courted by the Dutch, and perhaps tempted to change over, these judges remained firm until the end.[26]

Whereas the revolution in some ways reinforced the credentials of the Supreme Court, notably those of its chairman Kusumah Atmadja, the period in general was disastrous for the judiciary. The secretary-general of the Department of Justice, Besar Mertokusumo, later acknowledged that had he anticipated the hugely negative effect of so many judicial defections on the post-revolutionary standing of the judiciary, he would never have been so lenient in permitting them.[27] The judiciary was a small, clearly identifiable group, and the fact that many of its members had defected marred the image of the entire profession. The fact, moreover, that judges had left prestigious posts in the Republic in exchange for equally senior functions under the Dutch made their defections look all the more like outright treason. Not merely had they jumped ship when the going got tough, but they had denied the Republic the legitimacy it needed to survive and had instead provided the enemy with the legitimacy it so sorely lacked. In his historic account of the revolution, the Republican army chief of staff, General A. H. Nasution, singles out some of these turn-coat judges with barely concealed bitterness and contempt, noting that they "had to be tolerated as equals" by the Republican

---

This was Kusumah Atmadja's attitude also. Kort Verslag De Regt dated 5 January 1949, ARA-II, Algemene Secretarie no.4659.

[25] Dienstrapport 1B Uyt den Bogaard dated 18 January 1949 ARA-II, Algemene Secretarie no.3294.

[26] The Republican prosecutor general Tirtawinata was the sole member of the Court to have gone into hiding. Memo J. B. Kan no.346/49 dated 19 January 1949 ARA-II, Algemene Secretarie no.3294. Kusumah Atmadja in particular was interviewed by the Dutch, in part because he was the most senior judge and in part because the other remaining judges refused to budge unless Kusumah Atmadja gave the word. There are at least three extensive reports on interviews with Kusumah Atmadja, namely on 5 January 1949 (De Regt), 18 January 1949 (Uyt den Bogaard), and 19 January 1949 (Kan/Lemaire). ARA-II, Algemene Secretarie no.3294, 4659. On 29 January 1949, contacts with Kusumah Atmadja were cut off at the express instruction of Lemaire, then director of justice. The reasons are unclear. Memorandum Lemaire dated 29 January 1949 ARA-II, Algemene Secretarie no.4659. On the solidarity of this hard core, see De Regt: "Their sense of solidarity was remarkable. Nobody was prepared to take a decision without consulting Kusumah Atmadja. Everyone said that he was a good Republican..."

[27] Interview, Daniel S. Lev, Fall 1992.

leaders when the Dutch pushed them forward as "prominent" in the Indonesian-Dutch political talks.[28]

Thus, the judiciary's activities during the colonial period and the revolution damaged their political stock and undermined their authority later when their position was challenged in the 1950s.

2. PARLIAMENTARY DEMOCRACY (1950-1959): THE POLITICAL MOBILIZATION OF THE JUDICIARY

(a) The Beginning: The Struggle for Status[29]

Judicial status clearly reflects the place and role that the state is prepared to bestow upon the courts. The respect with which judges are treated is a significant indication of the political system's view of the courts' importance. Indeed, the political symbolism of status and respect are of particular relevance to the judiciary. Unlike government or Parliament, this weakest of government powers has no real instruments through which it can make its power felt, other than the respect with which it is endowed. A highly intimate relationship exists between the status of judicial office and the power which it can exercise. This makes the judiciary particularly concerned in upholding its public dignity and susceptible and vulnerable to public slights.[30]

In this context, it is not surprising that judicial status was the issue that unleashed the political debate and emerged as the first central item on the judiciary's political agenda. As the political assumptions underlying Parliamentary Democracy were increasingly questioned in the 1950s, the position of the judiciary was no longer taken for granted. During Parliamentary Democracy, initially by mere oversight but later by deliberate policy, the number of incidents humiliating to the judiciary rose steadily.

The most telling incident perhaps occurred in 1951 when the first Supreme Court chairman Kusumah Atmadja was not given a seat befitting his position at an official state banquet. A temperamental man with an acute awareness of the importance of the Supreme Court's institutional prestige, Kusumah Atmadja, to the dismay of the president, threw a tantrum and threatened to leave the banquet unless he was given a place befitting his august position—one right next to the

---

[28] A. H. Nasution, *Sekitar Perang Kemerdekaan Indonesia* (Bandung: Angkasa, 1979), pp. 10, 11, 199, 519.

[29] This section draws heavily on the best account of this period, D. S. Lev, "The Politics of Judicial Development in Indonesia," *Comparative Studies in Society and History* 7,2 (1965): 173.

[30] Judges typically cultivate the myth that their office figures as a source of not just law but profound wisdom. They attach importance to their own judicious behavior in and out of office, emphasize their great and objective technical expertise, preferably through the use of mystifying phrases and expressions in ancient tongues such as Latin, or by other handy status-boosting paraphernalia, such as gowns or wigs, or *in extremis* by instruments that in any other hands would be viewed as draconian and even unconstitutional, such as contempt citations. The problem with contempt is that it violates the basic tenet in the law that one may not judge one's own case. This arguably applies even if someone other than the affected judge were to decide a contempt case (which often is not the case), because of the strong bond of collegiality marking judiciaries particularly on status questions.

president.[31] It was an important incident because it showed that, even in those very early years, political leaders did not take the place and role of the Court for granted. Like Kusumah Atmadja, judges would have to fight to compel respect for their office, as indeed they were constantly subjected to similar slights.[32]

Yet not all judges were endowed with the force of personality of Kusumah Atmadja, who would grow into his role as a formidable Supreme Court chairman. Nor did all share his insights into the intricate links between personal status and institutional power. Many of his brethren on the bench, as one critical commentator described it, took the attitude that in the end such matters could not be forced, in other words that "if this is the way society wants to treat the Supreme Court chairman, well so be it."[33] Kusumah Atmadja's successor, Wirjono Prodjodikoro, adopted this attitude. An astute lawyer and a gentle person, Wirjono was out of his depth in politics and invariably preferred a compromise solution rather than standing up in defense of the Supreme Court's institutional interests. Subjected to the same treatment as his predecessor, Wirjono was steadily moved ever further down the hierarchical line at state banquets until he dropped off the end of the dinner table altogether and was no longer invited.[34] Similarly, when he joined President Sukarno on his 1959 state visit to the United States, Wirjono was given the status of a mere parliamentarian, as he was seated with senators and congressmen, while the American Chief Justice Earl Warren sat with Sukarno and Eisenhower.

The marginalization of the Supreme Court chairman in the 1950s indicated that respect for the judiciary, especially the Supreme Court, was waning. Increasingly unwilling to accord the institution the respect on which its authority was ultimately based, the government had ever less compunction about shunting it aside when it felt the situation called for it, as "Abdul Gani's breakfast" illustrates so well.[35] When, in 1959, President Sukarno heard that the Supreme Court had summoned minister Ruslan Abdul Gani for a hearing before it, the president invited Ruslan to breakfast at that same time. This was an intentional slight, showing how low the standing of the Court had sunk—not to speak of the fact that Sukarno was clearly obstructing the course of justice. "This would never have happened before the colonial Supreme Court," one commentator said, reflecting less on the quality of the Court itself than on the government's unwillingness to accord it respect and power.[36] Indeed, political power relationships enabled Ruslan to attend his presidential breakfast and thumb his nose at the judicial office. Incidents such as these revealed that the president himself deliberately undercut the judiciary, and that the judiciary's political room to maneuver was being restricted ever further.

---

[31] Daniel S. Lev, "Draft, Chapters on Post-Revolutionary Indonesian Legal History," (unpublished), ch. 2, p. 33; *Tempo*, 9 October 1971, p. 49.

[32] Thus, the later Minister of Justice Maengkom would relate that, when still a district court judge, he was invited to attend some official function by the governor, but upon his arrival found that his seat was a considerable distance away from the governor. Apparently Maengkom left the dinner also. DSL, 27 August 1960.

[33] *DSL*, 26 June 1960.

[34] *DSL*, 7 September 1959.

[35] *Tempo*, 11 September 1971, p. 24.

[36] *DSL*, 13 May 1959.

The ostensibly trivial matter of judicial salaries epitomized the dilemma. Government proposals in the early 1950s recommended reducing these salaries relative to those of other comparable government services, notably the public prosecution. Affecting all judges individually, these proposals focused judicial frustrations on the status issue and rapidly became the linchpin for politically mobilizing the judiciary. The judiciary came to perceive the salary issue as a matter of principle, whose outcome would determine their position in the modern Indonesian state.

The judiciary was easily mobilized, for in Indonesia's worsening postwar situation, their salaries were not very large in the first place. In fact, perceived hardship, both real and imagined, still unites the judiciary in conflicts concerning judicial salaries. Yet in the 1950s the hardship was very real and was an important factor in generating a sense of solidarity and bonding within the judiciary. In order to survive, even the Supreme Court chairman was forced to rent out his official car as a taxicab during office hours.[37] Nevertheless, judicial efforts were less geared toward securing larger incomes, as such, than to maintaining their senior position on the salary scale relative to other related professions, notably the prosecution. Judges were aware from the start that the relative size of judicial salaries measured against those of other state officials was a highly evocative symbol of the importance which the state attached to the judiciary. In the early 1950s in Indonesia, it was this symbolic and ultimately political aspect that mobilized the judges more than any other.

The salary issue in the 1950s became heavily politicized. In the competition over salaries, from the mid-1950s the government consistently backed other state officials against the judges, with the result that the comparative salary position of the judges steadily declined. Acutely aware that this erosion of prestige reflected immediately on their political status and power, the judges fought tooth and nail to improve their salary position, both absolutely and relatively.

In the late 1960s, the debate over the relative size of salaries was complemented by the issue of whether judicial salaries should be provided for by a distinct legislative regulation, or be determined as part of some general law on salaries for all government personnel.[38] On this issue, the status aspect touched upon questions of judicial autonomy from executive interference: the prevailing feeling within the judiciary was that a separate salary regulation was imperative not merely to maintain their prestige, but also to reduce the possibilities for government interference in the law's application.

The milestones in the salary debate can be briefly summarized as follows: in 1955 the judges lost their privileged salary position vis-à-vis the public prosecution; from 1968 onwards the lower judges were included with all regular civil servants in the national salary regulation (the so-called PGPS, Peraturan Gaji Pegawai Negeri Sipil, Salary Regulation for Civil Servants); and some years later their civil service status was established in Civil Service Law no.8/1974. And while the Basic Law on the Judiciary no.14/1970 stated that judicial salaries would be provided for by separate statute, it was not until almost a quarter-century

---

[37] Interview, Daniel S. Lev, Summer 1993.

[38] This was already defined as a long-range objective in 1953, but only became manifest in the 1960s. Daniel Lev, "Politics of Judicial Development," p. 184 note 37.

later that this was effected in a regulation that apparently did not actually improve the situation.[39]

Notwithstanding the important differences in the functions performed by judges and prosecutors, their physical proximity in the courtroom, their identical official attire, and their many apparent similarities in functions situated the struggle over status in each and every courthouse in the country. The role distribution in court, with the opposing prosecutor and disposing judge, gave the struggle a special edge and added to its fundamental symbolic value.[40]

However the roots of the conflict must be traced back to the colonial system of state justice, with its single judicial corps and dual system of prosecution.[41] This meant that, notwithstanding the differentiation among the courts for various population groups, the judiciary itself was an integrated corps, consisting of both Dutchmen and Indonesians (as well as Chinese). There was no comparable integrated service for prosecutors. Instead, the European courts were served by prosecutors operating under the European code of criminal procedure. These prosecutors, the so-called *officieren van justitie*, were invariably Dutch, and operated on a par in terms of status, responsibilities, and income with the judges. On the other hand, the Indonesian courts were served by an indigenous prosecution, operating under the much looser and more flexible Indonesian code of procedure (HIR, Herziene Inlandsch Reglement and Herziene Indonesisch Reglement).[42] In these courts, the prosecutor was the generally lowly educated *jaksa*, always an Indonesian, whose functions were much more restricted. Reflecting his relatively low status, the *jaksa* worked under the supervision of the judge.[43]

---

[39] Law no.14/1970 art.32 effected with Presidential Decree no.10/1995. This decree for the first time gave judicial salaries a separate statutory basis and in addition doubled them. There were some problems with this regulation, however. As judges immediately pointed out, presidential decrees come and go, and do not constitute a strong statutory protection against government manipulation of salaries. They would have preferred a Government Regulation (*Peraturan Pemerintah*) or an Act of Parliament (*Undang-undang*). In addition, the salary increase was to some extent offset by a drastic reduction in incidental benefits (*tunjangan*), so by 1995 it transpired that the effective income position of judges had not really changed. Indeed, there were calls to review the incidental benefit system because it was felt the measures unfairly benefited the judges. Yet the judges' whole purpose was precisely to claim special salary benefits to distinguish them from the other professions. It was not just that the 1995 salary measure misfired; the discussions on the measure showed that the views of the judges and the government were still far apart, and the government was unwilling to grant the judiciary special status. *Kompas*, 26 April 1995.

[40] This symbolic value should not be underestimated in reference to the Indonesian context. It was already a relevant factor during the Dutch administration. Another story told in later years relates that a young judge somewhere in Java regularly drove to work with the prosecutor, who owned a large car. One day the prosecutor's wife joined them, and the prosecutor asked the judge whether he wanted to sit in the back, so that his wife could sit beside him. The judge refused and got out of the car, stating that a judge would never sit behind a prosecutor. *DSL*, 16 July 1968.

[41] Here I am not speaking of the indigenous courts in self-governing territories (*inheemsche rechtspraak*), which, constitutionally speaking, were not colonial state courts.

[42] *Herziene Inlandsch* (later: *Indonesisch*) *Reglement* S.1941-44.

[43] This led to the curious situation in which the judge had to draw up the indictment whose validity he would later have to verify. Arts.83i and 250(4) HIR.

After independence, the Indonesian government adopted the colonial code of procedure for Indonesians (HIR) as the law of the land.[44] Thus, whereas the judges took over the prestigious functions of their European predecessors, the prosecutors followed their Indonesian institutional antecedents. As Lev put it:

> The end result was that Republican prosecutors inherited the organization of the former *officieren van justitie* but the limited responsibilities of the former *djaksas*.[45]

Reflecting this imbalance in power and prestige, after independence the judges were consistently ranked higher in the salary scales than their counterparts in the prosecution.[46]

Prosecutors resented the inequities and began to push for equality. In 1951 they organized in the Prosecutors' Union (Persatuan Jaksa) to lobby for salaries and status equal to the judges'.[47] The judges were slow to react. Traditionally unorganized individualists, imbued with a professional tradition that inclined them to look down on political mudfights, the judges felt that lobbying for their interests was beneath them. By and large, the judicial corps still displayed great professional self-confidence and appeared to share the expectation that its place and function within the Indonesian state would remain as secure and respected as it had been in colonial times. Still, there was a growing sense of unease, particularly in the lower courts, about the steady erosion of judicial standing.[48] When the prosecutors officially decided to push for equality at their Bandung 1951 general conference, the lower court judges were stung into action. Shortly afterwards, they began to organize, and in May 1953 they established the Judges' Association (IKAHI) to coordinate and serve as platform for their political interests.[49]

---

[44] This happened definitely with Emergency Law no.1/1951 art.6(1). There were some problems initially because the relevant article stated that the colonial code should be used as the "guide," not as an actual code. After Guided Democracy, it was given legal effect, however. The government feared that the complicated and strict European code of criminal procedure might prove unworkable for lack of skilled personnel and lack of familiarity.

[45] Lev, "Politics of Judicial Development," p. 177.

[46] Republican Regulation no.21/1948, Koesnodiprodjo, *Himpunan Undang2,* vol. 1948; Lev, "Politics of Judicial Development," p. 178, n. 15.

[47] Lev, "Politics of Judicial Development," p. 178.

[48] As pointed out by D. S. Lev, in ibid., p. 179, the main reason for this divergence of attitudes between junior and Supreme Court judges resided in the fact that the Supreme Court judges "enjoyed a sense of participation in government that the trial judges were beginning to lose." Prestige and standards of living were declining across the board, but the senior judges still were under the impression, mistaken perhaps, that they were among the torch bearers for the state.

[49] The first chairman was Soerjadi, chairman at the Surabaya district court. Apparently, Soerjadi became chairman because he had been one of the first to organize the judges in his district; this took place in 1952. The reason he had been so quick on the uptake was that Soerjadi was friends with Seno Adji, who was the prosecutor's spokesman in the salary debate. Seno Adji apparently gave Soerjadi a call after the 1951 Bandung meeting of the prosecutors, informing him that the prosecutors would fight to achieve equality. Soerjadi therefore was informed before the news officially broke and decided that something must be done. As a result, he began to mobilize and organize the judges in his district throughout 1952, thus laying the basis for IKAHI (Ikatan Hakim Indonesia, Judges' Association of Indonesia). Soerjadi would move on to become Supreme Court chairman during the turbulent transitory period from the Old

The prosecutors' call for equality in salaries and status was based on the argument that judges were losing both the professional and political edge which had established their superiority over the *jaksa*s in the colonial system and justified the differences in salary ranking.[50] There can be no doubt that this argument had merit. Professionally, judicial standards had been diluted by the many poorly trained judges whom the government had been forced to enlist in the early 1950s when faced with a pressing personnel shortage in the judiciary,[51] an action that undermined the judiciary's claim to be the better trained profession.[52] When the judges' supervisory powers over prosecutors were abolished in the late 1950s, the power imbalance between the two professions effectively came to an end.[53] This undercut the judges' arguments that their heavier burdens and responsibilities warranted higher status and salaries.

The judiciary's political stock was hardly in a better condition. As we have seen, their revolutionary record was poor, as many prominent judges sided with the Dutch, while many more were *"absen dari revolusi"* (absent from the revolution)—the rather negative euphemism for fence-sitters.[54] In addition, the

---

to the New Order 1966-1968, when he found himself in outright confrontation with the Judges' Association. D. Lev, "Politics of Judicial Development," pp. 178-79.

[50] One psychological reason was that the revolution unleashed a strong egalitarian movement within the country, and the judges' claims of special status did not go down well at the time. D. Lev, "Politics of Judicial Development," p. 181.

[51] Ibid., p. 183. The shortages resulted in part from the departure of the Dutch but notably also from the abolition of the autonomous courts in 1950 and the subjection of broad swathes of the country to the system of state justice.

[52] Another point was that the professional quality of the *jaksa*s improved. The prosecution offered good career prospects for law graduates in part because of its poor quality, which made it possible for educated newcomers to have some real influence, and because it was becoming clear that the service might benefit from prevailing political currents rather more than the judiciary. As a result, the prosecution attracted many new good law graduates who otherwise might have started their career in the judiciary. Seno Adji is one example.

[53] As pointed out by Lev, this development commenced about 1955 but was capped in 1961 when the authority to draw up the indictment was transferred from the judge to the prosecutor. Law no.15/1961 art.12.

[54] The prosecution survived the revolution in much better shape, in part no doubt because prosecutors simply were too unimportant to have comparable propaganda value and hence suffer similar political exposure. Note that this did not apply to the top prosecutors who, until the resignation of the hugely respected Prosecutor General Suprapto in 1959, were recruited from the judiciary. Indeed, in 1948 the top prosecutor on the Dutch side, the so-called *Procureur-Generaal*, was Oerip Kartodirdjo, a former judge. One reason why Indonesian judges were more inclined to support the Dutch than the prosecutors is that the judges were actually part of the Western (colonial) elite, and identified with it by training, professional occupation, and the social circles in which they found themselves. This also quite clearly tarnished their image after independence—unless they redeemed themselves by being fervent supporters of the Republic, as a few were. The *jaksa*s by way of contrast always stood in a relationship with their European superiors and the judges that was much more hierarchical, and without doubt much more colonial in terms of the underlying color bar. They were definitely not part of the elite. As a result, prosecutors by and large must have been more acutely aware of the many disadvantages inherent in the colonial state, which they indeed experienced at first hand. For them, supporting the revolution was a natural option, as they stood to gain from it much more than the judges. Regarding *jaksa*s, *jaksa*s were always Indonesians and, formally speaking, did not do any prosecuting or work as prosecutors. It was an abnormal situation that could only arise under colonialism. The persons who really conducted prosecution were exclusively Dutch prosecutors, called *Officier van Justitie* (. . .). It is clear that Indonesians were not sufficiently

judiciary's place in the modern Indonesian state had clearly declined, a fact demonstrated in the salary debate.

The principal argument of the judges, however, was that the salary issue concerned principle rather than professional standing or political antecedents. They argued that the judiciary should not be equated with any other government department because both constitutionally and ideologically it was special. The judiciary was on a par with government and Parliament, not subject to them, and therefore—as was the case for the president, government ministers, and members of Parliament—separate salary schedules were necessary to reinforce and reflect the judges' special status. If the government was serious about upholding the separation of powers doctrine and the rule of law, it should support the special position of judicial salaries.

> As a guide in determining the position of our judiciary under the Constitution, we must use the principles 1) that our state is a democratic state and 2) that our state is based on the rule of law . . . In a [democratic] state, the judiciary, as the guardian of the law and of . . . democracy, must necessarily be given considerable power; and [the judiciary] cannot be subordinated to any authority other than the Constitution and the law. This has been taught in the famous doctrine of *Trias Politika*, which gives the judiciary a position equal to that of the legislature and executive.[55]

According to this argument, abolishing special salary schedules for judges, or equating them with government officers, would weaken the courts and ultimately erode the constitutional ideology of the *Trias Politika* itself.

The judges made no real headway with their arguments. Indeed, with Minister of Justice Djody Gondokoesoemo supporting the *jaksas* rather than the judges, their position was slipping steadily.[56] The judges tried to lobby Parliament to reverse the situation, but that institution was increasingly tied down by its internal affairs, and though it is true that the judges encountered no disagreement, they were unable to generate real support, to paraphrase Lev. As a result, with the new salary law coming up for approval in 1954-1955, the judges were pretty much up against the wall and decided that a radical action was called for. In 1954 the Judges' Association decided that if the prosecutors won equality in salary ranking, the judges would go on strike.[57] Despite this decision, the new salary schedules,

---

trusted to do any work for the public prosecution. These positions were too important, for the colonial prosecutor defended society. See R. Soedarto, "Peranan kedjaksaan dalam penjelidikan, penuntutan dan pemeriksaan perkara pidana dalam sidang Pengadilan Negeri," *Varia Peradilan* 2,5-6 (1963): 5.

[55] Statement of the Judges' Association before Parliament, quoted in Lev, "Politics of Judicial Development," p. 184.

[56] As pointed out by Lev, in ibid., p. 186, this was in part because Djody Gondokoesomo's National People's Party counted quite a few prosecutors among its members, but hardly any judges.

[57] Officially the action was not called a strike, which was felt to be "undignified" and would be "subject to repression." Ibid., p. 186. Judges went to court, but simply refused to hear cases, which practically amounted to the same thing as a strike.

ranking prosecutors on a par with judges, were enacted in December 1955. As a result, in March 1956 the judiciary ceased work.[58]

It was a spectacular move, not only for what it meant, but also because it revealed how strong the Judges' Association had grown over the past couple of years. Support for it in the lower courts was total, as only the Supreme Court distanced itself from the strike. In fact, Supreme Court judges disapproved of the strike action, criticizing the judges for "violating their ethical code" and "the dignity of their office."[59] Unfortunately however, the poor timing of the judges' action effectively nullified its effect. The day after the strike began, the government resigned for unrelated reasons. The caretaker cabinet could make no important decisions, and the Judges' Association was forced to call off the strike to prevent the judiciary from collapsing altogether.[60]

Judicial efforts to retain their status had clearly failed. As would soon become apparent, the judges' fear that their loss of status would threaten their position in a much broader sense was all too well founded. This status debate, to be certain, started at a time when the judiciary still had a conception of what its position should be and understood the importance of status in securing the place and role of courts in the political arena. Later, particularly after the deceptions of the 1970s, the judiciary began to lose both its idealism and understanding of what was at issue here. With the emergence of a new generation of judges, the salary issue increasingly became a self-serving item on the judicial wish list. By the 1980s and 1990s, the low salaries ended up as a miserable justification for judicial corruption, which by then had become pervasive.

(b) New Emerging Issues: Autonomy and Power

The judges' failure in the salary debate in 1956 prompted some serious soul-searching. They gradually began to think in much broader terms about their constitutional place and role, and how these should be realized. This process was enhanced by the rapid derailment of the political system, as the nation began to topple from Parliamentary Democracy into patrimonial Guided Democracy. The failure of the judges in the salary debate was a prelude to even more severe losses, the result of more direct political challenges to the judiciary.

During the Guided Democracy era, generally accepted values and ideas on the place and role of courts were questioned, consciously ignored, and deliberately violated with increasing frequency. These challenges pushed the boundaries of the debate outwards, as the judges were compelled to explain, justify, and defend what hitherto had been taken for granted. In this painful process, judges began to

---

[58] According to some accounts of persons closely involved, the Judges' Association was tricked in the matter by Minister of Justice Djody Gondokoesomo. According to this version, Gondokoesomo actually promised the judges special salary status in the 1955 PGPS, but when the PGPS came out, there was nothing in it. Personal communication, 1 July 1994.

[59] Supreme Court judge Malikul Adil, "Hukum dan hakim in civilibus," *Hukum* 1-2 (1959): 6.

[60] D. Lev, "Politics of Judicial Development," p. 187. Some judges were furious about what they viewed as the half-hearted way in which the Judges' Association handled the strike. Thus, highly respected judge Mahadi continued to strike for more than two weeks after IKAHI had called it off. Some carried this action even further. Sumarjo thought a strike action was not enough and resigned from the Association because he felt all judges should have resigned rather than just gone on strike. *DSL,* 3 September 1960.

formulate new ideas on what a judiciary should be and do. In the status struggle, two new issues in particular made their appearance on the judicial agenda: autonomy from political interference, to be accomplished by transferring control over the lower courts to the Supreme Court; and increased power, to be achieved by granting the Supreme Court the power of judicial (constitutional) review.

These issues were not truly worked out in detail at the time, and as it happened this was never really done until *Reformasi* days. They were effectively slogans for change, reflecting more the dissatisfaction with the institution's current condition than a clear understanding of what the proposed change entailed. The foundation to this impressionistic and somewhat troubling process was laid in 1956, when the judiciary was groping for ways by which to offset the loss of terrain incurred in the salary debate and its institutional erosion.

In 1956, the Judges' Association began to lobby Parliament to improve the situation of the judiciary in Indonesia, presenting its own conception of the place and role of the judiciary. Its highly ambitious program claimed much more than had the original judicial arguments in the salary debate,[61] and, in contrast to the situation during that debate, this time the Judges' Association was backed by the Supreme Court. Supreme Court chairman Wirjono Prodjodikoro sent in his own proposal, which on all the important points was identical to that of the Judges' Association.[62] The proposals broke new ground in advocating the transfer of court administration from the Department of Justice to the Supreme Court[63] and increasing judicial power by granting the judiciary the right of constitutional review.[64] Referring explicitly to American constitutional law, they stated,

> ... in our opinion, it is desirable that the present condition in Indonesia be changed in such a way that the Supreme Court (rather than any other court) have the power to declare a law to be in conflict with the Constitution.[65]

Here, the 1956 proposals touched upon two fundamental characteristics of the separation of powers doctrine, as we previously noted (Chapter 1, section 1). The issues raised by the judges before Parliament did not just aim at recouping the terrain lost on the salary issue, but touched upon the heart of the judicial system prevailing to date. Since their failures the previous year, the political scene had changed in their favor. For a start, the Association now had Supreme Court backing on autonomy and power. Moreover, Parliament was finding itself in increasing opposition to the government, and was seeking a natural alliance with the judiciary. In 1956-57, there was extensive parliamentary support for introducing

---

[61] For a summary, see Lev, "Politics of Judicial Development," pp. 187-88.

[62] Wirjono Prodjodikoro, "Saran-saran untuk Konstituante tentang tempat pengadilan dalam ketatanegaraan," *Hukum* 5-6 (1956): 1.

[63] Wirjono put the Supreme Court at ministerial level, stating that " ... just as the Cabinet (or each minister) appoints the employees of his department, it must be the Supreme Court that appoints the judges and other officials in the lower courts." Wirjono Prodjodikoro, "Saran-saran untuk Konstituante," p. 3.

[64] I distinguish between constitutional and judicial review. The former refers to the authority of the courts to quash Acts of Parliament, the latter restricts their authority to reviews of inferior legislation.

[65] Wirjono Prodjodikoro, "Saran-saran untuk Konstituante," p. 3.

some form of constitutional review in the new constitution.⁶⁶ Indeed, the relevant parliamentary committee accepted the judicial proposals, which included the establishment of a special constitutional court to review legislation which would be composed in part of Supreme Court judges.⁶⁷

For a brief moment, it seemed as though the judges would prevail. Nevertheless, not unlike developments during the salary crisis, political events again overtook them. President Sukarno cut short the constitutional debate when he imposed martial law in 1957 and suspended the 1950 Provisional Constitution. Two years later, Parliament was suspended and the 1945 Constitution was enacted by decree. Guided Democracy had come, and the judges were out in the wilderness.

3. GUIDED DEMOCRACY (1959-1965): GOING DOWN

(a) Political Cooptation of the Judiciary and Legal Particularism

Guided Democracy completely redefined the constitutional parameters of the Indonesian state. It rendered meaningless the debate about judicial status, autonomy, and power, as it was oriented toward abolishing the separation of powers doctrine. Briefly summarized, this was through a process that commenced in 1957 with the imposition of martial law, and persisted through 1960, when the traditional symbol of justice—the blindfolded lady justice bearing sword and scales—was replaced as national symbol by a stylized banyan tree accompanied by the word *"Pengayoman,"* meaning "protection." That same year Supreme Court chairman Wirjono Prodjodikoro was appointed to the Cabinet with ministerial status, and Sukarno made a speech in the MPR(S) (Majelis Permusyawaratan Rakyat [Sementara], [Provisional] People's Consultative Assembly) proclaiming the end of the separation of powers doctrine. The process was capped by Laws 19/1964 and 13/1965, which allowed for direct government interference in the course of justice⁶⁸ and, as part of the general abolition of the separation of powers, explicitly ended judicial autonomy. As the official explanation to Law no.13/1965 states:

> This law with all its thrust aims at throwing out the spirit of liberalism, individualism, feudalism, and colonialism, in accordance with [modern] Indonesian law. It realizes the idea that the separation of powers doctrine (Trias Politika) no longer applies in Indonesian society. The concept that judges shall be impartial, independent from any external interference can no longer be upheld and has been buried. In this law, it is stipulated that judges are obliged to side with the truth as embodied in Pancasila and MANIPOL/USDEK.⁶⁹

---

⁶⁶ A.B. Nasution, *The Aspiration for Constitutional Government in Indonesia* (Jakarta: Pustaka Sinar Harapan, 1992), pp. 233-34.

⁶⁷ Lev, "Politics of Judicial Development," p. 188.

⁶⁸ Law no.19/1964 art.19. See also Law no.13/1965, art.23. These articles allowed for direct government interference in the course of justice on grounds of "revolutionary interests, the state or national honor, or pressing public interest."

⁶⁹ Official Explanation to Law no.13/1965. Manipol/Usdek: Manifesto Politik/Undang-Undang '45, Sosialisme a la Indonesia, Demokrasi Terpimpin, Kepribadian Indonesia, Political

Judges, to again borrow statutory wording, had become mere "instruments of the revolution."[70]

In a way, judges were the prime embodiment of the separation of powers that Guided Democracy aimed to abolish. This was notably the case after Parliament had been made into an instrument of the executive, leaving the judiciary in effect the only function of government not under executive control.[71] In addition, the judicial professional ethic, wholly imbued by ideas of legality and a professional bias toward the traditional, was anathema to revolutionary ideas of that period. To abandon these concepts and surrender their autonomy in order to become revolutionary instruments fundamentally conflicted with the judicial ethos. According to the judges' perspective, giving up their professional integrity really meant ceasing to be judges, as they understood the concept. Sukarno's exclamation, "You cannot make revolution with lawyers," often cited in Indonesia as a comment on the deep-rooted reactionism of the legal professions generally, also reflected deep-seated government exasperation at its failure to bring the judiciary into the government fold.[72]

After the suspension of the Provisional Constitution and the declaration of a state of emergency in 1957, judges were subjected to direct political pressure with increasing frequency. This involved military pressure in particular, as the army made a purposeful attempt to place army officers in the courts. From 1957, the army proposed that all court vice chairmen should be military officers.

> The army wants to control the courts because at the moment it cannot force the courts to try the cases the way it wants. The army seems to consider justice a matter of security, too, and so wants to extend its power into the sphere of justice.[73]

This army's takeover attempt was successfully resisted for the moment, but only at the cost of a compromise, whereby the Department of Justice (which controlled court administration) was to be placed under ultimate supervision of the Department of Defense in 1959.[74]

This setback did not prevent the army from undercutting court power, as judges would recount:

> Everywhere army pressure is brought to bear on the courts, so that the courts are suffocating. [. . .] In such areas as the Moluccas, the courts no longer try cases

---

Manifesto/1945 Constitution, Indonesian Socialism, Guided Democracy, Guided Economy, Indonesian Identity.

[70] Ibid.

[71] Parliament was suspended in 1957, and an executive-appointed Parliament, the so-called DPR-Gotong Royong (DPR-GR) was installed in its stead in 1959. DPR: Dewan Perwakilan Rakyat, People's Representative Assembly, i.e., the national parliament.

[72] President Sukarno quoted Liebknecht's famous phrase during the First Congress of Persahi (National Association of Indonesian Lawyers) in Yogyakarta, November 1961. *Varia Peradilan* 2,5-6 (1963): 3.

[73] *DSL*, 1 September 1959.

[74] Presidential Decree dated 5 July 1959.

involving the army in any way, because the army threatens the judges and continually applies pressure. [. . .] Thus, [. . .] the courts would not dare to decide cases fairly when they involve corruption in barter trade, which is run by the army.[75]

The judiciary fought back, even with some temporary success, as the government and the army were reluctant to precipitate an open confrontation. In the Moluccas case mentioned above, the Supreme Court tried to alleviate the plight of local courts by flying in special judges just to try the tough cases in which the army was involved. In theory, such judges would be less susceptible to local army pressures. They also developed procedures to help local judges stand up to army interference:

In outlying areas, when a judge is threatened by army interference he can send a protest to Wirjono, who will take it up with Minister of Defense Nasution. Nasution will then instruct the local commander to keep hands off. But it takes time, and generally is not very effective. Nevertheless, this procedure has been used by a number of judges in the outlying areas.[76]

One illustrative case in this period was the controversial *Schmidt case*, involving a Dutchman accused of attempting to overthrow the Indonesian government. The case was widely seen as part of the anti-Dutch propaganda effort that was coming to a head at the time. The appeals court, defying government and military pressure, freed Schmidt in 1959,[77] a decision that caused considerable public anger, but was applauded by the legal community as a brave judicial act. The fact that the judges were not harmed after the verdict was viewed as a sign that the courts had not completely lost their power. The judges in particular saw the *Schmidt case* as an indication that they still retained their political autonomy, and it gave them a moral boost.

It is clear that pressure was put on the court by government higher-ups to condemn Schmidt. But after Schmidt was freed, and despite many attacks on the court by newspapers and private individuals, no judge on the court was touched or threatened, etc. The real importance of the Schmidt case is that while courts evidently are subject to political pressure, there is enough respect for them that no one is willing to let them be harmed too much.[78]

The Schmidt case proved the strength of judges. . . . The government fears to touch the judges, and judges still feel free and strong to some extent.[79]

In reality, however, the case can be viewed as an indication of how far things had unraveled, in that the judges' reprieve from physical harm after deciding a sensitive case was cited to prove the autonomy of the judiciary. It was turning

---

[75] *DSL*, 12 August 1959.

[76] *DSL*, 18 August 1959.

[77] In fact the court imposed a prison term equal to his provisional detention, thus realizing the same result.

[78] *DSL*, 13 May 1959.

[79] *DSL*, 18 May 1959; *DSL* 26 May 1959; and *DSL*, 1 September 1959

constitutional principle on its head. Perhaps even more troubling, this was the first case in which the government, through the pronouncements of its prime minister, Juanda, publicly threatened the courts. Moreover, the highly respected chief public prosecutor, Soeprapto, was sacked as a result of the decision in the case.[80] Finally, few were aware that behind the scenes the government was preparing to move against the judges who had freed Schmidt, notably the courageous presiding judge, Lie Oen Hok. One of the participating judges recounted:

> ... the government ordered an investigation into the affairs of the presiding judge, Lie Oen Hok. Fortunately, the investigation was led by Soerjadi, who used to be a former judge but now was a Junior Chief Public Prosecutor. Soerjadi managed to redirect the investigation into a mere fact-finding mission. Also, while the judges were anxiously awaiting the aftershocks of their decision, they told Wirjono at the Supreme Court that if the Court were to be investigated or interfered with because of their decision in the Schmidt case, they would have to take action and resign. Apparently, Wirjono hurried off to Jakarta to try and stop things on that side also.[81]

So the judges in the *Schmidt case* emerged unharmed only after a good deal of string-pulling by various sides. Perhaps, as some observers argued, the government and the military still had sufficient respect for the judiciary and for its professional expertise to refrain from outright confrontation.[82]

The *Schmidt case* indicated that the judiciary teetered on the brink of losing all constitutional power, but resisted with some success. Several examples in the crucial 1957-1960 period further illustrate their resistance to government or military dictates.

> ... at the Douane Studie Club on November 4, 1959, [Surabaya judge] Mr. Soerjadi delivered a speech on Indonesia and the rule of law. The speech was well received. During the question period afterwards, Semadikoen gave a short speech by way of question in which he raised the point that at a time of revolution, as in the present period, leeway must be given to the executive, through the *"hukum revolusi"* [law of the revolution]. He said that at such times, judges have to submit to political circumstances or the needs of the state, even though this may mean deviating from the word

---

[80] Prime Minister Juanda said that, to protect national security, the government would use its martial law powers to ensure the political loyalty of the courts in the future, though he did admit that the government had no right to interfere with the judiciary. The important public figure who fell victim in the upheaval caused by the *Schmidt case* was the strong-willed chief public prosecutor, Suprapto. Suprapto played a peripheral role at best in the *Schmidt case* (he wrote a letter facilitating Schmidt's departure from the country). It was rather his success in protecting the prosecution from government interference that was the cause for his removal, as the government admitted in a report published after the event. It marked the end of the independence of the prosecution from government interference. Daniel S. Lev, *The Transition to Guided Democracy: Indonesian Politics 1957-1959* (Ithaca: Cornell Modern Indonesia Project Monograph, 1966), pp. 255-56; *Keterangan pemerintah mengenai penjelesaian soal Schmidt* (Jakarta: Ministry of Information, 1959).

[81] *DSL*, 27 June 1960.

[82] *DSL*, 13 May 1959.

and spirit of the law. This is a revolutionary time for Indonesia, and revolutionary needs are more important than the law per se, and judges must therefore follow along with those needs and support those leaders who are trying to fulfill them. After some thinking and nervous fidgeting for a few minutes, Soerjadi answered. His answer seemed honestly sincere in the form of an exposition of ideas about the task of the judge. His point was that judges should apply only what is the law. If there is no law, he cannot apply it. He must stick to the law under all circumstances. There was a considerable amount of applause for Soerjadi even before he finished his answer. The entire audience of 350-400 persons seemed to favor Soerjadi in the argument.[83]

Indeed, some judges dared to confront Sukarno directly in their support of the institutional interests of the judiciary—a step that was coming to be seen as outrageously daring. One such direct confrontation occurred in January 1960, when President Sukarno called a meeting with judges, prosecutors, and police to talk about economic conditions and the respective tasks for which they were each responsible when dealing with violations of economic regulations and so on. The president spoke for an hour or so on the Law of Revolution and the necessity to deal harshly with economic violators and persons who abused the system. Afterwards, during the luncheon, the president posed a rhetorical question about rice smuggling. He then called on some of the young judges present, seven or so of them, to answer the question and indicate what sort of sentence they would impose. He posed the question only to the judges, not to the prosecutors or the police. Most of the judges, rather impressed and cowed by the occasion, answered by saying that they would give sentences ranging from four to seven years. Sukarno found this unsatisfactory, complaining that the case he presented required a heavier sentence because of the prevalence of economic crimes. But when he asked Judge Suparni of the Jakarta special district court, he certainly didn't get the reply he expected. Judge Suparni made it clear that she thought the president was out of bounds in telling judges how heavy their sentences should be, and she emphasized the autonomy and independence of judges.

> **Judge Suparni**: I'm afraid I cannot answer that question, for it really depends on the specifics of the case.
> **Sukarno**: Well, I just gave you the specifics.
> **Judge Suparni**: Still, I would have to consider the full factual complexity of the case, before I could answer such a question.
> **Sukarno**: And what would you do if you got a direct instruction from the President?
> **Judge Suparni**: Well now, judicial independence forbids such a thing, doesn't it?[84]

---

[83] *DSL*, 8 November 1959.

[84] Personal communication, 30 June 1994; *DSL*, 2 February 1960. Apparently Judge Suparni was summoned before Minister of Justice Astrawinata the next day, but she didn't go because she expected that something might happen to her at the meeting. Nothing happened, but later Astrawinata told her that indeed, if she had turned up, some "ill would have befallen her"

Suparni's fellow judges were generally very impressed by her outspoken reaction, as word of it circulated quickly. Many said privately that they agreed with Suparni, but the situation had already deteriorated to a point where they did not dare express their opinion publicly, let alone face the president himself.[85]

In the view of some witnesses, it was at this point that Sukarno began to realize that the judges were a special group, who needed to be handled differently from the others. As Daniel Lev points out: "Under Guided Democracy, the courts caused President Sukarno some irritation, partly because a few judges refused dictation; but also because he supposed, quite rightly, that, on the whole, judges and private lawyers did not support the regime enthusiastically."[86] The opposition of the judiciary inevitably played its part in President Sukarno's determination to abandon the separation of powers doctrine altogether. There were constant brushes between Sukarno's political interests and the Supreme Court, as happened in 1960, for instance, when the Court convicted former Minister of Justice Djody Gondokoesoemo of corruption and imposed a prison term against the wishes of the president (who soon pardoned Djody). At the same time, it dismissed the Sosro case in which the president had been eagerly pushing for a conviction. In the opinion of a prominent judge, "It was these incidents that pushed the president toward making Wirjono a cabinet minister." These skirmishes occurred at a time, of course, when one could still appeal before the president to the separation of powers doctrine. By late 1960, the doctrine itself had come under attack, and the judges were up against the wall.[87]

The members of the Supreme Court had increasing problems as they were challenged by the willful revolutionary decisions of the president and his supporters. A law was enacted calling upon the Supreme Court to advise on the dissolution of the Masyumi and PSI (Partai Sosialis Indonesia) political parties (PP7). This caused considerable discomfort within the Court, which, true to its civil-law roots, felt it was being drawn into politics about which it knew nothing.[88] Amidst rumors that it was being pressured by the president, the Court advised that the dissolution could be validated on the basis of martial law.[89] During his national address on Independence Day that year, Sukarno suggested that the Court had effectively stated that the president could brush aside any statute, including the constitution itself.[90] Although this assuredly was not the case, the Supreme

---

(using the Indonesian expression to denote a child struck by sickness because it has been disobedient).

[85] *DSL*, 2 February 1960

[86] Daniel S. Lev, "Judicial Authority and the Struggle for an Indonesian Rechtstaat," *Law and Society Review* 13 (1978): 49.

[87] *DSL*, 27 June 1960.

[88] *DSL*, 11 September 1960.

[89] Apparently the Supreme Court advice stated that the Masyumi and PSI could be "struck" (*terkena*), but did not advise on what action to take. The advice was signed by chairman Wirjono Prodjodikoro and the court clerk Tamara only. *DSL*, 24 August 1960.

[90] Lev, "Draft, Chapters on Post-Revolutionary Indonesian Legal History," ch. 3, p. 63, n. 31.

Court could do nothing about it, thus strengthening the impression that the Court had joined the government's revolutionary bandwagon.[91]

In symbolic terms, things speeded up dramatically when Sukarno appointed Supreme Court chairman Wirjono Prodjodikoro to the Cabinet in 1960.[92] Wirjono was uncomfortable with the appointment and tried to reduce its importance by sending a Circular Letter to all judges justifying his acceptance. He argued that since constitutionally the Supreme Court must advise the president, it is easier for such advice to be offered by a judge who sits in the Cabinet. He stated that his appointment did not affect the separation of powers doctrine in any way, and that, indeed, judicial autonomy should continue to be upheld.[93] Nevertheless, Wirjono's logic was discredited when later in 1960 President Sukarno announced in the MPR that he would abolish the separation of powers altogether. Apparently, Wirjono felt he had been tricked into playing a part in all this, as was indeed the case, and he thought of resigning, but did not.[94]

After 1960, judicial identity and interests were rapidly eroded by a barrage of substantive and political steps and measures aimed at subjecting judges to the supreme and grandiose legitimating revolutionary ideology of the day.

Thus, the distinctive official attire of judges, their black gowns, was abolished in March 1963 and replaced by a military-style uniform which all civil servants were wearing at the time—in green camouflage colors with shoulder boards embossed with the *pengayoman* symbol.[95] The new uniform reduced the symbolic separation between judges and other civil servants, or, as the relevant statute phrases it, made judges "more aware of their responsibilities as instruments of the state and the revolution."[96] It was a move clearly inspired by President Sukarno, and also directed at severing the judges' ideological or emotional ties with their judicial roots:

---

[91] This image was not all that far from the truth, as the Supreme Court refused to hear any cases in which the constitutionality of the banning of the parties was challenged, and apparently instructed district courts to do the same. Ibid., ch. 3, p. 64, n. 31.

[92] Actually Wirjono was first appointed a member of the People's Consultative Assembly (MPRS), then a Minister/Legal Advisor and subsequently Minister/Chairman of the Supreme Court. Lev, "Draft, Chapters on Post-Revolutionary Indonesian Legal History," ch. 3, p. 25

[93] The Circular Letter was not published, and I am relying on interview material here.

[94] *DSL*, 3 September 1960.

[95] Decree Minister of Justice no.J.S.4/4/14 dated 6 March 1964. On the shoulder boards see *Varia Peradilan* 3,4-6 (1965): 31. Daniel S. Lev, "The Lady and the Banyan Tree: Civil Law Change in Indonesia," *American Journal of Comparative Law* 14 (1965): 282, notes the significance of this replacement as a symbol of change. This symbolism also extended to the substance of change. The Lady-Justice-with-sword-and-scales portrayed a depersonalized third party justice, but the Banyan Tree symbol combined with the word *pengayoman* (protection) carries a much more hierarchical, patrimonial, and discretionary connotation. The government of the day quite clearly saw it in those terms. Minister of Justice Sahardjo, who introduced the symbol, said in this context that the president was the "elder" (*sesepuh*) of the entire nation and responsible for *pengayoman*. His successor Astrawinata referred to the symbol as something "deeper, more glorious, more loving of people and society, more protective and comforting, more guiding and calming." See *Varia Peradilan* 3,7-9 (February-March 1964): 166-67, also referred to in Lev, "Draft, Chapters on Post-Revolutionary Indonesian Legal History," ch. 3, p. 58, n. 18.

[96] The uniforms were ceremoniously instituted when four judges, representing the entire judiciary, were presented at the Department of Justice with their new uniforms. *Varia Peradilan* 3,7-9 (February-March 1964): 166-167.

> Yes, it used to be, comrades, when we just acquired our independence, that I saw our judges still wearing gowns like Dutch judges. Why, now that we have our own country, a country with its own identity, a country in revolution, why should our judges still wear the same dress as during Dutch times? Why should they not also be clad in revolutionary outfit?[97]

Any resistance to these developments was fought with revolutionary fervor, as opposition was no longer tolerated in any form. Thus, Minister of Justice Astrawinata turned up at the Judges' Association reunion at Tretes in 1961 and gave a speech on "guided judiciary," to indicate that the judiciary was wholly subservient to the political goals of Guided Democracy.[98] Fielding questions on the separation of powers from the audience of judges, he brutally struck them down:

> After the talk, [Surabaya judge] Soerjadi got up and asked Astra about the separation of government powers. The Minister was wholly contemptuous in his reply, as if to say, you poor benighted bastard, even by asking about the separation of powers you reveal yourself to be still *oldefos*.[99]

The judges' role was subject to the goals of the revolution, as political leaders did not fail to impress upon the judiciary. In September 1964, during an address to a national judicial refresher course, Sukarno called for the judges each to "realize their duties as a people's and revolutionary judge."[100] They had to become true instruments of the revolution:

> Judges as instruments of the revolution must know who is friend and who is enemy of the revolution; they must be able to make a clear distinction and have the proper attitude towards friends and enemies of the revolution.[101]

And indeed, during the course, the judges resolved to be good revolutionary instruments,

> to give the heaviest punishments to those who obstruct the revolution, the reactionary group, the counter-revolutionary group,

---

[97] Sukarno, "Djalankan kewadjibanmu sebagai hakim rakjat hakim revolusi," *Varia Peradilan* 4,4-6 (1965): 33.

[98] This would be repeated during the National Conference on Development in the same year ("All courts must be guided, and the guidance is one . . . "), and the next year during a meeting with the regional conference of the Judges' Association in Prapat, North Sumatra. Direktorat Djenderal Pembinaan Hukum, *Kekuasaan kehakiman jang bebas* (Jakarta: Department of Justice, 1970), pp. 133-34.

[99] *DSL*, 7 December 1964. Astra was the nickname of Minister of Justice Astrawinata, and *oldefos* was the revolutionary epithet coined by Sukarno to denote anti-revolutionary forces or persons. It is an acronym of the English words Old Established Forces.

[100] Sukarno, "Djalankan kewadjibanmu," p. 32.

[101] Ibid., p. 31.

> the subversive group, in order to save and the necessity of the ongoing revolution ...[102]

Barely a month later, Sukarno reminded the judges that separation of powers was at an end. The sole sovereign authority was the revolution "and no one can be a good judge if he does not have the revolutionary spirit."[103]

The abolition of the separation of powers doctrine removed whatever qualms government might still retain about exerting direct political control over the judiciary. It rendered the judiciary quite powerless, as it could no longer argue, either ideologically or constitutionally, that it deserved a special place and role within the state. The political agenda to improve on its status, autonomy, and power, which the judiciary had progressively defined in the 1950s, no longer cut any ice under the post-1960 conditions. Indeed, regarding all political items on the judicial agenda, conditions worsened dramatically. Judicial status and autonomy reached a nadir, as judges sank steadily in the salary scales compared to other government officials:

> Our salary ranking steadily slips compared to other government officials. At first we were equated to a district head, then to a *patih* (vice-regent), then we were equated to a sub-district head, and so on.[104]

> The position of the prosecutors now is much stronger than that of the judges. The Junior Prosecutor General is ranked higher than Supreme Court judges, in fact. His rank is F6 to start with but moves up to F7 after a couple of years of competent service. Supreme Court judges are slotted in at F6 and always stay that way.[105]

Incidents of direct government interference in judicial personnel management became ever more frequent—though the campaign was not as structured as in later years. During this period, the first cases occurred in which the Department of Justice used its control over court administration to shift judges as it saw fit, disregarding Supreme Court requests.

---

[102] *Pernjataan kebulatan tekad* of the First Judicial Refresher Course, *Varia Peradilan* 4,4-6 (1965): 36. Judges in fact were giving way in this period, which damaged professional standards beyond repair. Lev recounts how revolutionary ideas of legitimacy eroded the binding force of statute, as judges "were encouraged to be creative, to embrace the revolutionary law [*hukum revolusi*] ... this formula began to be used by so many lower courts that Wirjono had to warn judges to support 'their own knowledge' with more substantial evidence ... " D. Lev, "The Lady and the Banyan Tree," p. 298.

[103] "Amanat P. J. M. Presiden R.I. kepada para Hakim Wanita se Indonesia pada penutupan Kursus Penggemblengan II, Desember 1964 di Bogor," *Varia Peradilan* 4,7-8 (1965): 63.

[104] *Varia Peradilan* 4,9-10 (1965): 116. This was noted during the brief preparatory Central Java IKAHI meeting in February 1965. Still in the midst of revolution, the text goes on with the somewhat baffling statement that this really is all the fault of liberalism, which might work all right in Western countries, but in Indonesia only worsened the condition of the judiciary.

[105] *DSL*, 21 September 1959.

As we have witnessed during Guided Democracy to such ill effect, in last instance the Minister of Justice has the final say over the appointment, placing, etc. of judges. [106]

One of the most insidious developments of Guided Democracy after 1960 was the government's loss of ideological inhibitions that had previously made it reluctant to impose its will on the judiciary. This *political cooptation* of the judiciary was embodied in a number of regulations.

In 1964, Supreme Court chairman Wirjono Prodjodikoro instructed judges to reach their verdict through deliberation with the prosecutor "in order to prevent the court verdict from differing too much from the indictment."[107] In cases where continuing differences of opinion divided the judge and the prosecutor, the issue had to be discussed in conference with the relevant appeals court chairman.[108] And, as we have seen, Law no.14/1964 allowed for direct government interference in cases before the court.

These measures legitimated interference in cases affecting government interests. While normally the judiciary might oppose such tactics, the weakness of Chief Justice Wirjono Prodjodikoro undermined its position. The *Cosmas case* (1962) illustrates his role dramatically.

> The *Cosmas case* involved a smuggler, and Sukarno wanted to have it tried as a subversion case to allow the imposition of the death penalty. Sukarno asked Supreme Court chairman Wirjono Prodjodikoro to instruct the handling first instance judge, Sri Widoyati Soekito, to impose the death penalty. Sri Widoyati refused to qualify smuggling as political subversion, and consequently refused to consider the death penalty. Wirjono insisted, referring to the pressure he was under, pleading with her, saying that she had been his favorite student at university, even crying at one point, but Sri Widoyati held firm. Finally, she could not take it any longer and said that she would look at the subversion angle if Wirjono could get her a presidential instruction telling her to do so. It was a ploy, because she never thought the president would dare

---

[106] Z. Asikin Kusumah Atmadja, *Menegakkan suatu kekuasaan kehakiman jang bebas* (Jakarta: LPHN, 1968), p. 13. I think that by New Order standards these cases were not very frequent, if only because the judiciary and the law were so unimportant. Thus, one of the prime channels of Department of Justice interference—recruitment—was practically nonexistent between 1957 and 1970. Some people say that no judges were recruited at all in this period. Personal communication, 28 June 1994. It seems that a handful of judges were in fact recruited during these years, including well-known judges such as Mrs. Sutadi (vice-chairman South Sumatra appeal court, later Junior Chief Justice), Din Mohammad (head of upgrading at the Supreme Court until 1998), and Winardi (chairman, appeal court Central Sulawesi). Still, judges recruited in those days testify to the fact that they were rare birds: "Appointment was a most summary procedure, which in fact consisted only of a letter of appointment and the oath of office. The reason was that no-one wanted to became a judge in this period, so they took whoever came." Personal communications, 11 May 1995, 12 May 1995.

[107] Circular Letter no.8/1964 dated 13 April 1964.

[108] That not the whole judicial apparatus was dead is revealed by the brief, but critical note in *Varia Peradilan* which said that this instruction might be all right for Javanese judges, but would the Supreme Court chairman please explain how district court judges in West Kalimantan might confer with their chief in the appeals court in Jakarta, or the Morotai judges might discuss with their boss in Makassar (Ujung Pandang)? *Varia Peradilan* 3,7-9 (1964): 163.

write her a letter asking her to impose the death penalty. To her amazement, however, Wirjono turned up the next day with such a letter.[109]

Sri Widoyati could not bring herself to decide the case, and asked for it to be transferred to someone else, which was done. The death penalty was imposed, but the case went up to appeal and, by the time it reached the Supreme Court, Guided Democracy had collapsed.

The importance of the *Cosmas* and similar cases was not just the political reality that the government instructed the courts on how to decide cases (see below, Chapter 6, sections 2 & 3). The political cooptation of the judiciary under Guided Democracy also had important effects on the appeal structure, conditioning the way the Supreme Court approaches its legal functions of ensuring legal unity and justice to the present day. In principle, Guided Democracy meant that, if cases involved political interests, the Court had to decide them as directed by the government, and bend over backwards to justify their decisions accordingly. If no political interests were involved, then normal cassation rules applied. This was theory. In practice, these distinctions were frequently blurred: the category of "political cases" broadened with increasing government engagement in society, and the distinction between state interests and the private interests of political leaders became vague. Also, in the end there were no outward defining marks distinguishing "political cases" from the normal ones. For society at large, and increasingly for the Court itself, cases decided on the basis of fact or on the basis of proper cassation rules were indistinguishable. Effectively, therefore, facts prevailed in Supreme Court decision-making, and cassation became a hollow concept. It was no longer clear which cases were decided on their legal merits and should therefore be viewed as authoritative statements on the law, and which were decided on the basis of their factual specificity generating political interest and pressures. This situation undercut the precedent value of Supreme Court decision-making, or its lawmaking authority, and in the end contributed to the unpredictability of the institution. Political interference in the courts, as a result, generated legal particularism in the decision making of the Supreme Court.

(b) The Judges' Association Moves Underground

Guided Democracy added trauma to the post-1950 demoralization of the Judges' Association. There was a widespread feeling within the organization, and in the Supreme Court also, that the judiciary had been betrayed, not least by the Court's own chairman, Wirjono Prodjodikoro.[110] The abolition of the separation of powers doctrine made all talk of improving the judicial condition pretty futile. Yet it was not just that the judges had lost a struggle, ideologically; now they were not even allowed to speak up for their interests. As the whole focus of the Judges' Association was to safeguard and strengthen the separate political identity of the judiciary, it was not clear after 1960 what its function would be. Wirjono's decision to join the Cabinet, viewed as a betrayal, together with Sukarno's 1960 speech

---

[109] *DSL*, 12 July 1967.

[110] *DSL*, 22 March 1960. This feeling was shared by Supreme Court judges, as judges such as Tirtaamidjaja and Wirjono Koesoemo roundly condemned the chairman. It severely divided the Supreme Court.

before the People's Assembly, destroyed everything the Association stood for and all but destroyed the organization itself. At a national level, the Judges' Association collapsed, with its central leadership ceasing operation altogether by 1961.[111] National conventions were no longer held after the fateful 1954 meeting, until a government-engineered gathering in Tugu in June 1964.[112]

The collapse at central level did not mean, however, that the Association folded entirely. At least in certain areas, it remained active at the local and regional levels, "if branches could manage and were willing to,"[113] although, as the Association readily admitted:

> Big steps could not be expected from these regional branches since there really was no contact between one branch and the other, a situation resulting from the blown fuses at central level.[114]

Nevertheless, the Association's regional and local level branches remained active and continued to advocate for judicial autonomy and more balanced government in a separation of powers structure. Through their professional organization, judges became a quasi-underground ideological opposition against the official Guided Democracy ideology. With the Judges' Association providing a focus and forum for their unofficial political activities and institutional loyalties, the judges were able to use it as a springboard in the turbulent first years of the New Order after the collapse of Guided Democracy.

Evidence of this low-level opposition against Guided Democracy, led by the Judges' Association, can be gleaned from a number of small activities, such as the fact that its regional branch at Semarang (Central Java) continued to serve as a caretaker of judicial interests, notably by continuing publication of the *Varia Peradilan* journal. The journal remained an important platform which, while following the official line in many of its articles, also provided a forum for advocating specific judicial interests.[115] Also, in 1962 the local Association branch

---

[111] *Varia Peradilan* 3,6 (1964): 135. One factor in the collapse of the central leadership was that one of the important movers (and first chairman) of the organization, Soerjadi, moved out of the judiciary to be appointed Junior Prosecutor General. *Varia Peradilan* 4,9-10 (1965): 118.

[112] Sukarno, "Kamu adalah hakim rakjat jang sebenarnja," *Varia Peradilan* 4,11-12 (1965): 140, refers to the fact that this is the first national meeting of the Judges' Association since the Second National Conference eleven years previously.

[113] *Varia Peradilan* 4,9-10 (1965): 118.

[114] Ibid., p. 118.

[115] *Varia Peradilan* 3,6 (1964): 135. The Central Java regional branch evidently played a crucial role both as caretaker and as guiding force behind the Purwokerto proposal. It is interesting to note that besides the important appeal court chairman Hapsoro, this branch of the Judges' Association was staffed by judges who would play a role in the judicial struggle in later years, notably Busthanul Arifin on the appeals court and Purwoto Gandasubrata, chairman of the Semarang district court (and also regional IKAHI chairman). Note that Purwoto originated from Purwokerto, that his uncle Bintoro was district court chairman there, and that it may have been no coincidence that it was there the blueprint for reform was drawn up. For a list of judges in the Central Java district cf. IKAHI, *Ajo berkongres* (n.d., n.p. [1965?]), pp. 15-17. Lev refers to an issue of the *Varia Peradilan* journal in which a Sukarno speech is published *in extenso*, replete with revolutionary slogans, but right in the middle of the speech the editors printed a quote from Arthur Vanderbilt which said, "It is in the courts and not in the legislature that our citizens primarily feel the keen, cutting edge of the law. If they have respect for the work of the courts, their respect for law will survive the shortcomings of every other branch of government

in Purwokerto on Java discussed ways of strengthening the judicial office, in the course of which it drew up a blueprint for reform, apparently based on the old ideas of splitting off court administration from the Department of Justice and instituting constitutional review.[116]

The judges' resistance against Guided Democracy became most apparent on another, most unexpected, occasion. In June 1964, the government suddenly called for a national convention of the Judges' Association. This was not an attempt to resuscitate the organization, but rather a step directed toward burying the judiciary once and for all. The convention was a prelude to the enactment of Law no.19/1964, the death knell of the judiciary if ever there was one, since it empowered the government to interfere directly in the course of justice. The conference was called, it would appear, to have the judges publicly support their own burial.[117]

Perhaps it was symbolic that the conference was organized in the immediate proximity of the Presidential Palace in Tugu (Bogor), with the decidedly non-judicious rallying cry "Let's have a congress" (*Ajo berkongres!*).[118] Officially, its thrust was to mobilize the judiciary in support of the revolution. In fact, the president's speech to the conference indicated that the judges were now definitely part of Guided Democracy: by 1964, according to Sukarno, judges had reached the exalted status of true revolutionaries. The speech refers to the suffering of the profession for lack of adequate material necessities, but also notes that judges continue to go to their offices and perform their functions for the sake of the revolution. For this reason: "Comrades, I as your President, as the Great Leader of the Revolution, give you the highest salute: you are true proletarian judges! (*Kamu adalah hakim rakjat jang sebenarnja*)" The presidential address left no doubt as to where the revolutionary loyalties and duties of the judges were supposed to lie.[119] The facade was upheld by the judges themselves, who officially resolved to overthrow colonial law, fully adopt the fighting spirit of the revolution, realize their integration with the people and the revolution, support "Guided Courts," and follow without reservation all "commands of the President/Great General of the Armed Forces/Great Leader of the Revolution/Supreme Protector Sukarno" and so on. It seemed that the government-inspired mobilization of the judiciary had finally reached its apotheosis, and that the judges were at last to be declared politically pure.[120]

..." Lev, "Draft, Chapters on Post-Revolutionary Indonesian Legal History," ch. 3, pp. 67-68, n. 35.

[116] These ideas were of course political heresy at the time. As IKAHI journal *Varia Peradilan* euphemistically puts it, they could not be discussed on a national level at the Tugu Conference "for technical and administrative reasons." *Varia Peradilan* 5,1-12 (1966): 9 caption.

[117] *Varia Peradilan* 3,6 (1964): 135. Officially the reestablishment of the Judges' Association's central leadership was to prepare for the III National Congress. In reality, the government wanted to use the Association to mobilize the judiciary. As the Association itself put it: the collapse of its central leadership in 1961 led to a situation in which "the statutes of the organization and its action program are not yet amended to bring them into line with the 1945 Constitution and the revolution." *Varia Peradilan* 4,9-10 (1965): 118. Note that the Central Java branch organized a preparatory meeting in February 1965. See *Varia Peradilan* 4,9-10 (1965).

[118] IKAHI, *Ajo berkonggres*. III IKAHI Conference Report.

[119] Sukarno, "Kamu adalah hakim rakjat," p. 140.

[120] *Varia Peradilan* 4,11-12 (1965): 150.

The official facade of revolutionary harmony was deceptive. Unwilling to be buried, the judges used their Tugu gathering to imbue the Judges' Association with new life by electing a new national leadership, an election that revealed that, for all their public support of the revolution, the judges were in fact unwilling to surrender.

> (. . .)
> . . . and as the conference opened on Tuesday evening,
> the rain and mountain cold went to the bone,
> yet all were overcome by the warmth
> which rose up from the many heart-felt stories,
> and the sorrows of the past eleven years.
>
> Oho, what is it that plays,
> behind the face full of emotions,
> and the sharp bespectacled look,
> of Supreme Court judge Soerjadi,
> the prime counselor of this Association?
> Perhaps the emotions on his face,
> relate the sorrows we have gone through,
> or is it a reflection of pride:
> this is a beautiful night!
> feelings are replenished with expectations!
> (. . .)
> Who will lead this association?
> This is the question that must be answered,
> by all those gathered in this small hall,
> And Sri Widoyati gives her advice,
> with her upright manner:
> He must be a progressive and revolutionary,
> with integrity and devoid of revolutionary faults,
> loyalty must run through his veins,
> this is the person we're looking for.
> this is the character we need.
>
> And together with the first crows
> of the roosters in the valley,
> the Association finds the person it has been seeking:
> Asikin Kusumah Atmadja,
> a man of character, with shining antecedents,
> on revolution, law and justice.
>
> Friends, take courage![121]

As it was restricted in its official statements, only through a poetic account such as this (published in the Association's journal) could the judiciary give some insight into what was really going on in the hearts and minds of the judges at the Tugu

---

[121] Ibid., pp. 151-52.

Conference. The poem reveals a strong commitment on the part of the judges to the law state. The few token references to the revolution are more than counterbalanced by references to the professional bonding within the organization, to the fact that the past consists of suffering, and that a strong leader, with judicial blood in his veins, must guide the organization. By so clearly stating that the current situation was lamentable, professional bonds of loyalty within the organization strong, and that a leader from its own circle must be elected to change things, the judiciary revealed that it remained quite determined to continue the struggle in behalf of its interests. This is all the more apparent if one considers the person elected Association chairman: Asikin Kusumah Atmadja.[122] Son of the first, highly independent Supreme Court chairman, Asikin was an outspoken and forceful character, firmly committed to the institutional values and interests of the judiciary and steeped in its legal traditions. The Judges' Association could hardly have chosen a more counter-revolutionary leader than it did during the Tugu Conference. The political chemistry surrounding Asikin Kusumah Atmadja's election, more than anything, perhaps, reveals that even while the Association dutifully repeated political formulas displaying loyalty to the revolution, its determination to hold on to its old ideals remained very much alive.

4. THE EMERGENCE OF THE MAJOR POLITICAL ACTORS

The debates in the 1950s had a lasting impact on the political scene. They cast a spotlight on the principal political actors in the debate on the Supreme Court, revealing the political fault lines separating these actors—most significantly, the Court, the Judges' Association, and the Department of Justice—and how they might develop in the future.

(a) The Supreme Court and the Judges' Association

The relationship between the Supreme Court and the Judges' Association has been variously combative and cooperative over the years, and has been affected by the evolution of the Association itself since Guided Democracy came to an end and Suharto's New Order regime established itself. By the 1970s, the Association had become the sole officially sanctioned professional organization for the judiciary.[123] This official recognition strengthened it in a number of ways. While during the 1950s its support within the judiciary had been strong, but not all-inclusive, from the 1970s on all district and appeal court judges automatically became members of the organization. From that time, the Association has held regular meetings, maintained a solidarity fund, scheduled tennis tournaments, and published its own journal, *Varia Peradilan*, which is distributed among all courts and has developed into one of the most authoritative law journals in Indonesia.[124]

---

[122] Ibid., p. 144. It also elected Jakarta district court Judge Ciel Suparni Moeliono as second secretary. She would later become the Association's secretary general and play an important role in the 1966-1970 period as Asikin's right-hand man, or woman.

[123] The Judges' Association merits closer attention than is possible in the context of this research, which only touches upon some basic elements. The Association remains one of the most vocal and interesting lobbies for law reform in Indonesia to date. Its changing shape and role throughout the years is a worthwhile topic of research.

[124] Insofar as could be traced, a number of issues of the journal *Varia Peradilan* appeared from 1962 until 1967. It seems to have ceased publication at that point, as in fact one of the

Politically, however, the official New Order sanction has also weakened the organization. This sanction was at least in part political, intended to control the judges, as, in fact, the leadership of the organization was often composed of judges whose background and loyalties allied them with the government rather than the judiciary. As a result, from about the late 1970s the Judges' Association lost the resolve, dedication, and aggressiveness that marked it earlier.

Even so, the Association has shown itself capable of resisting complete control. The New Order blunted its drive to some extent, but it remained remarkably outspoken and active even under Suharto's regime until the 1990s. One reason is that the government only managed to keep lower judges quiet through short term measures: scattered punishments and rewards, such as steering personnel appointment or offering incidental pay raises. Another important reason is that the Judges' Association until well into the 1980s was managed, or at the very least inspired, by judges who either belonged to the elite of the 1950s or closely identified with it. This group, though by no means immune to the vices and temptations of the New Order's patriarchal culture, at the same time retained a surprisingly tenacious commitment to the principles of judicial status, independence, and power they once knew. In the long run, the government failed to come up with a satisfactory alternative to the solutions the Association had in mind for the political problems facing the pretty cohesive judicial corps. Since over time the executive's short-term measures have lost their effectiveness, the Judges' Association remains for the government a politically restive organization with an unsettling history of getting involved in politics at the most unexpected and inopportune moments. In the end, therefore, official sanction did not fully dampen the political lobby which the Association in fact is.

The principal institutional actor to emerge out of the fragments of the 1950s struggle was of course the Judges' Association. Barely in existence a couple of years before, the Association revealed its political muscle in particular by bringing the justice machinery to a near-total standstill in the spectacular 1956 judges' strike. By that time, if not earlier, it had become absolutely evident that the Judges' Association was the prime actor in the political struggle of the judiciary, as it remains to the present day.

In the critical period of its establishment, the Judges' Association did not enjoy the support of the Supreme Court. This internal discord was a key element in the failure of the judiciary to secure its goals and in the decline of the institution as a whole. Even though both organizations presumably had ultimately the same interests at heart—that is, the political strengthening of the judiciary—the

---

resolutions of the National IKAHI Congress at Yogyakarta in 1968 (reiterated during its National Conference in Medan in 1971), was to resume publication (*menerbitkan kembali*) of the journal. This led to the publication of a single issue in 1972, the so-called special edition (*edisi khusus*), which concentrated on a working meeting between the Association's central board and regional representatives devoted to "The participation of judges in development." This special edition was meant to give a lift-off boost to the journal, but as far as could be traced there was no follow-up until 1985, when the first issue (*Nomor Perdana*) of the new series appeared, with financial support from the Supreme Court, the Department of Justice, and the Department of Information. The editorial in this first issue states: "After a long and winding road, in the end we are fortunate to publish the *Varia Peradilan* journal that we have intensely awaited for so long. This has been made possible with generous financial support from the minister of justice, the Supreme Court chairman and the minister of information." *Varia Peradilan*, No.Perdana, vol. 1 (1985): 3.

Supreme Court in fact actively obstructed the Association during the salary struggle, where it was instrumental in the Association's failure to realize its political goals. The Court opposed establishment of the Judges' Association, refused to back it once it got under way, and pulled the rug from under the strike action. As one judge stated:

> I have no doubts at all that our efforts failed because of lack of support by the Supreme Court. When IKAHI decided to strike at the Kaliurang meeting, Wirjono was there. Wirjono was in on some of the discussions pertaining to the IKAHI course of action, he absolutely knew what IKAHI wanted to do. It was clear all along that Wirjono opposed any strike action by the judges, holding that as judges they should uphold the rule of law, not oppose it. So, during the Kaliurang meeting, when IKAHI was ready to decide on the strike, Wirjono formally excused himself (and was excused by IKAHI members), so as not to be present officially when the decision to strike was taken.[125]

Another judge noted the tensions between the judges in the lower courts and the Supreme Court that resulted from the failure of the Court to support the strike:

> Mahadi wanted to continue the strike. He was furious with Wirjono because he felt Wirjono had quite simply botched up the whole thing.[126]

These tensions led to outright conflict between the Judges' Association and the Supreme Court in the early New Order years.

Throughout most of the New Order, however, the Court and the Association did not always stand in such outright opposition to each other, and in fact they have more often been mutually supportive. That said, they remain distinctly separate political actors. The Judges' Association really remains a political lobby for district and appeal court judges. After their appointment to the Supreme Court, these judges distance themselves both formally and figuratively from the Association—with a number of notable exceptions. Also, and well into the 1980s, the Association's leadership generally was recruited from among the most senior lower-court judges, rather than the judges of the Supreme Court. A variety of reasons underlie this institutional separation.

The first reason is the separation between insiders and outsiders with respect to the political elite. Notwithstanding their many disappointments, Supreme Court judges tend to identify strongly with the power holders with whom they interact. The erosion of political prestige and power over the years was much more evident in the lower courts, at the bottom rather than the top of the judicial pyramid.

---

[125] *DSL,* 4 July 1960. Apparently, the generally highly respected Supreme Court judge Wirjono Koesoemo was also at the meeting and didn't leave when the vote on whether or not to strike was taken. Nevertheless, when the strike actually began, Wirjono Koesoemo backed out and resigned from the Association.

[126] *DSL,* 30 June 1960. As I pointed out before, the highly respected Mahadi, who controlled Medan, apparently continued the strike for two weeks after the Association had called it off. In later years Mahadi was asked whether he would be prepared to move to the Supreme Court, but true to his roots he refused, saying that the appeals court was just as good as the Supreme Court.

First instance and appellate court judges took the initiative in organizing because they were hardest stung by the prosecutors' demands. They also suffered most from the decaying prestige and declining standard of living. Although a few Supreme Court judges sympathized with the Association, chairman Wirjono Prodjodikoro and others flatly opposed the Association's belligerency in the dispute with the prosecutors. The reason for this divergence of views between high and low judges seems to have been that Supreme Court judges enjoyed a sense of participation in the government that trial judges were beginning to lose. Moreover, members of the Supreme Court, particularly those who had been judges before the war, believed that the compelling dignity of their office denied them a right to engage in public skirmishes. This lack of solidarity and high level leadership disabled the Association . . . .[127]

The second reason, increasingly apparent recently, is that maintaining some separation serves both organizations. Simply put, the Supreme Court cannot speak as freely as the Judges' Association, and it benefits the judiciary as a whole to have an organization that can more or less freely express and promote ideas. The Supreme Court is held back by the variety of its functions, which include not just decision making, but also management. This necessarily involves wheeling and dealing in the political arena, compromising, agreeing to political trade-offs, and incurring certain liabilities. For example, while, as final appeals court, it must handle sometimes highly sensitive cases, at the same time it must also push for improvement in the salary conditions of lower-court judges. From the Court's perspective, therefore, a more or less independent Judges' Association can be useful because it can voice ideas which the Supreme Court may quietly support, but cannot express. For its part, the Association can formulate its political goals without having to compromise or accommodate broader political interests that restrain the Supreme Court and, as a result, can function more effectively as a lobby.

The third reason is that the Judges' Association and the Supreme Court are natural competitors. Simply put, they compete for political control over the judiciary. This is perhaps most crucially illustrated in the resignations of at least two Supreme Court chairmen, Wirjono Prodjodikoro and, later, Soerjadi, who had become Chief Justice during the earliest years of the New Order; both these men resigned after a power struggle with the Judges' Association leadership.[128]

In this context, it is clear that the people occupying the Supreme Court and Judges' Association leadership positions are very important in determining the relationship between the two organizations. Thus, when from 1974 the government began to appoint outsiders (i.e., nonprofessional judges) to the Supreme Court, this quite clearly exacerbated the political divide between it and the Judges' Association and strengthened the Association's roots in the system of lower courts. An example is when, in 1985, Supreme Court chairman Ali Said, who was an external appointee and a former general, angrily called the Association to heel when it urged Parliament to transfer the court administration from the Department of Justice to the Supreme Court. His attitude contrasts sharply with that of

---

[127] Lev, "The Politics of Judicial Development," p. 179.

[128] Particularly in Soerjadi's case, the Association deliberately obstructed Supreme Court control over the judiciary, for instance by scheduling meetings that overlapped with Supreme Court gatherings, and calling upon their members to attend their meetings.

Supreme Court chairman Purwoto Gandasubrata, himself a professional judge and former Association chairman, who in 1992 called for the court administration to be transferred out of the Justice Department.[129] It is evident that many Supreme Court judges, notably those recruited from the general court jurisdiction, strongly support the goals of the Judges' Association. The question of whether and how to support the Association as a result is very much a political issue within the Supreme Court.

The last decade of the New Order showed an important shift in the relationship between the Supreme Court and the Judges' Association, however. Basically, the Association was absorbed by the Supreme Court, and its political resolve vanished. From the 1990s, the Association has been led by Supreme Court justices. Its activities have become increasingly focused on a welfare-oriented agenda. The Supreme Court has become the sole architect and advocate of the political agenda, and has used the Association as a social organization and power base to serve its own (i.e., Supreme Court as opposed to general judicial) interests. As the last remnants of the generation of the 1950s fade from the scene and are replaced by intellectually more narrow and ideologically self-serving successors, the Judges' Association has really become little more than an unscrupulous power- and-money machine.

(b) The Department of Justice

The salary debate revealed the third major actor in the political debate: the Department of Justice, which played an important role alongside the Judges' Association and the Supreme Court. As the debate showed, the Department was no longer a natural political ally of the judiciary, but rather an opponent, having become a mouthpiece for government policies rather than a law lobby within government. In addition, the debate revealed some of the institutional weaknesses of the Department that made it particularly vulnerable to external pressures.

It may be recalled that, in the separation of powers system, the Department of Justice has an important role with respect to the judiciary. Briefly summarized, the system provides for courts managing only affairs relating to the decision-making process. All administrative matters, such as those concerning personnel management, office apparatus, and the like, are handled by government departments. This arrangement is traditionally justified with the argument that the separation of functions forbids the judiciary from running its own administration, while government may not meddle in court work. It also means that the Department of Justice runs the court administration "at the behest and request" of the judiciary, in other words, serving as an administrative conduit for judicial requests. Thus, if the judiciary needs more typewriters, or a personnel transfer, it proposes this to the Department, which then implements the proposal. Under politically balanced conditions, the system works as well as any other, as it presently does in the Netherlands and Germany, and did in the late colonial state. But if the political situation becomes unhinged, the arrangement potentially facilitates government interference in the affairs of the judiciary.[130]

---

[129] *Forum Keadilan*, 10 December 1992.

[130] While it is clear that the French-Dutch system opens the door to executive interference in judicial affairs under unstable political conditions, this is not to say that political instability actually results from that system, as some modern Indonesian authors are prone to argue. See for instance T. Mulya Lubis, *In Search of Human Rights* (Jakarta: Gramedia, 1993), p. 101.

The salary debate spotlighted the fact that the political role of government departments was undergoing a fundamental change as Parliamentary Democracy was replaced by Guided Democracy—and indeed, thereafter, by the New Order. The presidential system of government under the 1945 Constitution increasingly tied departments more closely to the central government. It was not merely that, according to that Constitution, ministers answered only to the president and indeed could be dismissed at his discretion, but that parliamentary control over government was much reduced. Rather than serving as lobbies for certain interests with the central government, departments became essentially passive conduits for prevailing political interests down the line. This had an important effect on the relationship between government departments and related services.

The Department of Justice is a case in point. Until the mid-1950s, senior Department officials showed a firm commitment to the interests of the law, and ministers were political operators in their own right. A natural alliance that transcended institutional boundaries united top officials from the Justice Department with senior judges and advocates. They all, by and large, shared basic ideas on the role of the law and its institutions in modern Indonesia. From about 1955, however, the Department became synonymous with government and adopted the government's ideas, and it evolved into a conduit for government control with regard to the legal community. There was a world of difference between, for example, the upright minister of justice, Lukman Wiriadinata, who fought for the law state, identified with its institutions, and tried to further its interests while dealing with an increasingly abrasive government, and his successors, Minister Djody Gondokoesoemo, a Sukarno sycophant, who ended up in prison for smuggling, or Minister Sahardjo, who actively destroyed the law in the name of prevailing revolutionary ideology, making himself obsolete in the process.

Such a change naturally had an impact on the relationship between the Department and related services. The Department and the various services of the legal community lost their shared basis of common interest and understanding on the role of the law and its institutions in the early 1950s. Simply put, from the mid-1950s, the Department evolved from an ally to an enemy of the judiciary, a development that fractured the working relationship between the Department and the judiciary, including the Supreme Court.

In addition to this political development, the Indonesian Department of Justice experienced deep institutional traumas that further complicated its relationship with the judiciary. Both the status and power of the Department of Justice were dramatically eroded after independence, and its administrative control over the (general and administrative) courts remains its only real political leverage. At the Declaration of Independence in 1945, the Department of Justice was placed third (after Interior and Foreign Affairs) in the list of departments, but it currently comes right at the bottom, a decline that reflects its loss of status, which perhaps matches the declining importance of the law generally in Indonesia.[131] Its prominent position in 1945 was in part based on the fact that it inherited the very broad functions of the colonial Department of Justice, which not merely controlled

---

[131] J. C. T. Simorangkir, *Sejarah Departemen Kehakiman Republik Indonesia 1945-1985* (n.p., n.d.), p. 19.

essentially all legal functions, but in addition functioned as Department of Social Affairs and of Information.[132]

Its power and position were subject to rapid diminution from the early days of the revolution. Practically all nonlegal functions were transferred to other departments immediately after independence, with the topographical service going to the Department of Agrarian Affairs, and the social and information portfolios to the newly instituted departments of that name. Over time, the legal portfolio of the Department was also cut, including a few of its somewhat peripheral functions, such as the responsibility for publication of the *State Gazette*.[133] Also, already in March 1946, control over the religious courts was given to the newly instituted Department of Religious Affairs.[134] But the Department's most important losses came when it was forced to transfer control over the police in 1947 to the Department of Interior (later to the Armed Forces), and when it had to surrender control over the Public Prosecution, which acquired independent status in 1957. As a result, the Department retained only functions that were at best peripheral, such as those concerning prisons, immigration, and legislation. Capping the marginalization of the Department and the interests it was meant to represent and promote, it lost its departmental status altogether under Guided Democracy. In 1962, the Department of Justice became subject to the Department of the Interior; its minister was demoted to become a junior minister who had to answer to the minister of the interior.[135] It recovered its departmental status only in 1968.[136]

The only function with effective political leverage which the Department retained after 1968 was its control over the administration of the general (and administrative) courts. As a result, the Department is inclined to view its link to the judiciary not just as another turf fight, but as a life line. But the Department's absolute determination to keep a grip on that life line transforms the link between Justice and the judiciary from an institutional advantage into a political liability, for in order to retain its control over court administration, the Department is prepared to go to great lengths to seek compromises on a variety of other issues. Both the Judges' Association and Supreme Court chairman Subekti commented somewhat scathingly that if the Department were to lose that function also, it

---

[132] S.1924:576.

[133] The *Lembaran Negara* for legislation and the *Berita Negara* for official news. With Government Regulation no.1/1950 this authority was transferred from the Department of Justice to the president and the State Secretariat. With Law no.2/1950, the Department of Justice regained control over publication, only to lose it definitely in 1960 with Presidential Decree no.234/1960.

[134] Governmental Decision (Penetapan Pemerintah) no.5/S.D./1946 dated 25 March 1946.

[135] Presidential Regulation no.4/1962 and 5/1962. As a result of these regulations, the Department of Justice had to be reorganized, but no regulation on this score was forthcoming—a further indication, no doubt, of the wholly eroded position of the former department. As a result, the (by then) junior minister for justice himself provided for the new organizational basis of the department in 1964—Ministerial Decision no.J.S.4/4/4 dated 12 February 1964 amended in the next year with Decision J.S./4/4/24 dated 27 January 1965.

[136] Pursuant to Decision Presidium Kabinet no.75/U/Kep/11/1966 dated 3 November 1966 and the Decision of the People's Congress TAP MPRS no.XIII/MPRS/1966, which constituted the organizational basis for the so-called Ampera Kabinet 1966-1967, Justice was subject to the minister of political affairs.

would no longer be worthy of its name, suggesting that it be renamed "Department of Legislation" in such a case.[137]

This perception that the survival of the Department is linked to its control over the courts has restricted the Department's approach to the debates with the judiciary and contributed to some of the modern tensions between the judiciary and the Department.[138]

(c) The Absentees: Parliament and the Special Courts

Throughout modern Indonesian history until *Reformasi*, the political debate on the role of the judiciary has been conducted by the three actors we have just considered, with Parliament and the special courts notable absentees. The reasons for their lack of participation in a matter that assuredly affects them closely are both political and historical. As both the Judges' Association and the Supreme Court have discussed the judiciary in broad conceptual terms, the absence of the other two actors has not profoundly affected the nature of the issues that were debated (though at least in the case of Parliament it has affected the results).

Parliament is the most notable absentee in these debates. It did not serve judicial interests particularly well during the period of Parliamentary Democracy, and from the time of Guided Democracy onwards does not figure as an independent political actor at all, except perhaps in the brief 1966-1970 interlude. The political fortunes of the Supreme Court appear to be intricately linked to the extent of Parliament's control over the government. In fact, Indonesian political scientists refer in the same breath to the political weakness of the judiciary and to the political insignificance of Parliament, as prominent Indonesian political scientist, Amir Santoso, has testified:

> The goal is that in the implementation of its tasks, the executive must be controlled so as to ensure that it does not transgress the boundaries of its authority, or to prevent it from an excessive accumulation of power. For this reason, both Parliament and the Supreme Court need to be adequately strengthened to control the executive.[139]

According to the author, this necessarily implies the right of constitutional review.[140]

In fact, at least when it really mattered, Parliament was a non-player throughout the period. It made interesting comments, organized fact-finding

---

[137] R. Subekti, *Kekuasaan Mahkamah Agung R.I.* (Bandung: Alumni, 1980), p. 53. Notwithstanding his own problems with the Department of Justice, in this book Subekti says that functions need not be divorced, as long as it is absolutely clear that the Department serves the Supreme Court and has no decisive power of its own.

[138] The Department of Justice is not the only department with a say in judicial matters, as in fact the administration of the religious courts rests with the Department of Religion, and that of the military courts with the Department of Defense. Nevertheless, in reality the political debate was steadfastly conducted by the Department of Justice, with the others hardly figuring at all.

[139] A. Santoso, "Institusionalisasi prosedur dan penciptaan checks and balances dalam sistem politik kita," in *Pembangunan politik situasi global dan hak asasi di Indonesia*, ed. H. Munandar (Jakarta: Gramedia, 1994), p. 85.

[140] Ibid., p. 86.

missions, heard declarations issued by government, the Supreme Court and professional organizations such as the Judges' Association on a regular basis, and its parliamentary reports are generally worth reading. The problem was that Parliament did little with any of this material, because, since the period of Guided Democracy, it was quite obviously not in a position to impose its will regarding any political item. More important perhaps, deep internal divisions and political machinations forced it into an almost perpetual deadlock, where it was informed but unable to act on that information.[141]

The general (and currently the administrative) courts are represented in the Judges' Association, but until 1995 the Association did not include the religious and military judges, who consequently never took part in the debates on fundamental political issues facing the judiciary. The number of military judges is so small that they barely count, but it is more important to examine the reasons for the absence of the religious judges in the political debate to date. First, the general court judges took over from the respected Dutch colonial judiciary, while the religious judges replaced colonial religious tribunals which had relatively low status and barely qualified as courts. For a long time, the general courts were seen, and saw themselves, as the true judiciary, while the religious courts were widely perceived as some sort of separate administrative institution. This perception was confirmed by the jurisdiction of the religious courts, which extended to cases of marriage, divorce, and inheritance, considered a marginal, "soft" sector by the hard-nosed general court judges, who had jurisdiction over criminal and complicated contract cases. Their sense of superiority was reinforced by a number of statutory rules or

---

[141] Besides meeting with all key players in the legal world on a quarterly basis, the parliamentary commission on law (Commission III, previously Commission B) conducts regional fact-finding tours. Commission hearings with the Department of Justice, the Prosecution, and the Police are based on accountability. In constitutional terms, they are different from hearings with the Supreme Court, which are based on constitutional tradition in which the Court voluntarily informs Parliament on its work and problems, since it need not account for its activities to Parliament or any other body. Nevertheless, it is clear that it serves the Supreme Court to have a smooth working relationship with Parliament. In practice, the difference is not very apparent, as the working order and procedures that characterize the Commission III hearings with the Supreme Court do not differ from those that typify hearings with the Department of Justice and the others. Moreover, on several occasions Commission III was very critical and incisive about Supreme Court performance, leading to frequent clashes and tensions. Thus, Supreme Court chairman Seno Adji repeatedly clashed with Commission III, and set the rule that he would not answer questions on individual cases pending before the Court, even if such questions dealt with how it was possible that cases were pending in the Supreme Court docket for more than seven years. *Tempo,* 27 September 1980. The most serious clash perhaps was between Supreme Court chairman Purwoto Gandasubrata and Commission III in 1993, when the chairman was grilled by the Commission on the Supreme Court practice of suspending the effectuation of a Court decision, which some Commission members thought was illegal. The questioning was so insistent that Purwoto raised the constitutional issue of whether he had to answer questions at all, since he was under no obligation to account for anything. Following this brush, parliamentary working order was changed for the first time in thirty years, as it was agreed that Supreme Court hearings would henceforth be conducted between the Supreme Court chairman and party leaders only, not the full Commission III. Personal communication, 19 July 1994. The logic behind this is that the pith of Commission III questioning depended very much on some members, notably the highly vocal and insistent V. B. Da Costa (PDI, Partai Demokrasi Indonesia) and the pressing O. Mahendra (Golkar). By restricting hearings to party leaders, these members would be excluded. The fact that parliamentary leaders agreed to this change in working routine testifies, to say the least, to that body's modest perception of its own political and constitutional function.

habits, partly of colonial origin. Thus, until 1989 a colonial provision subjected religious court decisions to general court approval before they could be enforced.[142] Also, until the 1990s recruitment to the Supreme Court remained the exclusive domain of the general court judges.[143] This not only strengthened the elite image of these judges within the judiciary, but also naturally inclined the Supreme Court to focus its political efforts on the general courts, rather than other jurisdictions. Moreover, religious court decisions could not be appealed to the Supreme Court until 1979, when Supreme Court chairman Seno Adji opened up the Court to such appeals. All these elements reinforced the image that religious courts were unimportant: inferior to the general courts in terms of professional quality and authority, marginal to the judicial process in terms of jurisdiction, and (seen as) more administrative in nature than autonomous courts. As a result, the religious judges were more interested in achieving equality with the general court judges than with debating the more fundamental political issues which preoccupied the Judges' Association. Indeed, religious judges did not organize themselves into the Religious Judges' Association (IKAHA, Ikatan Hakim Agama) until 1977, almost a quarter-century after establishment of the Judges' Association (IKAHI) and well after the crucial debates of the 1960s and the political course under the New Order had been set.

By the late 1980s, the efforts of the religious judges to achieve equality bore fruit, and they emerged from the professional wilderness. Their success became most evident with the Religious Courts' Law no.7/1989, which among other things abolished the enforcement construct in which general court judges supervised the religious courts, opening the way for further cooperation between the two groups. The religious judges argued that since the Religious Courts' Law equated the two jurisdictions and they both had identical goals, their professional organizations might as well cooperate.[144] Unable, perhaps unwilling, to stem the tide, the Judges' Association agreed in 1995, although it clearly remained the senior organization, not merely in size, but also because of its long history and political struggles, as Supreme Court chairman Soerjono impressed upon the religious judges.[145] So, in November 1995, IKAHA disbanded, and religious judges became members of the broader Judges' Association (IKAHI).[146]

---

[142] The provision said that religious court decisions had first to be submitted for approval to the general courts before they could be enforced. This rule originated from colonial times, when it served as a control mechanism by which European judges were able to supervise generally poorly educated religious judges.

[143] As shall become apparent, two judges from the religious courts were recently appointed to the Supreme Court. But it must be pointed out that these religious Supreme Court judges also are graduates from general law school, so that, even though their professional background is in the religious courts, in educational terms they fit into the general court judicial corps. This general law school education is in fact a condition for appointment to the Supreme Court, and religious law schools do not suffice. Personal communication, 21 April 1995.

[144] *Kompas*, 13 November 1995.

[145] Public Address, Supreme Court chairman to the extraordinary meeting of religious judges, 11 November 1995, *Varia Peradilan* 9 (January 1996): 5. Mr. Soerjono dwells for a long time on the forty-two-year history of IKAHI as well as its political struggle, and barely mentions the Religious Judges' Association in this address.

[146] Decision of the IKAHI and IKAHA central boards dated 11 November 1995, *Varia Peradilan* 11 (December 1995): 142.

This development will doubtlessly affect the Judges' Association, but as yet it is not quite clear how things will shape up. Suffice it here to say that, until *Reformasi*, the political debates were conducted by the general court judges, and that the special jurisdiction were effectively unrepresented.

The first Supreme Court Chairman Kusumah Atmadja (1945–1951).
A courageous and outspoken man, and a thorn in the side of Sukarno, he remains the example subsequent generations have tried to emulate.
(reprinted with permission, photo from Kusumah Atmadja Family)

Chapter Three

NEW ORDER (1965-1970): POWER STRUGGLE AND FAILURE

The abortive coup of 1965, the so-called GESTAPU affair, marked the end of Guided Democracy and the emergence of the New Order government under Suharto. It represented a radical change in the political climate that had a direct impact on the law and the judiciary. Shifting from the anti-legal revolutionary politics under Guided Democracy, the New Order government made legality a central item on its political agenda. Legality, which is not the same as justice, remained one of the hallmarks of the New Order government. But, particularly during the transitional years from 1966 until 1968, when emerging strongman Suharto was still involved in a power struggle with Sukarno, the New Order appealed very strongly to principles of legality, a restoration of the rule of law, and a democratic government.[1] Suharto himself stated this position in his widely publicized 1966 speech before the MPR(S) (Majelis Permusyawaratan Rakyat [Sementara], [Provisional] People's Consultative Assembly), in which he called for a return to the unadulterated "pure [*murni*] interpretation of the 1945 Constitution."[2] For this reason, insiders often refer to these early years of the New Order as the "pure New Order" (*Orde Baru Murni*). This period, during which the government backed the restoration of parliamentary democracy and the rule of law, is contrasted to later years when, in the eyes of the same insiders, the powerholders became corrupted and self-serving.[3]

---

[1] Daniel Lev convincingly argues that the emphasis on the law and its institutions was at least in part an ideological reaction against Guided Democracy. The change in political legitimacy made the New Order "resort to symbols of formal law and justice." Daniel S. Lev, "Judicial Institutions and Legal Culture in Indonesia," in *Culture and Politics in Indonesia*, ed. C. Holt et al. (Ithaca: Cornell University Press, 1972), p. 273.

[2] Suharto, *Kembalilah kepada kemurnian pelaksanaan sistim demokrasi terpimpin* (Jakarta: Ministry of Information, 1966).

[3] A considerable lack of clarity surrounds this concept of the "purity" of the New Order. In its early years, the New Order government gave unequivocal support to a restoration of constitutional government, so it is fair to speak about "purity" here. But in the drawn-out developments between the rejection of the first Bill on the Basic Principles of the Judiciary in 1967 and the imprisonment of many liberal thinkers and activists following the MALARI riots in 1974, the New Order government began to shift ground and use ideology and institutions for self-serving purposes. (MALARI, Malapetaka 15 Januari, Disaster of 15 January, the January 1974 riots triggered by the visit of the Japanese prime minister). It is difficult to pinpoint precisely the transformation from "pure" to "impure." The issue is not altogether irrelevant, because people use the concept of the "pure New Order" to legitimize and justify their own support for the Suharto government in the early years. The argument is that they were justified in supporting Suharto and his agents (such as the secret service, OPSUS) then because of their apparent purity. Here it is much less clear whether "pure" refers to some objective political standard ("government statements and actions support constitutional government") or whether it means that the government was pure in the eyes of the beholder ("I thought it was pure,

Apart from changing the political climate, the fall of Guided Democracy released pent-up frustrations in the legal world. All legal actors, not least the judiciary, forged ahead to recoup the terrain lost during the dismal previous years.[4] Their experiences under Parliamentary and Guided Democracy made the judiciary focus not merely on recovering losses and returning to the status quo ante, as they might describe the situation in the 1950s. In the bloody aftermath of the GESTAPU affair, the judiciary also took the view that its place and role could only be effectively secured in the fabric of the emerging political order if it were strengthened beyond its old boundaries. And so, rather than ask merely for the restoration of their former positions, judges clamored for greater rights, more power, higher status. For the judges in this period, this represented not just an institutional turf fight or a restoration of perks and status; it constituted the very essence of New Order constitutional and political reform. And indeed, the way in which the New Order government treated the judges was without doubt the most important indicator of the strength and sincerity of its political commitment to the law. With a new government proclaiming its commitment to the rule of law, with everything in flux and institutional boundaries being redrawn, this was clearly the

---

therefore support was justified even though it was in fact impure"), or that the beholder had self-serving motives from the start, and was just pretending ("I knew it was corrupt, but I pretended it was pure to justify my support"). As the sources referred to hereafter reveal, there is evidence that some of the prominent judges who were close to Suharto and his agents were in part, if not wholly, inspired by selfish motives. Their attempt to justify this cooperation ex post facto with reference to the purported "purity" of the New Order seems to be a sop. For the Indonesian government at present, the "pure-impure" dichotomy has taken on yet another meaning. Rather than referring to constitutional correctness, it uses the term to indicate political correctness, which is something different. Its reactions to A. B. Nasution's thesis (*The Aspiration for Constitutional Government in Indonesia* [Jakarta: Pustaka Sinar Harapan, 1992]), showed that by "pure" the New Order meant absolute loyalty to the government interpretation of the 1945 Constitution and the state ideology, *Pancasila*. "Impure" referred to what was politically unacceptable, and hence considered politically subversive, from the government perspective. *Forum Keadilan*, Edisi Khusus (August 1995): 102; Personal communication, 12 July 1995.

[4] An interesting side issue that cannot be dealt with here is that these exhilarating years created a solidarity between the legal professions that was unthinkable under Guided Democracy, embodied in a loosely structured organization, Pengabdi Hukum (Servants of the Law), which brought together advocates, judges, prosecutors, and police officials in a unique common attempt to restore the role of the law. Judges took the helm of the organization, and indeed judge Sri Widoyati Soekito (soon to be appointed to the Supreme Court) established the organization and became its first chairwomen in 1967. Pengabdi Hukum was meant to be a forum in which efforts between the legal professions might be coordinated and possible tensions ironed out. Yet, more important, participation in the organization could be interpreted as a sort of atonement for past wrongs to which the legal professions themselves had contributed. "A week ago or so, [X] said that Pengabdi Hukum represented in a sense the attempt by law officials to redeem themselves after their complicity in the ravages of Guided Democracy. All recognized, he said, that all were guilty for what had happened, and the Pengabdi Hukum was something like an attempt at atonement." Daniel S. Lev archives, 26 November 1971 (hereafter *DSL*. These are the personal interview notes of Daniel S. Lev; copies will be deposited in the University of Washington library [Seattle, WA], the Cornell University Kroch Collection [Ithaca, NY], and Pusat Studi Hukum dan Kebijakan [PSHK] in Jakarta). As a result, the organization was quite deliberately meant to serve as a political platform by means of which the place and role of the law and its institutions might be reasserted in the modern Indonesian state. Daniel S. Lev, "Draft, Chapters on Post-Revolutionary Indonesian Legal History," (unpublished), ch. 5; Daniel S. Lev, "Draft, The Political Journey of Yap Thiam Hien," (unpublished, 1995), p. 24.

time for the judges to pull out all the stops. Historical developments of the period can be roughly summarized as follows.

The first two years after GESTAPU, from 1965 until 1967, were auspicious. The judges' first major aim of achieving internal cohesion resulted in a power struggle between the Judges' Association (IKAHI, Ikatan Hakim Indonesia) and the Supreme Court, which ended in the Association's victory. They also strove to develop a comprehensive political program, which was essentially realized in 1966, with "the Soerjadi legacy," which laid down the three major goals of the judiciary: improvement of status through special salary provisions; realization of judicial autonomy from executive interference through transferring court administration from the Department of Justice to the Supreme Court; and strengthening judicial power by instituting the right of constitutional review.[5] There were other issues, but these were the three core points of attention.

The period after 1967 was marked by a progressive erosion of the political standing and influence of the judiciary. This was in part a result of increasing government interference in the Judges' Association through its secret service OPSUS (Operasi Khusus, Special Operations), which led to considerable internal tensions and a general loss of resolve within the judicial leadership. The decline also flowed from the fact that the judiciary lost control over the drafting process of the crucial Bill of the Basic Principles of the Judiciary. As a result, it was virtually excluded from the political process which would determine its role and place in the emerging new political order.

The final period, from 1968 until 1970, saw a brief but fierce fight over the Bill on the Basic Principles of the Judiciary. The fight started with a determined attempt by the judiciary to regain the initiative by opening up the debate to the public during the 1968 National Law Seminar. The judiciary hoped that, if public support could be rallied for its political goals at that meeting, Parliament might be induced to reconsider the Bill. In the face of determined government opposition, the judiciary failed to realize its goals at the 1968 Seminar, however. This led to a compromise, formulated during its subsequent National Congress in Yogyakarta (also in 1968), during which the judiciary laid down the blueprint that would eventually find its way into the 1970 law. With some small changes this compromise continued to apply throughout the New Order to the present day.

It is important to realize that from the outset the judges were not just aiming at improving their situation, but were actually suggesting (as indeed they still are today) a complete overhaul of the Indonesian constitutional system. Briefly summarized, this overhaul would change the system from a *separation* to a *balance*-of-powers system, which would strengthen the judiciary and Parliament and conceivably seriously curtail government power. As a result, the debates in the 1960s were very much a discussion of the constitutional and political principles that would determine the face of the modern Indonesian state. The 1970 law, in which the judges had to give way on all three key issues of their political agenda, is the watershed. This law became not just the legal, but more notably the ideological basis for the place and role of the judiciary in modern Indonesia, placing it firmly in the separation-of-powers tradition.

---

[5] As before, I distinguish between constitutional and judicial review. The former refers to the authority of the courts to quash Acts of Parliament, the latter restricts its authority to inferior legislation.

Developments in the late 1960s highlight a recurrent theme in Indonesian history (and perhaps not only in that country) that the strength of the judiciary relies heavily on the willingness of the government to respect it and uphold its ideals. If, in the first years of the New Order regime, the judiciary was able to recoup some of the terrain lost during Guided Democracy, this was because the regime presented itself as a strong supporter of the rule of law and robust legal institutions. The judiciary did not overcome political opposition, but rode a political wave.

What sets this period apart, particularly when compared to the thirty years that followed, is that the judiciary was willing to put up a fight when government support weakened. When it lost that fight with the 1970 law, this was more than just the loss of another battle; it destroyed judicial hope and basically destroyed the Judges' Association as a political fighting force. In retrospect, we can now say that the generation of judges active at the time never recovered their political idealism and mental energy after 1970, falling back instead into political acquiescence, professional apathy, and, in not a few cases, eventually, corruption. The demoralizing effect of the 1970 law is illustrated best by the sordid reality that almost all of the highly committed, idealistic, and talented leaders of the judiciary in the 1966–1970 struggle had within the next decade or two lost their integrity or their authority, or both. The judiciary would have to await not just a change in political regime, but also a new generation of judges, before there could be another attempt to redraw the parameters which the 1970 law had established.

On several occasions after institution of the 1970 law, there were flare-ups in the political debate—almost invariably initiated by political leaders rather than the judiciary itself. Nevertheless, these failed to generate the political mass required to challenge the basics of the 1970 law, and as time went on, such efforts barely even mobilized the judiciary itself. The judiciary clung to its reform agenda, which was routinely repeated during its annual gatherings and policy documents. But as the judiciary became increasingly co-opted and self-serving, the agenda ceased to serve as a platform for action, a set of operating principles, or as ideals that commanded real understanding or debate, obedience to its members, and perhaps confrontation with outside forces. Instead, references to status, power, and autonomy became a kind of ritual, devoid of meaning, and a justification for the judiciary's own deepening incompetence, and its lack of resolve and courage.

1. 1965-1968: REALIZING INTERNAL COHESION AND SHAPING THE POLITICAL AGENDA

In the aftermath of the GESTAPU affair, the judiciary found its situation transformed from one constrained by political duress into one that offered relative freedom. This led to two important developments in the following couple of years: a political power struggle between the Judges' Association and the Supreme Court, and the construction of the political program of the judiciary.

(a) Internal Cohesion within the Judiciary

(i) The Power Struggle between the Judges' Association and the Supreme Court

The first development was the strengthening of the internal political cohesion of the judiciary. This amounted to a power struggle between the Judges' Association, which supported the emerging New Order of Suharto, and the Supreme Court, which at the time was still controlled by Sukarno loyalists, notably chairmen Wirjono Prodjodikoro (1954-1966) and Soerjadi (1966-1968).

The opposition of the Judges' Association to Chairman Wirjono can be traced back to the salary struggle, where Wirjono had played a significant role in the Association's failure to protect judicial status. In contrast to other Supreme Court judges, notably Subekti, Wirjono was opposed to the Association's political activism and refused to support it during the 1950s salary struggle. He did little to redeem himself later, and instead became an integral part of Sukarno's entourage, inflicting a series of disservices on the judiciary.

When Sukarno came under fire after GESTAPU, Wirjono was the most exposed member of the judiciary. There are two accounts of his professional demise. According to one version, Wirjono's fall was linked to Sukarno's plan to suspend the MPRS. As Sukarno was being cornered in early 1966, he tried to work out a way to ensure his political survival. One of his ideas was to suspend the MPRS to prevent it from removing him. For this purpose he talked with the chairman of the MPRS and old PNI (Partai Nasional Indonesia, Indonesia National Party) stalwart, Sartono. It so happened that Supreme Court chairman Wirjono dropped by just as Sukarno and Sartono were discussing the matter, and Sukarno asked him casually what he thought of the plan, at which point Wirjono seems to have replied offhandedly: *"bisa saja"*—no problem. When this reaction was made public, it was presented as though President Sukarno were asking official advice from the chairman of the Supreme Court concerning whether or not the MPRS could be suspended, and being told that was that there were no formal legal obstacles. This comparatively trivial conversation was evidently blown up beyond proportion in the volatile political climate at the time.[6] According to the other version of the story, Wirjono's fall was related to Njono, one of the prominent Communist Party (Partai Komunis Indonesia, PKI) leaders arrested at an early stage of the 1965 political upheaval. It was said that Wirjono had advised the president to grant Njono amnesty.

In either case, as the political currents began to run clearly against the president, and as anti-Sukarno forces worked steadily to erode his power base, Wirjono, as one of the president's loyal supporters, became an opportune victim. With the students and various other associations at the forefront of the political liberalization movement responding fiercely to the accusations against Wirjono, the Judges' Association began to press for his resignation. Sri Widoyati Soekito, head of the influential Jakarta branch of the Association at the time, tried to warn Wirjono to step down before things got ugly, but he would not listen. So she went with Asikin Kusumah Atmadja, the son of former Supreme Court justice Kusumah

---

[6] DSL, 17 July 1967.

Atmadja, to inform him directly that he should step down.[7] Around the same time, the students' associations also came to Wirjono's house to demand his resignation.[8] It was an ugly meeting, and after it, Wirjono, totally upset, went over to see Besar Mertokusumo, the former secretary general of the Department of Justice and a highly respected, sincere man. Besar told Wirjono to resign, informing him frankly that he had weakened the Court, committed many errors, and failed to resist the incursions of Sukarno.[9] Wirjono returned home, and resigned the next day.[10]

Following the chief justice's resignation, a political struggle ensued between President Sukarno and emerging strong man Suharto, concerning the appointment of Wirjono's successor. When Wirjono resigned, Parliament put his succession to the vote, and after intensive lobbying by the Judges' Association, proposed the liberal-minded Subekti as his replacement.[11] Sukarno ignored this parliamentary candidate and selected Soerjadi instead.[12]

Sukarno said that he preferred Soerjadi because Subekti was "a poker player"—the president regarded poker as a degenerate activity—not "nationalistic."[13] In fact, Subekti did not play poker but bridge (though this

---

[7] *DSL*, 12 July 1967.

[8] Apparently, a large delegation of members of the KAMI (Kesatuan Aksi Mahasiswa Indonesia, Indonesian Students' Action Front) and KASI (Kesatuan Aksi Sardjana Indonesia, Indonesian Scholars' Action Front) first drove in two trucks to the Supreme Court building. The court clerk managed to convince them instead to send a small delegation to Wirjono's house. *DSL* 12 July 1967. Wirjono apparently said that the students came into the house acting coarsely and rudely at first, protesting in particular Njono's amnesty and one other matter, probably the suspension of the MPR(S). According to Wirjono, he managed to convince the students that in the first case he had advised against amnesty, but that the president had insisted on it, while on the second score, he had emphasized that the power of the Supreme Court was really very limited, that it only had an advisory function, and that this matter was all in the president's hands. According to Wirjono, the students then said, "Oh, well, if that is so, we are mistaken," and they left. *DSL*, 17 July 1967.

[9] *DSL*, 10 July 1967.

[10] Apparently, Sukarno, whose house of cards was collapsing all around him and who tried to rally his troops, pressured Wirjono to stay on, as did some others such as Adam Malik, according to reports. But Wirjono ignored the request.

[11] There are indications that the Judges' Association tried to preempt a regular appointments procedure precisely because it would in the end give President Sukarno the authority to appoint the Supreme Court chairman. During the famous Universitas Indonesia KASI conference in April 1966, Sri Widoyati called upon Suharto to use his March 11, 1966 presidential mandate to appoint a Supreme Court chairman. KASI (Kelompok Aksi Sardjana Indonesia), *Indonesia, negara hukum* (Jakarta: Seruling Masa, 1966), p. 151.

[12] By law, Parliament would draft a list with at least two names, from which the president would select one. Constitutional custom was that the president would always select the first name on the list. In this instance, the parliamentary list included two names, first Subekti and second Soerjadi. Subekti was so certain of his appointment that he had already resigned his university position in anticipation of being nominated. When the news came that Soerjadi had been appointed instead, Subekti apparently wept in disappointment. Though not a spiteful man, he has held a grudge against Sukarno ever since. *DSL*, 25 June 1967. This is the more plausible account. Nevertheless, there are reports from persons directly involved that Parliament did not in fact put Subekti first, or that, at the very least, there was very strong parliamentary support for Soerjadi, not just from his PNI bailiwick but also from such actors as the Partai Nasional and the Armed Forces (Alamsjah). Personal communication, 1 July 1994.

[13] *DSL*, 25 June 1967. In fact there may have been other reasons as well. Subekti's reputation as a liberal thinker was well-established. He was the one Supreme Court judge to support the

subtlety may have been lost on Sukarno), and everyone thought that the real reason was that Soerjadi was an old friend of Sukarno's from the PNI. There was a widespread feeling that Sukarno took the rather extraordinary step of ignoring the parliamentary recommendation to boost his own failing political support; as a result, more or less regardless of his own stance, Soerjadi was politically suspect from the beginning.[14]

As a result, Soerjadi almost immediately became a focus of opposition for New Order supporters. This opposition came first from Parliament, which felt slighted because its own recommendation had been bypassed by the president,[15] and which subsequently refused to nominate new members to the Supreme Court, even though the Court was seriously understaffed at the time. In 1966, it was reduced to only four members: Soerjadi, Subekti, Abdurrahman, and Hakim. Sutan A. Hakim, moreover, was soon to resign. This led to an uncomfortable situation in which, because of its chairman, the Supreme Court found it increasingly difficult to realize its functions.[16]

The strongest opposition to Soerjadi came from his own backyard, however. The Judges' Association, which he had established, was vehemently opposed to him, and from the start lobbied against him. In fact, almost on the day of his appointment, a delegation from the Association went over to talk him out of accepting the post, pointing out to him that he was being used. Soerjadi's refusal to change his mind led to a power struggle between the Judges' Association and the Supreme Court.[17]

---

judges' strike in 1956. His sons were known to have taken an active part in the students' movement that stood at the center of the political storm in 1965-1966.

[14] Several strong supporters of Subekti, such as Adnan Buyung Nasution, told me that they felt sorry for Soerjadi because he was very much a victim of circumstances. Personal communication, 12 July 1994. Soerjadi was a complex case, of course. On the one hand, he was the founder of the Judges' Association, had been their spokesman during the salary debate, and at various times had demonstrated his commitment to the separation-of-powers doctrine. Nevertheless, he was also a PNI man and had shifted between the judiciary and its traditional foe, the prosecutors. After the trauma of Guided Democracy, there were strong suspicions within the judiciary that Soerjadi was no longer "their man," and his loyalties were in doubt. But more than this ambivalent personal history, it was the struggle between Sukarno and Parliament that made Soerjadi an issue of political conflict. Thus, there was a rapprochement between Soerjadi and his staunch opponent Sri Widoyati after 1968, which may have been partly brought about by the latter's feeling that Soerjadi had not been treated fairly. Personal communication, 1 July 1994.

[15] DSL, 25 June 1967. Part of the problem was that Parliament had been bypassed. What lay behind it all was that Sukarno's party, the PNI, kept pushing for its candidates to be appointed to the Supreme Court, as happened with Soerjadi. So the DPR (Dewan Perwakilan Rakyat, People's Representative Assembly, i.e. Parliament), which began to ally itself more closely with Suharto from 1967 onwards, refused to do anything until a system had been worked out that would bypass the PNI. At the time, the DPR was in fact pushing for a system in which Supreme Court judges would be appointed by parliamentary majority vote and without any presidential role whatsoever.

[16] DSL, 20 June 1967.

[17] The talks were conducted by the Jakarta head of the Association, Sri Widoyati Soekito. Soerjadi tried to mobilize her family to convince her to draw back, as he knew her family was upset at seeing her name in the newspapers all the time. DSL, 12 July 1967. According to a slightly different account, Soerjadi was not officially informed of the presidential decision. It was broadcast on the radio and reported in the newspapers the next day, when he heard of it through his wife. He called State Secretary M. Ichsan, but Ichsan had not attended the cabinet

A good deal of personal friction between Soerjadi and a number of the Association's leaders, notably Asikin Kusumah Atmadja and Sri Widoyati Soekito, exacerbated the situation. This friction arose in part from the past troubled personal relationship between these judges, and was accentuated by professional conflicts when they served together on the same court.

On a personal level, things had started out fine. Soerjadi and Sri Widoyati at first had an excellent relationship. In fact, their respective families, though not related, were so close that when Sri Widoyati enrolled in the judiciary her family asked the older Soerjadi to take her under his wing. This he did, and while she served on the Semarang court, Sri Widoyati lived in Soerjadi's house.[18] It was then that Soerjadi came to the conclusion that Sri Widoyati might not be judge material. "Things happened there," Soerjadi would recount forty years later, refusing to go any further, "that convinced me she was not cut of the right wood to be a judge."[19]

These problems were intensified when Sri Widoyati, Asikin Kusumah Atmadja, and Soerjadi in the late Guided Democracy period served together on the same Jakarta courts, initially at the district level, and then on the appeals court. There, friction between them exploded a number of times into open conflict. The reason was that Asikin and Sri Widoyati felt that Soerjadi was letting political interests interfere with his work as a judge.[20]

---

meeting the previous day and was unable to say anything official. So they decided to meet the next day. Before Soerjadi met with Ichsan, however, the Association called him and made an appointment for that evening. About nine people came, including Asikin and Sri Widoyati. They asked him not to accept the nomination because it had not been the DPR's choice. Soerjadi, who professed surprise at the nomination since he was the most junior Supreme Court judge, said that he was not precisely aware of what was going on in the first place, had not asked for the job, and had not been officially informed about anything. He then suggested that the members of the delegation join him when he visited Ichsan the next day. The delegation withdrew to the veranda to discuss the best approach, and when they came back said that they would not join him. It later transpired that the Judges' Association bypassed Ichsan and went directly to Sukarno, asking him not to appoint Soerjadi. When Sukarno asked why, they answered that Soerjadi was PNI, admittedly not the most subtle argument, as in fact Sukarno threw them out and went ahead with the appointment. Personal communication, 1 July 1994.

[18] Personal communication, 1 July 1994.

[19] I was informed that the incident had nothing to do with either intellectual capabilities or money. Personal communication, 1 July 1994.

[20] One notable incident was the infamous 1962 Cosmas smuggling case. In this case, Supreme Court chairman Wirjono brought pressure to bear on Sri Widoyati at the Jakarta district court to impose the death penalty, as has been related earlier. When Widoyati refused to impose this penalty despite Wirjono's pressure and even a direct presidential order, Soerjadi intervened. He was chairman of the Jakarta district court, and reassigned the case to a more pliable judge, who duly imposed the death penalty. Asikin and Sri Widoyati were incensed by this. They felt that Soerjadi should have supported Sri Widoyati in her resistance to such blatant political pressures. The decision was appealed but, ironically, Asikin and Sri Widoyati had been appointed to the Jakarta court of appeal and when the case came up there, they overturned the district court verdict, choosing instead to impose a limited prison term. As the smuggler had already been imprisoned for the term imposed, he was effectively freed. The prosecution did not expect this verdict. It placed them in a tough spot because they had seized the goods of the defendant purportedly to serve as evidence during the trial. In fact, the goods were never used in evidence, but banking on a death penalty had been sold by the prosecution to line their own pockets. The prosecution decided to appeal in cassation to the Supreme Court, hoping that Soerjadi would let them off the hook. At that point, political events intervened, as the GESTAPU affair erupted. The case placed Soerjadi in a quandary. The defendant, a prominent

Following his appointment as chief justice by Sukarno, Soerjadi tried to counter opposition from the Association, bypassing it and creating his own network of followers within the judiciary. Thus, immediately after his appointment in 1966, he made a secret list of candidate judges for the Supreme Court and sent it off to the DPR (Dewan Perwakilan Rakyat, People's Representative Assembly). The list contained only rather junior and obscure judges, and did not include any of the Judges' Association leaders (and most senior lower-court judges), such as Asikin Kusumah Atmadja, Sri Widoyati Soekito, and Busthanul Arifin.[21] Thus, Lumbanraja was appointed to the Supreme Court directly from the peripheral court in the small Sumatran town of Balige. Soerjadi also tried to shift judges around within the system, with the aim of removing the vocal Association leaders such as Asikin Kusumah Atmadja and Sri Widoyati Soekito from their key positions in Jakarta and other large cities, replacing them by people loyal to him.[22]

The Association fought back. One of their members, Ciel Suparni Moeliono, got access to Soerjadi's list. On the basis of this, Association leaders approached judges on the list to persuade them to decline the promotions, which some of them did (for example the first instance court judge Rusli).[23] At the same time, the Judges' Association lobbied Parliament against Soerjadi's nominees and also against the proposed transfers. Seno Adji, minister of justice and a Suharto loyalist, called in Asikin Kusumah Atmadja and Sri Widoyati Soekito, whom Soerjadi had proposed transferring, and told them that, as minister of justice his hands were tied and he had to agree to any transfer request made by the Supreme Court chairman. Asikin and Widoyati argued that this was really a political struggle, that Soerjadi was a supporter of the old Sukarno regime, and Seno Adji should realize the way the wind was blowing. They also warned that groups supporting them, such as the Judges' Association, KASI, and KAMI, would take political action on their behalf. The minister of justice succumbed to the pressure and rejected the Soerjadi request that certain influential judges be transferred. This first documented case of a minister of justice denying a request by the Supreme Court chairman for a judicial transfer set a dangerous precedent for the future.[24]

In late 1966, the Judges' Association announced that it would hold a conference to discuss Soerjadi's appointments policies, and indeed Soerjadi himself. Soerjadi summoned the Association leadership to the Supreme Court, and because several of its members were out of town, its secretary-general, Ciel Suparni Moeliono, was

---

Chinese, had business links with Suharto. On the one hand, Soerjadi's loyalty to Sukarno and pressure from the prosecution inclined him to reimpose the death sentence, while on the other hand he recognized a need to accommodate the new political realities. *DSL*, 12 July 1967.

[21] *DSL*, 20 July 1968.

[22] Personal communication, 30 June 1994.

[23] *DSL*, 20 July 1968. Apparently, Soerjadi proposed Rusli because he wanted someone from the Sunda area on the Supreme Court. This is a rather curious argument, considering that Asikin was himself a Sundanese. Perhaps it was a device Soerjadi used to preempt Asikin's appointment to the Court—if Rusli were appointed, Soerjadi could argue that the Sundanese would be over-represented if Asikin became a Supreme Court judge also.

[24] Asikin apparently told Seno Adji that he would have agreed to his proposed transfer to Banjarmasin if it had been a matter of routine, but that it was really meant as punishment, and that on those grounds he had decided to resist it. He threatened to resign. Seeking a way out, Seno Adji apparently offered Asikin a position at the Department of Justice, but Asikin declined. Personal communication, 16 July 1994.

sent. Soerjadi did his best to unsettle her, addressing her before the full Court in the large and impressive session hall instead of in his own offices. Supported by Sutan Abdul Hakim, he gave vent to his anger, shouting at her that the Association's leaders should know better and would soon be taught a lesson.[25] Suparni, who had proven her worth during the confrontation with President Sukarno some years before, barely flinched, and calmly stated that the Association would go ahead with its conference as planned in November 1966. Soerjadi countered that the Supreme Court would organize an official meeting at Semarang at the same time. Unruffled, Suparni calmly replied that in that case, the Supreme Court conference would have to proceed without the Association's members. Soerjadi had to give way. The IKAHI conference was held as planned, and even Soerjadi attended for a while.[26]

The situation came to a head in 1968, after the fall of Sukarno. When rumors circulated that Asikin and Sri Widoyati were being considered for nomination to the Supreme Court, Soerjadi made it known that he would refuse to serve with them on the Court. The Judges' Association promptly advanced the two names (together with that of Busthanul Arifin) to Parliament for nomination as Supreme Court judges, and Parliament, eager to get its own back at Sukarno, nominated them. They were duly appointed, and Soerjadi resigned.[27] He was replaced by Subekti, who had been sympathetic to the Association all along.

As a result, the Judges' Association won its power struggle with the Supreme Court, and, as it took control of the Court in 1968, political cohesion between both principal political actors of the judiciary was achieved.

(ii) The Judicial Political Program

The second development marking this period was that the judiciary set about defining a comprehensive political program which would outline its objectives for reform. There was agreement that the role and position of the judiciary had to change, and the question then arose concerning where this change was to be effected.

As might be expected, the Judges' Association was the first to mobilize. Almost immediately after the GESTAPU affair, its active Central Java branch organized a conference in Semarang, together with Diponegoro University, to discuss the role and place of the judiciary under the 1945 Constitution. This May 1966 conference was led by able and committed judges such as Hapsoro, Busthanul Arifin, and Purwoto Gandasubrata (the regional Association chairman). Its conclusions effectively became the starting point for a national political agenda for the judiciary under the New Order.[28]

---

[25] *DSL*, 20 July 1968.

[26] When Soerjadi turned up at the conference, nobody dared to speak up against him. It was only after he left that judges began to berate him.

[27] Personal communications, 1 July 1994, 16 July 1994.

[28] Members of the conference basically proposed to split off the judiciary entirely from the Department of Justice. Apparently, this had already been discussed in a 1962 Association meeting in Purwokerto, but, as the journal *Varia Peradilan* puts it, the proposal could not be discussed on a national level for "technical and administrative reasons" at the III IKAHI General Conference in Tugu three years later. *Varia Peradilan* 5,1-12 (1966): 9 caption.

The meeting was tense. As the judiciary was emerging from a period of active government interference in its affairs, the main concern of its organizers was judicial autonomy from executive interference. Thus, the conference called for an abolition of the worst excesses of Guided Democracy legislation, which allowed for government interference in the judicial process, and in addition demanded that court administration be transferred from the Department of Justice to the Supreme Court. Rubbing not a little salt in the wound, in a manner that displays the Association's self-confidence at the time, the meeting also somewhat dismissively called for the Department of Justice to be renamed the Department of Law and Legislation, or some equivalent.[29]

This was the first time that the judges so openly called for separating court administration from the Department of Justice and dared to assert that judicial autonomy would benefit from such a separation, indicating thereby that the department was one of the main conduits through which political pressures had been brought to bear on them. Not one month after the Semarang meeting, in June 1966, the Association's central leadership fully adopted the meeting's conclusions.[30]

The Semarang conference, however, did not yet lead to a comprehensive political program for the judiciary, but merely placed one more item on the agenda. The autonomy issue completely overshadowed all other equally important items. Thus, the meeting made hardly any reference to improving judicial status by boosting salaries, and, although constitutional review was mentioned, it was only as a sort of afterthought.[31]

It was left to Supreme Court chairman Soerjadi to draw up the first comprehensive list of the judiciary's political demands. In November 1966, Soerjadi organized a meeting between the Supreme Court and all district and appeals court chairmen to discuss the role and place of the judiciary in the future state. At the end they issued a statement:

. . .

j.   . . . the technical management, organization, administration, and finances [of the courts] must be placed under the control of the Supreme Court and not under the Department of Justice . . . ;

k.   (1) The Supreme Court can nullify a central and regional government regulation for violating an Act of Parliament,
(2) The Supreme Court can nullify a law or a section of the law in the following cases:
    * in connection with a case serving in cassation before the court,
    * at the request of the Public Prosecutor,
    * at the request of an interested party.
(3) Any decision pertaining to the voiding of a law shall be taken by a Supreme Court chamber consisting of no less than five judges.

---

[29] For a report on the meeting, see ibid., pp. 8-15.

[30] Ibid., p. 9, caption. These developments were widely propagated, through the judges' journal *Varia Peradilan*, among others.

[31] Judicial review was merely mentioned as one of the conclusions of the conference by Busthanul Arifin in ibid., p. 15, item 5.

...
q. Matters relating to the scale, salary and social insurance of judges and other officers of the court shall be provided for in a separate regulation and in such a manner as to ensure the honesty and objectivity of judges in the realization of their function.[32]

It is a historical irony that whereas the Judges' Association publicly opposed Soerjadi because he was viewed as a Sukarno stooge, it was he, rather than the Association, who so cogently set out the political goals of the judiciary—and these remain its political goals to the present day.[33]

The Soerjadi testament, as we may call it, is a historic document in two ways. For a start, it is really the first time that the three principal political goals of the judiciary—namely the improvement of status, autonomy through a transfer of court administration from the Department of Justice to the Supreme Court, and finally, full powers of constitutional review—are comprehensively set out in unequivocal terms.[34] But in addition, the document also strikes at the heart of the separation-of-powers ideology that forms the basis of the role and place of the judiciary in Indonesia. It proposes abolishing almost all the important elements of that system in political and organizational terms and replacing them with elements that would firmly propel the judiciary, and by extension the constitutional system, in the direction of a balance-of-powers system modeled on that of the United States.

The Soerjadi testament, therefore, stood for the most fundamental political turn-about in the country since independence, one that, if implemented, would have seriously curtailed government power. It was clear that the political program of the judiciary was a matter that had the potential to stir up conflicts of the highest order.

(b) The 1967 Political Challenge: Constitutional Review

The government was spurred into action by the fact that the judges were taking the initiative not just in the debating clubs, but also in the courtrooms. By 1967,

---

[32] A separate attachment to the conference report made it clear that the authors intended to strengthen the relative salary position of judges and realize this with a separate regulation. "IV. The Supreme Court shall endeavor with all its power to realize a separate salary regulation for judges and court officers, with its own system of scales and social insurance that answer to their needs, so as to ensure an optimal performance of their functions based on honesty and objectivity."

[33] This development underscores the idea which a number of persons I interviewed also supported, that Soerjadi was in his own way quite committed to strengthening the role of law and its institutions, and was, at least to some extent, a victim of circumstances. Some prominent persons who strongly opposed Soerjadi at the time now express their regrets over this and accept that he was an essentially correct person, even though he may have been PNI. This feeling brought people like prominent human rights activist Buyung Nasution to offer Soerjadi a position as counsel at his law firm after Soerjadi's retirement, which he accepted. He also served as advisor to the human rights' organization Lembaga Bantuan Hukum (Legal Aid Institute). Personal communication, 12 July 1994.

[34] *Keputusan rapat kerdja para ketua Pengadilan Tinggi dan Pengadilan Negeri dibawah pimpinan Mahkamah Agung jang mewakili para hakim seluruh Indonesia*, no.1 tahun 1966 tentang "Kebebasan kekuasaan kehakiman dan hakim seluruh Indonesia sebagai penegak hukum, kebenaran dan keadilan" (Jakarta: mimeo, 27 November 1966).

their unprecedented challenge to the constitutional edifice was being translated from airy philosophizing into substantive legal action. This development made it clear that the matter would not die quietly, but had to be resolved.

The judges were too impatient to wait for change and instead set about actively trying to realize it, focusing on the political heart of their agenda, the right of constitutional review. They were perhaps inspired by the fact that one of the cornerstones of the 1967 MPR(S) report on the constitutional order under the New Order was that the Supreme Court be given this right.[35] While there were objections to this idea from government circles,[36] in 1966-1967 the judges evidently felt that they had sufficient political backing to pursue their aim.

The issue had in fact already arisen in 1960, when Supreme Court judge Tirtaamidjaja argued that, in the absence of an explicit prohibition in the 1945 Constitution against constitutional review, judges could avail themselves of the right to review Acts of Parliament.[37] He argued that if the idea conflicted with constitutional principle, it should have been disallowed explicitly, as indeed it had been in other constitutions.[38] In the turbulent early years of the New Order, this idea acquired new life. Indonesian judges began to refer with increasing frequency to the seminal *Marbury vs. Madison* case, in which the US Supreme Court accorded itself the right to constitutional review without waiting for any legislative approval or constitutional amendment. Sri Widoyati Soekito, a pivotal member of the Judges' Association, *Pengabdi Hukum*, and the Supreme Court, became an especially fervent supporter of the Tirtaamidjaja argument, asserting that in the absence of any constitutional provision, the right of constitutional review depended on the courage of the Supreme Court, nothing else. Referring to the history of the review in the United States, she argued that there was nothing to stop the Court from also proclaiming itself a constitutional court.

> . . . after all, in countries where constitutional review exists, it is not incorporated in the Constitution, as in America and even Japan. In Indonesia

---

[35] B. K. Harman, "Judicial review dan perjuangan untuk tegaknya konstitutionalisme," in *Konstitusionalisme, Peran DPR dan Judicial Review*, ed. B. K. Harman and Hendardi (Jakarta: Yayasan LBH Indonesia & JARIM, 1991), pp. 35-36.

[36] These objections were attached in a lengthy appendix to the MPR(S) report. Lampiran III: *Tanggapan terhadap hasil karya Panitia ad hoc II MPRS* no.SU 31-67 (mimeo). While the appendix mentions no author, Harman, "Judicial Review," p. 36 says that it was issued by Minister of Justice Seno Adji.

[37] M. H. Tirtaamidjaja, *Kedudukan hakim dan djaksa* (n.p., 1960). Tirtaamidjaja contrasts this with art.130(2) of the 1949 Federal Constitution and art.95(2) of the 1950 Provisional Constitution, which both explicitly disallowed judicial review. As pointed out by the well-known lawyer, S. Tasrif, in *Kompas*, 6 November 1968 (reprinted in S. Tasrif, *Menegakkan rule of law dibawah Orde Baru* [Jakarta: Peradin, 1971], p. 199), Tirtaamidjaja introduced this passage when his book was reprinted in 1960. The first edition of 1953 does not contain it.

[38] The Indonesian Federal Constitution of 1949 actually explicitly allowed the Supreme Court to review legislation made by federal member-states to determine if it violated the Constitution. Provisional Constitution 1950, art.95(2). See also, Gouwgioksiong, "De rechtsontwikkeling in Indonesië na de souvereiniteitsoverdracht," *Weekblad voor Privaatrecht, Notaris-ambt en Registratie*, no.4982 (1968). This article was translated into English in S. Gautama, *Essays in Indonesian Law* (Bandung: Citra Aditya Bakti, 1991), p. 434 passim.

courts must assert the same prerogative, and the Supreme Court obviously must take the lead.[39]

So, for the judges who wished to claim this power, it became a matter of just waiting for the right case to come along, at which point they could follow the *Madison vs Marbury* case, bypass government altogether, and lift the Supreme Court to the level of a constitutional court, with full powers of constitutional review. Such a case soon arose in September 1967. The authoritative leader of the Judges' Association, Asikin Kusumah Atmadja, on the Jakarta appeals court decided the case, which became a seminal case in Indonesian constitutional law.[40] Following the Tirtaamidjaja and Sri Widoyati arguments, Asikin gave his decision as follows:[41]

> . . .
>
> 1.5. that transitory provision no.2 [of the 1945 Constitution] states that legislation prior to 17 August 1945 still applies, unless it conflicts with the 1945 Constitution, in which case it is void by law, even though it has not been explicitly repealed;
>
> 1.6. that the judge, as a member of the judiciary, which is independent from government, has the task to give a binding decision on the question of whether an act conflicts or accords with applicable law; that as a consequence, it must first be determined whether or not the relevant law still applies;
>
> 1.7. that this means the judge must review whether the relevant law is in conflict with the 1945 Constitution (. . .);
>
> 1.8. that it should be added in further support of our views, that the 1945 Constitution bears no provision on the inviolate nature of acts of parliament, as can be found in art.124(2) of the Dutch Constitution or art.92(2) of the Provisional Constitution 1950, which stand at the basis of the idea that judges lack the right to constitutional review;
>
> . . .

Asikin was arguing quite simply that judges had the right to constitutional review. Even though the case only concerned colonial statute (admittedly an important one: the Civil Code), consideration 1.8. was so widely formulated that it might easily

---

[39] *DSL*, 13 July 1968. Sri Widoyati Notoprodjo said that people like Asikin and Busthanul had identical views. She indicated, however, that while on the face of it the judiciary was united, in reality these innovative views on judicial review still caused much discussion within the judiciary. Many of the older judges, as well as new appointees, remained to be convinced. They were conservative or merely reluctant to oppose the government generally.

[40] Jakarta Appeals Court no.25/1967 dated 15 March 1967. This case apparently did not go up for cassation.

[41] The decision, which is unpublished, could not be traced. Nevertheless, as the prominent commentator Gautama (Gouw Giok Siong) points out, it was the first in a series of judicial review cases which are all based "on the same reasoning." This quote was borrowed from the subsequent case, which was published. Mahkamah Agung no.105K/Sip/1968 dated 12 June 1969, *Yurisprudensi Indonesia* (1969): 609, quote from S. Gautama and R. N. Hornick, *An Introduction to Indonesian Law* (Bandung: Alumni, 1983), p. 189, n. 189. The passage quoted here fully accords with a summary given by Gautama (Gouw Giok Siong) of the 1967 case in "De rechtsontwikkeling in Indonesië."

be extended to Acts of Parliament enacted after independence. "It is clear," said one authoritative commentator, "that the chairman of the Judges' Association wanted to make full use of the opportunities which this case offered . . . "[42]

It was a momentous decision, hailed by the press as revolutionary.[43] This assessment certainly appeared to be correct, for the constitutional revolution unleashed by Asikin was continued in subsequent cases and affirmed by the Supreme Court. In June 1968, just a couple of months before the 1968 National Law Seminar, the Court reviewed a comparable case in cassation. In the interval, both Asikin Kusumah Atmadja and Sri Widoyati had been appointed to the Supreme Court, capping the Association's drive to clear the Court of Sukarno supporters. The Court now had no problem with the case.[44] A Supreme Court chamber composed of Chairman Subekti and Sri Widoyati (and Lumbanradja) upheld Asikin's decision on appeal, stating explicitly that no violation of the law was to be found.[45] In 1969, the Supreme Court affirmed a Jakarta appeals court decision that nullified the racial provisions of the colonial constitution.[46] Even as late as 1971, the Supreme Court declared several legislative provisions unconstitutional.[47] While all these cases involved colonial statute, and the step needed to give the Court explicit right to review independent statute was never taken, during the exhilarating late 1960s many thought that Indonesian judges had become John Marshalls in their own right and were in the process of overturning the constitutional order by themselves. It seemed that the judiciary had become the self-appointed custodian of the Constitution.

(c) Internal Problems: Leadership Conflicts and Government Interference

This image of a triumphant judiciary was not perfectly accurate, however. A number of thunderclouds packed the horizon, as the judges were facing several serious problems. Internally, the Judges' Association in particular was marked by increasing leadership tensions and rifts that held the organization back, weakened its political resolve, and frustrated its political struggle. By 1968, these rifts had developed into outright conflicts that had begun to spill into the open. The tensions were at least in part the result of government interference, which became increasingly geared toward reining in the aggressive and, from the perspective of government, overly ambitious judiciary.

---

[42] Gouwgioksiong, "De rechtsontwikkeling in Indonesië."

[43] See for instance *Kompas*, 15 April 1969, quoted in Tasrif, *Menegakkan rule of law*, p. 100.

[44] Unfortunately, the Supreme Court did not really have to address the fundamental constitutional issue raised by the Asikin appeals decision, because the appellant did not raise the matter in his grounds of cassation. The appellant instead rather lamely argued for review on the grounds that "the appellant in cassation has fought the case to exhaustion, to demonstrate the truth of his position, but is consistently ignored."

[45] Mahkamah Agung no.105K/Sip/1968 dated 12 June 1968, *Yurisprudensi Indonesia* (1969): 609; on the violation of law argument see p. 611. Setiawan, *Aneka masalah hukum dan hukum acara perdata* (Bandung: Alumni, 1992), p. 464.

[46] Mahkamah Agung no.105K/Sip/1968 dated 12 June 1969, *Yurisprudensi Indonesia* (1969): 609, also quoted in Gautama and Hornick, *Introduction to Indonesian Law*, pp. 189-190.

[47] Mahkamah Agung decision dated 14 April 1971, *Yurisprudensi Indonesia* (1971): 3; also quoted in Gautama and Hornick, *Introduction to Indonesian Law*, pp. 189-90.

Despite the Association's apparent unity, it was troubled internally by conflicting personal loyalties, weaknesses, and outstanding debts among members that, artfully exploited, had the potential of undermining that unity. In fact, from the immediate aftermath of GESTAPU, Suharto and his lieutenants were assiduous in exploiting these weaknesses through the government's principal agent in these matters, the regime's intelligence body, OPSUS (Operasi Khusus, special Operations).[48]

In the early years of the New Order, the principal function of OPSUS was to generate support for Suharto within society and state institutions and to undermine Sukarno. Patterned on US Special Operations (in fact a direct translation of it), this "personalistic, highly interventionist agency" was run by Suharto's long-time security chief, Ali Murtopo.[49] In the period 1966-1968, OPSUS focused its attention in particular on legal institutions, with the aim of bolstering the constitutional and legal image of the New Order government. At this time, many within the legal community were open to the agency's overtures. After the debacle of Guided Democracy, it seemed perfectly natural to associate with and receive support from the agency of a regime that continually proclaimed its support for restoring the 1945 Constitution to its "pure" form. Even the critical, independent, and newly established Legal Aid Institute (Lembaga Bantuan Hukum, LBH) was not above accepting gifts from OPSUS in this period.[50] OPSUS made its most spectacular

---

[48] OPSUS was one of the most pervasive secret services in operation from 1965 until the end of the 1970s. R. Tanter, "The Totalitarian Ambition: Intelligence Organisations in the Indonesian State," in *State and Civil Society in Indonesia*, ed. A. K. Budiman (Monash: Centre of Southeast Asian Studies, 1990), p. 218. The institutional roots of OPSUS reached exclusively to Suharto, and it operated outside the regular state administrative apparatus. Suharto established it in 1964 before the GESTAPU, when he was still commander of the strategic reserve KOSTRAD. Its aim at the time was to approach the Malaysian and British authorities to seek an end to the Sukarno-sponsored political and military confrontation between Indonesia and Malaysia—which was official government policy at the time. David Jenkins, *Suharto and his Generals* (Ithaca: Cornell Modern Indonesia Project, 1987), p. 22, J. Southwood and P. Flanagan, *Indonesia, Law, Propaganda, and Terror* (London: Zed Books, 1983), p. 58. Because of its personalistic character, its form and role are hard to define precisely. While there is general agreement that OPSUS played a significant role in the period under review here, there are no in-depth analyses of the organization. Still, there seems to be agreement on the fact that OPSUS had two different aspects. On the one hand, OPSUS was oriented towards the "illegal and violent end of the spectrum, often associated with death squads." Tanter, "Totalitarian Ambition," p. 218. Thus, OPSUS played an active role instigating the infamous public rioting during MALARI in January 1974 and the total disorder during the 1982 election campaign. Nevertheless, OPSUS also was the prime instrument of less violent, though no less effective, political maneuvering and manipulation. This was particularly apparent in the early years of the New Order, when OPSUS became the prime covert instrument through which Suharto increased his influence within the state apparatus. See the next note.

[49] As noted above, besides functioning at the illegal and violent end of the secret service spectrum, OPSUS was also geared towards political manipulation. Thus, in 1971 OPSUS steered the first general elections under the New Order in a direction favorable to the government. Apparently, OPSUS also took part in the original planning board of the 1975 Indonesian invasion of East Timor. L. Suryadinata, *Military Ascendancy and Political Culture* (Athens, OH: Ohio University Centre for International Studies 1989), pp. 26-27.

[50] Personal communication, 12 July 1994; *DSL*, 26 November 1971. As others in the legal world, Adnan Buyung Nasution, the chairman of the Human Rights Institute, was close to OPSUS head Ali Murtopo, because it seemed they still worked for the same cause. The gift consisted of five Vespa motorcycles. Although purportedly a gift from the government political party Golkar, they were probably funded by OPSUS, as indeed it was Ali Murtopo who handed them over

move with regard to the judiciary, however, when in 1968 it engineered the appointment to the Supreme Court of Asikin Kusumah Atmadja, Sri Widoyati Soekito, and Busthanul Arifin, all leaders of the Judges' Association.[51]

Asikin's ties with OPSUS and the military extended back to the very first days of the New Order. When in 1966 Suharto appointed (then) Colonel Ali Said as chairman of the special military tribunals for the political trials (the *Mahmillub*) following the GESTAPU affair, Ali Said was worried that he lacked the experience to draft proper verdicts and called on Asikin to help him behind the scenes. Throughout the existence of these tribunals, Asikin remained attached to the *Mahmillub* as a titular colonel and cooperated closely with Ali Said.[52]

With such close ties with the military, this powerful judge figured as an attractive potential ally for OPSUS, and he, together with Ciel Suparni Moeliono, was closely involved with the agency almost from the start.[53] Both judges openly

---

during an official ceremony to the LBH (Lembaga Bantuan Hukum, Legal Aid Institute). *Forum Keadilan*, 6 November 1995.

[51] Personal communication, 30 June 1994.

[52] "I was closely involved in all *Mahmillub* cases, including that of Njoto. I was made a colonel *tituler* to assist Ali Said, who had no experience drafting verdicts." Asikin Kusumah Atmadja, 16 July 1994. In foreign countries, *Mahmillub* is widely seen as a show trial court, purposely established to help legitimize physical annihilation of the Communist Party. This is correct, but it ignores the fact that the *Mahmillub* got under way at a time when the outcome of the political power struggle between Sukarno and Suharto was far from decided, and the trials themselves became part of the institutional power struggle in this confusing period. Ali Said undertook his task with great verve, so much so in fact that apparently he had to be reined in by Suharto. Nevertheless, it testified to some degree of courage that Ali Said was so firmly and overtly committed to Suharto when many were still hedging their bets. As a result, many who suffered under Guided Democracy still feel considerable goodwill toward him and the *Mahmillub*, notwithstanding its stage-managed character. "Ali Said is somewhat of a hero to many Indonesians for his role in the *Mahmillub*, which liquidated what to them was a terrible experience. Ali Said, as a result, has credit and goodwill with the older generation, which new ones such as Lopa have yet to acquire." Personal communication, 8 July 1994. Burhannudin Lopa was the popular director general for prisons and vocal member of the National Committee for Human Rights (Komisi Nasional Hak Azasi Manusia [KOMNAS HAM]) and became minister of justice in 2001.

[53] Asikin Kusumah Atmadja is generally known to have been ambitious to succeed his father as Supreme Court chairman. According to a number of accounts, his close association with OPSUS was at least in part based on the political gamble that it would deliver him the top job. Personal communication, 12 July 1994. In the end, he was very disappointed when he failed to secure the nomination. He had firmly expected to be nominated not just because he was the most senior judge, but particularly because of his firm commitment to the New Order through his OPSUS connections. Some have suggested that his failure to secure the top job may have generated a moral trauma, in that his justification for supporting OPSUS was redemption after securing the Supreme Court chair. With the reward withheld, he discovered he had just been used. He went into some sort of prolonged crisis after 1974, which strained to breaking point his ties with his old associates in the Judges' Association and isolated him politically. Personal communication, 12 July 1994. The 1974 Supreme Court nomination was a panic affair, coming as it did immediately after the MALARI riots, which shook the regime to its foundations. It brought the government to cut short the usual parliamentary debates and scrutiny of Supreme Court candidates, and instead confront Parliament with a ready-made batch of candidates—with Seno Adji as a surprise last minute addition for chairman. Seno Adji had, of course, proven his loyalty to Suharto before, while Asikin remained somewhat of an unknown factor. It may be therefore that it was this surprise development which foiled Asikin more than anything else. *DSL*, 14 November 1978. Note that OPSUS *agents provocateurs* are generally assumed to have played an important role in the MALARI affair, and that if this is correct Asikin's plans were

admitted their OPSUS ties because they felt there was really nothing wrong with such an affiliation during this "pure period" of the New Order.[54] They saw themselves as judges first and foremost, establishing links with emerging power centers to realize the goals of the judiciary. As Asikin put it:

> ... I have been accused of being too close to Ali Murtopo, of being an OPSUS man, of being the *kaki tangan* [henchman, lit. hands and feet] of the military, and so on. I admit I am close to Ali Murtopo, but I see nothing wrong with having connections with power centers. On the contrary, such connections are necessary for the institutional struggle.[55]

Or as Ciel Suparni somewhat dismissively argued:

> These judges were always so critical of OPSUS. But little did they realize that OPSUS funded their own IKAHI congresses in 1966 and 1968.[56]

Because of their close cooperation with OPSUS, it became unclear whether Asikin and Ciel Suparni were actually using OPSUS to further the goals of the Judges' Association, as they argued, or whether OPSUS was in fact using them. Their OPSUS involvement at the very least created the impression that they were working on the basis of a different political agenda than the Judges' Association. One later incident, which took place at an Association conference in Medan, illustrated the fact that, regardless of their actual intentions, Asikin and Suparni were perceived as operatives of the intelligence agency by their fellow Association judges.

> Asikin Kusumah Atmadja: ... when the 1971 IKAHI meeting in Medan came up, the IKAHI leadership invited Ali Murtopo to give a speech. Murtopo agreed, and I went to see him concerning the speech. Murtopo then asked me to accompany him to Medan, which I did. It may have caused some comment, but I see no reason for it.[57]

> Judges' Association leader: At the IKAHI Medan Conference, Ali Murtopo swept into the conference hall with a retinue of about ten persons, which to the

---

effectively foiled by his own secret service patron. Of course, the issue was wholly subsidiary to the political power struggle between OPSUS General Ali Murtopo and Chief of Staff General Sumitro, which figured as the basis of the riots. Harold Crouch, *Army and Politics in Indonesia* (Ithaca: Cornell University Press, 1978), pp. 315-17, n. 14.

[54] Apparently Ciel Suparni Moeliono cut her ties with OPSUS around 1970 because she realized that it was serving its own interests rather than that of the judiciary. Personal communication, 30 June 1994. She left the judicial scene in 1970, when she became a member of the People's Congress (MPR) as well as a prominent and successful advocate. Personal communication, 30 June 1994.

[55] *DSL*, 21 September 1971.

[56] Personal communication, 30 June 1994.

[57] *DSL*, 21 September 1971. Ali Murtopo's invitation signaled an important shift in Judges' Association policy and was revelatory of its problems after the 1970 law. Until then the Association had shunned contacts with OPSUS, notably its head, Ali Murtopo. See the next chapter.

surprise of the judges in the hall included Asikin Kusumah Atmadja. Busthanul Arifin bent over to me and whispered, "Isn't it embarrassing for a Supreme Court Judge to hold Ali Murtopo's coattails?"[58]

In fact, fellow Association leaders such as Sri Widoyati and Busthanul Arifin found it difficult to believe that one could retain one's independence and commitment to the judiciary's goals while being immersed in OPSUS affairs. Tensions developed within the Association, with Sri Widoyati and Busthanul in particular urging Asikin and Ciel to distance themselves from OPSUS. But the latter held firm.[59] These tensions came to a head when in 1968 OPSUS offered Asikin Kusumah Atmadja, Sri Widoyati Soekito, Ciel Suparni Moeliono, and Adnan Buyung Nasution a world tour purportedly organized to propagate New Order government ideas on law and constitutionality to the world at large.[60] It was unclear what the mission was meant to achieve, and many within the Association leadership saw it as a poisoned gift that ought to be firmly rejected. Thus, Sri Widoyati and Buyung Nasution declined the offer, but Asikin and Suparni agreed to go on the world tour.[61] The incident led to a breakdown within the Association's leadership, erupting into an open conflict during its 1968 meeting (an event that I will discuss later).

> ... Asikin was connected with OPSUS from the start in about 1966. He and Suparni really became OPSUS agents within IKAHI. This caused a split between Sri Widoyati and Asikin. At the National IKAHI meeting in 1968, plans put forward by Asikin as IKAHI chairman were rejected by the IKAHI Congress. This had never happened before. Sri Widoyati, as head of IKAHI Jakarta, was an opponent, and the split after that developed rapidly.[62]

Dispensing gifts was, then, a favorite OPSUS tactic to build up moral debts, or better still, create dependency.[63] As Soerjadi's testament and the judges'

---

[58] Personal communication, 30 June 1994. The term used was the Dutch *"rokkedrager."*

[59] DSL, 20 July 1968.

[60] Personal communications, 30 June 1994, 16 July 1994. The tour brought them to Hong Kong, Tokyo, Hawaii, Washington, New York, Holland, and Germany.

[61] Supreme Court chairman Soerjadi apparently was not informed. The Indonesian ambassador in the Netherlands was a relative of Soerjadi, and when Asikin and Suparni dropped in on him, he called Soerjadi to check what they were up to. It was only then that Soerjadi became aware of the tour. This tells us that communications between Soerjadi and the Association seem to have collapsed by then. Personal communication, 1 July 1994.

[62] DSL, 22 November 1971. Sri Widoyati also stated that, despite those differences, she and Asikin were coming together again. Nevertheless, when corruption engulfed the Supreme Court in the course of the 1970s, they again drifted apart, as Sri Widoyati's integrity isolated her ever further. Personal communication, 30 June 1994.

[63] Thus, in the early New Order, OPSUS channeled funds to Sukarno's party, the PNI, which was thus made dependent on the emerging strong man, Suharto, and weaned away from its old master. This final accomplishment was realized when OPSUS saved the PNI Bank Umum Nasional from collapse in 1967 by channeling massive financial infusions to that institution. The leverage OPSUS acquired in the process allowed its operators to exert voting pressure to get men favorable to Suharto on the PNI board when the PNI leadership came up for election. Similarly, OPSUS in 1970 engineered a leadership crisis within the Islamic Parmusi party to get a leadership more favorable to the government. Crouch, *Army and Politics*, pp. 259, 262.

increasingly strong advocacy of constitutional review opened the first rifts between government and judiciary at the end of 1966, OPSUS began to call in its debts. It revealed itself to have had no firm commitment to the law and constitutional state, as the judges had hoped, and only supported them when it was politically opportune.

OPSUS was chiefly motivated by its intent to co-opt the judges and prevent development of an independent judiciary. When some of the judges refused to cooperate, OPSUS began to apply pressure and undermined them. The strong-willed and independent Sri Widoyati recounts the effect this had on her:

> I was appointed [to the Supreme Court] because of OPSUS support and pressure in 1968. [. . .] But as my views became apparent, OPSUS became quite hostile to me. I am more silent now for fear of what OPSUS might do to my husband or me.[64]

Indeed, when OPSUS realized that Sri Widoyati could not be bought, they engineered a campaign to discredit her when she was proposed as a candidate to succeed Subekti in 1973-1974.

> When the retirement of Subekti came up, Sri Widoyati was proposed as a serious candidate to become the new Supreme Court chairman. Apparently she was supported by such prominent political figures as General Widodo, the General Chief of Staff. But OPSUS blocked her appointment by starting a whispering campaign. One of the most effective ways of killing someone's candidacy is by starting a whispering campaign that fields the candidate's name way in advance.[65]

In the end, it is not easy to determine the extent to which OPSUS was able to use its intimate involvement with some of the most prominent judicial leaders to steer the course of the Judges' Association.[66] It exerted direct pressure on the Association, to the extent that even the courageous Sri Widoyati admits that by 1970 she had begun to restrain herself quite simply because she was frightened. Asikin and Ciel Suparni, who were more closely involved, may also have been

---

[64] *DSL*, 22 November 1971. The secret service network also tried to get a grip on Sri Widoyati's husband, Wiratmo Soekito, a critical journalist, who was approached by OPSUS in 1966-1967 to suggest that he be appointed to Parliament. Although Wiratmo insisted that there were more qualified people around, OPSUS engineered his appointment in 1967. Still, Wirtamo continued to be critical of Parliament in his writing even after his appointment, distinguishing between the idea of Parliament which he supported strongly, and the practices in the existing Parliament, of which he was critical. OPSUS got upset about this, saying that he was ungrateful and so on, and apparently engineered his reelection defeat in 1970. *DSL*, 22 November 1971.

[65] Personal communication, 30 June 1994.

[66] Whilst secret service involvement was the major element weakening the Association's internal cohesion and contributing to its decline from 1968 onwards, other factors may have prevented its leaders from activism in the 1966-1970 period. Thus, it is somewhat surprising that Busthanul Arifin, who played such a major role in the Association in 1965-1968, should have been much more subdued after his OPSUS-engineered appointment to the Supreme Court, together with Asikin Kusumah Atmadja and Sri Widoyati in 1968. Only in the 1990s, just before his retirement, did he assume an important role in the Islamic recodification project. Personal communication, 30 June 1994.

influenced, if not directed, by OPSUS. This close OPSUS involvement in its affairs led to an internal split in the Association that clearly handicapped it in its political struggle.

> ... Ciel Suparni has many enemies, for personal and political reasons. Sri Widoyati is very strong against her, because Ciel is involved in OPSUS. Asikin and Widoyati are also at loggerheads because of political and other reasons. The problem is that much was expected from the Supreme Court as a result of the anticipated cooperation between these two.[67]

With cooperation among crucial judicial leaders breaking down, both the Judges' Association and the Supreme Court became steadily less active on the political scene, a situation that served government well.

(d) External Problems: Losing Grip on the Legislative Process

The internal problems within the Judges' Association were compounded by the fact that by 1967 the judges were losing their grip on the political process that was central to their political goals and institutional interests. If the Association were unable to make its voice heard adequately in the political fora, this would threaten everything the judiciary and the Supreme Court stood for.

In 1966, the government machinery was cranking up to review the controversial pieces of Guided Democracy legislation with regard to the judiciary. Laws no.19/1964 and 13/1965, which allowed for direct government interference in the judicial process, in particular, required the serious scrutiny called for by the People's Congress in 1966.[68] Three new bills were to be drafted: a Bill on the Basic Principles of the Judiciary, one on the Supreme Court, and a third on the General Courts. The first of these was to constitute the basic regulation determining the place and role of the judiciary in the modern Indonesian state; however debate on it was so acrimonious that it left everyone exhausted, so that neither government nor Parliament got around to dealing with the bills on the Supreme Court and the General Courts until fifteen years later. Although there were extensive debates on all three bills, particularly the one concerning the Supreme Court, this account will concentrate on the Bill of the Basic Principles of the Judiciary that was eventually enacted in 1970.

Pursuant to the 1966 resolution of the People's Congress, the Supreme Court and the Department of Justice established a committee in October 1966 to review the Guided Democracy laws. This committee would draft the first, highly influential, proposals for the new legislation, and as a result would have a big hand in determining the place and role of the judiciary under the New Order.[69]

---

[67] Personal communication, 30 June 1994.

[68] In Decree no.XIX/MPRS/1966, the People's Congress MPR(S) called for a revision of all Guided Democracy legislative instruments, so as to ensure a return to the "pure" 1945 Constitution.

[69] For a rather sanitized and summary description of the various committees and a list of their members, see Direktorat Djenderal Pembinaan Hukum, *Kekuasaan kehakiman jang bebas* (Jakarta: Department of Justice, n.d.), pp. 20-22. This account does not reveal anything about the work done by the first committee, suggesting indeed that no work was done at all, whereas in fact the first committee did come up with a bill. It does not relate anything about the conflicts between

Reflecting the political strength of the judiciary in these early New Order years, more than half of the members of the October 1966 committee were judges. What's more, many of these judges were political heavyweights, with Subekti as as chairman and Asikin Kusumah Atmadja and Sri Widoyati Soekito as delegates from the Judges' Association; other members included such prominent Association figures as Busthanul Arifin, Hapsoro, and Purwoto Gandasubrata. The committee came up with a bill for the Basic Law of the Judiciary that was remarkably liberal, as it eliminated Department of Justice control over court administration and granted the judiciary the right of constitutional review. If this bill were enacted, practically all the political goals of the judiciary would be realized.[70]

Minister of Justice Seno Adji thoroughly disliked the bill on both counts.[71] This attitude was in part the instinctive reaction of a department head who sees his portfolio more than halved, but it also reflected his strong loyalties toward Suharto and his agreement with the government's perspective on the place and role of the courts.[72] As Seno Adji attempted to sweep the committee and the bill under the carpet, his activities opened up an early division between the judiciary and

---

the judiciary and Minister of Justice Seno Adji, which stand at the root of the first committee's suspension in 1967 and its replacement with the interdepartmental committee from which judicial input was practically excluded.

[70] I could not lay hands on this first bill and must rely on interview material here.

[71] Before his appointment as minister of justice, Seno Adji built up a good record as a supporter of the rule of law. Thus, his forced retirement as assistant prosecutor general in 1962 came after a conflict with Prosecutor General Gunawan on the introduction of the consensual model of judicial decision-making which was being debated at the time. Gunawan pushed for this consensual model, which would compel judges to reach their verdict in cooperation with the prosecutors and not independently from them. Seno Adji opposed this proposal with arguments of principle based on judicial independence. Personal communication, 12 July 1994. His famous 1966 speech before the University of Indonesia reinforced the impression that Seno Adji was an advocate of a strong judiciary. O. Seno Adji, "Prasaran," in KASI, *Indonesia, negara hukum*. It was perhaps not so much what he said, as the fact that he said it at that particular time, which created the impression that he was courageous, as people wondered whether Seno Adji "had prepared a little suitcase with his pajamas, soap, and toothbrush ready for collection to be transported to the military detention centre at Budi Utomo Street after the meeting?" *Kompas*, 27 April 1966, also published in Tasrif, *Menegakkan rule of law*, p. 42. His record and reputation as a courageous man helped him secure the job as minister, for when Suharto consulted legal figures such as Asikin Kusumah Atmadja and Adnan Buyung Nasution to ask whom he ought to appoint, they supported Seno Adji. Personal communication, 12 July 1994; *DSL*, 13 October 1978. Only Sri Widoyati, who could not forget Seno Adji's role in the salary debate when he had served as the prosecutors' spokesman, distrusted the man and opposed his appointment, but she was overruled. *DSL*, 20 July 1968.

[72] Seno Adji was related to Suharto's wife, Ibu Tien, and in fact prior to 1965 was a long-time neighbor of the Suhartos' on Jalan Cendana. Their close relationship is indicated by the fact that Ibu Tien would give Seno Adji's family a traditional rice offering on ceremonial occasions. When Suharto rose to power, he told Seno Adji to find himself another place to stay. Seno Adji had the department buy him a house on Jl. Brawijaya in Kebayoran, and Suharto took over Seno's house on Cendana. Suharto knew that Seno could be manipulated, and that link in itself must have established his credentials. But in truth too much may have been made of Seno's support for the law state. On closer inspection, his famous 1966 speech for Universitas Indonesia quite clearly calls for a separation, and not a balance, of powers. He does not explicitly refer to separating court administration from the Department of Justice, nor does he call for judicial review. O. Seno Adji, "Prasaran."

the government.⁷³ Unable to pretend the committee never existed, he established another committee, this time with official sanction in the shape of a Presidential Decree.⁷⁴ Sri Widoyati Soekito has said that Seno's reaction to the first committee's bill confirmed her suspicions about him, namely that he was really a government man, rather than the law-state proponent he made himself out to be. These suspicions convinced her to oppose his candidacy for minister of justice, but prominent legal actors, such as Asikin Kusumah Atmadja and even Adnan Buyung Nasution, had great trust in Seno and supported him. If any point in time must be fixed in which the post-GESTAPU romance between the judiciary and the Department of Justice collapsed, it was when Seno rejected the first committee's bill in Spring 1967.

In order to avoid being caught in the same trap Seno Adji changed the composition of the committee. Seeking a means to limit the judiciary's influence, he came up with the "interdepartmental" formula, which by definition excluded non-government organizations. He was able to remove the Association's judges from the list, excluding from the committee the most vocal and assertive of them, such as Asikin Kusumah Atmadja, Sri Widoyati Soekito, and Busthanul Arifin, as well as Hapsoro and Purwoto Gandasubrata. Their replacements were all government loyalists, so that the judges were chronically underrepresented in the new interdepartmental committee.⁷⁵ Even though the remaining judges put up a fight in the committee, they were unable to get their political agenda reflected in the bill

---

⁷³ *DSL*, 13 July 1967. In presenting the bill to Parliament in 1968, Seno Adji said the first team was instituted to have consultations with relevant professional groups, the results of which were to be passed on to the official committees. "Keterangan pemerintah mengenai RUU Tentang Ketentuan-ketentuan Pokok Kekuasaan Kehakiman dan RUU Tentang Susunan, Kekuasaan dan Hukum Atjara Mahkamah Agung," in Direktorat Djenderal Pembinaan Hukum, *Kekuasaan kehakiman jang bebas*, p. 56. In personal interviews, Seno Adji had yet another story. Admitting that the first committee actually drafted a bill, he also said that he disagreed with some of its most prominent features. He told the committee that he would present the bill to Parliament, reserving the freedom to deliver his own statement as well. He then said in the interview that he managed to convince Parliament of his own views, which apparently were based on a comparative study of judicial systems, relying extensively on the 1961 UN Ecosoc report on the rule of law and freedom from arbitrary arrest and detention. *DSL*, 16 July 1968. I feel both of Seno Adji's accounts are only partially correct. His interview account doesn't state anything regarding any subsequent committees. Further, the bill presented to Parliament did not in any way reflect the demands of the judiciary. Also, as far as could be traced, the minister of justice had no commitment to the bill presented to Parliament. In addition, Seno Adji's interview account is altogether different from his statement in Parliament upon presenting the bill. And last but not least, the bill presented to Parliament differed on all essential points from the bill drafted by the first committee.

⁷⁴ Presidential Decree no.38/1967 dated 28 March 1967; *DSL*, 13 July 1967.

⁷⁵ The first committee included nine judges out of a total membership of seventeen, including all political leaders. The interdepartmental committee included three judges out of a total of thirteen members, of whom only Subekti could be regarded as an outspoken political supporter of the goals of the judiciary. When a definitive committee took shape in December 1967, there was just one more change. Presidential Decree no.271/1967 dated 29 December 1969. The composition of this group was practically identical with the composition of the interdepartmental committee, with only a single new name added to the old list, that of Professor I. Suny. As Professor Suny was known to be a supporter of the New Order government, this addition weakened the influence of the judiciary within the committee even further.

that eventually came out of its deliberations. From their perspective, this bill was definitely a poor product.[76]

2. 1968: THE POLITICAL TURN-ABOUT

(a) The Bill on the Basic Principles of the Judiciary

The Bill on the Basic Principles of the Judiciary was presented in July 1968 to President Suharto, who passed it on to Parliament the next month. The ensuing deliberations would last more than two years.[77]

As stated above, the final bill was not good for the judiciary, which had to give ground on all major points of its political program. The bill firmly placed court administration under the control of the Department of Justice[78] and denied constitutional review of Acts of Parliament. It did compromise on the latter issue in that, contrary to previous legislation, the Supreme Court was actually empowered to void inferior legislation, and thus was not restricted merely to declaring it inapplicable, as had been the case till then. Still, this legislation explicitly stopped short of allowing Court review of Acts of Parliament.[79] The only modest success realized by the judges was that the bill provided that the salaries of judges be regulated in a separate piece of legislation.[80] It would take almost a quarter century to implement this provision.

Other matters provided for by this bill and influencing the status, autonomy, and power of the judiciary were ambivalent. Thus, the Supreme Court was only named as the highest appellate tribunal for the general courts and not for the

---

[76] The final statement of the three members of the Supreme Court clearly shows that they only very reluctantly agreed with the bill. On considering the article placing court administration under the Department of Justice, Supreme Court delegate Sumoamidjojo says: "... this article and its separate paragraphs in the present form clearly do not guarantee the separation of the courts from government interference . . . But then this is a matter that is not easily resolved." On judicial review he blandly states: "... we feel that such a right is imperative, for which reason article 23 must be subject to serious study." See generally, Direktorat Djenderal Pembinaan Hukum, *Kekuasaan kehakiman jang bebas* (1970), pp. 29-30 and 32. While the bill rebuffed the judges on points of substance, Seno Adji added insult to injury by using the presence of prominent judges, such as Supreme Court chairman Subekti, on the various drafting committees to defend his bill against parliamentary questions later. At several points he argued that if Subekti agreed to it, then surely the judiciary would go along. See for instance ibid, p. 231. The judges thus not only failed to stop the government from drafting a bill that went against everything the judiciary stood for, but their presence was used by the government to give the bill the legitimacy which it obviously lacked.

[77] *DSL*, 14 July 1968; *DSL*, 16 July 1968.

[78] The revised bill can be found in Direktorat Djenderal Pembinaan Hukum, *Kekuasaan kehakiman jang bebas* (1970), pp. 36-53. The relevant article reads as follows: "art.10(3) The courts mentioned under the first paragraph of this article are under the organizational, administrative, and financial control of the relevant government Department, excepting the Supreme Court, which has organizational, administrative, and financial autonomy."

[79] "art.24 The Supreme Court is empowered to void any legislative instrument inferior to Acts of Parliament on grounds of violating higher legislation."

[80] "art.31: Matters relating to the hierarchy and salary of judges, court clerks, and court officials will be provided for by separate regulation."

special religious, military, and administrative jurisdictions.[81] This weakened the Court's position compared to Laws no.19/1964 and 13/1965, in which the Supreme Court was designated the single highest judicial tribunal of all jurisdictions. In fact, however, the Supreme Court had never been very enthusiastic about serving as highest appeals tribunal, in particular for the religious courts, so this was not felt as a great loss. Also, the bill envisaged the establishment of a special Judicial Council patterned on the French *Conseil Supérieur de la Magistrature* for the management of judicial personnel (*Madjelis Pertimbangan Penelitian Hakim*, MPPH).[82] While this council was meant to enhance judicial autonomy from political interference, it also gave the advocacy a say in the management of the judiciary, which the judiciary resisted.[83]

(b) The 1968 National Law Seminar: Open Conflict

The judges disliked the Bill on the Basic Principles of the Judiciary intensely. It still had to pass Parliament, of course, and the judiciary felt it imperative to rally political support in opposition to the bill. The 1968 National Law Seminar, a five-year event that assembled the legal *beau monde* of the country, seemed too good an opportunity to miss. At this seminar in December 1968, the judges presented their political program with great fanfare to the general public, hoping that they could turn the political tide. The 1968 National Law Seminar is important in the political history of the judiciary because it represented an open challenge by the judges which questioned the prevailing system of separation of powers. It also constitutes the high point of the judiciary's political hopes and expectations.

The seminar's keynote address on "the establishment of the autonomy of the judiciary" was given by the powerful, electric leader of the Association, Asikin Kusumah Atmadja. Asikin's speech touched upon the very essence of the constitutional order prevailing since independence. He pressed his basic argument upon the audience: "The Supreme Court must constitute the highest judicial authority in the country, on a par with the executive and legislative. . . "[84] Such equality remained a fiction, argued Asikin, so long as the improved status, autonomy, and power of the courts were not realized.

> Even though the New Order government acknowledges that the judiciary is a high body of state, of equal rank to the People's Congress, the President as mandatory of the People's Congress, [and] Parliament, (. . .), formally

---

[81] "art.10(2): The organization of the general courts culminates in the Supreme Court, while the organization of the other jurisdictions [religious, military, and administrative] shall be provided for by separate statute."

[82] "art.32(1): The Judicial Council shall consider and make final decisions on advice or recommendations pertaining to the appointment, advancement, transfer, dismissal and official measures/sanction of judges, which will be advanced by both the chairman of the Supreme Court and the minister of justice." "art.33(1): The Judicial Council consists of: 1. Supreme Court chairman (ex officio chairman), 2. Minister of Justice (ex officio vice chairman), 3. Supreme Court judge (member), 4. IKAHI representative (member), 5. Advocates representative (member)."

[83] Resolution no.18 Memorandum Ikatan Hakim Indonesia dated 7 November 1968 in IKAHI, *Menjongsong konperensi ke-VI IKAHI* (n.p., 1969), p. 130; *DSL*, 12 September 1971.

[84] Z. Asikin Kusumah Atmadja, *Menegakkan suatu kekuasaan kehakiman jang bebas* (Jakarta: LPHN, 1968), p. 16, item 10.

> speaking the law still qualifies Supreme Court judges at the rank of a department secretary-general (F.VII-F.VIII), whereas judges at the district and appeals courts are listed as Department of Justice officials. In the Regulation of State Salaries 1968, the separate status of judges does not transpire at all. It is not at all apparent from these regulations that judges within an overarching judicial power have separate status. On the contrary, this law rather emphasizes the role of the judge as an executive or administrative official, who is thrust into the executive structure with the rank of Junior Officer, Junior Officer First Rank, etc.[85]

Asikin pointed out that failing to provide the judges with a separate salary regulation was not just a matter that concerned status; it meant also that judges, by being including within the departmental salary structure, were subjected in appearance, if not in reality, to departmental hierarchies.

> All this means that, in fact, the status of judges as members of the judiciary is junior to that of section heads within the Secretariat General, the Directorate General, or the Inspectorate General of the Department of Justice.[86]

Acknowledging the rank of the judiciary as equal to that of the executive and legislative branches also reflected upon its autonomy. Equality of rank could never be realized as long as the judiciary was dependent on the executive for its administration, finances, and organization, according to Asikin.[87]

> Only one thing matters in the end: can the judiciary ever be independent from executive interference if judges are also Department of Justice officials? The answer is an emphatic "no." [. . .] Let me take an example. It is true that judges are positioned, transferred, or advanced by the Department of Justice at the request of the Supreme Court. But as far as I know, this practice is not based on law, and there is no sanction for it. How grateful must we be to the Department of Justice for the grand sense of responsibility guiding it, so that it doesn't mind being merely the administrator of Supreme Court requests! [But remember], people are just people. What if at some point the Department of Justice were to reject a request of the Supreme Court? This can all too easily lead to politically inspired appointments and transfers, as we have seen before GESTAPU with its disastrous results. And let me remind you, this can still happen now because in

---

[85] Ibid., p. 8. He also pointed out (p. 16, item 7) that on the whole judges were assigned a rank lower than their executive officer counterparts of equal experience and standing. He finally stated that, even though there had been attempts to upgrade the income of judges by complementing their relatively low salaries with comparatively high extra benefits (*tunjangan*), these measures did not in any way reduce their dependency on executive institutions. Indeed, he reported that, while the extra benefits had been approved by the Department of Finance, so far nothing had come down because the Central Bureau of Civil Service Administration had not yet handed down its decision (p. 14). So the extra benefits, instead of resolving, rather underscored the status problem.

[86] Ibid., p. 9.

[87] See on this point also S. Tasrif, "Kemandirian kekuasaan kehakiman," in *Loekman Wiriadinata SH—Kemandirian kekuasaan kehakiman*, ed. P. S. Baut and L. M. P. Pangaribuan (Jakarta: Yayasan Lembaga Bantuan Hukum, 1989), p. 70.

last instance the positioning etc. of judges is the responsibility of the Minister of Justice. [...] if the most important element of the structure and organization of the Judiciary is placed within and becomes the responsibility of the Department of Justice, its effectuation will also depend on that department. Yet is it not the entire purpose of this structure and organization to have a judiciary independent from any departmental interference ... ?[88]

Finally, regarding power, Asikin demanded the right of constitutional review, pointing out that the courts were in fact already on the way to acquiring the right for themselves. Quoting from recent Supreme Court case decisions, Asikin said:

... the Supreme Court is of the opinion that law development [...] must be effected through court decisions. Judges must be given the authority, if social conditions so require, not just to set aside legal provisions that are no longer in accord with modern developments, but also to introduce new rules.'[89]

Asikin's speech left no doubts about where the judges stood and what they really wanted. It reiterated the three basic points of Soerjadi's testament that would place the judiciary politically on par with the executive and Parliament. Formulated in such unequivocal terms and voiced so forcefully in public, it was a challenge that its opponents could not ignore. If the 1968 National Law Seminar stands out as the occasion in which the judiciary publicly threw down the gauntlet, it also marks the point where government took up the challenge. If there had ever been a honeymoon between the judiciary and government, the seminar marked its end. While at the beginning of the meeting, the judges perhaps still had reason to think that change was within reach, the conclusion of the seminar brought them back to reality.

Seno Adji led the government charge with a thundering speech, three times as long as that of the keynote speaker.[90] It was permeated with expressions, phrases, and quotations from English, Dutch, German, and French sources, riddled with an extraordinary wide and fairly indiscriminate collection of references.[91] Despite its almost tasteless exhibition of erudition, the speech is a contrived tangle, mixing theories, international comparisons, and semantics to justify opposition to Asikin's claims on behalf of the judiciary. If we cut through this underbrush, we discover that Seno Adji's arguments were as simple as they were predictable: they essentially advocated the French-Dutch legal system, in which characteristically

---

[88] Asikin, *Menegakkan suatu kekuasaan*, p. 13.

[89] Ibid., p. 12. The passage came from Supreme Court Decision no.182K/Sip/1967 dated 14 August 1968. While he referred in this context to colonial legislation, the quote was so broadly construed that it quite clearly extended to modern legislation also.

[90] Seno Adji's reaction numbered thirty-six pages compared to Asikin's twelve. Asikin, *Menegakkan suatu kekuasaan*, pp. 215-27; Seno Adji, "Prasaran," pp. 228-64 (with 49 footnotes).

[91] These ranged from the Swiss Civil Code to writings by the philosopher Kant and from the justice system in the Soviet Union to the Police Commission Van Bemmelen in the Netherlands. Indeed, as a long-time resident of Luxembourg, I was pleasantly struck by Seno Adji's reference to the case-reporting system in that country. Direktor Djenderal Pembinaan Hukum, *Kekuasaan kehakiman jang bebas* (1970), p. 233.

court administration is handled within the Department of Justice, and favored a limited form of judicial review, and perhaps some improvement in salaries.[92]

Despite their superficiality, the 1968 debates[93] were important because they manifested a divide between IKAHI and the government on the status, autonomy, and power of the judiciary that could not be bridged. Instead of rallying the legal community behind the judicial cause, the seminar revealed fundamental differences in perception on the place and role of the courts under the New Order. As one commentator said regarding the autonomy issue:

> Representatives of the Supreme Court and the IKAHI central leadership fought tooth and nail to free the judiciary from administrative control of the Department of Justice, while the representatives from the department did their utmost to keep the judges within the department. These conflicting views became most apparent during the Second National Law Seminar in Semarang in 1968.[94]

Daniel Lev acutely observed on constitutional review:

> . . . all these ideas, but particularly review, constituted a conception of political power and its conduct quite different from the one that had always governed Indonesia. Here was the essential reason why constitutional review was doomed to failure.[95]

---

[92] LPHN, *Seminar Hukum Nasional ke-II, Tahun 1968* (Jakarta: Gita Karya, 1968), pp. 110-12. In fact, only on the question of salaries was at least a semblance of agreement achieved, as the seminar recommended that salaries should be raised. Still, even here, nothing was said regarding a separate legislative regulation of those salaries.

[93] The apparent erudition displayed during the 1968 debates hides the poverty of the substantive argument that governs much of the political exchanges on the subject to the present day. In this sort of argument, which typically relies more on slogans than substantive analysis, references to US institutions are countered by references to French institutions, and vice versa. The one relevant point is that the government, which is pretty much on the defensive nowadays, generally legitimizes the prevailing system with reference to its French roots (not its Dutch ones, God forbid), whereas legal reformers who are on the offensive seek their inspiration in the US system. This pattern is in part caused by educational and economic factors, but whatever the reasons, the current Indonesian political debate on law is shaped by a basic dichotomy according to which the French-Dutch system stands for the old, colonial, politically reactionary order, and for government interests, and the US legal system stands for the liberal, democratic, and progressive alternative. The fact that in real terms this is an oversimplification, to say the least, and just plain wrong in terms of substance, does not invalidate its political reality and relevance. In that sense, the debates on the role and place of the judiciary during the 1968 National Law Seminar mark the beginning of a political discourse which, in terms of quality, is relatively poor compared to that of the 1950s, and which is determined less by substantive argument than by political symbolism.

[94] Ph. M. Hadjon, *Lembaga tertinggi dan lembaga-lembaga tinggi negara menurut Undang-undang Dasar 1945. Suatu analisa hukum dan kenegaraan* (Surabaya: Bina Ilmu, 1987), p. 69. The last sentence is the footnote attached to the passage in the text. Sri Soemantri makes a similar point about the judicial review debate during the Seminar. Sri Soemantri, *Hak menguji material di Indonesia* (Bandung: Almuni, 1986), p. 2.

[95] Daniel S. Lev, "Judicial Authority and the Struggle for an Indonesian Rechtstaat," *Law and Society Review* 13 (1978): 61.

The seminar was open ended, with both sides agreeing to disagree.⁹⁶ From the perspective of the judiciary, the 1968 National Law Seminar was a failure. Had the seminar concluded by supporting the judiciary's political program, it might have brought pressure to bear on Parliament, but ultimately it failed to deliver the political boost the judiciary was so desperately seeking.

3. 1968-1970: SLIPPING AND LOSING

(a) Cutting Losses and Opening Up for Compromise

Following the National Law Seminar, the Judges' Association organized its national conference at Yogyakarta in October 1968 to evaluate the situation. Upset and frustrated about losing their grip on such important developments, members focused their attention on their concerns about OPSUS interference and the failure of the Judges' Association during the National Law Seminar to persuade the other participants to accept its position. Emotions during the Yogya meeting ran high and centered on Asikin's leadership.⁹⁷ Suspicious of his OPSUS connections and disappointed at his failure to fulfill the Association's hopes, members challenged his leadership, and his star began to dim.⁹⁸ He was replaced as leader of the Judges' Association by Palti Radja Siregar.

---

⁹⁶ LPHN, "Hal-hal jang menimbulkan varietas pandangan," *Seminar Hukum Nasional ke-II*, p. 110.

⁹⁷ *DSL*, 22 November 1971. According to this account, Asikin's proposals were rejected for the first time by the Association's general congress in 1968 on a point of substance relating to the separation of court administration. On which see: Resolution I.3.c. *Pernjataan keluar: Musjawarah Nasional IKAHI ke-V jang diselenggarakan pada tgl.18 s.d. 20 Oktober 1968 di Jogjakarta* in IKAHI, *Menjongsong konperensi ke-VI IKAHI* (n.p., 1969), p. 44. In fact, it transpires that something altogether different was at stake. This related to Asikin's approach, which included active participation in demonstrations and direct confrontation. The Association felt that this approach exposed the judiciary politically, and in addition reduced the governing authority of the IKAHI National Congress by confronting it with *faits accomplis*. This seems to have been the crucial issue behind the conference members' rejection of the Association leadership's account, and their decision to replace that leadership. From then on, the National Congress insisted that the leadership follow its instructions and use constitutional methods to gain its ends, for instance by working through members of the parliamentary bodies who were also members of the Association. Purwoto S. Gandasubrata, "Derap-langkah IKAHI dari masa ke masa," *Varia Peradilan* 10,118 (1995): 147.

⁹⁸ Asikin was without doubt the most vocal and public judge during the 1965-1968 period and a political leader in his own right, marching in the streets, meeting with Suharto, and forcing Supreme Court chairmen to step down. But by 1974 he had lost his political grassroots contacts. This became painfully obvious when, during the 1974 MALARI troubles, the student rioters marched on the Supreme Court to demand the Court chairman read a statement. All the justices of the Court fled at that point, including Asikin, who a few years before would have stood up to the occasion. *DSL*, 30 October 1978. Asikin never recovered the proud political profile of his early days, and as the Supreme Court was progressively subdued by the post-1970 demoralization and increased bureaucratization, he was overshadowed by external appointees such as Seno Adji and Ali Said, and by less confrontational judges such as Purwoto Gandasubrata. In fact, there were inevitable latent tensions between Asikin Kusumah Atmadja and these "newcomers," as he perceived them. Tensions between Asikin and Purwoto in particular were high. Personal communication, 30 June 1994. These were exacerbated by the differences in their personalities, as Asikin was rather straightforward, outspoken, and confrontational, whereas Purwoto preferred the indirect approach. When, to the surprise of all,

At the Yogya meeting the Judges' Association began to realize that it would have to compromise. It made its first concession when it insisted only on separating the general and administrative court administration from the Department of Justice, leaving the other administration of the jurisdictions to their respective departments.[99] The general conference made its most important suggestion in its action program when it instructed the Association leadership that, until complete separation was realized,

> ... the Supreme Court shall endeavor to appoint a senior judge to become Director General for Court Affairs who shall be subjected to the Department of Justice in administrative terms, but with the specific task to realize in an autonomous manner all matters and needs relating to the courts, including personnel and financial matters, in the effectuation of Supreme Court instructions.[100]

This was a crucial event. Realizing that the Department would never concede complete separation, the Association put forward the idea that a separate Directorate General for court administration be created within the Department, and that to answer the concerns of the judiciary, the director general should be recruited from among the senior judges.[101] It was a construction which, the Association hoped, would on the one hand be acceptable to the Department of Justice, yet on the other would ensure as much judicial control as possible over court administration. At the Supreme Court, Subekti took up the point immediately, and within weeks began pushing for it with other state institutions.[102]

Purwoto was appointed vice-chairman in 1982 by Mudjono, he became senior in rank to Asikin, as indeed he was when later appointed Supreme Court chairman. This sharpened what became a real conflict, played out in various ways. Thus, Asikin was subject to mild hallucinatory fits during which he purportedly was entered by the spirit of his deceased father, the highly respected first Supreme Court chairman. He strongly believed in these occasions of possession, as did various others around him, including Purwoto. Asikin apparently would have such fits during leadership meetings (RAPIM, Rapat Pimpinan) at the Supreme Court, during which he would speak without reservation, to the embarrassment of all, some of whom would stalk out the room in a fury. Personal communication, 7 July 1994. Also, in the first *Kedung Ombo* case, Asikin overturned a previous decision taken in categorical and perhaps overly harsh terms. The fact that this earlier decision was taken by Purwoto may have played a role here. But Purwoto was tough, and through his seniority had greater leverage which he could use to counter Asikin, and did. Personal communication, 16 July 1994. Thus, the fact that Asikin's son, who is a judge, was parked for a relatively long period in a minor court in an outlying area may have had something to do with relations between his father and Purwoto. Personal communication, 16 July 1994.

[99] Resolution I.3.c. *Pernjataan keluar: Musjawarah Nasional IKAHI ke-V jang diselenggarakan pada tngl.18 d.s 20 Oktober 1968 di Jogjakarta* in IKAHI, *Menjongsong konperensi ke-VI IKAHI* (n.p., 1969), p. 44.

[100] *Program kerja keputusan Munas V tahun 1968* in ibid., p. 44.

[101] See also Tasrif, "Kemandirian kekuasaan kehakiman," p. 71.

[102] See for instance his letter to the Supreme Advisory Council (DPA, Dewan Pertimbangan Agung). The letter restates the political program of the judiciary "for which the judiciary already calls for many years," and asks the DPA to support the judicial struggle. Letter no.MA/Pemb/356/68 dated 23 December 1968. A copy of the letter can be found in Direktorat Djenderal Pembinaan Hukum, *Kekuasaan kehakiman jang bebas* (1968), p. 323. Subekti in his official correspondence revealed himself a vociferous fighter for the judicial cause.

The Association saw the Directorate General as a transitional phase on the road to full Supreme Court control over the judiciary. From its perspective, there would be a natural alliance between the judiciary and the director general, whose judicial background would inevitably incline him to the views of the Supreme Court. Thus, administration of the courts would in fact already be in the hands of the judiciary, and the formal separation would be just a matter of time. In a 1969 letter to Parliament, Supreme Court chairman Subekti expressed this opinion in so many words:

> In a transition period, and before the entire court administration is placed under the control of the Supreme Court, the Court agrees with the proposal of the Judges' Association that a Directorate General be established within the Department of Justice with the specific task of managing the courts, whose head will be appointed from amongst the senior judges, and who will endeavor to realize the above-mentioned transfer.[103]

Following a working meeting in Jakarta, in 1970 the Judges' Association emphasized the transitory character of the proposed Directorate General:

> In order to realize an independent judiciary, free from any extra-judicial factors, the aim is that the Directorate General within five years will release the organization, administration, and finances of the general and administrative courts, which it holds for the time being, and place them directly under the Supreme Court.[104]

(b) The "Compromise" Law No.14/1970 and Collapse

By breaching the impasse between the judiciary and the government, the Association's Yogyakarta compromise paved the way for the Bill on the Basic Principles of the Judiciary. Even though it would take an exhausting twenty-seven months of parliamentary debates before the bill was enacted, even though the judiciary tried to weight the process in its favor a number of times, and, indeed, even though some significant changes were made to the bill in the intervening period, the Judges' Association and the government had, in fact, already reached their basic understanding concerning whether the judiciary would be truly equal in status to the executive and Parliament, and whether it would manage its own court administration and have the power of constitutional review. The Department of Justice accepted the Association's proposal, and in 1970 the Directorate General was established as a preliminary step toward putting the Bill into effect through Law no.14/1970 on the Basic Principles of the Judiciary. The senior appeals court judge Hadipurnomo was appointed the first Director General.[105]

While the Judges' Association saw the Yogyakarta compromise as a step in the process of realizing full separation of court administration from the Department of Justice, it was nevertheless a significant retreat by the judiciary. This bill would

---

[103] Supreme Court chairman Subekti to the DPR no.Um/335/V/P/3/1969 dated 10 May 1969 in Direktorat Djenderal Pembinaan Hukum, *Kekuasaan kehakiman jang bebas* (1970), p. 343.

[104] S. Tasrif, "Kemandirian kekuasaan kehakiman," p. 71.

[105] Decision Minister of Justice no.J.S. 4/1/21 dated 27 January 1970.

determine the constitutional moorings of the judiciary under the New Order government, and the Association's willingness to compromise at that crucial juncture on such a pivotal issue turned out to be disastrous. It meant that the judges' goal of overhauling the constitutional system in order to replace separation of powers with balance of powers was off the books for the coming decades. Thus, the Association would have to continue to work within a system which, from its own perspective, had badly malfunctioned.

The strength of the IKAHI-government accord based on the Yogyakarta compromise is revealed by the failure of attempts to change this outcome. In 1969, Asikin Kusumah Atmadja and Busthanul Arifin thought that if some sort of "shock treatment" were applied during the parliamentary debates on the bill, this might wake people up and rally them behind the judiciary.[106] Asikin and Busthanul organized a meeting with all the appeals court chairmen, which led to the so-called "Law Report,"[107] detailing in stark terms some of the most pressing problems facing the judiciary. The report stated how thousands were imprisoned without court orders and how judges were frequently subjected to pressure by the military.[108] In this way, the authors of the report hoped to rattle society at large and Parliament in particular, making them realize the gravity of the situation. For a couple of weeks, the report did have an effect. Newspapers covered it extensively; the liberal newspaper *Indonesia Raya* serialized it on the front page. The Public Prosecution rushed to remedy the problems of unlawful detainees.[109] As Asikin and Busthanul hoped, with the press focused on the courts, other dirt began to spill out. Thus, when asked by the press about her working conditions, Judge Purbowati recounted that not only was her salary insufficient to live on, but in addition:

> I rarely receive my salary in one go, indeed, over the past couple of months I get only about half of the salary as officially listed.[110]

Still, the law report did not have enough shock value to alter the course of events. There was no groundswell of public reaction that could be used strengthen the position of the courts and turn the situation around in Parliament. Nor was there any serious follow-up, and the effects of the report soon ebbed. This failure discouraged the judges, pushing them even further down the road to compromise and, in the end, collapse.[111] More important, it revealed that the Yogyakarta compromise held firm.

Like the judiciary, Parliament basically conceded to the compromise, despite strong parliamentary debates and, indeed, despite a general feeling in that body that the judges merited support. For its own particular reasons, and on the basis of

---

[106] Apparently, it was Soedjatmoko who suggested to Busthanul Arifin that the courts needed "shock therapy. Something to rattle them out of their present position." *DSL*, 5 October 1971.

[107] "Laporan situasi hukum di Indonesia" (Djakarta, mimeo 1969).

[108] The report details how 2,129 non-political detainees were unlawfully detained. *Indonesia Raya*, 25-26 June 1969.

[109] *DSL*, 5 October 1971.

[110] *Indonesia Raya*, 29 January 1969.

[111] Apparently, Busthanul Arifin and Asikin were very discouraged by the limited effects of and follow-up subsequent to the report. *DSL*, 5 October 1971.

its procedural rules, the legislature could not settle these matters in a way that clearly favored the judiciary, despite all the fireworks.[112]

As a result, in breaking with the Guided Democracy legislation that allowed for active government interference in the course of justice, Law no.14/1970 reaffirmed the separation-of-powers ideology. It would realize judicial autonomy by separating functions of government, rather than by balancing them.

> The independent judiciary is based on the concept that the judiciary shall be free from any interference from any other power of government, as well as free from any force, directives, or recommendations from extra-judicial parties, except insofar as allowed by law.[113]

From here, it was inevitable that practically all of the major issues of the judicial political agenda went the government's way.

First, unlike the Bill on Basic Principles, Law no.14/1970 retained the idea of Law no.13/1965 that the Supreme Court would serve as highest appeals court to all jurisdictions, but stated that the government would retain its control over court administration.

> Art.10(3): On all court decisions given in final instance other than those of the Supreme Court, appeal in cassation can be lodged with the Supreme Court.

> Art.11(1): The courts as meant in art.10(1) [referring to all jurisdictions] shall be under the organizational, administrative, and financial control of the relevant government department.

The last, somewhat convoluted reference to "relevant government departments" refers to the fact that the various jurisdictions would be under the control of various

---

[112] The problems in the Parliamentary Commission (B) that advised on the matter to Parliament were symptomatic of the problems in that diverse body. In parliamentary commissions, decisions were not taken by vote, but by consensus. Thus, a minority could block a decision. In this case, the minority came from people like V. B. da Costa (Partai Katolik) and Tambunan (ABRI, Angkatan Bersenjata Republik Indonesia, Armed Forces of the Republic of Indonesia), who tended to side with Seno Adji. The reason was not that their parties wanted a weak judiciary, as indeed in later years Da Costa became one of the most vociferous critics of the weak judiciary, launching what effectively became a catchphrase in Indonesia: "the Supreme Court is rotten" (*brengsek*), and in 1992 was so insistent in his questioning of Supreme Court chairman Purwoto that parliamentary rules of procedure were changed. *Tempo*, 17 May 1980; *Tempo*, 20 September 1980. Personal communication, 3 September 1994. In the case of Da Costa, his non-Muslim party aimed at minimizing the influence of the Islamic courts within the judiciary. It wanted a structure that would isolate the religious courts, keeping them away from, and subservient to, the secular judiciary, that is the general courts and the Supreme Court. This meant that they favored placing the administration of these courts under the respective departments rather than the Supreme Court, and that they wanted to disallow, or at any rate restrict, appeal from the religious courts to the Supreme Court. Similarly the Army representative advocated the establishment of a separate court hierarchy for the military courts, under the administrative control of the Department of Defense. Of course, Da Costa and Tambunan were supported by Seno Adji, who saw this as a means to preserve his own control over the general courts. As a result, even though the majority of the Parliamentary Commission (B) favored the judiciary, because of people like Tambunan and Da Costa, the Seno Adji bill could not be changed by Parliament and was accepted *faute de mieux*. DSL, 5 October 1971.

[113] Official explanation Law no.14/1970 art.1.

government departments, the general and administrative courts under the Department of Justice, the religious courts under the Department of Religion, and the military courts under the Department of Defense.

Second, judicial review remained anchored in the French-Dutch separation-of-powers doctrine, with the law stating that Acts of Parliament would not be subject to review. The law denied that the Constitution's lack of provision for constitutional review meant that the courts could appropriate that right to themselves, as prominent judges had argued:

> If the 1945 Constitution does not provide [for constitutional review], this does not automatically mean that the power to review Acts of Parliament against the Constitution by the Supreme Court can be established by this law. If the Supreme Court is to be granted this right, this can only be realized by constitutional provision.[114]

There was compromise on a subsidiary point, whereby the Supreme Court was empowered to declare statutes inferior to Acts of Parliament inapplicable in general terms. Moreover, parties were allowed to apply directly to the Supreme Court for review of statute. Still, the law also clearly stated that the relevant government institution, not the Court, had the ultimate power to repeal the relevant statute, which again harked back to the French-Dutch system.

> Art.26(1): The Supreme Court may invalidate all statute below Acts of Parliament on grounds of violating superior law.

On the issue of status, i.e., salaries, a partial compromise was also achieved, under which a separate statute (art.32) would provide for all matters relating to salaries and special allowances of judges. The Judicial Council (MPPH, Majelis Pertimbangan Penelitian Hakim) envisaged by the Bill was withdrawn.

The judiciary's political retreat, set in motion two years earlier, was accelerated and ultimately sealed by the Law no.14/1970 on the Basic Principles of the Judiciary. The law determined the role and place of the judiciary in the New Order, and, both formally and effectively, still forms its basis to the present day. For all the fanfare with which the law was presented, its purported compromise character, and the high principle that it pretends to uphold, on close inspection, and compared to the better options desired and sometimes claimed by the judiciary in 1968, it represents a total defeat on all major points of the judicial agenda. If the judiciary had actually lost its grip on the political course of events with the National Law Seminar two years earlier, both ideologically and constitutionally, Law no.14/1970 confirmed that loss by firmly embedding the judiciary in the separation-of-powers tradition that was geared toward suffocating its political power completely.

---

[114] Official explanation Law no.14/1970 art.26.

CHAPTER FOUR

ENTRENCHED NEW ORDER (POST-1970): POLITICAL CO-OPTATION OF THE JUDICIARY

After the 1970 law, the political debate on the place and role of the judiciary in Indonesia effectively collapsed for many years. The law showed that the New Order government was not prepared to change fundamentally political relations in the country. Henceforth, the issue confronting the judiciary, and the Supreme Court in particular, was how best to survive in a political environment that clearly aimed at restricting the role of the courts as much as possible, if it was not outright hostile to its goals and interests.

This renewed political marginalization of the judiciary cut deeper and would last longer than anything before. In the thirty years from 1970 until *Reformasi*, an entire generation of judges grew up and made their careers in an environment that accorded neither respect nor relevance to their function. It deeply demoralized the judiciary, contributed to the dramatic weakening of its professional capabilities, and boosted corruption in a service that until 1970 had still been relatively clean (underpaid though it was even then). Under the New Order government, the judiciary never again was able to muster the will and mobilize the political clout to challenge seriously this condition. Its failure to play any role of significance during *Reformasi* in 1998 showed how deep the rot had spread.

Despite all this, the very concept of the judiciary invested its members with a basic tension that kept alive hopes for reform. No matter how demoralized, incompetent, and corrupt the judiciary was becoming, members of the profession could not fail to understand that the entire reason for its existence and function derived from basic concepts that the New Order government failed to honor. The fact remains that many judges knew that the New Order state was violating the fundamental principles from which the judiciary, and the judges themselves, in the end derived their existence and purpose. In its day-to-day operations, the judiciary became a loyal servant to the New Order government, but its ideology and basic culture remained one of resistance and opposition. This resistance may have been muted, rhetorical, and in part self-serving, but its consistency over the years is remarkable. The judicial political agenda that took shape in the period 1966-1970 and so totally failed to make its mark in Law no.14/1970 remains to the present day the yardstick by which progress is measured.[1]

---

[1] There are significant differences in the way judges approach their own political agenda, with a strong self-serving element emerging during the New Order. This is more problematic than may be apparent at first sight: the agenda, instead of becoming a vehicle for reform, became a shield for cover-ups. Some senior judges in the 1990s, and even after *Reformasi*, used the agenda when they sought to rationalize grossly corrupt behavior in the past and to strengthen corruption networks for the future. There has been little awareness of this, as most observers bought easily

Several phases in the evolution of Indonesia's judiciary can be distinguished in the aftermath of Law no.14/1970. The first phase runs until about 1974. Following the 1971 Judges' Association (IKAHI, Ikatan Hakim Indonesia) National Conference, in which the judges were effectively bought off, the Association lost political influence. The Supreme Court held out for a few more years under its liberal-minded and firm chairman, Subekti, but when he retired in 1974 and was replaced by Seno Adji, the Supreme Court caved in also. The second phase was marked by a progressive unhinging of the working relationship between the Supreme Court and the Department of Justice in the dual administration system of the judiciary (a development the Judges' Association had feared and predicted during the 1968 National Law Seminar). Despite ongoing lobbying and protests by the judiciary, the Court was unable to stop the Department of Justice from acquiring complete control over court administration, notably personnel management, and thereby excluding the judiciary from that decision-making process. This abuse of the system eroded professionalism and quality control within the judicial corps and was an important element in the moral and professional decline of the judicial profession that continues to the present. The third phase was the further weakening of the judiciary through the reappearance of the political fault line separating the Judges' Association and the Supreme Court. The rift was caused primarily by the fact that Supreme Court chairmen from Seno Adji onward came from outside the judicial corps. These outsiders by and large had little sympathy for the judiciary and significantly contributed to the erosion of its political standing and professional standards. This dissension became evident from time to time, notably during the debates on the Supreme Court Law no.14/1985. Conversely, when in the early 1990s Supreme Court chairmen were again appointed from the judicial corps, a cautious strengthening of the judiciary took place in certain fields. Nevertheless, by 1995 the political agenda of the judiciary was no closer to realization.

1. 1970-1985: THE POLITICAL CO-OPTATION OF THE JUDICIARY

(a) Medan 1971: The Last Ditch Attempt to Retain Judicial Autonomy

Law no.14/1970 played a crucial role in the rapid deterioration of the relationship between the judiciary and the government. Under the prevailing unstable political conditions, the judiciary could only have protected itself against government interference if it had equality in power, which would have been established through constitutional review.[2] Moreover, Law no.14/1970's continuation of the dual court administration gave the government a role in court administration that eased the way for political interference in the affairs of the judiciary.

---

into the political rhetoric that the judges were victims of the New Order regime, rather than its willing collaborators.

[2] As before, I distinguish between constitutional and judicial review. The former refers to the authority of the courts to quash Acts of Parliament, the latter restricts that power to inferior legislation.

The major factor in the rapid deterioration of judicial autonomy after 1970 was that the government, through the Department of Justice, used the system of dual court administration to bring the judicial apparatus under its political control. As we have already seen, this was one of the principal issues of the judicial struggle and the focus of the 1968 Yogyakarta compromise. The judges had made a crucial miscalculation in reaching this compromise. They expected that the appointment of a judge as director general for courts—a new position—would ensure that the Directorate General would be loyal to the judiciary and that the director general would work for the judiciary rather than government. The idea that the judiciary might maintain control of their administration through their director general proved to be a miscalculation. With political power (and funding) so heavily weighted in favor of the government, no judge after being appointed director general was willing to serve the judiciary rather than the government. This fact undermined the strategy of the Judges' Association, which was aimed at ensuring that the Directorate General would in the natural course of events be absorbed into the Supreme Court's jurisdiction after a five-year transition period. The expectation that eventually the Directorate General would effectively become a Supreme Court department and that the official transfer would be just a formality was completely frustrated. The director general never allied with the judiciary, and the Association's five-year plan fell apart.[3] Instead of being a transitional office, as envisaged in the 1968 Yogyakarta compromise, the Directorate General became a fixture within the Department of Justice and so represented a firm extension of government interests. Mrs. S. Soegondo's appointment as director general in 1992 broke new ground, as she was the first director general not to have come up through the judicial ranks, but to have been recruited directly from the departmental bureaucracy. The appointment severed the last ties, largely symbolic in any case, with the 1968 Yogyakarta compromise.[4]

In an action that revealed the members' desperation following passage of the 1970 law, the Judges' Association invited top political operator Ali Murtopo to address their 1971 National Congress in Medan. Until then, the Association had

---

[3] While the Department of Justice seems to have conveniently forgotten the Yogyakarta compromise on this point and never refers to it, the judiciary has not and keeps on referring to the establishment of the Directorate General as a temporary measure. " . . . the Directorate General on Courts which specifically caters for the needs of the judiciary, at some later stage will be transferred to the Supreme Court." Purwoto S. Gandasubrata, "Derap langkah IKAHI dari masa ke masa," *Varia Peradilan* 10,118 (July 1995): 147.

[4] Mrs. S. Soegondo came up through the regional offices (*Kantor Wilayah*) of the department. As she was a very capable administrative officer in her own right, her credentials for the Directorate General may have been strengthened by her strong personal and professional ties with the judiciary. Before her appointment, she had worked for many years as a senior administrative officer to the Supreme Court and thus knew the inner workings of the institution intimately. In addition, she had powerful family links with the judiciary. She is daughter-in-law to Supreme Court judge Satochid Kartanegara, and through that line a cousin of Supreme Court chairman Purwoto Gandasubrata. These factors may have helped her secure the top judicial job within the department and sweetened the pill for the judiciary. Personal communication, 23 August 1994. chairman Purwoto Gandasubrata in communications to the author said that he objected to her appointment as Director General, and there are in fact reports that their relations were frosty. But it remains striking that Mrs. Soegondo was part of the judicial family, broadly speaking, both in personal and professional terms. This made it less apparent that her appointment broke with precedent, and for the first time since 1970 placed a government official in direct management control of the judiciary.

shunned official contacts with Ali Murtopo, who was head of the secret service network OPSUS. Indeed, when Ali Murtopo had attacked judges in 1970 for being opposed to development, or just being generally useless, the Association had refused even to talk with him to clear up the matter, as some prominent OPSUS-connected judges proposed. Instead, the Judges' Association directly approached President Suharto, who merely directed them to discuss the matter with Ali Murtopo himself.[5] But in the aftermath of the 1970 law, they reversed themselves and called on Ali Murtopo to help them salvage the situation.

As was to be expected, nothing came of the Medan meeting. As in 1968, the official exchanges during the meeting were governed by conflicting principles, which failed to help participants resolve anything. The Judges' Association argued that separation of powers required that the management of the judiciary be controlled by the judiciary itself, while the presidential address to the conference, read and probably written by Minister of Justice Seno Adji, basically argued that courts should not assume administrative functions, but should leave such matters to the executive, i.e., the Department of Justice.[6]

Such discussions on principle only served to obfuscate what was at issue here, which was political control. A small conversation in the backrooms of the conference struck at the heart of the problem. Here, two protagonists in the debate, minister of justice Seno Adji and Supreme Court judge Busthanul Arifin, encountered each other. Seno Adji asked why the Judges' Association was making such a big fuss about the separation issue, commenting that, after all, in colonial times the Department of Justice had been run in the same way. Busthanul replied that, indeed, this had been the case, but in those times the Department of Justice was truly neutral and performed a strictly administrative function. Now, said Busthanul to an angry Seno, the department is just a political conduit, as indeed it was.[7]

At the Medan meeting, the judiciary struggled to keep the government out of its affairs, but under prevailing political conditions, they were no match for the executive. Already, prior to the meeting, the government was planning to deflect judicial demands quite simply by buying the judges off. For all the high-brow talk in Medan, Seno Adji admitted before the meeting that a lot could be accomplished with money:

> The main concern of the judges after all is salaries, income, security, etc. and the Department works for that, all the better now through the directorate of courts. Of course, there are principles, but these are of lesser importance now.

---

[5] Daniel S. Lev archives (hereafter *DSL*), 21 September 1971. (These are the personal interview notes of Daniel S. Lev; copies will be deposited in the University of Washington library [Seattle, WA], the Cornell University Kroch Collection [Ithaca, NY], and Pusat Studi Hukum dan Kebijakan [PSHK] in Jakarta.)

[6] *DSL*, 12 September 1971. Professor Daniel Lev believes the presidential speech was largely written by Seno Adji, who already in 1968 thought the judiciary's recommendations regarding administrative control—that the Supreme Court would have its own personnel budget, appoint and dismiss judges and so on, having nothing whatsoever to do with the rest of government—was rather "extreme." Seno said this was going too far, that nowhere in the world did judges enjoy such privileges, that there must be checks and balances. He wondered whether the Supreme Court would appoint its own new members, and so on.

[7] *DSL*, 5 October 1971.

(...) The judges are pushing for a separate salary schedule and the like, and this may take the heat off the autonomy issue.[8]

He was correct. After Director General Hadipurnomo announced in Medan that the judges would get a five-fold pay increase, the judges' determination began to crumble.[9] Hardly surprisingly, the IKAHI-Department of Justice meeting in Medan turned out favorably for the government.

The Medan gathering showed that the judges would have to wait a long time for the situation to improve. They might retain their agenda and political ambitions, but the government could afford to ignore them, and, increasingly, buy them off. Still, this failure did not kill the administrative issue, only postponed fruitful discussion of it. With prescience, one of the central players in the conflict, the controversial director general for courts at the Department of Justice, Hadipurnomo, said as much immediately after the Medan meeting:

I do not think that this will end the issue. The judges will continue to push for separation and placement of all responsibility under the Supreme Court. Indeed, Supreme Court judges see the Directorate General is only transitional to placing full administrative authority over the lower courts in the hands of the Supreme Court.[10]

(b) After Medan: The Justice Department Take-Over and Supreme Court Political Co-optation

For Minister of Justice Seno Adji, the 1971 Medan meeting could not have turned out better. The complete victory of the government amounted to a blank check that enabled the executive to tighten its control over the judges. Seno Adji's director general and former appeal court judge, Hadipurnomo, soon revealed himself to be the minister's loyal lieutenant. Understanding where political power rested, Hadipurnomo swiftly identified with departmental and government interests, and his judicial background and loyalties evaporated. As a result, the relationship between the department and the Supreme Court worsened drastically.

After Medan, the Department of Justice felt free to fully use, or rather abuse, the system of dual court administration for its own purposes. Holding all the political cards as well as the purse strings, the department simply refused to honor Supreme Court requests for judicial transfers and advancements. This had happened occasionally before, but from the early 1970s the practice became endemic and developed into a system in its own right. The department viewed Supreme Court requests for transfers and the like as mere suggestions to be followed or ignored as it pleased. And indeed, from Seno Adji's perspective, the system allowed him to propose his own candidates for judicial functions. The result was a complete breakdown of communications between the Supreme Court and the Department of Justice. The polite bureaucratic phraseology of the official correspondence between the Supreme Court and the department barely concealed

---

[8] *DSL*, 5 September 1971.

[9] The matter of the pay rise had been decided two weeks prior to the Medan meeting. *DSL*, 12 September 1971.

[10] Ibid.

the acrimonious relationships underneath, as Supreme Court chairman Subekti tried to insist that Minister Seno Adji cease meddling with his judges:

> I wish to make it absolutely clear, that the Supreme Court cannot agree with the transfer of Mr. Achmad Nasrul from the Chair of the Bengkalis District Court to the Tanjung Pinang District Court, and insists on its previous request of 12 March 1970 no.U.P.3/1464/1970 that he become chairman of the Sawah Lunto District Court, with the request that this receive your attention and further action.[11]

But Seno Adji was not impressed. He even cut out the Supreme Court formally from administration of the judiciary when, in late 1971, the Department of Justice enacted a regulation stating in unequivocal terms that the department, and not the Supreme Court, had final say in the personnel management of the judiciary.[12] This statement was a complete perversion of the dual administration system, and, at least in spirit, in outright opposition to Law no.14/1970, which guaranteed judicial autonomy.[13]

These developments forced the Supreme Court, together with the entire judiciary, against the wall. The Court made a last, desperate appeal to public opinion. In 1972, its chairman, Subekti, issued an extraordinary public statement in Parliament (which was becoming pretty much a paper tiger itself as a result of government actions):

> It should be pointed out here that the entire budget for personnel transfer is in the hands of the Directorate General for Courts at the Department of Justice. In theory, the Supreme Court suggests transfers, which subsequently are effected by the Directorate General. Nevertheless, many requests are simply ignored. Indeed, over the past two years only a few requests have been effected. The Supreme Court just has a stand-by role now, with such a backlog of requests that

---

[11] Supreme Court chairman Subekti to Minister of Justice Seno Adji no.U.P.3/5141/1971 dated 25 August 1971. This letter (in fact fifty copies of it) can be found in the parliamentary archives, to which it was presumably sent by Subekti to inform Parliament that the dual administration system was breaking down as a result of government abuse.

[12] As a result, and starting with Seno Adji, the department *by law* acquired final say in the personnel management of judges. Personal communication, 4 July 1994. This refers to Ministerial Regulation no.J.P. 18/14/23 dated 2 June 1971 as further effected with Regulation Director General for Court Upgrading J.Z.P. 18/67/19 dated 17 August 1971 of the Director General of Courts Upgrading. These regulations voided earlier regulations dating from 1953, which placed authority for the recruitment of non-judicial court personnel in the hands of the respective court chairmen. The 1971 regulation was followed in recent years by new regulations which are similarly based on the idea that the department has the authority to appoint, transfer, advance, or fire judges because of their status as civil servants. See notably Decisions Minister of Justice nos.M.2789-KP.04.11 and M.2790-KP.04.11 (1988), which both delegate power to appoint etc. judges without any reference to suggestions made by the Supreme Court. See also Department of Justice Regulation J.P. 18/14/23 dated 2 June 1967 which seems to be based on the same idea, cf. "Partisipasi hakim dalam pembangunan," *Varia Peradilan*, Edisi Khusus (1972): 14-15.

[13] In order to take control over the judges without violating the letter of Law no.14/1970, the Justice Department came up with a trick: it would regulate their civil servant status. Judges were both judges and civil servants, and in the latter capacity were subject to departmental control . . . control through the back door, as it were.

remain to be implemented by the Department. (. . .) We can essentially say that cooperation with the Directorate General currently is absolutely minimal. It is dismal that the Directorate General was proposed by the Supreme Court, and in fact, the Director General comes from Supreme Court circles. And indeed, the first two or three months we had regular meetings, with the Director General coming to the Supreme Court to discuss the situation. But then for some reason they thought it beneath them to be called to the Supreme Court, and relations worsened. Currently, meetings are discontinued; we just send in our requests. (. . .) This all works to the detriment of the Supreme Court, considering that it is they who have the funding and hold the money. Why, now even if we want to summon a judge to the capital, we must first get approval from the Director General. So we are under a great deal of pressure to supervise effectively the behavior of judges and the administration of justice. This is the situation.[14]

Parliament failed to respond, as it had in the past so often failed the judiciary. (One of the recurrent tragedies in Indonesian political and institutional history is the fact that since independence, Parliament has consistently failed to protect the judiciary adequately or provide it with the necessary instruments to perform its function.) The judges' loss of control over their own organization opened the floodgates to political interference. The Department of Justice had no conception of the special constitutional place and role of the judiciary, or its specific needs and requirements. Minister Seno Adji and his acolyte, Hadipurnomo, saw their control merely as a means of furthering the interests of the New Order government, not to speak of their own personal interests.[15]

A telling example of the careless, if not downright incompetent, management of the judiciary by the government was the recruitment drive of 1971-1973. During the Guided Democracy period, the judiciary had been severely depleted by an almost complete lack of recruitment. Come the New Order, the courts were one thousand judges short.[16] Consequently, it was decided in 1970 to begin recruitment of five hundred new judges, an extraordinary number. Advertisements were placed in various newspapers soliciting applicants, and the director general of the Justice Department, Hadipurnomo, informed potential candidates that even more new judges would be needed—so they were practically certain to obtain a position with good career prospects.[17] The five hundred new candidates were recruited on a temporary basis with minimum pay in April 1971, awaiting their definite presidential appointment. More than two years later, they remained in the same position: by summer 1973, they were still on probation and still receiving minimal

---

[14] *Catatan sementara rapat Komisi III DPR-RI dengan Ketua Mahkamah Agung (Subekti) no.4746/Kom.III/72* dated 23 November 1972, pp. 7-8, Supreme Court chairman R. Subekti speaking. The press expressed surprise at Subekti's straightforward declaration of his views during this meeting. *Tempo*, 30 September 1972.

[15] Minister of Justice Seno Adji at one point protested that government would never pressure judges in any way, but the press commented that this was precisely what a government official would be expected to say. See for instance *Tempo*, 9 October 1971, p. 46.

[16] *Tempo*, 2 June 1973, p. 14,

[17] Ibid.; *Tempo*, 26 October 1974, p. 38.

pay.[18] In fact, by that time only three hundred of the recruits remained; the others had had enough and simply left, often without giving notice.[19] When a delegation of the candidate-judges was dispatched to investigate what was happening, the Justice Department claimed that the Supreme Court had failed to send out appointment requests. The Court denied this, at which point the department claimed that the requests had been sent to the State Secretariat. When the State Secretariat denied receiving anything, the Department of Justice finally admitted that it had not processed the papers,[20] or in fact done anything else with regard to the candidates. The frustration among the remaining candidates was considerable, indeed so great that they rioted and smashed up the refectory of the Hadipurnomo's Directorate General of Court Upgrading.[21]

Another development in this period, one that had a devastating long-term impact, was the abandonment of the merit base for judicial personnel management. Until then, be it with some exceptions, quality assessment was the key element determining advancement in the judicial hierarchy. It was allowed to operate with a measure of objectivity, and in turn was an important factor in ensuring the professionalism of the judges themselves. The break down in cooperation between the Supreme Court and the Justice Department crippled this system. In reality, as judges to the present day never fail to point out, the department is poorly equipped to assess the quality of judges, and hence to handle personnel management. It does not work with the judges, does not handle cases on appeal, does not carry out the examinations of judges, and as a result cannot really make an independent, balanced assessment of their ability. If personnel management were to be based on the judicial abilities of any one person, argued the Supreme Court, how could the Department of Justice handle this at all without consulting the Court?

> Only the Supreme Court is in the position to gauge fully the professional skills of a judge. Let me be clear about this: the institution that knows whether a judge is bright or not, honest or not, hard working or not, is the Supreme Court, not the Department of Justice.[22]

It was a point the Supreme Court did not tire of making in Parliament also:

---

[18] *Tempo*, 30 September 1972, p. 40. In 1972, questions were raised in Parliament concerning the recruits in Ujung Pandang, who had been sleeping on their desks in the office for more than a year. The Supreme Court replied by saying that since the cooperation between the Court and the Department of Justice had effectively broken down, nothing could be done about the situation. *Catatan sementara rapat Komisi III*, pp. 9, 12.

[19] *Tempo*, 26 October 1974, pp. 38-42.

[20] *Tempo*, 2 June 1973, p. 14; *Tempo*, 26 October 1974, pp. 38-42.

[21] The rather conservative Hadipurnomo felt this to be unjudicial behavior and made a big fuss about collecting the names of the perpetrators, so as to strike them off the list of recruits. *Tempo*, 26 October 1974, pp. 39-42. This incident suggests that the Judges' Association had not really thought out the professional angle of their strategy, which perhaps is understandable, but may have weakened their bid for control over court administration when dealing with the government. Hadipurnomo showed that good judges (assuming Hadipurnomo was one) do not necessarily make good administrators. It would not be altogether surprising if his frequent administrative missteps influenced the government's perception that judges were not up to the task of administering the huge judicial apparatus.

[22] Supreme Court judge Asikin Kusumah Atmadja, quoted in *Tempo*, 13 May 1972, p. 34.

It is the function of the Supreme Court to supervise the judges, to assess their quality, honesty, the period of their tour of duty in any one spot, and if the Department is given authority in this field, i.e. to assess the quality of judges for transfer or advancement and so on, the system will get hopelessly messed up [*bentrokan*].[23]

Understandably, judges worried that if the department were unable to base its assessment of judicial personnel on criteria having to do with quality, then other more subjective criteria might be used—which would have their impact on the administration of justice.

Developments after Medan revealed the judiciary's concerns to be well founded. Minister of Justice Seno Adji effectively abolished the more or less neutral and professional system of judicial personnel management. The system, if system there was, became heavily personalized, as he eliminated quality assessment as a standard for transfers and advancements within the judicial apparatus. As a result, the cornerstone of quality control on which advancement had been hitherto based, namely the examination of court decisions by senior judges (*eksaminasi*), no longer served any serious function and ceased to operate.[24]

> ... the *eksaminasi* stopped in the early 70s. This change in procedure immediately led to the introduction of a system in which advancement was no longer based on quality, but on knowing people. It was a very bad development, not just because the *eksaminasi* system gave a more or less neutral indication of any judge's quality, but also because the process involved critiques of decisions, which would then be sent back for information. I learned a lot from the examination in my own time at the district court.[25]

Another judge testifies to the effect this had on his job:

> When I was still in Surabaya in the sixties, my decisions would be returned to me by the appeal court judges with firm comments, whole paragraphs would be struck down, question marks, comments such as "trash" or "nonsense." I accepted that and learned a lot from it. I remember how an appeal court judge told me that the prosecution had put in a *strikvraag* [question in which all answers can be found at fault] which I hadn't remarked, and a case in which statutory interpretation was plainly wrong. But after I was transferred to Jakarta in the

---

[23] *Catatan sementara Komisi III DPR-RI*, p. 23.

[24] It would appear that Supreme Court chairman Subekti tried to keep the examination system alive during his tenure, until his retirement in 1974, notwithstanding the fact that the Department of Justice by that time had effectively abandoned it as a criterion of advancement. For the Supreme Court, the examination served less as a criterion for personnel management (on which the Supreme Court was losing its grip anyway) than as an instrument for professional quality control. It may in fact have lost its edge there also, since the ultimate factor determining quality control (whether or not someone received a promotion) was no longer for the Supreme Court to decide. Nevertheless, it remained important as a means by which to uphold professional standards. As a result, examination was abandoned completely only after Seno Adji became Supreme Court chairman in 1974 and tried to keep up his patronage system in the face of Mochtar Kusumaatmadja's attempts to undermine it. While Mochtar tried to reintroduce quality control, he did not push it very hard, and the system was never reinstated.

[25] Personal communication, 12 May 1995.

early 1970s and served there for ten years, I never once received any comments. The supervisory system completely collapsed from that time onwards.[26]

Judicial personnel management came to depend essentially on how close one got to the minister of justice. To the present day, Indonesian judges call this the "like-dislike" system, which really is no system at all. Judges who are liked by and loyal to the minister of justice are placed in attractive positions, while those who fall out of favor are banished to the wilderness.

> . . . several district court chairmen are Seno men . . . Those are the judges he constantly favors and tries to protect from any attempt to move them . . . [27]

This personalized system greatly strengthened the power of the minister of justice, a development that Seno Adji welcomed, as did his successors, none of whom seriously threatened to reform his creation. Occasionally the system benefited the judiciary, but usually it worked to their disadvantage. Its effects depended to some extent on who headed the Justice Department, but since it had been created to protect political interests, the system invariably undermined the autonomy of the judiciary and its independence from executive interference.

In fact, when Seno Adji was transferred to the Supreme Court in 1974, he was hoist on his own petard. His successor at the Justice Department, Mochtar Kusumaatmadja, was a sharp and able administrator and disliked the mess created by Seno Adji, and indeed disliked the former minister for creating it.[28] He used Seno Adji's system to perpetuate direct interference in the management of judicial personnel, isolating Seno Adji as a member of the Supreme Court.[29] Following Seno's precedent, Mochtar rejected, as well as approved, judicial appointments and advancements proposed by the Supreme Court, and in many cases simply appointed his own candidates. Mochtar apparently did this with the deliberate purpose of breaking down the patronage system that Seno Adji had established. Heading the Court, Seno suddenly rediscovered his principles and balked at the purported interference in the affairs of the judiciary. An open conflict ensued between Seno Adji and Mochtar which could not be resolved and had to be brought to President Suharto for mediation. Seno, apparently afraid of the

---

[26] Personal communication, 5 August 1994.

[27] *DSL*, 30 October 1978. By the time of the interview, Seno had moved over to the Supreme Court and was trying to salvage the system of patronage which was being attacked by the new minister, Mochtar Kusumaatmadja.

[28] As discussed below, there were constant brushes between the able and analytical Mochtar Kusumaatmadja and the gregarious Seno Adji. Seno Adji spent a good deal of time trying to get in Mochtar's way, concocting ludicrous schemes to take away initiatives from the Department of Justice or otherwise obstruct it. But he was never a match for Mochtar's administrative capacity and, increasingly, his political leverage with the president.

[29] As Daniel S. Lev has commented, it was a typically astute move by President Suharto to transfer Seno Adji from the Department of Justice to the Supreme Court. Seno had tied himself in so many knots at the department and committed himself so completely to the government position that it would have exceeded the bounds of even Seno's redoubtable flexibility to become a pro-Court fighter now. *DSL*, 18 October 1978. The well-known lawyer Tasrif commented: " ... Seno has many problems at the Supreme Court, because he is tied to positions he took earlier as Minister . . . " *DSL*, 18 October 1978; "Seno is cornered by positions he took while minister of justice." *DSL*, 21 October 1978.

confrontation, claimed illness and sent a deputy to the meeting. Before the president, Mochtar Kusumaatmadja pointed out that he was merely continuing Seno's own policies, and the system was retained.[30]

Minister of Justice Mochtar Kusumaatmadja faced a hard decision. He could choose the constitutionally proper option of abolishing departmental control over judicial personnel management (and giving it back to Seno Adji as chief justice, with the near certainty that mismanagement would persist), or choose the unconstitutional option of retaining department control in order to be able to redress Seno Adji's worst excesses and prevent him from continuing as chief justice.

He opted for retaining departmental control over judicial personnel management. This undoubtedly brought some short-term benefits, as he was able to weed out some of Seno Adji's worst appointees, but in the long run this policy weakened the position of the judiciary. Mochtar Kusumaatmadja had inherited a constitutional aberration, a novelty that was not yet firmly rooted, and he was uniquely placed to correct it. His failure to do so, and his continued use of the imperfect system for practical purposes, made it harder to expose as the aberration it really was. What's more, its continued use under a new professional minister gave it a routine character and legitimacy, and consequently made it more difficult to uproot. In the end, this imperfect compromise strengthened calls for even more radical measures, such as the complete separation of court administration from the department.

In the process, Mochtar Kusumaatmadja also confirmed the personalistic government style that was emerging in this period. Rather than relying on clear and solid bureaucratic structures and institutional arrangements, he relied more on his own abilities and perception of the job as instruments through which the courts might be strengthened. Yet this personal approach hid important structural weaknesses. Mochtar failed to anticipate that his successors would not necessarily share his views or abilities, which in fact almost none of them did. More fundamentally, ministers of justice are political officers responsible for helping to realize the executive agenda, and by that very function are in many respects pitted against the judiciary. Full departmental control over judicial personnel management would inevitably invite political interference, if not with this minister then with the next. It is precisely for this reason that the role of the department was constitutionally conceived as an administrative extension of the judiciary, a kind of Supreme Court secretariat. The failure of Mochtar Kusumaatmadja to abolish departmental control over judicial personnel management established by Seno Adji and replace it with a structural institutional

---

[30] *DSL*, 27 November 1987. In fact, Seno Adji was able to protect many of his men even after his transfer to the Supreme Court. It was only when he retired as Supreme Court chairman in 1981 that his powers in this regard waned, and almost all courts in the big cities were cleaned out. Thus, within a year after his retirement, all senior judges in the Jakarta district court were convicted of corruption—the infamous Sumadiyono was caught red-handed. That year, seventy-one judges were up for corruption charges. *Pelita*, 12 February 1981. Interestingly enough, the anti-corruption sweep in a way was a blow to the Indonesian judiciary. While on the one hand a lot of dead wood was cut away (though not as much as some might have liked), the sweep also concentrated on some of the most senior and experienced district court judges. I have often heard complaints that, but for their own greed and Seno's manipulations, judges such as Loudoe, Staa, and Gunawan might have been highly talented jurists who could have greatly strengthened their profession. In fact, Loudoe continued to write useful publications on the law long after his forced resignation from the judiciary.

rearrangement was a missed opportunity and ended up by significantly contributing to the erosion of judicial autonomy.

From an aberration and abuse, therefore, the Seno Adji system evolved into a fixture that allowed his successors at the Department of Justice to meddle in the affairs of the judiciary for their own purposes. Thus, shortly after being appointed minister of justice, Mudjono in 1980 took disciplinary action against thirty-five judges for "commercializing their function," and transferred a large number of judges from central courts to outlying districts without consulting the chief justice.[31]

The system continued unchanged until *Reformasi*. In that period, the judiciary only challenged it twice—there was a small flare-up under Mudjono (who moved to the Supreme Court 1980-1982) and a more serious challenge under Purwoto (1992-1994), whose role we will discuss later. Mudjono is the same person who, as minister of justice, was not above using Seno Adji's policy to shunt judges about. But when Mudjono succeeded Seno Adji as chief justice in 1980, he suddenly called for court administration to be transferred fully from the department to the Supreme Court.[32] It was an unexpected proposal that took everyone by surprise, not in the least because Mudjono, as an external appointee and former general, was not expected to identify with judicial interests. Like Seno Adji before him, however, Mudjono had served as minister of justice immediately before his transfer to the Supreme Court, and people wondered why he had not put forward the proposal when he was actually able to implement it. Besides, he had been known to twist judicial arms himself during his tenure, as had been apparent in his handling of the *Jasin case* reviewed hereafter. Mudjono was now accused of acting merely out of frustration, and for that reason his ideas were dismissed.[33] The real point was, however, that he was challenging the system on a fundamental issue. By calling for a reassessment of the dual court administration, he questioned the very instrument by which political control was exerted over the judiciary. As a result, the government found it convenient to ignore his protestations, and probably even more convenient when he died soon thereafter.

The Department of Justice's ongoing control over judicial personnel management from the 1970s was a critical development in the erosion of judicial independence. It was matched by an equally important instrument that facilitated government interference. This was the political co-optation of the Supreme Court leadership through interference in their appointment. Seno Adji's appointment as chief justice demonstrates that the government was able from 1974 to appoint government loyalists to senior positions within the judiciary. Chapter 9 will look in greater detail at the co-optation mechanism that the government used in such cases. What matters here is that it changed the relationship between the Department of Justice (and by extension the government) and the Supreme Court from one of fundamental

---

[31] *Tempo*, 17 May 1980, pp. 56-57.

[32] *Kompas*, 10 August 1981.

[33] T. Mulya Lubis, *In Search of Human Rights* (Jakarta: Gramedia, 1993), pp. 104-105. There is some confusion as to whether Mudjono made his call before or after his transfer to the Supreme Court, as Mulya Lubis has pointed out. Mudjono apparently also suggested that the Directorate General for Prisons be transferred to the Department of Social Affairs, and Immigration to Foreign Affairs, so that the Department of Justice would only handle law proper. *Tempo*, 28 November 1992. Considering Mudjono's general disposition, he probably was honest and concerned about judicial interests when making the proposal. In the *Jasin case*, he was under as much pressure as the judge, as the judge himself admitted. *DSL*, 27 November 1987.

opposition and hostility to one of agreement on political essentials. The bottom line of this agreement between the Court leadership and the government was that political interests in cases arising before the Court had to be protected. As a result, all major political cases until *Reformasi* were decided by the Supreme Court in support of the government, and it was not necessary for the Department of Justice to intervene and "pack" the Court in order to gain its compliance—as in fact the department's authority did not extend to Supreme Court personnel management.

As the minister and the chief justice from 1974 served the same political interests, it became unnecessary to freeze the Supreme Court out of judicial personnel management. This was particularly so during the 1980s, when the minister of justice and chief justice (as well as the attorney general) shared the same professional background. As a result, the relationship between both institutions involving questions about personnel shifted from one characterized by arguments over constitutional principle to a more or less routine turf fight between departments. This still may have been cast in rhetorical terms referring to constitutional principle, but, insofar as the court leadership and minister were concerned, it was essentially a matter of nibbling at each other's institutional power and funding.

As the Supreme Court leadership was politically co-opted, the more principled debate regarding judicial autonomy shifted downward within the judiciary, so that it was now conducted by judges of a lower rank. Basically, rank-and-file judges held to the constitutional principle that court administration be separated from the Justice Department, and in response the Supreme Court leadership tried to keep the lid on. Initially the rank-and-file judges organized themselves through the Judges' Association (IKAHI), which for a while was an effective lobby, but by the 1990s, the Association itself had become self-serving, and the lower judges during those years just acted on their own. The situation was reminiscent of the conditions in the 1950s under Chief Justice Wirjono Prodjodikoro, another government loyalist.

The decline in the debate from one concerning constitutional principle to mere institutional infighting and the split between rank-and-file judges and the Supreme Court leadership became particularly evident from the 1980s onward, starting with Minister of Justice Ismael Saleh and Chief Justice Ali Said. Both were generals and government loyalists who controlled the judicial apparatus for more than a decade. Despite some minor bickering, both were in complete agreement that the judiciary should be kept on a leash. There were, however, some important personal differences between these two men that influenced institutional relationships. Besides being senior in rank, Ali Said was also a wily and astute political operator, while Ismael Saleh, by contrast, had a reputation as something of a bumbler.[34] While these two essentially cooperated in court administration, their differences allowed Ali Said to regain some managerial control over the judiciary for the Supreme Court leadership, as he himself recounts:

---

[34] In fact, Jakarta lawyers referred to Ismael Saleh as "a wandering black hole" on account of the fact that everything came to a standstill in his presence—though this may be too harsh an epithet for someone under whose administration a series of crucial laws on the judiciary were enacted. Personal communication, 8 July 1994.

> It is true that court administration is in the hands of the Department of Justice. They have carried out the administration for a long time. It has happened that their technical support did not match our requirements. Something was needed to overcome this. We agreed that the director general would always be a Supreme Court judge. It used to be an appeals court judge, but now he is from the Supreme Court circle... [When I was minister of justice] I talked about this matter with Mudjono, but it did not lead to substantive suggestions. But with [Minister of Justice] Ismael Saleh, in the end we managed to overcome problems in accordance with the position of the director-general. Currently, all decisions, whether relating to a transfer, technical matters, and so forth, are proposed by the director-general and subsequently brought to the minister and myself, and then we talk it over.[35]

Still, this did not mean that the judiciary could reassert its autonomy from the government in the handling of judicial transfers. As will be apparent in the next section, Supreme Court chairman Ali Said ensured from within that government interests would be adequately protected.[36]

(c) The Structure of Political Interference in the Course of Justice

A key factor in the erosion of professional standards in the judiciary was the personalized and essentially arbitrary management of the judiciary by the Department of Justice and the Supreme Court leadership. It allowed judges to be transferred at will, without reference to any consistent system or recourse on their part.

> A judge was informed by a friend in the Department of Justice that he was up for a transfer from an outlying court to a coveted post on Java. The judge was delighted and sent Minister of Justice Ismael Saleh a long telegram, thanking him profusely for the decision. It was a bad mistake. The minister was incensed because the transfer order, though drafted, had not yet been signed. So the minister transferred him instead to a place even further away.[37]

The vast archipelago with its wide variety of living conditions made transfers a highly effective instrument for dispensing or withholding favors. This subjective transfer system rendered judges vulnerable to political pressures in their decision making.

The practically unfettered power of the Justice Department and Supreme Court to ship judges around to more or less coveted situations in the archipelago became a powerful instrument of patronage. From the 1970s onwards, the judicial administration was marked by a spectacular rise of patronage systems, heavily

---

[35] *Tempo*, 18 July 1992. Ali Said used the institutional framework laid down by Mudjono, the regular consultative meeting called the "Mah-Dep forum."

[36] See below for a discussion of his role during the debates on Law no.14/1985.

[37] Personal communication, Summer 1992.

influenced by financial considerations.[38] Without objective standards in place, advancement in the judicial system, particularly advancement to coveted posts in the big cities, came to depend on favors rather than fair assessments of competence or seniority, and favors had to be curried. Aside from generating an atmosphere of subservience and deference to authority (not to speak of sycophancy) on the part of the junior judges, the system also gave rise to elaborate financial networks that linked junior judges, as clients, with their decision-making patrons in the Department of Justice and, increasingly, on the Supreme Court.[39] One Supreme Court judge, after stating that Seno would try to protect his men, went on to explain

> District courts have a line to Seno Adji through which part of their take is submitted. Thus, the Medan district court chairman was caught in a considerable corruption case and was to be subject to a disciplinary transfer. In fact, Subekti had already signed the order, but Seno Adji countermanded it.[40]

And a lawyer noted,

> ... the Supreme Court judges have their financial sources, with a line running through the appellate courts ... [41]

The principal result of the government's control over court administration, however, was that it enabled the executive to protect its political interests in cases arising before the courts. As we discuss in greater detail in Chapter 6, this required that cases be distinguished on the basis of the specific facts that characterized them (fact specificity), and it forced the Supreme Court to decide cases based upon their facts rather than upon the legal issues involved. Political interference as a result became a critical factor in the erosion of the lawmaking powers of the Supreme Court, as cassation became a practically meaningless concept. This condition took root rapidly. Despite losing the political battle in 1971, the judiciary was for a while still able to ward off political pressures through the Supreme Court. Led by the liberal-minded and dedicated Supreme Court chairman, Subekti, supported by judges such as Asikin Kusumah Atmadja, Sri Widoyati Notoprodjo, and Busthanul Arifin, the Court was still firmly committed to judicial autonomy from executive interference and served as an example to the judiciary as a whole. This became particularly relevant as the government increasingly began to pressure the judiciary to rule on cases as it instructed. While the lower courts were already beginning to feel the strain, the Supreme Court for a while was able to

---

[38] As a result, the Directorate General for Court Upgrading at the Justice Department handling court administration is viewed as a typically "wet" section of the Department. Personal communication, 4 July 1994.

[39] One long-time insider described the system as follows: "The corruption system works based on a mixture of tributary and target systems. The first is that judges must pay their superiors, the second is that prime locations are qualified in monetary terms and that is the amount judges posted there must generate for their superiors. If they don't, they will be transferred. Of course, it is likely they have to pay up to get there in the first place." Personal communication, 8 July 1994.

[40] *DSL*, 30 October 1978. The person interviewed was a Supreme Court judge, now deceased.

[41] *DSL*, 18 October 1978. The person interviewed is a top lawyer.

protect them from outright interference. As a Supreme Court high official would recount:

> Subekti led the Court firmly and refused outside interference. On several occasions, officials, either military or civilian, called to bring pressure on the Court. But Subekti refused even to see them, and instructed his clerk to tell them that he was busy or out, and if they persisted, he had to tell them just to wait for the decision.[42]

The Supreme Court's determination to fight for the law was notably apparent in two cases, the 1970 *Yap case* and the *1972 ILO cases*.

- In the *Yap case*, the well-known advocate Yap Thiam Hien was brought to trial for slander by prosecutors whom he had accused of corruption.[43] The case was heavily politicized, as in fact both the district and appeals courts caved in to external pressures and condemned Yap to prison. On cassation, the Supreme Court freed Yap, however, in what was widely applauded as a landmark decision reinforcing the institutional autonomy both of the Court and the advocacy.[44]

Similarly, the Supreme Court, to the dismay of the government, in 1972 declared a number of ILO (International Labor Organization) Conventions applicable in Indonesia.

When outsider Seno Adji was appointed chairman in 1974, however, this last judicial redoubt was breached. Seno Adji lacked a background as a judge and, more important, had no appreciation for the judiciary's specific needs or constitutional relevance. Throughout his career, his prime loyalties rested with the government, and as a result he allowed, and sometimes even guided, massive political interference in the courts.

As a result, during Seno Adji's tenure, the minister of justice and Supreme Court chairman, despite institutional competition, found themselves essentially on the same side. They worked together to ensure the political loyalty of the judiciary, manipulating arbitrary administrative policies in a way that enabled them to wield both carrot and stick.

- A typical example of such interference is the 1977 *Haris Murtopo case*. This case involved the son of General Murtopo, a top political operator for President Suharto, who also headed the secret service establishment. His son, Haris, shot and killed a fellow high school student during a fight over the way their cars were parked.[45] The judge freed him on the grounds that he was acting in self-defense, and accepted the contention that the illegal gun he used during the killing was owned by his driver. There were

---

[42] *DSL*, 30 October 1978.

[43] For a detailed discussion of the case, see Daniel S. Lev, "Draft, The Political Journey of Yap Thiam Hien," (unpublished, 1995), chapter XI. The *Yap case* also effectively destroyed the solidarity between the legal professions started with *Pengabdi Hukum*.

[44] Lev, "Yap Draft," p. 48.

[45] *Tempo*, 3 December 1977, 17 December 1977.

convincing rumors at the time, however, as well as barely veiled hints in the press, that the judge had been pressured to free Haris.[46] This was reinforced by the behavior of the parties, notably the lackadaisical attitude of the prosecutor, who was laughing and making jokes as he presented arguments in court. The prosecutor also accepted the court's decision straight away and thereby forfeited his right to appeal—though he would not admit this in public and suggested that he needed time to decide whether or not to appeal.[47] In fact, Supreme Court insiders recount that Court chairman Seno Adji called the district court judge in the Haris Murtopo murder trial and directly dictated the decision to him by which Haris was freed.[48]

The *Haris Murtopo case* illustrates that, after 1974, not just ministers of justice, but also Supreme Court chairmen loyal to Suharto intervened routinely in the course of justice. Seno Adji in particular went out of his way to demonstrate his loyalty to the government. Examples abound, but one notable case was his sudden decision to issue a Circular Letter on government tort actions—the only legal remedies against government decisions existing at the time. In the letter, Seno Adji "rectified" a seminal Supreme Court decision taken under his predecessor, Subekti, on the ground that it gave citizens too many rights.[49] His sole purpose for issuing the letter, say Supreme Court insiders, was to ingratiate himself with the government, notably the Suharto family.[50] Indeed, it is said that when, at the prompting of Mochtar Kusumaatmadja, the government party Golkar reacted negatively to the letter, Seno Adji was unable to sleep for three nights for fear that he might be dismissed.[51]

His efforts to control the judiciary were matched by those of the ministers of justice. Mudjono's role in the *Jasin case* (1980) provides a good illustration of departmental interference in the courts.[52]

- In 1979, the retired general M. Jasin, disenchanted by the rampant corruption of the late New Order, sent an open letter to Parliament accusing

---

[46] See for instance *Tempo*, 3 December 1977, p. 54: " . . . in criminal cases such as these, the judge . . . has the right to speak, as well as his own motives for speaking the way he does."

[47] *Tempo*, 17 December 1977, p 47.

[48] *DSL*, 30 October 1978. The informant was a Supreme Court insider close to Seno Adji.

[49] Seno Adji's Supreme Court Circular Letter no.MA/Pemb./0159/77 dated 25 February 1977 which states as follows: " . . . the Supreme Court decision no.838K/Sip./1970 (. . .) lays too much emphasis on individual protection against the state, and therefore is not in accordance with Indonesian thinking, which is oriented toward a balance between individual rights and collective interests, such as the state."

[50] *DSL*, 30 October 1978. The informant was a Supreme Court insider close to Seno Adji.

[51] Apparently, Mochtar Kusumaatmadja called his brother Sarwono, the then-Minister and member of the Golkar faction, to ask him to do something about Seno Adji's letter. Sarwono, a savvy political operator, apparently suggested that they wait for a week or two before reacting so as to give the impression that there was thought behind it. When, after two weeks, Golkar responded, it appeared as if it had consulted with the government concerning what stand to take, which decidedly was not the case. Nevertheless, Seno Adji thought such consultation had taken place. He was rather shaken by it all, a fact that illustrates once again where his loyalties rested. *DSL*, 19 November 1978.

[52] For more details on the case cf. David Jenkins, *Suharto and His Generals: Indonesian Military Politics 1975-1983* (Ithaca, NY: Cornell Modern Indonesia Project, 1987), pp. 164-67, 174-83.

the government, and quite notably President Suharto, of "hypocrisy," using the Indonesian word *"munafik."* It resulted in a general political crackdown. Soon, steps were taken to bring General Jasin to court for insulting the head of state. As it happened, no court case materialized because Jasin, who was under intense pressure, issued a statement retracting his letter. Nevertheless, the justice machinery had already been set in motion and the damage was done, as the judge directly involved recounts:

It was [then Prosecutor General] Ismael Saleh who decided that Jasin's word *"munafik"* would be given the religious meaning of "apostasy" rather than the conventional meaning of "hypocritical." The latter meaning was pretty light, to be used for someone who turns up late for an appointment or something. But in the former case, the implication was much more serious. I was assigned to the case when it came up a couple of years ago. Before the case was registered, I was called in by Minister of Justice Mudjono, who told me that I simply had to sentence Jasin. I didn't know what to do, but quite simply was instructed to convict. [The judge breaks down, crying.] It was a terrible experience, even though Jasin in the end withdrew his statement and the case never came about. There are numerous cases such as these in which both the minister of justice and the Supreme Court chairman directly instruct judges to convict, or as it happened, to acquit. The judges know they have to follow orders or lose their positions or worse. What can I do, I have a family and no money of my own.[53]

Such instances reveal that cases were no longer decided on their legal merits alone, but that if the facts were in any way politically relevant, this took preeminence. Therefore, regardless of legal guarantees concerning judicial independence, the dual administration system and political co-optation of the Supreme Court leadership that took shape in the mid-1970s ensured that government control over the judiciary was practically complete from that time until *Reformasi*. This was the critical element in weakening the professional standards and integrity of the judiciary.

While judicial autonomy was being progressively weakened during the 1970s by the executive's administration of and interference in the courts, the judiciary had to give ground also in the field of status and constitutional review. Law no.8/1974 firmly embedded the lower court judges in the civil service apparatus,[54] while designating the Supreme Court judges as "state officials."[55] Supervision of the lower judges by the state civil service apparatus not only subjected them to bureaucratic hierarchies, but also involved compulsory membership in the government-sponsored civil service union (KORPRI, Korps Pegawai Republik Indonesia, Indonesian Civil Service Corps) and demanded allegiance to the

---

[53] *DSL*, 27 November 1987. At the time of the interview, the judge to whom the Jasin case had been assigned was on the Supreme Court.

[54] Law no.8/1974 official elucidation art.2: "Civil servants of the central government are . . . judges at the general district courts and appeal courts." It should be noted that while the law specifically refers to judges in the jurisdiction of the general courts, the civil servant status by extension also applies to the judges of the other jurisdictions.

[55] Law no.8/1974 art.8: State official are: (. . .)4. The chairman, vice-chairman, junior chairmen, and judges at the Supreme Court.

"monoloyalty" (*monoloyalitas*) principle, which calls upon all civil servants to support the government.[56] As the dean of the Bandung Bar, Bob Nainggolan, put it:

> ... as civil servants, judges are government officials, which makes them side with the government in cases in which its interests are at issue ...[57]

This designation of judges as civil servants also signified that no adjustments in salaries were to be realized, though salaries remained one of the central items on the judicial political agenda. Despite contrary statutory provision in Law no.14/1970, judges were now firmly netted in the civil service salary regulations, according to which they were fully equated with other civil servants.[58] Admittedly, judges in the 1970s received special supplements (*tunjangan*) raising their income, which marginally strengthened their position in the civil service context,[59] however officials with comparable functions, such as the prosecutors, also benefited from special supplements.[60] The judicial supplements were slightly higher, but the difference was so insignificant that it neither boosted judicial self-confidence nor worried the prosecutors.[61]

Constitutional review will be considered in greater detail when we deal with the reforms in the 1990s. It can be stated here as a preliminary observation that the right was restricted even further in its implementation after Law no.14/1970. The major point in this period, however, is that the restricted interpretation of review became constitutionally more enshrined, effectively rooting the French-Dutch system more firmly in the political edifice of the New Order.

2. LAW NO.14/1985: AFFIRMING THE POLITICAL STATUS QUO

In 1985, the government somewhat unexpectedly launched two bills that were meant to constitute the legislative basis for the Supreme Court as well as the system of general courts for the coming decade. Essentially patterned on the bills that failed to pass in the 1960s, they were drummed through Parliament at great speed. In sharp contrast to the two years that it took to get the 1968/1970 Bill on

---

[56] *Kompas*, 23 October 1985.

[57] *Pelita*, 16 October 1985.

[58] A civil servant's income consists of a salary and supplements (*tunjangan*). Supplements can take different forms. Some are structural supplements that accrue to a civil servant on the basis of objective criteria, such as his family condition (child benefits) or geographic location. Thus, there is a special Irian Jaya supplement (Presidential Decree no.13/1977) and an East Timor supplement (Presidential Decree no.12/1979). Besides these, there also are special supplements accruing to functions on the basis of their relative importance. See for instance Circular Letter no.BAKN 02/SE/1977 point II.

[59] See for instance Presidential Decree no.17/1977, Circular Letter Head of the State Administrative Board no.BAKN 08/SE/1977.

[60] For the prosecutor supplements cf. Presidential Decree no.20/1977.

[61] The supplements for prosecutors with salary rankings II, III, and IV were Rp.30,000, Rp.45,000, and Rp.60,000 respectively, while for judges of the same rankings they were Rp.50,000, Rp.60,000, and Rp.70,000. This amounts to differences of approximately 7-14 US dollars measured by contemporary exchange rates.

General Judicial Principles enacted, the Supreme Court Bill was enacted as Law no.14/1985 within only three months, while the Bill on the General Courts did not take much longer (Law no.4/1986). The swift passage of these bills indicates two important aspects of both pieces of legislation. First, their basic elements stirred up very little political contest, so that there was little need for political bartering and compromises. Secondly, as a result, the bills were not legally very innovative. Consequently, the 1985 bills underscored the fact that between 1970 and 1985 the government had achieved dominance on the political issues relating to the judiciary: no new ground was broken, and the political status quo was affirmed. As the doyen of the Indonesian advocates, Harjono Tjitrosoebeno, remarked: "these laws just confirm existing conditions."[62]

(a) The Political Perspective: The Judiciary Silenced

The principal reason for the lack of a contest concerning the new legislation was that the judiciary was politically weakened and demoralized, and, as a result, was prevented from playing any role of significance in the 1985 debates. Aside from the generally unfavorable political climate, two factors in particular contributed to its weak position and that of its principal lobby, the Judges' Association. First, the Association leadership may have been dedicated to the political goals of the judiciary, but its members could not equal the forceful group that had led the Association in the 1960s. Its chairman Soerjadi was a somewhat self-effacing man, rather bureaucratically inclined. He was not noted for his table-hammering speeches or for taking part in civil protests (Asikin and Sri Widoyati had built up their credentials in the 1960s through participation in street protests). Secondly, and even more important, domination of the Supreme Court by external appointees meant the Association and the Court were split on all fundamental issues. The Supreme Court's chairman, Ali Said, as we have seen, was a former prosecutor general and minister of justice, in other words a government man with little interest in or commitment to the judiciary and its political goals. His refusal to back the Judges' Association effectively foiled whatever chances it may have had to realize its goals.

Both these weaknesses became painfully obvious when, in the run-up to the parliamentary debates on the two bills, the Association began to lobby in Parliament. In June 1985, it gave a presentation to Parliament in which it reiterated its political agenda, calling for separating the judges from the civil service, transferring court administration from the Department of Justice (though not to the Supreme Court this time but to the State Secretariat), as well as for the right of constitutional review.[63] Apparently, however, the Association had not consulted in advance with Supreme Court chairman Ali Said, who reportedly was quite taken aback when he heard about their presentation to Parliament—as indeed he told the press that he had forgotten the organization still existed.[64] Dissociating himself completely from their demands, he reportedly said, "it is no

---

[62] *Tempo*, 8 March 1986.

[63] Apparently the Judges' Association also suggested a transfer of court administration to the State Secretariat, which handles the administration of other high state organs. *Tempo*, 7 September 1985; 28 November 1992.

[64] *Tempo*, 8 June 1985.

use harking back to old songs."[65] He indicated that he would summon the Association's leadership to his office to call them to order. A couple of days later they caved in and apologized in public for what they called their "loose lips."[66] With the judiciary so eager to surrender, there was hardly any need for the government or Parliament to address the issues it raised; as a result, this pro-reform effort just evaporated.[67]

In fact, and unlike during the 1960s, the Association was at this time completely overshadowed by the Supreme Court, or at least by its chairman, Ali Said.[68] This became apparent when the Association made a new presentation to Parliament on the bills under discussion in November 1985, following its central-regional conference in Jakarta. While it did offer a forceful statement on one of the issues (whether or not to open up the judiciary for outside recruits), on all others it was mild, if not silent. Thus, the separation issue, which had been at the core of the Association's requests in June and had so angered Ali Said, was dropped altogether. Also, the Association abandoned its demand for complete constitutional review and merely suggested gently that, following the Decree of the People's Assembly no.TAP MPR/III/1978, the bills should allow direct action to the Supreme Court when a request is made for constitutional review, bypassing normal cassation procedure. Finally, it meekly proposed that judges be made state officials and thus separated from the civil service.[69]

This extraordinarily weak presentation nullified everything the Association had fought for over the years and made no impression on the continuing debates. Ali Said's message was clear: while he ruled the Supreme Court, the Judges' Association had no political role. The debates on the 1985 bills made it clear that he had achieved his goal.

(b) The Legal Perspective: Confirming the Status Quo

The absence of a strong judicial lobby throughout the 1980s made the debate with the government and Parliament concerning the place and role of the judiciary an empty performance: an exercise in one-hand clapping. Few changes could be expected from these actors, and nothing of importance altered with regard to the basic political issues on the judicial agenda. Nevertheless, the debates on Law no.14/1985 also revealed some interesting dimensions of the judiciary's political struggle that had hitherto remained generally unacknowledged. It seems that by 1985 the debate in Indonesia had become polarized to the point that it was nearly impossible to define the merits of the issues under consideration. This was made clear by former Supreme Court chairman Subekti when he addressed the issue of

---

[65] Ibid.

[66] *Tempo*, 7 September 1985.

[67] This happened even though Parliament was reportedly quite receptive to the idea of separating court administration from the Department of Justice. *Tempo*, 8 June 1985.

[68] At least two Supreme Court members were also leaders of the Judges' Association, namely Soerjono (Supreme Court chairman from 1994 onwards) and Iman Anis. These judges also took part in the June 1985 presentation to Parliament.

[69] IKAHI letter to the chairman of Parliament dated 19 November 1985, published in *Varia Peradilan* 1,3 (1985): 15-16.

the dual court administration and tried to break new ground by challenging the pre-set positions of both sides in the debate. His attempt was in vain, but the process provided some interesting insights that merit closer attention, if only because they indirectly revealed the extent to which the Supreme Court itself had become part of the political power games.[70]

(i) Power and Constitutional Review

The debate on constitutional review in 1985 differed fundamentally from that conducted in 1968-1970. In those early years, discussion addressed the merits of different systems of constitutional review. Such a debate was possible because political boundaries remained to be clearly defined, which led to greater openness. Also, key questions such as whether the 1945 Constitution allowed constitutional review remained unsettled. Law no.14/1970 constituted a government victory because it stated that such an important constitutional power required a constitutional amendment to be realized. The subsequent People's Assembly Decree no.TAP MPR/III/1978 moved even further away from granting constitutional review. It reiterated the rule laid down in Law no.14/1970 that constitutional review by the courts was restricted to statutes inferior to Acts of Parliament. This was one of the small but significant moves that weakened judicial standing even further.[71] It had the effect of embedding the institution deeper in the Indonesian governmental structures: following the decree, neither government, Parliament, nor the courts would, constitutionally at least, be able to alter constitutional review fundamentally. The *Madison v. Marbury* option that had seemed within reach in the 1960s was legally excluded as an option after 1978. This development helps explain why Supreme Court chairman Purwoto S. Gandasubrata in the 1990s would call for the People's Assembly—rather than any other institution and rather than the chairman himself—to change the rules governing constitutional review.[72]

The other change was more intrinsic and would condition the ideological aspect of the debate on constitutional review for years to come. The involvement of the People's Assembly, which embodies the sovereignty of the state, politicized the issue. While the idea that constitutional review might be accommodated within the framework of the 1945 Constitution was still accepted in the 1960s and under Law no.14/1970, the Decree of the People's Assembly no.MPR/III/1978 effectively declared it unconstitutional.[73] The New Order government made the 1945

---

[70] Indicative of the poor position of the Judges' Association, there really was no debate on the salary and status issue. The Bill on the General Courts only suggested, in line with Law no.14/1970, that the salary (and protocol) position of judges be effected by separate regulation (art.53 Bill).

[71] There was one aspect of the People's Assembly decision that favored the judiciary, at least from the perspective of the judges. Because the decision did not specifically provide for procedure, the judges held that it allowed for direct appeal to the Supreme Court, bypassing the lower courts and the lengthy contradictory procedures. See IKAHI statement in Parliament on the 1985 Supreme Court Bill, *Pikiran Rakyat,* 21 November 1985. As will be apparent, this question acquired considerable practical importance after the Supreme Court Bill was enacted.

[72] *Suara Karya*, 17 November 1992; see also M. F. Falaakh, "Mahkamah Agung dan judicial review dalam cita bernegara," *Varia Peradilan* 8,95 (August 1993): 126.

[73] It is this logic that underlies statements such as those of Member of Parliament Albert Hasibuan: "[The restricted judicial review] is correct, because it is founded on the concept of people's sovereignty embraced by the Indonesian state in People's Congress Decree no.TAP

Constitution the very key to its authority, so that any questioning of that statute approximated political criticism. The debate on constitutional review, as a result, could not be reopened where the parties had left off in 1970 because it was now politically out of bounds. Instead it would have to be expressed in technical and subdued tones, which in the end would lead to a subdued version of constitutional review.

Nevertheless, during the debates on the 1985 Supreme Court Bill, the Islamic PPP (Partai Persatuan Pembangunan, the Unity Development Party), the national PDI (Partai Demokrasi Indonesia), and the military fraction all called for more attention to constitutional review, and the issue was also being debated in the streets.[74] But while debate in the streets, like that in the 1960s, focused on the issue of whether review extended to Acts of Parliament,[75] the debate in Parliament focused on a comparatively subsidiary point: whether to allow for direct action before the Supreme Court in review cases, thus bypassing the cumbersome lower court procedure.[76] The government was not very enthusiastic about this proposal, because, as Minister of Justice Ismael Saleh put it, this would throw the doors wide open.[77]

In the end, Law no.14/1985 art.31 confirmed the restricted right of judicial review, yet remained ambivalent on whether direct action would be allowed. This ambivalence would have consequences for the future.[78]

(ii) Autonomy and Dual Court Administration

While the issue of dual court administration was raised during the debates on the 1985 Supreme Court Bill, only when the subsequent 1986 Bill on the General Courts was discussed did attention focus on administration. Few new ideas were expressed during the parliamentary debates, however, and the courts continued to be administered by the Department of Justice. Witness Law no.2/1986 on the General Courts:

Art.5(1): The technical management of the courts is effected by the Supreme Court.

MPR/III/1978." *Sinar Harapan*, 20 November 1985. A legal scholar argued along similar lines: judicial review is not in accordance with the ideas underlying the 1945 Constitution, "which places state sovereignty with the people, being the People's Congress [MPR]." *Kompas*, 16 October 1985

[74] *Varia Peradilan* 1,2 (1985).

[75] During a conference in Bandung leading up to the debates, former Supreme Court chairman Subekti revealed himself to be a fervent supporter of complete judicial review. *Sinar Pagi*, 12 October 1985.

[76] This is what the Decree of the People's Assembly TAP MPR/III/1978 was taken to mean. See, for instance, opening statement of the military (ABRI, Angkatan Bersenjata Republik Indonesia, Armed Forces of the Republic of Indonesia) fraction in *Varia Peradilan* 1,2 (1985): 88.

[77] Parties supporting direct access were the PDI, the PPP, and ABRI. *Angkatan Bersenjata*, 21 November 1985. Ministerial wording: "sangat besar dan luas" (very large and wide). The government party Golkar was not supportive, cf. *Varia Peradilan* 1,4 (1986): 84-85.

[78] As with Law no.14/1970, the 1985 law states that judicial review be effected in connection with normal cassation procedure. While this suggests that review must be commenced in the same manner as any other case, at district court level, the Indonesian verb used in the article is *dapat*, which can be read as either "must" or "can." *Merdeka*, 18 November 1992

Art.5(2): The organizational, administrative and financial management of the courts is effected by the minister of justice.

Art.5(3): The management referred to in paragraphs (1) and (2) may not interfere in the freedom of judges to handle and decide cases.

The official explanation adds that for all judicial appointments, dismissals, transfers, advancements, or other administrative actions concerning judges there will be cooperation, consultation, and coordination between the Supreme Court and the Justice Department.

If there was little action in Parliament on the issue of dual court management, outside those halls matters were bubbling. Since the 1971 Medan failure, the legal professions—particularly the judiciary and the advocacy—increasingly felt that the system had outlived its constitutional validity. Government interference and duplicity deepened the divide between the judges and the government over the question of whether administrative authority should be transferred from the Department of Justice to the Supreme Court. Over time, more judges became convinced that the system, rather than government abuse, was to blame for the breakdown. As a supportive Member of Parliament said:

> The dual system of court administration is inclined to reduce judicial values of independence, freedom, and autonomy.[79]

Viewed from this perspective, the system serves to legitimate government interference in the affairs of the judiciary, and abolition of the system is an essential prerequisite for restoring judicial autonomy. Placing court administration under the Justice Department effectively institutionalized government interference in court affairs, and thus one must abolish the executive's direct authority over the courts in order to solve the problem.

It is a logic tempting in its simplicity, and perhaps it was the only argument judges could offer in these political circumstances. But it denies some basic realities. One must recognize that judicial autonomy from executive interference works satisfactorily in other countries, such as the Netherlands, that have adopted the system of dual court administration, while judicial autonomy is seriously threatened in such countries as the Philippines, which adhere to the US system.

Former Supreme Court chairman Subekti raised this point obliquely during the 1985 debates[80] when, to the dismay of professional judges, he made clear his reluctance to transfer court administration to the Supreme Court. Some might have dismissed his view as merely traditional or unimaginative. In fact, it was based on a much deeper understanding of the political complexities of the situation than evidenced by the Judges' Association. According to Subekti, no system of dual management actually existed, for the Supreme Court was sovereign in its control over courts, with the department serving merely as an administrative extension. All that was necessary, he argued, was for the law to make the situation

---

[79] Soetomo for the PDI fraction, *Dewan Perwakilan Rakyat Republik Indonesia*, Persidangan O Rapat Paripurna Terbuka Ke-6 Tahun sidang 1985-1986, dated 17 September 1985, p. 44.

[80] *Pikiran Rakyat*, 11 October 1985; *Sinar Pagi*, 12 October 1985; *Kompas*, 14 October 1985.

absolutely clear.[81] In the course of unfolding his argument, Subekti indicated that prevailing political conditions ensured that a transfer of court administration to the Supreme Court would not in itself reduce or exclude government interference or strengthen judicial autonomy, as all judges seemed to believe. In his view, it was not the system of court administration that was at fault, but its political implementation. Nothing would be resolved by changing the system, quite simply because the government didn't need the dual court administration to achieve the desired results.[82]

This argument illuminated a further important reality, which judges were not at all eager to admit, namely that part of the problem rested within the judiciary itself. The Supreme Court was, and is, subject to political pressures, and moreover is a political and bureaucratic manipulator in its own right. Its personnel management is no less personalized than that of the Justice Department, and certainly is not free from (imposed) political considerations. As a result, transferring court administration to the Supreme Court would do little truly to improve autonomy. On the contrary, it might well destroy whatever restraints still exist in the management of judicial appointments and assignments, which has become so heavily dependent on political and personal connections. From the perspective of judges lacking such connections, the dual administration system might be better, in that it forces compromises on the Supreme Court and hence, perversely and however summarily, protects these judges. Indeed, some judges fear that were the Supreme Court to acquire complete control over court administration, nepotism would run rampant. Until political change is realized, perhaps the best way for a common judge to secure his position is by pitting one government force against the other.

The observation of one highly acute and observant judge—who long served at the Supreme Court level but has since retired—concerning this subject merits extensive quotation:

> The heavy administrative apparatus supporting the judiciary really has nothing to do with dogmatic French ideas, as is often argued in Indonesia. It is linked to a professional career judiciary, which inevitably stands for an extended and stratified judicial organization requiring an extensive bureaucratic supporting apparatus. It is nonsense to divorce such an apparatus from its social and political context, and to transfer court administration to the Supreme Court will, in my opinion, in the end, not add an iota to judicial status, or reduce political pressures on the judicial apparatus. (. . .) Indonesia is now in a post-development phase. The institutions are all there, political power centers multiply, and people are beginning to call for more clarity and for rules that reflect their aspirations and in the shaping of which they play their

---

[81] For this purpose, Subekti suggested that a common regulation be enacted by the Supreme Court chairman and the minister of justice in which their respective functions would be clearly defined and which would state that the Supreme Court would determine which functions were to be realized by the department. *Kompas*, 14 October 1985.

[82] It was an argument that apparently Professor Daniel S. Lev also made in Indonesia during a meeting with human rights' lawyers, raising a flood of protests. Consequently the point could not be properly analyzed, and the convenient fiction that the system was at fault persisted. It showed that the issue was politicized, and positions polarized to the point that a real debate of what was at stake had become impossible.

part. But until this is realized, there are distinct advantages in the present dual system of court administration. The advancement system is totally subjective and governed by the "like and dislike" motto. It may all seem neutral on paper, but in reality this is not so. Placing the system under full Supreme Court control makes each and every move of the system dependent on whether or not one is friends with Purwoto, and him only. The Supreme Court leadership meetings [RAPIM, Rapat Pimpinan] are under the complete control of the Court chairman. It is very hierarchical, and the input of the junior chairmen etc. is negligible. Currently, the Supreme Court meets once every three months with the Department of Justice. Both sides have their own list of demands, but compromises are necessary. The Court must give way on certain names, and so does the department. It really amounts to a sort of checks and balances system . . . [83]

The administration system issue clearly is not as simple as it may initially appear.

Whatever the validity of these arguments on grounds of substance, they did not really affect the political realities at work in 1985, or today. The fact is that, even under *Reformasi*, the modern debate in Indonesia on the system of dual court administration is conducted in terms of symbols and slogans, not in terms of a solid analysis of the substantive merits of the system, or of its alternatives.[84]

3. 1985-1992: THE OLD REGIME CONTINUED

In the final analysis, therefore, the 1985 laws affirmed the existing situation and did not in any way affect the weak political condition of the judiciary. The continuation of the old regime was evident in a variety of facts that all touched directly on the issues which the judiciary felt important.

Even the slight changes in judicial review did not affect the ways in which the Supreme Court approached the issue. It will be recalled that after Law no.14/1970, judicial review remained limited to colonial statute. Those in power probably adopted this approach because questioning colonial statute has little impact on modern government, or the modern state, and hence is not nearly as politically sensitive as review of modern legislation. Indeed, in modern Indonesian political psychology, questioning colonial statute strengthens nationalist credentials, and therefore is perfectly legitimate. For this reason, perhaps, the judges eagerly began to review colonial statute, striking down even colonial Acts of Parliament and treaties. Thus, in the 1970s and pursuant to its own Regulation no.2/1964, the

---

[83] Personal communication, 18 July 1994.

[84] Nevertheless Subekti's argument indicates a subtle undercurrent to the debate as it has come to be understood by some judges and their supporters. According to this perspective, political change will not perhaps be realized by reforming the system of court administration as such, but by means of the political symbolism and underlying power shifts that such a reorganization would necessarily entail. Thus, transfer of court administration in the face of government opposition would show that the political power balance between the government and the judiciary has shifted, and these modifications would ultimately make judicial independence viable. So it is actually useful to make the system a political issue and polarize the debate. There is considerable validity to this argument, yet I submit that most participants would find it too subtle for their tastes.

Supreme Court nullified colonial statute HIR art.209, under which persons could be imprisoned as security in the case of a contractual default (*gijzeling/sandera*).[85] In 1989, it similarly nullified a colonial ordinance on interreligious marriages for allegedly violating Marriage Law no.1/1974, and subsequently created a new procedure for concluding such marriages.[86] In 1985, the Court declared an international treaty on the enforcement of foreign arbitral awards to be quite dead. The treaty had been concluded in the Dutch period and was generally assumed to have been accepted in Indonesian law after independence, until the Supreme Court decided otherwise.[87]

Judicial activism with regard to colonial law was, however, more than counterbalanced by its reticence in reviewing modern statute. The consistent refusal of Indonesian courts to subject modern statute to serious scrutiny undermined their authority. It created the image of a politically compliant judiciary ("toothless" as the press called it[88]), both unprepared and unable to challenge the government, and as a result not truly independent.[89] This image was strengthened by the judges' excessive restraint. Thus, in 1972 the Supreme Court stopped short of reviewing Government Regulation (Peraturan Pemerintah) no.49/1963 on the Housing Boards (Kantor Urusan Perumahan). In its decision, the Court stated that, according to that law, the Housing Boards rather than the general courts were empowered to decide housing disputes, even though Law no.14/1970 art.10 had in fact abolished the jurisdiction of Housing Boards altogether.[90]

After 1985 the Supreme Court basically remained unable or unwilling to check the government. It consistently refused to hear cases in which it was asked to quash executive regulation. A notable example is the 1990 *Pedicab case*.[91]

---

[85] Mahkamah Agung no.951K/Sip/1974. In nullifying the colonial legislative provision, the case goes much further than Supreme Court Regulation nr.2/1964, which instructed the courts not to avail themselves of the provision in deciding cases. This Regulation effectively suspended the article, without nullifying it, therefore. After *Reformasi* and in the middle of the economic crisis, the Supreme Court reinstated civil detention with Regulation nr.1/2000. This Regulation said it only lifted the suspension of Regulation nr.2/1964. In so doing, it ignored Supreme Court decisions by which the relevant colonial statute had been nullified, such as the case cited above. It raises the interesting constitutional question whether the Supreme Court can revoke its own jurisprudence (which, after all, constitutionally is a source of law) by regulation and whether and how the constitutionality of Supreme Court regulations can be determined.

[86] Mahkamah Agung no.1400K/Pdt/1986 dated 20 January 1989.

[87] This decision and the previous one are noteworthy because they reversed even established Supreme Court jurisprudence on these issues. Both also were controversial decisions that have tended to confuse matters rather than resolve them.

[88] "Mahkamah ompong," *Tempo*, 18 July 1992.

[89] As the chairman of LBH (Lembaga Bantuan Hukum, Legal Aid Institute), A. H. Nusantara said in 1992: "The weakness of the Supreme Court is not because of technical problems, such as the backlogs or corrupt judges, but because of the political system." *Kompas*, 8 August 1992.

[90] Mahkamah Agung no.1078K/Sip/1971 dated 26 July 1972; see also Falaakh, "Mahkamah Agung," p. 128; S. Mertokusumo, *Hukum acara perdata Indonesia* (Yogyakarta: Liberty, 1981), pp. 22-23. Both publications also refer to a Supreme Court decision no.1205K/Sip/1971 dated 17 January 1973, in which the Court questioned the validity of Law no.49/Prp/1960 because it conflicted with Law no.14/1970. This is perhaps the closest the Supreme Court ever came to reviewing modern statute, but here, as both authors point out, it was actually questioning the validity of an Act of Parliament, which by law it is not allowed to do.

[91] This contradicts the argument, sometimes heard in judicial circles, that the courts cannot practice judicial review for lack of cases. As Purwoto S. Gandasubrata said: "Judicial review

- The *Pedicab case* arose out of the 1990 decision of the Governor of Jakarta to cleanse the city of its famous pedicabs (*becak*), on the grounds that driving a pedicab was degrading work.[92] The measure was strongly resisted by the pedicab drivers, whose livelihood was taken away from them. Indeed, resistance was so strong that the only way by which the local government in the end was able to enforce its decision was by throwing the pedicabs into the sea.[93] As a result, the Legal Aid Institute (LBH, Lembaga Bantuan Hukum) brought a direct action before the Supreme Court in which they asked that the Governor of Jakarta Decision be nullified for conflicting with the Constitution as well as various labor and social security laws. Supreme Court chairman Ali Said refused even to hear the case. In his letter of reply the Secretary General of the Supreme Court suggested that the problem rested with the direct application to the Court: " . . . after careful study, we herewith inform you that the review as mentioned would be better presented through normal appeal channels."[94]

From a legal perspective, the *Pedicab case* showed that the Ali Said Court interpreted Law no.14/1985 art.31 to mean that no direct action for judicial review could be brought to the Supreme Court, which would hear such cases only if they came up through the lower courts as a normal contradictory procedure. Yet the blunt terms in which the Supreme Court denied even a hearing on the case created the impression that it was unwilling to review any government regulation. As a result, the Jakarta LBH concluded that such actions were futile and gave up on the *Pedicab case*: after filing a pro forma claim at the Jakarta district court (which was rejected), the organization lost track of it altogether.[95]

The *Pedicab case* was only one of several that reinforced the impression that the judiciary was on a government leash.[96] Thereafter, Supreme Court chairman Ali Said consistently rebuffed parties hoping to submit cases directly to the Court for review. During this period, there was a series of prominent cases based on complaints that publishing licenses had been withdrawn by the government in apparent conflict with the law, yet while Ali Said was chairman, none of these cases was brought to the Supreme Court. When the weekly *Prioritas* was banned in 1986, the editor, Surya Paloh, approached Ali Said to check whether the case

---

is not used because nobody asks us to." *Kompas*, 14 October 1992. This statement by Purwoto can be read two ways: as an awkward apology for judicial inaction, or as a call for more cases.

[92] Decision Governor of Jakarta no.850/1990.

[93] This process was called "to Tanjung-Priok pedicabs," after the Jakarta harbor, Tanjung Priok. Other cities followed suit, and in Surabaya pedicabs were "Tanjung-Perakked" by being tossed in the Surabaya harbor, Tanjung Perak.

[94] Letter Supreme Court Secretary General no.354/SK/YLBHI/XII/1990, quoted in *Kompas*, 15 October 1992.

[95] Ibid. In December 1992, the LBH wondered about the "fate of this case," which showed that it had given up on it. *Kompas*, 15 December 1992.

[96] When looking back at the eve of his retirement in July 1992, Supreme Court chairman Ali Said had a somewhat selective memory of events and underwent a complete change of heart. He suddenly began to call for the right to review Acts of Parliament, and said that the present procedure, which, according to him, necessitated going through the lower courts first, was unduly burdensome. *Tempo*, 18 July 1992; *Media Indonesia*, 9 December 1992.

might be brought directly before the Supreme Court. Ali Said refused, telling Surya Paloh to take his case to the district courts instead. Surya Paloh saw this as a ploy that would lead nowhere and consequently did not initiate an action before the district court. The duplicitous Ali Said later told reporters that if Surya Paloh didn't bring any action, why, how could the Supreme Court be blamed for failing to act on judicial review, as it never got any cases?[97] Ali Said also reined in the Judges' Association when it lobbied for complete constitutional review in 1985, and denied the possibility of direct action for judicial review when he refused to hear the *Pedicab case*. Regardless of his statements to reporters, Ali Said's actions made it clear that, so long as he was the top judge, it was no use bringing actions against the government. Indeed, parties became so convinced that requests for review were hopeless that in a number of other prominent cases they did not even bother to bring any action at all.

- This happened in the *Monitor case* (1990). The journal, the *Monitor*, published a popularity poll that listed the Prophet Mohammad far down in the line of names. This poll caused great unrest in the predominantly Muslim Indonesian society, and the publishing license of the journal was withdrawn based on the accusation that it had offended the religious sensitivities of the community. In this case, nobody bothered to bring any action to protest the loss of the license, though the journal's prima facie case was certainly not without merit.[98]

With respect to the dual court administration system, again, there was little change: as before, the system after 1985 facilitated political interference in politically sensitive cases before the court. As during the late 1970s, during the 1980s both the Department of Justice and the Supreme Court leadership used the leverage of the court administration to pressure judges into political compliance. Intervention of this sort was apparent in a number of notable cases that drew public attention, such as the *Dharsono case* (1986).[99]

- This well-known case, tried before the Central Jakarta district court, involved another disenchanted general, H. R. Dharsono, formerly secretary-general of ASEAN (Association of Southeast Asian Nations). Dharsono was accused of participating in an Islamic organization aimed at overthrowing the government. Significantly, even though the court chairman S. had already been transferred to Medan, the actual transfer was delayed, with the specific instruction that S. was to try the Dharsono case before departing. As his replacement had already been appointed a few months earlier, the Central Jakarta district court had two chairmen.[100] A Supreme Court judge monitoring the case gave an explanation for this curious course of events:

---

[97] *Tempo*, 18 July 1992; *Media Indonesia*, 9 December 1992.

[98] *Tempo*, 18 July 1992.

[99] For reports on the case, see for instance *Tempo*, 18 January 1986; *Tempo*, 8 March 1986; *Tempo*, 29 March 1986.

[100] *Tempo* 18 January 1986.

In the *Dharsono case,* the presiding judge S. was already up for a transfer to Medan. Nevertheless, through an intermediary he offered himself to the Department of Justice to try the case, with the implied promise to convict. The reason was that S. had a couple of shady deals behind him and wanted to clear his name with the department. Trying the Dharsono case was his way out. He was already appointed to the Medan court, but the minister said all right, you handle the case. So he tried the case, obviously with the understanding that he would convict, which he did.[101]

Yet it was not just in relatively high-profile cases, where evident political interests were at stake, that politics interfered. Political interference in the course of justice became a routine matter. Even in the most ordinary cases, the Department of Justice, working through its head office in Jakarta or its extensive network of local branches (KanWil, Kantor Wilayah), routinely intervened as it saw fit, sometimes without any prompting from the political center.[102] Indeed, it was not clear at all whether interventions by the Department of Justice and the Supreme Court were politically inspired or occurred merely because personal interests of departmental big shots so dictated. As a result, departmental or Supreme Court intervention also influenced petty cases, in which, for some reason or other, important Justice Department officials or the Supreme Court leadership defined an interest. Interference in such run-of-the-mill cases indicates the pervasiveness of this practice even after 1985..

The prevalence of executive interference also meant that government officials no longer felt the need to keep up constitutional pretenses and hide their meddling in the course of justice. Instead, official instructions to judges on how to decide cases were given openly and on paper.

- The routine nature of executive interference after 1985 can be illustrated with the *Maumere nationalization case* (1990), a unexceptional nationalization case implemented by court order in a small island in the Eastern half of the archipelago. Notwithstanding its mundane character, Minister of Justice Ismael Saleh intervened in the case and directly instructed the judge to nullify his former decision granting nationality: " . . . Considering the result of the team of the Inspectorate General of the Department of Justice dated X 1990 in the Maumere District Court and the Immigration Office in Maumere, the Minister of Justice herewith instructs the Chairman of the District Court of Maumere to annul the declaration of nationality no. [X].[103]

The judge is quite open in acknowledging such executive instructions, a response that indicates not merely their routine character, but also in subtle ways the fact that

---

[101] *DSL,* 27 November 1987. A. B. Nasution, defense counsel for Dharsono, would later recount that he never stood a chance with the presiding judge S., who cut him short at every turn.

[102] In 1985, Judges' Association chairman Soerjadi pointed out that the regional offices (KanWil) of the Department of Justice were important sources of interference in the course of justice. *Tempo,* 8 June 1985; *Tempo* 8 March 1986.

[103] Documents in the possession of the author. The file was given to me by an Indonesian member of Parliament. Number kept anonymous on request.

the sole public protest a judge can make is to point out in his decision that his arm is being twisted:

> Having read the Instruction of the minister of justice of the Indonesian Republic xxxxx (1992) (. . .) it is herewith decided that the declaration of nationality is annulled. . . . [104]

In fact, given the arbitrary transfer and advancement system, district court judges were poorly placed to defend their autonomy and independence. As the wife of a prominent district court judge told me:

> The reality is that the big fish from the Supreme Court or the Department of Justice routinely instruct district court judges on how to decide cases and constantly mess about in their affairs. And then, when the balloon bursts in the press, they play the innocent and hide behind the doctrine that no one may interfere in the judicial process and such hash. Or they even put on the thumb screws and punish the district court judge for the corruption that they themselves were instrumental in setting up in the first place. Some prominent judges once said that it is the small district court judges who have the toughest job of all.[105]

Clearly, the judiciary after 1985 was in no better position to resist this political pressure from the top than before.

4. 1992-1995: PURWOTO GANDASUBRATA'S ATTEMPTS AT REFORM

The most serious attempt at political change after 1970 came during the brief tenure of Supreme Court chairman Purwoto S. Gandasubrata from 1992 until 1994. Purwoto was the first Supreme Court chairman to be appointed from the professional judiciary since Seno Adji in 1974, and his professional background helped him identify more closely with judicial as opposed to government interests. In fact, the political gap existing between the Supreme Court and the Judges' Association under Ali Said narrowed perceptibly under his successor. Aside from introducing a number of important changes in the operation and internal structure of the Court (which will be considered in Chapter 8), Purwoto was the first Court chairman to challenge the political place and role of the Court since Subekti had done so two decades earlier. Addressing all major issues of the judicial political agenda, he stirred up waves that rocked the political boat.

Nevertheless, Purwoto was unable to realize substantive political change during his tenure. A number of political incidents undercut the chairman's power and thwarted his reforms. Also, on several occasions the government openly confronted the judiciary and subjected it to impressive pressures to ensure its loyalty. In fact, in Purwoto's pre-appointment hearing, he was made to wait for one

---

[104] Ibid. It is not unlikely, considering the involvement of the Inspectorate General, that the preceding nationalization procedure was legally flawed in some way. Nevertheless, this should call for a retrial, not for executive instruction.

[105] Personal communication, 20 July 1994.

hour before being received by state secretary, Mr. Moerdiono.[106] This poor start was widely interpreted as a deliberate slight, an impression that was reinforced when real change did not materialize, exposing Purwoto to criticism that he "was just a talker."[107] All this showed the political constraints under which judges in modern Indonesia operated: the real lesson to be learned from Purwoto's failure was that judicial reform still depended on larger political developments.

(a) Fall 1992: Autonomy

Purwoto was scheduled to retire less than two years after his appointment and had to move quickly to issue his challenge. During parliamentary hearings in November 1992, shortly after his appointment, Purwoto asked for court administration to be transferred from the Department of Justice to the Supreme Court.[108] In the context of the time, it was a remarkable request. Apart from Mudjono's somewhat spurious interjection in 1981, no high state official had publicly questioned this basic feature of Indonesian judicial organization, let alone demanded that Parliament do something about it.[109] Purwoto's arguments were identical to those used by the Judges' Association during the II National Law Seminar in 1968. Challenging the arguments of the minister of justice, Ismael Saleh,[110] that the system had been in operation during colonial times, Purwoto responded that the department had then only served as an administrative extension of the Supreme Court. Since that time, stated Purwoto, the Court and the department had often been in conflict for the simple reason that:

> the department refuses to serve as a mere administrative extension of the Court. If previously the Supreme Court was in functional-operational control, currently there is dualism.[111]

The political constraints on Purwoto were clear, in that he was not prepared to argue his case based on the contention that the Supreme Court must have autonomy

---

[106] *Forum Keadilan*, 27 October 1994.

[107] Some commentators, not without justification, noted the fact that Purwoto had been Supreme Court vice-chairman for more than ten years, and that if he hadn't realized fundamental change during that time, how could one expect him to do better now that he held the top job? This criticism persisted after his retirement, when it was said that Purwoto may have talked about reform but accomplished little. This criticism was so insistent that Purwoto felt obliged to deny that he was "just a talker." *Forum Keadilan*, 24 November 1994, p. 94.

[108] An integral report can be found in *Varia Peradilan* 8,88 (January 1993): 5-13.

[109] *Tempo*, 28 November 1992 states that this was the first time the matter had been formally raised, which does not of course take into account the debates on Law no.14/1970.

[110] According to newspaper reports, Minister of Justice Ismael Saleh argued that the department only handled administrative and organizational matters, whereas matters relating to the judicial function "have to be realized together with the Supreme Court." *Forum Keadilan*, 10 December 1992, p. 85. This may be the result of sloppy editing by the journal, and it would be interesting to see the original parliamentary records on the matter. Constitutionally the department must handle all judicial matters in cooperation with the Supreme Court, and it may be that this task description by Saleh reveals the way things actually work.

[111] *Forum Keadilan*, 10 December 1992, p. 85.

from executive interference. Indeed, when queried by the Parliamentary Commission III as to whether the department interfered with the judges, Purwoto denied this,[112] perhaps fearing that to reveal these manipulations was politically too risky. Instead, he argued that dualism created budgetary constraints for the judiciary by channeling money away from the courts. He pointed out that the budget of the Department of Justice was among the lowest, if not the lowest, of all government departments,[113] while the Public Prosecution had a much higher budget, "even though it does less work than the courts."[114] If the Public Prosecution's budget was any indication, said Purwoto, then funding for the judiciary would improve if it were channeled directly to the courts, instead of by way of the department. Pressing home his point, Purwoto then publicly asked the People's Assembly to issue a decree calling for the transfer of court administration to the Supreme Court.[115] He was supported by the Judges' Association, which as usual expressed itself in rather more explicit terms than the Supreme Court, as it called for the end of government intervention in the management of the judiciary.[116] This challenge suggested that the judiciary had not forgotten its objectives and would keep harking back to "these old songs," as Ali Said called them, until they were realized.

Minister of Justice Ismael Saleh defended his department with pragmatic arguments: that other departments were involved, that the system had been in operation since colonial times (which presumably was some indication of quality), and that the existing departmental structure, with the separate Directorate General, had been advocated in the Judges' Association's own proposal.[117]

Although Purwoto's proposal failed, his broadside on the dual administration system showed that this was an enduring issue. And while nothing was achieved for the time being, a subtle shift in the political power balance became evident. Purwoto's call for greater autonomy was part of a much more general movement within Indonesian society demanding more control over the government, fueled in part by such court cases as the *Kedung Ombo case*, which we shall consider later. While clearly still the stronger party, the government seemed somewhat defensive in its arguments justifying the system of dual court administration.

---

[112] *Kompas*, 17 November 1992.

[113] By Purwoto's own account, it was second from the bottom, but according to press reports it stood at the absolute bottom. See *Varia Pengadilan*, Th. I-XVII, 1993 ([Jakarta]: Pengurus Pusat Ikatan Hakim Indonesia, 1986-2002), p. 5. See *Berita Yudha*, 2 March 1992.

[114] *Varia Pengadilan*, Th. I-XVII, 1993 ([Jakarta]: Pengurus Pusat Ikatan Hakim Indonesia, 1986-2002), p. 10; *Forum Keadilan*, 10 December 1992, p. 85.

[115] *Merdeka*, 16 October 1992; *Media Indonesia*, 17 October 1992.

[116] *Media Indonesia*, 16 October 1992. The Judges' Association was also supported by the Advocates' Association, Peradin.

[117] *Tempo*, 28 November 1992; *Forum Keadilan*, 10 December 1992. Saleh conveniently forgot about the fact that the Judges' Association only suggested this as a transitional measure.

(b) 1992-1994: Judicial and Constitutional Review

The second issue to emerge during Purwoto's administration was that of constitutional review, which was, as we have seen, one of the cornerstones of the political struggle of the judiciary.

After an enthusiastic start in the 1960s, the courts became extremely cautious in applying even their limited right of judicial review. They were not prepared to go as far as the 1967 Asikin Kusumah Atmadja decision. Despite the broad wording of that decision, and even though the judiciary at the time clearly intended to include modern statute in its review powers, indeed despite Law no.14/1970 and Law no.14/1985, which permitted review of Government Regulations, Presidential Decrees, and lower regulations, the courts always stopped short of reviewing modern statute.[118]

The legal professions saw government loyalist and former general Ali Said's replacement by professional judge Purwoto S. Gandasubrata as an opportunity to resume efforts to secure the right to judicial review. Purwoto himself announced in the press that if a case of judicial review were brought to court, he would consider it.[119] His statement suggested that he would take a more lenient approach toward judicial review than had been the case under Ali Said.[120]

It fact, a review case, the *Prioritas case* (1993), had for some time been ready for launching. Ali Said had fobbed the case off, but it was still pending when Purwoto issued his open invitation for judicial review cases.

- The daily newspaper, *Prioritas*, had been banned in 1984 for publishing sensitive material. The ban was implemented by a Decision of the Minister of Information, which revoked the publishing license of the journal, the so-called SIUPP (Surat Ijin Usaha Penerbitan Pers, Permit to Operate a Press Company). The owner of the journal, Surya Paloh, decided to challenge this decision on grounds that the underlying regulation concerning the SIUPP (Minister of Information Regulation no.1/1984) was in conflict with the national press law that disallowed censure and prohibition of publication, and of the constitutional provision that guaranteed freedom of

---

[118] It did come close at times, however. Thus, with decision no.275K/Pid/1983 the Supreme Court held that, notwithstanding art.67 jo.244 of the modern Code of Criminal Procedure, appeal or cassation could be lodged against court decisions in which a suspect was freed. While this decision was directly opposed in substance to statute, it didn't actually review the relevant statutory articles. Similarly, Law no.1/1950 was repealed by Law no.13/1965 art.70, which law did not, however, provide for the law of procedure before the Supreme Court. The Court as a result steadily held that art.70 had to be interpreted in such a way as to exclude the rule of procedure of Law no.1/1950. Here again, the Supreme Court skirted the issue of judicial review, but never actually nullified, art.70 Law no.13/1965.

[119] *Media Indonesia*, 3 November 1992.

[120] Even so, Purwoto was unlikely to go as far as Asikin and Sri Widoyati had hoped in the 1960s. He notably refused to countenance reviewing Acts of Parliament, and stated repeatedly that this was a matter for the MPR (Majelis Permusyawaratan Rakyat, People's Consultative Assembly) to decide. *Suara Karya* 17 November 1992. This approach was forced upon him by MPR Decree TAP/MPR/III/1978, which stated that judicial review be restricted to regulations inferior to Acts of Parliament. This effectively precluded change unless the MPR so provided. See also Falaakh, "Mahkamah Agung," p. 128.

opinion.¹²¹ It was a fundamental challenge to the government, questioning as it did the instruments by which the government ensured the loyalty of the national press.

Surya Paloh first lobbied with Parliament. When Purwoto issued his invitation, however, he decided to bring a judicial review case before the Supreme Court, asking for the annulment of the underlying regulation and the return of his permit.¹²² The *Prioritas case* caught the public imagination and received broad press coverage. A group of prominent advocates decided to work together on the case and established the so-called "Judicial Review Team." Chaired by the chairman of the National Bar, Harjono Tjitrosoebeno, the advocates hoped that their association with the case would strengthen its cause both in and outside court.¹²³ As in the *Pedicab case*, the Judicial Review Team brought the *Prioritas case* directly to the Supreme Court, asking for the nullification of the underlying Decision of the minister of information. The Supreme Court decided the case with a very strong chamber of judges, reflecting its importance.¹²⁴ The decision consisted of a number of elements. First, unlike in the *Pedicab case*, the Supreme Court in the *Prioritas case* allowed direct appeal before the Supreme Court action in judicial review cases, on grounds of their "special constitutional" character.¹²⁵ Second, the Court felt that the defending government instance should have the opportunity to present its view, and that as a result procedural rules for direct action for judicial review were required. In this case, and failing procedural rules, the claim had to be dismissed. Third, the Supreme Court said that it would

---

¹²¹ Minister of Information Regulation no.1/1984 art.33 says that the minister can nullify the publication permit without recourse to the court. The main conflict rests with the National Press Law no.21/1982 art.4, which says that the press will not be censured nor their publication hampered. The court case can be found in *Varia Peradilan* 8,95 (August 1993): 27. For publications, see, for instance, B. R. Wibowo, "Kedudukan, wewenang dan acara Mahkamah Agung dalam menguji secara materiil peraturan perundang-undangan," *Pro Justitia* 12,4 (October 1994): 64; Falaakh, "Mahkamah Agung," p. 126; J. Z. Loudoe, "Judicial review: sistem perlindungan hukum terhadap tindakan penguasa," *Varia Peradilan* 8,95 (August 1993): 149.

¹²² *Media Indonesia*, 3 November 1992. Parliament was only too happy to pass on this hot potato and appealed to the public to take their concerns to the Supreme Court. *Media Indonesia*, 4 November 1992.

¹²³ The Judicial Review Team consisted of the most prestigious litigation lawyers in town, many of whom had a background in legal aid circles: Harjono Tjitrosoebeno, R. O. Tambunan, T. Mulya Lubis, Abdul Hakim Nusantara, Nursyahbani Katjasungkana, and Luhut M. P. Pangaribuan.

¹²⁴ Mahkamah Agung no.01P/TN/1992 dated 15 June 1993. The case was decided by a three-judge panel consisting of Supreme Court chairman Purwoto S. Gandasubrata as presiding judge, and Supreme Court junior chairmen Asikin Kusumah Atmadja and Olden Bidara as members.

¹²⁵ The logic was based on an interpretation of the relevant article 31 Law no.14/1985. This article stated that judicial review was to be effected through normal cassation procedure, using the Indonesian term *dapat*, which can mean either "can" or "must." In the *Monitor* case, the Supreme Court interpreted the term to mean "can." Following this decision, judicial review can be brought in two ways before the Supreme Court, either through a regular court procedure starting out at district court, or through direct appeal to the Supreme Court, bypassing the lower courts altogether.

forthwith enact procedural rules for direct action before that Court in judicial review cases.

Ultimately the Court elected to dismiss the *Prioritas case*, an action that suggested nothing really had changed. Surya Paloh was reportedly dumbstruck by the decision.[126] Nevertheless, the decision did shift ground on the issue. First, by allowing direct action, the Supreme Court broke new ground and rid itself of the cumbersome Ali Said legacy. Second, as became evident within two weeks after the Court had rendered its verdict in the *Prioritas case*, rules of procedure in judicial review cases were now provided by the Court. These rules provided both for direct action before the Supreme Court and for cases begun at district court level (Supreme Court Regulation no.1/1993 dated 15 June 1993). The press reported, as a result, that despite its dismissal, the *Prioritas case* and ensuing events generated a feeling of excitement and expectation in the legal profession.[127] They eagerly awaited a new case in which both Regulation no.1/1993 and the resolve of the Supreme Court would be put to the test. Such a case arose in the course of 1993 and became known as the *Unlawful Dismissal case*.

- The action for review in the *Unlawful Dismissal case* was brought by four employees on grounds of arbitrary dismissal. The Supreme Court heard the case on the basis of Regulation no.1/1993, yet it dismissed it on arguments of substance. In fact, it transpired that the claimants had asked for the annulment of a Regulation of the Minister of Labor no.342/1986, which, even as the trial was under way, had been replaced with a new regulation no.15A/1994. The Supreme Court felt there was no cause for action on this ground, adding that even if there were, no substantial conflict existed between the relevant regulation and superior law.[128]

After the opening created with the *Prioritas case*, the failure of the Supreme Court to uphold the judicial review action in the *Unlawful Dismissal case* left advocates of judicial review despondent. They got the impression that the Supreme Court was just window-dressing and that the political environment was simply too constrictive. Everything, in fact, pointed in that direction. Almost three years after the *Prioritas case* and the establishment of Regulation no.1/1993, the Supreme Court had yet to grant its first action, all applications for such action in that period having been dismissed.[129]

Nevertheless, the Judicial Review Regulation had the effect of placing both the Supreme Court and the government on the defensive, forcing them to justify their rejection of judicial review actions. Indeed, the *Unlawful Dismissal case* was immediately succeeded by a case that concerned the banning of the three journals: *Tempo*, *Detik*, and *Editor*. Sooner or later, this case would land before the Court, as in fact it would, as we shall see. Purwoto's regulation had made it inevitable that

---

[126] *Tempo*, 26 June 1993, p. 74.
[127] Ibid.
[128] *Forum Keadilan*, 8 December 1994, p. 98.
[129] There were six such actions. *Kompas*, 29 August 1995.

the Supreme Court would eventually have to play its part on the political scene and quash some government regulation.[130]

It may perhaps appear slightly bizarre that the Indonesian judiciary should clamor for a full right of constitutional review when even the limited right of review that it actually does possess is not used. This is all the more true because in practice the emphasis in lawmaking rests with the government. In Indonesian legal practice, as in so many other countries, presidential (Keputusan Presiden) and ministerial regulations (Keputusan/Peraturan Menteri) are far more frequent and relevant than the hierarchically superior Acts of Parliament (Undang-undang) or even government regulations (Peraturan Pemerintah). These presidential and ministerial regulations can actually be subjected to judicial review under the present system, and legally the judiciary, therefore, is even now empowered to strike at the heart of the governmental system, should it so desire.[131] The question can therefore be raised whether, if the current judiciary is too weak to exercise even the limited rights it does have, can it possibly be expected to exercise the more extended right of constitutional review it aspires to? The *Prioritas* and *Unlawful Dismissals cases* suggest that if the judiciary lacks the political clout to exercise even the limited powers it currently has, its problems could not be resolved by increasing its powers.

This argument ignores the symbolic value of the debate on constitutional review. Both the judiciary and social forces have targeted constitutional review precisely because the judiciary is so weak. What matters is, after all, not just the outcome, but the process by which it is achieved. The Indonesian government fiercely opposes constitutional review, and therefore to realize that power over and above government opposition by its very nature involves a major realignment of political forces. If the court were to exercise those review powers and nullify legislation, it would express that realignment.

Constitutional review thereby stands for a reordering of the structure of the Indonesian state. It would not only change the prevailing constitutional doctrine from one that follows a separation-of-powers model into one that follows the balance-of-powers model. More important, perhaps, it would challenge official ideology, which embraces ideas of shared responsibilities, collectivism, and ultimately the indivisibility—and hence unaccountability—of power and authority, establishing instead a system in which power might be truly shared, accounted for, and could be effectively checked. From this perspective, the struggle for constitutional review is vitally important, as it leads to an entirely new concept of the Indonesian state.

---

[130] Pressure has been building up, as in 1992 the PPP, supported by the PDI, proposed in Parliament revision of TAP MPR/III/1978, with the aim of giving the Supreme Court full rights of constitutional review. While the motion was rejected, it suggests that in Parliament also old axioms and clichés are being increasingly questioned. *Forum Keadilan*, 24 December 1992, p. 76.

[131] Indeed, as the cases on judicial review illustrate, the Supreme Court need not depend on cases brought before it, but can take the initiative by issuing a Circular Letter or a Regulation.

(c) Fall 1994: Status

The final initiative of Purwoto S. Gandasubrata related to the issue of status, harking back to the old salary debate. As we have seen, very little had changed on this score since the late 1950s, and the position of the judges as part of the civil service had become ever more firmly entrenched. In a move that took everybody by surprise, Supreme Court chairman Purwoto Gandasubrata, on the occasion of his retirement in 1994, announced Presidential Decree no.10/1994, a separate salary regulation for judges that gave them a 100 percent increase in salaries.[132] As the prosecutors would not benefit from a comparable salary increase, the judges in 1994 seemed to have recovered the privileged position they had lost in 1955. It was, as initial press reactions put it, an extraordinary farewell gift that fully realized the salary goals that the judiciary had been pursuing for over the past forty years.[133] The separate legislative regulation and higher salaries gave them their coveted status vis-à-vis other branches of the state administration.

This, to all appearances, was a total victory, and the implication, therefore, a recognition that the judiciary was moving to the political center stage.[134] It also was accomplished so effectively and smoothly that the traditional competitors had no time to react. The prosecutors did mount a rear-guard action to have their own scales upgraded, but were unsuccessful.[135] There were some complaints that the law, in fact, required a separate Act of Parliament for any adjustment of judicial salaries rather than just a Presidential Decree.[136] But these did not lead to anything. Against the backdrop of the virulent 1955 debates, the 1994 salary issue generated surprisingly few reactions, for or against. Purwoto's parting gift looked like a silent revolution.

But when time had passed, closer inspection showed it to be less spectacular than it appeared. The real question, after all, is whether the regulation improved the material position of the judges in both absolute and relative terms. And here the whole picture became progressively more murky. In April 1995, it transpired

---

[132] Government Regulation no.33/1994, becoming effective as of 1 January 1995.

[133] *Forum Keadilan*, 24 November 1994.

[134] The 1994 salary measures also revealed that national and international pressures apparently strengthened the position of the judges to the point that the government thought it necessary to improve their status. In fact, State Secretary Moerdiono quite clearly referred to the international dimension of the judicial salary. *Kompas*, 4 November 1994. According to Purwoto Gandasubrata and State Secretary Moerdiono, the increases in judicial salaries were the result of a long and hard struggle. Ibid. Still, other factors were also in play. The Supreme Court was handling the highly controversial *Kedung Ombo case* at the time, which attracted much public attention and was decided favorably to the government within days of the salary increase. If not actually proving anything, the timing creates at least the suspicion of a trade-off. Moreover, Indonesia had problems with the image of its legal establishment abroad at the time, notably with regard to the United States, which was reconsidering its privileged trade status according to GSP rules on account of Indonesia's poor labor law record. There are suggestions that the improvement of judicial salary scales, plus the selection of non-military judge Soerjono to succeed Purwoto Gandasubrata (in place of the presumed favorite, the former general and Supreme Court vice-chairman, Djaelani), were both steps to improve Indonesia's international image in the field of law.

[135] *Kompas*, 17 December 1994. The prosecutors and police argued that the salaries of all law enforcement officers of the state needed to be raised to strengthen the rule of law.

[136] Comment of the vice-chairman of the Parliamentary Commission III on legal affairs Djupri, referring to Law no.14/1985. *Kompas*, 26 April 1985.

that the judges would retroactively suffer cuts of up to 45 percent in their additional benefits (*tunjangan*), traditionally a considerable chunk of their income. What they won in terms of salaries, therefore, they lost in terms of benefits. The judges may have their own regulation, but in material terms they hadn't moved an inch relative to the other professions, or to where they themselves had been shortly before. It rendered the entire thing quite meaningless. It transpired that the opposition from other agencies, after all, had had the better of the judiciary and had offset the salary increases with sharp reductions in the benefits. Adding insult to injury, it turned out that the judges might have to return the benefits received over the period January-April 1995, which rather underscored that nothing in fact had changed.[137] Purwoto's parting gift did not amount to anything after all. Far from enjoying a revolution, the judiciary found itself in the familiar role of vainly protesting injustices even after the decree was passed. It all underscored that in political terms, also, nothing had really changed.

(d) Broken Mirrors: The Kedung Ombo Case

While Purwoto was struggling to book some progress on court autonomy, power, and status, perhaps the most important challenge confronting him and the judiciary was the increasing number of high-profile cases that the Supreme Court was coming to face in this period. The importance of these cases, notably the *Kedung Ombo case*, is hard to underrate in Indonesian legal and political history. Purwoto inherited the case when he became chairman in 1992, and he decided it two days before his retirement in 1994. He therefore carried the case with him like a millstone through his full two years as chairman. It mortgaged all his initiatives for reform and seriously strained relations between the Supreme Court, the government, and society. Its unsatisfactory conclusion left all parties dissatisfied, and its effect was "traumatic," as the press described it. President Suharto reportedly stated: "Let's not have another Kedung Ombo again,"[138] which reflects on the damage the case did to the government.

- Briefly summarized and insofar as is relevant here, the *Kedung Ombo case* arose out of a project funded by the World Bank to build a hydroelectric plant in a Central Javanese valley. The project envisaged an artificial lake that would flood land, which at the time was partially cultivated and inhabited by 5,268 families and required the expropriation of land. The compensation offered to the farmers was small (Rp.800), and generally acknowledged as inadequate, given the actual value of the land. No agreement was reached concerning compensation, and the price was imposed unilaterally by the Central Java regional government. Under pressure, and after a protracted period of time during which the building of

---

[137] In April 1995, it was reported that the judges' structural benefits (*tunjangan*), which constitute a significant part of their income, would be reduced by 30-45 percent, becoming effective with the enactment of Presidential Decree no.10/1995 on 1 January 1995. According to press reports, this meant that the benefits the judges received from January-April 1995 might have to be returned. *Kompas*, 26 April 1995.

[138] *Forum Keadilan*, 19 January 1995; *Republika*, 27 December 1994.

the dam was begun, most of the farmers eventually accepted the compensation offered. A hard kernel of thirty-four families continued to reject it, however, and remained on their land, which was now actually being flooded. These farmers claimed damages of Rp.10,000 per square meter. The case was taken up by the local branch of the LBH. The farmers lost their case at the district court and appeal court, and in 1992 it landed on the Supreme Court docket. By that time, and as pictures of flooding village sheds with farmers on their roofs were televised across the globe, the case had attracted both national and international attention.

The case had great symbolic power, as all were well aware. The televised images did not just broadcast the fight of the simple man against the all-powerful state. Even more important, perhaps, was that the case revealed the social cost of the determined development drive pursued by the New Order state. In this sense, the protest and subsequent publicity challenged not merely the patrimonial government attitudes, but cut at the very roots of the New Order's economic and political ideology. Public exposure was extensive both within Indonesia and abroad, to the point that a number of books were written on the issue, including three doctoral dissertations.[139]

The Supreme Court's decision in the *First Kedung Ombo case* (1992),[140] with the Court's junior chairman, Asikin Kusumah Atmadja, presiding, had been a shocker for the Indonesian political establishment.[141] Asikin, who himself was also just two days from retirement, awarded compensation of Rp.80,000 per square meter to cover both the actual value of the land as well as "immaterial damages." It was a decision completely out of step with the Supreme Court's customary deferential behavior and that of the Indonesian judiciary in general over the previous two decades. The farmers and those supporting political reform could hardly believe their luck, and the government had great difficulty in coming to grips with a disobedient court. In fact, when informed of the decision, the Central Java military commander and former Suharto adjudant, Soejono, was unable to believe it and said that the Supreme Court decision surely must have been falsified.[142]

The government, including some of the most senior political officers of the country, exerted formidable and public pressure on the Supreme Court to reopen and nullify the case in a special review procedure. President Suharto had in fact already expressed his displeasure with the Kedung Ombo farmers, calling them *mbalelo*—troublemakers[143]—a potent term referring to someone who places himself

---

[139] M. Pakpahan, *Menarik Pelajaran dari Kedung Ombo* (Jakarta: Forum Adil Sejahtera, [1990]); Stanley [Y. A. Prasetyo], *Seputar Kedung Ombo* (Jakarta: Lembaga Studi dan Advokasi Masyarakat, 1994); Y. de Adelhart Toorop, *Kedung Ombo door de bank genomen*. George J. Aditjondro, "The Media as Development 'Textbook': A Case Study on Information Distortion in the Debate about the Social Impact of an Indonesian Dam" (PhD dissertation, Cornell University, 1993). Other dissertations were written by J. Tukiman Taruna at the University of the Philippines and A. Rumansara from the International Forum for Indonesian Development. These could not be traced, however.

[140] Mahkamah Agung no.2263.K/Pdt/1991 dated 18 July 1993, *Varia Peradilan* 9,108 (September 1994): 5.

[141] *Forum Keadilan*, 4 August 1994.

[142] Ibid.

[143] *Forum Keadilan*, 10 December 1992.

outside the group and who therefore deserves to be isolated and punished.[144] At another opportunity, the president referred to the protesting farmers as former Communists.[145] President Suharto directed more overt pressure on the Supreme Court after the publication of the first Kedung Ombo decision, when he declared in public that the damages awarded to the farmers "should be realistic," suggesting that those awarded in the *First Kedung Ombo case* were not.[146] He summoned Supreme Court chairman Purwoto to the palace. Feeling perhaps that he had little choice, Chairman Purwoto paid the visit, but it was a bad tactical mistake, for it alienated the Indonesian public. One Supreme Court judge stated:

> Purwoto's visit to the president as well as the reaction of the governor of Central Java to the first Kedung Ombo decision created the impression that the Supreme Court is being pressured by the government to overturn the first decision in review.[147]

This impression was reinforced, if not proven, by a statement of the president during the meeting that was made public afterwards. He said that he hoped the Court would take "the most just decision" (*putusan seadil-adilnya*) in the review procedure, reminding the Supreme Court chairman that the Kedung Ombo project was for the public good.[148] In the Indonesian context, there was no mistaking this statement: it was an executive directive to Purwoto demanding that the first Kedung Ombo decision be overturned in review. As one member of Parliament commented:

> This presidential statement on Kedung Ombo cannot be misunderstood. It says that the previous decision was wrong, that's what it means. Isn't that outrageous, that the President tells the Supreme Court that it was wrong and now would they please review their decision?![149]

A former Supreme Court judge put it as follows:

> In the Javanese context, if the King calls for a review decision that must be *seadil-adilnya*, this by definition implies that the former decision must be unjust.[150]

---

[144] One prominent Jakarta advocate said that in a bureaucratic context, the term had considerable importance. Talking about how difficult it was for judges to remain honest, he said: "Judges must play the game. If they don't they may be qualified as *mbalelo* [Javanese], or *pembangkang* in Indonesian, which literally means troublemakers. In bureaucratic jargon, it refers to the fact that they are up for dismissal, and one sees, in fact, that once judges are so qualified they resign sooner or later." Personal communication, 9 July 1994. In fact, both terms were used in reports documenting Suharto's comments on the Kedung Ombo farmers. *Forum Keadilan*, 4 August 1994.

[145] *Forum Keadilan*, 4 August 1994.

[146] *Forum Keadilan*, 18 August 1994.

[147] Personal communication, 3 August 1994.

[148] *Forum Keadilan*, 18 August 1992, p.29.

[149] Personal communication, 4 August 1994.

[150] Personal communication, 5 August 1994.

As a result, a review procedure was started and decided by Purwoto S. Gandasubrata just two days before his retirement (the *Second Kedung Ombo case*, 1994).[151] In this second case, a Supreme Court panel chaired by Court chairman Purwoto S. Gandasubrata nullified the earlier decision essentially on the grounds that a court may not award damages in excess of what is claimed by parties; this panel called for a retrial.

There were strong doubts concerning the legal soundness of Supreme Court reasoning in the *Second Kedung Ombo case*, not least because of a line of precedent decisions going back to the 1970s in which the Court had upheld the principle that courts could award more than claimed by parties.[152] Indeed, barely one year after the *Second Kedung Ombo case*, a powerful Supreme Court panel led by the Court's new chairman, Soerjono, in the *Small Credits case* (1996) explicitly upheld the principle that more could be awarded than claimed.[153] In addition, fundamental procedural rules were violated in the *Second Kedung Ombo* case.[154] There are many more significant aspects to the case, such as the fact that both decisions were taken two days before the retirement of the presiding judges, making it relatively easy for them to face the political flak that might come their way.[155]

---

[151] Mahkamah Agung no.650.PK/Pdt/1994 dated 29 October 1994, *Varia Peradilan* 9,112 (January 1995): 8.

[152] Mahkamah Agung decisions no.499.K/Sip/1970 and no.556.K/Sip/1971 referred to in the case cited in the next footnote, and in which the Supreme Court stated "that the lower judge may award more than has been claimed, as long as it accords with the factual conditions of the relevant case."

[153] Mahkamah Agung no.3714.K/Pdt/1992 dated 22 February 1994, *Varia Peradilan* 11 (March 1996): 126. Briefly summarized, this case arose out of a dispute resulting from the action of a claimant who had given the certificate of ownership for his land to a bank as security for a loan and protested when the bank refused to return the certificate after the loan had been repaid. The case focused on the fact that the claimant failed to demand a return of the certificate in his court plea (*petitum*). In its decision, the Supreme Court, referring to earlier decisions, upheld the view that more could be granted by the judge than claimed by parties, but said that this could only be effected if the claimant had entered a subsidiary plea for a "just decision" (*ex aequo et bono*). This not being the case here, the Court took the view that the claim should be denied. It will be recalled that in the *Kedung Ombo cases* the claimants had actually asked for a "just decision."

[154] As indicated by several legal observers, it was not clear whether by law there was sufficient ground for review. The Supreme Court took the view that, because the *First Kedung Ombo case* awarded more than claimed, this constituted grounds for review on the basis of art.67(c) law no.14/1985. Others said, however, that because the claim of the villagers in the *First Kedung Ombo case* was based on equity (*ex aequo et bono*), technically speaking the *First Kedung Ombo case* did not in fact award more than was claimed. The point is that, as shall become apparent in Chapter 6, the grounds for review, while tightly defined by law, are loosely applied by the Supreme Court, with the result that any case can be reviewed as the Court sees fit. *Forum Keadilan*, 1 September 1994, p. 28

[155] With no career prospects to speak of, and feeling pretty secure, Supreme Court judges are known to make fairly wild jumps shortly before their retirement. Some of these actions may be meant to assert their independence, perhaps also as a form of atonement for having been leashed by the government over the years (this may have been Asikin's motive). In Purwoto's case, there may have been a tradeoff, in that his political loyalty in the *Kedung Ombo case* was subsequently rewarded by the government, which appointed a non-military successor to the Supreme Court chair on his retirement and granted salary raises for all judges. One letter-writer to the journal *Forum Keadilan* suggested this also; see *Forum Keadilan*, 22 December 1994. But there also are cases in which Supreme Court judges used the security of their imminent retirement as a vehicle for utter corruption: emptying the till, as it were, while they still could.

These legal aspects were of little importance to the public, which understandably was convinced that something more fundamental was amiss. When deciding the *Second Kedung Ombo case*, the Supreme Court opted for the government in terms that could not be mistaken. As a result, the case strengthened the prevailing feeling that the Supreme Court merely served as an extension of the politically dominant executive, or at the very least, could still be pressured into obedience.

The case undermined the Supreme Court's prestige and generated great disappointment with Court chairman Purwoto. With litigating farmers now thrown back "to square one," as the press put it,[156] the Court was subjected to severe criticism. Asikin was praised to heaven,[157] but Purwoto's reputation was shattered. He was accused of being just an ineffective "talker";[158] his compensatory gift of the salary hike to the other judges was ridiculed.[159] The press described *Kedung Ombo* as "a broken mirror of the judiciary."[160]

(e) Causes of Failure

Purwoto's administration is special. In contrast to his predecessors, Seno Adji and Ali Said, or his successors, Soerjono and Sarwata, all of whom in their own way served the judiciary badly, Purwoto's tenure marks a serious attempt at strengthening the judiciary and improving the condition of the judges. Why then did he fail? It serves to spend some time looking at the causes of this failure because these tell us something about the challenges facing judicial reform and, more generally, about the changing dynamics in Indonesian society in the decade prior to *Reformasi*. I believe the causes for failure are to be found in the person of Purwoto, the role of the government, social dynamics, and the judiciary itself.

Purwoto is an intriguing character, a tragic hero of sorts. As a professional judge who had long served on the Supreme Court, he knew well what was wrong. In his short tenure, he made a valiant effort at changing this. He despaired at his failure to turn the situation around—after his retirement he often would lament missed opportunities and times passed. He was also torn by his own role in these events, and his figure is somehow enhanced by the way in which he struggled with his own shortcomings.

A slim tall man, Purwoto exuded a dignity and a natural reserve that made him a quintessential judge in the eyes of his peers and not a few foreigners also, who would comment on this. His refinement and soft voice made it easy to mistake him as a pliable character. Yet he had grit and commanded authority, and I saw him swing around an unresponsive audience with determination, intelligence, and

---

Personal communication, 4 July 1994. The *Sugar Lee case* (1991) and the *Gandhi Memorial School case* (1996), discussed in chapter 8, point in this direction. Indeed, in the *Gandhi Memorial School case*, both the judge who raised the corruption issue (junior chairman Adi Andoyo Soetjipto) and the Supreme Court judge accused of corruption were nearing retirement. *Forum Keadilan*, 22 April 1996.

[156] *Forum Keadilan*, 8 December 1994.

[157] *Forum Keadilan*, 22 December 1994 (letter).

[158] *Forum Keadilan*, 24 November 1994.

[159] *Forum Keadilan*, 22 December (letter).

[160] *Forum Keadilan*, 19 January 1995.

raw power. There were accusations that he had been involved in improprieties, as he himself admitted, but these did not seem to have an excessive impact on his public authority or standing, which were further supported by a track record that showed how he valued integrity and hard work.[161] If conditions had been more favorably disposed to the rule of law and the judiciary, he might well have developed into a prominent figure in his country. As it was, he faced a government that vacillated between the hostile and the contemptuous, a judiciary that was itself seriously degraded, and a general environment that was getting progressively more difficult, as we shall see.

But there was, in fairness, something to the man himself that complicated the situation. Not unlike Wirjono Prodjodikoro or even Subekti before him, Purwoto's best qualities were most apparent in discussions on technical issues and in small settings in which his position of authority was accepted. He was less at ease in larger groups and was not the man to secure backing from broader constituencies for the political or institutional reforms that were needed. As such, he followed developments rather than shaping them. Had the position and role of the judiciary been secure, his judicial qualities assuredly would have played in his favor. But with the judiciary under constant challenge, these very same qualities turned out to be a bit of a handicap. The judiciary was pretty close to the bottom of the political pile, and this would only change through a major redistribution of political power. Purwoto, who was reserved and dignified and looked down on the mud fights of politics, was not the type of person to achieve this redistribution. Purwoto may have been a good man and judge—he did take more initiatives than his predecessor or successor—but in the end he remained on the defensive because he could not free himself from his quintessential judicial qualities. As a result, Purwoto found himself in a position like an advanced version of the proverbial Hans Brinker, trying to plug a dike that sprang ever more leaks. In an increasingly frantic struggle to stave off the inevitable, he eventually was overwhelmed.

Moreover, he was facing a situation of greater complexity than most of his recent predecessors had had to face. By the 1990s something new had came in play that made the role of the courts different from the previous decades.

Ever since the New Order government came into power, it was directed to keep major political issues out of the courts. The government never shed its distrust of the judiciary, which in the end it could not fully control, even though it never lost a case, as we have seen. Also, court cases were a public affair in which events, and rights and wrongs, were expounded in stark colors and exposed to public scrutiny. Almost regardless what the government did, high-profile cases ended up damaging its political stock, exposing interference, ineptitude, or failed policies. For the New Order, controlling the courts was not simply a matter of managing claims and disputes, it was also a means of controlling public perceptions.

For a long time, the New Order government was successful in this approach. But by the early 1990s, the policy of keeping high-profile cases out of court was

---

[161] Thus, it was widely known that he had facilitated the appointment of Mrs. Retnowulan Sutianto to the bench. Mrs. Retnowulan was a first-rate lawyer, but being a woman of Chinese descent, stood little chance of making it to the top. Purwoto pushed her in part for her outstanding legal skills, and in part because she was absolutely incorruptible. He knew that she had rejected her portion of the inheritance of her parents, when it proved to be difficult to split it with her siblings. On Purwoto's own admission to being accused of improprieties, cf. *Forum Keadilan*, 6 May 1996, p.94

collapsing. It is not quite clear what triggered this, but what can be said for certain is that an increasing numer of high-profile cases ended up in court. Also, the government ended up with mud on the face in almost all these cases.

There had been high-profile cases before, but with *Kedung Ombo* it seemed that a corner had been turned. The statement of President Suharto—"Let's not have another Kedung Ombo again"—which followed the dramatic court case should not be narrowly understood as just a call for better management of the court process, since, after all, once such disputes ended up in court there was little the government could do that would not, in the end, backfire. Instead, Suharto exhorted his government to ensure that such politically sensitive disputes would not get to the courts in the first place—just like in the good old days. As subsequent events were to show, the government was unable to reclaim this sort of control. *Kedung Ombo* unplugged a vat filled to the brim with societal grievances, and it poured into the courts like a bag of dung. Something was changing in society, and it seems the good old New Order days of backroom deals had gone.

What distinguishes these new cases is that the parties went to court as part of a deliberate political strategy to embarrass the government. They assuredly did not expect to win, but instead used the court process to expose the abuses of the regime. These cases were particularly sensitive for the government because they touched on the fundamentals of its policies for over three decades. The *Kedung Ombo case* struck at the heart of the economic development ideology on which the New Order based its legitimacy. It cut a path for later cases, such as the *Tempo case* (challenging the banning of a respected weekly by the government, involving freedom of speech principles) and the *Megawati case* (involving the fraudulent ouster of Megawati as leader of the PDI party in its 1996 Party Conference in Medan, which exposed government manipulation of the political process). There had been incidental political cases before, but it is fair to say that by the 1990s society was discovering that the courts could be used as a political platform and people were breaking through government attempts to keep them out. The number of high-profile cases increased and, presaging what was to come, government credibility was beginning to suffer death from a thousand cuts.

In this emerging struggle between society and the government, Purwoto and the courts were caught in the middle. They responded like deer caught in the headlights. In the cross beams of media exposure and sudden political responsibility, the judiciary froze. With leadership, vision, and courage, the Supreme Court might have bolted for the political high ground, for after all each of these cases presented a clear-cut opportunity to challenge the political status quo. Instead, the court stuck to its administrative routines and ossified procedures. Above all, it followed its political compass favoring regime loyalty. It is here where Purwoto and his successors had a choice and failed to make their mark.[162]

The government and the political elite did not lose a single case of the many high-profile cases filed in the 1990s prior to *Reformasi*. This reality is all the more salient because one of the distinguishing features of the well-publicized cases that made their way to the courts is that they involved the disenfranchised.

---

[162] This is not just hindsight. In some of these political cases, Supreme Court judges did try to change course, reflecting internal tensions. Thus, in first hearings of the *Kedung Ombo* and *Tempo* cases, the claims were upheld. Also, in later years in the Philippines, the great Supreme Court chairman Davide did strike out for reform in a comparable setting.

Those who lost were the small farmers in the *Kedung Ombo case*, the Papua tribesmen who had been denied compensation in the *Ohee case*, the labor activist in the *Pakpahan case*, the victims in the *July 26, 1996 riots case*, and so forth.[163] If there was any doubt at all, the years preceding *Reformasi* firmly and unequivocally established the Supreme Court, not as a victim, but as a collaborator in the political oppression of the New Order. The Supreme Court's performance in the 1990s is unqualifiedly dismal and shameful; it is one of unprecedented failure.

For the courts, the developments of the 1990s were disastrous. They revealed the deep flaws within the judiciary itself and exhibited its failure to mobilize in the face of the political challenges presented in these high-profile cases. Purwoto was not just struggling with the political elite, he was also struggling with his own institution. This internal struggle within the judiciary, to a large extent, came down to a conflict between idealism and cynicism, divided largely along generational lines. Strikingly enough, many of the older judges, for all their flaws, continued to be idealists. Perhaps they believed in change because they had lived through it and therefore had the reference points and knew it to be possible. For these older judges, the three elements of the judicial agenda were cornerstones to rebuild a world they recalled with affection—autonomy, status, and power were approximations of a much broader and deeper process of political and institutional change. Older judges such as Subekti were always suspicious when issues such as salaries or even the one-roof system would come up. Purwoto belonged to that group. He would rarely say simplistic things, for example, that higher salaries would solve everything, and instead saw such comparatively minor reforms as first steps towards restoring professional values and standards, something the young judges hardly ever mentioned.

But Purwoto, who would refer to himself as "the last of the Mohicans," and his generation were fading out, and in truth, their world had disappeared long ago. The younger judges had seen only the wasteland of the New Order and could not imagine things being different. By the 1990s, nearly all judges had spent their entire careers in the New Order. They lacked the reference points of the elders and generally their quality also. They had lived their entire lives in conditions marked by steady marginalization, institutional patronage, low incomes, weak professional standards, and weak legal thinking. They may have been dissatisfied, but had few ideas concerning the objectives for change. And in truth, few were motivated to press for reform. The political agenda of the judiciary was developing into something of a sop. Talk about status (meaning higher salaries), autonomy (meaning transfer of court administration), and power (meaning constitutional review) belonged to the rhetoric of public venues and meetings of the Judges Association. The judges grew to regard these as perks that should rightfully be theirs, but they did not look beyond those perks. Unlike the older judges, who

---

[163] The dismal record of the Supreme Court is underscored by the way the decisions were taken, which was wobbly at best or in some cases manifestly illegal. In *Kedung Ombo*, the case was overturned in a highly irregular review procedure by the Chief Justice a couple of days before his retirement. In the *Pakpahan, Tempo,* and *Megawati cases*, similar review procedures were filed. In the *Gandhi Memorial School case*, the whole corrupt process involved a massive cover-up, and dirt was heaped on the senior judge who flagged the problem. In *Ohee*, an award for damages to the Papua tribe was suspended by administrative order of the Supreme Court chairman, in violation of the law. The 1996 riots, which it is generally known were engineered by outside forces, involved massive scapegoating.

saw these three big ideas as the beginning of reform, for the younger judges they were the ends. They would take their pay increase, their power, and their autonomy, thank you very much, and that would be it.

The younger judges are an utterly modern group and a reflection of their times, unhampered by ideology and willing to pocket their winnings where they can. They know that the judiciary is rotten through and through, and most of them are active participants in this. They barely understand the reform process and care little for it, except when it will benefit them. They repeat the political agenda because it is politically correct and because it justifies their unhappy practices. They are an utterly cynical group. Thirty years of political marginalization, erosion of professional standards, corruption, and the patronage system have crushed the willingness of the judges to reform the institution.

There is a certain facile convenience at work when New Order judges present themselves as victims of the system. This they assuredly are. But the judiciary's portrayal of itself as the victim is increasingly not part of a struggle to reform, but is a convenient excuse for the judges' role as collaborators within the system. It is a condition of self-serving irresponsibility, of inaction. Presented cynically, they live in a comfortable world in which they cannot lose: their corruption can be blamed on their salaries, and their political weakness on government pressure. If they take money or support the powerful, they are victims of the system. The occasional judge who supports the weak is proclaimed a hero (or just barking mad). The New Order judges are tempted by the image of being either victims or heroes because it absolves them from responsibility, either for what they actually do in the day-to-day grind in the courts or for failing to shape their future. The projection of themselves as victims or heroes absolves them from responsibility and the need to take action.[164]

Purwoto remains an intriguing last survivor of a defunct order. Unlike his immediate predecessors and successors, after his retirement Purwoto continued to command considerable respect. His successors, Soerjono and Sarwata, crawled under a stone and didn't reappear until it was time to write their obituaries, but Purwoto remained a respected public figure. When the Suharto regime collapsed, he played an active and influential role in managing a judicial reform process with the new commercial courts, which for some time stood at the forefront of the initiative to renew and reform the institution.

As the last representative of a generation of "parliamentary judges," all recruited in the 1950s, after his retirement Purwoto would often hark back to his days as a young judge. Assuredly his memory gave the 1950s a gloss that was misleading, and certainly the conditions he described could not be recreated. Even so, the 1950s were in many ways a better time for the judiciary. Compared to the monstrous organization created under the New Order, in the early decades of the Republic the judiciary was relatively small, manageable, and professional. It was propped up by living memory and by the respect bestowed on legal institutions under the parliamentary state, and it had an intellectual discipline as yet undamaged by political radicalization, military intrusion, and the collapse of professional standards.

Here perhaps lie some of the roots for the continued respect Purwoto enjoys. More than serving merely as the representative of a generation and a political order that had disappeared, Purwoto represented a set of professional concepts that had been lost. The young were politely dismissive of his occasional historical "escapades" and doomed attempts to recreate a mythical past; indeed some of them might have been politely dismissive of his seniority. Yet at the same time there was the recognition that he had emerged from a service and a generation that at one time had maintained standards that they wanted to recapture. As a young Indonesian lawyer once told me: "We are exasperated by grandmas and granddads [such as Purwoto]. But this is in part because they know things that we suspect are important for the legal reform process and that we can no longer access."

Despite his failure therefore, Purwoto was a symbol. He stood for something valuable that had been lost and that needed to be rediscovered and reconstituted in order to move forward.

5. 1995-1998: Into the Vortex—Soerjono and Sarwata

(a) Soerjono

For all Purwoto's skills, his stature was undeniably boosted by the contrast with his two successors. Purwoto may not have been an unqualified-success story, but by comparison to Soerjono and Sarwata he seemed brilliant, as indeed anyone would. It is difficult fully to do justice to the last two Chief Justices of the Suharto regime, Soerjono (1995-1996) and Sarwata (1996-2001), whose incompetence is remarkable even by the grim overall standards of the Indonesian Supreme Court.

Soerjono, a self-effacing, unspectacular candidate, was a surprise appointment to head the Supreme Court after Purwoto Gandasubrata's tenure. Everyone had believed that the forceful vice-chairman and reputed presidential favorite, Djaelani (a former general), was the natural successor. On closer inspection, Soerjono's appointment should not have generated the surprise it did. Neither a great institution-builder nor an assertive political leader, Soerjono was unlikely to rock the Supreme Court or to steady it. He was a chairman in the Wirjono Prodjodikoro tradition that the government favored: someone who gently fitted into a situation and was both ready to compromise and politically deferential.

Subsequent developments confirmed that Soerjono was indeed unable to stand up to the government or advance the political program of the judiciary. In fact, from the first weeks of his appointment, he became enmeshed in a politically sensitive case, and even before the dust had settled on that case, another even more controversial case burst into the media. Soerjono's poor handling of these cases lost him whatever political goodwill he had.

The case that tripped up Soerjono at the very beginning of his administration was the *Ohee case* (1995).

- The *Ohee case* involved compensation for unlawful occupation of land in Irian Jaya (New Guinea).[165] The land had been leased by the owner, Mr. Hanoch Ohee, to the former Dutch colonial government for a period of ten years. After the transfer of sovereignty, the Indonesian local government took over the contract, but continued to occupy the land even after the contract expired. The owner of the land, Mr. Ohee, acting on behalf of his

---

[165] *Forum Keadilan*, 27 April 1995; *Forum Keadilan*, 11 May 1995.

clan, brought action against the local government in 1984, on grounds of unlawful occupation of land. After an exhausting procedure involving twenty-two court sessions and ten postponements (and costing him a fortune), Ohee won the case in a special review procedure before the Supreme Court in 1992. He was awarded the spectacular amount of Rp.18.6 billion in damages (approximately US$ 11 million).

Unlike the *Kedung Ombo case*, the *Ohee case* had attracted little attention before it was decided, perhaps because it was an individual action in a geographically remote area and the issues involved did not touch upon the ideological fundamentals of Indonesian state ideology. What brought the case to public attention was that after Ohee had won and was seeking enforcement against the local government, Soerjono intervened and annulled the enforcement of the Supreme Court decision by simple fiat.[166] The official ground for annulment was flimsy: the decision could not be enforced because the case had been brought against the provincial governor of Irian Jaya, who was no legal person. This was wrong, if only because the law itself stated that the governor represents the province.[167] There was strong evidence that the letter had been secured by government pressure, for the amount of the compensation exceeded the annual budget of the provincial government and would have forced it to close down for the year.[168]

Even within the Supreme Court and closely related circles, the decision to annul generated criticism and opposition. Within a few weeks of the case, prominent Supreme Court staff member Setiawan published a lead article in the weekly *Forum Keadilan* in which he bluntly faulted the Court on the central point of its reasoning. It quite simply was not true, he stated, that the local government rather than the governor should have been summoned as defendant.[169] No less significant, a Supreme Court junior chairman expressed his disagreement with the verdict in no uncertain terms.

> The *Ohee case* was a disaster. The Court should have upheld the law and forced the local government into a settlement.[170]

The case also had an important impact in the politically restive Irian Jaya province. It fueled feelings in the region that Jakarta was not truly committed to the province's interests. In fact, not long after the *Ohee case*, the separatist movement in the region began a prolonged hostage affair, and observers close to the scene believed this to be, at least in part, a reaction against the *Ohee* decision.[171]

---

[166] When questioned by the press, Supreme Court chairman Soerjono tried to hide behind others, arguing that his instruction was only a recommendation to the district court chairman, who was ultimately the person to decide whether or not to enforce. Not surprisingly, the district court chairman rebutted this claim, saying, "To my regret I must inform you that we must defer to the Supreme Court chairman. Because [in matters such as these] we are merely the implementing officers." *Forum Keadilan*, 11 May 1995.

[167] art.23(1) Law no.5/1974.

[168] *Forum Keadilan*, 11 May 1995.

[169] *Forum Keadilan*, 25 May 1995.

[170] Personal communication, 10 May 1996.

[171] Ibid.

In the aftermath of the *Ohee case,* there were public calls for Supreme Court chairman Soerjono to resign,[172] and the increasingly personal invective heaped on his head reflected disillusionment with the Court and with its chairman.[173] The Court had no time to recover and regain the initiative in what effectively became a media battle. Very quickly, another even more troublesome case attracted media attention. This case was to usher in a new phase in the political debate on the Supreme Court.

This was the *Gandhi Memorial School case* (1996). Its facts were unremarkable. (We will examine this case in greater detail in Chapter 8.) What is important here is that the defense lawyer, a former Supreme Court judge and Judges' Association chairman, was accused of having put his Supreme Court contacts to good use; it was said that he steered the case to a friend on the Supreme Court with the agreement that a decision favorable to his client be handed down. There were strong suspicions of money having changed hands. The possibility of internal fraud and collusion came to the notice of junior chairman Adi Andoyo Sutjipto, who wrote an internal confidential memo requesting that the case be investigated and reopened. The letter was leaked to the press, and by the next day the court and the political establishment faced a full-blown crisis. It is not every day that high agencies of state leak internal memos on corruption, and, what is more, the corrupter and corrupted were (former) senior Supreme Court judges, as was the accuser.[174]

Chairman Soerjono mishandled the situation completely. A stronger and more insightful leader along the lines of a Kusumaatmadja might well have taken the incident as an opportunity for institutional reform. The crisis assuredly should have been tackled by addressing the internal corruption in the court, and if it had played out well, it might have even boosted the court's position and power.[175] A more wily and self-serving operator, taking his cue from Ali Said, might have announced a public investigation and then smothered it. Instead, Soerjono took the incident as a personal challenge and spent much of his tenure plotting and scheming against Adi Andoyo Soetjipto. Blaming him for "soiling his own nest,"[176] Soerjono publicly disavowed the junior chairman and imposed a gag order on him. Under pressure to order an independent outside investigation, he instead ordered an internal investigation, which was controversial and never commanded any authority.[177] Neither the public nor, by Soerjono's own admission, even the

---

[172] *Media Indonesia,* 17 May 1996.

[173] Thus, the press referred to Supreme Court chairman Soerjono as a *banci*. This term can be translated to mean either an impotent person or a hermaphrodite. *Forum Keadilan,* 27 April 1995.

[174] *Forum Keadilan,* 22 April 1996; *Gatra,* 20 April 1996; *Forum Keadilan,* 6 May 1996; A. Andoyo Soetjipto, "Uraian kronologis terjadinya masalah 'kolusi' di Mahkamah Agung RI" (unpublished, 1996).

[175] Media coverage at the time recommended this option, and Soerjono could have taken his cue from the media if it didn't come naturally. *Forum Keadilan,* 6 May 1966, p.99.

[176] *Gatra,* 20 April 1996.

[177] Indonesian NGOs and Bar Associations had called for an independent investigation. *Forum Keadilan,* 6 May 1996, p. 100. The internal Commission was very slow out of the starting block. It took almost a month to even start hearing Adi Andoyo Soetjipto. This was remarkable, because Junior Chairman Sarwata, who headed the commission, actually had his offices next door to Adi Andoyo Soetjipto. *Forum Keadilan,* 20 May 1996.

President, got to see the full version. Its conclusion that there was no evidence of corruption was ridiculed, not least because Adi Andoyo Soetjipto had hardly been heard. Even so, Soerjono submitted a request to the President for a dishonorable dismissal of Adi Andoyo Soetjipto. It was a wasting and senseless battle and completely self-defeating. Far more than missing the opportunity for reform, it was also a disaster for the image of the Supreme Court, making it appear protective of corruption.[178]

Adi Andoyo Soetjipto was hard to ignore in the best of times. He was, after all, a senior judge with a forceful and outspoken character.[179] He was outraged by the treatment to which Soerjono exposed him and was not the kind of character to take this lying down.[180] Making public appearances and giving interviews and speeches, he soon became part of the pantheon of leaders of the emerging student movement; in fact, students in various places in the country went on hunger strikes in his support.[181] His stature grew as the crisis deepened, and he developed into a public hero.[182]

The position of the government was complicated. No senior judge in the history of the republic had been dishonorably dismissed with forfeiture of pension rights. And here was one of the most senior judges in the land, with more than thirty years under his belt, of unquestioned high standing, and a public hero to boot. Also, what would be the grounds for dismissal? After all, Adi Andoyo Soetjipto could hardly be blamed for identifying possible corruption in the court. (This might have been different only if he had intentionally leaked the internal memo; he steadfastly denied responsibility for the leak.) The political fallout would be terrible. Soerjono's request for a dismissal placed the government in a Catch-22 situation—it could hardly openly deny or ignore a request from the Supreme Court chairman, yet dismissing a senior judge and public hero who had come out against corruption did

---

[178] Indeed, some explained Soerjono's disproportionate vehemence in this case as an indication that he himself had benefited from the corrupt transaction. *Forum Keadilan*, 29 July 1996, p.26.

[179] Adi Andoyo Soetjipto's status as an independent judge shortly before the *Gandhi Memorial School case* was enhanced by his decision in the high-profile *Pakpahan case*, which will be discussed later. In the *Pakpahan case*, a panel chaired by Adi Andoyo Soetjipto dismissed all charges and freed the suspect, who was a well-known labor activist and had been a thorn in the side of the New Order for some years.

[180] Personal communication, 10 May 1996. What was particularly hurtful to Adi Andoyo Soetjipto in the *Gandhi Memorial School case* was the fact that he was so purposely put down by the Supreme Court leader. The senior Adi Andoyo Soetjipto had apparently strongly backed Soerjono's appointment to the Supreme Court, and later his appointment as the Court's junior chairman. The pressure on Adi Andoyo was significant. Besides the publicity and the internal and political pressures, he received threatening phone calls saying that a contract had been put out on his life. Personal communication, 10 May 1996; *Kompas*, 3 May 1996.

[181] *Forum Keadilan* August 12, 1996, pp. 103-104. The hunger strike was held in different regions, and on occasion was pushed pretty far, to the point that three students from Purwokerto had to be hospitalized, with one in a coma. Adi Andoyo Sutjipto had to go out to the regions to convince the students to break the strike.

[182] As a result of his new status as a hero, Adi Andoyo Soetjipto after *Reformasi* became chairman of the first independent and multi-party Election Committion (KPU) in 1999, and two years later chaired the interim Anti Corruption Commission called the Joint Investigating Team (TGPTPK, Tim Gabungan Pemberantasan Tindak Pidana Korupsi). Adi Andoyo Soetjipto tried to re-open the *Gandhi Memorial School case* at the time, but was obstructed by the Attorney General's Office. Shortly thereafter, his commission was declared unconstitutional by the Supreme Court.

not seem like a great alternative. As Soerjono persisted, the fracas confirmed his reputation for bottomless stupidity, and calls for his own resignation grew.[183]

The *Gandhi Memorial School case* raised basic questions about whether the Supreme Court was able to resolve its problems on its own. The ineptitude of Chairman Soerjono, while important and remarkable, was only part of the problem. Perhaps just as damaging was a petition signed by almost all of the Supreme Court judges and submitted to the President, in which they asked for Adi Andoyo's dismissal. Also, the result of the subsequent internal investigation cleared all major parties from wrongdoing.[184] The report looked like a cover-up, and no one outside the institution took it seriously. All this created the image of an institution whose leadership, general culture, and institutional dynamics conspired to protect their own interests, condone corruption, and prevent change.

As a result of the *Gandhi Memorial School case*, the general public and senior officials, perhaps for the first time, began openly to discuss placing the judiciary under some sort of outside supervision. It had always been accepted as a constitutional principle that the courts could not be subjected to outside supervision, particularly not the Supreme Court. The fact that this principle was now being openly questioned, not just by activists, but by senior state officials, indicated the depth of the crisis.

Thus, commenting on the *Gandhi Memorial School case*, the vocal director general of the Department of Justice, Sunaryati Hartono, called for an MPR (Majelis Permusyawaratan Rakyat, People's Consultative Assembly) body to supervise the Supreme Court.[185] Similarly, a prominent member of Parliament, Albert Hasibuan, proposed a new body, partially composed of government appointees, that would have controlling powers over the Supreme Court.[186] And Parliament began to hold more pointed regular hearings with the Supreme Court.[187] Supreme Court secretary general Toton Suprapto felt compelled to state repeatedly that this was an internal affair and that constitutional principle opposed meddling from outside the Court.[188] The Judges' Association enclosed a flyer in the May issue of its journal *Varia Peradilan* strongly objecting to outside supervision.[189]

Despite this resistance, even within the Court, there was a certain feeling of despondency and a corresponding call for extreme measures. While reform-minded Supreme Court judges were aware that their recommendations favoring supervision might, in effect, pull a Trojan horse within their gates, they also realized that the Court leadership's apparent unwillingness to investigate strong allegations of improprieties involving the Court left them no alternative.

---

[183] *Forum Keadilan* August 12, 1996, p. 100. The government was aware that both judges were close to retirement age and resolved the issue by sitting it out. Soerjono retired on August 31, 1996; Adi Andoyo in early 1997.

[184] *Forum Keadilan*, 10 June 1996

[185] *Kompas*, 2 May 1996.

[186] *Kompas*, 3 May 1996. The defense lawyer causing all the problems worked at Albert Hasibuan's law firm, but there were no calls for subjecting the advocacy to stronger supervision.

[187] *Kompas*, 13 May 1996.

[188] See for instance *Kompas*, 16, 17 April 1996.

[189] *Varia Peradilan* 11,128 (May 1996).

Supreme Court Judge: With the *Gandhi Memorial School case*, I have become convinced we need outside supervision.
SP: Aren't you afraid that this will institutionalize outside interference?
Supreme Court Judge: It is choosing between two evils. But in the face of our evident inability to resolve our own problems, I think outside supervision is the lesser one.[190]

By 1996, therefore, with the credibility of the institution sunk to abysmal depths, it made little sense even to think of moving ahead on the different issues of the judicial political program.

As Soerjono tottered to the end of his mercifully short tenure, he and his agency were completely discredited. Many other state agencies must have had problems much like those at the Supreme Court, but, politically, the judiciary turned out to be one of the most exposed institutions by the end of the New Order. The media, never slow to focus on a chink in the state's armor, kept up an unrelenting attack. By the mid-1990s, reports were coming out almost daily about improprieties up and down the judicial line. These improprieties were outrageous, including the falsification of Supreme Court decisions, judges hiding evidence, senior judges bribing junior judges on the same panel, and so on.[191] Also, it transpired that despite the fallout from the *Ohee case*, Soerjono continued the highly controversial and unlawful practice of suspending court orders by simple letter.[192]

By 1996-1997, the political pressure on the court system was unrelenting. The New Order policy of keeping cases out of court had collapsed completely, and ever more high-profile cases ended up in the court system. They almost invariably seemed to end up in a mess. The first exorbitant financial fraud cases appeared in the lower courts, most notably the *Golden Key case* with Eddy Tansil. While financial fraud was not unprecedented in Indonesia, to say the least, the 1990s stand out for the sheer magnitude of the fraudulent transactions. The *Golden Key case* involved an alleged illegal siphoning off of Rp.1.3 trillion (US$520,000,000 against contemporary exchange rates). With so much money spinning around, increased corruption of the law enforcement agencies, notably the Attorney General's Office and the courts, became inevitable. These major cases involving financial fraud stirred up a wake of corruption allegations as they made their way through the court system. Besides damaging the authority of the court system as a whole, and the Supreme Court by direct association, they also set a troubling precedent for the financial crisis in later years.[193]

---

[190] Personal communication, 10 May 1996.

[191] For an overview see *Forum Keadilan*, 15 January 1996, p. 32. Also, *Forum Keadilan*, 29 January 1996, pp. 34-35.

[192] *Forum Keadilan*, 22 April 1996, p. 31.

[193] The infamous *Golden Key corruption case* involving the infamous businessman Eddy Tansil began its rumbling journey through the lower courts in 1996. See for instance *Forum Keadilan*, 26 February 1996, pp. 22-23; *Forum Keadilan*, 11 March 1996, pp. 12-28; *Forum Keadilan*, 22 April 1996, p. 107. The district court judge, who actually had convicted Tansil, ended up being suspended. *Forum Keadilan*, 15 July 1996, p. 31. The outcome of that case was unsatisfactory, in that the principal suspect was convicted but escaped under suspicious circumstances, and no assets were recovered. The case set the tone for the period after *Reformasi*, when asset recovery became a major issue with the dissipation of bank liquidity support funds. The Attorney General's Office after 1998 consistently refused to start criminal proceedings against the tycoons, despite strong indications in some cases of improprieties having occurred, on grounds

Since the lower courts were being pummeled, the Supreme Court under Soerjono could not escape. More and more high-profile cases moved up through the appeal system and ended in his lap. They added to the pressure and exposed Soerjono's own weaknesses, as well as those of the system as a whole. Caught between the temerity of its leader (and the court's institutional limitations) and the vice of the political regime, the court simply could not handle these highly publicized cases properly. It was a grueling and painful process, to which there seemed no end.

- One high-profile case that came up before the Court under Soerjono was the *Mochtar Pakpahan case*. Under the late New Order, Mochtar Pakpahan was, without a doubt, Indonesia's most widely respected and internationally recognized labor activist. He spent much of his life trying to establish and run an independent labor union, the SBSI.[194] Pakpahan's union was recognized by the ILO (International Labor Organization), which disavowed the official SBSI union because it was politically co-opted. The government harassed Pakpahan relentlessly. In 1994, action was brought against him for engineering a massive strike in Medan in April of that year. The District and Appeal Courts imposed penalties of three and four years imprisonment, respectively. But in 1995 he was freed of all charges by a Supreme Court panel chaired by Adi Andoyo Soetjipto. On October 25, 1996, in a special review procedure chaired by Chairman Soerjono, this decision was overturned and a penalty of four years re-imposed.[195]

The *Pakpahan case* captured public imagination for obvious reasons: it was a traditional stand-off between well-connected entrepreneurs and the disenfranchised; it challenged the New Order policies of encouraging growth and stability at the expense of labor rights; and it focused attention on the tensions between international agencies (and some governments), and the Indonesian authorities. From a legal perspective, the internal review procedure whereby the Supreme Court reviews its own decisions in itself was cause for debate. Also, the Supreme Court deviated from the Criminal Code principle that if a person has been freed from criminal charges, his case cannot be re-filed by the prosecution. Most remarkable, however, the Attorney General's Office had never before filed a special review procedure with the Supreme Court. The Indonesian Code of Criminal Procedure made no provision for this, which implied that this right was available only to suspects.[196] It underlined the strong impression that Pakpahan

---

that the *Golden Key corruption case* clearly showed that criminal enforcement did not assist in securing asset recovery. The government was one of the principal duped creditors in many such cases, and the fact that even it became concerned and began consultations with the law enforcement agencies after this case reflects a significant shift in the magnitude of corruption in the 1990s. For the government concerns and consultations with the law enforcement agencies cf. *Forum Keadila,n* 6 May 1996, p. 108.

[194] SBSI—Serikat Buruh Sejahtera Indonesia, the Indonesian Welfare Labor Union.

[195] Breaking with established Supreme Court tradition in which difficult cases are decided and announced very shortly before the retirement of the chairman, Soerjono's decision in the *Pakpahan case* was announced almost six weeks after he retired. It was an act of ineptitude tinged by cowardice. *Forum Keadilan*, 16 December 1996, p.76.

[196] *Forum Keadilan*, 20 May 1996, p. 33.

was being specially targeted and harassed by the state. Pakpahan added absurdity to Soerjono's procedural perversity by subsequently submitting a special review of the special review, though, with politics being what they were, this ended up going nowhere.[197]

- The case to come up after the Pakpahan debacle attracted perhaps even greater attention. It arose out of the banning in 1994 of the Indonesian weekly *Tempo*, which no doubt was the best-known independent weekly in the country. *Tempo* brought a case challenging the government's ban.[198] *Tempo* did not rate its chances very highly, but it felt it had no choice, "because it involves the principle of press freedom," as the editor Goenawan Mohamad explained. *Tempo* unexpectedly won in the district court, which gave its judge, Benjamin Mangkoedilaga, instant-hero status in the country (and resulted in a prompt punitive transfer to the outpost of Medan). The decision was upheld on appeal, and the government was forced to bring it all the way to the Supreme Court, where the *Tempo case* was fated to have Soerjono decide it. Recognizing the importance of the occasion, the Court, little known for transparency, held an unprecedented public hearing of the case.[199] Soerjono upheld the government appeal, and *Tempo* was banned. Attendance was huge, and the case caused an instant uproar. The journal knew the odds were against it, and it must have anticipated what was to come. Goenawan Mohamad made a prepared statement on the steps of the Supreme Court, challenging the decision, in which he said that the Supreme Court was not able to overcome political oppression and that the chairman should resign.

There is nothing to add. Soerjono knew he was hardly a success story, and slipped out the back door even while lawyers, students, and activists were converging now almost daily on the front steps of the Supreme Court building, conducting vocal protests, and holding up banners calling for his resignation.[200]

For its part, the government assuredly gave very little help to the Supreme Court. Government practice of using the dual court administration to pressure judges into political compliance continued unabated into the 1990s. Numerous incidents reflect the complete dependence of judges on the mercy of the minister of justice and Supreme Court chairman, as well as the government's willingness to use its leverage as it saw fit. Thus, when a promising senior appeals court judge, Winardi, annoyed the minister of justice, Ismael Saleh, he was passed over at the last second

---

[197] *Forum Keadilan*, 10 February 1997, p. 39. Reviewing a review procedure confused the court administration no end, and they didn't know whether or not to accept it. Adding spice the situation, they first rejected it, and then accepted it after all. As Pakpahan said: "If you file a crazy review procedure, you get another crazy one back." *Forum Keadilan*, 8 September 1997, p. 37

[198] The government withdrew publication permits of three weeklies, *Detik, Editor,* and *Tempo*. *Tempo* was the only to challenge this in court.

[199] www.tempo.co.id/mingguan/27/n_utama2.htm

[200] Soerjono ended up issuing so few public statements that the press dubbed him commander of the "Shut Up Brigade." *Forum Keadilan*, 6 May 1996, pp. 102-103. For photographs of the protests, see pictures in *Forum Keadilan*, 12 August 1996, p. 101.

for advancement to the post of appeals court chairman. As one Supreme Court junior chairman related:

> It was decided to transfer Winardi to become appeals court chairman in Palu. The decision was already typed up. But then suddenly, for some reason I don't know, someone else was appointed, and Winardi was sent off to Riau province. It was all done so clumsily. They had just whitened Winardi's name out with Typex from the Ministerial order, and typed the name of the other guy over it. But when you held up the decision to the light, one could see Winardi's name shine through.[201]

The Justice Department and Supreme Court chairman continued to abuse their leverage to secure compliance from the judges in cases involving major interests. Thus, when in 1995 the daring and outspoken administrative court judge, Benyamin Mangkudilaga, upheld the weekly *Tempo*'s action to contest its banning, he was moved from Jakarta to the outback of Medan within two weeks:

> There can be no doubt that Mangkudilaga was transferred to Medan because he dared to speak up in the *Tempo* case.[202]

It was clear that if change were to come, it would require a fundamental and wholesale political reform that included not just the court, but also the government.

(b) Sarwata

Sarwata, who became Supreme Court chairman in November 1996, was hardly the man to bring about that kind of reform. Firmly embedded in the military bureaucracy, he shared with fellow administrators of military extraction (such as Ali Said) the mild contempt for civilian institutions and for anything that detracted from command unity. He was the kind of man President Suharto understood and could handle.[203]

Sarwata passed through history with a dimness that matches his brethren. It is tempting to describe him as the last night watchman of the court before *Reformasi*, a caretaker who turns out the lights at the end, except that he lacked the basic qualities of a caretaker. He was rarely present in the court and showed little knowledge or interest in legal issues, whether substantive or technical. He never met an official visitor if he could prevent it, and would leave much of the daily business to his second-in-command, Judge Ketut Suraputra. On management issues, his style exasperated even die-hard old timers. As one senior judge once commented:

---

[201] Personal communication, 16 July 1994. Later, however, Winardi secured the job.

[202] Mangkudilaga himself is said to be convinced that there was a connection between his sudden transfer and his decision in the *Tempo case*. Medan was relatively mild retribution, as he could have been sent to Ujung Pandang, which in administrative terms is an even less prestigious court. Personal communication, 3 November 1995.

[203] Sarwata spent much of his entire career as a military judge, gaining his kudos as a judge in the extraordinary anti-communist tribunals in 1966 (Mahmilub). *Forum Keadilan*, 16 December 1996, p. 102.

If someone comes up with an idea or a suggestion, Chief Justice Sarwata invariably says: good idea, let's have a commission. This kills off whatever initiatives were undertaken. Nothing happened, nothing at all."[204]

A status quo loyalist, Sarwata was dubbed as "controversial before doing a thing" by the press.[205] He had chaired the commission that investigated the Gandhi Memorial School scandal and signed a demand for Adi Andoyo Soetjipto's removal from the court. When journalists queried him on his role in the case, Sarwata responded by saying that, after all, this was an issue concerning command loyalty, that this was crucial to him, and how could one do differently? It was a silly response that ignored the issue of institutional integrity and corruption and showed a lack of understanding about the intellectual nature of what courts do and the inherently pluralist nature of complex modern societies. His reply is indicative of both his feeble intellect and his basic intuitions.

But the reasons why Sarwata was described as "controversial before doing a thing" run deeper and make it even more clear why he was no caretaker of the courts. Sarwata was the first Supreme Court chairman to be openly accused of corruption.[206] He served for a while as secretary general at the Department of Agrarian Affairs and had been pursued by persistent rumors of involvement in improprieties since that time. He was unable to dispel them. It was not that his predecessors were all spot clean, and the accusation says much about the climate of political openness as the New Order was unraveling. But when the subject involves a sitting Supreme Court chairman, there is a quantum leap separating rumors of corruption from accusations of corruption made openly in the media.

Nor would the corruption charges leave him after he became Supreme Court chairman. There were constant rumors of improprieties, claiming, for instance, that he used family to link up to parties in important cases serving before the court.[207] These rumors further fractured a court little known for its solidity, as some judges who were trying to maintain their integrity refused to serve on panels with their own chairman for fear of being drawn into unsavory transactions.[208] Others would

---

[204] Personal communication August 25, 2000.

[205] *Forum Keadilan*, 16 December 1996, p. 102

[206] *Berita Keadilan* 29 December 1998, pp. 3-8.

[207] Personal communication, July 13, 2000.

[208] Personal communication, July 7, 2000. One senior judge (who is still serving on the bench, so let's call him Judge X) recounted how he was asked to be a member in a panel with Sarwata and another senior judge, widely suspected of being in cahoots with Sarwata. During the deliberations, Judge X says that Sarwata and his pal were pushing for dismissal of the case. There was in fact already a draft decision to that effect attached to the file. The senior judge told Sarwata and his foot soldier that he had not read the case, which was a thick file, and that he would not agree to any decision until he had read the file. The whole thing smelled bad, recounts Judge X, for there never is a typed decision available before the first deliberations and without one of the judges having read the file. While Judge X was working through the file, a task that took a couple of days, the draft decision somehow ended up with the Supreme Court administration without him knowing it. The administration reworked it into the definitive decision with the proper heading and the signatures of the judges at the bottom. His own signature was there also, it was not falsified but appeared with the standard caption for signature. So the suspect in the case received the decision and claimed it to be the right one. The senior Judge X didn't know any of this had happened, and after having read the file went into the second deliberations, stating that on the basis of the documents the suspect was guilty as hell and should go to jail. There was opposition, notably from the judge supporting Sarwata,

recount how, in internal discussions, he would deliberately scuttle cases, saying that the next chairman would set it right no doubt.[209] His management of the court system involved all sorts of basic irregularities, as one respected senior judge recounted.

> In one incident, a supervisory Supreme Court judge during a visit to Bali heard complaints about an extra Rp.15.000 levy for the registration of cases that had to be redirected to Jakarta. He was not aware such a levy existed, and on asking, he could not find a regulatory basis. Upon his return to Jakarta, he raised the issue during a pleno meeting. Sarwata then admitted that he had issued an unwritten rule that a levy should be imposed for the "general welfare of the judges." Even though this was unwritten, it applied nationwide. It was generating billions [bilyun] for the Supreme Court treasury. It caused a bit of an uproar during the pleno, with members calling that this was unlawful, that it was defrauding litigants and society and such. Questions were asked concerning how this was spent, and it was admitted that there was separate bookkeeping for this income, and that it was spent to cover expenses like dinner parties for the new justices who were recruited. But no one got to see the books.[210]

Sarwata reinstated with vigor the unlawful practice of suspending the enforcement of court decisions, the same illegal action that had tripped up Soerjono in the *Ohee case*. In some cases, Sarwata would actually suspend the enforcement of his own decision if exposure became too risky, and thus would play out the system against itself.

One case involved a well-known Jakarta mafia boss who was squeezing the rightful owner out of the Hard Rock Café in Bali, in the process violating every law in the book. Sarwata was finagling the case as it came to court. His approach was to grant the mafia boss his manifest fraudulent claim, but allow at the same time for suspension of enforcement if the media exposure happened to spin out of control. One senior Supreme Court judge (who is still serving with him on the bench, so I will call him Judge Y) protested the actions of Sarwata. He recounts the conversation as follows:

> **Judge Y**: We cannot enforce this contract. It violates the terms, it violates basic contract law principles, and it violates the permits.
> **Sarwata**: What do you make a fuss about? We can simply enforce, and then suspend enforcement subsequently if it is challenged. [eksekusi jalankan saja, nanti batalkan eksekusi kalau ada keluhan]

---

with Sarwata not committing one way or the other. The senior Judge X said, essentially, "Well if you want to put this to the vote, that's fine, you will outvote me, and I have to accept that because that's the way the system works, but my opinion stands." In the end, Sarwata came down on the side of Judge X, and in the valid decision the suspect was convicted to a prison term. When the valid decision came out, everyone discovered that there were two conflicting decisions in the same case. The suspect then said that the second decision was false, and that he was holding the right one. The story broke and created a magnificent mess. Judge X says he had no doubt that Sarwata had set it all up, and when things did not go the way he had planned, he felt no compunction about burning his client.

[209] Personal communication 28 October 2000.
[210] Personal communication 8 December 2000

Judge Y: But that would be making a deliberate and basic mistake.
Sarwata: Why do you create such a headache about this? Let's do this and then the next Supreme Court chairman can fix it, if there is any need. [kenapa kita pusing-pusing tentang ini, KMA nanti yang batalkan saja.][211]

The above example suggests that Sarwata had no standards at all, except those guiding his efforts to line his pockets. He would contradict himself if the occasion called for it, or reverse his predecessor by suspending enforcement of a court decision that had been given the go-ahead.[212] This battle between successive Supreme Court chairmen with conflicting enforcement letters destroys everything court decisions stand for.[213] Much more than that, they destroy the cornerstone of legal certainty and the deep sense of responsibility that judges should have. When confronted, Sarwata denied that he had issued suspension letters at all, recognizing explicitly that these were unlawful. Yet barely two weeks later, copies of these letters signed by him were published in the press, which showed that he had lied through his teeth.[214] After *Reformasi*, Sarwata's corruption would be openly discussed in Parliament and at the government level, and the careers of some judges were ruined because they were thought to be too close to him.[215]

Meanwhile, the societal onslaught on the justice system continued unabated. More and more cases that never would have made it to the courts before now crashed heavily into the justice system. The lower courts, in particular, were assailed by high-profile cases, many of which were increasingly and overtly political in nature. Thus, as the relationship between the future President Megawati Sukarnoputri and the government became more overtly confrontational, the courts came to play a central part in the conflict. In 1996, the government through fraudulent means ousted Megawati as PDI Party Chief. She decided to challenge this in the courts, filing a case jointly against the government stooge Soerjadi, who replaced her, and against the government itself, including the Minister of the Interior, the Chief of Staff of the Armed Forces, and the Chief of Police. And with her, throughout the country all regional PDI chapters loyal to her filed cases before the local district courts. Hundreds of cases were filed within

---

[211] Judge Y concluded the Sarwata must have been in the pay of the mafia boss, so that there was nothing he could do, and as a result he pulled out.

[212] "Sarwata batalkan eksekusi yang 'disetujui' Soerjono" (Sarwata nullifies the enforcement that had been approved by Soerjono), *Kompas* 23 July 1998.

[213] In *Suara Pembaruan* 13 July 1998, the chairman of the Denpasar District Court complained about being bombarded with letters from Sarwata during the enforcement process of a court order against another big hotel.

[214] Sarwata denied issuing letters suspending enforcement in *Merdeka*, 1 May 1998, but a copy of such a letter was published front page in *Kontan*, 20 July 1998.

[215] During the Parliamentary fit and proper test for new Supreme Court judges before Commission II, Commission member Sahetapy asked candidate judge Gde Sudharta: "You are nothing less than the '*kaki tangan*' of Sarwata's corruption networks." Commission member Panda Nababan asked: "Have you ever been approached by Sarwata's son?" Personal communication July 18, 2000. One junior minister expressed his surprise to me at how Sarwata had changed since his days at the Department of Agrarian Affairs. Then, he said, Sarwata was known to be "quite strict," but now he seemed to have "messed up." Personal communication July 4, 2000. It was clear, however, that Sarwata had been problematic even during his time at the Department of Agrarian Affairs, and this may have been an attempt by the minister to distance himself from Sarwata when it became apparent that he was, in fact, a total disaster.

the span of two or three days; the Surakarta district court alone faced 78 individual claims. District courts in places as diverse as Surabaya, Medan, Makassar (Ujung Pandang), Banjarmasin, Magelang, Denpasar, Kebumen, and Cianjur faced political claims challenging Megawati's ouster and asking for her reinstatement. What had been brewing since *Kedung Ombo* came to the boil with the *PDI crisis cases*, which showed that courts had become fully involved in the political process. With rumors abounding that Chairman Sarwata had been instructed by the Chief of the Armed Forces General Feisal Tanjung to have the courts dismiss the cases, the Supreme Court—ever the regime loyalist—was going in overdrive trying to control the situation.[216] In fact, various district courts were defying instructions and upheld the petitions, which says something about the limited credibility and authority of the Supreme Court and the general mood in the country.[217] Dissident judges were sanctioned.[218] When the Supreme Court itself heard the appeal, Megawati's claim was dismissed on the ground that this was an internal party matter.[219]

For its part, the government itself increasingly managed political tensions through the courts. While it was successful in the sense that it did not lose a single case in court, the effect also was that the courts became part of the political process as they had never been before. In that sense, their political complicity and lack of independence was ever more glaring. In another case relating to Megawati, the government brought a case against 124 Megawati supporters who were arrested subsequent to major riots in Central Jakarta surrounding the PDI headquarters. It was widely believed that these riots were government engineered, and in fact there were dozens of deaths—all suffered by Megawati's supporters—yet it was her supporters who were brought to court. The district courts toed the line, and the supporters were convicted.[220] Further cases were filed against the political maverick Sri Bintang Pamungkas on grounds that he had insulted the head of state and set up a new political party. These cases attracted much attention, in part, because Pamungkas himself was a disaffected member of the political establishment, and, in part, because he was so open in setting out his challenge, including his call for Indonesians to deny Suharto a further term as president.[221] Not long afterwards, the challenge of the left-wing student movement led by

---

[216] http://www.library.ohiou.edu/indopubs/1996/12/26/0033.html.

[217] The District Courts of Bekasi, Marabahan, Tebing Tinggi, Menado, Pontianak and Denpasar upheld the actions in support of Megawati. While the other courts dismissed the actions, no court went as far as to uphold the legality of Soerjadi, who had replaced Megawati. *SiaR* 31 July 1998.

[218] *Forum Keadilan*, 20 October 1997, p. 38.

[219] *Forum Keadilan*, 4 November 1996, p. 31.

[220] Of the 124 defendants, eight could prove they had been at another location at the time of the incident. The remaining 116 defendants were found guilty and convicted to the term of detention, meaning they were freed on the spot. While lenient, this decision still was felt to be an injustice, particularly by the families of the persons who had died or disappeared. The setting in court was very emotional—some people lost control entirely. *Forum Keadilan*, 16 December 1996, p. 17.

[221] In May 1996, Sri Bintang Pamungkas was sentenced to a prison term of two years and ten months for insulting the head of state. He was free pending his appeal. The next year, he was sued for subversion for having established a political party outside the existing legal framework, and calling for Suharto's resignation. *Forum Keadilan*, 24 March 1997, pp. 100-105.

Budiman Sudjatmiko came up in the courts. The court procedure was marked by an almost total breakdown in order and discipline as witnesses loyal to Budiman refused to testify, witnesses to the prosecution did not turn up, and the judges, not daring to back down, hardly knew how to move forward either.[222] The judge desperately tried to manage the situation with some chatty questions to Budiman, asking him about his trip from Surabaya to Jakarta and such. Budiman, known as a man who does not suffer fools gladly, interrupted the judge, asking him what, for goodness sakes, this had to do with the case, and would he please get on with it? This response left the judge even more frazzled. What do you expect, commented the press, the courts are held in total contempt.[223] Budiman and his colleagues incurred brutal prison terms, which if anything reflected an increasing lack of self-confidence on the part of the courts, and perhaps the regime as a whole.[224] As these things go, these decisions did little to enhance the authority of or respect for the judiciary.

The Supreme Court limped into *Reformasi* in a miserable condition. The institution itself was in deep trouble. The chairman and much of the Supreme Court leadership had serious problems with professional standards and integrity. Younger judges, with such examples to follow, and subject to the unpredictable wiles of their elders, dedicated themselves to honing their skills in opportunistic maneuvering rather that legal scholarship and mastery. The government was very much part of the problem, abusing its controls over court administration to shunt judges about and thus ensure their political compliance. And all the while, a thoroughly dissatisfied and unhappy society was increasing the pressure with highly publicized cases. This was not going to last.

Sarwata, and the people who put him there, were at the very root of the problem. The authority and effectiveness of the judiciary depends in large part on its being perceived as independent, honest, and capable. To appoint someone so manifestly controversial and unqualified to become top judge invited problems. As a military bureaucrat, Sarwata may have been intended to serve as part of the barricade that the increasingly embattled New Order was building to bolster its position. But if he was chosen to serve this purpose, the decision was a mistake, because both by action and reputation he proved himself to be part and parcel of the political liabilities that actually helped bring everything down.

6. CONCLUSION

Developments after 1970 reveal a continuing erosion of the place and role of the courts in Indonesia. The outstanding feature of this period was a steady decline of judicial autonomy in the face of political interference. Instrumental in this

---

[222] *Forum Keadilan*, 21 April 1997, p. 31.

[223] "Ketika Pengadilan tak lagi berwibawa" (When the courts have no more authority), *Forum Keadilan*, 21 April 1997, p. 31.

[224] Budiman Sudjatmiko incurred a prison term of thirteen years, and the Secretary General Petrus Hariyanto six years—by most standards brutal terms to impose on young people for publishing a political tract criticizing the government. When he was offered an amnesty by President Habibie three years later, Budiman refused on grounds that to do so would to acknowledge fault. He said that he would only agree to an unconditional release. This was duly offered by President Abdurrahman Wahid a year later. It was in effect an acknowledgement of four years' wrongful imprisonment.

development was the fact that the 1968 Yogyakarta compromise misfired completely. The judiciary had agreed to the establishment of a separate Directorate General for Court Upgrading within the Department of Justice, in the expectation that if it were chaired by a senior judge, it would develop into an extension of the judiciary within the executive. It did nothing of the sort. From the time of its first director general, Hadipurnomo, it became an executive instrument through which the department acquired leverage over the judiciary.

Minister of Justice Seno Adji laid down the basis for this executive leverage over the judiciary. In the early 1970s, he decreed that henceforth the department would not automatically realize Supreme Court requests in the field of judicial personnel management, but would manage judicial personnel autonomously. This decree was crucial in hastening the decline of professional standards within the judiciary for two reasons. First, unlike the Supreme Court, which actually handled cases, the department was not able to make balanced assessments of the professional performance of judges. Second, the department was basically unwilling to make such assessments; indeed Seno Adji used control over the judges to ensure their political compliance and his own personal benefit.

This system, which gave ultimate control over judicial management to a department of the executive branch, was perpetuated after Seno Adji. Admittedly, the sharp edges of the department-Court conflict regarding the issue were blunted somewhat as government loyalists replaced professional judges at the helm of the Supreme Court. From the early 1980s, both institutions managed judicial personnel problems in regular meetings through a so-called "consultative forum." Nevertheless, the idea was retained that the department could reject requests for transfers or advancements made by the Supreme Court, and professional achievement remained a subsidiary criterion in judicial career assessments.

Just as the Court's control over its own personnel was restricted, so were possibilities for implementing judicial review. Until 1970, in the absence of an explicit constitutional prohibition, constitutional review was possible, but that year Law no.14/1970 was passed, decreeing that the right to constitutional review required explicit constitutional authority, and this interpretation prevailed thereafter. This change put an end to the series of cases developed under chairman Subekti, in which the Supreme Court quashed colonial superior legislation and seemed well on its way to secure full powers of constitutional review. More generally, it again marginalized the judiciary on the political scene.

This poor situation continued unchanged until the reform attempt under Supreme Court chairman Purwoto S. Gandasubrata, the first career judge to be appointed after two decades of external appointees. His reforms were directed toward all three points of the judiciary's political agenda, regarding autonomous court administration, constitutional review, and salaries. His actions showed that the career judges were still committed to their program of political reform more than twenty years after their defeat. Yet at the same time, Gandasubrata's efforts had limited success. The principal cause rests with the political constrictions under which the judiciary continued to operate. But it lies also with the internal weakening of the judiciary in capacity, professional standards, and commitment. Also, Gandasubrata's reforms bogged down in the increased number of high profile cases that society brought to court starting in the early 1990s. These cases were an enormous burden to the court, both in the way they monopolized human resources and affected the Court's political standing, and they effectively blocked the broader reforms. These high-profile cases also point at emerging weaknesses within the government and bureaucracy, particularly a progressive breakdown in the bureaucratic control mechanisms whereby societal conflicts are depoliticized and de-juridified but are resolved through internal bureaucratic processes. The role of the Supreme Court and the lower courts became more overtly political as a result. The government managed to keep the judiciary in place principally through the political cooptation and singular ineptness of the last two chairmen under the old regime, Soerjono and Sarwata.

Supreme Court Chairman Seno Adji (1972–1980) installs Appeals Court chairmen, March 7, 1974. Minister of Justice Mochtar Kusumaatmadja (no relation of the first Chief Justice) stands to his side.
(reprinted with permission, personal collection)

Supreme Court Chairman Seno Adji (1972–1980) installs Appeals Court chairmen, March 7, 1974. Gregarious, sophisticated, intelligent, and better read than almost all of his successors, Seno Adji was also weak. The erosion of professional standards and integrity at the Supreme Court began with him. (reprinted with permission, personal collection)

Chapter Five

The Supreme Court and Judicial Organization

The Supreme Court's present august position at the head of Indonesia's entire judiciary is not a birthright. The 1945 Constitution does not unequivocally designate it as the highest court of the land, or exclude the possibility that there might be other supreme courts for special jurisdictions. It took two decades for the Court to reach the apex of the judicial system, and it was only a quarter century after independence that it began to hear appeal cases from all Indonesian courts.

This evolution occurred within the context of a larger reorganization of the Indonesian judiciary. The principal feature of this reorganization was abolition of the plural colonial judicial system in favor of the present four jurisdictions: general, religious, military, and administrative courts. These reforms posed some formidable institutional challenges to the Indonesian judiciary that remain relevant even today. The reforms also influence the way in which the Supreme Court currently exercises its functions, as will be apparent in later chapters.

Here we will first give a brief legal history of the development of Indonesian judicial organization and the position of the Supreme Court within it, and will then consider the problems that grew out of the reforms.

1. JUDICIAL ORGANIZATION

Modern Indonesian judicial organization underwent a series of significant changes after the colonial period. The basic features of judicial organization will be outlined below, followed by a consideration of the Supreme Court's place in it.

(a) Judicial Evolution: Unification and Simplification

The first stage of judicial development was that of unification. It can only be understood against the background of the two characteristic features of the colonial judiciary that post–1942 reforms sought to nullify.[1]

First was the colonial legal system's racial criterion, under which each population group was subject to its own specific law and jurisdiction. Two separate judicial hierarchies co–existed, one administering the law for Europeans and

---

[1] See generally J. H. Carpentier Alting, *Grondslagen der rechtsbedeeling in Nederlandsch-Indië* (The Hague: M. Nijhoff, 1926); Ph. Kleintjes, *Staatsinstellingen van Nederlandsch-Indië* (Amsterdam: De Bussy, 1933), pt. 2, ch. 23; G. André de la Porte, *Recht en rechtsbedeling in Nederlandsch-Indië* (The Hague: Belinfante, 1933); Supomo, *Sistem hukum di Indonesia sebelum Perang Dunia II* (Jakarta: Pradnya Paramita, 1982).

another the law for Indonesians.² Even during the colonial period, the evident racial characteristics of this system had been much debated, although they were never changed. Under the impact of the Ethical Policy, steps had been taken at the beginning of the twentieth century to abandon the dualist structure of government courts and replace it with a single unified law for the colony, and by the same token institute a unified court system. The strong opposition to these initiatives was itself at least partially based on the Ethical argument of respecting the indigenous legal system (*adat*). The proposed wholesale abandonment of the plural legal system and judicial organization was consequently replaced by a more equivocal approach. In the late colonial period, steps to unify law and judicial organization were in many cases counterbalanced by measures fostering plurality. Particularly after the 1920s, the role of Indonesian courts and Indonesian indigenous law (*adat*) was by and large strengthened rather than weakened. Thus, as late as 1935, judges deciding cases involving Indonesians were instructed (S.1935:102) to inform themselves whether the case had already been decided by the Indonesian village chief, and if this had not happened, then refer the parties to such a chief.³

The second feature was that in the colonial system involving direct and indirect rule, indigenous courts within those districts under indirect rule were retained as part of the indigenous government. As a result, one system of courts derived its authority from the colonial government, the other from indigenous communities.⁴

The revolution released pent-up frustrations among Indonesians, notably the political elite, regarding the discriminatory elements in the colonial judicial system. There was a concerted drive to rid the judiciary of the elements of diversity it had inherited from the colonial era, starting with its discriminatory character, "in which judicial pluralism inevitably contained an invidious distinction between 'advanced' Europeans and 'backward' natives."⁵ Initiated under the Japanese and

---

² See above Chapter 1. The European judicial hierarchy consisted of a hierarchy of three courts: the small claims and misdemeanors Residents' courts (*Residentiegerechten*) at the bottom; the major first instance council of justice courts (*Raden van Justitie*); and the colonial Supreme Court (*Hooggerechtshof*) at the top. These courts had their own law of civil and criminal procedure, which closely followed the corresponding codes in the Netherlands. The Indonesian judicial hierarchy was diverse. At the bottom of this judicial hierarchy stood a variety of small-claims and misdemeanors courts (for example, *regentschapsgerechten, districtsgerechten*). Unlike the other courts, these petty courts were presided over not by professional judges, but by colonial administrators. The *landraad* was the central judicial institution, chaired by a judge in all but a few isolated spots. It was subjected to a different law of procedure, the *Herziene Indonesisch Reglement*, a loosely structured code that applied in both civil and criminal procedure.

³ *Indisch Tijdschrift van het Recht* 142 (1935): 109; J. F. Holleman, "Volksrecht in Leiden," *Nieuwsbrief voor Nederlandse Rechtssociologen, Rechtsantropologen, en Rechtspsychologen* (hereafter *NNR*) 2 (1981): 22-23. See also Daniel S. Lev, "Judicial Unification in Post-colonial Indonesia," *Indonesia* 16 (October 1973): 4. For a brief overview of the initiatives for unification and impediments that frustrated their realization, see P. Burns, "The Netherlands East Indies: Colonial Legal Policy and the Definitions of Law," in *Laws of South-East Asia,* vol. II: *European Laws in South-East Asia,* ed. M. B. Hooker (Singapore: Butterworth, 1988), p. 179; A. D. A. de Kat Angelino, *Staatkundig beleid en bestuurszorg in Nederlandsch-Indië* (The Hague: M. Nijhoff, 1931), part 2.

⁴ See notably Daniel Lev, "Judicial Unification." Lev uses the terms *vertical* and *horizontal* to denote the racial and the governmental differentiation respectively. Note that in some directly governed districts, such as Aceh, the system of indigenous courts was retained also.

⁵ Ibid., p. 1.

advanced in the early 1950s, these moves led to the dissolution of the system of separate courts for separate population groups.[6] At the same time, Indonesia's political leaders were seeking to strengthen national unity and realize the Republic's control over the whole country. The indigenous courts were swept aside in this broader political process through which the system of direct and indirect government, and later Dutch-implanted federal structures, were replaced by a unitary state, a development not altogether different from what happened in nineteenth-century Europe.[7] From 1951 onwards, a state court system steadily replaced the dual structure of state and indigenous courts. As shall be apparent later, this change was essentially dictated by an interest in furthering political control:

> Courts were unified not first of all because of the principle, dear to lawyers, that rules ought to be the same for everybody, but because the state itself had to be unified.[8]

---

[6] Ibid., p. 5 and passim; Sebastiaan Pompe, "Between Crime and Custom: Extra Marital Sex in Modern Indonesian Law," *Bijdragen tot de Taal-, Land- en Volkenkunde* 150,1 (1994).

[7] It is strongly reminiscent of the replacement of European eighteenth-century class society, with its varied privileged groups of persons, by a more egalitarian political structure. Essentially a central state development, the central state sought to impose its control over the land by destroying the various autonomous legislative and judicial authorities. Thus, the reference in the Dutch 1814 Constitution that all justice was to be effected "In the name of the King" in fact was meant to indicate that the administration of justice henceforth would be a matter regulated by central government, rather than by the various provinces or local authorities, as had been the case up till then. See E. M. H. Hirsch Ballin, "Onafhankelijke rechtsvorming. Staatsrechtelijke aantekeningen over de plaats en functie van de Hoge Raad in de Nederlandse rechtsorde," in *De Hoge Raad der Nederlanden: De plaats van de Hoge Raad in het huidige staatsbestel* (Zwolle: W. E. J. Tjeenk Willink, 1988), pp. 211-37, esp. p. 214. The reference is to art.99 of the 1814 Dutch Constitution. Hirsch Ballin also points out that the wording of the expression was not new and came from a wholly unexpected quarter. It originated from the French Ancien Régime, where the adage applied that "Toute justice émane du Roi," meaning that ultimately (in France, not in Holland) the king could override any decision taken by his courts. Following the French Revolution, this authority was vested in a council attached to Parliament, and that developed later into the Cour de Cassation. In the 1983 Dutch Constitution, the article was scrapped for the first time for being "superfluous," which presumably means that the principle after more than 150 years is so well established that it no longer requires specific constitutional mention. Currently in the Netherlands, court decisions, as well as other authentic law documents, must still be embossed with the heading "In the name of the King." This practice was adopted by Indonesia, which requires authentic legal documents be embossed with the heading "In the name of God Almighty" (*Demi Ketuhanan yang Maha Esa*). Like the Dutch construct, this formula serves to affirm the authority of the central state over the administration of justice (and the law apparatus as a whole).

[8] Daniel S. Lev, "Draft, Chapters on Post-Revolutionary Indonesian Legal History," (unpublished), ch. 1, p. 9. The unification drive is "a paramount objective in many new states," as noted by Antony Allott, precisely because it is seen by the political elite as an instrument by which to consolidate the unity of the state and build a nation. Traditional authority is perceived not just as an obstacle to development, but as a political competitor that weakens the fragile loyalty of citizens to the new state. Antony Allott, *The Limits of Law* (London: Butterworths, 1980), p. 176. As Martin Shapiro has indicated, the judiciary is one of the instruments by which political elites aim to control society and mold it to their image. This results in a natural downward extension of the judicial apparatus into the social fabric and an abolition of competing sources of authority and value systems. In Shapiro's words: "New courts might compete with indigenous modes of conflict resolution. To the extent that they won the competition, they would aid the central authorities in breaking into the cake of local custom

During their Occupation, the Japanese instituted legal reforms which in effect abolished the racial criterion of the colonial system and eliminated the distinction between European and Indonesian courts.[9] A single judicial hierarchy and a unified law of procedure replaced the plural colonial courts.[10] Consequently, everyone now went to the same first instance courts.[11] The *landraad* (renamed *Tihoo Hooin*) became the general first instance court, and the *Raad van Justitie* (renamed *Kootoo Hooin*) was made a general court of appeal. The original jurisdiction of the *Tihoo Hooin* as principal first instance court for Europeans (and Foreign Orientals) was abandoned. A number of courts in the European judicial hierarchy, such as the *residentiegerechten*, became superfluous and were abolished. As the judicial organization was straightened out, the *Tihoo Hooin* found itself firmly placed under the Supreme Court (*Saikoo Hooin*), to which Indonesians were now appointed.[12] Leaving aside the Supreme Court for the moment, the Japanese reforms did not extend to other elements of the judicial organization. They did not affect the indigenous court system (*inheemse rechtspraak*) and retained the specialized jurisdictions, most notably the religious courts.

After the proclamation of Indonesia's independence in 1945, the Japanese reforms were retained and extended. Revolutionary Laws no.23/1947 and no.19/1948 laid down the basic structure of judicial organization envisaged by the leaders of the new Republic.[13] Law no.23 abolished the indigenous courts on the islands of Java and Sumatra, and was the first step in a process of eliminating the indigenous jurisdictions altogether, eventually completed in 1960. Law no.19 of 1948 simplified

---

and bringing government influence down into the villages. Judicial services, like medical services, are a way into the countryside. Such new courts would provide a body of more specific, uniform, and flexible law that would appeal to those locals inhibited by the old customary law. They would provide an 'independent' judge freer of local dominant interests than the village elders or the folk courts. Thus, what we often mean by an independent judiciary is one that serves upper-class and nationalizing interests rather than dominant local interests and thus one more satisfying to persons trying to break through the web of local interests." Martin Shapiro, *Courts: A Political Analysis* (Chicago: University of Chicago Press, 1981), pp. 23-24.

[9] See generally O. Kartodirdjo, "De rechtspraak op Java en Madoera tijdens de Japansche bezetting 1942-1945," *Indisch Tijdschrift van het Recht* 156 (1947): 8; S. Mertokusumo, *Sedjarah peradilan dan perundang-undangannya sedjak 1942 dan apakah kemanfaatnja bagi kita bangsa Indonesia* (Yogyakarta: n.p. 1971), ch. 1; A. A. Zorab, *De Japanse bezetting van Indonesië* (Leiden: Universitaire Pers, 1954). In reality, the Japanese administration followed a zigzag course, in which they first abolished the dualism of the colonial court administration, reinstated it for nine months in 1943, only to abolish it for a second time later that year.

[10] *Osamu Seirei* no. 3/1942, no. 21/1943. As the dual judicial hierarchy prevailing during colonial times was supplanted by a single one, the Japanese had to choose a single law of procedure as well. This they did by making the colonial *Herziene Indonesisch Reglement* (HIR) the law of procedure for both criminal and civil cases.

[11] Though it may be recalled that the Japanese themselves were subjected to separate courts.

[12] Three Indonesians were appointed to the *Saikoo Hooin*: Soepomo, Sastromoeljono, and Noto Soebagio. Only Noto Soebagio had been a professional judge in colonial times. *Orang Indonesia jang terkemoeka di Djawa* (Jakarta: Gunseikanbu, 2604/1944), pp. 150, 155, 159; O. Kartodirdjo, "De rechtspraak op Java en Madoera tijdens de Japansche bezetting 1942-1945," *Indisch Tijdschrift van het Recht* 146 (1947): 14.

[13] Koesnodiprodjo, *Himpunan Undang2, Peraturan2, Penetapan2 Pemerintah Republik Indonesia 1947* (Jakarta: S. K. Seno, 1951), pp. 88-89; Koesnodiprodjo, *Himpunan Undang2, Peraturan2, Penetapan2 Pemerintah Republik Indonesia 1948* (Semarang: Van Dorp, n.d.), pp. 51-61.

the several jurisdictions and judicial hierarchy, distinguishing only three instances: general, administrative, and military (art.6). The Supreme Court (Mahkamah Agung) was designated the supreme court only for the general branch of the judiciary (art.7 jo. art.50), while a transitory provision made it also the highest court of appeal for the administrative courts (art.66). Its role as instance of appeal for the military courts was not specified, as a supreme military court had already been established in 1946 (Law no.7/1946). The law did not mention the religious courts, except to imply that they would be abolished, with their jurisdiction transferred to specially constituted general courts, as indicated in special provisions of the law dealing with the adjudication of Islamic cases by the general courts (art.35 and 45). This purpose, a reflection of the nationalist ethos of the Republican leadership, was eventually foiled by the religious leaders.[14] Both the religious courts and their appellate tribunal, established in the 1930s (S.1937:610), remained in operation during the revolutionary period; a legislative provision moved the appeals tribunal from Jakarta to Surakarta.[15] In the interests of simplification, the law proposed introducing a single first instance court for each jurisdiction, thus eliminating the various colonial small–claims and misdemeanors courts (*districtsgerecht* and *regentschapsgerecht*). This was the first law after independence in which the lower courts were actually given Indonesian names: *pengadilan negeri* (first instance general court) and *pengadilan tinggi* (appellate general court).

This Law, no.19/1948, never went into effect, partially as a result of the military conflict with the Dutch, partially because regulations to implement the law of proceeding before the Supreme Court were not forthcoming.[16] Nevertheless, it is an interesting piece of legislation that indicates the policy goals of the nationalist leadership in reforming judicial organization. If we consider it together with other legislation, a picture emerges of a policy directed toward abolishing the indigenous courts altogether and simplifying the structure of the government courts by limiting the number of jurisdictions and instituting a three–layered hierarchy.

Following the transfer of sovereignty at the end of 1949, the government pushed ahead with unification of judicial organization along these two lines. Laws no.1/1950 and no.1/1951 were the main legislative foundations of the Supreme Court and of the judicial organization of the Indonesian Republic as a whole until 1965, notwithstanding its return to the 1945 Constitution in 1959.

With regard to judicial organization, apart from some slight discrepancies in nuances, Law no.1/1951 had identical aims to those of the 1948 law. Rejecting half measures, in its first article it abolished the mish–mash of government courts that had survived the revolutionary and federal periods. The only exceptions were the courts established by the Republic itself, the Supreme Court (Mahkamah Agung) (Law no.1/1950), the district court (*pengadilan negeri*), and the appeal court (*pengadilan tinggi*) in the capital, Jakarta (Emergency Law no.27/1950), as well as the specialized military jurisdiction. The statute did not mention the religious

---

[14] Daniel S. Lev, *Islamic Courts in Indonesia* (Berkeley: University of California Press, 1972), p. 62.

[15] Decision of the Minister of Justice no.T2 dated 2 January 1946.

[16] J. J. de Jongh, *Het nieuwe cassatie instituut van Indonesië bezien in zijn verband met de rechterlijke organisatie hier te lande* (Jakarta: n.p., 1951), pp. 27, 58.

courts except in the elucidation, which expressed the hope that the government would take up the matter in Parliament in order to determine whether the functions of the religious courts should be transferred to the general courts.[17] Until that was done, the religious courts were to be preserved; as it happened, political realities soon made their disappearance unthinkable. The newly instituted Department of Religious Affairs strengthened the political standing of the religious courts, and in fact, from 1950 onwards the department began to regulate them, introducing them in various regions of the archipelago where they had not previously existed and thus rooting them ever more firmly into the legal landscape.[18]

The more formidable impact of Law no.1/1951 was delivered in its second article, which provided for the progressive abolition of indigenous courts throughout the land. The Indonesian judiciary was to be unified under the central state. In the absence of adequate means, particularly of trained judges, the law envisaged a progressive unification.[19] Over subsequent years, the old courts were gradually replaced by the new district courts in a process that, leaving aside the special case of Irian Jaya, was not completed until a decade later.[20]

After the reinstatement of the 1945 Constitution as the basis for Indonesia's government in July 1959, a new law on the judicial organization (no.19/1964) was enacted to replace Emergency Law no.1/1951. Compared to the earlier legislation, it was very brief, and it is chiefly remembered for its negative aspects, notably that it allowed the executive to interfere in judicial process in the public interest (art.19). Nevertheless, and for all its drawbacks, it also introduced a number of important organizational (and procedural) reforms that have lasted to the present day. It was the first law to state unequivocally that henceforth the only courts to be recognized would be state courts (art.1), an article that destroyed the foundation of the indigenous courts, which were legitimized by customary communities, not the state.[21] It also distinguished the four jurisdictions—general, religious, military, and administrative (art.7[1]).

The New Order, initiated at the end of 1965, completed the process of judicial unification and simplification, adumbrating a new national judicial organization in

---

[17] J. H. Scheers, V. F. M. den Hartog, W. Sidabutar, *Susunan pengadilan dalam Negara Republik Indonesia* (Jakarta: Pustaka Rakjat, 1952), pp. 104, 107.

[18] See generally Mertokusumo, *Sedjarah Peradilan*, p. 113. Note however, that well into the 1970s there was talk in some quarters of abolishing the religious courts and transferring their jurisdiction to the general courts. See, for instance, *Tempo*, 20 January 1979.

[19] art.1(2) law no.1/1951, cf. also J. H. A. Logemann, *Het staatsrecht van Indonesië* (The Hague: Van Hoeve, 1954), p. 128.

[20] The Bali courts were abolished in March 1952 (Decree Minister of Justice no. J.S. 4/8/16 Supplement State Gazette 231); the Sulawesi courts were abolished in August 1952 (Decree Minister of Justice no.J.B. 4/3/17 Supplement State Gazette 276); the Lombok courts in September 1953 (Decree Minister of Justice no.J.B. 4/4/7 Supplement State Gazette 462); the courts in Sumbawa, Sumba, Timor, and Flores in May 1954 (Decree Minister of Justice no.J.B. 4/2/20 Supplement State Gazette 603); and the courts in Kalimantan in August 1954 (Decree Minister of Justice no.J.B. 4/4/20 Supplement State Gazette 642). Mertokusumo, *Sedjarah peradilan*, pp. 88-89. The last regions to undergo this process were Bengkulu, the Rejang, and lastly Jambi, Riau, and the Moluccas, where the indigenous courts were abolished in 1960. D. Lev, "Judicial Unification," p. 31.

[21] As stated in the Official Explanation to the law: "It must be emphasized that the courts now are state courts. As such, there no longer is a place for indigenous or *adat* courts."

Law no.14/1970, which remains in force today. This law was specifically intended to repeal the controversial 1964 law, replacing the article on executive interference with extensive references to the independence of the judiciary.[22] For the rest, however, the 1970 law proposed no significant revision to the previous law. It reiterated the 1964 provision that all courts were to be established by the state (art.3[1]), with the explicit purpose of ridding the country of old "feudal and non–state courts."[23] It also retained the four jurisdictions (art.10[1]).

National judicial organization, then, had finally crystallized into four jurisdictions (general, religious, military, and administrative), each with three tiers culminating in the Supreme Court (Mahkamah Agung) as the single instance of final appeal.

(b) Between Pyramid and Minaret: The Supreme Court in the Judicial Organization[24]

The Mahkamah Agung's current status as the supreme court of the land, which receives cases from the lower courts of all jurisdictions, was not always unchallenged. It was only gradually achieved and not without political complications.

As an Indonesian parliamentarian aptly put it during the debates in the late 1960s, there were really two options for the Supreme Court within the judicial organization: it could be a pyramid or it could be a minaret, or rather one minaret among several others.[25] The first figurative term indicates a structure in which the Supreme Court serves as supreme appellate court to all courts in the land, while the second would restrict its judicial function to the general courts only, more or less following the colonial system.[26] If the "minaret" option were chosen, the special courts would have their own special supreme appeal courts.

---

[22] Law no.14/1970, ch. 1.

[23] Direktorat Djenderal Pembinaan Hukum, *Undang-undang tentang ketentuan-ketentuan pokok kekuasaan kehakiman* [hereafter DDPH, *Undang-undang*] (Jakarta: Departemen Kehakiman, n.d.), p. 47.

[24] This paragraph deals with the debate which took place between 1945 and 1970 on whether the Supreme Court should be the sole supreme court of appeal for the four specialist jurisdictions. This debate in some respects boiled down to working out whether there should be a single Supreme Court or more of such courts, much as in France, German, or the Netherlands there are, in fact, various Supreme Appellate Tribunal for different categories of cases. For the four specialist jurisdictions, the issue was resolved with law nr.14/1970, which confirmed that the Mahkamah Agung would serve as sole ultimate court of appeal for all lower courts. After *Reformasi*, a separate Constitutional Court was established, at a constitutional par with the Mahkamah Agung, to decide constitutional review and comparable issues of constitutionality

[25] Ibid., p. 106. The MP was Kuntjoro Jakti of the Karya Pembangunan party.

[26] The debate focused particularly on whether the Supreme Court should serve as appeals tribunal to the religious courts. The military courts were a special category, as they remain today, small in size, with limited social impact and closely tied in to the military establishment in Indonesia. The progressive emergence of the Mahkamah Agung as the sole Supreme Court of the land in a way reflects the constitutional emancipation of the religious court system, which in colonial times was of a wholly subsidiary character.

Though this issue has some historical roots—in the colonial[27] rather than the Japanese[28] period)—uncertainty about the Supreme Court's role in the judiciary primarily derived from a lack of clarity in the constitution that raised questions after independence. The single article in the 1945 Constitution on the Supreme Court (Mahkamah Agung)(art.24) provides that it and other judicial organs will be established by law, yet it is equivocal on the Court's place in the judicial organization. The article does not seem to preclude the possibility that there might be other supreme courts, nor does it specify that the Mahkamah Agung itself shall be superior to all others. Those who supported the establishment of a "pyramidal" Supreme Court repeatedly denied this point during the debates of the 1960s, as was to be expected.

Still, with some vacillations, by and large the development of judicial organization in the first two decades after independence did in fact make the Mahkamah Agung the sole Supreme Court of the land, which heard appeals from all courts.

A slightly more substantial regulation on judicial organization was added to the 1945 Constitution in 1947 (Law no.7/1947). Primarily intended to reform the judicial organization, this regulation does not deal with powers of appeal. The official explanation indicated that the law was intended to abolish the Japanese system in which, by the end of the war, each administrative region effectively had its own supreme court of appeal. Instead, judicial organization was now to consist of a unified system in which all courts were under the supervision of a single Supreme Court, the Mahkamah Agung; the law states definitively that the Mahkamah Agung stands at the pinnacle of judicial organization, supervising all courts of the land (art.2[1]). In that capacity, it may give instructions to the lower courts, either individually or collectively, with circular letters (art.2[3]).[29]

Nevertheless, in the subsequent year, Law no.19/1948 stated that the Supreme Court would only serve as highest appeal court to the general courts; it said nothing about other courts. In fact, as was mentioned earlier, the law envisaged abolition of the religious courts, which made it superfluous to accommodate them

---

[27] The colonial Supreme Court was the supreme judicial tribunal in the colony and had supervisory powers over all government courts, but as a general rule only handled appeals (and cassation cases) from the European courts. It took only a select number of cases from the courts serving Indonesians—the *Landraden*—and never handled cases decided by the religious courts, the *Priesterraden*. So in terms of its judicial function, the colonial Supreme Court was definitely tied to the system on which the general courts were based in post-independence Indonesia, rather than to specialized jurisdictions, such as the religious courts. This organizational link was reinforced by the fact that some special jurisdictions, such as the religious courts, were considered to be unequal and decidedly inferior in status to the government courts. Government court judges resisted the religious courts, as indeed they still do today.

[28] In the short run, the Japanese had a distinctly negative impact on the place and role of the Mahkamah Agung in the judicial organization, but in the long run their impact was negligible. The unification of the court system did not really affect the appeal system, which the Japanese were at a loss how to handle. On the impact of the Japanese on judicial organization, see Zorab, *De Japanse bezetting*, p. 55; Kartodirdjo, "De rechtspraak op Java en Madoera," pp. 14, 16; R. D. Kollewijn and R. van Dijk, "Staatsrecht en rechterlijke organisatie van Indonesië in de overgangstijd" (Leiden: mimeo, 1948), pp. 23-24; and M. Aziz, *Japan's Colonialism and Indonesia* (The Hague: M. Nijhoff, 1955), p. 159.

[29] Koesnodiprodjo, *Himpunan Undang2, 1947*, pp. 14-18.

organizationally.[30] As it happened, however, the religious courts were not abolished, and without clear legal provision the idea took root that the Supreme Court might not serve as highest appeal court to the special courts.[31]

The 1949 Federal and 1950 Provisional Constitutions were much clearer than the 1945 Constitution in designating the Supreme Court as the highest court of the land. Art.147 of the Federal Constitution established this in so many words, stating further that the Court was to exercise control over all other federal courts (art.15/0), as well as over all supreme courts of the member states (art.153). The federal system was abrogated within seven months of the enactment of the Federal Constitution, but this did not basically affect the position of the Supreme Court.[32] The new Provisional Constitution explicitly provided for the Supreme Court to be "the highest court of the state" (art.105[1]).

Legal statute concerning the position of the Supreme Court was further amplified by Law no.1/1950, which gave effect to the constitutional provisions on the Court's position. In unequivocal terms, Article 12 established the Supreme Court at the pinnacle of the judiciary. It stated that the Court was to supervise all federal courts as well as all supreme judicature of the member states; was to ensure that there would be a proper administration of justice; would heed the behavior and professional conduct of courts and judges and give them individual or collective instructions; and finally, the Court was permitted to demand information and advice of all judicial instances, including the military courts, as well as the public prosecution. The Supreme Court was also to advise the government in all legal matters (art.13/2), while it could complement rules of procedure where necessary (art.131). The law stated quite clearly that the Court would decide cases originating not just from the general courts (art.14, referring to the appeal courts of the general jurisdiction), but also decisions taken in final instance by all other courts (art.16). This would appear firmly to establish the Supreme Court as the highest court of the land in terms of both judicial organization and functions. This 1950 law was reinforced by Law no.1/1951, which stated that the Supreme Court would serve as the highest court of appeal for all courts (art.7[2]). Nevertheless, this provision was not enacted, as we shall see, and well into the 1970s appeals from the religious and military courts were denied by the Supreme Court. That said, the 1950s clearly brought the judiciary closer to a pyramidal structure.

The return to the 1945 Constitution (1959) did not much change the situation until new laws regarding the judiciary in 1964–1965 established the Supreme Court as superior to all others in the nation, authorized to hear appeals from all jurisdictions. Law no.19/1964 stated that all courts were subject to the Supreme Court (art.7[2]), a point reiterated by Law no.13/1965, under which the Court "gives leadership to all courts in all jurisdictions" (art.47[2]).

The 1964–1965 laws opted firmly for the pyramidal judicial organization, but the motives of the government in imposing this structure were suspect. Indeed, after the fall of Guided Democracy, the 1964–1965 laws came to be generally discredited

---

[30] "The statute made no mention at all of a distinct sphere of Islamic justice, thus implying its demise. Instead it provided that Islamic litigants contesting Islamic legal issues would be tried by first instance or appellate courts with a Muslim chairman and two judges expert in Islamic law." Daniel Lev, *Islamic Courts*, p. 65.

[31] DDPH, *Undang-undang*, p. 206.

[32] Logemann, *Het staatsrecht van Indonesië*, p. 125.

for specifically allowing political interference in the course of justice. There were strong indications, in fact, that the pyramidal structure had been proposed by Sukarno's regime not for the benefit of the judiciary, whose interests were of little concern to the government at the time, but in order to strengthen political control over the judicial apparatus. Giving the Supreme Court a pivotal position would tighten lines of control in the sprawling judicial structure and allow the government to create a "guided judiciary."[33] Minister of Justice Sahardjo in 1961 put it as follows:

> All courts must be guided, and guidance is one. The MA [Mahkamah Agung] serves as the guide of the four jurisdictions. [. . .] With the central guidance of the MA after, as well as before, an occurrence or a court case, we have now a system of justice that can be called "guided justice."[34]

The establishment of this "guided" judiciary did not necessarily mean that the courts were placed under direct political control, though Guided Democracy would not have raised fundamental political or ideological objections to such a practice. Still, it was a construct that created, to quote the later Minister of Justice Seno Adji, "a strong hierarchical relation, with the result that the courts internally can no longer be viewed as independent."[35] Consequently, when Guided Democracy gave way to the New Order, the pyramidal judicial structure, together with the 1964–1965 laws, came under close scrutiny.

When the Bill on the General Principles of the Judiciary (later to become Law no.14/1970) was presented to Parliament in 1968, judicial organization and the role of the Supreme Court were extensively debated. The bill proposed that the Court serve only as a final appeal instance to the general courts, and that separate provisions would decide whether appeal to the Supreme Court should be allowed in each district, a provision that tended toward establishing a "minaret" rather than a "pyramidal" system. The government argued that under Guided Democracy, the proposal to make the Supreme Court the appeal court for all the nation's courts was meant to facilitate political control, and this by itself disqualified the concept under the New Order. Nevertheless, the government proposal was broadly resisted in and out of Parliament, as well as in the judiciary.[36]

A number of arguments were advanced. One was that the 1945 Constitution dealt with a *Supreme Court*, which must refer to a single court and preclude the existence of other supreme courts.[37] Another argument was that only a single Supreme Court could ensure a uniform application of law.[38] Yet the basic idea behind these technical arguments was that judicial independence was best secured

---

[33] DDPH, *Undang-undang*, pp. 57, 75.

[34] Ibid., p. 134.

[35] Ibid., p. 133.

[36] For a discussion of resistance outside Parliament cf. S. Tasrif, *Menegakkan rule of law dibawah orde baru* (Jakarta: Peradin, 1971), p. 134.

[37] DDPH, *Undang-undang*, p. 64. Such was also the argument of Supreme Court chairman Subekti and IKAHI (Ikatan Hakim Indonesia, Judges' Association) in letters they sent to Parliament cited in ibid., pp. 343, 354.

[38] Ibid., p. 69 (Tuti Harahap—Christian Party), p. 114 (Soedijono—Catholic Party).

by a streamlined judicial apparatus, with a Supreme Court in complete control.[39] Ultimately this concept found its way into the law, as the place of the Mahkamah Agung as the highest appeal tribunal to all jurisdictions was established (art.10[2] jo.10 [3]). These articles are still the basis of judicial organization, and of the position of the Supreme Court, as was subsequently confirmed in the Supreme Court Law no.14/1985.[40]

It is ironic that, whereas the pyramidal construct clearly was advanced by the Guided Democracy government to realize political control over the judicial apparatus, under the New Order the defenders of the judiciary worked hard to realize an identical construct in the face of government opposition. This switch in positions was no doubt motivated by the idea that the principle of judicial independence envisaged by Law no.14/1970 would be best served and defended by a strong judicial organization. This assessment motivated law advocates to call for a more monolithic, rather than diverse, judicial organization, with an absolutely pivotal role for the Supreme Court therein. Advocates believed that the Mahkamah Agung's dominant role in controlling the nation's courts would be undercut if alternative, possibly competing, supreme judicial tribunals were allowed. The judicial motto clearly was that a pyramid gives greater political protection, and that minarets topple more quickly.

Figure 1: Modern Indonesian Judicial Organization *

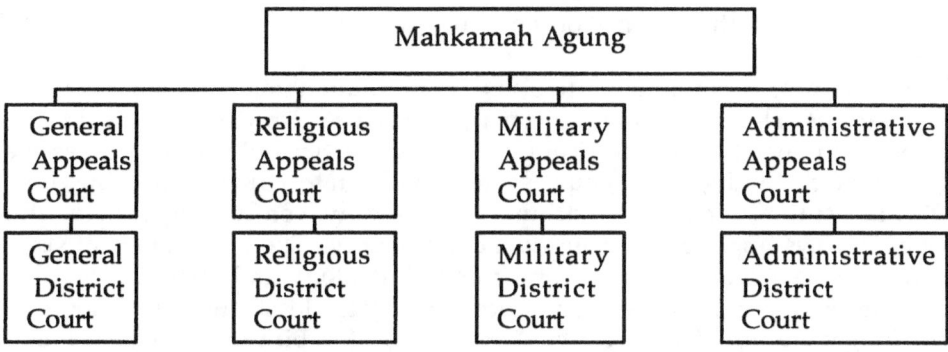

* This is the judicial organization that exists currently. The major change of *Reformasi* is the addition of a new and distinct Constitutional Court.

---

[39] This is in fact what the Nahdlatul Ulama representative Zain Badjeber said. Ibid., p. 180.

[40] The law states that the Mahkamah Agung is the highest court in the land (art.2) and hears appeals from all jurisdictions (art.29). It may be added that Law no.14/1985 put an end to a curious situation in which, well into the New Order, the legislative basis for the Supreme Court itself was weak. The Guided Democracy legislation on the Supreme Court was repealed in 1969 (Law no.6/1969, attachment III, no. 5), but for a long time no law was enacted to replace it. Since earlier legislation on the Mahkamah Agung, notably Law no.1/1950, had itself been withdrawn by the 1965 law, technically speaking the Supreme Court had no legislative basis at all—aside from the meager constitutional provisions. This caused considerable procedural problems, as will be apparent in the next chapter, but had little effect on the position of the Court in the judicial organization. Law no.14/1985 remedied this situation.

This structure did not work as intended, however. Despite legal guarantees established in theory, the New Order government flouted judicial independence. The pyramidal judicial structure laid down in Law no.14/1970 played an important role in this process, allowing the government to extend its control over the entire judicial apparatus by co-opting the Supreme Court. As Seno Adji had anticipated, the strong hierarchical structure of the judiciary in the end helped reduce judicial independence.

2. THE IMPACT OF UNIFICATION ON JUDICIAL STRUCTURES AND SOCIETY

Initially, the unification of the judiciary had a disastrous impact on the administration of justice in Indonesia. It confronted the Indonesian state with unprecedented institutional problems that required massive investments of both human and financial resources. The judicial organization came close to physical disintegration, from which it did not begin to recover until well into the 1970s. Until then, in many parts of the archipelago, whatever hold the courts may previously have exerted on society became tenuous indeed. Unification of the judiciary led to a condition in which the court system, and through it the government, was close to losing control over dispute settlement in Indonesian society, and its legitimacy was weakened accordingly. As a result, in the 1970s, organizational reinforcement and improvement of the judicial apparatus became a political imperative. Strengthening judicial institutions through the construction of new courthouses and transport facilities placed a great burden on the state budgets in the 1970s, at the expense of the badly needed professional upgrading of the judges.

The issues were complex and involved more than a mere retooling of the judicial apparatus. The changes in judicial infrastructure also deeply affected the role of courts in society. The unification process, particularly the progressive replacement of the indigenous court system with state courts following Law no.1/1951, thrust the state justice machinery into society, confronting society with state justice in ways unprecedented in Indonesian history. The penetration of state justice—with its new symbols and reform-minded ideology and instruments—into local communities has not been an easy process, to say the least, and is still far from complete. Judges are forced to negotiate between local aspirations for justice and state-imposed demands that are not always easy to reconcile. Unlike local government officials, judges, by the nature of their function, cannot withdraw from such a position or compromise. As a result, the apparently sterile development of the judicial organization has become one of the prime areas of friction in the complex and politically sensitive relationship between the state and its citizens. This in turn inevitably reflects on the way in which the Supreme Court realizes its functions.

(a) The Impact on the Courts: Institutional Problems

Until the New Order, the modern Indonesian state was both economically unable and politically unwilling to respond seriously to the demands generated by its drive to unite the judiciary into a single hierarchy. Replacement of the indigenous court system, in particular, called for investments in manpower, infrastructure, organization, management, and, in the end, funding, that, until well into the 1970s, went far beyond the capacities of government.[41] Notably, the unification drive caused a severe shortage in the number of judges needed to staff the new courts. During the colonial period, it had been possible to keep the European judiciary small precisely because the East Indies government relied on the indigenous courts to absorb the bulk of petty cases involving Indonesians. Consequently, abolition of the indigenous courts led to shortages in judicial personnel, making it necessary to expand the judiciary, not only because new state courts had to be established to replace the indigenous courts, but also because, in the absence of an absorptive mechanism for petty cases, caseloads in the new state courts increased. Thus, in 1972, with reference to the Sulawesi district courts, the Supreme Court specifically cited the abolition of the indigenous courts as the main reason for their sudden backlogs:

> ... the dual cause of these backlogs is first the large jurisdiction of those courts and second the large number of indigenous courts brought under their jurisdiction. The number of judges is minimal ...[42]

In addition to the personnel shortage, there were insufficient courthouses, too few communications and administrative personnel to manage such an organization, and no funds to pay for it all. Law no.1/1951 had in part anticipated this situation and called for "a step-by-step realization."[43] Nevertheless, problems were without doubt underestimated and in time revealed themselves to be formidable. Daniel Lev recounts that, even in the 1950s, in the face of a potential collapse of the administration of justice, indigenous courts and their judges had to be retained, or even reinstated in several areas. And while the transitional phase during which all indigenous courts were to be abolished legally came to an end in 1960 (except for the special case of Irian Jaya), in reality many of those courts continued to function.

If under Parliamentary Democracy the government was unable to resolve this problem, under Guided Democracy it was unwilling to do so. In fact, the infrastructural problems increased beyond measure during the political derailment of the early 1960s. The chief question no longer concerned how to expand the

---

[41] The abolition of the indigenous courts meant that new courts had to be established rapidly, a challenge that came on top of existing institutional problems resulting from the replacement of the Dutch judges and other personnel in existing courts. The number of district courts, and especially appeals courts, was in fact increased. In 1964, the government set an official target that each district (*kabupaten*, of which there currently are around 290) would have its proper district court, and each province (*propinsi*, which, including East Timor, numbered twenty-seven) its own appeals court. Nevertheless, realization of these goals during Parliamentary Democracy was slow and problematic. After the collapse of Guided Democracy, only 191 district courts were in existence, while appeals courts numbered nine—both well short of the government target. Soerjadi, "Jang datang & jang pergi," *Varia Peradilan* 6,6-8 (1967): 88.

[42] *Tjatatan rapat Komisi III DPR-RI pada sidang pleno DPR-RI tentang follow-up laporan peninjauan Komisi III ke-Sulawesi Selatan, Sulawesi Utara dan Kalimantan Selatan no.4810/Kom.III/72* dated 21 December 1972, p. 8. See also Supreme Court chairman Subekti: "... the backlogs arise from the fact that there used to be numerous indigenous courts which originally fell under the authority of the governor, without possibilities of appeal or cassation. With Law no.1/1951, these were transformed and now fell under the district courts, the decisions of which are subject to appeal before the appeals court, and thus increase the tasks of that court." *Tjatatan rapat Komisi III DPR-RI dengan Ketua MA (Subekti) no.4746/Kom.III/72* dated 23 November 1972, p. 3.

[43] art.1(2) law no.1/1951, cf. also Logemann, *Het staatsrecht van Indonesië*, p. 128.

machinery of state justice into the countryside, but how to keep it running at all. In the 1960s, working conditions in the courts were appalling even by Guided Democracy standards, as President Sukarno felt called upon to acknowledge:

> . . . court officials have no office furniture, whatever is there is their own property, which they take from their homes in order to realize their official duties. Their office doubles up as office for the prosecutors. The Jepara District Court doesn't have any mode of transport, and from time to time judges must hold court session while sitting on the floor. In other courts, such as in Kupang, Mana, Bengkulu, Bali, Endeh and so on, the situation is no different.[44]

Under the New Order in the early 1970s, parliamentary reports fully exposed the havoc that legislative demands, together with the unfavorable economic and political climate, had created for the Indonesian judiciary. These reports depict the bleakness and near-total devastation of the entire judicial machine. They reveal the failure of the judiciary to realize the unification drive that would have enabled state courts to become effective forums for the settlement of conflicts. The problems were elementary and extremely serious, touching upon the most basic and elementary aspects of court work, or indeed any work at all. It was clear that if the state was to retain at least a semblance of control over social conflict, it had to do something dramatic about the court system.

In the early New Order, conditions had grown desperate, exceeding even the problems of an earlier stage, when judges had to take their own chairs to court. Physical disintegration stared the judiciary in the face; for instance, the Langsa district court ceased operations altogether during the rainy season for the simple reason that it lacked a roof and had to hold court in the open air. Since the court also had to do without toilet facilities, "this rather obstructs a smooth flow of cases."[45] The Kandangan district court building was in such a poor condition that at one point the floor collapsed altogether while the court was in session.[46] Needless to say, aside from the corrosive effect this situation had on the professional morale of judges, such conditions were hardly conducive to a smoothly functioning judicial apparatus.

Breakdown of the system was all the more evident when it became nearly impossible, even for courts with roofs, floors, and toilets, to comply with the formalities prescribed by law. The wheels of the justice machinery in those years appeared to be clogged by everything from tiny, mundane grains of sand to huge misfit spokes.

An example of such grains of sand: Supreme Court judge Asikin Kusumah Atmadja has the distinction of making typewriters an issue of parliamentary debate in 1973:

---

[44] Sukarno, "Kamu adalah hakim rakjat jang sebenarnja," *Varia Peradilan* 4,11-12 (1965): 141.

[45] *Tjatatan rapat Komisi III dengan Menteri Kehakiman (Seno Adji)* dated 23 March 1972, p. 14.

[46] *Tjatatan rapat Komisi III DPR-RI dengan Ketua MA (Subekti) no.4746/Kom.III/72* dated 23 November 1972, p. 25; *Tjatatan rapat Komisi III DPR-RI pada sidang pleno DPR-RI tentang follow-up laporan peninjauan Komisi III ke-Sulawesi Selatan, Sulawesi Utara and Kalimantan Selatan no.4810/Kom.III/72* dated 12 December 1972, p. 6.

The material condition of the courts is instrumental in reducing their efficiency and building up backlogs. Various district courts have no typing machines, and simple guards without any legal knowledge whatsoever are appointed as court clerks.[47]

It appears unlikely, perhaps, that typewriters could cause the justice machinery to break down, but this was in fact the case, for if documents were to be acknowledged as authentic (and hence enforceable), the law required them to be typed. For example, the Tanggerang district court in 1974 was experiencing serious backlogs simply because it only had one typewriter in working order.[48] The situation was even worse in the Garut district court, where all typewriters had broken down irreparably, bringing work to a complete standstill by the mid–1970s.[49]

Ongoing personnel shortages constituted the major spoke in the judicial wheels. Well into the 1980s, courts had to dispense with the legal requirement that a three-judge panel decide cases.[50] Many courts were staffed by only one or two judges. As the Supreme Court pointed out in 1972:

> The situation is so bad that even statutory requirements on court order cannot be realized. The law requires decision making by a panel of three judges, but many of the outlying courts only have a single judge. Should cases so decided come up for cassation, technically they must be nullified, but the Supreme Court can do little else but add some water to the wine.[51]

The challenges posed by these shortages were compounded by other difficulties. It was not just a matter of there being "too few judges to go around," as one minister of justice put it,[52] but also a matter of getting available judges distributed to the regions where they were needed. Minister of Justice Mochtar Kusumaatmadja recounted in 1974 that on a fact-finding mission to southern Sumatra, he found that the Muara Enim district court was overstaffed, with judges loafing about, while other courts were dramatically understaffed. Thus, for lack of personnel, the appeal court for Central Java was forced to employ a candidate judge as a full judge

---

[47] *Tjatatan sementara rapat Komisi III DPR-RI dengan Mahkamah Agung (Subekti)* no.1119/Kom.III/1973 dated 9 February 1973, p. 9.

[48] *Tjatatan sementara rapat Komisi III DPR-RI dengan Menteri Kehakiman (Kusumaatmadja)* no.3812/Kom.III/74-019 dated 19 June 1974, p. 17.

[49] *Laporan Peninjauan Komisi III DPR-RI ke Jawa Barat* no.3130/Kom.III/74 dated 30 August 1974, pp. 3-4.

[50] Law no.19/1964 art.8(1). It was an interesting requirement. I have been unable to trace what triggered this requirement in 1964, but it certainly increased the anonymity of judges and reduced opportunities for forceful personalities to make themselves known and gain influence. It also is quite curious that this requirement was put into the 1964 law at a time when the judiciary was not even able to keep its head above the water with *unus iudex* courts. The requirement was also adopted by Law no.14/1970 art.15.

[51] *Tjatatan rapat Komisi III DPR-RI dengan Ketua MA (Subekti)* no.4746/Kom.III/72 dated 23 November 1972, p. 5; *Tjatatan sementara rapat Komisi III DPR-RI dengan Menteri Kehakiman (Kusumaatmadja)* no.3812/Kom.III/74-019 dated 19 June 1974, p. 17; *Kompas*, 5 June 1974. Even in 1993 circuit judges in the Moluccas were allowed to sit in single judge courts—cf. Authorization Supreme Court Chairman no. KMA/1079/IX/1993.

[52] Seno Adji in *Tjatatan rapat Komisi III DPR-RI dengan Menteri Kehakiman* dated 23 March 1972, pp. 12-13.

for more than three years.⁵³ The budget was simply too small to allow for transporting judges to new posts on a regular basis. And there was no transfer system to speak of. For the year 1972, the budget allowed for the transfer of only fifty judges, and moreover it was so tightly calculated as to permit judges to be transferred only to a court located in the immediate vicinity of their former posting, this in order to limit travel costs.⁵⁴ Even in 1976, only 35 percent of all judicial transfers crossed provincial boundaries.⁵⁵ It was an unworkable transfer rate: with approximately two thousand district court judges (in the general jurisdiction) in function at the time, it meant that, on average, a judge had to serve twenty years at any one court, a prospect so unappealing that it could hardly be expected to work.⁵⁶ The situation was miserable. Numerous reports noted judges idling away their time in isolated, faraway places for up to twenty years,⁵⁷ being transferred without funding,⁵⁸ or even getting lost in the transfer process altogether.⁵⁹ Supreme Court judge Sugianto calculated in 1978 that, if the standard term of office for two thousand district court judges was to be five years at any single court, the system would have to ship four hundred judges around each year. The money was simply not there, he stated dryly, so "we must prioritize."⁶⁰ Only

---

⁵³ *Tjatatan sementara rapat Komisi III DPR-RI dengan Menteri Kehakiman (Kusumaatmadja) no.3812/Kom.III/74-019* dated 19 June 1974, pp. 9, 17. Subekti noted the same thing two years previously when he found a number of Sumatran courts to be overstaffed compared with courts in the eastern provinces, which were dramatically understaffed. *Tjatatan rapat Komisi III DPR-RI dengan Ketua MA (Subekti) no.4746/Kom.III/72* dated 23 November 1972, p. 4.

⁵⁴ *Tjatatan rapat Komisi III DPR-RI dengan Ketua MA (Subekti) no.4746/Kom.III/72* dated 23 November 1972, p. 4. Admittedly, it is not completely clear from the report whether the Supreme Court had to limit geographic range when transferring judges because of budgetary constraints or whether it voluntarily did so in order to allow for as many transfers as possible. I have opted for the first interpretation on account of the fact that Subekti refers to fifty transfers only.

⁵⁵ *Tjatatan sementara rapat kerja Komisi III DPR-RI dengan Ketua MA (Seno Adji) no.3804/Kom.III/76* n.d., p. 1.

⁵⁶ In fact, in the first Five Year Plan (Pelita), half of the judges transferred (196 out of 361) were so desperate to get away that they paid for their transfers out of their own pockets. J. C. T. Simorangkir, *Sejarah Departemen Kehakiman 1945-1985* (Jakarta: Departemen Kehakiman, 1985), p. 348.

⁵⁷ In February 1977, a number of judges in Jambi province sent a joint letter to the president, the chairman of Parliament, the minister of the interior, the minister of justice, and the Supreme Court chairman, pointing out that Judge Hutabarat had served thirty years in the same place, Judge Haji Ahmad nineteen years, Judge Abdussamad eighteen years, Judge Ati Karim ten years, and both court clerks an astounding thirty years. Parliamentary archives no.452/BI/77. *Tjatatan sementara rapat kerja Komisi III DPR-RI dengan Ketua MA (Seno Adji) no.3804/Kom.III/76* n.d., p. 1: " . . . there is one judge who served in Belang Kejeureun, some place in Aceh, for more than ten years. . . . " The records also relate stories of judges being kept in physical, not to speak of mental, isolation for twenty-five years. *Tjatatan sementara rapat kerja Komisi III dengan Ketua MA (Seno Adji) no.3608/Kom.III/76* dated 22 September 1976, p. 6.

⁵⁸ *Tjatatan rapat Komisi III dengan Menteri Kehakiman (Seno Adji)* dated 23 March 1972, p. 16.

⁵⁹ " . . . in the District of Kutai, in the Tenggarong region, the district court chairman was allocated three candidate judges, the order of their appointment was effected in September 1973, funding for their travel was allocated, but so far the judges have not yet reported for duty . . . " *Tjatatan sementara rapt Komisi III DPR-RI dengan Menteri Kehakiman (Kusumaatmadja) no.3812/Kom.III/74-019* dated 19 June 1974, p. 11.

⁶⁰ *Catatan sementara rapat kerja Komisi III dengan Ketua MA (Seno Adji) no.3128/Kom.III/78* dated 7 February 1978, pp. 33-34. It is not clear what the priorities were. With many eager to get away and so few travel slots available, the system lent itself to manipulation, and it was

toward the end of the 1970s did the transfer system begin to approach Sugianto's numbers, with an average of 250 judges being transferred annually from 1979 onwards.[61] This was still, of course, a low transfer rate, which meant that judges had to serve, on average, seven to eight years in the same court.[62] As late as 1983, the goal of a five–year transfer system remained unrealized.[63]

The transfer system was complicated by a variety of exacerbating factors, such as the absence or inadequacy of official housing. It was impossible really to induce judges to move unless they were either provided with housing or received housing allowances. The budget was inadequate to meet such demands. Judicial reports are riddled with examples of housing problems. The chairman of the Ambon appeals court, Jusran Saifuddin, for instance, recounted in 1972 that, lacking any housing whatsoever, he had been sleeping in the office for close to two years.[64] In that same year, the first batch of five hundred new judicial recruits was so poorly provided for that they were unable to afford hotels and had to sleep on their desks even two years after their recruitment.[65] It was difficult at times to fine–tune improvements to the situation. Thus, in 1972 the district court chairman in Ujung Pandang had a car and housing, but the appeals court judges in the same place had to do without.[66]

Aside from the personnel shortages and transfer problems, there were problems with infrastructure that had a direct, negative impact on judges' professionalism. Judges needed not only roofs and floors and regular transfers; they also required access to the tools of their trade—statutes, court decisions, books—to ensure their competence. It was also essential that they be properly trained. By the 1970s, it

---

only under Minister Mochtar Kusumaatmadja that the Justice Department, at least, seemed to develop organizational transfer priorities. While Seno Adji was minister, and when he later became chairman of the Supreme Court, the transfer system was applied very selectively. Such Seno appointees as Sumadiyono, Loudoe, Staa, and Gunawan, all served for up to ten years in the coveted posts in the large Indonesian cities and seemed to be exempt from transfer. They were all swept away in the anti-corruption drive that coincided with Seno Adji's retirement in 1980-1981. *Tempo*, 6 December 1980, p. 49.

[61] *Catatan sementara rapat kerja Komisi III DPR-RI dengan Menteri Kehakiman (Mudjono) no.1182/Kom.III/79* dated 12 December 1978, p. 4, gives the following figures: 1979/80: 298 judges; 1980/81: 254 judges; 1981/82: 289 judges; 1982/83: 234 judges; 1983/84: 233 judges. In the report, Mudjono estimated the number of judges transferred in 1977/78 and 1978/79 to average 180. These figures differ slightly, but not significantly, from the data furnished in Simorangkir, *Sejarah Departemen Kehakiman*, p. 348. The wording of the relevant paragraph there is slightly equivocal, but according to my reading states that during the first Five Year Plan (Pelita), which expired in 1973/74, a total of 361 judges were transferred. Thus the transfer rate in those early years would be approximately seventy judges a year, a singularly low rate for the judiciary, which numbered 1,731 judges at the time.

[62] It is difficult to assess the size of the judiciary, as sources conflict. According to Simorangkir, *Sedjarah Departemen Kehakiman*, pp. 346-47, the number of judges at the general courts were as follows: 1,731 (1974), 2,150 (1979), and 2,238 (1984). Currently the number of judges at the general courts stands at approximately 2,600. These figures are supported by a 1969 Supreme Court report (referred to in Mertokusumo, *Sedjarah peradilan*) that puts the number of general court judges in 1969 at 1,686.

[63] *Kesimpulan hasil rapat kerja Komisi III DPR-RI dengan pasangan kerja dalam membahas RAPBN 1983/1984 no.578/Kom.III/83* dated 11 February 1983.

[64] *Tempo*, 15 July 1972, p. 15.

[65] *Tjatatan rapat Komisi III DPR-RI dengan Ketua MA (Subekti) no.4746/Kom.III/72* dated 23 November 1972, p. 9.

[66] Ibid.

was apparent that the system had failed on all these points. The unification drive begun by Law no.1/1951 had encountered such shortages that the drive itself became an important factor in the erosion of professional standards within the judiciary.

Courts without exception lacked adequate source materials. It was thus quite impossible for judges to know the law or learn about legal developments. In 1971, the weekly *Tempo* reported that W. A. Engelbrecht's compilation of statutes, commonly referred to as the "Bible for lawyers," "is harder to come by than the Old Testament and is one hundred times more expensive than the Koran."[67] Indeed court libraries simply did not exist: " . . . maybe some books from the 1930s float about here and there, but no one can read them," reported the Supreme Court to Parliament in 1972.[68] Trying to fill the gap, the Department of Justice that same year sent twenty-two books to each court to constitute its basic library.[69] But there was no follow-up,[70] and the situation remained pretty dismal well into the 1980s, when fact-finding missions of the Indonesian–Dutch Legal Cooperation Program found court libraries to be badly in need of the most elementary materials.[71]

---

[67] *Tempo*, 9 October 1971, pp. 46-51. This may not be true nowadays, when both the Koran and the Bible are easy to obtain, but it certainly was in the 1970s.

[68] *Tjatatan rapat Komisi III DPR-RI dengan Ketua MA (Subekti) no.4746/Kom.III/72* dated 23 November 1972, p. 5.

[69] Twenty of these books were written by former Supreme Court chairman Wirjono Prodjodikoro and the remaining two by former Supreme Court chairman Subekti. Hadipurono, "Pidato uraian Direktur Djenderal Pembinaan Badan2 Peradilan pada Konperensi Dinas dengan para Ketua Pengadilan Tinggi seluruh Indonesia dan para Ketua Pengadilan Negeri jang mendjadi Pimpinan Projek tahun anggaran 1972/1973, pada tanggal 15 Djuni 1972 di Djakarta," in *Varia Peradilan*, Edisi Khusus (1972): 23.

[70] In 1974, judges reported they had received nothing from the Justice Department. *Tempo*, 26 October 1974, pp. 38-39. Only in 1983 did the department send books to augment court libraries. Simorangkir, *Sedjarah Departemen Kehakiman*, p. 343.

[71] Taking court decisions as an example, the case-law series published by the Supreme Court (*Yurisprudensi Indonesia*) ceased publication between 1958 and 1969, and was later only continued on a project basis. This situation continues to the present day and effectively nullifies the role of court decisions as a source of law or as an instrument ensuring legal harmony within the judicial apparatus. Irregular and inadequate funding causes both wide variation in the number of volumes published and haphazard distribution. It is thus very difficult for lower courts to learn of important legal developments through court decisions. When Subekti succeeded in resuming publication of Supreme Court decisions in 1969 on a project basis, he had to reapply for funding to support publication every year. Uncertainty about funding, aside from hampering effective distribution, affected the number of copies published. For instance, in 1975/76 the Supreme Court planned to print eight thousand copies of its *Yurisprudensi Indonesia*, but because the budget was not fully approved, it was forced to cut publication to three thousand copies. *Catatan sementara rapat kerja Komisi III dengan Ketua MA (Seno Adji) no.3128/Kom.III/78* dated 7 February 1978, pp. 29-30. As a result of this situation, district courts failed to build up a comprehensive case-law collection. There were also evident problems within the Supreme Court relating to the selection of cases. For example, in the budget year 1982/83, the Supreme Court only managed to publish records of fifteen of the two hundred cases it had planned to make available. This was part of the Seno Adji legacy of mismanagement. Indeed, the new Supreme Court chairman Mudjono expressed surprise at the fact that the Court had not managed to do better. *Rapat kerja Komisi III DPR-RI dengan Ketua MA (Mudjono) no.2115/Kom.III/82* dated 11 February 1982, pp. 52-53. The sorry conditions created by poor funding reveal the relatively limited importance attached to court decisions as a source of law in Indonesia, and undermine the ability of the Supreme Court to ensure legal unity within the judiciary through its decisions.

Aside from inadequate libraries, there were also problems with the training of judges. As indicated by Supreme Court Justice Asikin Kusumah Atmadja, staff shortages led to the recruitment of large numbers of poorly trained personnel. In terms of university training, the periods of Parliamentary Government and Guided Democracy fundamentally eroded professional standards within the judiciary: in 1969, nearly half of the 1,686 district court judges were non–law graduates.[72] Some regional concentrations of these unqualified personnel were quite high: only 25 percent of judges in all Sulawesi courts were law graduates, with figures in Aceh reportedly even smaller, at 20 percent.[73] The prominence of non–law graduates in the judiciary effectively precluded a speedy resolution of the quality problem, a point made all the more apparent by the fact that by the early 1970s untrained judicial recruits had achieved sufficient seniority to move up in the hierarchy. Thus, in 1969 an astonishing 80 percent of all appellate judges were non–law graduates (seventy-nine out of a total of ninety-six).[74] While the quality problems were acute in their own right, the fact that the law prescribed that judges should be law graduates further complicated the situation:

> ... another problem we have is that if we want to comply with the legislative provisions of Law no.14/1970 that all judges must be law graduates. Well, at this moment at least in one provincial capital 80 percent of the judges are non–law graduates. This doesn't mean that they do not deserve respect. Indeed, their history cannot be divorced from the abolition of the indigenous courts with Law no.1/1951, which were replaced with the state district courts. This happened at a time that we were really short of judges, so that many new judges were recruited from the SHD [Sekolah Hakim Djaksa, vocational law schools]. (. . .) So the non–law graduates I referred to already have professional experience of ten to twelve years, while some law graduates have only just been appointed. What do you expect us to do? We cannot just kick the former out, where would they go to, and besides they are already senior judges. But at the same time they block the conduits [literally, "flow-through"] and restrict new law graduates to the back country.[75]

Until the many judges who did not hold law degrees retired, there was no hope of improving professional standards.[76] In the meantime, the judiciary would have

---

[72] There were 792 non-law graduates in the general courts. Supreme Court report 11 June 1969, referred to in Mertokusumo, *Sedjarah Peradilan*, p. 158.

[73] *Tjatatan rapat Komisi III DPR-RI dengan Ketua MA no.4746/Kom.III/72* dated 23 November 1972, pp. 4, 7. Seno Adji denied the accuracy of these figures and put the number of law graduates in the Aceh province at 45 percent. Ibid., pp. 8-9.

[74] General court figures. Supreme Court report 11 June 1969, referred to in Mertokusumo, *Sedjarah Peradilan*, p. 158.

[75] *Catatan sementara rapat kerja Komisi III dengan Ketua Mahkamah Agung (Seno Adji) no.3128/Kom.III/78* dated 7 February 1978, pp. 34-35. I could find no requirement in Law no.14/1970 that judges be law graduates, and the judge must have erred on this point. His remark was based on Supreme Court chairman Instruction no.JZP 17/13/25, which stated that by 1975/76 all judges had to be law graduates. This instruction seems to be based on Law no.13/1965, which, unlike Law no.19/1964, was explicitly repealed in 1970 (cf. Official Explanation law no.14/1970 I. Umum, pts. 2 & 3).

[76] The non-law graduates were deeply troubled by the 1972 Supreme Court chairman's Instruction, in which he stated that all judges must be law graduates by 1975. Many non-law

to try to upgrade available personnel, but the lack of funds rendered this effort difficult. When the Supreme Court started its professional development (upgrading) courses in the early 1970s, the budget would only allow fifty judges to participate annually. Justice Kusumah Atmadja sarcastically commented in Parliament that it would take the Supreme Court "thirty to forty years to get through the entire judiciary this way."[77] In 1970, an attempt was made to conduct upgrading courses for district court judges through radio broadcasts, which would benefit a greater number of judges and ideally also have a bonding effect. Since many district courts lacked electricity, cheap battery–powered transistor radios had to be distributed throughout the archipelago. The project collapsed altogether, however, because the radios did not receive the wavelength on which the courses were being transmitted.[78]

This problem concerning judges' training would just have to run its course and expire in due course. This it did, though perhaps not quite in the way the judiciary had hoped. Pressed by the requirements of the New Order government, universities in the 1970s began to churn out ever greater numbers of law graduates. The process was facilitated by curriculum changes that shortened the prescribed term of a legal education and narrowed the educational base. On paper, the goals of the judiciary were achieved fairly rapidly, as by 1983 practically all of the 2,238 general court judges were law graduates.[79] Yet it soon became apparent that, in the process, the quality of legal education had suffered considerably, and the endemic problem created by inadequate judicial training had not in fact been resolved. As one critical law professor who lived through the process put it:

> . . . there was evident political pressure to increase the number of law graduates. The law curriculum is being reduced left and right, and there is a true inflation in academic degrees with the sole purpose, I suspect, that Indonesia can boast about the number of its graduates. Nonetheless, this all goes forward at the cost of quality. This is a reality that even the government acknowledges. There is a Department of Education Circular in fact stating that students who graduated before 1970 may go on directly for their PhD, but graduates after 1970 must first do their masters. Apparently even the government recognizes that law graduates are not up to snuff.[80]

---

graduates would not have reached retirement age by then and feared that they might be dismissed or demoted to mere administrative staff positions. During a trip of Parliamentary Commission III to Sulawesi, non-law graduate judges literally cried when they pleaded with the Members of Parliament to support them. Subekti cut the issue short by stating that there was no question of dismissing anyone, and that the measure was aimed merely at restricting new recruitment. *Tjatatan rapat Komisi III DPR-RI dengan Ketua MA (Subekti) no.4746/Kom.III/72* dated 23 November 1972, pp. 9, 15.

[77] *Tjatatan rapat Komisi III DPR-RI dengan Ketua MA no.4746/Kom.III/72* dated 23 November 1972, p. 5.

[78] *Tjatatan rapat Komisi III DPR-RI dengan Ketua MA (Subekti) no.4746/Kom.III/72* dated 23 November 1972, p. 19. It is not clear whether there was any follow-up to this failure, and whether different radios were later distributed.

[79] Simorangkir, *Sedjarah Departemen Kehakiman*, pp. 346-47, says that only 251 non-law graduate judges remained.

[80] Personal communication, 16 August 1994. I could not trace the circular. In another interview, a law professor at another university said that when, after his retirement, Supreme Court chairman Seno Adji moved over to the prestigious Universitas Indonesia, he pushed for as many

Thus the expansion of the judiciary was instrumental in the long-term erosion of its professional quality. It had an impact on both the standing and work of the judiciary.[81] The poor quality of the judges greatly increased the number of errors at the district-court level. As one Supreme Court junior chairman related:

> District court judges nowadays make the most elementary mistakes in the law—actually I'm quite desperate about it. I mean just now the vice–chairman of the Central Jakarta district court qualified the colonial Civil Code as the *adat* governing land law in Jakarta. It is hard to believe that someone like that is vice-chairman, too.[82]

Despite the evident shortcomings of the system, the higher number of law graduates testifies to a government commitment under the New Order to tackling the institutional problems of the lower courts. Improvements began to materialize under Minister of Justice Mochtar Kusumaatmadja in the late 1970s. Mochtar's contribution, which contrasted sharply with the haphazard approach of his predecessor, Seno Adji, was to lay down a blueprint for the ideal judicial infrastructure, in the process defining the goals at which reforms had to aim.[83]

Looking back in 1977, Kusumaatmadja described the changes he wrought in plastic terms (revealing in the process that the days of Seno Adji acolyte, Director General Hadipurnomo, were numbered):

> The first year I came into the department, I asked for the Director General for Court Upgrading. It was still Hadipurnomo at the time. I asked about court buildings: if new ones were to be built, how many square meters should these be? The director general, taken aback, answered: how can I tell, there are 260 of them and this must be thought out first, Sir. All right, I said, that's easy. I was a new minister, and new ministers always say easy. And usually of course, high civil servants, when they get a new minister, they think, now what does this guy want? On the other hand, the minister asks the director generals, how did you do things up to now? So in this case I wanted to know about court buildings,

---

PhDs as possible, and tried to have them all accorded the highest honorific of *cum laude*. His actions threatened to undercut the quality of the university's PhD program, which could be partly resisted by the staff. Personal communication 29 June 1994.

[81] It is hardly surprising, considering these problems, that the prestige of the judicial profession and its popularity with law students declined. Thus, according to a 1981 poll conducted among 167 law students, 83 percent stated that they had no intention whatsoever of becoming a judge. They gave these reasons: that there was no living to be made, and that judges did not contribute to legal development. *Tempo*, 28 February 1981, p. 55.

[82] Personal communication. 7 July 1994.

[83] Admittedly, Mochtar had the advantage over Seno Adji in that the Indonesian state budget had increased following the rise in oil prices after the 1973 international oil crisis. Yet, it was not just this financial windfall that made his administration a success. Seno Adji just was a poor manager, and Mochtar was not. The gregarious Seno Adji was fundamentally disorganized and had a tendency to ignore problems in the hope that eventually they would disappear. Mochtar was a completely different character. An archetypal Weberian, he was tough and structured. The parliamentary reports show someone who, disliking loose ends and ad hoc approaches, aggressively tackles the problems he faces, seeking pragmatic solutions, while in the process establishing general guidelines.

and ordered the director general to work out the square meters. Now that was a difficult job. The method was to establish guidelines, for an appeals court so many square meters, so many rooms, how large the toilets, how did it compare with other courts, are there to be different classes of courts, with each a different type and so on.... So within one, two, or three weeks, back came the director general with his answer. It was decided then to build so many, to improve so many. And then I said, you do the same with the housing for judges. If you know the general picture, it's handy, you can determine the budget required, you don't have to go back and forth striking out this and that, wondering what to do if money is left over and so on.[84]

This process was repeated for all other aspects of court work, and led to the important "Guidelines on the Improvement of Court Upgrading," a series of regulations that laid down the basic directives concerning the physical aspects of the courts.[85] These rules addressed issues ranging from internal court order, to the optimal size of each courtroom in square meters, the number of courts and personnel, official transport and housing, and the transfer system. Thus, for the first time the rules stated that judges generally should be transferred every five years.[86] These effectively remain guidelines for reform to the present day.

While these guidelines were in many ways refreshing, clearly they could not be realized overnight. In fact, the minister, with typical directness, pointed out that his guidelines would be useless unless they were matched by adequate funding:

> ... I hope that Parliament will help me realize the [guidelines] with a larger budget. I should remind Parliament that if it calls for a smoothly functioning transfer system without providing matching funds, this becomes a pretty empty call. Thus, currently there are 264 district courts with more or less 2,600 judges. So if people complain about cars, well, the calculation is easily made: a car costs 3 million, multiplied by the number of judges, this would mean 780 million Rupiahs. We're not talking peanuts here.[87]

Nevertheless, with the state budget boosted by the increasing oil revenues, rapid progress was made. Already in 1977, Mochtar Kusumaatmadja happily reported to Parliament that judges no longer had "to bow to the prosecutors or the police":

> They drive fair cars now, and district court chairmen and vice-chairmen all now have official housing. This currently also is effected at the appeals court level, and in the future hopefully will be true for all judges.[88]

---

[84] *Catatan sementara rapat kerja Komisi III dengan Menteri Kehakiman (Kusumaatmadja) no.3639/Kom.III/77* dated 7 November 1977, pp. 8-9.

[85] Decisions of the Minister of Justice no.J.S. 4/2/13 dated 28 February 1976; no.J.S. 1/7/5 dated 4 August 1977; no.J.B. 1/1/5 dated 23 March 1978; and no.J.S. 1/3/16 dated 18 February 1978.

[86] Decision Minister of Justice no.J.B. 1/1/5 dated 23 March 1978, paragraph V (*Pola tentang peningkatan jabatan/mutasi hakim*).

[87] *Catatan sementara rapat Komisi III DPR-RI dengan Menteri Kehakiman (Kusumaatmadja) no.3812/Kom.III/74-019* dated 19 June 1974, p. 18.

[88] *Catatan sementara rapat kerja Komisi III dengan Menteri Kehakiman (Kusumaatmadja) no.3639/Kom.III/77* dated 7 November 1977, p. 9.

The effect of Mochtar's reforms was to give the unification drive the bite it had hitherto lacked. The abolition of various colonial courts and court systems following the unification drive in the 1950s had created a void, and Mochtar filled it from the 1970s onwards. His reforms fundamentally changed the relationship between the state courts and society, as became progressively apparent during the New Order. It is to this issue—the authority of the state courts—that we shall turn next.

(b) The Impact on Society: Problems of Judicial Authority

It was only under Minister of Justice Mochtar Kusumaatmadja in the second half of the 1970s, then, that unification actually materialized and state courts began to take over the administration of justice throughout the land. This development had important consequences as it affected both the geographical and psychological distance separating the state courts and society.

Looking first at geography, it must be pointed out that, before the New Order, the principal effect of the unification drive had been to increase the geographical distance between courts and society. This was a natural result of the fact that a new state district court had not replaced each of the colonial courts, especially in the case of the autonomous courts. Indeed, only thirty-five new district courts were built between 1951 and 1965, a small number in view of the demands that Law no.1/1951 imposed on the judiciary.[89] Instead, the legal authority of centrally located district courts was expanded to include the old indigenous court jurisdictions. This meant that most district courts acquired jurisdictions that in geographic terms were much larger than those managed by the old indigenous courts or the colonial *landraden*. This was particularly evident in the Outer Islands. Thus, the Balikpapan district court (Kalimantan) took over the jurisdictions of four indigenous courts; Denpasar (Bali) replaced six indigenous courts; and Kupang (West Timor) acquired twenty-one old indigenous court jurisdictions.[90] By and large, therefore, people had to travel longer distances to bring their cases to court.

The widening gap between the state courts and local populations was physically exemplified throughout the sprawling eastern half of the archipelago. In the province of the Moluccas, Law no.1/1951 effectively abolished all administration of justice on several island groups, such as the Aru and Tanimbar islands. The indigenous courts on these islands (located in the small towns of Dobo, Larat, and Saumlakki), the so-called Council of Elders,[91] were closed down, and their jurisdiction transferred to the sole state court in this area, the district court in

---

[89] In 1942, there were 162 colonial *landraad* courts, whereas in 1966 district courts numbered 196, hardly a significant increase considering the fact that the colonial judiciary relied on the indigenous courts. *Regeeringsalmanak voor Nederlandsch-Indië* (1942), pt. 2 (Batavia: Landsdrukkerij, 1942); *Varia Peradilan* 6 (1967): 99.

[90] These were, for Balikpapan: Balikpapan, Sambaliung, Gunungtabur, and Bulungan; for Denpasar: Tabanan, Badung, Gianjar, Bangli, Klungkung, and Karangasem; and, for Kupang: Kupang, Amarasi, Fataleo, Amfoan, Mionofo, Beboki, Insana, Amanuban, Manantun, Molo, Belu, Barmesa, Pantar matahari naik, Alor, Kui, Kolana, Batulolong, Pureman, Erana, Roti, and Sabu.

[91] *Raad van Hoofden*, cf. *Regeeringsalmanak voor Nederlandsch-Indië* (1942), pt. 2, pp. 154-56.

the small town of Tual in the Kai (Ewav) island group. Tual is about 200 km. away from the northern tip of the Tanimbar islands as the crow flies, and up to 320 km. from the more heavily populated southern regions of the group. In fact, the route by sea is circuitous and sometimes dangerous, and for a long time these groups of islands were not serviced by regular sea transport. Even in the 1970s, a ship berthed only once a month in Tual itself for its return voyage to Ambon, where the appeals court resided and which itself lies 3,500 km. from Jakarta.[92] With only six state courts in the huge Moluccan archipelago, the impact of the state administration of justice on society was at best marginal.[93]

In order to deal with this problem, the Supreme Court impressed upon judges the necessity of reaching deeper into society by running circuits. This meant that judges had to tour their sprawling jurisdiction and conduct sessions in a number of places. According to the government, circuits "would bring justice closer to the people."[94] Courts had to be "mobilized," which meant that they had both to engage themselves in society and also to keep moving physically.[95] Everybody agreed in fact that this was imperative if the courts were to maintain contact with society.

Nevertheless, as the Supreme Court acknowledged, circuits could only be realized "insofar as possible,"[96] and as we have seen, little was possible until the 1970s. Circuits were obstructed by both natural and financial conditions. In the absence of adequate transportation facilities, such as cars or boats, and of funding, it was deluded to expect that circuits could be effectively achieved. Indeed, if the province of the Moluccas revealed in starkest terms how abolition of the indigenous courts loosened the grip of the courts on society, difficulties of physical access were manifest in varying degrees across the Indonesian archipelago. Swamps, hills, seas, rivers: it seemed as though nature itself conspired to frustrate the judiciary's attempts to reach the people it was meant to serve after the indigenous courts were closed down.

All over the country, courts complained about being physically unable to serve their districts, which is another way of saying that people were not taking their conflicts to state courts. In 1972 in Tenggarong, where the district court's jurisdiction covered a very large geographical area, the court had to make do with two broken bicycles, and, lacking an office of its own, had to borrow three rooms from the local government. The courthouse was hard to reach because it lay near a river where there was no bridge, and no boat to ferry people across.[97] For the Purwakarta court

---

[92] *Tempo*, 15 July 1972, p. 15.

[93] Such long lines of communication also were instrumental in building up backlogs, cf. *Tjatatan sementara rapat Komisi III DPR-RI dengan Ketua MA (Subekti) no.1797/Kom.III/73* dated 24 May 1973, p. 5.

[94] *Tjatatan rapat Komisi III DPR-RI dengan Ketua MA (Subekti) no.4746/Kom.III/72* dated 23 November 1972, p. 24.

[95] In the Indonesian: " . . . adanya Pengadilan Negeri secara mobil." *Tjatatan rapat Komisi III DPR-RI pada sidang pleno DPR-RI tentang follow-up laporan Peninjauan Komisi III ke-Sulawesi Selatan, Sulawesi Utara dan Kalimantan Selatan no.4810/Kom.III/72* dated 21 December 1972, p. 4.

[96] *Tjatatan rapat Komisi III DPR-RI dengan Ketua MA (Subekti) no.4746/Kom.III/72* dated 23 November 1972, p. 24.

[97] *Laporan peninjauan Komisi III DPR-RI ke Jawa Barat no.3130/Kom.III/74* dated 30 August 1974, lampiran, p. 1.

in West Java, the single office vehicle was a sixteen–year-old broken-down car.[98] A district court in Riau province was so isolated that it could only be reached after a sea trip that took a full day and had no regular schedule.[99] Judges, in fact, had considerable trouble reaching their own courts, as some reportedly went to their office "by hitching rides on the back of passing lorries," and it was not clear at all how they were expected to run circuits.[100] Indeed, well into the 1970s, judges still applied for horses to help them better serve their districts because roads were few and other modes of transport lacking.[101] All these difficulties weakened the state's ability to adjudicate and control local conflicts.

Mochtar Kusumaatmadja's reforms improved these conditions. As the court-building program was getting under way, the progressive introduction of district courts into every district "tighten[ed] the relationship between the officers of the law and the justice seekers," as the Supreme Court put it.[102] By the late 1980s, the process was nearing completion, with nearly all districts served by district courts, presently numbering 290, while all provinces with the exception of East Timor had their proper appeals court.[103] In addition, the infrastructure of the circuit courts was improved,[104] as were transportation facilities (" . . . currently nineteen courts have been provided with water-going modes of transport [1978]"[105]), and this clearly reduced the physical distances separating the courts from society. The transfer system was smoothed out: ever greater numbers of judges were moved around,[106] and official housing mushroomed across the country.[107] When, in the

---

[98] Ibid., pp. 3-4.

[99] *Tjatatan sementara rapat Komisi III DPR-RI dengan Menteri Kehakiman (Kusumaatmadja) no.3812/Kom.III/74-019* dated 19 June 1974, p. 3.

[100] DDPH, *Undang-undang*, p. 63.

[101] *Tempo*, 15 July 1972, p. 15.

[102] *Catatan sementara rapat kerja Komisi III dengan Ketua MA (Seno Adji) no.3128/Kom.III/78* dated 7 February 1978, pp. 3-4.

[103] The program of building an average of six district courts a year was phased out in about 1987, by which time courts saturated the country. It was replaced by a much more modest building program for administrative courts. See *Jawaban Direktur Jenderal Pembinaan Badan Peradilan Umum Departemen Kehakiman pada acara dengar pendapat Komisi III DPR-RI dengan Direktur Jenderal Pembinaan Badan Peradilan Umum Departemen Kehakiman* dated 17 May 1985, pp. 5-7, which states that the Directorate General planned to build thirteen district courts in the 1984/85 budget year, and four in 1985/1986. In 1995, Minister of Justice Oetoyo Oesman announced that East Timor would get its own appeals court also. *Media Indonesia*, 7 November 1995.

[104] The upgrading/building of courts of session for circuit judges proceeded as follows: 1979/80: 34; 1980/81: 72; 1981/82: 38; 1982/83: 137; 1983/84: 57; 1985/86: 14. *Catatan rapat Komisi III DPR-RI dengan Menteri Kehakiman (Ali Said) no.23/Kom.III/83* dated 9 November 1982, p. 41; *Jawaban Direktur Jenderal Pembinaan Badan Peradilan Umum Departemen Kehakiman pada acara dengar pendapat Komisi III DPR-RI dengan Direktur Jenderal Pembinaan Badan Peradilan Umum Departemen Kehakiman* dated 17 May 1985, pp. 5-7.

[105] *Catatan sementara rapat kerja Komisi III DPR-RI dengan Menteri Kehakiman (Mudjono) no.1182/Kom.III/79* dated 12 December 1978, pp. 6-7.

[106] Thus, in 1980 a total of 556 judges were transferred, though admittedly as many as 209 still paid their own moving expenses. Simorangkir,*Sedjarah Departemen Kehakiman*, p. 348.

[107] This process was also nearing completion around 1987. In 1985/86, 280 official houses were built for judges, and the next year ninety-five were constructed. *Jawaban Direktur Jenderal Pembinaan Badan Peradilan Umum Departemen Kehakiman pada acara dengar pendapat Komisi III*

mid–1980s, the judiciary began to call for comparatively nonessential accoutrements, such as new judicial robes (which were provided), it became evident that the pressure was easing.[108]

As a consequence of Mochtar's reforms, state courts were able to reach out and make contact with society to an unprecedented degree. In the late 1980s, nearly thirty years after the beginning of the unification drive, the impact of state court justice on local communities became more evident.

One result was to raise the issue—previously muted if it existed at all—of how to accommodate state ideology and law to diverging local norms and values. This question was all the more urgent during the New Order, when state ideology and local values tended to grow apart. The New Order government was much more "development"-oriented than either Parliamentary Democracy or Guided Democracy had been, as "development" was one of the regime's principal ideological pillars.[109] In its active pursuit of its development goals, the government was not—in fact could not be—particularly responsive to local conceptions of justice. Indeed, development almost by definition involved interfering in and changing local communities, rather than responding to their ideas of justice and equity.[110]

The physical proximity of the state judicial machinery to society, realized in the 1980s, also began to reveal a broadening psychological distance dividing state justice from local values and normative systems, and, indeed, from local realities. The unification of the judiciary therefore ultimately complicated interactions between the courts and society.

That the situation was confrontational in its inception was perhaps most vividly expressed by the symbols involved. The new court buildings sprouting up throughout the archipelago were all built in the same style, purposely designed "so that they will be known as courts by the people."[111] What this meant, of course, was that the buildings would be recognizable as national, state courts. The model was a neo–classical building with pillared front and a frieze. Strongly reminiscent of the colonial building style, it could hardly have been further removed from indigenous and local architectural forms.[112] This symbolic remoteness from local

---

DPR-RI dengan Direktur Jenderal Pembinaan Badan Peradilan Umum Departemen Kehakiman dated 17 May 1985, pp. 5-7.

[108] In 1986, the Department supplied the judges with 2,180 new robes. The fact that the department bothered at all about such things as robes testifies to the improved situation. *Jawaban Direktur Jenderal Pembinaan Badan Peradilan Umum Departemen Kehakiman pada acara dengar pendapat Komisi III DPR-RI dengan Direktur Jenderal Pembinaan Badan Peradilan Umum Departemen Kehakiman* dated 17 May 1985, pp. 5-7.

[109] The official ideological trilogy of the New Order was development (*pembangunan*), equity (*pemerataan*), and stability (*stabilitas*). Hal Hill, ed., *Indonesia's New Order* (Sydney: Allen & Unwin, 1994), p. xxix.

[110] Again, this characteristic behavior suggests that the New Order government complied with Antony Allott's typology of governments in developing countries as being *impatient* because the regime has a sense that there is no time to waste, *seeking fundamental and irreversible changes*, and being *command oriented* rather than interested in working through persuasion, conversion, or the offering of options. Allott, *The Limits of the Law*, p. 175.

[111] Supreme Court chairman Subekti's words, quoted in *Catatan sementara rapat Komisi III DPR-RI no.1797/Kom.III/73* dated 24 May 1973, p. 6.

[112] These court buildings were constructed at a time when pillars were *en vogue*, but happily new architectural models have since emerged, which better accommodate Indonesian architectural modes, as a number have multilayered roofs, or even the *yoni* shapes (see, for

society perhaps was meant to indicate the interests which the judiciary was expected to uphold. As one Jakarta lawyer observed: "It seems as though the pillars of European antiquity follow the Justinian Codes."[113] In fact, this Western architectural form, bolstered by judicial robes, by judges who had arrived from faraway places, and by curious symbols, all served to impress both upon the judges and upon all those who entered that the court was an institution of the central state. District courts, as both the law and the Supreme Court put it, using the even more remote Dutch terminology, "are the advance posts [*voorposten*] of the Supreme Court in the regions."[114] As pillared buildings and robed magistrates multiplied throughout the archipelago, Mochtar's reforms revealed in the most physical terms what unification stood for—the creation of a judicial apparatus ultimately representing central state objectives and interests. District courts were the "advance posts" of that machinery, purposely designed to replace indigenous courts and, in the end, the local and regional interests these embodied.[115]

The messages conveyed by these symbols, which essentially identified state courts as instruments of the national government, were reinforced by the substance of the law. Admittedly, legislation such as Law no.14/1970 required judges to accommodate state law to local norms and values: it said that while enforcing national law, judges should also delve into, follow, and seek to understand values existing in local society.[116] Yet while the judiciary was being portrayed as a bridge between state law and local values and norms, developments made it clear that the state very much intended this bridge to carry one-way traffic. Government inevitably exhorted and pressured judges to impress national law upon society. As the Guidelines of State Policy 1983 put it:

> The legal information services must be strengthened so as to achieve high legal awareness in society, so that all will be aware of their rights and duties as citizens in the context of legal certainty, justice, and the protection of human dignity and integrity, law and order in accordance with the 1945 Constitution.[117]

This drive to impress state law on the social fabric also resulted in various government programs purportedly aimed at bringing state judges and local society together. The 1985 "Judges enter the village" (*Hakim masuk desa*) program is an

---

instance, the Bank Bumi Daya in Central Jakarta). Interestingly enough, in the 1930s the colonial law scholar Ter Haar recommended that court architecture be redesigned to better harmonize with purported Indonesian perceptions.

[113] Personal communication, 8 July 1994.

[114] *Catatan sementara rapat kerja Komisi III dengan Ketua MA (Seno Adji) no.3128/Kom.III/78* dated 7 February 1978, p. 3. It is tempting to infer deeper associations from such symbols: perhaps the judiciary clings to the familiar with greater tenacity than other government services, or perhaps it intuitively feels affinity with the authority and role accorded to the judiciary in Western democracies and their colonies, however perverted.

[115] D. S. Lev, "Judicial Unification," pp. 22-37.

[116] Law no.14/1970 art.27 following law no.19/1964 art.20. The first article states: "Judges as officers of law and justice are under the obligation to find, follow, and understand legal values living in society."

[117] TAP MPR no.II/MPR/1983.

example.[118] On the face of it, this program was intended to make judges better aware of the needs of local society by asking them to participate physically in village work, "by building fences, gates, small bridges and so on."[119] Yet in fact the whole thrust of the program was to introduce state law into local communities. Judges were called upon to "increase the knowledge and understanding in society of the law, and increase legal awareness within society."[120] When the program was replaced in the early 1990s with the Family Legal Awareness Program (Keluarga Sadar Hukum, Kadarkum), accommodation was less important: the new program merely instructed judges to tell the people about the law, without requiring them to participate in building gates or bridges.

All these measures provide evidence of a strong tendency within the Indonesian state to view the judges less as mediators between different normative systems, or between state law and reality, than as conduits meant to convey state norms and state interests to local society.

The resultant tensions between state law and local realities, and the difficult balancing acts required of district court judges, have been amply documented, perhaps most extensively by C. E. von Benda–Beckmann.[121] The one limitation of these studies for our purpose, perhaps, is that they approach the issue exclusively from the perspective of local communities, and therefore provide little insight into the role of state courts in either generating or bridging this gulf; they tend merely to view state law and state judges as failing to accommodate local society. It is beyond the ambit of the present study to look into this problem in detail. Certainly judicial behavior varies across a wide range; in dealing with local situations, certain judges simply make mistakes (one judge exhorted a suspect, "why don't you just admit it, because you're wrong you know"[122]), others are unreliable because corrupt, and others may choose to subvert local norms for quite justifiable reasons. Such matters are often not unequivocal, as in fact local norms are sometimes based on conceptions of justice that by present–day standards are rightfully considered antiquated and unacceptable, such as the practical exclusion of women from inheritance, or vendetta–like revenge murders. Indeed, one frequent problem is that Indonesian state law and state courts quite simply are inadequate to resolve a broad category of real life problems that have evolved over time. We shall return to this later. Suffice it here to quote briefly from Supreme Court chairman Seno Adji on this particular challenge:

> As far as the effectuation of court decisions is concerned, it sometimes happens that a decision is in accordance with the law, but gives rise to insurmountable problems in the field. (. . .) Thus, we just had a case from Sulawesi in which land owned by an individual had been occupied by an entire village since the

---

[118] Instruction Minister of Justice no.M.20–UM.06.02/1985.

[119] *Tanggapan/jawaban Menteri Kehakiman Republik Indonesia atas laporan kunjungan kerja/pertanyaan Komisi III DPR-RI pada rapat kerja Komisi III DPR-RI dengan Menteri Kehakiman* dated 9 February 1987, p. 25.

[120] Instruction Minister of Justice no.M.20–UM.06.02/1985, part A sub 1.

[121] C. E. von Benda-Beckmann, *The Broken Stairways to Consensus: Village Justice and State Courts in Minangkabau* (Dordrecht: ICG Printing, 1984).

[122] *Tjatatan public hearing Komisi III DPR-RI dengan IKAHI no.3156/Kom.III/72* dated 9 June 1972, p. 7.

Japanese period. Legally speaking, the claimant was the rightful owner, and the villagers should be evicted. But this would lead to important social and political problems.[123]

It is clear that, for various reasons, tensions between state law and local realities can be very difficult for judges to resolve, particularly at the district court level.

This disjunction is an important factor in generating local resistance against state justice and corresponding pressures on district court judges to comply with local values and norms concerning justice rather than to the values of a remote and anonymous state. Public resistance is evident from a broad range of collective displays of anti–court behavior, which, if anything, have become more frequent over the past decade or so. This behavior ranges from public demonstrations of large–scale opposition to a court decision or expressions of contempt for judges to outright physical intimidation and assault. Dismay at the frequency of attacks such as these (intensified, no doubt, by their own underlying sense of inadequacy) brought judges to push for contempt of court powers from the late 1980s.

Local resistance to state law is hard to quantify precisely, and indeed would merit a detailed comparative study to be conclusive. At the same time, reports of such disturbances are so frequent that they do provide us with significant evidence of widespread public dissatisfaction. Let me cite just two examples: the Kipas incident and the *Nuku Suleiman case*. The first refers to a bankruptcy trial in Surabaya in which the judge, for no apparent reason, constantly delayed the trial date, thus infuriating the duped creditors. Suspecting corruption, they all turned up one day, and when the judge began to remit the date once again, all members of the court audience started fanning themselves with bank notes.[124] The *Nuku Suleiman case* involved a popular student activist arrested for insulting the head of state. The case was a riotous affair, in which a campaign of hoaxes repeatedly interrupted the trial.[125] Thus, an ambulance was ordered, on the pretext that Nuku had fallen ill and needed urgent hospitalization. A medic came running into the courtroom with a stretcher, only to have the judge tell him that it was all a hoax. The case later dissolved into contemptuous hilarity when an unsuspecting florist suddenly arrived with a large bouquet to be delivered to the presiding judge (a woman), only to be followed by a baker with a large cake inscribed with the judge's name. Such instances reveal a broadly shared view among both spectators and litigating parties that the court's concept of justice is not theirs. As Nuku Suleiman shouted at one point, banging the table: "I am not expecting justice from this court!"[126]

At the other extreme, resistance expresses itself in direct collective violence or acts of intimidation. District court judges have for a long time been subject to physical intimidation and aggression, while the incineration of courthouses has developed into a routine. A report in 1974 stated:

---

[123] *Catatan sementara rapat kerja Komisi III dengan Ketua MA (Seno Adji) no.3608/Kom.III/78* dated 22 September 1974, p. 12.

[124] *Forum Keadilan*, 11 November 1993.

[125] *Forum Keadilan*, 3 February 1994.

[126] *Inside Indonesia*, March 1994, p. 12.

Maybe six months ago, in the Palopo area of Sulawesi, which is hard to reach by car, judges were threatened. The Supreme Court just received a report of an incident in which the ring around a judge's finger suddenly left his hand, and flew four meters through the courtroom. The judge died within three weeks of deciding the case. The police investigating the incident say that such things often happen there because it is a very mystical area. In fact, the police have strong ideas about who might have perpetrated the act, but cannot arrest him for lack of evidence.[127]

In the same year, judges were stabbed in both the Pemakasan[128] and Bandung district courts,[129] while in the Polewali district court the judge was so intimidated that he agreed to suspend the enforcement of his decision.[130] The problem continues to the present day. For instance, protestors staged a "karate party under the judge's nose" (1974);[131] the entire Lahat district court was beaten up and the courthouse burned down; a judge was lynched by women at the Sungai Penuh district court, and that courthouse too destroyed; and courthouses in such faraway places as Sumatran Lubukpakam and the Central Sulawesi appeals court were torched during riots.[132] In May 1991, the district court in Ruteng (Flores) was burned down during massive rioting, one judge was knifed, and the rest were intimidated to the point that they fled to the neighboring island of Timor.[133] It appears that it took more than a month to restore the administration of justice in the Ruteng district. In 1995, the Bekasi district court faced massive rioting, and two weeks later the Kediri district court was destroyed by hundreds of visitors.[134] As Supreme Court judge Kusumah Atmadja put it in Parliament: "Being a judge is not always attractive because one's safety cannot be guaranteed."[135]

(c) Judicial "Error" and Adaptation

It is sometimes said in Indonesia that district court judges have the hardest job in the judiciary. One important reason is that they must walk a thin line, if such a line even exists, between state law requirements and diverging local norms and values, or realities. They cannot win: if they fail to apply state law, this exposes

---

[127] *Tjatatan sementara rapat Komisi III DPR-RI dengan Ketua Mahkamah Agung (Subekti)* no.4746/Kom.III/72 dated 23 November 1974, p. 14.

[128] Ibid., p. 25.

[129] *Tjatatan sementara rapat Komisi III DPR-RI dengan IKAHI* no.3156/Kom.III/72 dated 9 June 1974, p. 7.

[130] *Tjatatan sementara rapat Komisi III DPR-RI dengan Ketua Mahkamah Agung (Subekti)* no.4746/Kom.III/72 dated 23 November 1974, p. 11.

[131] *Tjatatan sementara rapat Komisi III DPR-RI dengaan Menteria Kehakiman (Kusumaatmadja)* no.3812/Kom.III/74-019 dated 19 June 1974, p. 5.

[132] *Tempo,* 11 May 1991; *Suara Pembaruan,* 13 May 1991; *Merdeka,* 31 May 1991.

[133] With the exception of the district court chairman, who died the morning after the incident, "while putting on his socks," according to the newspapers. *Pelita,* 8 May 1991.

[134] *Forum Keadilan,* 9 October 1995; *Kompas,* 26 October 1995.

[135] *Tjatatan sementara rapat Komisi III DPR-RI dengan Ketua Mahkamah Agung (Subekti)* no.4746/Kom.III/72 dated 23 November 1974, p. 14.

them to the accusation that they oppose development, and a lack of respect for local values or realities exposes them to reprisals at the hands of litigants or local communities. Notwithstanding state expectations, district court judges must add some water to the legal wine and mediate between local reality and pressures on the one hand, and state law and pressures on the other. These efforts at mediation can result in a rather loose interpretation of state law, to put it mildly. This dynamic helps explain why, in a divorce case, the judge upheld the validity of a divorce conducted by customary ritual, notwithstanding explicit statutory provisions that only a divorce in court is valid.[136] Similarly, a Lombok judge held a boy criminally liable for backing out of a marriage and condemned him to an astonishing twenty-one days in prison.[137] These cases are interesting because judges explicitly cite the reference in Law no.1/1951 to local norms and values in order to justify their decisions. And so, whereas these provisions were included in 1951 with the aim of absorbing traditional customary law into state law and thereby reducing its influence, by the 1980s the situation was reversed. In the face of public pressure, district court judges used these provisions to escape the statutory law's effect, rather than bring local values within the law's ambit.[138]

Judged by state law, this often results in "judicial error." Sometimes, of course, the (perhaps poorly trained) judge has erred. But sometimes, his "error" is a willful misapplication of the law resulting from external pressures, as one Supreme Court judge pointed out to me.

> **Supreme Court judge**: The first case I handled after being appointed to the Supreme Court was a murder case, with nine suspects. The district court judge declared them guilty, but there was not a shred of evidence, and I acquitted all of them.
> **SP**: Why do you think the district court judge found them guilty?
> **Supreme Court judge**: I don't really know, but it is very possible that he was threatened.[139]

The process of judicial unification, described above, is also at the root of tensions existing between state law and local perceptions of justice and reality. These tensions have influenced the Supreme Court's role, as we will see later. Confronted with the judiciary's problematic infrastructure and the difficulties of adapting state law to local conditions, as well as difficulties resulting from political interference, the Supreme Court tends to rely on fact-specific decision making, which reaches down into the judicial apparatus to solve constantly arising problems on an ad hoc basis. The Court's role, as we shall see, developed after it opened up the appeal system and allowed almost any case to come up for review in order to control and correct errors. This appeal system generated backlogs, and it

---

[136] Sebastiaan Pompe, "De invloed van het adatrecht bij de toepassing van het strafrecht in Indonesië," *Bijdragen tot de Taal-, Land- en Volkenkunde* 143,4 (1986): 499.

[137] District Court Mataram 23 March 1988, *Varia Peradilan* 39 (1988): 68.

[138] S. Pompe, "Between Crime and Custom." This in itself is a complex development. In this article, I tried to indicate that judges in applying law no.1/1951 need not always refer to actually existing local norms and values, which assuredly are hard to ascertain, but may impose their own idea of what these local norms and values are, which is not the same thing.

[139] Personal communication, July 1994.

explains the failure of the Supreme Court to ensure a unified application of state law throughout the country.

Chapter Six

The Judicial Function

As a logical result of both the political pressures and institutional problems under which the Supreme Court operated after independence, its control over the lower courts was strengthened. Under Guided Democracy and the New Order, the government's tendency to safeguard its political interests in the courts, combined with the litany of errors and injustices in the poorly staffed and trained lower judiciary, compelled both the government and the Supreme Court to seek instruments to strengthen their grip on the lower courts.[1]

This strengthening of Supreme Court control applies notably to its core judicial function. The prime instrument by which its control over the lower courts was realized and extended was the appeals institution of cassation. The prevailing trend in the past fifty years, both in statute and the varied Supreme Court realization thereof, has been a continuous reinforcement of the appellate tasks of the Supreme Court over the lower courts.

There are two major parallel elements in this development. First, in organizational terms, as we have seen, the unification of the judicial organization after independence solidly placed the Supreme Court at the top of a tier-structured judicial pyramid. This made it possible for the Court to broaden its powers of appeal to include appeals to decisions originating from all courts and concerning a much greater variety of disputes than had been the case under the colonial regime. So we find that, in a development matching the organizational reforms of the judiciary after independence, the Supreme Court evolved from a highly selective, primarily European-oriented judicial tribunal into an appeals court covering the entire judicial apparatus.

Second, and as regards the substance of cassation, we will find that in its interpretation of its statutory powers, the Supreme Court consistently lowered procedural and substantive thresholds with the aim of facilitating appeals. Indeed, perhaps the single outstanding feature of cassation in modern Indonesia is that it has come to resemble closely an appeal instrument. Many procedural hurdles and dogmatic restrictions specific to the cassation instrument were dropped, in practice if not in theory, so that at present practically any case can be appealed before the Supreme Court. Both these elements will be considered in this chapter.

---

[1] From this perspective, the Supreme Court is a prime example of the political logic underlying the appeals system as defined by Martin Shapiro; that is, it functions as "an important political mechanism both for increasing the level of central control over administrative subordinates and for ensuring the authority and legitimacy of rulers." If the autonomy of the courts is weak, such a mechanism can then be used as an instrument to facilitate direct political intervention in the judicial system, as we have seen, but it also serves as a "mode of ensuring against the venality, prejudice, and/or ignorance of trial court judges." Martin Shapiro, *Courts: A Comparative and Political Analysis* (Chicago: University of Chicago Press, 1981), pp. 52-53, 49.

Cassation was not the only way by which the Supreme Court strengthened its grip over the lower courts. Supreme Court judicial powers other than cassation all evolved in the same direction. Their effect was to "pull up" cases from the lower courts into the Supreme Court's jurisdiction and facilitate the Court's intervention even outside normal appeals channels, such as in the enforcement of court decisions. As shall become apparent in later chapters, broadening both cassation and other judicial powers has had a number of important institutional consequences for the Court; for instance, it contributed to the Court's backlog problem and helped determine the organizational response to that problem.

According to the latest legislation, the Supreme Court's judicial function, while defined as a single task, in fact consists of a variety of tasks. Their common denominator is that they all deal with the core function of the Court: *decision making*, or the settlement of disputes. The latest law with regard to the Supreme Court (Law no.14/1985) lists five judicial tasks: cassation (art.28); settlement of jurisdiction problems between courts (art.28); special review of cases decided in final instance (art.28); judicial review (art.31); and the seizure of foreign vessels (art.78). This clearly is a partial list, as the law specifically allows the Supreme Court to assume any other task as provided by law (art.39). This is no empty clause, as exemplified by the fact that the Supreme Court in 1993 provided that foreign arbitral awards could only be enforced in Indonesia after being affirmed (*exequatur*) by the Supreme Court itself (Regulation Supreme Court no.1/1990). Moreover, we will find that some of the Court's ostensibly subsidiary procedural powers, such as stay of action pending appeal, evolved into important judicial powers in their own right. Nevertheless, there is little use in dealing with all these tasks separately. Practically all tasks in some way or the other are covered by the legal mechanics governing normal appeal mechanisms for lodging cases before the Supreme Court. Moreover, some of these tasks are highly exceptional. Thus, the six judicial review cases that were heard in the last decade of the New Order government, despite their political importance, are hardly a match for the more than twenty thousand cassation cases that burden the docket on an *annual* basis during the same period. More important, they tell us little about the development of the appeal mechanism and its underlying motives. So it serves us to focus here on the core judicial task of the Supreme Court: that it is a court of cassation.

1. THE ORGANIZATIONAL STRENGTHENING OF THE SUPREME COURT'S JUDICIAL FUNCTION

(a) Colonial Complexity and Japanese Reforms[2]

We have seen that the colonial judicial organization was exceedingly diverse, organized as it was according to essentially racial distinctions. This diversity had an important impact on the judicial tasks of the colonial Supreme Court. These

---

[2] See generally G. André de la Porte, *Recht en Rechtsbedeling in Nederlandsch-Indië* (The Hague: Belinfante, 1933), p. 134; Ph. Kleintjes, *Staatsinstellingen van Nederlandsch-Indië* (Amsterdam: De Bussy, 1933), pt. 2, p. 272; J. H. Carpentier Alting, *Grondslagen der rechtsbedeeling in Nederlandsch-Indië* (The Hague: M. Nijhoff, 1926), §34,114, 119, 127.

tasks were varied in their own right and, no less important, essentially oriented toward serving European interests by largely excluding appeals from the Indonesian courts.

The colonial Constitution granted the colonial Supreme Court the power to ensure that the law be properly applied by the courts, for which purpose it was empowered to nullify judicial decisions.[3] The Constitution did not determine the way in which the Court should effect this provision, nor did it determine that any lower court decision might be appealed to the court. It is important to keep in mind that in the last decades of colonial rule the appeal system was based on a two-tier construct, which meant that, as a general rule, there could only be a single appeal from any court decision. Thus, the *landraad* served as final court of appeal for the inferior courts, and the *Raad van Justitie* as final court of appeal for *landraad* decisions taken in first instance. As regards the colonial Supreme Court, it sometimes served as a first instance court, most often as a regular court of full appeal, and only residually as a court of cassation. These triple tasks can be briefly described as follows.

In first instance, the colonial Supreme Court determined *forum priviligiatum* cases, being actions brought against high colonial officers.[4] It also decided jurisdictional conflicts between different courts in first and final instance.[5] Moreover, civil cases, which normally would be decided by the lower *Raad van Justitie* and would be liable for appeal before the Supreme Court, could, upon agreement between the parties, be directly presented to the Supreme Court, bypassing the lower court. The Supreme Court would then decide the case as a first and final instance court (*prorogatie*).[6]

In second instance, being full appeal, the colonial Supreme Court decided cases determined by the *Raad van Justitie* as first instance court,[7] and decided appeals from arbitral awards[8] and certain decisions of residents' courts.[9]

The Supreme Court acted as court of cassation only in cases in which all other legal remedies were exhausted. This included decisions which, for a variety of reasons, were not liable to full appeal before the Supreme Court, such as in small civil cases or because the *Raad van Justitie* itself decided a case as an appellate tribunal.[10]

---

[3] art.158(1) *Indische Staatsregeling*: The Supreme Court will ensure the proper course and administration of justice, as well as the obedience to laws and other regulations having general effect in all court and judicial instances. (2) In accordance with the law, it may nullify and render ineffective judicial actions, decrees, and decisions if these are not in accord with laws and other regulations having general effect.

[4] For a list of these officers: art.155 *Indische Staatsregeling*, and art.165 *Reglement op de Rechterlijke Organisatie en het Beleid der Justitie*.

[5] art.162 *Rechterlijke Organisatie* (S.1847:23).

[6] art.164 *Rechterlijke Organisatie* (S.1847:23).

[7] art.126, 129, 130(2) and 163 *Rechterlijke Organisatie* (S.1847:23).

[8] Only when in excess of five hundred guilders—art.163(2) *Rechterlijke Organisatie* (S.1847:23).

[9] art.163(3) *Rechterlijke Organisatie* (S.1847:23).

[10] See generally art.170 *Rechterlijke Organisatie* (S.1847:23). For some curious exceptions cf. S.1905:445 art.IX referring to annulment of decisions from the Ternate *rijksraad*.

The diverse jurisdiction of the colonial Supreme Court was bounded, however, by the division between the colonizers and the colonized. Certain incidents aside,[11] some broadly defined categories of court decisions were excluded from review by the colonial Supreme Court. These notably included a broad category of decisions from the Indonesian courts, as indeed we will find that the courts which most affected the Indonesian community were not supervised or evaluated by the colonial Supreme Court.[12]

The most notable exclusion concerned court decisions in which unwritten Indonesian indigenous law (*adat*) applied. On the face of it, the reason for disqualifying *adat* cases from appeal in cassation to the colonial Supreme Court was a matter of doctrine. The logic ran more or less as follows. The principal first instance court in Indonesian cases was the *landraad*, with the possibility of appeal before the *Raad van Justitie*. Since there already was an appellate court, these cases were only liable for review before the Supreme Court by means of cassation. Review in cassation (at least until the late 1940s) was limited to statute, however, and as *adat* law was largely uncodified, such decisions were for reasons of doctrine excluded from review in cassation by the colonial Supreme Court. From the late nineteenth century, the colonial Supreme Court, acting as court of cassation, refused to hear cases on uncodified *adat* law, as cassation and *adat* were regarded as "mutually exclusive."[13] There was an underlying reason for this division, which had to do with the racial diversity on which the plural colonial court system, and indeed the colonial essence, was really, politically grounded. This reality became evident when in 1901 *all* cases decided by the *landraden* were excluded from appeal to the colonial Supreme Court, even if they were based on statute (as criminal cases were),[14] demonstrating that the judicial function of the colonial Supreme Court was primarily conceived as serving the interests of the European community rather than Indonesians.

The exclusion of the bulk of cases involving Indonesians from appeal to the colonial Supreme Court was further complemented by the exclusion of a broad category of cases that intimately affected the Indonesian community. These were the decisions of the Islamic courts (*Priesterraden*). Decisions from these courts were subjected to a separate appeals tribunal, the *Mahkamah Islam Tinggi*, and from

---

[11] Thus, cassation was limited in a number of ways, cf. art.126 *Rechterlijke Organisatie* jo. art.170 (2) *Rechterlijke Organisatie*, as well as art.95 (3) *Rechterlijke Organisatie* jo. art.170 (2) *Rechterlijke Organisatie* (S.1837:23).

[12] Carpentier Alting, *Grondslagen*, p. 279.

[13] Hooggerechtshof (colonial Supreme Court, hereafter HGH) 21 October 1880, *Indisch Tijdschrift van het Recht* 35: 324; HGH 1 March 1883, *Indisch Weekblad van het Recht* 21,1032 (9 April 1883): 57-59; HGH 1 May 1884, *Indisch Tijdschrift van het Recht* 43: 111; HGH 7 April 1892, *Indisch Weekblad van het Recht* 30,1511 (13 June 1892): 95; HGH 18 December 1897, *Indisch Tijdschrift van het Recht* 70: 148; HGH 16 February 1899, *Indisch Weekblad van het Recht* 37,1865 (27 March 1899): 49. J. J. de Jongh, *Het nieuwe cassatie instituut van Indonesië bezien in zijn verband met de rechterlijke organisatie hier te lande* (Jakarta: n.p., 1951), p. 18. Wording of the colonial Bar Association, *Handelingen der Nederlandsch-Indische Juristen Vereniging* (1885), pt. 3, p. 254; J. J. de Jongh, *Het nieuwe cassatie instituut van Indonesië*, p. 18.

[14] S.1901:124. See also Advice Dutch colonial Bar Association 1885, *Handelingen der Nederlandsch-Indische Juristen Vereniging* (1885), pt. 3, p. 268.

there directly to the Governor-General.[15] There was no chance of appeal to the colonial Supreme Court.

The Japanese administration did not quite know how to handle the colonial Supreme Court; it initially curtailed its jurisdiction, and finally, in 1944, suspended it altogether. This ambivalence reflected the fact that the archipelago was carved up into different regions, controlled by various army and navy groups. In administrative terms, these administrations were highly autonomous, with the result that the country as a whole effectively ceased to function as a single administrative unit. The Supreme Court's nationwide jurisdiction did not fit in with the Japanese administrative reforms, and the Japanese therefore paid little attention to its jurisdiction.[16] Suspension of the Supreme Court in 1944 was the inevitable outcome.

Nevertheless, and however unintended, the Japanese reforms of the judicial organization laid down a blueprint for important reforms in the jurisdiction of the Supreme Court after independence. As we have seen, they made the *landraad* the general first instance court and the *Raad van Justitie* the general appeals court, reforms which were retained after independence. This change had two important effects. The first was that the first instance and appellate tasks of the Supreme Court, rooted as they were in organizational diversity, lost much of their relevance. Thus, when the organizational reforms were retained and even extended after the war, this quite naturally also simplified the jurisdiction of the Supreme Court. The second effect was that, by making the *landraad* court the general first instance court in an integrated judicial structure, the Japanese established the basis for bringing these courts under Supreme Court control, as in fact would be realized after independence.[17] As a result, their reforms were indirectly conducive to an extension of the Supreme Court's judicial control over the lower, and particularly Indonesian, courts.

(b) The Revolutionary Period (1945-1949): Erosion of Appeal, Cassation Broadened

The post-independence reforms aimed to replace the complex jurisdiction of the colonial Supreme Court with an appeals system that embraced all courts. The Indonesian Republic unified the judicial organization, with the Supreme Court at its apex. The impact of this organizational reform was to erode the full appeal and special judicial tasks of the Court, replacing them with a cassation mechanism that was all-embracing.

From the start, the Supreme Court was clearly envisaged as the head of the judicial organization, with responsibility for ensuring the unified administration

---

[15] Daniel S. Lev, *Islamic Courts in Indonesia* (Berkeley: University of California Press, 1972), p. 30.

[16] In fact, it seems that the Japanese also did not understand the distinction between full appeal and cassation, and apparently never fully grasped the use of a third appeal.

[17] This does not deny that in some cases the Japanese quite consciously abrogated the courts' judicial powers, as in the case of the *forum privilegiatum*. See generally A. A. Zorab, *De Japanse bezetting van Indonesië* (Leiden: Universitaire Pers, 1954), ch. 4; O. Kartodirdjo, "De rechtspraak op Java en Madoera tijdens de Japansche bezetting 1942-1945," *Indisch Tijdschrift van het Recht* 156 (1947): 14; R. D. Kollewijn and R. van Dijk, "Staatsrecht en rechterlijke organisatie van Indonesië in overgangstijd" (Leiden: mimeo, 1948), p. 23.

of justice in all courts. The first substantial regulation with respect to the Supreme Court, Law no.7/1947, stated that the Court shall "supervise the administration of justice in any court throughout Indonesia" [art.2(1)] and ensure a "proper and fair administration of justice" [art.2(2)]. It quite clearly abolished the Japanese system under which the former *Raden van Justitie* had developed into supreme judicial tribunals in their own right. The Official Explanation to the law states that "such a situation works to the detriment of a unified administration of justice, and of the ultimate goal of a united Indonesia."[18] These ideas were reiterated in the later Law no.19/1948 (art.55).

While the Supreme Court was restored as head of the judiciary and guardian of the unified administration of justice, the essence of the Japanese reforms was retained, which would eventually ease the way for simplifying the complex colonial jurisdiction of the Supreme Court. The Court's judicial tasks as first instance and appellate court were, almost by implication, becoming redundant, a fact apparent even during the Japanese Occupation.

The simplification did not materialize during the revolution, which, on the contrary, witnessed a partial restoration of colonial complexity. Thus, Law no.7/1947 explicitly retained the Court's power to determine jurisdiction conflicts between lower courts as first and final instance tribunals (art.5). Law no.19/1948 proposed reinstating the Supreme Court as a court of first instance, full appeal, and cassation. As a first instance court, the Supreme Court would decide *forum privilegiatum* cases against senior state officials (art.60) and conflicts of jurisdiction between appeal courts (art.58); as an appellate court, it would hear appeals in all cases that had been decided by the appeal courts as first instance tribunals (art.59); while, finally, it would also function as an institute of cassation (art.61-62).

If on the surface this 1948 law went some way toward restoring the prewar complexity of the judicial system, on closer inspection important differences are manifest, pertaining particularly to the appellate responsibility of the Supreme Court. The law formulates this task so broadly that it makes it look like a copy of the colonial system, but in reality the Court's role was much more limited than it had been previously. In colonial times, the appeal courts as *Raden van Justitie* were the principal first instance tribunals for Europeans. The sheer volume of these cases meant that the appellate task of the colonial Supreme Court constituted its main judicial power. According to Law no.19/1948, however, the appeals courts only served as first instance tribunals for jurisdictional conflicts of the lower courts [art.47(1)]. Thus, the Supreme Court's appellate task was reduced in importance and essentially restricted to a minor procedural issue. The 1948 law, then, in effect abolished appeal as a means by which the Supreme Court might ensure a unified administration of justice. The result was an important change in emphasis: whereas in colonial times the Court's primary task was in the field of appeals, after independence this task became residual, and cassation took its place.

The most important aspect of the 1947/1948 legislation is perhaps that it greatly extended the Supreme Court's cassation net. Not only did Japanese and subsequent reforms firmly place the former *landraad* courts in a hierarchical relationship to the Supreme Court, more important, perhaps, they redefined the

---

[18] Official Explanation Law no.7/1947, Koesnodiprodjo, *Himpunan Undang2, Peraturan2, Penetapan2 Pemerintah Republik Indonesia 1947* (Jakarta: S. K. Seno, 1951), p. 17.

cassation instrument itself with the effect that unwritten law might be subject to cassation. Thus, cases involving traditional *adat* law, and eventually Islamic law (which was not mentioned in the 1947-1948 statute) became actionable before the Supreme Court.

According to Law no.19/1948 art.63, a case could be reviewed on the grounds that a "statute had not been applied or had been erroneously effected" (*kesalahan dalam melaksanakannya*). This article was apparently inspired by developments on the Dutch side of the political divide. In 1947, the Dutch reconstituted the colonial Supreme Court in the territories they controlled.[19] The constituting regulation reflected ideas that had been voiced in the Netherlands as early as 1909, to the effect that limiting cassation to statutory law was overly restrictive.[20] The purpose of cassation was to ensure unity of the law, it was argued, and law was not to be found in statute alone. This argument reflects the demise of the French revolutionary idea that legislation is to be seen as the sole expression of the law, and it affirms the lawmaking function of the judiciary.

It is essentially on the basis of these ideas that the 1947 Dutch statute concerning the Supreme Court in Indonesia states that henceforth cassation will no longer respond to violations of a statute (*wet*), but to violations of the law (*recht*); this was a revolutionary break with the law on cassation that had been prevalent in the Netherlands to that day. It is an example, by no means unique, of the way in which developments in the colony anticipated developments in Europe, as the Netherlands changed its rules on cassation along the same lines only in 1963,[21] and France's similar revisions of it own legal system occurred as late as 1979.[22] Pursuant to the Official Explanation of the 1947 law, cassation had to ensure uniformity in the application of legislation, as well as uniformity of law created through precedent by court decisions.[23] The effect of this regulation was that from 1947 onward there were no longer any conceptual obstacles to extending cassation to cases of indigenous Indonesian *adat* law and indeed of Islamic law, and, in fact, a special *adat* chamber was instituted in the colonial Supreme Court in 1947.

Art.63 of Indonesian Law no.19/1948 was a literal copy of the Dutch law, leading commentators to conclude that the Indonesians now also had adopted the view that cassation should not be limited to statute only.[24] This development was important not merely in the conceptual leap it represented, but also in its considerable practical effect. The drive to unify the judicial organization, discussed in the previous chapter, effectively limited the appeals task of the Supreme Court to cassation. After the 1948 regulation widened the scope of the cassation concept, decisions from any court could come up for cassation, a development that strengthened the Supreme Court relative to the lower courts.[25]

---

[19] S.1947:20, *Bijblad* 15077.

[20] Advice from E. N. de Brauw to the Dutch Bar Association, *Handelingen van de Nederlandse Juristen Vereniging* (1909), pt. 1, pp. 222, 246; pt. 2, p. 187; D. J. Veegens, *Cassatie in Burgerlijke Zaken* (Zwolle: Tjeenk Willink, 1989), pp. 56-58.

[21] Law 20 June 1963 Dutch S.272.

[22] art.604 Nouvelle Code de Procédure Civile replaces the much vaunted "*loi* "with "*règle de droit.*" R. Perrot, *Institutions judiciaires* (Paris: Montchrestien, 1992), p. 181.

[23] Bijblad 15077.

[24] J. J. de Jongh, *Het nieuwe cassatie instituut*, p. 26.

[25] R. D. Kollewijn and R. van Dijk, "Staatsrecht en rechterlijke organisatie," p. 31.

(c) After Independence: Appeal Supplanted by Cassation

It is not surprising that the Republic stayed this course as it sought to define the nation's legal system after the transfer of sovereignty. Both the 1949 and 1950 Constitutions emphasize that the Supreme Court's goal is to ensure uniformity in the administration of justice,[26] a charge most clearly formulated in the important Law no.1/1950 on the Supreme Court (art.12 jo.art.16).[27]

Under this law, the Court retained its first instance jurisdiction both in conflicts of jurisdiction [art.14(I)][28] and as regards the *forum privilegiatum*.[29] The old colonial regulation stating that the court could adjudicate conflicts arising out of the seizure of ships and airplanes was also retained [art.14(II)]. Its appellate jurisdiction was reduced ever further. As the Republic was determined to root out the indigenous administration of justice, the Dutch reference to the residents' courts was not adopted, and the appellate jurisdiction was restricted so that it only called for review of arbitral awards (art.15). This effectively left cassation as the only appellate instrument by which the Supreme Court could attempt to assure uniformity in the administration of justice (art.16-21).

The 1959 reinstatement of the 1945 Constitution strengthened the cassation role of the Court and further simplified its jurisdiction. Law no.13/1965 on the Supreme Court emphasized that its prime role remained that of safeguarding uniformity in the administration of justice (art.47). But the return to the 1945 Constitution was deemed to have abolished the *forum privilegiatum*. In 1950, the prominent legal scholar, Soepomo, had argued that the unitary republic's replacement of the federal structure had removed the basis for such special jurisdictions;[30] during the parliamentarian period this view was not accepted, however, and indeed the *forum privilegiatum* was extended to new categories of state officials, such as members of the Constitutional Committee (*Konstituante*).[31] When the 1945 Constitution was reintroduced, this situation was reconsidered, and in 1959 the Supreme Court decided that the special procedure no longer existed.[32] As a result, the sole first instance jurisdiction remaining with the Court was the adjudication of jurisdictional conflicts (art.48). Moreover, the Supreme Court's appellate task was now fully abolished, as even arbitral awards were no longer liable for appeal before that Court, so that its only function remained cassation (art.49-50). So, from

---

[26] art.153 Federal Constitution; art.105 Provisional Constitution.

[27] The specific federal powers of the Supreme Court under the Federal Constitution will not be considered in detail here, as they had little practical effect because the Constitution was soon replaced and the federal system abolished.

[28] The Court itself qualified art.14 insofar that jurisdictional conflicts between first instance courts would be dealt with by the appeals court. Mahkamah Agung Regulation (PERMA) no.2/1954. E. Bonn, "Enkele aantekeningen op de wet op de Hoge Raad van Indonesia," *Mededelingen van het Documentatiecentrum voor Overzees Recht* 5 (1955): 1.

[29] art.106 Federal Constitution, Emergency Law no.29/1950, Law no.22/1951.

[30] R. Soepomo, *Undang-undang Dasar Sementara Republik Indonesia* (Jakarta: Noordhoff-Kolff, 1954), p. 136.

[31] Law no.23/1956; S. Mertokusumo, *Sedjarah peradilan dan perundangan-undangan di Indonesia sedjak 1942 dan apakah kemanfaatnja bagi kita bangsa Indonesia* (Bandung: Kilatmadju, 1971), p. 80.

[32] *Hukum dan Masjarakat* 3-6 (1960), p. 187; Mertokusumo, *Sedjarah peradilan*, p. 157.

its hybrid colonial origins, characterized by a varied jurisdiction, the Supreme Court had by 1965 evolved into what was essentially a court of cassation, no more and no less.

Under the New Order, this transformative process was pushed ahead. The Supreme Court was firmly ensconced in its principal cassation task of ensuring a uniform administration of justice in the lower courts, a principle reiterated time and again in the new legislation.[33] Currently, under the present legislation (art.28-30 Law no.14/1985), this remains its principal task, while its first instance jurisdiction has been limited to jurisdictional conflicts (art.33 Law no.14/1985) and such exceptional cases as the seizure of foreign vessels (art.78). In recent years, the Court has acquired other first instance powers, such as the review of foreign arbitral awards,[34] and judicial review of regulations having general effect other than Acts of Parliament.[35] These effectively restored some diversity to the Court without affecting its principal task of cassation. In 1979, the Supreme Court also began to hear appeals from the religious courts, capping the process by which the cassation instrument was broadened to include all courts.[36]

2. THE CASSATION MECHANISM

In view of its importance, it is worth looking more closely at the cassation instrument and the way in which it evolved after independence.

A closer study of the application of cassation will show that the Supreme Court deliberately and consistently sought to reduce and abolish procedural barriers that might hamper the flow of cases to the Court. This pattern supports the argument that the Supreme Court used the cassation instrument to extend its control over the lower courts. Therefore, while the organizational reforms provided the necessary infrastructure for appeal, the procedural reforms of cassation used this infrastructure to "pull up" cases from the lower courts to the Supreme Court.

---

[33] art.10 Law no.14/1970.

[34] Regulation of the Mahkamah Agung (PERMA) no.1/1990 states in art.3(4) that foreign arbitral awards can only be executed in Indonesia after an enforcement order (*exequatur*) has been obtained from the Supreme Court.

[35] Regulation of the Mahkamah Agung (PERMA) no.1/1993 in fact creates a separate jurisdictional venue by allowing claims to nullify regulations other than Acts of Parliament (*Undang-undang*) to be presented directly to the Supreme Court. See also *Forum Keadilan*, 8 July 1993, pp. 5, 25.

[36] The administrative courts established in 1991 fitted in smoothly with a well-established system.

(a) Basic Characteristics and Historical Origins[37]

Historically, cassation originated in France, from where the Netherlands acquired it, then passed it on to their colony, whence it was adopted by the Indonesian Republic. Nevertheless, as the geographical distance from its conceptual roots increased, the concept of cassation underwent important changes. Filtered by the Dutch legal tradition and the colonial condition, from the start cassation in the colony differed in some notable ways from its French original. Briefly, the chief difference was that colonial cassation had more muscle than its European antecedents.

The essence of the French antecedents can be summarized as follows.[38] The legal reforms of the French Revolution were based on the idea that the law ought to be codified so that it would be uniform and applied equally to everyone. A logical extension of this idea was that a tribunal be instituted to ensure the uniform application by the courts of that codified law. If the courts applied codified law incorrectly, this tribunal would quash these decisions, hence the word *cassation*.[39]

Originally this tribunal was set up as part of the legislature—or at least *not* as part of the judiciary.[40] In this way, the legislature meant to ensure its supremacy as the sole source of the law. Moreover, on a more fundamental level, the ideas on the

---

[37] Cassation is traditionally contrasted with the Anglo-Saxon, and notably American, system of full appeal (subject to certworthiness and other appeal barriers, of course). See for instance J. H. Merryman, *The Civil Law Tradition* (Stanford: Stanford University Press, 1985), p. 39. The US system of full appeal is more open than cassation, or so are we led to believe. This may be true in theory, but legal and institutional realities are different. It would go beyond the ambit of this study to deal with this matter in depth, but suffice it to point out here that the actual use of appeal barriers in the supposedly less restrictive US appeal system actually pushes that system more in the direction of a cassation system than is generally believed, and in some respects makes it even more restrictive. In fact, the US Supreme Court shows a propensity to deny cert not just in cases that are "fact-specific" (and thus apply cassation rules), but also in cases that are "law-specific" or in other respects fail to respond to the somewhat hazy standards demanded by US Justices for certworthy cases. See H. W. Perry, *Deciding To Decide: Agenda Setting in the US Supreme Court* (Cambridge: Harvard University Press, 1991), p. 223 on the strong tendency of the court to refuse cases that are "fact specific." See also ibid., p. 230 on "percolation," which refers to the US Supreme Court practice of allowing a case that raises an issue of law to pass if it has not been fleshed out enough in the lower courts, in the hopes that a clearer case raising the same issue will come along later. Perry incidentally also refutes the oft-heard argument that the typical cassation court by definition is more overburdened than, say, the US Supreme Court, in that the former must take all cases coming its way while the latter can refuse cases. (In fact, the US Supreme Court rejects more than 95 percent of the cases coming its way. See ibid., p. 22.) The relatively small number of cases decided by the US Supreme Court compared to most cassation courts suggests that the US Court actually has more time on its hands. Nevertheless, US figures obscure the fact that the 95 percent of cases rejected must all be considered and advised upon by the full Court. The certworthiness procedure is, in fact, very burdensome to the Court, and this burden is not represented in the number of cases it actually decides. It is similar to the summary dismissals in cassation courts, where cases are rejected on very weak grounds for violating procedural rules, such as rules having to do with fact specificity, insufficient evidence, and the like.

[38] See generally P. Bellet, A. Tunc, A. Touffait, *La Cour judiciaire suprême* (Paris: n.p., 1978); Perrot, *Institutions judiciaires*; G. Picca and L. Cobert, *La Cour de Cassation* (Paris: PUF, 1986); Veegens, *Cassatie in Burgerlijke Zaken*; Merryman, *Civil Law Tradition*.

[39] From the basic *casser*, meaning to break or quash.

[40] In the words of the famous Revolutionary Decree of 27 November–1 December 1790: Il y aura un Tribunal de cassation établi auprès du Corps législatif (art.1).

separation of powers prevailing in France at the time stated that it was the function of the legislature to make the law, and of the judiciary to apply it. Consequently, the judiciary was denied any lawmaking function, and thus could not issue regulations of a general nature[41] nor engage in the interpretation of statute. Its tasks were limited to ascertaining the relevant facts in an individual case[42] and applying the law. Decisions to restrict the Tribunal de Cassation in this manner sprang from the high expectations at the time that codification might provide for each and every case to come before the courts.[43] Moreover, in France the pre-revolutionary courts, *parlements*, had revealed themselves to be bastions of conservatism and inequality, and the new order was determined to abolish their role.

As a result, the powers of the tribunal were limited: it could quash court decisions on grounds of violating the law, but was bound by the facts as ascertained by the courts. Moreover, it could not decide the dispute itself, since that was a judicial function. For that reason, after consideration by the Tribunal de Cassation, decisions would be sent back for reconsideration and adjudication to the judiciary (*renvoi*).

In France, the role of the Tribunal de Cassation and its decisions have changed since the French Revolution. In the course of the nineteenth century, the tribunal moved from the legislature to the judiciary and was in fact renamed the *Cour de Cassation*. Moreover, as reality took over and the shortcomings of codification became evident, the lawmaking role of the judiciary could not be denied. Initially, the court could only quash decisions on grounds of erroneous interpretation of the law, but by 1837 it could impose its own legislative interpretation ("imposer l'interprétation de la loi"). This established the foundation of the authority of the court's decisions, *jurisprudence*. This authority increased with time, and at present the authority of *Cour de Cassation* decisions effectively can be compared to that of superior courts in Anglo-Saxon countries, notwithstanding formal differences.[44]

Nevertheless, the basis of the concept of cassation was not fundamentally affected by these developments. Cassation is still essentially based on these two points: (i) appeal is based on questions of (codified) law and not of fact, which must be determined by the lower courts; (ii) cases must be referred back to these lower courts for final adjudication.[45]

---

[41] Law of 16-24 August 1790 (art.12): Ils ne pourront faire des règlements ...

[42] In the wording of Cambacérès: "Aujourd'hui, il n'y aura que des questions de fait, faciles à saisir, plus faciles encore à terminer." Quoted in Veegens, *Cassatie in Burgerlijke Zaken*, p. 8.

[43] In the words of Merryman, it was believed that codification could be made judge-proof, as in fact Frederick the Great in Prussia adopted a Code containing 17,000 articles in a sublime effort to exclude any judicial interpretation. Merryman, *Civil Law Tradition*, p. 39.

[44] The most notable formal difference is that *Cour de Cassation* decisions do not constitute a source of law. Thus, in the *renvoi* procedure, the lower court was technically not bound by the decision of the *Cour de Cassation*, and it was possible for the same case to come up for retrial by the *Cour de Cassation* on identical grounds, a not infrequent occurrence in the early nineteenth century. In 1837, this situation was remedied to the effect that should the same case come up for retrial before the *Cour de Cassation* on identical grounds, the court would decide it in plenary session and the lower court would be bound by that decision.

[45] This does not deny the considerable developments in the grounds of appeal and in the nature of the *renvoi* procedure in France, as well as in the organization of the court itself. The grounds of cassation, defined as violation of the law or procedure, have been extended. Art.131-135 and 627 Nouveau Code de Procédure Civile have qualified the *renvoi* in the sense that the Court

The Netherlands adopted cassation during the Napoleonic period.[46] With its different legal background, the country did not adopt the strict French interpretation of the concept, except during the first turbulent years after its introduction. In fact, cassation remained a subject of debate until the beginning of the twentieth century, and on several occasions there were serious efforts to abolish cassation altogether and replace it with full appeal. Such a change would allow the Supreme Court to review both facts and law and decide the case by itself. There was general agreement that in any individual case it was preferable to go for full appeal by the more senior, and presumably experienced, judges. The reason for retaining cassation was, then, because it seemed the best method of achieving the Supreme Court's ultimate goal of ensuring a uniform administration of justice. With time, debate ceased, and indeed nowadays the Dutch Supreme Court (*Hoge Raad*) seems stronger than ever.

Until World War II, the essence of the Dutch concept of cassation followed the French ideas. Like the French, the Dutch Supreme Court could only review cases on points of (codified) law and not on the facts, which were left to the lower judges to determine.[47] A major difference which soon became apparent between the two countries concerned the *renvoi* procedure, which the Netherlands all but abandoned. In 1838, the Dutch Supreme Court was allowed to decide a case by itself unless it concerned a violation of proper forms.[48] The Supreme Court's ability to give a final decision in a legal dispute itself, and thus impose its interpretation of the law on all parties, constituted a recognition of the Court's lawmaking capacity and enhanced the function of its decisions as authoritative statements of the law.

The colony of the Netherlands Indies adopted the Dutch concept of cassation, further strengthening the position of the Supreme Court.[49] It copied the Dutch system of review of the (codified) law[50] and, like the Netherlands, limited the necessity of referring cases back to the lower courts after cassation.[51] However, the

---

need no longer refer a case back to the lower courts if it can apply the proper rule on the facts as ascertained by the lower judge.

[46] See generally Veegens, *Cassatie in Burgerlijke Zaken*.

[47] art.99 *Rechterlijke Organisatie* (S.1847:23) "verkeerde toepassing of schending der wet"; art.105 *Rechterlijke Organisatie*.

[48] art.106 *Rechterlijke Organisatie* (S.1847:23).

[49] See generally J. J. de Jongh, *Het nieuwe cassatie instituut*.

[50] art.171 *Rechterlijke Organisatie* (S.1847:23): "The colonial Supreme Court shall quash, upon a request in cassation, the acts and decisions of the *Raden van Justitie* (. . .) 1. on grounds of violating proper forms as provided for by law on pain of nullity; 2. on grounds of erroneous application and violation of legislative provisions; 3. on grounds of exceeding powers; 4. on grounds of lack of powers (incompetence)."

[51] art.173 *Rechterlijke Organisatie* (S.1837:23): "If a decision of a court has been quashed on grounds of erroneous application and violation of legislative provisions, of exceeding powers, or of lack of powers (incompetence), the colonial Supreme Court shall decide the case itself . . . "; art.174: "If a decision of a court has been quashed on grounds of not respecting proper forms prescribed on pain of nullity, the Supreme Court shall issue an instruction to recommence proceedings . . . , which instruction can be effected by the Supreme Court itself which then shall decide the case, or by the original judge . . . ."; art.175: "If the decision of a court has been quashed on grounds of lack of powers (incompetence), the colonial Supreme Court shall refer the case to the competent judge." It seems that practical reasons were important in limiting *renvoi* in the colony, as the costs and the administrative burdens of referring a case heard in cassation from the *Raad van Justitite* Batavia to Semarang would be difficult to effect. A. J. Immink, *De rechterlijke organisatie van Nederlandsch-Indië* (The Hague: Stemberg, 1882), p. 410.

colonial Supreme Court could in addition instruct an investigation into the facts of the case if it thought this to be necessary. The case would then come up for retrial by the colonial Supreme Court on the basis of these new facts.[52] This power was limited to criminal cases, though it had originally been intended to cover civil cases as well. The reason for this distinction rested in the fact that the colonial government thought it unnecessary to take note of new facts when adjudicating civil cases in cassation, whereas the same could not be said for criminal cases. In criminal cases, the measure of punishment within the framework of the law depends on the relevant facts and differs in accordance with the way each article of criminal legislation qualified liability. If the colonial Supreme Court were to quash the decision of the lower court and find someone criminally liable on different grounds, the relevant facts would have to be reascertained to decide the measure of punishment.[53] In the field of criminal law, therefore, cassation in the colony approached full appeal.[54] Moreover, as we have seen, during the turbulent revolutionary period, the Dutch introduced a new statute that no longer limited appeal by the colonial Supreme Court to statute only, but extended it to uncodified law.

The Indonesian Republic adopted the diluted colonial cassation concept, which had effectively abolished *renvoi* and blurred the distinction between law and fact questions in criminal matters. It granted greater authority to Supreme Court decisions as a source of law, effectively giving them precedential value akin to those in the Anglo-Saxon legal tradition. This made the Supreme Court's control over lower courts stronger than in the original French situation, where, as we have seen, lower courts could blithely ignore superior decisions in *renvoi* procedures. In addition, the Supreme Court's authority to demand a further fact-search much reduced its dependence on lower court fact finding.

(b) Cassation After Independence

This significant departure from European cassation procedures was further reinforced after independence by a reduction in procedural barriers.

(i) Haphazard Legislative Development, the "Magic Formula" & Two Basic Features

Since the transfer of sovereignty, there have been only three laws which have covered cassation in Indonesia. The most influential of these was the first law on the subject, Law no.1/1950. The period of its formal validity from 1950 until 1965 was probably the most formative for cassation. Its active influence, however,

---

[52] art.173(2) colonial *Rechterlijke Organisatie* as distinct from art.105 Dutch *Rechterlijke Organisatie*. J. J. de Jongh, *Het nieuwe cassatie instituut*, p. 14.

[53] This does not exclude the possibility that the colonial Supreme Court could hold a suspect criminally liable on the same grounds as the lower court and that if the facts were sufficiently clear, the Supreme Court would proceed to final decision. See, for instance, HGH 4 March 1880, *Indisch Weekblad van het Recht* 875, quoted in Immink, *De rechterlijke organisatie*, p. 409.

[54] Although it must be pointed out that the colonial Supreme Court could not review the facts that had already been established by the lower instances, cf. art.326 colonial Code of Criminal Procedure.

extended beyond that period. The law was repealed with the introduction of Law no.13/1965 (art.70), which focused on the function and organization of the Supreme Court. As will become apparent, however, the grounds of cassation were essentially identical to those outlined in the 1950 law. What is most important here, no rules of procedure were provided for, as the Department of Justice failed to follow up with procedural rules as envisioned in art.49 of the 1965 law. If it was to hear cases at all, then, the Supreme Court was compelled to apply the rules of procedure from the previous 1950 law, notwithstanding the fact that this law had been explicitly repealed. Consequently the Supreme Court informed all courts of the land that the relevant procedural rules of the 1950 law still applied.[55] From 1965, all Supreme Court decisions included the "Supreme Court formula" stating that, in the absence of new rules on procedure, the old 1950 law was to be applied.[56] The basic law on the judiciary (no.14/1970) further muddied the waters. This law repealed the 1965 law, but, like that law, did not provide for either procedure or grounds of cassation. Following up on its earlier steps, the Supreme Court decided to adhere to the 1950 law and changed its "magic formula" accordingly.[57] Consequently, with respect to procedure, the 1950 law effectively remained in force until the new Supreme Court Law no.14/1985.[58] At least as regards cassation, this law did not constitute a major

---

[55] Mahkamah Agung Circular Letter (SEMA) no.3/1965 to the effect that the cassation rules for civil (art.112 pass. Law no.1/1950) and criminal cases (art.121 pass. Law no.1/1950) still applied. Soedirjo, *Kasasi dalam perkara perdata* (Jakarta: Akademika Pressindo 1983), pp. 15-16.

[56] This formula ran as follows: "Considering first, that even though art.70 of Law no.13/1965 repeals the previous law on the Mahkamah Agung, nevertheless because Chapter IV of the aforementioned law only provides for the constitutional function, organization, and powers of the Mahkamah Agung, and in the absence of legislation providing for procedural rules as envisioned under art.49(4) of this law, the Mahkamah Agung holds the view that art.70 of the aforementioned law should be interpreted to the effect of not applying to the entire 1950 law of the Mahkamah Agung, but only as regards the constitutional function, organization, and powers of the Court, so that matters pertaining to the rules of procedure in cassation are still to be found in the law on the Mahkamah Agung." All fifty-three Supreme Court decisions included in one of the first publications to record court decisions after 1965 have this formula: see *Yurisprudensi Indonesia* (1969). R. Subekti, *Kekuasaan* Mahkamah Agung R.I. (Bandung: Alumni, 1980), p. 4.

[57] The somewhat convoluted formula now ran as follows: "Considering first that the enactment of Law no.14/1970 on the Basic Principles of the Judiciary repeals Law no.19/1964 on the Principles of the Judiciary, and that the law of procedure for cassation as meant in art.49(4) Law no.13/1965 until now has not materialized, the Mahkamah Agung deems it necessary to emphasize once again the law of procedure to be used; that regarding this matter on grounds of art.40 Law no.14/1970, art.70 Law no.13/1965 must be read in such a manner, that Law no.1/1950 is not repealed in its entirety, but only insofar as covering matters which have been provided for in Law no.13/1965, except when conflicting with Law no.14/1970." This formula incidentally became standard only in 1976, until which year the Mahkamah Agung persisted in using the old formula with its references to laws long suspended and repealed. Mahkamah Agung no.1225K/Sip/1976 dated 30 October 1976, *Yurisprudensi Indonesia* (1976): 449. The formula began to fall into disuse in the two years predating the new i Law no.14/1985, which was to make it superfluous. Thus, in the course of 1984, some Court decisions still refer to the formula (Mahkamah Agung no.588K/Sip/1983 dated 28 May 1984), but others disregard it (Mahkamah Agung no.20PK/Perd/1983 dated 29 September 1984). See generally *Yurisprudensi Indonesia* (1984-II). By 1985, the formula had largely disappeared (for an exception see Mahkamah Agung no.277K/Pdt/1984 dated 29 May 1985, *Yurisprudensi Indonesia* [1985-I]: 105).

[58] Neither the formula used nor the literature on the subject is fully clear as to whether the Supreme Court reverted back to the 1950 law merely with regard to procedure of cassation, or

break with previous law, as it was not meant to introduce important changes but merely to end the twisted situation resulting both from the 1965 and the 1970 laws.

It may be pointed out here as a prelude that all Indonesian statutes lack two important restrictive features that prevail in most appeal systems. The first is that none of the laws provide for an appeal barrier of material interest. Only Law no.7/1947, which, as we have seen, never came into effect, restricted appeals in cassation to claims in excess of 200 Rupiah—an amount which corresponded to approximately US$100 at the time. Subsequent legislation did not repeat this article, nor for that matter did the Supreme Court provide for this, as it might have. Even if the 1947 law were to be applied on this score, devaluation measures and inflation of the Indonesian currency obviously would later have rendered it meaningless, as (the Supreme Court vice-chairman) Purwoto Gandasubrata pointed out in 1982:

> The problem is that according to a 1947 law any case with a material value in excess of 200 Rupiah can appeal. And if appeal is allowed, well then naturally cassation must be allowed also. But then there are no cases valued at less than 200 Rupiah.[59]

As a result, any case, irrespective of how trivial the actual claim at issue, can be appealed right up to the Supreme Court (within cassation rules).

The second restrictive feature missing in Indonesian statutes is that there is no mandatory party representation by an advocate when proceeding before the Supreme Court. Mandatory party representation did exist before the colonial Supreme Court, but when Indonesia opted for the HIR (Herziene Inlandsch [later Indonesisch] Reglement, Indonesian Code of Procedure) as the national procedural law during the Japanese administration, this removed that rule. This situation has been allowed to continue to the present day, notwithstanding the passage of four laws pertaining to the Supreme Court. As a result, parties can argue their own case before any Indonesian court, including the Supreme Court. Advocates' expert advice on whether to appeal or not, and more important perhaps, advocates' fees are not part of the process, and, as a result, obviously spurious claims and weak or insignificant cases are not weeded out.[60]

The absence of these barriers to appeal, needless to say, greatly facilitates access to the Supreme Court. The evident absurdity to which this can lead is best illustrated perhaps by the recent *Chinbuckle case* (1996).

---

also with regard to grounds of cassation. This is, however, largely an academic issue, since the grounds of cassation in the 1950 and the 1965 law are nearly identical. See for instance: H. M. Husein, *Kasasi sebagai upaya hukum* (Jakarta: Sinar Grafika, 1992), p. 45.

[59] *Tempo*, 6 November 1982, p. 12.

[60] Supreme Court chairman Seno Adji in 1977 specifically referred to the absence of mandatory party representation as a factor conducive to case flow: "One of the reasons for the Supreme Court backlog without a doubt is the fact that there is no mandatory legal representation, which reduces costs." *Catatan sementara rapat Komisi III DPR-RI dengan Ketua Mahkamah Agung (Seno Adji) no.02/Komisi III/78* dated 3 November 1977, p. 32. As pointed out by Bruinsma, advocacy can pay a significant role in reducing the caseload of the highest court by effectively blocking spurious or hopeless cases. F. Bruinsma, *Cassatierechtspraak in civiele zaken* (Zwolle: Tjeenk Willink, 1988), p. 39.

- The case arose out of the fact that a motorcyclist was fined by the police because, even though he wore the mandatory helmet, his chin-buckle was unfastened. The motorcyclist refused to pay the fine and was brought to court. The district court imposed a penalty of Rp.7.500 (being the equivalent of US$3 at the time). In the absence of an appeal barrier on material interest and of any requirement that the plaintiff be represented by a costly advocate, there was nothing to prevent him from taking the case all the way up to the Supreme Court—which he did.[61]

The mere fact that the *Chinbuckle case* was reported suggests that there is a growing awareness in Indonesia that the appeal system should not be burdened with trivial cases, unless perhaps they raise issues of legal principle. The evident absurdity of this case strengthened recent calls for instituting material interest appeal barriers.[62]

(ii) The Procedure of Cassation

The most important impact of the 1950 law was that it fundamentally altered the procedure of cassation by changing the way one entered a plea, with the effect of making this form of appeal available to each citizen. Under the old law, the claimant had to present the defendant with a summons within twenty-eight days of the final decision of the lower court. This summons had to be registered at the Supreme Court.[63] Under Law no.1/1950, this summons procedure was replaced with a procedure of request to be presented not at the Supreme Court itself, but at the court which last decided the case.[64] In 1963, the Supreme Court provided "in the interest of the parties before the court" that henceforth claimants would be allowed to deposit their claim of cassation before the court that decided the case at issue in first instance, that being the district court.[65] These provisions were continued under Law no.14/1985, which stated that requests for cassation must be presented to the original first instance (i.e., district) court,[66] a determination that further reduced traveling distances for litigants, and thus facilitated appeals.[67]

---

[61] *Forum Keadilan*, 15 January 1996.

[62] It was reported in 1992 that a Bill on Civil Procedure was being completed. According to the reports, the government and Parliament agreed on instituting appeal barriers along these lines. Thus, it was suggested that appeal be excluded on interlocutory judgments and on cases of small material value. So far the bill has yet to materialize. *Kompas,* 19 August, and *Kompas,* 12 October 1992. Note that the Dutch law on civil procedure excludes appeals on decisions from magistrates' courts unless they exceed the amount of $f2,500$, although these can be subject to review in cassation by the Supreme Court if issues of legal principle are involved (art.39 *Rechterlijke Organisatie*).

[63] *Burgerlijke Rechtsvordering,* Chapter 12 (S.1847:23).

[64] art.113. The claim must be presented within fourteen days of the relevant court decision to the court clerk.

[65] Regulation Mahkamah Agung (PERMA) no.1/1963. Still, the Court has decided that claims in cassation cannot be presented directly to the Supreme Court itself: Mahkamah Agung no.29K/Kr/1969, *Yurisprudensi Indonesia* (1969): 95.

[66] art.46(1). This must be effected within fourteen days.

[67] In a case predating the 1985 law, the Supreme Court has accepted a claim of cassation addressed directly to itself on grounds that the first instance court clerk had refused it. It may be

The aim of these measures was clearly to facilitate access to cassation. Under the new procedure, travel expenses were cut, and administrative difficulties and the related costs of going to Jakarta and presenting a claim in cassation before the Supreme Court itself were much reduced.

It is important to note here that Law no.1/1950 encountered considerable problems in its implementation. The problem was that the 1950 law required the lower courts to register the request and grounds of cassation, notify the other party, and send the whole file to the Supreme Court, a series of tasks beyond the capacity of the lower courts.[68] The law threatened to have a counterproductive effect, as cassation claims in many cases were presented to the wrong court, often resulting in their being struck down because they had failed to meet the deadline. Indeed, claims were sometimes presented to the Supreme Court directly, a procedure not countenanced by Law no.1/1950, on account of which such claims had to be dismissed.[69] Finally, it became apparent that after the Supreme Court had decided a case and sent it down to the lower courts for notification to the litigants, such notification often did not occur. The Supreme Court complained that litigants regularly asked about the progress of a case that had been decided long before, in some cases more than one year earlier.[70] It was clear that a strict application of Law no.1/1950 would force the Supreme Court to deny actions in massive numbers, and bring the justice machinery to a halt.

The Supreme Court sent out a constant stream of Circular Letters and Regulations in an effort to make the lower courts stick to procedure. Nevertheless, it was swamped by an unrelenting number of problems and forced to be lenient on procedure, accepting cases which technically should have been dismissed for basic procedural flaws. This problem continues to plague the Supreme Court to the present day. Law no.1/1950 facilitated appeals by lowering appeal barriers, in the process generating problems that pushed the Supreme Court toward lowering appeal barriers further, as we shall see.[71]

In a clear break with colonial law, in post-independence Indonesia the request of cassation can be exceedingly informal. Thus, it can be made either orally or in writing,[72] and the court clerk must register the claim and inform the opposing party

---

that this case has survived the 1985 law—Mahkamah Agung no.03K/Ag/1979 dated 14 March 1979, *Yurisprudensi Indonesia* 1 (1979): 270.

[68] For example, many requests were never reported to the defendant, or were presented to the Supreme Court without being properly registered by the lower court as required by law. Mahkamah Agung Circular Letter (SEMA) no.3/1951

[69] Mahkamah Agung Circular Letter (SEMA) no.1/1953.

[70] Mahkamah Agung Circular Letter (SEMA) no.2/1955 and Circular Letter (SEMA) no.1/1961. This does not even touch upon administrative fees, which were left unregulated by the 1950 law, a situation that created its own problems. See for instance, Mahkamah Agung Circular Letter (SEMA) no.1/1955 requiring advance down-payment on pains of dismissal of a claim, the size of which was determined anew in Regulation (PERMA) no.1/1959.

[71] The time limits are problematic. Art.115 states that the claimant in cassation must deposit his written plea of cassation within two weeks of his declared intention to appeal, while a defendant must also respond within two weeks [art.115(3)]. Within one month of the declaration to appeal, all relevant documents must be forwarded by the clerk of the lower court to the Supreme Court (art.116). This article cannot be effected if both parties avail themselves of the maximum period of time allowed to them by the law.

[72] The claimant in cassation, however, must present his written pleas with motivation within two weeks: see art.115 Law no.1/1950 and art.46(1) Law no.14/1985. Nevertheless, the

"as quickly as possible."[73] This procedure was tightened up somewhat under art.46(4) Law no.14/1985, which provided that the court clerk must inform the defendant of the action within seven days.[74] Within thirty days, the written pleas with motivation must be sent to the defendant [art.47(2)], who then has fourteen days to react [art.47(3)]. The case can be withdrawn at any moment until the final decision by the Supreme Court, in which case it is excluded from retrial (art.49).[75]

The Supreme Court is not bound by the grounds advanced by the claimant in his written pleas,[76] and can itself determine whether there has been a violation of law or forms, irrespective of the arguments forwarded by the claimant.[77] This provision smoothed the road of appeal to the Supreme Court from 1950 onwards, as cases could be presented to the Court with very little motivation.[78]

Supreme Court loosened statutory requirements facilitating appeals. It provided that if litigants are unable to write, the whole procedure can be conducted orally, with the district court clerk making a note of the grounds of cassation. Subekti, *Kekuasaan Mahkamah Agung R.I.*, p. 6.

[73] art.113 Law no.1/1950. Before 1985, the Supreme Court interpreted this to mean that the court clerk would be allowed to wait until the claimant had presented the written motivation of his claim; this gave the clerk fourteen days. Mahkamah Agung Circular Letter (SEMA) no.3/1951. It should be noted that this Circular Letter does not allow the court clerk to reject claims of cassation on the grounds that deadlines have expired, on grounds that "only the Supreme Court has the right to consider whether the claim has been presented within the proper time." A series of cases strictly uphold these time limits, despite the difficulties faced by claimants trying to respond within such brief periods of time. cf. Mahkamah Agung no.306K/Sip/1970 dated 23 December 1970 in C. Ali, *Yurisprudensi hukum acara perdata Indonesia* (Yogyakarta: Nur Cahaya, 1985), p. 19; Mahkamah Agung no.5K/Kr/1966, *Yurisprudensi Indonesia* (1968): 19; Mahkamah Agung no.33K/Kr/1966, *Yurisprudensi Indonesia* (1968): 16; Mahkamah Agung no.266K/Sip/1968 dated 27 November 1968, in A. T. Hamid, *Kamus yurisprudensi dan beberapa pengertian tentang hukum (acara) perdata* (Surabaya: Bina Ilmu, 1984), pp. 173-74.

[74] There is authority to the effect that the Supreme Court upholds this rule and denies actions in which the motivation was entered after the fourteen days' deadline. Retnowulan Sutianto and Iskandar Oeripkartawinata, *Hukum acara perdata dalam teori dan praktek* (Bandung: Mandar Maju, 1995), p. 172.

[75] This constitutes a change from the old law, where, once the case had been sent off to the Supreme Court, one could not withdraw from the procedure of cassation but had to fight it out until the end [art.114(1)] and 124(1) Law no.1/1950].

[76] art.119 Law no.1/1950.

[77] This rule, which in colonial times only concerned criminal cases (art.323 Criminal Procedure), after 1950 was extended to civil cases and has been upheld by the Supreme Court in several cases, such as Mahkamah Agung no.45K/Sip/1954 dated 9 May 1956, *Hukum* 3-4 (1957): 38; also Mahkamah Agung no.1381K/Sip/1971 referred to hereafter.

[78] Already in colonial times, it was general practice to present very summarily motivated criminal cases in cassation. J. J. de Jongh, *Het nieuwe cassatie instituut*, p. 169. This now also applied to civil cases. In fact, however, the Supreme Court reaffirmed on many occasions the provision in art.115 Law no.1/1950 that required motivation. See Mahkamah Agung no.639K/Sip/1970 dated 9 January 1971 [an unmotivated complaint in cassation must be dismissed for violating art.115 Law no.1/1950]; Mahkamah Agung no.468K/Sip/1971 dated 25 July 1973; Mahkamah Agung (no registration number) dated 22 October 1975 in C. Ali, *Yurisprudensi hukum acara perdata Indonesia* (Bandung: Armico, 1984), pt. 3, pp. 75, 313, 323; Mahkamah Agung no.8K/Sip/1967 dated 29 April 1967; Mahkamah Agung no.15K/Sip/1973 dated 7 February 1973 in Hamid, *Kamus yurisprudensi*, pp. 177, 178. See for criminal cases Mahkamah Agung Circular Letter (SEMA) no.1/1965, which states that if a claim in cassation is completely unmotivated it will be declared inadmissible before the Court, and for civil cases Mahkamah Agung Circular Letter (SEMA) no.3/1973, giving an inventory of the documents to

Because of the resultant steady stream of inadequately motivated cases,[79] in 1965 the Supreme Court instructed the district court clerks who registered the claims in cassation to inquire also regarding the motives of the litigant entering the claim. The clerk was also required to make a note of these objections, which, failing a written motivation, would be regarded as the motivation by the Supreme Court.[80] Subsequently, the Court was able to determine whether to quash a decision of a lower court and on what grounds. In addition, however, and unlike colonial law,[81] the law no longer allowed the Court to dismiss a claim in cassation on the mere ground that it was improperly motivated, even where in fact the lower court had erred in applying the law.[82]

In presenting his claim of cassation before the Supreme Court, the claimant had to rely upon the same facts and arguments used in proceedings before the lower courts. As can be seen from a number of Supreme Court cases, he could not advance new facts or evidence,[83] while the defendant could not change his line of argument.[84]

For its part, however, the Supreme Court does have the power to call for parties, witnesses, and the like to amplify the facts where deemed necessary [art.117 and 127 Law no.1/1950; art.50(1) Law no.14/1985]. The colonial Supreme Court held comparable power, but was tied to the evidence as determined by the lower courts and could only seek additional information in criminal cases.[85] Under the 1950 law, the Supreme Court is not bound even by the facts as determined by the lower courts. It can, at its own discretion and in both civil and criminal cases, itself call for evidence that might or might not override the evidence presented to it by

---

be sent to the Supreme Court by the lower court clerk and dealing extensively with the motivation.

[79] One of the problems with motivating claims for cassation was that by law such motivation was not required for the procedure before the court of appeal. See Subekti, *Kekuasaan Mahkamah Agung*, p. 17, who states that at least in his days it was regular practice for the sole motivation for a claim of cassation to be "I am not satisfied with the decision of the court of appeal." p. 18.

[80] Mahkamah Agung Circular Letter (SEMA) no.1/1965.

[81] art.425 *Burgerlijke Rechtsvordering*.

[82] This has not restrained the Court from dismissing spurious claims of cassation based on totally irrelevant motivations, cf. Mahkamah Agung no.19K/Sip/1973 dated 29 October 1975 in Hamid, *Kamus yurisprudensi*, p. 174.

[83] Mahkamah Agung no.51K/Sip/1955 dated 7 March 1956, *Hukum* 5-6 (1956): 87. See also Mahkamah Agung no.422K/Sip/1959 dated 28 November 1959; Mahkamah Agung no.93K/Sip/1969 dated 12 April 1969; Mahkamah Agung no.152K/Sip/1969 dated 28 November 1969—all of these laws are referred to in Soedirjo, *Kasasi dalam perkara perdata*, p. 50; Mahkamah Agung 18 April 1955, *Hukum* 1-2 (1957): 104; Mahkamah Agung dated 7 March 1956, *Hukum* 5-6 (1956): 87.

[84] Mahkamah Agung no.59K/Sip/1958 dated 7 February 1959.

[85] art.173 *Rechterlijke Organisatie*. Unlike the 1950 and 1985 laws, this article also limited those situations when additional evidence could be called to include (a) times when when it was necessary to determine the validity of the claim of cassation and (b) during the final decision. The restrictive role of the old Supreme Court in determining the facts was reaffirmed by the Court as late as 1948, when it stated that it could not determine the validity of facts as determined by lower courts. *Hooggerechtshof* dated 16 September 1948, in *Indisch Tijdschrift van het Recht* (1949), p. 86. J. E. Jonkers, Korte aantekening op de cassatieregeling in de "Wet op de Hoge Raad van Indonesië," Mededelingen van het Documentatiebureau voor Overzees Recht (1951), pp. 30-44.

the lower courts.[86] The 1985 law is formulated slightly more restrictively, stating that the case is decided by the Supreme Court on the basis of the documents forwarded to it by the lower courts. Only if the Supreme Court deems it necessary after consulting those documents can it call for additional information. Yet it evidently is not tied to the facts determined by the lower courts.

It is clear from the above that procedural restrictions have been loosened considerably. Yet the most important underlying development is that the basis on which the Supreme Court decides a case has moved from procedural issues to issues of substance. Thus, the Court hears even cases in which procedure has been violated, as long as the substance warrants their attention. In fact, it appears that in dealing with cases, Supreme Court judges nowadays routinely pass over procedural issues and move on directly to study the substance of a case. In 1995, one Supreme Court judge recounted how, in the working routine of most Supreme Court judges, procedure effectively had ceased to play any role whatsoever:

> I think I am one of the last Supreme Court judges who still looks at procedural issues. So I check whether the power of attorney is in order, time bars are respected and so on, and if they are faulty I just dismiss the case. Practically all other Supreme Court judges pass over these procedural issues. They directly study the Memory of Cassation and look at the substance of the case. Why, if these judges, or their clerks, are confronted with my approach, they are quite astonished.[87]

(iii) Object of Cassation

Legislation generally states that only *court* decisions are liable to cassation. This refers to decisions from the general courts. If decisions derive from some special jurisdiction, cassation is denied unless the law specifically allows for such cassation.[88] As a result, decisions emanating from quasi-judicial tribunals are not liable for cassation. Thus, there is long line of Supreme Court decisions stating that decisions from such tribunals must be rejected.[89] The restriction of cassation to judicial decisions also means that one cannot appeal decisions by other officers of the court, such as the court clerk.

---

[86] Regarding the 1950 law, it should be noted that Jonkers argues that while the law gives considerable leeway to the Supreme Court to determine the facts, the very essence of cassation implies that this function will be interpreted restrictively. J. E. Jonkers, Korte aantekening op de cassatieregeling in de "Wet op de Hoge Raad van Indonesië," (1951), pp. 35-36.

[87] Personal communication, 24 April 1995.

[88] Setiawan, "Several Notes Concerning the Indonesian Legal System: Role of Judges in Civil Court Proceedings," in *BW-Krant Jaarboek 1989: Een Internationale Code* (Arnhem: Gouda Quint, 1989), p. 53.

[89] Mahkamah Agung no.2K/Sip/1951 dated 7 June 1951, *Hukum* 1 (1951): 23 [Tribunal for House Rent—*Panitia Sewa-Menyewa*]; Mahkamah Agung no.42K/Sip/1952 dated 9 June 1952, *Hukum* 3 (1952): 27 [Commission for the Settlement of Labor Disputes—*Panitia Penyelesaian Perselisihan Perburuhan*]; R. Supomo, *Hukum atjara perdata pengadilan negeri* (Jakarta: Fasco, 1958), p. 171. It may be pointed out that, pursuant the Government Regulation no.49/1981, the power to decide housing problems was shifted from the above-mentioned tribunal back to the general first instance court, so that currently decisions affecting housing are again subject to cassation.

The law is not fully consistent on the type of court *decision* that is subject to cassation. Law no.1/1950 refers to decisions, findings, and acts, whereas later legislation merely refers to decisions and findings. The addition of the term "acts" in the 1950 law was an innovation.[90] The precise meaning of this term cannot be established,[91] a fact that doubtlessly contributed to its exclusion from the 1985 law, which refers merely to decisions and findings.

"Decisions" refers to court decisions in contradictory proceedings and "findings" to court decisions in unilateral actions. Findings need not be motivated. While the Supreme Court in various cases reviewed findings in cassation pursuant to the law,[92] findings concerning the administrative order within a court seem to have been generally denied.[93]

There are few restrictions regarding court decisions in contradictory proceedings. On the contrary, there is at least one case in which the Supreme Court determined that the entire decision of the lower court was subject to review, not just the part which had been advanced as subject to cassation.[94]

The law provides that a court decision can come up for cassation only after *all appeals have been exhausted,* unless, of course, the law provides otherwise [art.113(1) Law no.1/1950; art.43 Law no.14/1985]. After 1970, this has generally meant that cases must have gone through first instance (district court) and appellate instance (appeals court) before being submitted for cassation. Nevertheless, some exceptions apply.

First, only final judicial decisions can be submitted for cassation. Thus, the Supreme Court took the view in a number of cases that preparatory or interlocutory decisions of the court are excluded and can only be submitted to cassation together with the final decision.[95] Moreover, there is authority stating that decisions taken in a defendant's absence cannot be directly subjected to appeal or cassation by him.[96]

---

[90] Though it may be noted that the original Dutch text until 1912 also used the term. It was abolished with S.1912:253.

[91] J. J. de Jongh, *Het nieuw cassatie instituut*, pp. 158-59 refers to the sealing and unsealing of official documents as a possible action; also J. E. Jonkers, Korte aantekening op de cassatieregeling in de "Wet op de Hoge Raad van Indonesië," (1951), p. 38. In the words of Soedirjo, *Kasasi dalam perkara perdata*, p. 31: "The meaning of acts, besides decisions and findings, is altogether unclear." He refers to the possibility that in his decision a judge may recommend appeal erroneously (in cases where it is not allowed) as falling within this category.

[92] Such as Mahkamah Agung no.130K/Sip/1957 dated 5 November 1957, in R. Subekti, *Hukum adat Indonesia dalam yurisprudensi Mahkamah Agung* (Bandung: Alumni, 1978), p. 9; Mahkamah Agung no.951K/Sip/1974 dated 6 February 1975, *Yurisprudensi Indonesia* (1975): 638; Mahkamah Agung no.156K/Sip/1967 dated 1 May 1968, *Yurisprudensi Indonesia* (1969): 678.

[93] These concern findings such as the determination of the day of court session or the calling of witnesses. In several decisions, the Court denied review in cassation of findings required for the effectuation of a court decisions. Mahkamah Agung no.580K/Sip/1975 dated 12 May 1976, *Yurisprudensi Indonesia* (1975): 635.

[94] Mahkamah Agung dated 9 May 1956, *Hukum* 3-4 (1957): 38.

[95] Mahkamah Agung no.1400K/Sip/1974 dated 18 November 1975; Soedirjo, *Kasasi dalam perkara perdata*, pp. 33-34; Setiawan, *Aneka masalah hukum dan hukum acara perdata* (Bandung: Alumni, 1992), p. 359.

[96] art.190 *Herzien Indonesisch Reglement*. The defendant must first enter a plea of objection before the original first instance court, which will then reconsider the case.

Second, certain cases are excluded from appeal by special legislative provision, and hence can be submitted for cassation immediately after the first instance judgment. This is most evident in trademark law, for instance, and in bankruptcy proceedings (after 1998).[97] On other points, there is a certain ambivalence, notably with regard to general rules on appeal. While there actually is legislation stating that appeal in civil cases should be limited to the size of the claim, I would argue that these provisions have effectively become a dead letter and that cases must be submitted to the appellate courts regardless of the size of the claim.[98]

(iv) Grounds of Cassation

The grounds of cassation with some small changes have remained essentially the same throughout the Court's modern history. They can be briefly summarized as violation of the law, violation of forms, and transgression of judicial powers.

Violation of the law. The statutory wording on violation of the law is practically identical in all three laws (1950, 1965, 1985).[99] Pursuant to this provision, the Supreme Court can review cases only on points of law, not of fact. Statute consistently refers to the Supreme Court as a court of cassation, as indeed the Court itself retains its traditional reference to the lower court as the *iudex facti*—the fact judge. The law/fact distinction is intricate under even the best of circumstances. In Indonesia, however, this technical intricacy is overshadowed by two more fundamental developments. The first is that the definition of "law" was expanded, with the effect that issues that previously were "fact-specific" are nowadays "law-specific." The second is that, notwithstanding statutory restrictions, the law/fact distinction these days is largely ignored by the Supreme Court, and issues are accepted in appeal even if they are fact-specific.

We have already noted that the definition of the "law" concept was significantly broadened after independence. In large part, this was accomplished by extending its scope beyond statute to include non-codified law rules. But in its actual application, the Court acquired enormous freedom in defining "law" under

---

[97] Thus, conflicts pertaining to trademarks have to be submitted in cassation to the Supreme Court directly after the first instance judgment. Law no.21/1961 art.9,10,12 (excluding appeal). Mahkamah Agung no.455K/Sip/1972 dated 17 January 1973; Mahkamah Agung no.314K/Sip/1973 dated 31 December 1973. The new trademark law no.19/1992 art.52 and 53 is drafted along similar lines. C. B. Kaehlig and G. J. Churchill, *Indonesian Intellectual Property Law* (Jakarta: Tatanusa, 1993).

[98] Thus, art.96 *Rechterlijke Organisatie* (S.1847:23) jo. art.188 *Herzien Indonesische Reglement* and art.199 *Rechtsreglement Buitengewesten* (the procedural code for the Outer Islands) states that only claims exceeding the value of ƒ100 (guilders) or of indeterminate value are liable for appeal. See de la Porte, *Recht en Rechtsbedeling*, p. 120. Law no.20/1947 art.6 stated that on the islands of Java and Madura, no appeal should be allowed for civil claims exceeding Rp.100. Needless to say, with inflation and devaluation measures, these amounts have become so small as to render these legal provisions inoperative, quite aside from the fact that at least the latter regulation has been long since repealed. Soedirjo, *Kasasi dalam perkara perdata*, p. 32.

[99] Law no.1/1950 art.18(1): A rule of law has not been applied or if there is an error in its application; Law no.13/1965 art.51(c): The law has been erroneously applied or applicable law has been violated; Law no.14/1985 art.30(b): The law has been erroneously applied or applicable law has been violated. The differences between the 1950 law and the later laws can be attributed to the linguistic development of legal language in modern Indonesia, rather than to conceptual differences.

both statute and uncodified law, primarily because a lack of statutory clarity gave the Court great freedom in its application, while it also acquired broader powers to establish non-statutory law rules, notably in the field of *adat* law.

The main problem with modern Indonesian statutes is their general vagueness, which is most apparent in the modern legislator's reluctance to repeal unequivocally old statutes. This uncertainty generally casts doubts on the validity of statutes in Indonesian law, particularly those originating in the colonial period. These statues are already politically suspect for their colonial origins, and questions concerning their applicability are further complicated by their complexity and the language barrier, which have had the effect of both restricting and widening the Supreme Court's role. The restrictive effect is that the Court has been both unwilling and unable to resolve unclear legislative issues. We have noted in previous chapters that the Court lacks the power of constitutional review, that is, the power to quash Acts of Parliament (*Undang-undang*), so its authority in this area is in any case restricted.[100] For fear of treading on politically sensitive ground, the Supreme Court has been very reluctant even to review any legislative instrument, developing instead a practice in which a statute is quietly ignored rather than actively invalidated. Thus, in a long series of cases, the Supreme Court quietly dismissed the validity of the colonial Gold Clause Ordinance without once explicitly repealing it.[101] Instead, it allowed contractual liabilities to be secured against fluctuating money value with reference to the gold standard, which the Gold Clause Ordinance specifically aimed to prevent.[102] Such an approach is inadequate to resolve existing uncertainties, for it is not always evident whether the Court has chosen to ignore a certain statute because of judgments concerning its general validity or merely in response to specific aspects of the case under review.[103] At the same time, the lack of legislative clarity has given the courts considerable leeway in exercising their judicial tasks. The Supreme Court and the lower courts have a long tradition of determining which statute applies and what it says, not least as regards the extensive body of colonial law. Colonial law was marked by a variety of regulations pertaining to the same issues for different population groups. After the war and in the absence of legislative intervention, the

---

[100] Asikin Kusumah Atmadja, until recently one of the vice-chairmen of the Supreme Court, determined in 1967, when he was chairman of the Jakarta appeals court, that judges could review the validity of colonial legislation, regardless of whether these were Acts of Parliament or lower legislative instruments. Jakarta Appeals Court no.25/1967 PT Perdata dated 15 March 1967. Gouwgioksiong, "De rechtsontwikkeling in Indonesië na de souvereiniteitsoverdracht," *Weekblad voor Privaatrecht, Notaris-ambt en Registratie* (1968), no. 4982-4984. Nevertheless, this power was specifically denied by subsequent legislation, which stated that judicial review should be limited to legislative instruments lower than Acts of Parliament, and moreover restricted it to the Supreme Court alone. Law no.14/1970 art.26 affirmed in Law no.15/1985 art.31. This does not deny the fact that judges at all levels routinely ignore statute in the course of their normal line of work.

[101] Ordinance on the Gold Clause S.1937:585.

[102] For a review of the cases, see Sebastiaan Pompe, "Some Comments on the Depreciation of Currency Value in Indonesian Law," *Varia Peradilan* 6,70 (1991): 102.

[103] However, the general authority of a particular statute is obviously weakened as the number of cases that clearly contradict or fail to apply such a statute increases.

judiciary had to determine which colonial legislative provision to apply. As a result, it has a tradition of shaping legislation applicable in the country.[104]

The Supreme Court's flexibility in the application of statute is compounded by an even greater leeway in determining the applicability and meaning of non-statutory laws. This particularly applies to the traditional normative systems in the archipelago, the so-called *adat*, which, as we have seen, became subject to cassation during the revolutionary period.

The main characteristic of *adat* is that it is generally unwritten. In colonial times, the Dutch conducted an extensive and ongoing study and documentation of *adat* rules, but this practice was discontinued for the most part after independence. As a result, it is not quite clear how the existence of an *adat* rule is determined. Unlike customary rules in the Netherlands, for instance,[105] there seems to be no fixed test for this determination.

Aside from the factual opaqueness that makes it difficult to know whether an *adat* rule exists, the conceptual problem arises as to how the Supreme Court should review such rules. A variety of options present themselves: a claim based on *adat* could be reviewed by first checking on the *adat* rule's existence, in which case review amounts essentially to reascertaining the facts of a case; alternatively, such a claim could be reviewed by reference to statute or to basic principles of law, such as good faith, public order, or basic legal principles, such as equality before the law.

Supreme Court actions in this field suggest that it gradually shifted from reviewing a claim on the basis of *adat* (i.e., reascertaining the facts) to reviewing it on the basis of general principles of law. Inheritance law can serve as an example here. As Daniel Lev has pointed out,[106] the Supreme Court in the 1950s reasoned that a claim relying upon an *adat* rule had to be reviewed on the basis of that very rule, meaning that the validity of that rule had to be ascertained. As early as 1952, the Surabaya appeals court determined an *adat* rule on the basis of the judge's "own experience" and "pre-war *adat* law studies."[107] The same reasoning (though with different effect) is reflected in the concurrent Supreme Court cases. Thus, in 1953 the Court stated that a rule in *adat* law had to be established on the basis of clear and unequivocal evidence.[108] Although by the end of the decade the Court was softening this stance, it still based its power of cassation regarding *adat* rules essentially on reascertaining their factual validity. In 1959, it determined:

---

[104] Thus, the so-called "Kort Geding" (Summary Proceedings) provided for in the colonial code of civil procedure for Europeans (*Burgerlijke Rechtsvordering*) was declared inapplicable, and there is general agreement now in Indonesia that this is in fact the law, Mahkamah Agung no.145K/Sip/1953 dated 13 November 1954, *Hukum* 1-2 (1955): 56. At the same time, however, other instruments of the same code, such as review (*rekes-sipil*) were declared applicable—cf. First Instance Court Surabaya no.211/1953 dated 29 September 1953, *Hukum* 2-3 (1954): 88 and First Instance Court Jakarta no.1231/1955/G. dated 30 January 1957, *Hukum* 5-6 (1957): 113.

[105] Veegens, *Cassatie in Burgerlijke Zaken*, pp. 160-61.

[106] Daniel S. Lev, "The Supreme Court and *Adat* Inheritance Law in Indonesia," *The American Journal of Comparative Law* 11 (1962): 215.

[107] Ibid.

[108] *Hukum* (1955): 38; D. Lev, "The Supreme Court," p. 219.

> ... in Central Javanese society the feeling has begun to grow that because of the equal participation of women in the national struggles, it is just that a widow get half of the community property, so that this has become the *adat* law of Central Java.[109]

It was never fully established whether the court had called for evidence from the field to support its assertion regarding the actual content of the *adat*. But this seems unlikely, as the Supreme Court soon established that the rule applied not merely in Central Java, but throughout the land.[110]

As time passed, the Court's increasingly rare use of the term *adat* came to refer to some general concept that seemed to exist primarily in the minds of the Supreme Court judges, or the political establishment, with little relationship to the rules actually applied in the field. By 1960, the Supreme Court was dropping any reference to factual evidence, merely making such bland statements as " . . . according to the *adat* law in the whole of Indonesia, a widow is the executor of her husband's estate . . . "[111] The Court did not deny that this *adat* might be something altogether different from the regional *adat* laws that had been followed previously, in one instance admitting

> ... that according to the *adat* which still applies today in the Simalungun community, neither female children nor the widow can inherit from the deceased . . . but [that] according to the new *adat* inheritance law, a widow and female children do inherit.[112]

In later cases the Supreme Court refers increasingly to its own earlier decisions and indeed, "justice,"[113] as guidelines motivating current decisions. This suggests that the Supreme Court increasingly reviews *adat* cases on the basis of general principles of law, rather than on the mere factual issue as to whether the rule of *adat*, as asserted by the claimant, does in fact exist.

Islam differs in fundamental respects from *adat*. Its laws are written, and there is fair agreement on the meaning of some its basic rules. It is also politically much more sensitive. Treading carefully, the Supreme Court consistently refused to get involved in debates on substantive religious issues. Consequently, it never reviewed such cases concerning their interpretation of Islamic rules. Neither has it followed the reasoning in the *adat* cases, to consider whether religious rules somehow have changed, or if general principles of justice should prevail over such rules. Instead, and without exception, it has followed a legalistic course and reviewed cases coming up through the religious courts only on the basis of statute. Thus, there are several Supreme Court decisions to the effect that divorces must be conducted before

---

[109] *Hukum* 5-6 (1959): 54; D. Lev, "The Supreme Court," p. 217.

[110] R. Subekti and J. Tamara, *Kumpulan putusan Mahkamah Agung mengenai hukum adat* (Jakarta: Gunung Agung, 1961).

[111] Mahkamah Agung no.302K/Sip/1960 dated 2 November 1960, in A. Samsudin, Y. Anwar, and A. Sulaiman, *Yurisprudensi hukum waris* (Bandung: Alumni, 1983), p. 140.

[112] Mahkamah Agung no.284K/Sip/1975 dated 18 November 1976, in Samsudin et al., *Yurisprudensi hukum waris*, p. 314.

[113] Mahkamah Agung no.1589K/Sip/1974 dated 15 March 1978, ibid., p. 388.

a judge and polygamy be restricted pursuant to the marriage law and notwithstanding contrary Islamic rules.[114]

At the same time that it broadened the "law" concept and granted itself such leeway in defining and applying the law, the Court effectively began to deny the validity of the law/fact distinction altogether. This is a highly important development, which cuts at the very roots of the cassation instrument.

We have already seen that in procedural terms, the distinction between fact and law questions was significantly eroded by statute. The most notable point in this context is that the Supreme Court is no longer bound by the facts as established by the lower courts and may itself call for additional fact finding. Supreme Court practice further eroded the distinction, a development indicated by the minute number of cases the Court has dismissed on the grounds that they deal with questions of fact, rather than law.[115] Moreover, these cases concern relatively trivial issues, such as which of the two divorced parents is best equipped to look after the children[116] or whether a two-year-long argument is sufficient to dissolve a twenty-year-old marriage.[117]

This suggests that, despite unequivocal references to cassation in law, the Court in actual fact has broadened the appeal instrument to the point that it currently approaches full appeal—i.e., it includes both questions of law and of fact. Judges and legal commentators have themselves confirmed this change. According to a prominent Jakarta lawyer, the current Supreme Court is a full-blooded third instance of appeal, reviewing cases irrespective of their triviality, fact-specific nature, or relevance.[118] Even Supreme Court judges themselves informally acknowledge the change, generally dating it to 1974, after the retirement of Supreme Court chairman Subekti.[119] As one Supreme Court judge put it:

> Cassation has been vastly broadened. I think only in one out of a hundred cases, at best, are cassation rules an issue, for instance with a referral to the lower courts. For the rest, the Supreme Court just deals with a case as if it were a normal appeals court.[120]

A junior chairman on the Supreme Court expressed it in stark terms:

---

[114] See for a line of such cases: Sebastiaan Pompe and J. M. Otto, "Some Comments on Recent Developments in Indonesian Marriage Law with Particular Respect to the Rights of Women," *Verfassung und Recht in Übersee* 23,4 (1990): 415.

[115] Of a total of 235 dismissals over the years 1969-1979, only fourteen cases were dismissed on grounds of dealing with points of fact, rather than law. Soedirjo, *Kasasi dalam perkara perdata*, pp. 231-32.

[116] Mahkamah Agung no.8K/Sip/1950 dated 25 January 1951.

[117] Mahkamah Agung no.277K/Sip/1979 dated 7 August 1975. Cases cited in Soedirjo, *Kasasi dalam perkara perdata*, p. 232.

[118] Personal communication, 8 June 1994.

[119] According to one Supreme Court insider. Personal communication, 18 July 1994.

[120] Personal communication, 24 April 1995.

Formally speaking, the distinction between fact and a law-specific question still exists, of course, but we have abandoned it in substance. References to the *iudex facti* in Supreme Court decisions are only a facade.[121]

Another Supreme Court judge explained the increasing tendency of the Court to approach its judicial function on an ad hoc, "casuistic" basis as follows:

Several reasons can be advanced for this casuistic approach. For a start, many matters that used to be fact-specific have become legally unsettled or questionable, and as a result are subject to Supreme Court appeal in cassation. Thus, the authority of authentic notary deeds or the binding nature of contracts on the basis of art.1338 Civil Code clearly were fact-specific in the old days, but nowadays have become subject to cassation and are verified on such criteria as fairness and equity (*redelijkheid en billijkheid*). This "juridification" of fact-matters is enhanced by unclear and conflicting legislation. Thus, legislation on the age of majority is a total mess, with the Civil Code putting it at twenty-one years, legislation on marriage at sixteen years, and sometimes nineteen, parental responsibility at twenty-five or thirty years, child welfare at twenty-one, nationality at seventeen, criminal law at sixteen, etc. etc. So the age of majority cannot be accepted as an established fact by the Court. But perhaps the most insidious problem is that the Supreme Court in the end is at a loss regarding what justice to dispense. Justice in this country is too dependent on circumstances, which vary broadly between the procedural, substantive, economic, and political, compounded by the poor quality of the district courts.[122]

Indeed, Supreme Court judges evidently feel that political reality and the poor quality of the district courts, in particular, require them to broaden cassation to the point of abandoning the rule that distinguishes between law-based and fact-based questions altogether. In fact, it is said that, in one of its decisions, the Supreme Court stated in so many words that the distinction between law and fact has become irrelevant in modern Indonesian law and should be abandoned.[123] The senior Supreme Court judge who allegedly made the decision could not quite remember it —which rather underscores the fact that the law versus fact issue has become a matter of peripheral importance in the thinking of prominent Supreme Court judges. Moreover, when queried on the matter, this judge confirmed the underlying logic for abandoning this cornerstone of the cassation system and appeal barrier and said that he supported full appeal.

SP: I was told that you decided a case that actually said that the distinction between law and fact could no longer be maintained.
Supreme Court judge: (after searching his memory a bit) That may be so, I do not quite remember. In any case, it is plainly unfair to stick too closely to the

---

[121] Personal communication, 7 July 1994.

[122] Personal communication, 9 September 1994

[123] I was unable to trace this decision, but its existence was repeatedly confirmed in interviews, for example in personal communications of 18 July 1994 and 4 August 1994.

law/fact distinction in cases in which the district court judge plainly erred on the facts. We must deal with these cases also.[124]

In describing his first experiences on the Supreme Court, one judge pointed out how lower court errors forced Supreme Court intervention, even though in his first case he was able to review it without violating the law versus fact rule.

> The first case I got to handle after my nomination to the Supreme Court was a case in which nine suspects were accused of murder. The nine were condemned by the lower courts. Nevertheless, there only was one witness, which by law is insufficient for condemning them. It was a clear-cut, simple matter, and I freed them.[125]

Even though, in this instance, the Supreme Court was able to free the suspects on the basis of an erroneous application of the law, the case still illustrates quite clearly that the lower courts (including the court of appeal) allows errors of the first magnitude to pass, thus necessitating Supreme Court intervention.

Violation of Forms. A court decision may also be appealed in cassation on grounds that it does not respect the proper forms. On this score, the 1950 law is slightly different from subsequent legislation, as it does not limit review on this ground only to forms prescribed on pain of nullity (art.18).[126] Thus, the 1950 law allowed that any mistake, however trivial, was sufficient grounds to bring a case up for cassation. This did not exclude the possibility, of course, that the Court itself would interpret this power restrictively along lines prevalent hitherto, as in fact was pointed out by some contemporary authors.[127] The general assessment is that this was what the Supreme Court proceeded to do until the situation was redressed in 1965, and formalized in 1985.[128]

Nullity may be determined by legislation or by the judge himself, and can be based on a variety of points. For example, proceedings must be held in open court unless the law allows otherwise,[129] and court decisions must be taken by a panel of

---

[124] Personal communication, 21 September 1994.

[125] Personal communication, 28 June 1994.

[126] art.18 Law no.1/1950: The grounds of cassation are: (1) . . . (2) not respecting proper forms as prescribed by law. Compare the 1950 law with subsequent legislation: art.51 law no.13/1965: "In cassation the Supreme Court shall quash decisions and findings of lower courts: (a) because proper forms which have been prescribed by law on pains of nullity have not been respected . . ." Compare also art.30 Law no.14/1985: "The Supreme Court in cassation shall quash decisions or findings of courts from all jurisdictions on grounds of: (a) . . . ,(b) . . . (c) because proper forms which have been prescribed by law on pain of nullity have not been respected." Note that the rule stating that only forms prescribed on pain of nullity could be advanced for cassation prevailed also during the Dutch period: art.174 *Rechterlijke Organisatie* (S.1847:23)

[127] J. E. Jonkers, Korte aantekening op de cassatieregeling in de "Wet op de Hoge Raad van Indonesië," (1951), p. 31; de Jongh, *Het nieuwe cassatie instituut*, p. 162.

[128] See generally Setiawan, *Aneka masalah hukum*, ch. 7.

[129] The Supreme Court has quashed decisions that violated this principle. Art.17,18 Law no.14/1970 confirmed with Mahkamah Agung no.334K/Sip/1972 dated 4 October 1972, *Yurisprudensi Indonesia* (1971): 195; Soedirjo, *Kasasi dalam perkara perdata*, p. 66.

three judges on pains of nullity.[130] The decisions must be embossed with the official caption "In the name of Justice based on God Almighty," if they are not to be found null and void.[131]

The major issue with respect to violation of forms is undoubtedly the motivation of the court decision.[132] The 1950 law stated in rather general terms that the reasoning, the legal basis, and the relevant articles must be stated in the court decision, which moreover must bear the signature of the judge, but though the law's wording suggests that this is a mandatory requirement, it does not say that in so many words. Subsequent Supreme Court decisions spell out in unequivocal terms that this is, in fact, a mandatory provision,[133] which the Court has defined more closely in a series of cases. It has provided that absence of motivation is a clear violation of the requirement,[134] and that each individual rejection by the court of the points advanced by the plaintiff must be motivated.[135] It is insufficient for a court merely to express approval of the plaintiff's written pleas and repeat them, without evaluating the evidence advanced therein on the basis of the material advanced by the defendant.[136] If the appeals court in its final decision reviews a point which it has decided differently in an interlocutory decision, forms are violated on grounds of contradiction.[137]

Transgression of Judicial Powers. Authors seem to be united in their assessment that the transgression of judicial powers is "an obscure concept."[138] They refer to it alternately as meaning that the Court may not exceed its judicial powers and tread on the domain of the legislature or executive, or that it may not exceed its powers as described by law. As shall be apparent in the next chapter, in Indonesia the Supreme Court had in fact been given a quasi-legislative authority.[139] With the ambit of judicial authority so widely drawn, it has become nearly impossible to determine whether the Supreme Court has in fact transgressed its authority. The same, however, does not apply to the lower courts, which do not share a

---

[130] art.15(1) Law no.14/1970. This principle had been established earlier by judicial intervention, cf. Mahkamah Agung no.25K/Kr/1964 dated 7 July 1964; Husein, *Kasasi sebagai upaya hukum*, p. 80.

[131] art.4(1) Law no.14/1970; Mahkamah Agung no.104K/Kr/1973 dated 8 August 1974. Sutianto and Oeripkartawinata, *Hukum acara perdata*, p. 129.

[132] art.23 Law no.14/1970. See generally Setiawan, *Aneka masalah hukum*, ch. 7; and Soedirjo, *Kasasi dalam perkara perdata*, p. 65.

[133] Mahkamah Agung Circular Letter (SEMA) no.14/1977 to the effect that if the motivation of the court decision is insufficient, unclear, confusing, contradictory, or altogether absent, this qualifies it as a violation of forms leading to cassation of the decision of the court.

[134] Mahkamah Agung no.672K/Sip/1972 dated 18 October 1972; Mahkamah Agung no.588K/Sip/1975 dated 13 July 1976.

[135] Mahkamah Agung no.698K/Sip/1969 dated 18 December 1970.

[136] Mahkamah Agung no.9K/Sip/1972 dated 19 August 1972; Mahkamah Agung no.638K/Sip/1970 dated 22 July 1970.

[137] Mahkamah Agung no.117K/Sip/1975 dated 8 May 1957.

[138] Soedirjo, *Kasasi dalam perkara perdata,*, p. 46, closely following Veegens, *Cassatie in Burgerlijke Zaken*, p. 240.

[139] art.131 Law no.1/1950 states that if an issue pertaining to the judiciary is not regulated by law, the Supreme Court can itself determine how this issue must be approached. This is reiterated in the recent Law no.13/1985 art.79.

comparable quasi-legislative authority. Nevertheless, it is understandable that the Supreme Court should tread cautiously on this point, and in fact no decisions could be found where court decisions were quashed on cassation with reference to this ground.

(v) The Decision

The Supreme Court can make three forms of decisions: declaring the claim in cassation inadmissible (*tidak dapat diterima*); rejecting the claim of cassation (*ditolak*); or annulling the lower court judgment (*dikabulkan*). This is the terminology used by the Court itself, as the relevant legislation does not appear consistent on this score.[140]

A claim in cassation is declared inadmissible if procedure has not been respected. Thus, the Court has held that failure to give an authenticated mandate in writing for a legal representative, failure to enclose a motivation, violation of time limits, or the absence of registration at the first instance court are all reasons for declaring cases inadmissible before the Court.[141] If the claim of cassation has passed this procedural hurdle, it can still be rejected on the basis of substantive arguments. This means that the Court would uphold the decision of the lower court as the correct interpretation of the law and deny the claim. Finally, the Supreme Court can annul the decision of the lower court.

The obligation to refer cases back to the lower courts, characteristic of cassation, is very limited in Indonesia. *Renvoi* basically makes sense only when the court of cassation has to rely upon the evidence presented to it by the lower courts and is unable to go further. This, as we have seen, did not apply to post-independence Indonesia. Indeed, this procedure was never very firmly established in the Netherlands, and had been even weaker in the colony, but after independence it was watered down even further. This was the natural consequence of the extensive power granted the Supreme Court to ascertain new facts. Consequently, both the 1950 and 1985 laws only obliged the Court to refer cases back to the lower courts in situations where the judge had exceeded his authority.[142] This is evidently a procedural issue which does not in the end touch upon the essence of the dispute and hence calls for a retrial.

---

[140] The wording of art.30 Law no.14/1985 regarding the grounds of cassation states that the Supreme Court may quash (*membatalkan*) decisions on such and such grounds. Art.50, which deals with the power of the Court to call for additional evidence and hear witnesses, uses the same wording. The term "quash" is not used by the Supreme Court in its own decisions, however, and the precise meaning of the term in the law is uncertain. Art.51, says that that Court may annul (*mengabulkan*) a decision on the grounds mentioned there. The Indonesian terminology used in the law derives, it is submitted, from the Dutch "*niet-ontvankelijk*," "*verwerping van het beroep*," and "*de bestreden uitspraak vernietigen*."

[141] On these, see respectively Mahkamah Agung no.24K/Sip/1967 dated 18 February 1967, *Yurisprudensi Indonesia* (1969): 792; Mahkamah Agung no.8K/Sip/1967 dated 29 April 1967, *Yurisprudensi Indonesia* (1969): 558; Mahkamah Agung no.208K/Sip/1973 dated 14 April 1973 and no.379K/Sip/1971 dated 5 March 1975, both quoted in Soedirjo, *Kasasi dalam perkara perdata*, pp. 70-71; and Mahkamah Agung no.1104K/Sip/1972 dated 21 January 1976, quoted in Soedirjo, *Kasasi dalam perkara perdata*, p. 71.

[142] art.20 Law no.1/1950; art.51 law no.14/1985. In colonial times, *renvoi* was extended also to include cases in which proper forms were not respected. Art.163-175 *Rechterlijke Organisatie*, in de Jongh, *Het nieuwe cassatie instituut*, p. 162.

This restricted *renvoi* procedure does raise some problems, particularly as not all violations of form permit final review by the Supreme Court. Thus, when the presiding judge is challenged on grounds of family bonds or personal interest (*ingkar/mengundurkan diri*), and when that challenge is dismissed, there may have been an error of form which cannot be redressed in final instance but calls for a retrial.[143] The law does not allow for that possibility.

In actual fact, there is a clear tendency on the part of the Supreme Court to decide all cases itself. *Renvoi* is very rarely effected in Supreme Court procedure, with only one in a hundred cases, at best, being referred back to a lower court.[144]

3. THE POLICY ON APPEAL BARRIERS: THE ELEVATION OF CASES TO THE SUPREME COURT'S LEVEL

Besides facilitating appeal to the Court by lowering cassation barriers, the Supreme Court actively boosted case-flow to its docket in two more ways. The first was that the Court made certain kinds of procedures actionable before it and promoted these, giving litigants a strong incentive to appeal. Secondly, it created new procedures that bypassed the lower courts altogether and were dealt with directly by the Supreme Court.[145]

(a) Making Procedures Subject To Litigation

This refers to a tendency on the part of the Supreme Court to open the possibility of litigation on issues that previously were excluded from judicial control. Three notable examples of this tendency can be given here: the enforcement of court decisions pending appeal (*putusan serta merta/pelaksanaan lebih dahulu*,

---

[143] de Jongh, *Het nieuwe cassatie instituut*, p. 163.

[144] Personal communication from a Supreme Court judge, 24 April 1994.

[145] No attention has been paid to the procedural venue specific to cassation, in which an action is brought by the Chief Public Prosecutor. This procedure is directed toward inviting the Court to express itself on a civil or criminal legal issue raised in lower court decisions which has not been appealed and which is considered to have great practical and legal significance. This procedure is specifically directed toward ensuring the unified administration of the law, and for that reason is referred to as "cassation in the interest of the law." It is specifically not concerned with determining the rights and obligations of the parties in the case on which this cassation is requested, and its outcome does not affect them or affect the implementation of the lower court decision. Art.45(1) Law no.14/1985; Mahkamah Agung no.186K/Kr/1979 dated 5 September 1979; Husein, *Kasasi sebagai upaya hukum*, p. 147. Indonesian law adopted this procedure for all jurisdictions except the military. For the old law, see: art.17 Law no.1/1950. As regards the new law, art.45 Law no.14/1985 referring to art.44(1)(a) says that only first instance and appellate decisions in the general, religious, and administrative jurisdictions may be subjected to this procedure. The Code of Criminal Procedure provides in greater detail for the procedure in criminal cases (art.259-262 Code of Criminal Procedure, Law no.8/1981). The Chief Public Prosecutor initiates this at his discretion. It is not a contradictory procedure in that parties are not called before the Court; instead, a one-party plea is made before the Court. It is only open with respect to final court decisions of first and second instance, meaning court decisions which are no longer liable for appeal. This type of cassation consequently is not bound by time limits (Mahkamah Agung no.25K/Kr/1964 dated 7 July 1964). The grounds of cassation are identical. cf. Husein, *Kasasi sebagai upaya hukum*, p. 150; Y. Harahap, *Pembahasan permasalahan dan penerapan KUHAP* (part II) (Jakarta: Kartini, 1988), pp. 1195-1196. There have been very few cases advanced on this procedure. E. Bonn, "Enkele aantekeningen op de Wet op de Hoge Raad van Indonesia," *Mededelingen van het Documentatiebureau voor Overzees Recht* 5 (1955): 1.

uitvoerbaar bij voorraad); expedited enforcement of security rights (*grosse akte*); and in the field of criminal law, appeal on freeing suspects (*bebas murni*).

(i) Enforcing Court Decisions Pending Appeal (Provisional Enforcement)

The first example concerns the enforcement of a lower court decision pending appeal. The Code of Procedure art.180(1) HIR allows for such provisional enforcement by special court order on clear and pressing grounds. The unwritten rule is that the judge must take into account whether provisional enforcement of a court decision will result in a situation that cannot be undone if his decision were to be overturned on appeal. Despite this understanding, the procedure has led to gross injustices in practice. A great number of cases arose in which lower courts allowed provisional enforcement, but when the decision was overturned on appeal it was discovered that the situation prior to enforcement could not be reinstated, or there were innumerable complications. Such was the case, for instance, when provisional enforcement allowed property to be officially auctioned off and it was acquired by a third party in good faith.[146] Also, there were cases in which houses were destroyed pursuant to court decisions that had been provisionally enforced, but were then quashed on appeal. In the words of a respected former Supreme Court law clerk: " . . . the problem of provisional enforcement cannot be divorced from the problem of the quality of court decisions themselves . . . "[147]

Faced with an excessive use of provisional enforcement by first instance courts, the Supreme Court sought to restrict their authority to grant provisional enforcement pending appeal. In so doing, it opted for a system in which the higher courts acquired strong supervisory authority over the procedure of provisional enforcement, and the authority of the lower courts was seriously curtailed in substantive terms. The Supreme Court raised the procedure on provisional enforcement from lower court jurisdiction, as it were, to bring it under its own control. This pattern was clearest in 1964, when the Supreme Court stated simply that henceforth provisional enforcement would be allowed only with prior approval of the Supreme Court itself.[148] In later years, the high Court's supervision of provisional enforcement was diluted somewhat, and a system was progressively introduced allowing the first instance courts to decide provisional enforcement pending appeal, but granting the higher courts strong powers to suspend such enforcement.[149] In addition, restrictions were placed on the circumstances under which provisional enforcement was allowed.

---

[146] This brought the Supreme Court in 1975 to require the applicant to provide security if he applied for the provisional enforcement of a court order allowing for auctioning off property. See Circular Letter no.6/1975 dated 1 December 1975.

[147] Setiawan, *Aneka masalah hukum*, p. 442.

[148] Mahkamah Agung Circular Letter no.13/1965 dated 10 July 1964.

[149] Mahkamah Agung Circular Letter no.5/1969 dated 2 June 1969 transferred the main burden of supervision to the appellate courts. Both the 1964 and 1969 letters were repealed with Circular Letter no.3/1971 dated 17 May 1971, which transferred the authority of provisional enforcement back to the first instance courts, but instructed them to handle it with the utmost care, and, moreover, granted the Supreme Court itself the authority to suspend enforcement. With Letter no.6/1975 dated 1 December 1975, the Supreme Court said that the authority could only be used in the most exceptional circumstances, and only to prevent egregious results. The Supreme Court also made it a condition that the applicant give security should the decision be overturned on appeal. Finally, it granted authority to the appellate court to suspend

Consequently, provisional enforcement has become very rare in Indonesian procedural law. This quite clearly is the direct result of the restrictions the Court imposed on art.180 HIR. According to former Supreme Court vice chairman Purwoto Gandasubrata:

> On the basis of Circular Letter no.3/1978 the first instance courts are effectively not allowed to grant provisional enforcement of their decisions. This applies even in cases in which the conditions listed in art.180 HIR are complied with (. . .). Still, in the most pressing circumstances, this highly exceptional procedure may be allowed . . . [150]

An additional factor obstructs provisional enforcement. For nearly thirty years, the Supreme Court has quite clearly discouraged the imposition of such enforcement, and this has inevitably influenced the way in which the instrument is viewed by lower court judges generally. Fearing a Supreme Court rap on the knuckles, lower court judges are slow to grant provisional enforcement, even when confronted with a clear-cut case, and, should they do so, are hesitant to allow the order to be actually enforced.[151] In an atmosphere of legal uncertainty, they fear making a mistake, and play it safe as a result.

This feeling of insecurity and caution is not altogether surprising, because when it comes down to actual cases, the Supreme Court is less than consistent. Neither are the Court's various Circular Letters on the subject wholly consistent, nor is the law unequivocal.[152] In addition, the Supreme Court has vacillated on the issue in individual cases; we note, for instance, the 1992 *Bali Kuta Cottage case*, in which the Supreme Court first allowed provisional enforcement, but then disallowed it barely a month later.[153] In this context, it takes a daring judge to allow provisional enforcement of his decision and actually implement it as well. One Supreme Court judge put it as follows:

> Courts actually dare decide [for provisional enforcement]. But generally they do not actually effect this decision. From the x number of cases which are purportedly *uitvoerbaar bij voorraad* [the Dutch term for provisional

---

enforcement should it deem this necessary. This approach was maintained in 1978, when the Supreme Court with Circular Letter no.3/1978 dated 1 April 1978 returned the authority to decide the enforcement of court decisions pending appeal to the first instance courts, but also instructed them to report to the appellate courts and the Supreme Court, allowing both courts to suspend provisional enforcement.

[150] *Forum Keadilan*, 23 July 1992, pp. 89-90.

[151] For a case in which the lower judge was reprimanded for granting provisional enforcement, see for instance *Tempo*, 18 January 1986, p. 28. Here Appellate Judge Aslamiyah Sulaiman, who later moved to the Supreme Court, stated blandly that " . . . after appeal is lodged, the first instance judge can no longer allow provisional enforcement."

[152] This need not be dealt with extensively here, but to summarize briefly, Circular Letters nos.3/1978 and 6/1975 conflict on a number of issues. Mr. Purwoto S. Gandasubrata argued that Circular Letter no.6/1975 essentially covers procedure and no.3/1978 deals with substance. *Forum Keadilan*, 23 July 1992, pp. 89-90.

[153] *Forum Keadilan*, 23 July 1992, p. 89.

enforcement], hardly any is actually effected. I think the ratio is at best one out of a thousand.[154]

These developments caused cases to be elevated to the Supreme Court in two ways: first, Supreme Court control over provisional enforcement itself raised cases, as parties began to appeal such matters; in addition, as provisional enforcement became increasingly rare, appeal inevitably stayed enforcement. As a result, appeal became a handy delaying tactic for litigants who used it not because they expected to win, but because enforcement would be stayed thereby and the opposing party might abandon the case as a result.

(ii) Expedited Enforcement of Security Rights (grosse akte)

The second example of the way in which the Supreme Court "raises" cases into its jurisdiction concerns the expedited enforcement of debts based on the so-called *grosse akte*. The *grosse akte* refers to a copy of a notary deed testifying to either of two debt instruments: a mortgage (hypothec) or an acknowledgement of debt.[155] These are the pivotal instruments of Indonesian credit and security law, and vitally important in Indonesian commercial life. One publication estimated that by 1986 the banking world availed itself of the *grosse akte* as a debt instrument approximately 500,000 times a year, although it is a mystery how that figure was reached.[156] The special legal authority of the *grosse akte* resides in the fact that, according to art.224 Indonesian Code of Procedure (HIR), it has the same authority as a court decision. As a result it can be enforced in an expedited form, effectively bypassing the court system.

The right of hypothec is a registered security right on immovable property. It is particularly strong because as a matter of general practice it is coupled to the right of first avail based on art.1178 Civil Code. This means that the creditor in the case of a default can bypass the courts and auction off the property to secure his credit. The case of an acknowledgement of debt has the same effect. As the term implies, it is the acknowledgement of a debt by notary deed. In the case of a default, it can be enforced if the creditor simply applies for an enforcement order.

Even though both debt instruments were clearly meant to bypass the court system, the Supreme Court progressively brought them under control of the courts.

> ... the idea was that the debt could be enforced without having to go through a lengthy court procedure, precisely because the *grosse akte* is enforceable like a court order. Nevertheless, in practice it appeared that many debtors objected

---

[154] Supreme Court Judge M. Yahya Harahap, "Permasalahan eksekusi," *Varia Peradilan* 3 (October 1992): 119.

[155] As noted earlier, according to art.224 HIR, this must be a formalized copy embossed with the heading "In the name of Justice based on Almighty God." There is some theoretical debate on whether only these two debt instruments can establish a *grosse akte*, or if any notarial document will suffice. As pointed out by Hadi, this is not really the salient issue. The issue is what (formalized copies of) notarial deeds allow for expedited enforcement; by law, these are the ones relating to hypothec and acknowledgement. While a formalized copy may perhaps be made of any notarial deed, this does not always mean that these can be enforced in an expedited manner. M. Hadi, "Grosse akte," *Varia Peradilan* 1 (August 1986): 146, 150-51.

[156] Hadi, "Grosse akte," p. 154.

to such expedited enforcement based on art.224 HIR, and brought action on grounds that the deed was invalid.[157]

The point is that the Supreme Court held that such actions should be accepted, thus vitiating the effect of art.224 HIR and adding to its caseload.

Regarding hypothec, this happened in the well-known *Kandaga Shopping Center* case.[158] Here the Supreme Court held that the creditor could only realize the collateral after approval of the district court chairman.[159] The decision effectively rendered art.1178 Civil Code inoperative, which had the effect henceforth of subjecting enforcement of hypothec to court control—further adding to the courts' workload.[160]

As regards the acknowledgment of debts, developments were slightly more complicated, but had the same effect of bringing the matter under court control and eventually landing it on the Supreme Court docket. Originally, the acknowledgement of debt was viewed as an "exceptional institution."[161] By the late 1970s, however, it suddenly gained popularity, after a prominent Jakarta notary public, Kartini Muljadi, began to use this legislative debt instrument for more general purposes. She discovered that art.224 HIR offered a way of bypassing the cumbersome and unreliable judiciary in the enforcement of debts. If the limits of the instrument were broadened, it might be used to pour increasingly complicated transactions into the simple cast of debt acknowledgment and secure expedited enforcement in the case of a default. Once the construct took root in the legal professions, an increasing number of agreements came to be structured as "acknowledgements of debt," which subsequently became ever more complex.[162] Instead of the debtor simply acknowledging a clear and precise debt by notarial deed, these instruments became complex credit agreements—"complete with drawdown schedules, floating interest rates, representations, covenants, and

---

[157] Purwoto S. Gandasubrata, "Penerapan hukum jaminan dalam praktek di Indonesia," *Varia Peradilan* 3 (January 1988): 163.

[158] Supreme Court no.3210K/Pdt/1984 dated 30 January 1986. It is also known as the *Golden City Textile Industry* case—cf. I. Fachruddin, "Terobosan terhadap prinsip hipotik," *Varia Peradilan* 7 (February 1992): 138.

[159] See for instance Setiawan, "Eksekusi hipotik," *Varia Peradilan* 7 (December 1991): 134; A. W. Sudiono, "Grosse akta pengakuan hutang dalam teori dan praktek," *Varia Peradilan* 8 (July 1993): 127.

[160] Setiawan, *Aneka masalah hukum*, pp. 141-42, relates that there is some discussion in Indonesia concerning whether the *Kandaga Shopping Center* case should be seen as an incident, or whether it sets out a new line of cases. The case is frequently referred to in recent publications and has evident authority, yet at least one Supreme Court judge has stated in public that this must not be taken to mean that art.1178 is vitiated. Supreme Court judge T. Boestomi quoted by Setiawan, "Eksekusi hipotik," p. 141.

[161] Wording of Supreme Court junior chairman Asikin Kusumah Atmadja in his letter to the Board BKPH Perbanas dated 1 April 1986 published in *Varia Peradilan* 1 (August 1986): 158.

[162] Letter, Supreme Court junior chairman Asikin Kusumah Atmadja to the Board BKPH Perbanas dated 1 April 1986 published in *Varia Peradilan* 1 (August 1986): 158. "It should be explained that the acknowledgement of debt (...) is being misused nowadays in that practically every agreement (sale and purchase, credit agreements, and so on) are made up in the form of an acknowledgement of a debt. This practice changes the exceptional character of art.224 HIR to one of becoming general practice since every agreement can be enforced in an expedited form, as long as it is in the shape of an acknowledgement of a debt."

acceleration clauses."[163] By the late 1970s and early 1980s, it seemed as though every sizeable commercial transaction was drawn up in the form of an acknowledgement of debt, from straightforward "purchase and sale" agreements to credit agreements, and so on."[164] Of course, in the enforcement stage, these agreements invariably bypassed the judiciary, requiring only summary court approval to be legally effective.

The effect of this development was that the original intent of art.224 HIR to ascertain the existence of a "simple loan, barely exists anymore."[165] Indeed, the main element of art.224 HIR, i.e., a debt that could be clearly ascertained, was lost. Lost also was the ability of the debtor adequately to defend himself. As a result, the Supreme Court felt it could not allow this development to go unchecked. Its decision to intervene was justified by some lower court decisions on debt acknowledgment that were confusing, to say the least. In one spectacular case, a lower court held that the debt could not be precisely ascertained because the debtor had repaid part of it, and expedited enforcement was denied. As one commentator put it:

> In effect the court seemed to say that a debtor could defeat the special status of an acknowledgement of debt merely by repaying part of the debt—an absurd result.[166]

And so, in 1986 the Supreme Court in the well-known *Nichimen case* seriously restricted the use of debt acknowledgements,[167] establishing a number of criteria that had to be realized before a notary deed might qualify as an acknowledgement of debt under art.224 HIR.[168] What this also meant is that all acknowledgements of debt based on art.224 HIR now must be scrutinized by the courts to see whether they comply with the criteria laid down in the *Nichimen case*.

(iii) Appeal on Freeing Suspects (bebas murni)

The third category of case that the Supreme Court has pulled into its jurisdiction comes from the field of criminal procedure. It concerns the *bebas murni* situation, generally known in most legal systems, which refers to the rule that the

---

[163] S. Gautama and R. N. Hornick, "Indonesia—Supreme Court Sets Tougher Standards for Expediting Enforcement of Acknowledgements of Debt," *Varia Peradilan* 3 (April 1988): 142.

[164] Supreme Court junior chairman Asikin Kusumah Atmadja to the Board of the Bank Negara Indonesia 1946 dated 18 March 1986, published in *Varia Peradilan* 1 (August 1986): 157.

[165] Asikin Kusumah Atmadja, *Beberapa yurisprudensi perdata yang penting serta hubungan ketentuan hukum acara perdata* (Jakarta: Mahkamah Agung, 1992), p. 14.

[166] Gautama and Hornick, "Indonesia—Supreme Court Sets Tougher Standards," p. 142.

[167] *PT Waringin Metal Printing v. Nichimen & Takegawa* Mahkamah Agung no.3454K/Pdt/1985 dated 4 March 1987, *Varia Peradilan* 2 (June 1987): 83.

[168] It stated that art.224 HIR only extended to straight debt acknowledgements, in which the sum was clearly mentioned and no other conditions were imposed apart from the obligation to repay. In addition, it held, perhaps as an *obiter*, that, in the case of substantial debts (in the *Nichimen* case the amount involved was US$3.167 million), the defendant should be given the opportunity to defend himself. This lack of clarity is itself grounds for appealing to the courts, and litigation on the article clearly is not over yet, a situation that threatens to further burden the courts.

state cannot appeal a court decision that frees the suspect in a criminal case. This rule is known in Indonesian law also,[169] yet a number of developments in Indonesia have brought it under scrutiny. The *bebas murni* cases emerged in the 1980s, when it transpired that suspects in criminal cases were being freed by the lower courts on improper grounds. The problem was that these were not incidental cases involving judicial error, but were instead a whole series of highly controversial cases that attracted much public attention. There was a strong suspicion that this procedural protection of the suspect in criminal cases was being consciously abused by judges to free suspects and, at the same time, preempt the state from taking any further action against them.

- One notorious example was the 1984 *Sutomo case*, which arose as part of an anti-corruption sweep in which thirty-four suspects were brought to trial, including the well-known, high-living reputed smuggler, Jos Sutomo. Sutomo was freed by the district court amid speculations that the judge had colluded with the rich suspect. According to the prosecutor:

... to take just a couple of examples, during the entire trial the judge was steering toward freeing Sutomo. He refused to summon several important witnesses for the prosecution. And some think the court decision was known to Sutomo before being handed down, as the day prior to the court session his employees had a large ceremonial party [*selamatan*] in his factory.[170]

As a result of this public exposure, the matter was subsequently raised in Parliament, when the 1985 Supreme Court Bill came up for debate. One member of Parliament described the issue as follows:

Let's say that in a corruption case the state is defrauded of ten billion Rupiah, of which the suspect hooks one billion with his fishing rod, which he dangles in front of the judge. It is not at all inconceivable that the judge snaps it up and decides to free the suspect. And if the suspect is freed, then in accordance with the law, no appeal or cassation can be lodged. I ask you, is this fair?[171]

Both the minister of justice and public prosecutor clearly thought it was not, suggesting that there might be more to these cases than meets the eye.[172] As a result, and notwithstanding the Code of Criminal Procedure, the prosecutor decided to appeal the *Jos Sutomo case* to the Supreme Court directly. The Court allowed the action, and early in 1985 handed down the first guilty verdict in this special

---

[169] Code of Criminal Procedure art.244. It goes too far to deal with some of the complexities of Indonesian—and Dutch—criminal procedure in this context. See for instance, Soenoto, "Putusan bebas tidak murni," *Varia Peradilan* 10 (March 1995): 141.

[170] *Tempo*, 1 October 1988, p. 76. Curiously enough, after all the public racket and official suspicions at first instance, Sutomo was found not guilty by the Supreme Court four years later. In another notable smuggling case involving a wealthy entrepreneur, the action was allowed by the Supreme Court, but the case dismissed on procedural grounds, apparently making the prosecutor absolutely furious. *Tempo*, 8 October 1988, p. 101.

[171] *Kompas*, 7 December 1985. As a result of the debates, the draft art.37 of the bill was altered to allow such cases to be brought. *Kompas*, 13 December 1985.

[172] *Tempo*, 20 October 1984, p. 60.

category of cases.[173] This opened the door to direct appeals from district courts to the Supreme Court, bypassing the appeal courts,[174] in such *bebas murni* cases. The *bebas murni* cases therefore constitute a further illustration of the tendency on the part of the Supreme Court to elevate cases to a level that brings them under its direct control.

(b) New Actions Directly to the Supreme Court

The second development by which the Supreme Court actively boosted movement of cases is by creating new actions which the Court handles exclusively. In such actions, litigants can address themselves directly to the Supreme Court, bypassing the lower courts. A notable example is the special review procedure (*peninjauan kembali, request civiel/herziening*). In some cases, authority originally rested with the lower courts, but was transferred to the Supreme Court, excluding the lower courts, which consequently no longer served as filters reducing case-flow to the Supreme Court. Examples are judicial review and arbitration. Finally, some novel procedures were called into existence, such as stay of enforcement of Supreme Court decisions (*eksekusi*).

(i) Reopening Cases: Special Review

The special review procedure would allow the Supreme Court to reopen cases that had acquired force of law (i.e., in which all legal remedies are exhausted), including its own decisions in cassation. It was thought that this option was disallowed under Indonesian procedural law.[175] By 1969, chronic errors in the lower courts pushed the Supreme Court to begin lobbying for a special review procedure. In fact, Court chairman Subekti issued a number of Circular Letters that opened the door to special review.[176] They caused quite an uproar because the matter was thought to be too important to be decided by the Supreme Court alone.[177] And so, by

---

[173] *Tempo*, 2 February 1985, p. 62.

[174] The Supreme Court several times explicitly denied the authority of appellate courts to handle "*bebas murni*" cases—see for instance Supreme Court no.170K/Pid/1985 dated 27 May 1986, *Varia Peradilan* 2 (March 1987): 60.

[175] As was established in the previous chapter, the courts did accept the institution in the 1950s, but it had fallen into disuse a decade later. Moreover, it was not quite clear what procedure governed it.

[176] Circular Letter no.1/1969 as amended by Circular Letter no.18/1969 and replaced by Regulation no.1/1971. The authority of these letters and regulations was based on Law no.19/1964 art.15, which provided for review, but said that this matter would be dealt with in greater detail by law. When this enacting law had not materialized even by the late 1960s, the Supreme Court started issuing the letters. The important Law no.14/1970 in art.21 explicitly allowed for review to the Supreme Court. Supreme Court chairman Subekti recounts that he expected effecting legislation, and that was why he suspended review with Regulation no.1/1971. Subekti, *Kekuasaan Mahkamah Agung R.I.*, p. 26.

[177] One MP recounts that Subekti was questioned quite seriously in Parliament on his Circular Letter no.1/1969. Subekti apparently argued that judicial errors in the lower courts were frequent, and that after appeal terms had expired, injustices caused by such cases could not be remedied. When the MP asked how many cases had come to light so far, Subekti answered truthfully that there were three at the time (1970). At that the MP sat back and laughed, for he

the early 1970s, the procedure was suspended as an option,[178] and later disallowed altogether[179]—the one hundred review cases pending before the Supreme Court were simply discarded.[180]

Nevertheless, after a couple of years the special review issue reemerged. Against a background of constant complaints about judicial errors in the lower courts, the problematic *Sengkon-Karta case* (1980) acted as a catalyst.

- The case concerned the murder of a small shopkeeper and his wife. Before dying, the shopkeeper managed to whisper the name of Sengkon to witnesses carrying him to hospital. Sengkon's sandal was also found in the courtyard. Sengkon was a well-known hoodlum in the area, invariably operating together with his partner, Karta. Both Sengkon and Karta were arrested and eventually convicted. Sengkon appealed, but to no avail. Karta decided not to appeal. Then, six years later an entirely new figure appeared on the scene, as a third party arrested in a totally unconnected case suddenly confessed to having murdered the shopkeeper and his wife. In fact, there was not a shred of evidence to establish his guilt, but the self-incriminating character of the testimony was found to be so convincing that it brought Supreme Court chairman Seno Adji to seek ways to reopen the case.

The *Sengkon-Karta case* resulted in Supreme Court Regulation no.1/1980, which now definitely introduced the special review procedure into Indonesian procedural law. The regulation allowed for a review of court decisions having force of law (lacking legal remedies). Actions under this regulation had to be brought directly before the Supreme Court. As a result of that regulation, the *Sengkon-Karta case* was retried and Sengkon and Karta were freed, while in a separate case the person who had confessed was convicted.[181] Regardless of the factual correctness of the case, about which there is some debate,[182] it had the important long-term legal

---

said that if Subekti answered so honestly, giving such a low figure and still thinking it an important matter, all argument stops. According to this account, Subekti was coaxed by Parliament to reconsider. Regulation no.1/1971 first suspended the review before it was definitely repealed with Regulation no.1/1976. In fact, however, between 1971 and 1976 review was a dead letter. Personal communication, 19 July 1994. Yet as the number of review cases by 1976 and later developments reveal, the MP may have underrated the relevance and importance of the review procedure.

[178] Regulation no.1/1971.

[179] Mahkamah Agung Regulation no.1/1976.

[180] *Tempo*, 4 September 1976, p. 17.

[181] Both subsequently brought action for damages against the Indonesian state for false imprisonment. Before their case was decided, however, Sengkon died of tuberculosis and Karta was run over by a truck. *Forum Keadilan*, 29 September 1994, p. 103.

[182] The *Sengkon-Karta case* is now said to be one in a series of cases in which innocent persons, pushed either by fear or greed, are said to have taken the rap for serious crimes, letting the real perpetrators go free. One of the most famous cases is the Diece murder, in which a movie star was rumored to have been killed by politically very well-connected persons, and a totally innocent bystander, Pak Deh, was pressured to take the blame. At least one Supreme Court judge expressed his doubts to me regarding the *Sengkon-Karta case*. He believed that the evidence against Sengkon and Karta was solid and that this was further shown by the acquiescence of

effect of reviving the review procedure. Currently a number of cases have emerged that strongly resemble the *Sengkon-Karta case*.[183]

The special review procedure before the Supreme Court is now a fixture of modern Indonesian procedural law. The Supreme Court Law no.14/1985 (art.66 passim) established its legislative basis; this law also states explicitly that review cases shall only be heard by the Supreme Court, thus bypassing all lower courts [art.70(2)]. As it happened, review turned out to be much more popular than expected, and in course of time became a serious burden for the Supreme Court. The reason was that, notwithstanding explicit legal provisions that review would *not* stay enforcement [art.66(2)], in reality this did occur, essentially because lower judges were afraid to enforce judgment of cases still subject for review by the Supreme Court. The situation is not basically different from that discussed with provisional enforcement. The fact that some Supreme Court judges argue that enforcement of a Supreme Court decision pending review should in fact be stayed has not helped in these matters.[184] This led to a situation in which litigating parties commenced review procedures just for their nuisance value: i.e., because instituting appeal to review the case effectively stayed enforcement even of Supreme Court decisions—"review to manipulate enforcement," as a Supreme Court judge put it.[185] Thus, rather like provisional enforcement, review added to the Supreme Court workload not only because it elevated a new procedure to be directly considered by that Court, but also because of the advantages which this procedure gave litigants. Instead of an exceptional instrument, review came to be used with increasing frequency in the course of the 1980s. As a result of this development, as Indonesian lawyers are apt to say, the Indonesian judiciary in the 1980s effectively evolved from a three-layered structure into a four-layered one.[186]

Karta, and that the third man was just a fall guy who feared for his life in prison. Personal communication, 9 September 1994.

[183] Thus, in the *Lingah-Pacah-Sumir case* (1994), three suspects called Lingah, Pacah, and Sumir were convicted by the Supreme Court of a murder in 1987. Five years later, a wholly unknown figure suddenly emerged, one Asun, claiming that he was the murderer. He said he decided to give himself up because he felt remorse and pity for the innocent Lingah, Pacah, and Sumir in prison. The case also created waves, because the *Lingah-Pacah-Sumir case* had been tried by a Supreme Court bench, chaired by the respected criminal expert junior chairman, Adi Andoyo Soetjipto. *Forum Keadilan*, 29 September 1994, p. 100. A similar incident occurred again in 1995, in the *Adnan Kopli case*. By this time, cases in which suspects were erroneously convicted on a murder charge, with the actual murderer presenting himself later, had become so common that they were referred to as "Sengkon-Karta cases." Thus, the *Adnan Kopli case,* which occurred in Palembang, was referred to in the press as "Sengkon-Karta in Palembang." *Forum Keadilan*, 11 May 1995, p. 87.

[184] Several Supreme Court judges have argued in print that enforcement of a court decision can be stayed for "good" reasons. See for instance Y. Harahap, *Ruang lingkup permasalahan eksekusi bidang perdata* (Jakarta: Gramedia, 1988), p. 298; R. Sutianto, "Wewenang Mahkamah Agung untuk menangguhkan eksekusi sehubungan dengan permohonan peninjauan kembali," *Varia Peradilan* 1 (August 1986): 140; and Ngurah Adi (Judge Central Java appeals court), "Surat perintah penundaan pelaksanaan putusan pengadilan," *Varia Peradilan* 5 (June 1990): 130.

[185] Harahap, *Ruang lingkup*, p. 300.

[186] Many of these cases were spurious, but they had to be reviewed anyway. Harahap, *Ruang lingkup*, p. 140 estimates the ratio of well-founded review applications to spurious or "irrational" ones was approximately one out of a thousand.

(ii) Shifting the Burden to the Supreme Court: Judicial Review and Arbitration

Under the New Order, specific procedures have been removed from the first instance courts and brought under direct Supreme Court control, thus creating an "original" Supreme Court jurisdiction. Responsibility for both judicial review and arbitration procedures has been shifted into the Supreme Court's jurisdiction, once again expanding the variety of tasks the Court is expected to handle.

As regards judicial review, in the original law all courts were allowed to review legislation inferior to formal laws (i.e., Acts of Parliament) and declare them non-binding on grounds of violating superior law. In fact, in some notable cases lower courts proceeded explicitly to void (semi-)legislative acts for purportedly violating superior law.[187] Nevertheless, Law no.14/1970 art.26(1) restricted the power of judicial review to the Supreme Court only and disallowed lower courts from questioning the validity of any legislative instrument whatsoever.[188]

Arbitration is another case in point. It will be recalled that, in the remarkable *Navigation Maritime Bulgare case* of 1984, the Supreme Court found that foreign arbitral awards could not enforced in Indonesia.[189] In 1990 the Supreme Court again provided for the matter by issuing a regulation that reopened the possibility of enforcing foreign arbitral awards. This time, however, it was the Supreme Court itself which had to approve enforcement, rather than the first instance court in the district where the award was to be effected, as had been previously the case.[190] As a result, arbitration cases were no longer filtered through the first instance courts, but were handled directly by the Supreme Court, adding to its caseload.

(iii) Enforcement of Supreme Court Decisions

It also happens that entirely new procedures are sometimes called into existence by the Supreme Court. These procedures may have little or no source in law, but blossom unexpectedly and then spread. The enforcement of Supreme Court decisions is a typical case in point.[191]

---

[187] In a highly important 1967 case (no.249/1967 PT Perdata, in *Yurisprudensi Indonesia* [1969]: 609), the Jakarta appellate court stated explicitly that judges had the authority to review legislation inferior to Acts of Parliament, and in fact the court proceeded to void a number of articles of the Civil Code (while upholding its general legal validity). The case was upheld on appeal by the Supreme Court. Gouwgioksiong, "De rechtsontwikkeling in Indonesia na de souvereiniteitsoverdracht," *Weekblad voor Privaatrecht, Notaris-ambt en Registratie* (1968), no.4982; Setiawan, *Aneka masalah hukum*, p. 464.

[188] This was reiterated in Law no.14/1985 art.31.

[189] Mahkamah Aagung no.2944K/Pdt/1983 dated 29 November 1984.

[190] Perma 1/1990 requires the application to be registered at the Central Jakarta first instance court (art.1), with the Supreme Court giving approval [art.3(3)]. For the old law, see S.1933:132.

[191] Another example in this context is amnesty. It is not a legal procedure as such, but a matter that requires the Supreme Court to advise the president, who must choose whether to grant or withhold amnesty. The problem is that amnesty can be, and in fact is, requested with respect to any form of court-imposed punishment. A tradition has developed in Indonesia whereby even the shoplifter condemned to a single day in prison appeals for an amnesty. See *Tempo*, 6 November 1982, p. 12.

As the law stands, there is no real remedy against the enforcement of a Supreme Court decision. Nevertheless, that is not what happens in reality. Over time, the Court adopted a practice in which, in certain cases, it allowed a stay in enforcement of its own decision, sometimes indefinitely.[192] In defending this approach, it sometimes argued that serious disorder would threaten if its decision in certain cases were enforced, or contended that a particular situation simply could not be corrected, arguing essentially that the law clearly required the opposite from what reality imposed.[193] Such cases place the Supreme Court in a difficult position: it can either pervert the law, or uphold the law but delay enforcement and hope for a settlement—a choice between blowing up the law or "torpedoing itself," as the press put it.[194]

- A typical example of such auto-destruction is the *Ohee case* (1995) in Irian Jaya. A peasant brought a case against the Irian provincial government on grounds that the government had illegally used his tribal land for an extension to an airport. After long and complicated litigation, which reportedly cost the peasant US$450,000, he won the case in final instance before the Supreme Court. The Irian provincial government was ordered to pay the peasant and his tribe US$8.5 million damages, a prohibitive amount that approximated the total budget of the province and would have caused its quasi bankruptcy. As a result, and instead of pushing for a settlement, the Supreme Court with one of its "holy letters" instructed the district court not to enforce the decision.[195]

A number of problems attach to this procedure. For a start, and in the absence of legal provisions, it is not quite clear what the shape of the decision should be. Sometimes the Supreme Court stayed execution of its own verdict by official letter (*Surat Sakti*—"holy letters"), but there have been instances in which enforcement was stayed by telegram, or even with a mere phone call.[196] In addition, it is not

---

[192] For examples see, for instance, *Tempo*, 4 October 1980 (concerning a case where parties were involved in litigation for twenty-seven years); *Tempo*, 28 February 1981; and *Tempo*, 9 July 1983, p. 25, which referred to a case in which parties had been waiting for more than ten years for a Supreme Court decision to be enforced.

[193] Thus, one Supreme Court judge gives as an example, a situation in which it transpires that the title to land is flawed after the purported owner constructed a high-rise office block on it. Sutianto, "Wewenang Mahkamah Agung," p. 141. While Mrs. Sutianto, herself a Supreme Court judge, made the point in connection with a review procedure, the essence of the argument related to postponing enforcement and, by extension, also applies to the enforcement of the Supreme Court decision for review procedures.

[194] *Kompas*, 24 April 1995.

[195] *Jakarta Post*, 12 April 1995; *Forum Keadilan*, 11 May 1995, pp. 97-105; *Gatra*, 22 April 1995, pp. 42-43. Letter of the Supreme Court chairman Soerjono no.KMA/126/IV/1995 dated 5 April 1995 states simply that the Supreme Court decision "cannot be enforced" (*tidak dapat dieksekusi*). In 1992 a very similar case occurred, the *Fistus Yom case*, also involving land in Irian, with Supreme Court chairman Purwoto apparently staying the execution with the same argument. See *Kompas*, 24 April 1995.

[196] *Tempo*, 17 May 1980, p. 54; *Tempo*, 10 September 1990, p. 10. In one case, a convicted criminal was kept in prison after serving his full term because the Supreme Court phoned the prison officials to tell them that his case might be reopened and asked them to hold the defendant until further notice. *Tempo*, 9 May 1987.

quite evident why stays of enforcement are granted in the first place. While there may be cases in which enforcement might cause great hardship or threats to public order, in numerous stays of execution such factors did not seem to be in play at all. Thus, the Supreme Court at times first instructed enforcement of a decision, but then for no apparent reason subsequently allowed a stay. There even were cases in which the Court order for a stay of enforcement only reached parties after the Court decision had already been enforced with no apparent difficulties.[197]

When questioned concerning its policies, the Supreme Court argued that it was just deciding these cases on the basis of the law. "Stay of execution is based on legal considerations," said former Supreme Court vice chairman, Purwoto Gandasubrata, in 1986.[198] The problem was that there simply was no law on the matter, leading commentators to argue that what determined the relevant law was the Chancellor's shoe size, as the English put it. Member of Parliament V. B. da Costa expressed it as follows: "Many of the things done by the Supreme Court lack a legal basis—they are just the personal opinion of the Supreme Court judges, or even the chairman."[199] A law professor and sharp legal commentator, Satjipto Rahardjo, made the following comment with respect to stays of enforcement in the absence of clear laws or institutional policies: " . . . there really is not a single Supreme Court. Rather we have the Supreme Court of Purwoto, the Supreme Court of Asikin, and now the Supreme Court of Soerjono, and so on . . . . "[200]

In fact, there are no distinct rules on stay of enforcement. One Supreme Court judge said that institutional policy on this matter was typically realized on a "case by case basis" and "by way of exception."[201] In 1994 chairman Purwoto Gandasubrata was so strongly questioned about stays of enforcement that a row between the Supreme Court and Parliament ensued, and the order of parliamentary hearings was changed.[202] Purwoto argued that only 0.1 percent of all applications for stays in execution were awarded. But what matters most here is that it also transpired that the Supreme Court had to handle seventeen thousand such applications.[203]

---

[197] *Tempo*, 14 June 1986, p. 20. For other examples see, for instance, *Tempo*, 7 April 1990, p. 73; *Tempo*, 31 May 1980, p. 25; and *Tempo*, 27 September 1980, p. 26 on the well-known *PT Asa v. Hufco* and the *PT Lima Tujuh v Citibank* cases.

[198] *Tempo*, 14 June 1986, p. 20.

[199] Ibid.

[200] *Kompas*, 24 April 1995.

[201] Harahap, *Ruang lingkup*, p. 397. In 1990, Supreme Court chairman Purwoto Gandasubrata admitted as much. *Tempo*, 7 April 1990, p. 73.

[202] From 1994 onwards and following the open confrontation between Supreme Court chairman Purwoto and member of Parliament Da Costa, it was agreed that parliamentary hearings with the Supreme Court would no longer be conducted by the complete Parliamentary Commission on law, the Commission III, but only by party leaders. The row was widely publicized in the press, but no parliamentary record of it has yet been published. Copies of the parliamentary tapes of the debate are in the author's possession.

[203] *Tempo*, 9 October 1993, p. 84. Purwoto did not specify whether these were yearly or total figures. He said that only twenty-five out of a grand total of 17,000 were awarded.

4. CONCLUSION

As a result of political and organizational pressures, the judicial function of the Supreme Court has changed considerably since independence. Most significantly, the Court's powers have vastly increased as a result of its purposeful efforts to strengthen its control over the lower courts. This translated primarily into easing appeal restrictions and barriers, and thus promoting the appeal flow of cases to the Supreme Court. As the Court became the sole, all-encompassing, supreme appeals court for the entire Indonesian judiciary, it also broadened the cassation instrument to the point that any court decision currently can be appealed. Moreover, the Supreme Court has watered down the restrictions having to do with cassation to the point that it can now review any case, no matter how trivial and banal, or factual. In addition, the Court boosted the upward flow of cases by actively intervening in what has been called here "raising" cases to its own level. This was effected through various instruments and means, broadly directed toward making actions that previously were excluded from court control subject to litigation, as well as toward instituting direct appeals to the Supreme Court which bypassed the lower courts.

Generally speaking, the whole thrust of Supreme Court reforms in this field reflects a considerable lack of trust in the lower courts. As shall become apparent in the next chapters, the extension of its judicial control over the lower courts did come at a price. The Supreme Court seems to have opted for ensuring justice in each and every case, rather than realizing a uniformity in the administration of justice throughout the Indonesian court system that could be expected to promote legal certainty and broader justice. This has led not just to a flood of cases and resultant backlogs, which now figure as the Court's principal institutional problem (as we shall see in Chapter 8). No less important was the loss of the lawmaking power of court decisions. We turn next to this issue.

CHAPTER SEVEN

THE SUPREME COURT FUNCTIONS OF REGULATION AND SUPERVISION

The development of judicial function had an important impact on the way in which the other Supreme Court functions evolved. As the judicial function was increasingly directed toward resolving individual disputes between the two parties before the Court, Supreme Court decisions became less and less effective as instruments by which to ensure a uniform application of the law by the lower courts of the land. Supreme Court decision making, as a result, progressively lost what Martin Shapiro calls its "lawmaking" effect,[1] namely the power to shape the law for future application for Indonesian society at large. The Supreme Court drive to strengthen its control over the lower courts reduced its ability to guide the judicial apparatus as a whole. The Court might have an increased ability to set things right in an eventual cassation procedure, but the lower courts did not become any more predictable (or uniform) for it—quite the contrary.

This chapter will show that when Supreme Court decisions generally lost their effectiveness as lawmaking instruments, the Supreme Court compensated by boosting its other functions. As the Court became increasingly unable to ensure legal uniformity and predictability in the lower courts through its decisions, it turned to other instruments to realize this aim. The intensified use of its other functions, notably regulation and supervision, was a natural consequence of the manifest shortcomings of its judicial function.

The regulatory function refers to the Supreme Court's authority to issue "Regulations" (*Peraturan*) to supplement gaps in the law of procedure.[2] Yet the supervisory function also generates a form of regulation. It refers to the authority of the Supreme Court to supervise courts and judges in the exercise of their professional duties. In this context, the Court is empowered to issue "Instructions, Reminders, and Reprimands" to judges individually or collectively. The collective form is generally referred to as Circular Letters (*Surat Edaran*) and closely resembles quasi-legislation.[3]

---

[1] Martin Shapiro, *Courts: A Comparative and Political Analysis* (Chicago, IL: The University of Chicago Press, 1981), p. 28.

[2] R. Subekti, *Kekuasaan Mahkamah Agung R.I.* (Bandung: Alumni, 1980).

[3] Law nr.14/1985 art.32 refers only to "instructions, reprimands, and reminders." Earlier legislation refers to general decisions, being instructions etc. other than those directed towards judges individually, such as "Circular Letters" (*Surat Edaran*)—see for instance Law nr.13/1965 art.47. The colonial Regulation on Judicial Organization (*Reglement op de Rechterlijke Organisatie*) art.157 states in so many words that the colonial Supreme Court is allowed to give general instructions to the courts "by circular letter" (*bij rondgaande brief*). In colonial times, such general instructions consequently were consistently referred to as *Circulaire*, or *Rondschrijven*, which was also the word embossed in the heading. After

This quasi-legislation was used with greater frequency and with a steadily broadening ambit as the authority of Supreme Court decisions declined. In fact, regulation and supervision became instruments for shaping the law, and the legal professions increasingly viewed them as authoritative statements on the law. Reinforced by such practices as regular publication (unlike the case with Court decisions),[4] they command great authority in current Indonesian legal practice. In many ways they effectively have replaced Court decisions as the mainstay of the Court's lawmaking power.

Implementation of these functions has clearly strengthened the Supreme Court's grip on the lower courts, supported by several steps evidently directed toward tightening the Court's supervision. Lower courts are now required to report to the Supreme Court much more often and in more detail. Also, the Court gave bite to its supervision by strengthening its control over individual judges: first, by widening its oversight of "judicial acts" to include not just judges' professional acts, but also their private behavior; and second, by replacing the relatively neutral and objective system of assessing the professional performance of judges (and determining their careers) by a much more fluid and subjective system. Neither criterion is clearly defined. The resultant uncertainty concerning the precise criteria for individual performance assessment gives the Supreme Court considerable discretion in handling lower court judges, and increases their dependence on the Court.

1. REGULATION AND PROCEDURAL LAW

In statutory terms, regulations are meant to be instruments for lawmaking, i.e., to be binding upon courts and citizens alike. Issuing such regulations is a remarkable power for a court to possess, though the Supreme Court is not wholly unique in this respect.[5] When the power was first introduced with Law no.1/1950, the judicial system was completely reorganized, and as a result gaps in procedural law became likely. It was decided, therefore, that the Supreme Court would have residual legislative powers to fill procedural gaps which the 1950 legislation might have

---

independence, the Indonesian translation, *Surat Edaran,* has acquired general usage and usually, though not always, is also embossed in the headings of official instructions.

[4] Note in this context also that, unlike Court decisions, exhaustive lists of Circular Letters and Regulations are currently published on a regular basis by the Supreme Court. See for important compilations of Circular Letters: Mahkamah Agung R.I., *Himpunan Surat Edaran Mahkamah Agung (SEMA) Tahun 1951-1978* (Jakarta: Mahkamah Agung, 1979); Mahkamah Agung R.I., *Himpunan Surat Edaran Mahkamah Agung (SEMA) Tahun 1979-1985* (Jakarta: Mahkamah Agung, 1986); Mahkamah Agung R.I., *Kumpulan Surat Edaran Mahkamah Agung (SEMA) Tahun 1981-1991* (Jakarta: BP Tunas Agung, 1986). This is not to say, incidentally, that all Circular Letters are published in such compilations. Some important letters are to be found in separate publications, such as Circular Letter nr.MA/Pemb/0807 dated 20 August 1975 on marriage, which is published in (among other sources) Abdurrahman, *Himpunan peraturan perundang-undangan tentang perkawinan* (Jakarta: Akademika Pressindo, 1985), p. 219.

[5] As pointed out by Subekti, the Japanese Supreme Court has a comparable power. Nevertheless, the very fact that Subekti apparently feels obliged to justify this power with reference to foreign legal systems rather underscores its exclusivity. Subekti, *Kekuasaan Mahkamah Agung,* p. 45.

overlooked.⁶ These powers were clearly circumscribed, however. The regulatory function could only be used in matters of procedural law, and only in cases where the law is "insufficient." Law no.14/1985 art.79 in fact restates the Court's authority to enact quasi-legislation in the field of procedural law, while specifically precluding regulation of substantive law, or, for that matter, of the law of evidence.⁷

It is noteworthy that this power has been retained to the present day. Both in organizational and procedural terms, the judiciary is evidently now much more institutionalized and regulated than it was during the transitional 1950s, yet the validity of this regulatory function has never seriously been re-evaluated or questioned. This does not deny the fact that a number of observant commentators have privately expressed their surprise and concern about this power, and, as we shall see, the way in which it has evolved. As one Court insider put it to me:

> It is odd that the Supreme Court's regulatory function has been retained to the present day, and I do not view this as either desirable or constitutionally correct. It is quite understandable that it was instituted in 1950 as some sort of stopgap measure in the transitional phase of reforms of the judicial organization, but that phase is over now, as things now are clearly much more settled. But more fundamental to me is the fact that the Supreme Court as a court should only be allowed to effect internal, bureaucratic rules, and not "norm-setting" regulations that are binding upon Indonesian society as a whole.⁸

Possibly as a result of the unequivocal legislative requirements restricting the application of the Court's regulations, this instrument is not very frequently used. In fact, only fourteen such regulations have been published, and to my knowledge, issued between independence and *Reformasi*.

Still, as shall become apparent, legislative restrictions do not prevent these regulations from having a broader effect in two other respects. In the first place, these regulations are often used to clarify conditions that have been obscured by hazy, inconsistent, or otherwise problematic court decisions. In such cases, the Supreme Court enacts regulations to clear up the mess it itself created through inconsistent applications of the laws in its decisions. In that sense, regulations obviously help to compensate for the loss of lawmaking power of Supreme Court decisions. The second point is that, while statute clearly restricts this function to the domain of the law of procedure, in fact its influence has spilled over into substantive law. The effect of regulations thus is broader than intended by law, making it even more a replacement for decision making, a tendency that is clearly illustrated in Regulation no.1/1993 on judicial review and Regulation no.1/1990 on the enforcement of foreign arbitral awards in Indonesia.

---

⁶ Law nr.1/1950 art.131. J. H. A. Logemann points out that there is no requirement in law for publication of Supreme Court Regulations. J. H. A. Logemann, *Het staatsrecht van Indonesië* (The Hague: Van Hoeve, 1954), p. 136.

⁷ Official elucidation to art.79 Law nr.14/1985.

⁸ Personal communication, 5 August 1994

It will be recalled that discussions concerning the issue of individual review in Indonesia[9] have questioned whether, as a result of Law no.14/1985, a judicial review action might be brought directly before the Supreme Court or would have to pass through the lower courts. Supreme Court chairman Ali Said withheld comment on the matter, but chairman Purwoto S. Gandasubrata publicly stated that he would consider direct actions. This led to the *Prioritas case* (1993), which was heard by the Supreme Court, but dismissed because procedural rules for judicial review were lacking. Regulation no.1/1993 on judicial review filled this procedural gap, and in that way dealt with an issue that the Supreme Court was apparently unable or unwilling to resolve with its decisions.

The more striking example of such an action is no doubt Regulation no.1/1990 on arbitration. The regulation responded to a 1984 Supreme Court *volte-face* on the issue of enforcement of foreign arbitral awards. Up until the 1980s, authority for such enforcement seemed to be as strong as it could be: Indonesia ratified the 1958 New York Convention on the enforcement of foreign arbitral awards in 1981.[10] Moreover, in 1933 the government of the Netherlands had acceded to the 1927 Geneva Convention on behalf of its colony, and it was generally understood that this treaty had survived the transfer of sovereignty.[11] Indeed, well into the 1980s, Indonesian courts enforced foreign arbitral awards on the basis of, and with reference to, these treaties.[12] Then in 1984, the Court's decision in the *Maritime Bulgare case* changed everything. When this case had been brought before the Jakarta district court in 1981, enforcement was granted with reference to the international treaties.[13] Then, in a surprise development, the Supreme Court overturned the district court's decision with totally novel arguments.[14] The Court stated that the Geneva Convention had not in fact survived the transfer of sovereignty. What's more, because there were no enacting rules, the New York Convention could not be enforced. Lacking any procedure for enforcement, foreign arbitral awards could not, as a result, be enforced in Indonesia.

Flying in the face of precedent and what seemed to be established law, the case created much confusion and did little to bolster the authority or lawmaking power of Supreme Court decisions.[15] Criticism of the Court was vociferous, as the legal

---

[9] See generally chapter 4, section 3.

[10] Presidential Decree nr.34/1981.

[11] *Colonial State Gazette* (*Indisch Staatsblad*), 1933: 132 jo.133. S. Gautama, *Indonesia dan arbitrase internasional* (Bandung: Alumni, 1986), p. 67; S. Gautama, *Perkembangan arbitrase dagang internasional di Indonesia* (Bandung: Eresco, 1989), p. 31; R. N. Hornick, "The Recognition and Enforcement of Foreign Judgments in Indonesia," *Harvard International Law Journal* 97 (1977): 102.

[12] For instance, District Court South Jakarta nr.64/Pdt/G/1984 cited in Gautama, *Indonesia dan arbitrase internasional*, p. 90.

[13] Jakarta First Instance Court nr.228/1979P dated 10 June 1981.

[14] Mahkamah Agung nr.2944K/Pdt/1983 dated 20 August 1984, published in *Varia Peradilan* 103 (1987).

[15] The decision was criticized from various quarters, most notably by the highly authoritative S. Gautama, in a number of publications, some of which have been quoted above. The criticism impelled the presiding Supreme Court judge, Asikin Kusumah Atmadja, to defend his position in a number of public statements. Cf. A. Kusumah Atmadja, "Konvensi/ratifikasi dan eksekusi putusan arbitrase," paper presented at the Seminar Sehari Arbitrase, Jakarta, 16 November 1988.

community struggled to find a way around the problems that had suddenly emerged. This fierce reaction prompted the Court to correct the problems it had itself created.[16] It did so with Regulation no.1/1993, which again made it possible to enforce foreign arbitral awards in Indonesia. Here again, then, a regulation clarified the obscurity which Supreme Court decision making had generated in the first place.

Nevertheless, Regulation no.1/1993 also illustrated the broadening scope of the regulatory function. The regulation not only provided for procedure, but also established a normative standard with which foreign arbitral awards must comply if they were to be enforced. In that sense, the regulation crossed boundaries into the domain of substantive law. As one former judge told me:

> The Arbitration Regulation is an example of how the Supreme Court crosses procedural boundaries, and also regulates on matters of substantive law. The regulation doesn't just give procedural rules defining how to effect foreign arbitral awards in Indonesia, it also defines the basic normative criteria that foreign arbitral awards have to comply with. That is not procedure at all, but substantive law.[17]

These developments are certainly not without risk. The commentator quoted above had absolutely no doubts that the broadened use of the regulations, combined with its unclear status, made it inevitable that "sooner or later things will go wrong," as he put it. What he meant was that Supreme Court regulations sooner or later would find themselves in conflict with statute. Aside from the damage this might do to the reputation and status of the institutions involved, it would erode the authority of the regulation or statute, as the case might be, and thereby undermine legal certainty.

2. SUPERVISION

In statutory terms, supervision is altogether different from regulation, though as we shall see there are many similarities in practice. The Supreme Court has an extensive supervisory function, with broadly drawn powers extending over both the way courts operate and judges behave.[18] In this context, the Supreme Court can issue "Instructions, Reminders, and Reprimands" to courts collectively or judges individually. The collective form is generally referred to as a Circular Letter

---

[16] Yahya Harahap, himself a Supreme Court judge, indicates that the regulation was issued at least partially in reaction to the criticism leveled against the *Maritime Bulgare* decision. Y. Harahap, *Arbitrase* (Jakarta: Pustaka Kartini, 1991), p. 436.

[17] Personal communication, 5 August 1994

[18] The various legislative provisions on this function have barely changed at all since independence. They will be considered in greater detail below. See for the most recent legislation art.32 Law nr.14/1985, replacing art.47 Law nr.13/1965, which replaced art.12 Law nr.1/1950, which finally replaced art.157 Colonial Law on the Judicial Organization S.1847:23. All legislation referred to distinguishes between supervision over the judiciary, on the one hand, and over the legal profession, on the other—cf. for the latest law art.36 Law nr.14/1985. At a conference held April 2, 1980, involving the Supreme Court and the chairmen of the appellate courts, this distinction was identified by the terms "judicial" and "non-judicial" supervision, cf. Mahkamah Agung Circular Letter nr.3/1980 dated 23 September 1980. Supervision over the legal profession will be dealt with in another chapter.

(*Surat Edaran*). On this score, the Supreme Court is an institution far more daunting and mighty than the French *Cour de Cassation,* for instance, which has barely any supervisory powers,[19] or the Dutch Supreme Court, whose supervisory powers are essentially limited to matters of judicial discipline.[20]

Indonesia's Supreme Court is no paper tiger in this regard, as its bite is felt by courts and judges alike. Moreover, the Court has displayed a notable tendency to increase the scope of its supervisory function.

(a) Supervision over Courts and Circular Letters

The legislative mandate states that the Supreme Court shall supervise the judiciary on matters of court administration, or, in the words of a former Court chairman, "the methods of effecting justice."[21] The idea behind this supervisory power, which has colonial and European roots,[22] is that appeal might well serve as an instrument to correct erroneous application of the law in the lower courts; however, it is an ineffective instrument for correcting in these courts administrative problems that affect the administration of justice, yet do not concern an issue of legal dispute. If a supreme court is to have control over the administration of justice in its broadest sense, it must not just serve as the highest appeals tribunal, but must also have powers to provide for the administration of the courts.

The central legislative concept is that the Supreme Court ensure a "judicial process"[23] that is "precise and fair."[24] Since the 1960s, this has been defined to

---

[19] In France, comparable supervisory powers have been granted to a special institution, the *Conseil Superieur de la Magistrature*, in which the government is prominently represented. A. Pouillie, *Le pouvoir judiciaire et les tribunaux* (Paris: Masson, 1985), ch. 3.

[20] See on the historical development, J. T. Buijs, *De Grondwet: Toelichting en kritiek* (Arnhem: Gouda Quint, 1887), pt. 2, p. 458 on art.162; and for the present, J. Remmelink, "De Hoge Raad als toezichthouder," in *De Hoge Raad der Nederlanden 1838-1988: Een portret* (Zwolle: Tjeenk Willink, 1988).

[21] Subekti, *Kekuasaan Mahkamah Agung*, p. 34: *"cara-cara menjalankan peradilan."*

[22] Buijs, *De Grondwet*, p. 458 on art.162. The colonial Regulation on the Judicial Organization (*Reglement op de Rechterlijke Organisatie*) art.157 says that the colonial Supreme Court shall "supervise the administration of justice in the entire territory of the Netherlands-Indies, and ensure that this administration shall be effected properly and correctly. It will supervise the work and actions of the courts . . ."

[23] This is the most adequate translation for the Indonesian concept which is the *"jalan peradilan"*—the "way of justice." The Indonesian term is a literal translation of the Dutch *"rechtsgang,"* which corresponds more or less with the English "judicial process" concept. See for instance, Subekti, *Kekuasaan Mahkamah Agung*, ch. 2. The wording differs slightly between the 1950, 1965, and 1985 laws of the Supreme Court, but are all based on the same idea. The relevant section of art.32(1) Law nr.14/1985 states that the Supreme Court has supervision over "the effectuation of justice by all jurisdictions in performing the function of the judiciary," with the Official Elucidation referring in its introductory note (point 2 sub a) to the *"jalan peradilan"* clause. The few publications dealing with the subject use the terms of the 1985 law and previous legislation without distinction. See for instance, Soedirjo, *Mahkamah Agung, Uraian singkat tentang kedudukan, susunan dan kekuasaannya menurut undang-undang nomor 14 tahun 1985* (Jakarta: Media Sarana Press, 1987), p. 45.

[24] The Indonesian wording is *"seksama dan sewajarnya."* Cf. art.12(2) Law nr.1/1950 and art.47(2) Law nr.13/1965, which follows the Dutch *"behoorlijk en onvertogen,"* and *"nauwkeurig"* ex art.157 Colonial Law on the Judicial Organization S.1847:23.

mean without "obstacles, without delays, and without (excessive) costs."[25] The legislature conceived the Supreme Court's supervisory function as an internal nuts-and-bolts affair directed at ensuring the smooth flow of cases through the judicial apparatus. The most recent legislation cuts cleanly through the somewhat high-minded and elusive thicket of statutory formulae and unequivocally states the goals that have been the legislative mainstay over the past century: "efficiency and effectiveness."[26]

However, in its attempts to realize these statutory goals of efficiency and effectiveness, the Supreme Court went beyond mere nuts and bolts—whatever these may be. Buffeted as it is by political and institutional forces, the Indonesian judicial machinery has a history troubled by breakdowns, blockages, frictions, and overheating of various sorts. In an attempt to remedy these, the Court has intervened in situations as varied as they are unexpected, often quite clearly reaching beyond the statutory mandate of court administration.[27]

Thus, the Court has intervened in such eminently important issues as fundamental due process principles,[28] the settling of backlogs, and a variety of

---

[25] As a general principle for the administration of justice in its entirety, this was first established in art.2(2) Law nr.19/1964. See also S. Mertokusumo, *Sedjarah peradilan dan perundang-undangan di Indonesia sedjak 1942 dan apakah kemanfaatnja bagi kita bangsa Indonesia* (Yogyakarta: Gadjah Mada, 1971), p. 135. It was later repeated in art.4(2) Law nr.14/1970, which constitutes the legislative basis for the judicial organization to the present day. The official elucidation of this law adds a number of criteria, including "just." Neither in the 1970 law nor in the 1985 law on the Supreme Court is there reference to the "precise and fair" concept. Nevertheless, Law nr.2/1986 on the General Courts specifies that the principles of the 1970 law are an elaboration of the "precise and fair" concept—cf. Official Explanation to art.53(2) law no.2/1986. See also Soedirjo, *Mahkamah Agung*, p. 46.

[26] Law nr.14/1985 Official Explanation point 3 sub c.

[27] It may be pointed out, however, that from colonial times onward the supervisory power has been broadly construed. Thus, the colonial Supreme Court exhorted colonial judges on such varied subjects as the treatment of suspects, procedural costs, reporting duties, court composition, terms of appeal, and so on. See generally *Circulaires van het Hooggerechtshof van Nederlandsch-Indië (1866-1916)* (n.d., n.p.). Of particular note is *Rondschrijven* colonial Supreme Court nr.44/94 dated 1 June 1916, stating among other things: "It has come to the attention of the colonial Supreme Court, that—albeit, fortunately, only in incidental cases—there have been occurrences in which judges have lost the dignity of office from view by strongly scolding witnesses or suspects during session, swearing at them, or even becoming physical, for instance, though possibly without hurting them, briefly pulling their ear, or pushing up a bowed head, or striking them with the court mallet . . . " The famous colonial commentator and administrator, G. L. Gonggrijp, described the behavior of a particularly choleric judge who, in fixed order and with few exceptions, would throw his shoe, his cigar, and his law book at suspects. Another judge, described by Gonggrijp as definitely more dangerous, would throw his court mallet at a suspect, which in one case actually cost the defendant his two front teeth. Fearing worse, the court clerk came to the government administrator, who happened to be Gonggrijp, for advice. Gonggrijp told the court clerk to tie the mallet to the bench. This advice was apparently taken, and when the judge in the next case again threw his mallet, "it returned to him as quickly as he threw it," which apparently cured him of the habit forever. G. L. Gonggrijp, *Brieven van Opheffer* (Maastricht: Leiter-Nypels, 1944), pp. 206-207.

[28] Apparently, the Supreme Court has repeatedly intervened in cases involving denial of justice. Such cases typically do not involve difficulties in gaining access to court, but rather concern excessive delays on the part of the court in delivering judgment. Such cases may be brought before the Supreme Court through normal appeal channels, as pointed out by Setiawan, who bases this view on Dutch Supreme Court decision *Nederlandse Jurisprudentie* 1929:847. See Setiawan, *Aneka masalah hukum dan hukum acara perdata* (Bandung: Alumni, 1992), pp. 424-26.

matters in civil procedure, such as appeal or stay of action, as we have noted elsewhere. It also has provided for such ostensibly mundane issues as what dress to wear in court, where to sit,[29] what pictures to put on the walls,[30] what official headings to give to court decisions,[31] the shape, size, and colors of the Supreme Court judicial seal,[32] or the authority of fingerprints in lieu of signatures.[33] Finally, its supervisory power extends to the mundane, addressing questions such as how to bind case-files sent up for cassation.[34] At last, it would be no exaggeration to say that the Court through supervision has touched on practically every issue in the administration of courts and the terrain beyond. Through this function, the

---

Yet this author notes that such cases have never arisen before the Supreme Court, notwithstanding their frequent occurrence in Indonesian judicial practice. As a former associate judge at the Court and a highly respected scholar, Setiawan is well placed for such an observation. In his view, the absence of court decisions in such cases can be explained on grounds of the highly effective supervisory function of the Supreme Court. He argues that plaintiffs successfully invoke the Court's intercession in order to prod the lower courts into action. A recent example illustrates the point. Apparently first instance and appellate courts of Medan were deliberately obstructing the course of justice in a particular case. The party involved appealed to the Supreme Court in its supervisory function, not through normal appeal channels. As the press descended on the Court chairman, Purwoto Gandasubrata, to get his opinion, the Court dispatched one of its own members, the judge responsible for the Medan district, to investigate and settle the issue (*Media Indonesia*, 27 December 1993). It may be added that in colonial times, the Supreme Court intervened publicly in a number of cases involving gross errors of procedure. This was done in part to further its political goal of fully separating judicial and administrative functions in the administration of justice. [Anonymous], *De magistratuur in Nederlandsch-Indië* (Semarang: De Groot, 1878), p. 62; A. J. Immink, *De Regterlijke Organisatie van Nederlandsch-Indië* (The Hague: Stemberg, 1882), p. 197 passim. Circular Letters colonial Supreme Court no.2 dated 10 December 1863; no.1 dated 27 February 1861, in *Het Regt in Nederlandsch-Indië*, pt. 21, p. 76 and pt. 19, p. 155.

[29] Mahkamah Agung Circular Letter nr.22/1969 dated 2 December 1969.

[30] See Mahkamah Circular Letter nr.4/1959 dated 1 March 1959 stating that each court must have the state seal put on the wall behind the court chairman without any other sign or symbols. Though this directive may seem trivial, it must be remembered that this development coincided with the progressive abolition of the autonomous courts left over from colonial times. Unlike state courts, these autonomous courts derived their authority from the various semi-autonomous states within the national framework. The imposition of the state seal in all courts by this letter of 1959 symbolized the definite collapse of these semi-autonomous states and their replacement by a unitary republic in which all administration of justice derived its authority exclusively from that republic.

[31] Mahkamah Agung Circular Letter nr.10/1985. The practical effect of this letter is extremely important. The law states that legal documents, including court decisions but also such documents as notary deeds, only have legal effect if certain formal requirements are fulfilled, one such requirement being that the document be headed with an official caption. The absence of that caption meant that the document had no executory effect and as a result could not be implemented. The problem had arisen earlier with notary deeds—cf. Mahkamah Agung Circular Letter nr.MA/Pemb/0951/80 dated 20 October 1980.

[32] Mahkamah Agung Circular Letter no.MA/Pemb/7873/84 dated 28 November 1984. This is important for the authentication of documents, though skilled craftsmen on Jakarta street corners can create exact replicas of such stamps within minutes.

[33] Mahkamah Agung Circular Letter nr.1/1959 dated January 1959. The letter purports to ensure stricter rules for ascertaining the authenticity of fingerprints in lieu of signatures on official appeal documents. Needless to say, in a country in which analphabetism exists, the option of signing documents with fingerprints is important for ensuring equitable treatment of citizens by the courts.

[34] Mahkamah Agung Circular Letter nr.4/1969 dated 26 April 1969.

Supreme Court plays a significant role in shaping the administration of justice in Indonesia as a whole.

A few examples illustrate the significance of Supreme Court Circular Letters. Following the end of Guided Democracy, Circular Letters addressed ostensibly mundane administrative matters—concerning the judiciary's wardrobe and seating arrangements—that in fact had great symbolic and political significance. It will be recalled that revolutionary politics under Sukarno's Guided Democracy in the early 1960s seriously weakened the position of the courts, a condition reflected in some elementary practices in the courtroom. Thus, in 1964 judges were instructed to replace their official judicial robes, the so-called *toga*, with the standard civil servant uniform, demonstrating that judges were part of, rather than separate from, the civil service, and hence subject to civil service regulations and ultimately executive control. Another indication of changed power relationships was that public prosecutors, who had acquired considerable political power during Guided Democracy, shifted their position in the courtroom; whereas previously the prosecutor had stood obliquely to the bench, now he sat behind the bench and next to the judge. This new arrangement reflected an actual shift in power, for judges henceforth had to reach their verdict *in agreement* with the prosecutors, not independently from them. The prosecutor was now on a par with the judges and operating within a clear hierarchical relationship as representative of his political boss, the Chief Public Prosecutor. When Guided Democracy ended, the Supreme Court intervened swiftly to restore the old situation, issuing in 1966 a Circular Letter that sternly instructed all the judges of the land to wear judicial robes again.[35] Then in 1969, the Supreme Court issued another Letter directing the judges to sit apart from the public prosecutors,[36] and issued a further instruction that the lower judges reach their verdict independently from the prosecutors, not in agreement with them.[37]

These Circular Letters were obviously important both constitutionally and politically, as they were aimed at restoring judicial independence, not just on paper, but in the eyes of the general public. The return to robes set the judges apart from the civil service hierarchy and symbolized their independence. Restoring the old court layout reestablished the physical distance between judge and prosecutor and symbolized the rearrangement of their constitutional positions relative to one another. This action was reinforced by abolishing the procedure that required a judge to reach a consensual verdict with the prosecutor.

---

[35] Mahkamah Agung Circular Letter nr.6/1966 dated 11 September 1966 followed by Mahkamah Agung Circular Letter nr.121/70/518/1970/Pid. dated 17 September 1970. Subsequently, the Supreme Court also issued directives outlining proper court dress for advocates—cf. Mahkamah Agung Circular Letter nr.MA/Pemb/999/71 dated 26 May 1971 (on advocates). The judicial gown was abolished in 1964—cf. Instruction Minister of Justice and Minister of the Interior no.I.S. 4/19/22 jo.2195/Menko/64 dated 3 October 1964; Instruction Minister of Justice no.J.S. 1/9 A/16 dated 24 October 1964. Lately, and in line with the general practice in Indonesia, where public officers are expected to wear standardized clothes when on duty, the specificities of the official judicial gown and normal working dress have been laid out with minute precision—cf. Mahkamah Agung Circular Letter nr.MA/Pemb/8364/84 dated 18 December 1984.

[36] Mahkamah Agung Circular Letter nr.22/1969 dated 2 December 1969.

[37] Mahkamah Agung Circular Letter nr.11/1969 dated 14 August 1969.

Circular Letters have also proven important in the administrative sphere, most notably in the Court's efforts to reduce case backlogs clogging the lower courts. Both the colonial and independent Supreme Courts have focused on backlogs in their attempts to supervise the judiciary. Backlogs in the lower courts have been caused at least in part by a constant understaffing of the judiciary from the nineteenth century onwards. Only under the New Order government in the 1970s was this problem effectively resolved. The colonial Supreme Court had intervened on numerous occasions and in various ways by issuing Circular Letters to get rid of backlogs, sometimes at the expense of justice. As described in the dismissive comment of one contemporaneous critic, it was like selling justice by the yardstick.[38] After the transfer of sovereignty, the Indonesian lower courts were faced almost immediately with serious backlog problems. Availing itself of its supervisory power, the Supreme Court tried to resolve the issue essentially in two ways: first by improving discipline within the judiciary; and second, by changing the courts' composition.

As regards judicial discipline, the Supreme Court followed the colonial example of imposing a minimum workload on each judge, if need be at the penalty of administrative sanctions. Thus, when in 1951 the Court was faced with a mounting backlog of cases in the lower courts, particularly in the criminal sphere, it issued a Circular Letter instructing the district courts to decide at least sixty criminal cases a month.[39] Despite this directive, backlogs continued to accumulate in the 1950s and early 1960s, caused in part, no doubt, by the increasing workload which the existing judicial structure was not equipped to handle. In addition, however, as judges became increasingly demoralized, their working discipline and performance steadily declined. It appears from the records that by 1960 judges were barely able to keep abreast of the cases coming in each month, let alone settle backlogs, which in some courts began to run into the thousands. Again in 1960, the Supreme Court intervened with a Circular Letter reminding the courts of the 1951 instruction.[40] The Court's increasingly frantic exhortations reflect the growing pressures on the judiciary, as, barely two years after the 1960 missive, another Circular Letter informed the judges that they were doing even worse than before, for the courts were settling on average no more than ten cases a month, a disappointing performance that prevailed regardless of the number of cases registered or existing backlogs, and that was exacerbated by the inadequate

---

[38] A. J. Immink, *Iets over de tegenwoordige onafhankelijkheid van de Nederlandsch-Indische rechterlijke ambtenaren* (Amsterdam: De Bussy, 1880), p. 21. One example recounted by this author was the appointment, in 1876, of an additional judge to the Semarang *Raad van Justitie*, an action which was meant to deal with the backlog there. The new judge was reputed to be very efficient in eliminating backlogs, and in fact proceeded to settle cases with such alacrity that counsel was unable to present argument. The backlog was settled in six months, to the considerable satisfaction of the colonial Supreme Court, and the judge in question was duly promoted. See also M. C. Piepers, "Iets over de rechterlijke macht in het algemeen, hare verhouding tot de andere staatsmachten en tot de maatschappij," *Indisch Weekblad van het Recht* (1878), nr.773-780 at nr.779, p. 86. Reflecting the importance attached to the speedy settlement of cases, the colonial Supreme Court successfully pushed for the government to enact a regulation stipulating that the Indonesian *landraad* courts must settle at least four hundred criminal and civil cases a year (S.1875-12 *Bijblad* 3068). This regulation inspired later interventions of a similar nature by the post-independence Supreme Court.

[39] Mahkamah Agung Circular Letter nr.5/Db/1951.

[40] Mahkamah Agung Circular Letter nr.4/1960 dated 11 July 1960.

implementation of the verdicts that were decided.[41] In fact, the Court had discovered that even after a judge had rendered his verdict in a case, it could take several years before his decision was properly issued to the parties.[42] In 1964, the Supreme Court asked judges at least to go to their offices.[43]

While the situation improved in the early years of the New Order in terms of political environment and judicial organization, the impact of the improvements was slow, and cases kept coming in. The Supreme Court found in 1969 that in some courts cases were ten years behind schedule. With improved prospects for the judiciary, and with a more confident Supreme Court, the Court took sterner measures, threatening the lower courts with disciplinary action.[44] Even though backlogs in the lower courts decreased from the 1970s onwards, this did not reflect increased efficiency of those courts, as might be expected. On the contrary, Circular Letters well into the 1990s reveal Supreme Court concern about lower court sloppiness in handling cases and the resultant, unacceptable delays. Relying on the time-honored practice that cases should be dealt with without delay, Chairman Purwoto Gandasubrata issued Circular Letter no.6/1992, in which he instructed lower courts that cases had to be completed within six months. The continued problems are evidenced by the fact that Chairman Sarwata had to reissue the letter six years later.[45]

The other method by which the Court tried to solve bottlenecks was by changing the court's composition. Thus, it allowed single-judge panels, rather than the three-judge panels prescribed by law, to decide cases "if circumstances so dictate."[46] Clearly, backlogs constituted such circumstances. This remained "general practice" until the accumulation of undecided cases declined by the end of the 1960s,[47] enabling the Supreme Court in 1969 to allow a single-judge panel only "under exceptional circumstances,"[48] which might include excessive backlogs.

---

[41] Mahkamah Agung Circular Letter nr.4/1962, in which the Supreme Court expressed its concern (among other things) that the courts seemed to have left all executory matters to the court clerk (*griffier*), reflecting the fact that courts no longer bothered about the enforcement of court decisions and orders.

[42] Mahkamah Agung Circular Letter nr.2/1963.

[43] Mahkamah Agung Circular Letter nr.1/1964 dated 20 January 1964. Two years earlier, a similar despairing Mahkamah Agung Circular Letter was issued, cf. Circular Letter nr.3/1962 dated 7 May 1962.

[44] Mahkamah Agung Circular Letter nr.12/1969.

[45] Mahkamah Agung Circular Letter 3/1998. Also *Media Indonesia*, 27 December 1993. See also Chapter 8, paragraph 2.

[46] The requirement that three judges hear a case was instituted with art.8(1) Law nr.19/1964 and reaffirmed with art.29(1) Law nr.13/1965. The Court allowed single judges to continue hearing cases with Circular Letter nr.19/1964 dated 23 December 1964. The Supreme Court was inspired to adopt this measure in part because a fair number of courts were staffed by less than three judges at the time and a strict application of the 1964 law would have quite effectively killed off whatever spark there was left in the judicial apparatus. Nevertheless, as is clear from Circular Letter no.3/1965 dated 1 February 1965, the backlog was at the forefront of the Court's concerns.

[47] Wording by the Supreme Court: Mahkamah Agung Circular Letter nr.M.A./Pemb./720/1970 dated 30 March 1970 ad 3.

[48] The Court cited the increased number of judges as the primary motivation for this Letter. Mahkamah Agung Circular Letter nr.10/1969 dated 9 August 1969.

During this period, in fact, backlogs were exceptional.[49] By 1970, the Supreme Court issued an unequivocal instruction to return to collegiate decision-making if sufficient judges were available.[50] In 1975 the development was capped with an instruction that the judiciary practice decision making without exceptions.[51]

The Supreme Court's use of Circular Letters to address problems created by excessive backlogs was typical and thus illustrative; it would confront problems in other spheres with this same instrument. The ambit of such intervention encompassed issues ranging from forced workloads, through fixed office hours, to the size of the judges' panels. At the same time, such examples illustrate the limitations of administrative intervention: the quasi-disintegration of the judiciary during Guided Democracy led to a series of frantic Circular Letters which could do little to alter the general political atmosphere in which the courts operated.

For all their scope, Circular Letters remained internal bureaucratic instruments directed toward ensuring administrative discipline within the judiciary. As a result, by law they had no binding effect upon the general public. They were also precluded from intervening in issues of substantive law. On these two points there have been subtle but important changes in the last two decades.

(b) Intensifying Supervision

(i) Multiplication of Reporting Duties

Since about the 1960s, the Supreme Court has increasingly resorted to instruments of supervision, with the clear purpose of intensifying its control over the lower courts.

One notable result of intensified supervision has been that reporting duties have multiplied. Lower courts did report to the Supreme Court in colonial times, but the practice was limited and skeletal; it expanded after independence.[52] As a result, lower court judges spend most of their time, when not engaged in decision making, drafting detailed reports of their activities. Until the 1990s, district courts had to report on the number of cases registered, pending, and decided both to the Supreme Court and to the appeals court under whose jurisdiction they resided. In addition, they had to send a monthly list of cases that had been appealed in cassation. Finally, they had to submit quarterly reports incorporating the same data, as well as a list of the number of cases decided by each judge. A comparable system of reporting was required by the appeals courts that sent records of

---

[49] The letter refers to art.29(3) Law nr.13/1965. In an oblique reference to backlogs, the Official Explanation to this article states that single-judge panels may be instituted "to smooth the judicial process" by "speeding up the administration of justice."

[50] Mahkamah Agung Circular Letter nr.M.A./Pemb./720/1970 dated 30 March 1970 only allowed single-judge panels in cases where three judges had been presiding but one or two of them had dropped out for various reasons along the way.

[51] Mahkamah Agung Circular Letter nr.2/1975 dated 28 August 1975.

[52] The inherited colonial legislative system prescribed only quarterly reports to the Supreme Court, and only criminal cases were to be included in those reports—though in practice the principle was extended to civil cases as well. cf. C. W. Margadant, *Het Regeeringsreglement van Nederlandsch-Indië*, 3 vols. (Batavia: J. Kolff, 1894-97), p. 220.

activities to the Supreme Court, supplemented by an area report on the district courts' performance.[53]

From 1992 onwards, reporting duties increased, as each district court was from that time required to send in at least fifteen reports annually, with a breakdown as follows:

A. To the Supreme Court, the relevant Appeals Court, and the Department of Justice: two annual reports on the number of cases
B. To the Supreme Court
   1. Monthly: • report on civil cases • report on the finances regarding civil cases • report on criminal cases
   2. Every Four Months: • report on civil cases that have been appealed • report on civil cases submitted for cassation • report on enforcement of cases • report on criminal cases that have been appealed • report on criminal cases submitted for cassation • report on criminal cases submitted for special review • report on criminal cases in which amnesty has been requested
   3. Every Six Months: • assessment report on judges in civil cases • assessment report on judges in criminal cases • report on activities of the supervisory judges

Although their mandated assessments were not as extensive, the appeals courts still also had to send in six reports annually.[54]

---

[53] Soedirjo, *Mahkamah Agung*, pp. 46-47; Subekti, *Kekuasaan Mahkamah Agung*, pp. 35-37. It may be recalled that in colonial times the *Raad van Justitie* could, on its own authority or at the request of the colonial Supreme Court, examine decisions of the Indonesian *landraad* courts that could not be appealed—cf. art.129a colonial Regulation on the Judicial Organization. This effectively was a delegation of the supervisory function of the colonial Supreme Court. G. André de la Porte, *Recht en rechtsbedeling in Nederlandsch-Indië* (The Hague: Belinfante, 1933), p. 134. Nevertheless, an essentially one-step system that involved direct reporting from first instance courts to the colonial Supreme Court—and, after independence, to the Indonesian Supreme Court—prevailed. See for instance Circular Letter nr.8/Db/1950 dated 14 November 1950; Circular Letter nr.2/Db/1951 dated 10 January 1951; and Circular Letter nr.58/P/860/Db./60. Two-step reporting was progressively introduced. Thus, in 1954 the Supreme Court stated explicitly that the appellate courts were themselves allowed to issue guidelines and give instructions to first instance courts within their area of jurisdiction, provided that power was delegated to them. See Mahkamah Agung Circular Letter nr.1/1954. In 1965, Law nr.13/1965 art.39 established supervision by appellate courts of first instance courts. This effectively introduced a two-step reporting system. See also Circular Letter nr.5/1966 dated 7 September 1977; and Circular Letter nr.1/1967 dated 7 February 1967. This decision was affirmed in 1969, when, during a conference between the Supreme Court and the chairmen of the appellate courts (June 9-11, 1969), it was decided henceforth to transfer supervision over first instance courts to the appellate level throughout the country. Because they function as the district courts on other issues, the appeals courts are referred to as the *voorpost* of the Supreme Court in the regions. *Voorpost* is the Dutch term for "advanced posts" or feelers, which indicates that ultimate judicial responsibility continued to rest with the Supreme Court. See Mahkamah Agung Circular Letter nr.MA/Pemb./929/1970 dated 22 April 1970. In 1986, the two-step reporting system was ensconced in law: art.53(3) Law nr.2/1986.

[54] Circular Letter no.5/1992, elaborating on the Decision of the Chairman no.KMA/012-SK/III/1990[?] and KMA/019-SK/VIII/1991. These regulations refer to the reporting duties of the general district courts. Reporting duties of the special jurisdictions, though still impressive, are not as intensive. See most recently Circular Letter nr.2/1993 on the religious courts, which requests nine reports annually.

(ii) Broadening Circular Letters

The clearest evidence of intensified supervision by the Supreme Court over the lower courts is that Circular Letters came to be used with increasing frequency and with a steadily broadening scope.[55] In the process, they clearly were no longer limited to the administrative domain, but extended to matters of substantive law. Like regulations, Circular Letters began to serve as authoritative statements on the law.

Rare in the 1950s, Circular Letters became much more frequent in later years. Thus, in the period 1951-1960, the total number of Circular Letters published was only twenty-six, yet by 1981-1990 this number had risen to 128. The increase was not constant, however, as the underlying figures indicate.

Figure 1: The Number of Published Supreme Court Circular Letters[56]

	1960: 4	1970: 19	1980: 9	1990: 5
1951: 3	1961: 7	1971: 10	1981: 6	1991: 1
1952: 1	1962: 6	1972: 6	1982: 3	1992: 7
1953: 1	1963: 4	1973: 13	1983: 36	1993: 6
1954: 3	1964: 13	1974: 4	1984: 24	1994: 6
1955: 3	1965: 5	1975: 8	1985: 28	1995: 1
1956: 0	1966: 5	1976: 5	1986: 5	1996:
1957: 1	1967: 6	1977: 4	1987: 8	1997: 2
1958: 2	1968: 6	1978: 4	1988: 6	
1959: 5	1969: 28	1979: 4	1989: 4	

Clearly, the Supreme Court exercised very active supervision in some years, yet in others it was relatively quiet. Notable "peak" years are 1969 (29 Circular Letters), 1983 (36 Circular Letters), and 1985 (28 Circular Letters). It may be noted that these peak years often occur just after the appointment of new Court chairmen,

---

[55] These Circular Letters originated from colonial times, when it was felt necessary to give the colonial Supreme Court additional powers to control the sprawling judicial apparatus. It must be pointed out that the colonial Court sometimes used these letters for external effect also. Thus, in its struggle to separate judicial from administrative functions at the *landraad* courts in the late nineteenth century, the colonial Supreme Court issued a number of Circular Letters noting blatant errors committed by administrator-judges concerning the most elementary principles of justice. Unable to quash these decisions in appeal, the Circular Letters were used to express public disapproval of administrative performance by the court. Margadant, *Het Regeeringsreglement*, p. 221; Philip Kleintjes, *Staatsinstellingen van Nederlandsch-Indië*, 2 vols. (Amsterdam: J. H. de Bussy, 1927-29), part II, p. 273; [Anonymous], *De magistratuur in Nederlandsch-Indië* (Semarang: De Groot, 1878), p. 62; Immink, *De regterlijke organisatie*, p. 197 passim; Circular Letters colonial Supreme Court nr.2 dated 10 December 1861; nr.1 dated 18 February 1863; nr.1 dated 27 February 1861, in *Het Regt in Nederlandsch-Indië*, pt. 21, p. 76 and pt. 19, p. 155.

[56] These are the Circular Letters as published by the Supreme Court itself—cf. Mahkamah Agung R.I., *SEMA Tahun 1951-1978*; Mahkamah Agung R.I., *SEMA Tahun 1979-1985*; Mahkamah Agung R.I., *SEMA Tahun 1981-1991*; Mahkamah Agung R.I., *Himpunan Surat Edaran Mahkamah Agung Republik Indonesia 1951-1999* (Jakarta: Mahkamah Agung, 2000).

with 1969 being Subekti's first full year of tenure, 1983 that of Mudjono, and 1985 that of Ali Said. This suggests that Court chairmen avail themselves of Circular Letters to shape the judiciary to their image and ideas. It also indicates that Circular Letters function as instruments of reform or repair; when conditions are stable, they remain unused. Still, the overall figures show that the Supreme Court has used the instrument with increasing frequency.

In addition, the scope of Circular Letters was gradually broadened. Rather than remaining tied to matters of court administration, Circular Letters also began to encroach on matters of substantive law. Though it happened gradually, the paper wall dividing administrative matters from substantive legal matters was ultimately breached, I would submit, with Circular Letter no.3/1963. Issued at the height of the revolutionary politics marking Sukarno's Guided Democracy, this letter purported to do away with the Civil Code, stating that the code violated the revolutionary spirit and hence should no longer have the binding authority of law, but should only serve as a guideline. Some particular articles of the code were singled out for violating the Indonesian revolution and nullified in this letter.[57]

After the fall of Guided Democracy, legal commentators strongly criticized the Circular Letter. In fact, in 1967 a court decision at appeals level presided over by one of Indonesia's most authoritative appeal court judges, Asikin Kusumah Atmadja, voided the Circular Letters. The judge accepted the argument of the claimant that such letters are no more than "cat's bells" (after the Dutch *kattebelletje*—a mere scrawl) and denied that they had any binding force whatsoever.[58] Moreover, he stated that laws could not be voided by Circular Letters. This argument was accepted by the Supreme Court in cassation.[59] While this decision settled the matter as far as the law was concerned, the Circular Letter had a remarkable afterlife that should trouble conscientious lawyers. The Kusumah Atmadja and Supreme Court decisions are hardly ever quoted and barely known in modern Indonesia, while the controversial 1963 Circular Letter is still routinely cited as if no contradictory decisions had intervened;[60] both these conditions confirm the court decision's relative loss of authority and the Circular Letter's comparable gain. Indeed, while the Supreme Court accepted the validity

---

[57] See generally, Gouwgioksiong, "De rechtsontwikkeling in Indonesië na de souvereiniteitsoverdracht," *Weekblad voor Privaatrecht, Notaris-ambt en Registratie* (1968), nrs.4982-4984; Setiawan, *Aneka masalah hukum*, ch. 8.

[58] Jakarta Appellate Court nr.249/1967 PT. Perdata, published in *Yurisprudensi Indonesia* (1969): 609.

[59] Decision Mahkamah Agung no.105K/Sip/1968 dated 12 June 1968 published in *Yurisprudensi Indonesia* (1969-I): 609. In the wording of the Supreme Court, "there are insufficient grounds to conclude that the decision of the *iudex facti* in this case violates the law ..."

[60] The letter is listed in the most authoritative compilation of modern Indonesian law regulations: *Himpunan peraturan perundang-undangan Republik Indonesia* (Jakarta: Ichtiar Baru-Van Hoeve, 1989), p. 597. It also is listed rather indiscriminately in the Supreme Court compilation Mahkamah Agung R.I., *Himpunan Surat Edaran SEMA Tahun 1951-1978*, p. 69. It may be noted that Indonesian legal commentators often refer to a 1972 speech of Supreme Court chairman Subekti at Gadjah Mada University as a basis for voiding Circular Letter nr.3/1963. Speeches are a rather flimsy basis, if basis at all in law, to void anything, and the alleged importance of this speech underlines the decline of Court decisions as a source of law.

of Kusumah Atmadja's argument in its own decision, it consistently refused to draw the logical conclusion and explicitly void the 1963 Circular Letter.[61]

Yet the more important feature of Circular Letter no.3/1963 for our purposes here is that it dealt in no uncertain terms with substantive law and thus clearly exceeded the legislative mandate that restricted its application to "court administration." It created an important precedent that was soon followed. From being internal bureaucratic instruments of a purely administrative nature, Circular Letters became important indicators of the way in which the Supreme Court interpreted the law, or wished lower courts to interpret the law. These Letters thus acquired external influence in that they affected the rights and duties of individual citizens.

As regards substantive law, although Supreme Court chairman Subekti maintained in the late 1960s that Circular Letters dealt with "administrative matters only," even during his tenure these letters quite clearly encroached upon the areas of substantive law. For instance, in response to the ongoing value loss of the Indonesian currency, the Rupiah,[62] the Court from the 1950s onwards declared the colonial statute prohibiting the securing of contractual financial liabilities with reference to the gold standard[63] (intended to guard against currency fluctuations) to be null and void. In a rare example of consistent decision-making, the Court allowed the securing of contractual liabilities against the gold standard, with a risk-sharing proviso, and decided more than twenty cases along this line.

The relevant point here is that almost fifteen years after the matter had been firmly settled by this series of published Supreme Court decisions,[64] in 1969 the Menado appeals court chairman asked the Supreme Court for instructions on how to deal with the matter of currency loss in contract law.[65] The Court responded with a letter referring to its latest decision, and repeated the passage containing the relevant legal argument verbatim.[66] As a result of the subsequent correspondence between the Menado appeals circuit and the Supreme Court, in 1970 the Court issued a Circular Letter for all courts, referring to its earlier decision regarding contract liabilities and the gold standard, along with the risk-sharing proviso, and declaring that these should be regarded as the law of the land.[67] It is worth recalling that by that year at least thirteen cases on the issue had already been decided by the Supreme Court and published.

This example testifies to the increasing scope and importance of Supreme Court Circular Letters, as well as the dramatic decline in the authority of the Court's decisions, whether or not they were published. It would appear that the Menado appeals court, as well as many other courts, were quite simply unaware of a

---

[61] While the Supreme Court at times repeals its own Circular Letters (see for instance Circular Letters nr.11/1969 and nr.12/1985), it did not do so with the Circular Letter nr.3/1963.

[62] See above, chapter 6; see also Sebastiaan Pompe, "Some Comments on the Depreciation of Currency Value in Indonesian Law," *Varia Peradilan* 6,70 (1989): 102.

[63] Ordinance on the Gold Clause S.1937-585.

[64] As far as I could trace it, the first decision was issued on 11 May 1955 and published in the journal *Hukum* 3 (1955).

[65] Letter no.2273/KPT/1969 dated 28 August 1969 referred to in the response of the Supreme Court.

[66] Letter nr.Um/660/X/950/P/I/1969 dated 20 October 1969.

[67] Circular Letter nr.4/1970 dated 2 March 1970.

consistent line of Supreme Court cases on this contractual issue, even though these decisions had been published. The Court had to employ a Circular Letter to settle the issue.

That Letter unquestionably dealt with substantive law, legitimizing this apparent transgression of authority by referring to the Court's own decision. It is a technically interesting nuance, demonstrating that, at this juncture at least, the Court denied the lawmaking function of Circular Letters. It still perceived these Circulars as essentially internal administrative instruments, serving merely as a conduit, i.e., to notify lower courts of Supreme Court decisions in answer to queries or problems.

This approach persisted into the 1970s. During this period, the Supreme Court as a matter of common practice began to provide for matters of substantive law by Circular Letter, but when it did so it invariably referred to its own Court decisions. Thus, by way of example, Circular Letter no.8/1980 referring to Supreme Court decision no.349 K/Kr/1980 dated 26 December 1980 extended the ambit of art.284(1) Criminal Code on adultery to persons who marry polygamously without court authorization as required by law. Sometimes, these court decisions constituted an attachment to the Circular Letter.[68]

The emergence of Circular Letters as a conduit for Supreme Court decisions in the 1970s altered their role and significance in Indonesian legal practice in a number of important ways. By acting as a conduit, Circular Letters arguably speeded up rather than countered the declining authority of Court decisions. It appeared that Supreme Court decisions carried no weight at all if they lacked Circular Letters to confirm them. Circular Letters were now used to notify the public and the lower courts of the Supreme Court's opinions concerning the law and, ultimately, to establish that law, which meant that they no longer served as mere internal, administrative instruments. For all their internal intent as far as the law is concerned, Circular Letters had an external effect.

Developments in the 1980s reinforced this pattern. During this decade, Circular Letters ceased to refer to Court decisions when providing for substantive law. Often they made no reference to their source of legitimacy, and if they did, it was to such vague concepts as "government policy." Circular Letters began to provide for substantive law matters not merely as a continuation of the Court's decision-making role, but independently from it. As a result, these letters developed into instruments for shaping the law in their own right. Thus, in a 1988 Circular Letter on illegal fishing, the Supreme Court quite simply extended the meaning of the legislative terminology, thus broadening criminal liability.[69] A 1989 Circular Letter blandly

---

[68] See for instance Circular Letter nr.4/1975 dated 1 December 1975 (civil procedure); Circular Letter nr.1/1980 dated 5 March 1980 (labor law); Circular Letter nr.4/1980 dated 23 September 1980 (criminal procedure); Circular Letter nr.8/1980 dated 31 December 1980 (marriage law); Circular Letter nr.1/1981 dated 22 January 1981 (criminal procedure).

[69] Circular Letter nr.3/1988 dated 20 February 1988. The letter states that the term "use" (*menggunakan*) in Presidential Decision nr.39/1980 must be interpreted to encompass "do" (*membuat*), "master" (*menguasai*), "carry" (*membawa*), "store" (*menyimpan*), "use" (*menggunakan*), and "trade" (*memperdagangkan*). The last is important, as it suggests that owners of trawling vessels can be held criminally liable for illegal fishing even though they may not be the masters of the ship. The Letter also requests the courts to impose higher punishments for such violations.

stated that in certain cases unmentioned in the law, traffic violators may be imprisoned.[70]

Perhaps the clearest illustration that Circular Letters had acquired lawmaking power, not merely as an extension of Court decisions but independently from them, was when the Court started to qualify its own decisions with Circular Letters. In 1970 the Supreme Court issued a decision that allowed citizens a fairly wide latitude in their recourse against the state on grounds of government tort (art.1365 Indonesian Civil Code).[71] In the 1980s, a Circular Letter was issued which seriously qualified and restricted this ruling on the grounds that "it overly emphasized the protection of the individual as against the state."[72]

As perceived by the Supreme Court, therefore, by the 1980s, Circular Letters had effectively supplanted the authority of Court decisions. This happened not as a result of a previous Court decision, but by virtue of the authority that these Circular Letters commanded in practice. It is indicative, perhaps, that the large compilations of Circular Letters came to be published during this period, not before.[73] The Letters were used with ever greater frequency,[74] and, while continuing to emphasize court administration, they began also to cover matters of substantive law and, in time, to undercut the power of the Court's own decisions.

(iii) Effectiveness

It is easy to understand the Supreme Court's gravitation toward Circular Letters as instruments by which to shape the law. Compared to Court decisions, such letters are much more efficient instruments for controlling the lower courts. This comparative efficiency rests on a number of factors, namely clarity, lower cost, focus, and ease of enforcement. In addition, Circular Letters have the advantage of initiative.

Clarity. Circular Letters are much more easily formulated and digested than court cases. Court decisions are still tied down by the cumbersome forms inherited from colonial times and the French system, which involve a long enumeration of the relevant facts and positions by both parties, followed by a list of legal considerations, leading then to a decision. The language and terminology is cluttered with historical forms, making for convoluted, winding sentences that are usually difficult to digest. Decisions are formulated so briefly and generally that it often requires close reading and analysis to make out what actually has been decided. Circular Letters do not suffer from such problems. Their terminology is clear and unambiguous. They rarely exceed a single page; some are no longer than one or two sentences. They amount to little else but directives or instructions.

---

[70] Circular Letter nr.3/1989 dated 29 May 1989.

[71] Decision Mahkamah Agung nr.838K/Sip/1970 dated 3 March 1971.

[72] Letter Mahkamah Agung no.M.A./Pemb/0519/77 dated 25 February 1977 listed in C. Ali, *Himpunan peraturan hukum agraria* (Bandung: Binacipta, 1980), p. 577. Quotation at point 6, p. 581.

[73] The first of the compilations was published in 1979. See footnote 4 above.

[74] According to the publications cited, the growing significance of Circular Letters was matched by their ever more frequent use: while only twenty-six letters were published in the first decade, their number had increased to 128 in the period 1980-1990.

Lower Cost. Single-paged Circular Letters are handier and cheaper to distribute than full reports of Court decisions, which can run to tens, sometimes hundreds, of pages.

Focus. The Supreme Court is not tied down by the specifics of a particular case when writing and issuing a Circular Letter, but can intervene in an issue it both chooses and defines. Rather than having parties decide the issue or purpose of the intervention, the Court chooses its own focus and response. As a result, it can more effectively address what it considers to be core problems, and at the same time evade questions that it might find problematic or of peripheral importance.

Ease of Enforcement. Finally, Circular Letters are bureaucratic instruments of control, wielded by the Supreme Court in its supervisory function and coupled, as a result, with a wide array of disciplinary sanctions. Unlike Court decisions, with their vague precedent value, Circular Letters actually have force. We will examine this issue more closely in the next section.[75]

And Circular Letters have another significant advantage over decision making. This is the advantage of initiative: unlike Court decisions, the Supreme Court can take the initiative in responding to what it perceives as pressing problems, not needing to wait for a case to present itself. This is an important possibility for pulling the initiative for law reform or legal development toward the institution, and tightening the leashes of control throughout the judicial apparatus.

Indeed, as we have seen, sometimes the Supreme Court very busily oversees the lower courts, while at other times it is much less active, apparently because it sees little reason to intervene. Court supervision, then, is essentially reactive, as it responds to problems when they manifest themselves, rather than anticipating those problems. This image of a "reactive" rather than proactive Court is supported by interviews, as one Supreme Court judge put it, "In 1993-1994 we didn't issue any Circular Letters because the lower courts are doing fine and there were no serious problems."[76]

The fact is that for all the information coming up through the extended reporting system, the Supreme Court is only rarely fully aware of what goes on in the field, and thus is unable to act on that information. To some extent, this is a problem of structure. One major problem for the Court (as well as the Department of Justice) has been to manage the information load generated by an expanding judicial apparatus and an intensified reporting system. We will look at this dilemma more closely in Chapter 8, section 4.

---

[75] One Jakarta lawyer suggested that the role of Circular Letters was changing, and that recently the Supreme Court has been issuing Letters not only to keep the lower courts in line, but also to keep government out of its affairs: "The Circular Letter should not just be looked at for what it is. It really is part of a much wider struggle for power between the Supreme Court and the Department of Justice. It is a bureaucratic instrument par excellence in that it is, in effect, 'a direct order' from the Supreme Court to the lower judges. This explains the widening use and impact of these Circulars. The Department of Justice is in constant retreat and effectively has become wholly inactive on the score of judicial organization, with the old civil and criminal directorates becoming some sort of registration office." Personal communication, 8 July 1994. This may be so, but to my mind is not yet clear cut. It should be noted that in the past, the Supreme Court issued Circular Letters deliberately to protect and further government interests within the judiciary, such as in the case of tort actions against the government.

[76] Personal communication, 16 April 1994.

(c) Supervision over Judges

At the same time that the Court has used Circular Letters as handy, flexible instruments to tighten its supervision of the judicial system and even shape the law of the land, it has also adopted a number of policies that have intensified its direct supervision of lower court judges. In fact, in its supervision of the lower courts, the Supreme Court has available a wide array of sanctions that can be applied against judges. In short, if judges do not comply with its instructions, their careers suffer.

The Supreme Court has tended to increase its control over judges by exercising supervision over a broader range of judicial actions and by replacing previously objective, neutral criteria for professional performance and career advancement with more fluid and subjective criteria. Both methods are hard to define precisely, with the result that lower court judges have become more insecure and dependent on the favors of Supreme Court decision makers.

(i) Judicial Acts and Behavior

The range of judicial behavior falling under Supreme Court supervision has broadened to include private, rather than exclusively professional, behavior. The law requires the Supreme Court to supervise "the behavior of judges," but the definition of that concept has clearly been revised over time.[77] Originally, statutory wording explicitly limited supervision to actions taken by judges in their professional capacity only.[78] Law no.1/1950 imposed that restriction in so many words. This restriction is less evident in subsequent legislation. Law no.13/1965 art.47(3) still referred to "acts," but dropped the explicit reference to the judges' professional capacity, only stating somewhat ambiguously that this supervision was meant to ensure a proper functioning of the courts. In fact, former Supreme Court chairman Subekti in 1980 still maintained that judges who gambled, incurred excessive debts, or had extramarital affairs did not fall within the scope of Supreme Court supervision so long as these acts did not affect judicial performance—though he did add that such actions might be prejudicial to a judge's appointment.[79] Then legislation in the 1980s broadened the Supreme Court's oversight powers, permitting them to consider a judge's private behavior in their assessment of his or her performance. Law no.14/1985 no longer referred to "acts" alone, but stated that supervision should extend over "behavior and acts."[80] Moreover, Law no.2/1986 on the General Courts made judges answerable for "ignominious" behavior outside the court,"[81] obviously suggesting that a much wider range of actions were being scrutinized by the Supreme Court. Commentators say that such private behavior as adultery, gambling, regular drunkenness, and physical aggressiveness can be considered by the Court in its professional

---

[77] art.32(2) Law nr.14/1985; art.47(3) Law nr.13/1965 and art.12(3) Law nr.1/1950.

[78] The reference in art.12(3) Law nr.1/1950 to "acts" points at a restriction of supervision to acts undertaken by judges in their professional capacity. The law adds between brackets that these "acts" must be work related.

[79] Subekti, *Kekuasaan Mahkamah Agung,* pp. 35-36.

[80] Art.32(2) Law nr.14/1985.

[81] Law nr.2/1986 art.18(1) jo. art.20(1) and Official Explanation point 4.

assessment of a judge.[82] Clearly, judges may now be called to answer for actions wholly unrelated with their professional work.

The lines are not clearly drawn; only when they are transgressed do they manifest themselves. One judge acutely described the vague rules of this game and the ultimate political result:

> ... rules are set, but nobody quite knows what the rules are and only discovers them after they are crossed. It is on that uncertainty that political power is based.[83]

This uncertainty promotes a feeling of dependence amongst lower court judges.

(ii) Judicial Performance: Examination, Conduite, and the Black Book

The second method by which the Supreme Court increased its supervisory control over personnel in the lower courts was by reducing the role of neutral, objective standards as the yardsticks for measuring judicial performance and in the end determining advancement. Instead, criteria for assessing judicial performance have become more fluid, flexible, and difficult to define.

In the original system adopted from colonial times and prevailing in the 1950s, judges were assessed based on their professional performance: they had to complete their share of work capably. Performance was evaluated quantitatively by reviewing the number of cases each judge had handled, and qualitatively by the so-called *examination*, a critical appraisal of a judge's decisions. The decisions chosen to be evaluated were sometimes the ones coming up through regular appeal channels; alternately the reviewers might select cases that impressed them as relevant. Sometimes cases were selected to be examined on grounds of having attracted public attention.[84] The results of both the quantitative and qualitative supervision are noted in the judge's personal file, the so-called *conduite*. This file is important in determining a judge's career within the judicial apparatus, though exactly how important is difficult to tell. Bad errors are registered in the *black book*. As a result, in the words of one judge:

> ... even though the judge is independent, he must take care in deciding a case, because any decision he takes also determines his advancement.[85]

The importance of the examination and the resulting *conduite* as the principal standard for determining judicial careers has declined over the years. It was still the principal yardstick for advancement under Chairman Soerjadi, who attached

---

[82] Soedirjo, *Mahkamah Agung*, pp. 49-50

[83] Personal communication, 18 July 1994.

[84] Soedirjo, *Mahkamah Agung* p. 50. It may be that, in these cases, examination is not so much intended to be an instrument for evaluating the professional performance of the judge, but rather as a way to mitigate the impact of the decision in the executory phase.

[85] *Kompas*, 6 June 1991, quoting Judge M. S. Lumme: " ... mesti hakim itu mandiri, namun ia tetap harus berhatihati dalam memutuskan suatu perkara, karena semua putusannya akan menentukan pula promosinya."

great importance to it.[86] He raised the matter during a 1966 meeting between the Supreme Court and the appeals courts, after which it was decided that the district court judges would be supervised by the appeals courts, and that Supreme Court supervision would essentially be restricted so that it extended only to the appeals court judges. The examination was based on three recent criminal and three civil cases.[87] In the early 1970s, Supreme Court chairman Subekti still advocated the examination and the *conduite* as the criteria by which the performance of judges was to be evaluated and promotions determined,[88] notwithstanding problems in implementation.[89] The incumbent Supreme Court chairman, Purwoto S. Gandasubrata, when queried on the subject in 1971, stated that in the 1950s the appeals courts and Supreme Court were incomparably more stringent in reviewing district court cases. District court decisions would be sent back heavily marked with blue pencil notes and demands for correction. But now the appeals courts are less stringent, Purwoto said, and they accept all sorts of errors in order to get the cases finished, preferring to settle disputes and eliminate backlogs rather than to uphold formal principles of law.[90]

The system became more flexible under chairman Seno Adji. In 1976 the Supreme Court stated in so many words that the *conduite* was but one of many criteria which could be used to determine judicial promotions and transfers. The other criteria were not specified, however.[91] In 1978, the Supreme Court referred to the examination as a "complementary condition."[92] As noted in Chapter 4, according to one Supreme Court Judge, "the *eksaminasi* ceased in the early 70s," and during this same decade, review and critique of judges' written decisions by their peers became markedly less stringent.[93] The *eksaminasi*, a comparatively objective

---

[86] Personal communication, July 1992. Mr. Soerjadi said dismissively that the kind of active supervision which was prevalent when he was chairman, whereby superior judges would actually call for lower court decisions and comment upon them, was discontinued in modern times. He stated that this was an indication of the declining performance of the Supreme Court.

[87] Mahkamah Agung Circular Letter nr.1/1967 dated 7 February 1967.

[88] In a parting shot by Subekti, the Supreme Court that he chaired supplemented earlier Circular Letters with an exhaustive list of criteria on the basis of which the judges' performance was to be determined. Circular Letter nr.2/1974 dated 16 September 1974.

[89] In 1970, the Supreme Court was forced to acknowledge that supervision of district court judges by the appeal courts was spotty. In fact, the appeal courts failed to carry out examinations, as a result of which no district court judges could be advanced. Circular Letter nr.5/1970 dated 23 March 1970.

[90] Daniel S. Lev archives, (hereafter *DSL*) 15 October 1971. (These are the personal interview notes of Daniel S. Lev; copies will be deposited in the University of Washington library [Seattle, WA], the Cornell University Kroch Collection [Ithaca, NY], and Pusat Studi Hukum dan Kebijakan [PSHK] in Jakarta.) The interview notes indicate that after being appointed PT chairman, Gandasubrata called for an inspection of the courts under his authority and found that, as a result of diminished supervision, now a wide variety of procedural methods were being used in the first instance courts. Thus, in some courts, cases would be allotted to judges by the court clerk, in others by the court chairman, and in others by member judges. This situation prompted him to write a short standard summary of procedural law in 1969 for the first instance courts. This document came to the attention of the Ministry of Justice, and after some revisions, the ministry published the statement and sent it to all the courts under its own imprimatur.

[91] Mahkamah Agung Circular Letter nr.5/1976 dated 15 June 1976.

[92] Mahkamah Agung Circular Letter nr.2/1978 dated 6 April 1978.

[93] Personal communication, 12 May 1995.

method of assessment, was not replaced by clear and unambiguous instruments for evaluating the quality of judicial performances. In the 1980s, the Supreme Court feebly reminded the appeals courts of their supervisory function, drafting this reminder in terms of "education," of the critical evaluation that goes with an examination.[94] All this indicates that judicial performance was no longer being evaluated by objective, neutral criteria.[95]

The result is that lower court judges are currently more dependent on ill-defined and hence arbitrary criteria that determine their professional fate.

(iii) Vague and Arbitrary Rules as Instruments of Control

Supreme Court supervision over judges does work to resolve concrete problems and discipline errant judges, yet in its overall operation the system tends to be vague, changeable, and as a result, unreliable. Rather than explicating what judges should and should not do, it leaves the rules indefinite, and by this means increases the powers of those who are supposed to be supervising the judiciary.

The absence of precise criteria for assessing a judge's professional performance gives the Supreme Court (and the Department of Justice) considerable discretion in deciding how judicial careers will unfold. Dependent on subjective, personal factors to win promotion or appointment to an attractive post, judges are exposed to a variety of pressures and manipulations. Judges can be arbitrarily transferred from prestigious and pleasant postings in the big cities to distant out-of-the-way hamlets, causing considerable personal discomfort, loss of prestige and power, loss of intellectual challenge, and, in many cases, the loss of a comfortable living situation. Following the shake-up of the Central Jakarta district court after allegations of malfeasance in May 1987, many judges were transferred to the provinces. Two of these judges resigned shortly afterwards because, as one said: "Kupang is too quiet, I only get to try horse thieves here"; another was dismissed within a year on corruption charges; a fourth was imprisoned not long afterwards; a fifth committed suicide. The press commented dryly that it does not augur well to be transferred out of Jakarta.[96]

In technical terms, transfers to the Outer Islands might be represented as advancement: junior judges in a big city may be promoted to become chairman or vice-chairman of a provincial court, or be promoted from an urban district to a

---

[94] Mahkamah Agung Circular Letter nr.MA/Pemb./7955/84 dated 18 December 1984.

[95] Few people acknowledge to what extent discretion and preference affect decisions concerning transfers and advancements; most maintain the fiction that the examination remains essential to the evaluation process. See for instance *Kompas*, 6 June 1991: " . . . the examination or annotation of the decisions of a judge to the present day remains instrumental in determining the transfer or advancement of a judge."

[96] According to official sources, this was a routine transfer, rather like shifting the team at bat in a cricket match, intended to let those who had been in Jakarta out and those who had been out in (*Bisnis*, 4 June 1987; *Kompas*, 6 June 1987; *Suara Karya*, 6 June 1987). Some of the judges involved were—and indeed still are—so prominent that it becomes impossible to draw easy conclusions. It may be noted that one of the judges transferred, who soon after resigned from the judiciary, had sat on the notable political trial of Dharsono some years before. Furthermore, the one judge who (according to press reports) had been accused of corruption was not transferred to the provinces but was promoted to the Supreme Court. *Merdeka*, 25 May 1987; *Prioritas*, 2 June 1987; *Bisnis*, 4 June 1987; *Suara Karya*, 6 June 1987; *Kompas*, 6 June 1987, transfer list in *Varia Peradilan* (October 1987); Personal communication, 13 June 1991.

provincial appeals court. Nevertheless, the formal hierarchy does not necessarily correspond to a judge's personal priorities. Most judges want to go to the big cities, preferably the ones on Java, rather than preside over officially superior provincial courts located in regions that lack such big city benefits as good schools, good hospitals and cinemas, and attractive opportunities for making money on the side. The Supreme Court is well aware that all judges covet big city postings. A transfer to the Outer Islands is often viewed as and, indeed, meant as a blot on one's career, or even some sort of punishment. It may bring a judge to resign from the service altogether as his hopes for advancement are crushed.

As a result of all these developments, as supervision has begun to encroach on substantive law, the Supreme Court has gained more power to direct judges' decisions in cases—generally by Circular Letters, or individually by Instructions, as the case may arise. This is not only an important personal and professional problem for judges, but is also a constitutional problem, since the broadening of supervision undermines a judge's independence in reaching his decision as specifically warranted by law.[97] Although many Indonesian justices are understandably too preoccupied with their careers to worry about this much, some thoughtful and concerned individuals do point out that Circular Letters instructing them on how to read the law lack a solid legal basis. As one put it to me:

> The fact is that the Circular Letters [as instructions] really lack a solid legal basis. The way I try to justify them is that they help shape the inner conviction of judges, and in that sense serve as an indirect source of law. In reality these are direct instructions, of course. As regards their encroachment on the field of substantive law, I try to see this as "restatements" of the law, as in the US: a sort of summarizing confirmation of the state of the law, and notably court decisions, on a specific issue at a certain point of time.[98]

This, to be certain, is an elegant argument. Still, it would appear that the judges' inner conviction in complying with a Circular Letter is determined less by the intrinsic theoretical persuasiveness of such an instrument than by their justifiable apprehension concerning what might happen to their careers should they disregard it. Supervision definitely constitutes outside interference in the autonomy of judges in reaching their decision.

3. CONCLUSION

In the past half century, the regulatory and supervisory functions of the Supreme Court have increased significantly in importance. The Court has resorted to these functions with greater frequency, while at the same time broadening the scope of their application, thereby exceeding the restrictions mandated by the legislature, which intended them to be used for court administration, not for shaping substantive law. This development matches the decline of the judicial

---

[97] art.32(5) law nr.14/1985. This proviso does not recur in earlier legislation on the Supreme Court, cf. for instance, art.47 Law nr.13/1965.
[98] Personal communication, 18 July 1994

function as an instrument by which to shape the law. The increasingly fact-specific nature of Supreme Court decision making reduced the ability of the Court to keep the judicial apparatus in line through its decisions and forced it to resort to these other methods. The appeal of the various instruments used by the Court to implement regulation and supervision rests in a number of elements, such as their conciseness and the fact that, with them, the Supreme Court can take the initiative in voicing its opinions and issuing directives on a number of issues, rather than waiting for a relevant case to arise. Notably as regards supervision, the grip of the Supreme Court on the lower courts is particularly strong because through that function the Court can determine judicial career patterns. In the past fifty years, the criteria by which judicial careers are determined have become less clear. As a result, judges concerned about their own professional futures have become more dependent on the Supreme Court's wishes and demands.

CHAPTER EIGHT

THE ORGANIZATION OF THE SUPREME COURT

Over the years, the organization of the Supreme Court altered in a number of important ways, partly in response to the Court's changing position within Indonesia's judiciary. We have already noted that one of the important results of the unification of the court system was to place the Supreme Court at the pinnacle of the judicial organization, which consisted of four jurisdictions (general, religious, military, and administrative). This unification took shape with Law no.13/1965, a controversial law perhaps on constitutional principle, and for that reason short-lived, but one that was innovative and long-lasting as regards the reforms it initiated in judicial organization.[1] The law also envisaged an adaptation of the internal Supreme Court organization to accommodate the revisions in the court system. As the various jurisdictions were to be brought under the Supreme Court's control, separate Court chambers were to be established for each of the jurisdictions.[2] Each chamber was to be headed by a Supreme Court junior chairman, who would fill a new hierarchical slot just under the Supreme Court chairman and vice-chairman.[3]

These provisions were realized very slowly, and when they were it was as a result of an altogether new development. In fact, changes in the Supreme Court's judicial and supervisory functions, discussed in the previous chapter, probably had the most important impact on the Court's internal organization. The Court's expanded control over the lower judiciary increased its workload enormously, as we have seen. The Court at first tried to overcome these problems with a variety of measures, such as increasing the judicial corps and delegating supervisory duties

---

[1] Aside from the results of the law under consideration here, one of its long-lasting effects was to introduce the principle that each province (or Daerah Tingkat I, as the law puts it) should have its appellate courts, and each district (Daerah Tingkat II) its own first instance court. This was the policy yardstick during the first years of Guided Democracy and remains official policy to the present day, being effectively realized at least as regards the general and religious courts—cf. art.25 & 33, Law no.13/1965. Note also that despite the fact that the law was officially repealed in 1969, the Supreme Court subsequently held that this repeal did not apply to Court rules of procedure and, considering parliamentary and government references to the law, certainly not as regards judicial organization. Thus, parliamentary sources reveal that judicial appointments to the Supreme Court right up to the new 1985 Supreme Court law were effected on the basis of Law no.13/1965, see for instance *Dewan Perwakilan Rakyat Republik Indonesia Periode 1971-1977* (Jakarta: DPR, n.d.), pp. 41-44; *Dewan Perwakilan Rakyat Republik Indonesia Periode 1982-1987* (Jakarta: DPR, n.d.), p. 39. Keppres no.75/1985, which provided for the Supreme Court administration, also refers to Law no.13/1965 as its legal basis. Law no.13/1965 was repealed for the second time with Law no.14/1985 (art.81) and that hardy piece of legislative work must be taken to be wholly dead and fully buried as of December 1985.

[2] Law no.13/1965 art.46(2).

[3] Law no.13/1965 art.41(2)(b).

both within the Supreme Court itself and from the Supreme Court to appeal courts. These stopgap measures had an effect on court structure, but did not overcome the workload difficulties. The Court's failure to keep up with decision making developed into a problem of the first order, and by 1981 the backlog of undecided cases at the Supreme Court level had risen to unprecedented levels. When Chairman Mudjono took office that year, he decided to overhaul the Supreme Court's internal organization completely.

The 1981 Mudjono reforms, known as OPSKIS,[4] were based on the idea that the workload problem, particularly backlogs, should be overcome by increasing personnel and realizing the long-delayed provisions of Law no.13/1965 regarding internal Supreme Court organization. They consisted of three major changes: the number of Supreme Court justices was tripled; a new hierarchical structure was imposed with the introduction of junior chairmen; and a new structure for chambers organized along jurisdictional lines was instituted. The present Court is still essentially based on the Mudjono reforms.

These organizational changes did create some problems. First, it remains to be seen whether enlarging the Court effectively helped address the workload dilemma. Although in the short run this increase did alleviate some of the pressures, when Chairman Ali Said retired in 1992 the backlog of undecided cases was larger than ever before—indeed, twice the size of the 1981 backlog that had prompted Mudjono's reforms. Another consequence of the reforms has been even more damaging to the reputation and standing of the Supreme Court. The increase in the size of the Court created problems of coordination and control within the institution that cut at the very roots of the way its functions were realized. Both the judges and the administration were affected.

Most judges were organized in chambers, which, as their number increased, came to operate with increased autonomy. This aspect of the Mudjono reforms fundamentally weakened the Court's organizational cohesion. From the early 1980s, there were serious inconsistencies in the Supreme Court's decision making, a situation that was worsened by the overloaded docket and the lack of legislative clarity. As decisions became increasingly inconsistent, the potential for judicial malfeasance increased. The bloated court bureaucracy suffers from comparable problems of control. In its handling of cases before, during, and after judicial decision making, it does not function as the passive and neutral machine it is supposed to be. On the contrary, the bureaucracy guides and influences the judicial process, sometimes decisively. The extent of this problem became most brutally apparent in a painful incident during the months preceding Supreme Court chairman Ali Said's retirement. At this sensitive juncture, when media and public attention focused with greater intensity on the institution, it came to light that Supreme Court decisions were being falsified by the courts's own bureaucracy.

By 1992, it had become overwhelmingly clear that something was amiss with the Court's internal organization and mode of operating. Mudjono's structural reforms, far from being a remedy, had in fact generated problems that could not be ignored. This situation prompted the Supreme Court to carry out a fairly radical process of self-examination. In 1992, the Court, together with the Faculty of Social

---

[4] OPSKIS is an acronym from the Indonesian *Operasi Kikis*—Clean-up Operation.

and Political Sciences of the University of Jakarta, conducted an internal audit.[5] Although there had been internal audits before, the university team stipulated that the results be made public—an event without precedent in the history of the institution.[6] At the time, the 1992 Internal Audit seemed a breakthrough, and the promise of change was in the air. In fact, the audit was realized in the face of ardent opposition from within the Court, and it is not certain whether any of the members expected it would lead to serious reforms—as someone closely involved relates.

> It was clear from the start that the majority on the Court resisted the idea of an outside party conducting a Supreme Court audit, it was like washing your dirty linen out in the open. If it were to be proposed within the leadership meeting, the proposal would be voted down. So backed by the shock waves generated by the falsified decision, [. . .] went to see Supreme Court chairman Ali Said personally and put the idea to him. [. . .] said that this was his chance to make a mark on the history of the institution etc. etc. and in the end Ali Said said, "all right, just do it."[7]

Still, opposition within the Court managed to block the report's recommendations. Until *Reformasi* six years later, and even beyond that, the reforms remained cosmetic at best. Steps were taken to increase judicial coordination and tighten administrative control, but it was clear that these measures just scratched the surface. The Court's structure did not fundamentally change, and its problems remain essentially unresolved. As a disillusioned and disgruntled Supreme Court junior chairman exclaimed in 1994: "What has come of the report, I ask you? Nothing has changed, nothing has been done."[8]

To be certain, and despite the significant and debilitating problems to which this gave rise, the increased size of the Court was part of a broader strategy. The impetus for adding personnel was at least partially based on the Supreme Court's resolve to take over control of the judiciary from the Department of Justice. Its increased bureaucratic bulk and specialist expertise have given the Supreme Court some of the administrative potential and political clout it badly wants and needs. The enlarged Supreme Court administration is not used merely to serve the immediate needs of the Court itself, but to reach down and extend its control over the judiciary as a whole. Thus, in order to regain the initiative over the management of judicial personnel in its meetings with the Department of Justice, the Supreme Court began to develop its own personnel management system,

---

[5] Mahkamah Agung R.I. & LPPIS FISIP UI, "Masalah dan faktor yang mempengaruhi pelaksanaan tugas administrasi dalam proses penyelesaian perkara di Mahkamah Agung Republik Indonesia," (mimeo, Jakarta 1992), p. 34. In the text, it will be referred to hereafter as the 1992 Internal Audit. (LPPIS—Lembaga Penelitian dan Pembangunan Ilmu Sosial, Institute for Research and Development of the Social Sciences.)

[6] Personal communication, July 1992. I was informed that LPPIS only agreed to cooperate on the condition that the results be made public. In the event, the report was never published, but it could be obtained through university offices. The project was initiated within the Supreme Court by the Court's junior chairman, Adi Andoyo Soetjipto—who also played an important role in uncovering the falsification of the Supreme Court decision in 1992.

[7] Personal communication, 10 May 1996.

[8] Personal communication, 16 July 1994.

organized training courses, summoned judges to the capital, and so on. Whereas in the past, shifts of control from the Department to the Supreme Court may have been hampered for the very practical reason that the Supreme Court's administrative capacity was insufficient, now it seemed to have that capability. Ultimately, the enlarged Court administration was to become a basis for a shift of control over the judiciary from the Department of Justice to the Supreme Court.

1. THE TRANSFORMATION OF THE SUPREME COURT'S FORMAL STRUCTURE[9]

As an organization, the Supreme Court has changed in a number of important ways over the years, most obviously in size, as it has increased almost tenfold over the past half century. The number of Supreme Court judges expanded from about five judges in the 1950s to fifty-one judges at present, while the supporting staff exploded from a mere handful in the 1950s to more than 1,300 at present. This formidable aggrandizement of the Supreme Court has inevitably had an impact on its organization, which is based on the twin pillars of the judicial corps and the administration.

The organization and function of the judicial corps is not fully regulated. Only very general legislative provisions exist stating that there must be chairmen and judges. The law does not specify how these are to be organized and what their functions are to be. Some of these matters were regulated in Supreme Court chairman decisions, the so-called KMA's,[10] but most have been based on "convention," as the 1992 Internal Audit put it. Still, the basic organizational outlines of the Supreme Court's judicial corps are fairly clear. Roughly speaking, the institution has been reshaped in two significant ways.

First, the structure of the judicial corps has changed from being relatively flat to being one organized on clear hierarchical lines. Starting out as an organization with little specialization of functions and, at least by convention, minimal hierarchy, the Supreme Court judicial corps became more hierarchical, first in practice and then legally. The Court started out from a *primus inter pares* basis in which by law and convention the chairman had few substantial prerogatives over the other judges. Even in the 1950s, however, Supreme Court chairmen began to operate with increasing independence from the other Court judges. In 1965, the size of the Court's leadership was augmented by law and its powers expanded. From the 1970s onwards, hierarchy was increasingly apparent and functions became specialized—as indeed judges themselves began to resemble deferential civil

---

[9] Data are based on the government appendix to the Presidential Account to Parliament under the New Order, complemented by other sources. There are some problems with these figures, which were apparently provided by the National Bureau of Statistics (Biro Statistik) and the National Development Planning Board (BAPPENAS, Badan Perencanaan Pembangunan Nasional). First, some closely involved persons have argued that, at least under Seno Adji, the data forwarded by the Supreme Court to the Bureau of Statistics were falsified at the behest of the Court chairman to hide the Supreme Court's disastrous institutional performance. Secondly, when speaking before Parliament in 1993, Chairman Purwoto argued that Supreme Court institutional data were different from those in the government appendix, and he defended the accuracy of his data even when questioned on the matter by Parliament. In both cases, divergences are not so significant as to fundamentally affect the validity of the data provided by the government.

[10] From the Indonesian *Keputusan Ketua Mahkamah Agung*—Supreme Court Chairman Decisions.

servants. From 1985, the law distinguished the "Court leadership"[11] (consisting of all the chairmen) from other members of the judiciary, and gave the former specific powers.

Second, the structure of the Court, which had been comparatively simple, became more vertically differentiated. A number of supervisory functions (though not all) were progressively delegated by Supreme Court chairmen to various senior Court judges. In the field of decision making, the Court shifted from a fairly unified structure, in which cases were decided by the full, so-called *pleno,* Court, into a much more differentiated one based on *chambers.* The practice of deciding cases by the *pleno* Court was progressively abandoned, and the judges came to be organized in smaller groups that settled cases conjunctly — as is done in almost all civil law supreme courts.[12] One feature of such chambers is that they are organized not on an *ad hoc* basis but with a fixed composition, although this sort of organization never quite took root in the Indonesian Supreme Court. Chambers therefore allow for professional specialization within the Court, as they enhance the development of specific legal expertise on the part of its individual justices. Also, as similar cases tend to be directed toward the most appropriate and "expert" chambers, decision making becomes more consistent.

As the Court has evolved, so has its bureaucracy. The Supreme Court bureaucracy transformed itself from an administrative backup service supporting the justices in their primary function of decision making into a much more broadly oriented bureaucracy with a variety of functions. In the process, it became more diverse, powerful, and difficult to control. From the political perspective and notwithstanding the legal primacy of the judicial corps, the bureaucracy changed from being a servant of the judicial corps into a full-fledged partner.

(a) Consequences of the Increasing Workload

The immediate cause for the increase in the size of the Supreme Court was its formidable workload. Its responsibilities consisted of essentially two elements: supervision and decision making.

(i) Supervision

Supervision over the lower courts became ever more burdensome for the Supreme Court, in part as a natural result of the expanding judicial apparatus. In 1942, there were 224 government courts, which, together with the colonial Supreme Court, were staffed by a grand total of 291 professional judges.[13] After independence, new first instance courts were rapidly created. By 1969, the number of general first instance

---

[11] Law no.15/1985 art.5(1).

[12] There is no legislative provision in the history of the Supreme Court requiring it to decide cases with all judges attending. The law only requires cases to be decided by a minimum of three judges. Over the years, a standard practice developed in the Supreme Court so that cases were usually decided by just three judges. They are organized in so-called chambers, which may number more than three judges, in which case the justices sit on the bench in a rotating order. See art.154 colonial Judicial Organization (*Rechterlijke Organisatie* S.1847:20); art.3(1) Law no.1/1950; art.46 Law no.13/1965; art.40(1) Law no.14/1985.

[13] *Regeeringsalamanak voor Nederlandsch-Indië* (1942), pt. 2. The numerous indigenous courts are not included in these numbers.

courts had reached 260, with thirteen appeals courts.[14] Fifteen years later, in 1983, the figure had increased to 290 general first instance courts, with twenty-six appeals courts.[15] To these should be added courts in the other jurisdictions, which were progressively brought under the Supreme Court's control, or, in the case of the administrative courts, newly established. The religious courts, most notably, added to the Court's supervisory burden. In colonial times, these courts were a judicial backwater of little consequence, but by 1983 they had reached the same level as the general courts, with 292 first instance religious tribunals and fifteen appellate courts.[16]

As the number of courts increased, so did the number of judges. From 291 in 1942, by 1983 there were close to 2,500 judges in the general courts alone, while there were almost two thousand judges in other jurisdictions; that number had increased to almost 2,900 judges staffing the general courts by 1997, with other figures fairly constant, so that the grand total amounted to approximately five thousand judges.[17]

(ii) Decision Making

Yet more than anything else, the Court has been hobbled by its bloated docket and resultant backlogs, which have forced it to reconsider the way in which it is organized, and operated.

As we have seen, unification of the judicial organization led to an important downward expansion of the judicial apparatus into the country and society, generating a massive increase in the number of cases decided by the district courts. According to official figures, from 1970 onwards, the turnover of cases at the district court level never stopped increasing, starting from a modest forty to fifty thousand cases annually, but accelerating rapidly in later years, increasing by as much as 700,000 cases between 1984 and 1985.[18] Over the past twenty-five years, the turnover of cases in the general courts increased twentyfold: the district courts

---

[14] These are Mahkamah Agung figures provided by S. Mertokusumo, *Sedjarah peradilan dan perundang-undangannnja di Indonesia sedjak 1942 dan apakah kemanfaatnja bagi kita bangsa Indonesia* (Yogyakarta: Gadjah Mada, 1971), p. 168. It is not quite clear how these figures were reached but they are sufficient to illustrate the point of this paragraph. There may be some lack of clarity on the breakdown, however. Thus, it may be noted that these figures list the number of general appellate courts at thirteen, whereas at least by law, there should be fifteen. Between 1959 and 1966 nine new appellate courts were instituted to join the six already in existence in colonial times. The new courts were Central Java (Emergency Law no.7/1959), Kotabaru—presently Jayapura (Presidential Regulation no.12/1963), Palembang (Law no.11/1964), Denpasar (Law no.1/1965), Bandjarmasin (Law no.20/1965), Bukittinggi (Law no.21/1965), Ambon (Law no.4/1966), Banda Aceh (Law no.16/1968), and, finally Bandung (Law no.1/1969).

[15] Mahkamah Agung Circular Letter no.MA/Pemb./1285/84 dated 29 February 1984.

[16] Ibid.

[17] There are constant fluctuations in the numbers cited and imprecision in the figures quoted, as sources often do not specify whether they are referring only to general court judges or judges in all jurisdictions. See for instance, Soerjadi, *Varia Peradilan* 6 (1967): 84, 88; Mertokusumo, *Sedjarah peradilan*, pp. 158, 168; J. C. T. Simorangkir, *Sejarah Departemen Kehakiman* (Jakarta: Departemen Kehakiman, 1985), pp. 346, 356; data on the late 1990s received directly from the Department of Justice and Human Rights.

[18] See Appendix B. Between 1984 and 1985, the number of cases at district court level almost doubled from 766,880 to 1,482,624 cases.

decided 95,000 cases in 1969 and close to two million in 1994. This enormous volume of cases suggests that an increasing number of Indonesians are taking their conflicts to court.

This increased turnover in the district courts could not fail to have an impact on appeal structures. With more cases being decided at first instance, more cases inevitably found their way up the appeals ladder (case-flow). Indeed, the appeal rates increased so rapidly under the New Order that the Indonesian public and the judiciary came to believe that hardly any dispute was conclusively settled in the lower courts. Thus as early as 1972, the Judges' Association (IKAHI) noted somewhat disconcertedly: " . . . it seems that almost 90 percent of the cases are appealed."[19] This idea remains firmly planted in the Indonesian legal psyche today: " . . . generally all litigants want to go on until cassation," Haryono Tjitrosoebeno, chairman of the Bar Association, stated recently.[20] MP Albert Hasibuan expressed a similar opinion:

> The general rule is that if someone loses in the district court, he will appeal. If he loses on appeal, he'll push on for cassation and so on until review. It is this mentality that causes increasing backlogs.[21]

Although this image may require some qualification,[22] it is evident that a connection exists between the massive increase in the turnover of cases in the lower courts and the increase in the Supreme Court workload under the New Order. This

---

[19] *Tjatatan public hearing Komisi III DPR-RI dengan IKAHI no.3156/K.III/72* dated 9 June 1972, p. 3, the Judges' Association representative speaking.

[20] *Editor*, 18 July 1992.

[21] *Kompas*, 31 August 1992. Political scientist Amir Santosa added in the report that people might also appeal because, whether right or wrong, they hope that the result "can be fixed," or perhaps in order to "play for time."

[22] See Appendix B for data. It is not clear whether, in fact, appeal rates in Indonesia are extraordinary. Based on the 1993-1994 figures, out of the annual district court docket of between 1.5 and 2 million cases, only about eight thousand end up before the Supreme Court, i.e., less than 0.5 percent. This rate is not noticeably higher than rates in systems with effective appeal barriers, a fact that challenges the widespread assumption in Indonesia that all cases are appealed. In fact, in the US federal judiciary the appeal rate between Federal District Courts and the Federal Supreme Court is around 2.5 percent (excluding bankruptcy cases). In the US Federal Courts, therefore, six times more cases are appealed than in the Indonesian general courts. Note that the Supreme Court's yearly intake is identical to the number of cases decided by the appeals courts, so it seems that once parties decide to appeal, the large majority of them will automatically move on the cassation. Litigants in Indonesia are most likely to drop or concede a case after it has been heard by the district courts, before moving to the appeals courts; at least by the 1990s, nearly every case heard by the appeals courts proceeded on to the Supreme Court. This is one reason why Supreme Court judges sometimes dismissively refer to the appeals courts as "letter boxes." Personal communication, 5 August 1994. Still, to the present day the idea exists in Indonesia that parties just keep on litigating until all remedies are exhausted. This is rooted in a variety of factors, notably the very rapid increase in the Supreme Court docket in the early 1970s, the relatively minor importance of many of the cases coming up for cassation, and the 1972 parliamentary fact-finding mission to Aceh, when it was found that practically all cases were appealed from the district courts to the appeals courts. While this finding may have been peculiar to Aceh at that particular time, it was taken to apply broadly to the entire judiciary, and for months afterwards these data were referred to in general terms. *Laporan penindjauan Komisi III DPR-RI ke Daerah-daerah Sumatera Utara, Atjeh dan Djawa Timur* (1972).

development was strengthened as new jurisdictions were progressively brought into the Supreme Court's domain in this period. Though hardly as significant as the general courts, the military, religious, and administrative courts all contributed to the situation. Thus, by the early 1990s the Supreme Court had to deal with approximately six hundred cases annually that had originated from these special courts, which was three times the entire Supreme Court docket under the Old Order.[23]

This boost in case-flow might have been blocked by the various appeal barriers proper to cassation, or any other appeal instrument.[24] One prominent Indonesian lawyer suggested in fact that a strict application of the cassation system would be quite effective in restricting the tremendous case-flow generated by the expanding judicial apparatus:

> What the Supreme Court should do is just review cases on legal or procedural errors. It shouldn't become a second court of appeal, which is what it does at present. [. . .] The backlog will never be resolved if cases are fully reviewed [both on the law and the facts] by the Supreme Court. [. . .] People call for restricting appeals to the Court. Why should this be? The main thing is for the Court to realize its function as it should.[25]

Nevertheless, as we have seen, the whole thrust of statutory and Supreme Court intervention in the appeals system has been to facilitate rather than restrict appeal, as the Supreme Court strove for control over the lower courts. To give just one indication, by the early 1990s the special review procedure that allowed decided cases to be reconsidered alone generated around 650 cases a year (backlogs of special review cases numbered 550).[26] "Half of all Supreme Court decisions are reconsidered in special review," exclaimed an exasperated Supreme Court judge in 1994.[27] This may be an exaggeration, but nevertheless this peripheral procedure by

---

[23] The 1990 breakdown is as follows: *religious*: 440 cassation cases (including a 366 backlog), thirty-six review cases; *military*: forty-eight cassation cases, five review cases. *Catatan rapat Komisi III DPR-RI dengan Ketua MA (Ali Said) no.2156/K.III/90* dated 10 September 1990, pp. 18, 20. In 1992, there were close to one hundred administrative cases pending before the Supreme Court, bringing the total from the special courts to approximately six hundred cases.

[24] It has been argued that the workload is proper to the cassation system generally. *Tempo*, 10 April 1982, p. 25. This is really a matter that would require further study. As a first observation, there are strong indications that cassation is more burdensome to supreme courts than "leave to appeal" systems, in which, within broad legislative limits, lower judges determine whether an appeal should be allowed. It is not at all clear, however, whether cassation is more burdensome than the US *certiorari* system, in which the US Supreme Court, after a summary scrutiny of cases, determines whether or not to hear them. *Certiorari* figures are rarely reported, which may contribute to the idea that the US Supreme Court's workload is much less than that in other systems. Such is not the case, however, as four thousand petitions for *certiorari* are filed with the US Supreme Court every year, and the system is creaking under the burden. See generally H. W. Perry, *Deciding to Decide: Agenda Setting in the United States Supreme Court* (Cambridge, MA: Harvard University Press, 1991), pp. 11-12; for a comparison between the three systems T. Koopmans, "Hogere voorziening naar rechterlijke goedvinden," *Nederlands Juristenblad*, 28 December 1985, p. 1417.

[25] Haryono Tjitrosoebeno quoted in *Kompas*, 15 August 1992.

[26] H. Franken, "Draft report to the Asia Foundation," June 1993, pp. 7-8.

[27] Personal communication, 22 August 1994.

itself in the 1990s generated more cases than the entire court docket in the 1950s. The backlog problem consequently may be partly the result of increased turnover in the district courts, but it derives no less from the way in which the Supreme Court handles the appeal system.

It is interesting to note that the backlog problem passed through all levels of the judicial apparatus in a direction that apparently matched the movement of funds allocated under the New Order to improve judicial infrastructure.[28] In the 1960s the problem was very much restricted to the district courts.[29] As conditions in these courts gradually improved, by the early 1970s the problem manifested itself in the appeal courts,[30] which in turn overcame their backlogs by 1975.[31] By that time backlogs increasingly began to accumulate at the highest level.

---

[28] The colonial Supreme Court also suffered from these problems. Still, this Court had a much larger docket, since its cassation jurisdiction was augmented by a direct appeal jurisdiction for cases originating from the *Raden van Justitie*—these cases constituted the larger part of its jurisdiction. In 1880 there apparently was a backlog of two thousand cases. See *Indisch Weekblad van het Recht* 886 (1880). The colonial government exhorted the Supreme Court judges to work harder and thought of dispatching *Raden van Justitie* judges to the Supreme Court to help handle the many pending cases. The press commented that, in fact, judges were working flat-out, but that there simply were too few of them. *De Indische Gids* 2,2B (1880), p. 1092. Note that the workload of the Court in 1881 was 9,760 cases, increasing in 1892 to 10,630 cases, which is not unlike modern day figures. *Dutch Parliament Session 1899-1900* no.135 item 4, footnote. The staff assigned to the task was small and overburdened; the yearly intake of ten thousand cases had to be handled by just two deputy chief public prosecutors (*advocaten generaal*) attached to the Court at the time, whose weekly caseload was at least seventy-seven cases per person. A. J. Immink, *Iets over de tegenwoordige afhankelijheid van de Nederlandsch Indische rechterlijke ambtenaren* (Amsterdam: De Bussy, 1880), p. 22. The workload did not fail to take its toll, and in September 1879, for instance, all six judges on the colonial Supreme Court took ill. *Indisch Tijdschrift van het Recht* 847 (1879). The situation improved significantly in the twentieth century, however.

[29] Under the New Order, the district courts could only resolve around 65 percent of their caseload until 1973-1974, when the effects of the improvement to the judiciary were felt. By 1974, percentages of resolved cases jumped to 97 percent and have barely dropped from that level since then. See the various *Lampiran Pidato Kenegaraan Presiden Republik Indonesia di depan sidang Dewan Perwakilan Rakyat* from 1970 onwards as summarized in Appendix B.

[30] The parliamentary reports from the early 1970s are filled with debates that express concern about the backlogs in the appellate courts, which deeply troubled both the Supreme Court and Parliament at a time when backlogs were a relative novelty. Subekti describes how undecided cases accumulated in different parts of the country: "In the appellate courts of Banda Aceh, Medan, Semarang, and Ujung Pandang, backlogs are in excess of one thousand cases. The Medan appellate court now has a backlog of about two thousand cases, which is partly inherited from the Bukit Tinggi court, which used to be the sole appellate court for the whole island of Sumatra. Also, when the appellate court of Banda Aceh was established, one thousand cases were immediately transferred to it from the Medan docket. We should add that Banda Aceh had some staffing problems that took half a year to resolve, all of which certainly did not help things move along. Presently there are 1,190 cases pending in Medan, with 490 new cases coming in for 1972, while in Banda Aceh 1,090 cases are pending, with three hundred new cases. Semarang underwent exactly the same experience. Its backlog really is a leftover from the appellate court in Yogyakarta, which used to be the sole appellate court for Java during the RIS period [Republik Indonesia Serikat, Republic of the United States of Indonesia, the period of the Indonesian Federal Republic in 1949], and which subsequently moved to Surabaya. When the Semarang court was established, it inherited some of the backlog from Surabaya. So if at present the situation in Surabaya is under control, with 443 cases pending and 369 cases coming in for 1972, in Semarang there is a backlog of 1,100 cases, with four hundred new cases coming in. Ujung Pandang is the same story, which can be traced back to the times when Ujung Pandang was the sole appellate court for the whole of Eastern Indonesia. There currently is a backlog of

(b) The Judicial Corps: From Equality to Hierarchy, from Unity to Diversity

The Supreme Court responded to its burgeoning caseload by making two parallel changes in the formal structure of the Court, as well as in its working order. First, in order to reduce the backlog of pending cases, the number of judges was increased; judges were organized into chambers with teams operating conjunctly; and fixed targets were set specifying how many cases ought to be decided by these chambers. The second change was oriented towards overcoming the burden of supervision. It involved a delegation of supervisory tasks (though not all of them, as shall become apparent) to special supervisory judges within the Supreme Court, and from there to the appeal courts. These institutional responses ultimately created a larger and organizationally more complex institution.

(i) The "Flat" Organization of the First Twenty Years

The Supreme Court started out as an exceedingly simple organization, for the 1950 law instituting the Court for the new republic only mentioned judges and a chairman and vice-chairman,[32] who had no clear powers except with regard to a number of essentially administrative matters.[33] The 1950 law apparently conceived the chairman, in the tradition of the colonial court, as a *primus inter pares*, a first among equals, not a superior. This signified that all the important matters were to be decided by the entire Supreme Court judicial corps. As always, the reality was more complex, with the first sign of hierarchical structures emerging even at this early date. In fact, in the early 1950s the Supreme Court chairmen increasingly disregarded the collegiate principle underlying the proposed structure of the judicial corps. Wirjono Prodjodikoro, in particular, began to make important decisions affecting the Court and the judiciary independently, without consulting his brethren on the bench.[34] In later years, the tendency of Supreme Court chairmen

---

1,400 cases, with three hundred new ones coming in. For this reason new appellate courts are being established in Ambon and Denpasar." *Catatan sementara rapat Komisi III DPR-RI no.1797/Kom.III/73* dated 24 May 1973, p. 3.

[31] Between 1972 and 1975, the appeals courts managed to improve decision-making percentages from 30 percent to 95.8 percent. Though the rate has not been entirely constant since then (in 1981 they dropped to 76.8 percent for instance), backlogs never arose as they did for the Supreme Court. See the various *Lampiran Pidato Kenegaraan Presiden Republik Indonesia di depan sidang Dewan Perwakilan Rakyat* from 1970 onwards as summarized in Appendix B. It is interesting to note that backlogs did not accumulate seriously from 1975 onwards either in the district or the appeal courts. This may indicate, in part, that the lower courts, their number having increased, are now properly equipped to deal with the workload. It is also possible, perhaps likely, that the lower courts simply pass the buck and do not seriously study cases. This attitude may be rooted in a generalized irresponsibility and insecurity fostered by low appeal thresholds and arbitrary interventions by the Supreme Court, which we will deal with later. This helps explain why Supreme Court judges dismissively describe lower courts sometimes as mere "letter boxes." The alleged "letter box" character of the lower courts is both the cause and the result of the low appellate thresholds, which the Supreme Court had a hand in determining.

[32] Law no.1/1950 art.2(1). This law allows for more than a single vice-chairman to be appointed; it was never realized.

[33] Thus, the Supreme Court chairman could decide internal work order.

[34] Such as the Supreme Court regulation abolishing the Civil Code, or his decision to enter the cabinet as a minister. See below, Chapter Nine.

to identify with interests outside the Court would be reinforced by presidential decisions to appoint chairmen who had not previously served in the judiciary.

During these early years, the workload of the relatively small judicial corps was still manageable. As a result, under Kusumaatmadja and the early tenure of Wirjono the Court's modest supervisory functions were usually implemented directly by the chairman and the registrar (*panitera*).[35] This practice of relying on "one-step supervision" was qualified to some extent when, in 1954, the Supreme Court stated explicitly that the appeals courts could issue guidelines and give instructions to district courts within their area of jurisdiction if that power were delegated to them.[36] This ruling planted the seeds for a two-step supervision system, as indeed Law no.13/1965 established that appeals courts could supervise district courts (art.39).

With respect to cases, the Court generally decided them in *pleno* sessions, and there was no chamber structure, even though under Wirjono a practice developed in which the chairman would take on civil cases and the vice-chairman criminal cases. The other Supreme Court judges were not organized along such lines, however, and served on any case, regardless of its character, on a rotating basis.[37]

As we have already seen, the 1965 law provided that all jurisdictions would be progressively brought under Supreme Court supervision. As a result, the law proposed revising the Court's formal structure, whereby it would be reconstituted in four chambers, one for each jurisdiction (i.e., general, religious, military, and administrative) [art.41(2)]. The law also stated that each chamber would be chaired by a junior chairman [art.41(2) & art.46], a new function that made the Court hierarchy more diverse. It would, however, take almost twenty years to realize these provisions.

At first (from 1965 until 1974), the main reason for the delay in implementing this reform was that the Court was simply too small, making it impossible even to retain Wirjono's civil/criminal working order, let alone think about extending hierarchies. As a result, the comparatively simple structure, involving a single chairman and vice-chairman, was retained under Soerjadi and Subekti, while cases continued to be heard in full (*pleno*) session. Also it served no purpose to create Supreme Court chambers and junior chairmen for jurisdictions that still had to be brought under Supreme Court control, such as the religious courts, or did not even

---

[35] See for instance Circular Letter no.8/Db/1950 dated 14 November 1950; Circular Letter no.2/Db/1951 dated 10 January 1951; and Circular Letter no.58/P/860/Db./60 no date.

[36] Circular Letter no.1/1954.

[37] Anonymous copy, no date, p. 28 in possession of the author. During the colonial era, a specific regulation provided for the internal organization of the colonial Supreme Court (S.1901:126). It stated that there would be three chambers arranged according to civil/criminal distinctions. This provision was repealed in 1947 (S.1947:20), when the broadened grounds of cassation made it necessary to review the internal organization of the colonial Supreme Court in its entirety. There were no new legislative provisions outlining internal Supreme Court structure in Indonesia; Law no.1/1950 did not refer to this issue at all. The first Indonesian legislative provision was art.41(2) Law no.13/1965. The chairman of the colonial Supreme Court could arrange for working order pursuant to art.154 colonial Judicial Organization (*Rechterlijke Organisatie* S.1847:23), and this practice was perpetuated under Law no.1/1950, which lacked a comparable provision. The provision that the Supreme Court chairman could provide for internal working order was reiterated in Law no.13/1965 (art.42) and again in Law no.14/1985 [art.28(2)]. As we shall see, the chairman has availed himself of this power repeatedly in the past decades.

exist, such as the administrative courts. Finally, the New Order tended to scrutinize all Guided Democracy products, including Law no.13/1965. The law was repealed in 1969, and there were indications at the time that new legislation would be introduced aimed at limiting the role of the Supreme Court so that it dealt with general jurisdiction only.[38] As a result, both the means and the logic were lacking to change the Supreme Court's organization.[39]

Nevertheless, during this period the Supreme Court's workload began to rise steeply. Even though it was really only servicing the general courts, the Supreme Court could barely keep abreast of its rapidly increasing work in terms of supervision and decision making. Something clearly had to change and Chairman Subekti was the first to start tinkering with the Court's organization. With respect to supervision, he began to delegate, placing the main burden for supervising district courts at the appellate level, while appellate courts themselves were supervised by all Supreme Court judges.[40] The two-step supervision system was introduced from 1967 onwards,[41] and in 1969 it was decided that henceforth appeals courts would be totally responsible for supervising district courts.[42] In 1986 this would be confirmed in statute.[43]

As regards decision making, it seems that Subekti managed to keep abreast of the rising intake, "doubling even during my tenure as Supreme Court chairman,"[44] but only with the greatest difficulty. Speed was his prime concern—"there is no meeting in which I do not impress upon the judges the absolute necessity of speeding up case settlement."[45] To increase case turnover, Subekti aimed at reintroducing the

---

[38] In 1968 Government presented a Supreme Court Bill to Parliament that re-opened the entire issue of whether the Court would serve as the supreme court to all jurisdictions, or only to the general courts. The Bill provided that the Supreme Court would hold authority over the general courts only, and that the other jurisdictions would have their own supreme courts. Note that the Supreme Court judges had an important say in the drafting of the Bill. Direktorat Djenderal Pembinaan Hukum, *Undang-undang tentang ketentuan-ketentuan pokok kekuasaan kehakiman* (Jakarta: Departemen Kehakiman, n.d.), chapters 3, 12 & 14.

[39] Law no.13/1965 was officially repealed in 1969, although, as we have established, in the absence of a successor it remained in force in practical terms as regards procedure and judicial organization.

[40] Subekti delegated supervision over the lower courts by creating six districts, one for each Supreme Court judge. Nevertheless, he pointed out several times that this was an imperfect remedy, making the best of what was, in effect, an unworkable situation. *Catatan sementara rapat Komisi III DPR-RI dengan Ketua Mahkamah Agung (Subekti) no.4746/Kom.III/72* dated 23 November 1972, pp. 2-3. Note that by 1973, the number of appellate courts had increased to fourteen, and they were facing important case handling problems that required constant Supreme Court attention. As Subekti stated in Parliament: "... *presently* the [MA] workload is becoming heavier by the day. We hope that the number of judges will be increased in the future ..." *Catatan sementara rapat Komisi III DPR-RI dengan Ketua Mahkamah Agung (Subekti) no.1119/Kom.III/73* dated 9 February 1973, p. 14.

[41] See for instance Circular Letter no.5/1966 dated 7 September 1966, and Circular Letter no.1/1967 dated 7 February 1967.

[42] *Conference between the MA and the Appeal Court Chairmen 9-11 June 1969*. It indicates that the ultimate responsibility and control continues to rest with the Supreme Court, on which topic, see for instance Mahkamah Agung Circular Letter no.MA/Pemb./929/1970 dated 22 April 1970.

[43] Law no.2/1986 art.53(3).

[44] *Tempo*, 16 February 1974, p. 35.

[45] *Tempo*, 2 February 1974, p. 8.

old civil and criminal chambers. As in the old days, these chambers would be presided over by the chairman and vice-chairman, respectively. However, the plan could not be immediately realized because there were too few Supreme Court judges. In 1973, exclaiming that "we're as tight as one can get,"[46] Subekti began to push for an increase in the number of Supreme Court judges.[47] He was unsuccessful. It was largely due to the outstanding professional discipline of his administration that no backlogs developed during his tenure. Nevertheless, this situation clearly could not last for long.[48]

(ii) Seno Adji: More Hierarchy and Diversity, and the First Collapse

It was essentially on grounds of work efficiency therefore, that the number of Supreme Court judges was increased from seven to seventeen when Seno Adji took over in 1974.[49] The larger crew of judges, with its mystical authority in the

---

[46] *Catatan sementara rapat Komisi III DPR-RI dengan Ketua Mahkamah Agung (Subekti) no.1119/Kom.III/73* dated 9 February 1973, p. 14.

[47] Subekti planned to have a five-judge civil chamber under the chairman and a four-judge criminal chamber under the vice-chairman. For this purpose he proposed increasing the number of Supreme Court judges from seven to nine. According to parliamentary reports, the proposal was favorably received by the Department of Justice, but Subekti's retirement intervened. *Catatan sementara rapat Komisi III DPR-RI dengan Ketua Mahkamah Agung (Subekti) no.1797/Kom.III/73* dated 24 May 1973, p. 4. If we follow the parliamentary reports, the Department of Justice played a duplicitous game here. Other sources reveal that on 5 April 1973 the Department of Justice suggested there be a total of seventeen Supreme Court judges, to which the Supreme Court replied on 24 April 1973 that it preferred to have nine Court judges. The parliamentary report quoted above indicates that in May 1973, the Department agreed to the Court proposal. Nevertheless, while the Supreme Court made up a list of four candidates pursuant to filling the two vacancies, in September 1973 Parliament, after lobbying from the Department of Justice, came up with a list of twelve candidates (including the then minister of justice, Seno Adji), all of whom were selected. *Dewan Perwakilan Rakyat–RI Periode 1971-1977* (Jakarta: DPR, n.d.), pp. 41-42. This suggests that between May and September 1973, Seno Adji was approached concerning the possibility that he might become the new Supreme Court chairman, and he may have changed his opinion on the number of Court judges as a result. Finally, on p. 31 of the Anonymous document (n.d.) referred to in a previous footnote, it is said that Subekti did manage to establish the chambers he had proposed, but the parliamentary reports show that at least by May 1973 this had still not been realized.

[48] There is some confusion on whether backlogs actually began under Subekti or under Seno Adji. In fact, there were rumors that Subekti was unable to keep abreast of the rising number of cases, as indeed records of the percentages for cases settled during his tenure are not complete. Nevertheless, Subekti reported to Parliament in 1973 that there were no backlogs: "Persistent rumors suggest that the current Supreme Court has a backlog of about nine hundred cases. We conducted an internal investigation into this question and concluded that during this year, 1,200 cases have come in, of which seven hundred are still pending. So the situation can be described as normal." The batch of undecided cases, according to Subekti, was remitted by parties themselves, not left in abeyance by the Court. *Catatan sementara rapat Komisi III DPR-RI br.1797/Kom.III/73* dated 24 May 1973, p. 3.

[49] On the official correspondence and various proposals concerning the enlargement of the Court, cf. *Dewan Perwakilan Rakyat RI Periode 1971-1977* (Jakarta: DPR, n.d.), pp. 41-45. Given the administrative logic of the Indonesian cassation system, lacking as it does "leave to appeal" or "certiorari" systems which allow the judiciary itself to filter out appeals, it becomes natural to increase the number of judges in response to growing workloads. Parliament queried Seno Adji soon after the 1974 increase in judges to ask how he planned to organize them efficiently in order to deal with the backlogs. See for example Member of Parliament Oka Mahendra, *Catatan*

Indonesian context, allowed Seno Adji to carry out some of the organizational reforms which Subekti had hoped to achieve. Thus, Seno Adji maintained and expanded Subekti's structures for supervision, according to which Supreme Court judges, as a general rule, only supervised appeals courts. At the same time, he withdrew from their portfolio personnel management of the district courts, a power he retained for himself. The supervisory function of the other Supreme Court judges was limited to technical matters, such as training and upgrading, which, albeit increasingly important, brought little political leverage.[50] These actions set a precedent that effectively continues to the present day.

Still, Seno's most important measures concerned the caseload. When Seno Adji established various chambers to handle cases independently, the Supreme Court's organization began to diversify. He did not, however, follow guidelines set forth in the 1965 law, but distinguished his five chambers along old civil/criminal lines, with four civil and one criminal chamber, a ratio that reflected the nature of the caseload at the time.[51] As before, cases were allocated to different chambers according to the legal issues involved, not depending on the jurisdictions from

---

sementara rapat kerja Komisi III dengan Ketua Mahkamah Agung (Seno Adji) no.3608/Kom.III/76 dated 22 September 1974, p. 10. An additional reason for the increase in the number of Supreme Court judges was to supervise the expanding judicial organization in the field more effectively. Nevertheless, the surprising size of the 1974 increase, as well as the nature of the recruits, some of whom had military backgrounds, suggests that the government did not just have efficiency and effectiveness in mind, but was at least in part motivated by reasons of political manipulation.

[50] In this context, the distinction is made between technical-legal supervision (*tehnis-judicial*) and administrative-personal (*administrative-personil*). *Catatan sementara rapat Komisi III DPR-RI dengan Ketua Mahkamah Agung (Seno Adji) no.3608/Kom.III/76* dated 22 September 1974, p. 12; *Catatan sementara rapat Komisi III DPR-RI dengan Ketua Mahkamah Agung (Seno Adji) no.02/Kom.III/78* dated 3 November 1977, p. 42. Note that while Seno Adji emphasized that administrative-personnel matters were his domain, he did install a commission of Supreme Court judges in 1976 to advise him. *Catatan sementara rapat kerja dengan Ketua Mahkamah Agung (Seno Adji) no.3804/Kom.III/76.06* n.d., p. 2.

[51] Seno Adji indicated that he introduced a dual chamber structure in 1974 under the Supreme Court chairman (i.e. himself) and the vice-chairman. Nevertheless, he admitted that this structure, with just two chairs acting as supervisors, created congestion at the top of the hierarchy, and so by 1975 he established the five chambers. *Catatan sementara rapat kerja Komisi III dengan Ketua Mahkamah Agung (Seno Adji) no.3804/Kom.III/76.06* dated 11 February 1976, p. 2. Seno Adji pointed out several times that, unlike in many Western countries, the Supreme Court in Indonesia handled many more civil cases than criminal ones. He was not quite consistent in his reports on the breakdown, however. Thus, in 1976, he reported that the Court dealt with eight civil cases for every one criminal case, i.e. 1,775 civil vs. 179 criminal (*Catatan sementara rapat kerja Komisi III DPR-RI dengan Ketua Mahkamah Agung no.3804/Kom.III/76.06* dated 11 February 1976, p. 2), but in 1979 he gave the civil/criminal breakdown as 4:1—perhaps to justify the chamber structure (*Laporan singkat rapat Komisi III DPR-RI dengan Ketua Mahkamah Agung (Seno Adji) no.2120/Kom.III/79* dated 5 February 1979, p. 14). It is possible that the proportions changed, but I find it unlikely that they changed as much as Seno Adji reported over barely three years. As civil cases are generally more complicated and burdensome to the judges, they added disproportionately to Supreme Court's workload. The 1981 figures given by the new Supreme Court chairman Mudjono are as follows: 7,921 civil cases and 525 criminal cases. *Rapat kerja Komisi III DPR-RI dengan Mahkamah Agung (Mudjono) membahas RAPBN 11* dated February 1982, p. 13. In 1993, the breakdown of the backlog was reported to stand at 14,041 civil cases versus 5,875 criminal cases. *Konsultasi Komisi III DPR-RI dengan Ketua Mahkamah Agung (Purwoto)* dated 23 June 1993 [taped recording].

which they originated, as had been envisaged by the 1965 law.[52] Also, Seno Adji retained the old hierarchical structure, with a chairman *and* a vice-chairman only; he introduced no junior chairmen. In fact, though Seno talked about at least implementing the chamber structure proposed by the 1965 law, at the same time he claimed that "it was giving rise to all sorts of problems,"[53] and refused to push the matter.[54]

A variety of reasons explain why the introduction of the court structure envisaged by the 1965 law was such a drawn out and fragmented process under Supreme Court chairman Seno Adji, notwithstanding the fact that the Court was now staffed by a sufficient number of judges. The first reason was that, at least when Seno Adji took office in 1974, the judicial organization was still pretty much as it had been under Subekti. Aside from the rising workload, nothing really called for more drastic action. What's more, the proposed reform of the Court's chamber structure seemed to make little sense since the Court effectively still served as supreme court to the general jurisdiction only.[55] (It did not allow appeals from the religious courts until 1979, while the administrative courts were established only in 1986, under a law that was not implemented for some years.[56])

This organizational reality was compounded by the fact that, as had been true under Subekti, the Seno Adji Court itself resisted the proposed organization reform, particularly the inclusion of a special religious chamber. The Supreme Court judges saw themselves as the backbone of the judicial edifice, legally more skilled than the religious and military judges, and professionally better equipped to act as the legal and political custodians of the judiciary's interests. They did not want to handle religious or military cases, and worried lest such a development might also break their monopoly on Supreme Court recruitment—as had already occurred with

---

[52] See for instance, the following statement by Seno Adji in Parliament: "Up to now the distinctions between chambers are not based on the various jurisdictions reflected in our legislation [. . .], that is the general courts, the religious courts, the military courts, and the administrative courts. The internal system that has been followed to date distinguishes between chambers based on the legal issue [*materi*] facing the Supreme Court . . . " *Catatan sementara Komisi III DPR-RI dengan Ketua Mahkamah Agung (Seno Adji) no.02/Kom.III/78* dated 3 November 1978, p. 5. This meant, as Seno Adji would point out, that cases coming up through the military courts, for instance, would be allocated to the criminal chamber. *Laporan singkat Rapat Komisi III dengan Ketua Mahkamah Agung (Seno Adji) no.2120/Kom.III/79* dated 5 February 1979, p. 39.

[53] *Catatan sementara rapat kerja Komisi III DPR-RI dengan Ketua Mahkamah Agung (Seno Adji) no.3804/Kom.III/76* n.d., p. 2.

[54] In 1977, for example, Seno reported to Parliament that the civil/criminal chambers structure was already established in the Court, and that there were plans afoot for introducing a chamber system organized according to judicial hierarchy (general, religious, military, and administrative). *Catatan sementara rapat Komisi III DPR-RI dengan Ketua Mahkamah Agung (seno Adji) no.02/Kom.IIII/78* dated 3 November 1977. It is clear, however, that one of the most crucial elements of the proposed reform was the appointment of junior chairmen to the various chambers, which did not take place until 1982 under Chairman Mudjono; at that time, the action was termed "the biggest devolution of *ketua* power" by the press. *Tempo*, 10 April 1982, p. 25.

[55] Note that when the chamber structure outlined in 1965 was in fact introduced by Chairman Mudjono in 1982, the junior chairman for the administrative courts, Indroharto, was effectively unemployed, since the administrative courts were not yet established. As a result, he handled labor and housing cases. *Rapat Komisi III dengan Ketua Mahkamah Agung (Mudjono) no.798/Kom.III/83* dated 10 February 1983, p. 17.

[56] See Chapter One.

the military courts. During his February 1979 meeting with Parliament, Seno Adji obliquely expressed his continuing reservations and explained how adhering to the prevailing civil/criminal distinction could defuse the issue:

> Do we need administrative Supreme Court judges, do we need military Supreme Court judges [. . .], do we need religious Supreme Court judges . . . ? [. . .] The question is not whether there must be Religious or Administrative Supreme Court judges, or whatever, because the organization of the Supreme Court is based solely on the substantive issue of the case, not on the jurisdictional sphere.[57]

In this address, Seno Adji indirectly reminds his audience that maintaining the old structure would circumvent the politically divisive issue of what sorts of Supreme Court judges—religious? administrative?—would be recruited.

There was also a third reason for not fully enacting the 1965 law. Seno Adji apparently was not eager to introduce junior chairmen because he would then have to delegate functions, thus diluting his own power in the Court. Records indicate that Seno liked keeping a grip on things, holding the leash of leadership as tightly as possible. He was not particularly keen even on the civil/criminal chamber structure that he himself had introduced, and he took a number of measures that undercut the efficiency this reform was supposed to bring about. For instance, he retained *pleno* sessions in which cases were heard by the full Court.[58] In addition, he generated all sorts of extra-judicial activities that made it impossible to have five chambers fully operative at all times. With great frequency, Supreme Court judges were sent off to conferences, to the regions under their supervision, to foreign countries, or to play host to foreign dignitaries.[59] As a

---

[57] *Laporan singkat Rapat Komisi III dengan Ketua Mahkamah Agung (Seno Adji) no.2120/Kom.III/79* dated 5 February 1979, pp. 38-39. As later developments would show, his view that chamber structure based on jurisdictions would generate pressures to broaden recruitment was quite correct. Seno Adji's predecessor as Supreme Court chairman, Subekti, shared these concerns. Apparently Subekti dreaded that the government sooner or later would force him to accept judges from the military. Following the philosophy that this illness might be best cured by contracting another, Subekti apparently thought of advocating the recruitment of religious judges in hopes that they might neutralize the impact of military judges. As it happened, Subekti retired before having to deal with the issue.

[58] Seno reported to Parliament that the Supreme Court sat in *pleno* "if the Supreme Court expects the case to set out a new line in the law," or "if a case receives much public attention." *Catatan sementara rapat Komisi III DPR-RI dengan Ketua Mahkamah Agung (Seno Adji) no.02/Kom.III/78* dated 3 November 1977, p.34. Seno Adji's *pleno* sessions continued right up to his retirement; see for instance *Tempo*, 20 September 1980, pp. 44-45.

[59] The parliamentary reports during Seno Adji's tenure as Supreme Court chairman are a travel agent's delight. Just to take some examples: in 1974 Seno Adji visited Holland. *Laporan singkat rapat kerja Komisi III dengan Ketua Mahkamah Agung (Seno Adji) no.2120/Kom.III/79* dated 5 February 1976. The next year Seno Adji with three Supreme Court judges attended the Chief Justices Conference in New Zealand, afterwards visiting Australia, and then making a comparative study tour of the Philippines, Thailand, Malaysia, and Singapore; they were absent from the Court for almost six weeks. *Catatan sementara rapat kerja Komisi III dengan Ketua Mahkamah Agung (Seno Adji) no.3628/Kom.III/97* dated 10 February 1975. In spring 1976, he regretfully informed Parliament that he could only attend for a couple of hours because he was hosting the minister of justice of the Philippines. *Catatan sementara rapat kerja Komisi III dengan Ketua Mahkamah Agung (Seno Adji) no.3804/Kom.III/76* dated 11 February 1976. The same year, Supreme Court judge Asikin Kusumah Atmadja was sent off for a lengthy period to

result of such frequent absences by one or two of their members, the three-judge chambers were unable to decide cases and sometimes the entire Court would go for a month without holding any sessions at all. In 1980, Purwoto Gandasubrata, when still a regular Supreme Court judge, reported such a breakdown to Parliament:

> ... we can say that the chamber system rather ties us down. What this boils down to is that if a single judge doesn't appear, the entire chamber collapses. Let me give you an example: if five Supreme Court judges are invited to follow an upgrading course, and all chambers are asked to send out one of their members, well, then all chambers must cease operations. In fact, it happens that for such reasons chambers stop operations for one week, and that sometimes even for up to three weeks no court sessions are held at all.[60]

Adding yet another obstacle to the system, Seno insisted that he himself check cases before the decisions were made public. Measures such as these did not just undercut the efficiency of the chamber structure, but also reinforced hierarchical divisions within the Court.[61] In the end, therefore, Seno Adji's reforms failed to make the Court more efficient, and responsibility for that failure rested, in part, with the chairman himself. A lackadaisical, easygoing man, as one Supreme Court judge recalled, "Seno Adji was just partying along, rarely held court sessions, and landed Mudjono with the backlog."[62]

---

study court congestion. *Laporan singkat rapat kerja Komisi III dengan Ketua Mahkamah Agung (Seno Adji) no.2120/Kom.III/79* dated 5 February 1976, p. 15. In 1976 also, several Supreme Court judges were sent abroad to countries such as France, Germany, England, and Japan for up to six weeks for "upgrading" and "legal comparison." *Catatan sementara rapat kerja Komisi III DPR-RI dengan Ketua Mahkamah Agung (Seno Adji) no.3804/Kom.III/76*, n.d., p. 3. In 1979, some of the Supreme Court judges attended the Asian Law Conference. *Laporan singkat rapat kerja Komisi III dengan Ketua Mahkamah Agung (Seno Adji) no.2120/Kom.III/79* dated 5 February 1976. Seno Adji himself, together with two other Supreme Court judges, went to England, Holland, and France, besides attending the World Conference of Peace through Law. *Risalah sementara rapat Komisi III dengan Ketua Mahkamah Agung (Seno Adji) no.423/Kom.III/80* dated 27 September 1979, pp. 2-3. Parliament displayed some irritation with all this traveling. Thus, when it was announced that Seno Adji had asked to host the Asian Judicial Conference in June 1978, an arrangement that would potentially halt work at the Supreme Court for ten days—"five days talking business" and the rest "visiting the Borobudur and so on"—Parliament asked whether this was not just a "personal and social" meeting, and questioned the Court regarding the benefits of these many conferences. *Catatan sementara rapat Komisi III dengan Ketua Mahkamah Agung (Seno Adji) no.3128/Kom.III/78* dated 7 February 1978, pp. 11, 15.

[60] *Catatan sementara rapat kerja Komisi III DPR-RI dengan Ketua Mahkamah Agung (Seno Adji) no.3804/Kom.III/76* n.d. Purwoto was probably referring to the ideological upgrading course P4. See for example p. 31 of the same report, in which he noted that working breaks lasted up to four weeks. In this context, he also pointed out that when Supreme Court judge Lumbanradja died in office, his chamber ceased operations for a lengthy period of time. *Risalah sementara rapat Komisi III DPR-RI dengan Ketua Mahkamah Agung (Seno Adji) no.423/Kom.III/80* dated 27 September 1979, pp. 10-11.

[61] In 1977, Parliament asked Seno why the backlog of undecided cases was rising rapidly despite his organizational reforms. Member of Parlement Sihombing, *Catatan sementara rapat Komisi III DPR-RI dengan Ketua Mahkamah Agung (Seno Adji) no.02/Kom.III/78* dated 3 November 1977, p. 22. Seno Adji responded that the problem was caused by the great number of complicated civil cases, by the fact the Public Prosecution took its time in presenting its conclusions, and that there was no obligatory party representation by legal counsel.

[62] Personal communication, 11 July 1994.

Court performance collapsed almost overnight under his leadership. Within one year of Seno Adji's appointment, the active MP Oka Mahendra began to ask the chairman how he planned to reorganize the Court, given the fact that, according to his information, of the 2,914 pending before the Supreme Court in 1974 only twelve cases had been finished.[63] In fact, backlogs built up rapidly: to one thousand undecided cases in a year. The erosion in institutional performance was both obvious and embarrassing.[64] By 1978, the Supreme Court administration was fully aware that the situation was little short of disastrous, yet Seno Adji was able to keep the lid on and maintain secrecy.[65] By 1980, the truth could no longer be hidden, and Seno Adji was forced to cite the same difficulties Subekti had six years earlier, namely that the Supreme Court docket had doubled during his tenure.[66] Only this time, he also had to admit that the workload was too much for the Court to handle, despite increases in personnel. By the time of Seno Adji's retirement, the backlog had reached an overwhelming ten thousand undecided cases—a shocking situation that only gradually seeped through in the media.[67]

(iii) Mudjono's OPSKIS Reforms

Court structure changed dramatically with the advent of Supreme Court chairman Mudjono, who took office in 1981. His reforms, which completely

---

[63] *Catatan sementara rapat kerja Komisi III dengan Ketua Mahkamah Agung (Seno Adji) no.3608/Kom.III/76* dated 22 September 1974, p. 10.

[64] The Supreme Court was not eager to admit the size of the backlog before Mudjono came in and threw open the windows. Seno Adji in 1981 admitted to a backlog of only three thousand cases, "or perhaps five thousand," adding that this was a pretty good record compared to the performance of courts in other countries, such as the Pakistani Supreme Court, with its backlog of sixteen thousand cases. Still, when asked, another Supreme Court judge said: "There are many [cases awaiting trial], really many . . . more than seven thousand, but not quite ten thousand." *Tempo*, 28 February 1981, p. 58.

[65] A Supreme Court insider, very close to Seno Adji, was ordered by him to falsify the annual reports sent to BAPPENAS on the Court's institutional performance, and in fact at one point was instructed not to send any report at all. Seno Adji also manipulated figures to make the backlog seem much smaller than it was, for instance by excluding cases that had been decided but in which final verdict remained to be given, or by reporting percentage patterns over the years, rather than exact figures. Thus, for 1978 Seno Adji reported a backlog of only three thousand cases, whereas it had apparently already reached seven thousand cases. Daniel S. Lev archives, (hereafter *DSL*) 30 October 1978. (These are the personal interview notes of Daniel S. Lev; copies will be deposited in the University of Washington library [Seattle, WA], the Cornell University Kroch Collection [Ithaca, NY], and Pusat Studi Hukum dan Kebijakan [PSHK] in Jakarta.)

[66] *Tempo*, 20 September 1980, p. 44. It was a rare example of Seno Adji understating his case: in fact between 1974 and 1980 the Supreme Court docket more than tripled, growing as it did from 2,914 to 10,425 cases.

[67] As we have seen, in February 1981 Seno Adji himself admitted only to "three thousand or perhaps five thousand cases" pending and another Supreme Court judge was prepared to acknowledge "more than seven thousand but less than ten thousand cases." By April the next year, the backlog was put at 9,400 cases (*Tempo*, 10 April 1982, p. 25), and by August at 10,800 cases (*Tempo*, 14 August 1982). By January 1984, the Seno Adji inheritance was reckoned to be nine thousand pending, undecided cases (*Tempo*, 7 January 1984). It may be that this backlog built up in the couple of months before Mudjono's reforms became effective, but this could not account for the overly modest figures presented by Seno Adji. It may also be that actual data were only gradually released.

overhauled the institution, effectively constitute the basis of the present Court. They were implemented in response to the crisis inherited from Seno Adji. The most obvious problem was the large backlog, but in addition, the Court's supervisory functions were seriously run down,[68] and the religious courts that had been brought into its fold in 1979 added a new burden to the already foundering institution.[69] Radical measures were in order, and Mudjono set out to introduce them: upon entering office he reportedly stated that, if necessary, he would bring in tanks to do the job. This was not perhaps the most diplomatic statement to be made by the first army general to be appointed to the highest judicial office in the land, but at least it left no doubt about his determination to get the job done.[70]

Mudjono's reforms had a lasting impact in three areas: the size of the Court; its hierarchical structure; and the organization of teams and chambers of Supreme Court judges. His reforms put Law no.13/1965 into effect with respect to hierarchy and organization. The core of these reforms, OPSKIS (Operasi Kikis), was directed toward resolving the backlog problem.[71] It called for an increase in the number of judges, who would then be divided into a variety of teams and chambers operating under an expanded Supreme Court leadership. The judges would be supported by clerks, and have a target of fifty cases decided a month per team.[72] Discipline and speed were of prime importance: "cases may only float about in the Supreme Court building for a month," said Mudjono.[73]

Increasing the Number of Judges. In the first fifteen months of Mudjono's tenure, the Supreme Court tripled in size. The first increase occurred at the time of his appointment, when the number of judges was augmented from seventeen to twenty-four. After less than a year in office, Mudjono reported that caseload projections in particular revealed that the twenty-four-judge Court would continue to accumulate backlogs, and he called for a further increase in the bench.[74]

---

[68] Thus, already in 1977 legal commentator R. Syahrani pointed out that the court system had really become too big and that the Supreme Court was having problems supervising the judiciary. *Suara Karya*, 30 May 1977, reprinted in: R. Syahrani, *Masalah tertumpuknya beribu-ribu perkara di Mahkamah Agung* (Bandung: Alumni, 1980), p. 60.

[69] Seno Adji opened up cassation for military and religious cases in 1977 despite opposition from other Supreme Court judges (*Peraturan MA no.1/1977*). The regulation took some time to become effective, notably as a result of opposition from the Department of Religious Affairs, which saw its control over the religious courts reduced. The Department promptly issued a regulation blocking appeals to the Supreme Court (Circular Letter Director Court Upgrading, Department of Religious Affairs no.DIV/Ed/1978). The Supreme Court and the Department settled the matter in early 1979 in favor of the Court, which began to hear appeals from the religious courts later that year.

[70] *Tempo*, 28 February 1981, p.56.

[71] OPSKIS was distinguished by a number of phases. The first OPSKIS, which commenced on June 1, 1981, was directed toward resolving the backlog of eight thousand cases. The second OPSKIS, also called the "pure OPSKIS" (OPSKIS *murni*), started on July 23, 1983 and aimed at settling all the current cases, which numbered 4,556. Finally, a "Post-OPSKIS *murni*" was conducted to clean all slates. *Suara Pembaruan*, 26 August 1992.

[72] *Tempo*, 6 November 1982, p. 12; *Tempo*, 7 January 1984, p. 60.

[73] *Tempo*, 7 January 1984, p. 60.

[74] The increase of judges from twenty-four to fifty-one was implemented in response to substantive projections of the Supreme Court's caseload made in February 1982. They were based on an assessment that proposed each chamber ought to be able to handle sixty cases per month, or six hundred cases per year, allowing for the fact that "even judges must rest, sleep,

If we stay with the present formation of twenty-four judges, then it is not a matter of opinion but of raw fact that we will retain a backlog of 6,600 cases. It is absolutely clear that we must have more personnel to solve the backlog.[75]

His plans were favorably received in Parliament[76] and a second increase was effected in 1982, when the number of judges was raised from twenty-four to fifty-one—its present level.[77]

New Junior Chairmen: The RAPIM and the Pleno. As regards hierarchy, Mudjono finally introduced the positions of junior chairmen in what the press called "the biggest delegation of chairman power yet."[78] Each of the new chairmen covered one of the four jurisdictions (general, religious, military, and administrative). To deal with the increased number of cases coming up for appeal from the general courts, three junior chairmen were appointed exclusively for this jurisdiction: one for written civil law, one for unwritten (*adat*) civil law, and one for criminal law.[79] This brought the total of junior chairmen to six.[80]

These additional chairmen changed the shape of the Court, creating a distinct leadership group. While the Supreme Court chairman, and to a lesser extent the

---

play with their grandchildren and have a day off or so," as Mudjono put it. See *Rapat kerja Komisi III DPR-RI dengan Ketua Mahkamah Agung (Mudjono) no.650/Kom.III/82* dated 1 December 1982, p. 9. According to these projections, the Supreme Court could not both overcome existing backlogs and keep abreast of projected incoming cases, but instead would run up an additional backlog of 5,400 cases per year. On the basis of these data, an additional nine chambers would have to be instituted, that is, twenty-seven new judges would have to be added.

[75] *Catatan rapat kerja Komisi III DPR-RI dengan Mahkamah Agung* dated 1 December 1981, p. 24.

[76] See for instance member of Parliament Situmorang of the Parliamentary Commission III: " . . . with the difficulties in settling cases and with the backlog expected to grow in coming years, I suggest that the present number of judges be increased. I also heard, in fact, that there are quite a few members of this commission interested in becoming Supreme Court judge [laughter], so maybe the Supreme Court chairman can indicate who in the front, middle, and back rows stands a chance . . . " *Catatan rapat kerja Komisi III DPR-RI dengan Mahkamah Agung* dated 1 December 1981, p. 15.

[77] It is interesting to note that Mudjono quite specifically saw this increase as a stopgap measure to overcome the existing backlog. He clearly did not exclude the possibility of reducing the size of the Supreme Court again once the backlog had been overcome. This idea smoldered throughout the term of his successor, Ali Said, when the backlog almost doubled to 22,000 cases. Nevertheless, some parties on the Supreme Court remained strong advocates of reducing the number of judges. Junior chairman Adi Andoyo, for one, is reported to have been a steady advocate of bringing the Court back to about seventeen judges, arguing that it is more important to make good decisions than many decisions. His suggestion apparently was in part motivated by the fact that, in his view, the many Supreme Court functions increasingly served as end-of-career slots for burnt-out loyal lower court judges, rather than attracting young, bright energetic judges. But, referring to the backlog, Ali Said and Purwoto Gandasubrata dismissed his ideas. Personal communication, 10 May 1996.

[78] The first junior chairmen were appointed on March 27, 1982. *Tempo*, 10 April 1982, p. 25.

[79] *Rapat kerja Komisi III dengan Ketua Mahkamah Agung (Mudjono) no.682/Kom.III/82*, p. 10.

[80] As stated above, the administrative courts still had to be established in 1979; the junior chairman appointed in 1982 and assigned to the administrative courts (Indroharto), as a result, handled cases not allocated to any of the other teams, notably those having to do with housing and labor. *Rapat Komisi III dengan Ketua Mahkamah Agung (Mudjono) no.798/Kom.III/83* dated 10 February 1983, p. 17.

vice-chairman, clearly retained their central functions, legislation began to refer to the "Court leadership" by the mid-1980s.[81] This leadership included all the chairmen. Gathering weekly in the so-called "leadership-meeting," abbreviated RAPIM (*rapat pimpinan*), the Supreme Court chairman, vice-chairman, and six junior chairmen constituted the most important policy-making body of the Court. Aside from the RAPIM's management function, it also was intended to serve as the central instance panel to ensure a unified application of the law by the various Supreme Court teams.

Figure 1
The Supreme Court (Mahkamah Agung) Leadership after the Mudjono Reforms

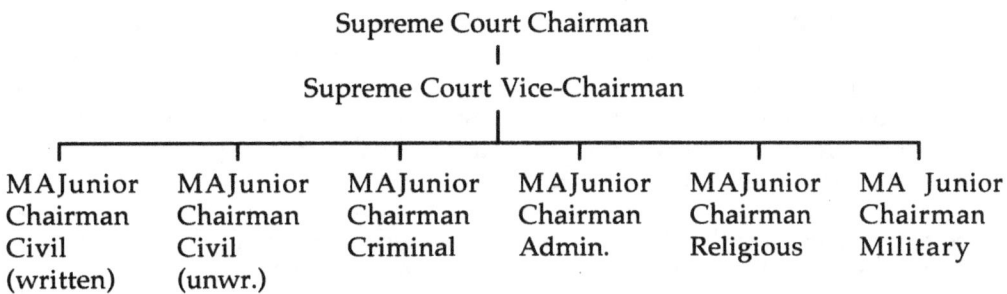

Compared with the pivotal Supreme Court chairman and the RAPIM, the full court, the *pleno*, retained only a residual function. According to regulations, the chairmen could bring important matters before the *pleno* for debate;[82] however the wording of the various regulations indicate that Mudjono's reforms had rendered the *pleno* powerless in running the Court. The *pleno* meetings were reduced to a forum where general policy issues might be debated, but they lacked decisive force.[83] The regulations do not specify which issues are important, nor do they indicate whether *pleno* decisions are binding on the Court leadership, nor whether common Supreme Court judges might themselves take the initiative to call for a *pleno* meeting. While there are occasional reports of confrontational *pleno* gatherings, the fact that these are specifically mentioned underscores the fact that the common Supreme Court judges retained little power. Notably from the Ali Said administration onwards, *pleno* meetings became increasingly infrequent and largely ceremonial gatherings.[84] There may not have been all that much left of the *primus*

---

[81] For instance Law no.15/1985 art.5(1).

[82] *Surat Keputusan Ketua Mahkamah Agung no.KMA/06/SK/V/1982*, art.6 & 9.

[83] Thus, the *pleno* would gather to consider such issues as review of Supreme Court decisions (*peninjauan kembali, herziening*), which emerged just as Mudjono took office, or indeed matters of internal court organization. *Rapat kerja Komisi III DPR-RI dengan Ketua Mahkamah Agung (Mudjono) no.650/Kom.III/82* dated 1 December 1982, p. 22. Supreme Court regulations invariably refer to the fact that the *pleno* was *consulted*, not that it *agreed*. See, for instance, *Surat Keputusan Ketua Mahkamah Agung no.KMA/06/SK/V/1982* dated 31 May 1982.

[84] The idea that the Supreme Court *pleno* was a club of yes-men dependent on favors from the leadership is supported by a particular event. During a *pleno* gathering in 1994, one common Supreme Court judge engaged in an active and insistent discussion with the Court's leaders

inter pares rule under Seno Adji, but the Mudjono reforms certainly killed it off for good.

Teams and Chambers. The new hierarchical structure was intricately linked to a new arrangement of Supreme Court chambers. As Mudjono broke with the civil/criminal distinction prevailing since the first days of independence, he progressively reorganized the Court along the jurisdictional lines set out in Law no.13/1965.[85] The 1982 increase in the number of Supreme Court judges allowed Mudjono to reconstruct his edifice. The judges were organized into eight teams, presided over by all chairmen. The teams were listed alphabetically from A to H, each letter denoting an Indonesian bird,[86] and were subdivided into chambers, one each for the chairman and vice-chairman, and one or two for each of the junior chairmen.[87] The presiding chairman of each team essentially determined its internal organization. As a result, various constructs were introduced to decide who would preside over chambers within each team: in some cases, the chairman headed all chambers, while in others he would chair just one chamber and a senior judge would preside over the other.[88] These teams were autonomous in handling cases, which were no longer decided in *pleno* sessions, even though that possibility seems not to have been fully excluded.[89]

---

concerning administrative law. This infuriated the leaders and apparently destroyed whatever hopes the judge may have had to succeed an incumbent junior chairman.

[85] Regulations reveal the quick development of Mudjono's ideas on this issue. In March 1981, barely a month after his arrival on the Court, he issued a regulation in which he combined the old civil-criminal structure with the new jurisdictional structure envisaged by Law no.13/1965, a proposal reiterated in May 1981. In November 1981, however, Mudjono abandoned that idea and eliminated the civil-criminal structure altogether. Thus, in KMA/02/1981 dated 16 March 1981 art.1 and KMA/06/SK/V/1982 dated 31 May 1981, art.1, Mudjono proposed that there would be two chambers organized along civil and criminal lines, and chaired by the Supreme Court chairman and vice-chairman. Still, the civil chamber would consist of four "sectors" organized along 1965 jurisdictional lines: civil, *adat*, religious and administrative. The criminal chamber would consist of two "sectors": general and military. By November 1981, Mudjono reported to Parliament that he was working to establish eight chambers along jurisdictional lines, disregarding the old civil-criminal distinction. There were some staffing problems that made it more difficult to get things under way, however. One chamber never got off the ground for unknown reasons. In addition, one judge died, one judge (Sri Widoyati) became grievously ill (and soon died), and one judge by bureaucratic convention was dispatched to serve as director general of court upgrading at the Department of Justice. So only six groups of judges were operating in the fall of 1981. *Catatan rapat kerja Komisi III DPR-RI dengan Ketua Mahkamah Agung (Mudjono) no.685/Kom.III/82* dated 8 November 1982, pp. 5-6.

[86] *Tempo*, 6 November 1982, p. 12. The teams are called: **A**lap-alap, **B**uraq, **C**endrawasih, **D**adali, **E**lang, **F**alcon, **G**aruda, **H**antu. Apparently, there were some problems with naming the "F" team, since the name of no Indonesian bird apparently started with that letter, so the English *Falcon* was used.

[87] Note that within one chamber judges double up in teams.

[88] Mahkamah Agung RI & LPPIS FISIP UI, "Masalah dan faktor yang mempengaruhi pelaksanaan tugas administrasi dalam proses penyelesaian perkara di Mahkamah Agung Republik Indonesia," p. 27.

[89] *Surat Keputusan Ketua Mahkamah Agung no.KMA/06/SK/V/1982*, art.6 says that "important issues or matters of principle may be brought before the Supreme Court in *pleno* for resolution." It is not fully clear whether this article refers to problems of an organizational nature, or also

Figure 2
Teams and Chambers after Mudjono's Reforms

8 Chairmen
|
8 Teams
|
17 Chambers

The Quota System. The main thrust of the OPSKIS reforms was to solve the pressing backlog problem. The program consequently also imposed a minimum quota of fifty cases per month for each chamber. The emphasis on case turnover effectively nullified the established distinctions between teams, whereby they were to handle only those cases coming up through "their" respective specific jurisdictions.[90] From the time of Mudjono's reforms, cases were allocated to teams with little regard to developing their specific legal expertise. The practice of spreading the bulk of cases from the general courts indiscriminately among all teams and chambers continues to the present day. By and large, only cases coming up through the special jurisdictions were and are allocated to the teams of the special, designated chairmen.[91] Criminal cases, in particular, were generally viewed as easy and a means for achieving a high turnover. The civil teams, because of their expertise, receive most civil cases, but they also deal with criminal cases. As a result, Mudjono's team structure to some extent broke down the professional distinctions within the Supreme Court that had been determined by judges' special areas of expertise. Now this specialization applied only to the small number of religious and military cases, and not to the civil and criminal cases that constituted the bulk of Supreme Court work, nor, by the end of the 1980s, to the administrative cases.

Supervision: The Supervising Supreme Court Judges (HAWASDA, Hakim Agung Pengawas Daerah, Judges Supervising the Regions*).* Supervision was only a residual feature of the OPSKIS program. Nevertheless, Mudjono also took steps with regard to the steadily expanding judicial apparatus (in 1982 alone, seven new appeal courts were added). All new judges appointed in 1981 were made supervisors of the appeals courts, with the exception of the chairman and vice-chairman. Because of the rapid increase in the number of such courts, some Supreme Court

---

to legal issues. Note that art.11(3) of that same regulation states that organizational problems relating to supervision may be brought before the *pleno* for resolution.

[90] This is further supported by the fact that junior chairmen often are appointed to certain functions because of their specific technical expertise. Thus, the junior chairman for written civil law, Asikin Kusumah Atmadja, was a highly respected civil jurist; the junior chairman for religious courts, Busthanul Arifin, had a strong Islamic background and had just been on the *haj*; and the chairman for military courts was a former general, Piola Isa. *Rapat kerja Komisi III dengan Ketua Mahkamah Agung (Mudjono) no.682/Kom.III/82* dated 8 November 1982, p. 45.

[91] Religious cases went to Busthanul Arifin's team, military cases to Piola Isa's team, and administrative cases to Indroharto's team.

judges initially had to supervise more than a single appellate court,[92] but this situation was remedied in 1982.[93] The subsequent expansion of the Supreme Court has meant that almost half of the judges do not share in the supervisory burden, nor in its privileges. The supervisory judges must visit their regions occasionally, with travel expenses paid, and they constitute an important—and thus influential—conduit of information for the Supreme Court leadership in personnel management. The supervisory function thus introduced an informal hierarchy in the Supreme Court, with senior or favored judges serving as regional supervisors, while junior or less favored ones were not granted these powers.

The OPSKIS program was successful in the short run, though it stretched the Court to the limit, with the justices in the early 1980s working frantically even during the summer holidays to liquidate the Seno Adji legacy.[94] Supreme Court judge Karlinah described the judges' ordeal:

> I can do three or four small cases a day. But the heavy ones sometimes take me more than an entire day. Sometimes I get so tired, I no longer understand what I'm reading.[95]

Though there were some calls for stricter rules on appeal and cassation to control case-flow to the Supreme Court,[96] the OPSKIS program was oriented toward cleaning out the Supreme Court docket, and it was highly successful in that regard. By 1984, Mudjono was able to report to the president, who apparently took an interest, that the backlog was practically settled. He died a few weeks later.[97]

---

[92] *Catatan rapat kerja Komisi III DPR-RI dengan Ketua Mahkamah Agung (Mudjono) no.2115/Kom.III/82* dated 11 February 1982, p. 14. *Surat Keputusan Ketua Mahkamah Agung no.KMA/06/SK/V/1982* dated 31 May 1982, art.8 states that the areas of supervision for each Supreme Court judge might include one *or more* appellate courts, which is the reason why instead of being called "regional" (*daerah*) courts, they were called "sector" (*wilayah*) courts. This explains why originally supervising judges were called HAWASWIL (Hakim Agung Pengawas Wilayah), the WIL standing for *wilayah* rather than *daerah,* which is associated with the provincial structure.

[93] In the process, the supervising Supreme Court judges acquired their definite name of HAWASDA (Hakim Agung Pengawas Daerah). *Surat Keputusan Ketua Mahkamah Agung KMA/012/SK/VIII/1983* dated 11 August 1983, art.3(1): " . . . the MA leadership will be assisted by a number of Supervising MA judges (HAWASDA) for each appellate court region . . ."

[94] *Tempo,* 7 January 1984, p. 60.

[95] Ibid.

[96] Ibid.

[97] *Tempo,* 21 May 1983, p. 20; *Tempo,* 7 January 1984, p. 60; *Tempo,* 21 April 1984, p. 13. Dismissively referred to sometimes as a mere "clerk" because of his alleged lack of imagination, Mudjono had several admirable qualities. A workaholic, he stayed at his office until late at night with strong coffee and cigarettes, habitually taking work home with him (four attache cases full) and returning before dawn. "I work twenty-four hours a day," he said, "You know, I've a real modest background." When he became a minister, he bought a little Japanese van, rather than the customary Mercedes Benz, and when he went to be hospitalized abroad, he purchased a cheap plane ticket so he could take his loyal chauffeur with him to see Europe. Mudjono was a heavy smoker (five packs a day) and died of cancer.

(iv) Ali Said and After: The Second Collapse

Mudjono laid down the formal structure of the present-day Supreme Court; subsequent changes did not fundamentally alter it. Only one feature was added, the KORWASSUS (Koordinator Pengawas Khusus), a somewhat obscure internal supervisory body that attracted little notice until 1996.[98] This relative stability in institutional structures, however, was not a result of the Court successfully resolving the problems it was meant to address, but rather of the fact that problems had become so formidable that organizational changes were no longer effective in overcoming them. Mudjono's court structure was retained by default, not thanks to its proven strengths.

Ali Said came into office in 1982 under much more favorable circumstances than his predecessor, and settled in for a comfortable ride. Wondering what he ought to do with "fifty-one empty-handed Supreme Court judges," he vaguely philosophized about "doing something about quality control."[99] For a while it did look as though the backlog issue had been solved once and for all, as attention was drawn to other matters, but troubling signals soon appeared. In 1985, Ali Said mentioned in passing that the number of cases decided by the Court that year was about the same as the number of new cases coming in. In other words, the Court was fully occupied in coping with the docket of new cases and could not address the backlog. Although little attention was paid to the situation at the time, it later became clear that already by 1987 the backlog had returned to the pre-OPSKIS level of ten thousand cases.[100] Again, the press was kept from discovering this troubling reality.

Only when Ali Said's tenure ended in 1992 was the performance of his administration subjected to public scrutiny, and news reports of the problem exploded like a series of firecrackers. In July 1992, Supreme Court judges modestly reported that "about twelve thousand" cases were awaiting decision.[101] The press tentatively put the backlog at fourteen thousand cases,[102] which was in fact the number Chairman Ali Said reported to the president.[103] Yet skeptical observers smelled a rat. "It's a mountain," declared a prominent lawyer,[104] and by the fall of 1992 Parliament was asking questions about a backlog of sixteen thousand cases.[105]

---

[98] Instituted under Ali Said in 1987, it was a team of Supreme Court judges operating under a junior chairman with the special task of ensuring internal discipline. It did not jump into action, at least not noticeably so, until the *Gandhi Memorial School case* (1996). Personal communication, 10 May 1996.

[99] *Tempo*, 16 June 1984.

[100] By April 1987, the backlog stood at ten thousand cases, 7,918 of which were the particularly burdensome civil cases. *Suara Pembaruan*, 26 August 1992.

[101] *Forum Keadilan*, 20 August 1992, p. 71.

[102] *Tempo*, 4 July 1992, p. 36.

[103] *Angkatan Bersenjata*, 25 June 1992.

[104] *Forum Keadilan*, 17 September 1992, p. 68

[105] *Daftar pertanyaan tertulis Komisi III DPR-RI pada rapat konsultasi dengan Ketua Mahkamah Agung no.1088/K.III/92* dated 16 November 1992, question 3; and *Daftar pertanyaan tertulis Komisi III DPR-RI pada rapat konsultasi dengan Ketua Mahkamah Agung* dated 19 September 1991, question 2. Note that Parliament stated in both cases that it was prompted to ask these questions by reports in the press. Judging by its questions in June 1991, it failed to appreciate the magnitude of the backlog problem before Fall 1991, notwithstanding the fact that the Supreme Court reported to it extensively on the matter. *Daftar pertanyaan tertulis Komisi III*

It finally transpired that when Ali Said retired, the cases waiting to be decided by the Supreme Court numbered around twenty thousand— twice the pre-OPSKIS levels.[106]

The new chairman, Purwoto Gandasubrata, essentially reinstituted Mudjono's OPSKIS program, tightening time limits for handling cases,[107] adding personnel,[108] and thus raising the monthly quota of cases for each chamber. As a result, the monthly turnover of cases increased from an average of five hundred to seven hundred under his administration.[109] Indeed, as Purwoto recounted with a mixture of pride and exasperation, not even during Mudjono's years had the Supreme Court handled cases at the rapid rate achieved during 1992 through 1994.[110]

Nevertheless, despite this all-out effort, the Court's accomplishments were outpaced by the ever-increasing case-flow. In fact, by late 1992 the *monthly* intake of cases reportedly stood at eight hundred.[111] In 1993, Purwoto admitted in Parliament that notwithstanding official reports that the backlog had been reduced to 17,500 cases, it in fact still stood at 20,210.[112] One year later, as Purwoto's tenure as Supreme Court chairman came to an end, it was clear that his efforts had barely dented the mountain of cases pending before the Court, which in November 1994 was still estimated to number around twenty thousand.[113] In fact, the Court seemed to have given up on the issue under Purwoto's successors Soerjono and Sarwata: in 1997, it decided only slightly more than half of the cases it had tackled in 1994 (5,199 for 1997, compared to 9,608 for 1994).[114] Despite all the investment of effort and manpower, nothing had changed since 1991-92, and the

---

DPR-RI pada rapat konsultasi dengan Ketua Mahkamah Agung no.960/K.X/91 dated 2 July 1991; *Catatan rapat Komisi III dengan Ketua Mahkamah Agung no.2156/K.III/90* dated 10 September 1990, pp. 16-19; *Konsultasi Pimpinan DPR, Pimpinan Komisi III, Wakil Fraksi dengan Ketua Mahkamah Agung no.284/K.III/90* dated 31 January 1990, p. 3, putting the backlog at 15,800 cases. In August 1992, the press reported a backlog of 17,128 cases. See *Suara Pembaruan*, 26 August 1992.

[106] According to official data in the *Lampiran Pidato Kenegaraan Presiden Republik Indonesia di depan sidang Dewan Perwakilan Rakyat 16 August 1994* XX/24, the backlog in 1991 was 18,571 cases, and in 1992 (the year of Ali Said's retirement) it stood at 20,495 cases.

[107] Mahkamah Agung Circular Letter (SEMA) no.1/1992.

[108] Purwoto appointed seventeen senior law clerks to increase team productivity. *Merdeka*, 14 October 1992; *Suara Karya*, 15 October 1992.

[109] *Forum Keadilan*, 8 August 1992, p. 42.

[110] Personal communication, 21 April 1995.

[111] *Suara Karya*, 15 October 1992, reports the monthly intake as eight hundred cases.

[112] *Konsultasi Komisi III DPR-RI dengan Ketua Mahkamah Agung (Purwoto)* dated 23 June 1993 (taped recordings).

[113] *Forum Keadilan*, 24 November 1994, p. 94. Purwoto described how, with the help of the new senior clerks, cases resolved by each chamber had been increased from sixty to eighty a month, which meant the Supreme Court in 1993 completed about 9,200 cases, and in 1994 expected to decide 10,400 cases. Nevertheless, new cases in 1993 and 1994 numbered seven thousand a year, so the gross total was only reduced by about two thousand cases.

[114] On the problematic relationship between the backlogs and the laid-back attitude of the Court itself, see Sebastiaan Pompe, "Recent Data on the Backlogs within the Indonesian Supreme Court," *Indonesian Law and Administration Review*, 3,2 (1997): 62.

Supreme Court had clearly reached the limit of its institutional capacity to resolve the backlog issue.[115]

(c) The Bureaucracy

The changes in the judicial organization not only led to an overhaul of the Supreme Court judicial corps, they also deeply affected the Court's bureaucracy. Under the New Order, the work pressures generated by the cases flooding the Supreme Court docket and by the need to supervise an ever-expanding judicial apparatus could not fail to affect the bureaucracy. In due course, the functions of the Court administration had to change in response to the situation.

In essence, the bureaucracy developed from being primarily a back-up service for the Supreme Court's judicial corps in its decision-making function to being a policy-shaping organization for the entire judiciary. From the pivotal figure of the Supreme Court registrar, who was the Court's top administrator, three distinct administrative branches extended like spokes of a wheel: the registry proper, with its primary function of case management; the general administration, oriented toward such matters as personnel and the budget; and, finally, the law clerks, who were closest to the judicial corps and were organized in their own, so-called "functional group." Over time, these administrative branches acquired bulk and clout, so that now in some respects, and at least from the judicial perspective, the Supreme Court's bureaucracy has practically become a shadow Department of Justice.

There is actually little legislation governing the Supreme Court administration. Until 1985, no separate piece of legislation existed to establish the structure and functions of the Court bureaucracy at all—though there were a series of Supreme Court chairmens' instructions. Then in 1985, a Presidential Decree on the subject was introduced (Presidential Decree no.75/1985). It came about under somewhat curious circumstances, as it was enacted barely three weeks before the 1985 Supreme Court Bill was accepted by Parliament and at the very moment that Parliament was debating the organization of the registry that would be outlined in that bill. It is not quite clear why the executive decided to intervene at this precise juncture, causing unnecessary political exposure, particularly as the Supreme Court administration was really a peripheral issue in the debate, an issue which had, in fact, been essentially dormant for forty years. Perhaps the Decree was simply intended to "push debates along nicely," as the press put it; if that was the aim, the government was successful. In response to the government's show of force, Parliament caved in completely: "Who dares question a Presidential Decree," said an exasperated MP.[116] Despite parliamentary complaints about such "unethical behavior,"[117] the debates on Supreme Court administration were singularly brief,

---

[115] By 1995, the appeals structure was being discussed and reconsidered. A commission was installed by the Department of Justice to review procedural law, and also consider how to restrict appeal to the Supreme Court. As I have argued in chapters seven and eight, this effort is more complicated than it may seem, as any solution to the problem must take into account both the Supreme Court's responsibilities for supervising the rather weak lower courts and its limited capability to handle the resultant, huge case-flow.

[116] *Kompas*, 7 December 1985.

[117] *Kompas*, 3 December 1985. It was political reality rather than the law that caused the problems. Legally, Parliament could, of course, have changed the law. The Presidential Decree

and the eventual 1985 Supreme Court Bill was an outright copy of the Presidential Decree no.75/1985 on this score.

(i) The Supreme Court Registrar (Panitera/Sekretaris Jenderal)[118]

The civil law system left its imprint on the Supreme Court by setting a precedent granting the Court registrar relatively high status within the judicial system. The registrar in Indonesia is appointed by special procedure, by the president,[119] and when the Supreme Court still held official sessions, he sat on the bench in judicial robes. Under the 1950 law, the Supreme Court registrar even had judicial decision-making powers, i.e., he could function as a full Supreme Court judge. Although this practice was discontinued under Law no.13/1965, the position retained at least a shadow of its old authority into the 1980s.[120] The registrar's proximity in status to the Supreme Court judges is reinforced by their shared professional background: this bureaucrat is traditionally recruited from the judiciary itself, as Law no.14/1985 specifies identical recruitment requirements for the registrar and the Supreme Court judges.[121] It is not surprising that the majority of Supreme Court registrars, such as Pitoyo, Bismar Siregar, Mohammad Iman, and Toton Suprapto, were also appointed to the Supreme Court bench. Subekti himself

---

75/1985 was based on the old Law no.13/1965, which the 1985 Bill was designed to replace. In constitutional terms, there was nothing to prevent Parliament from going against the Presidential Decree, which is an instrument of inferior status—though, of course, some agreement with the government would have to be reached. The 1985 provisions concerning the Supreme Court registry were not really revolutionary, except insofar as they combined the functions of registrar and secretary general. This item did generate some debate, but it hardly qualified as a fundamental issue meriting such a show of force that invited political exposure. The government could have weathered the debates without problems, as it did on much more controversial issues, waited a week or two, and then enacted the Presidential Decree. Based on the new law, the decree could have been presented as evidence of government efficiency and concerns regarding the rule of law.

[118] No distinction is made in Indonesian between the person of the registrar and the office he heads—both are referred to as *panitera*. From 1985 onwards, the law distinguishes between the section of the Supreme Court bureaucracy that handles cases, called the *panitera* or "case administration" (*administrasi perkara*), and the section handling general affairs, called the general administration (*administrasi umum*). See art.2 Presidential Decree no.75/1985.

[119] Law no.1/1950 art.6, and Law no.15/1985 art.21. Law no.13/1965 is not clear on the matter. It says in art.55 that registrars should be appointed by the minister of justice. The official elucidation explains that this rule only applies to the lower courts, however, without specifying what procedure ought to be followed for the Supreme Court. Art.4 and 41 suggest that the registrar is appointed by the Supreme Court chairman, but this is rather equivocal. Note further that while Presidential Decree 75/1985 explicitly equated the Court registrar with a secretary general in a government department, in fact regular secretary generals are legally appointed by their minister, not by the president.

[120] Law no.1/1950, art.2(2). The 1985 Supreme Court Bill proposed granting the registrar judicial decision-making powers "if deemed necessary" by the Supreme Court chairman (art.14). This article was scrapped in Parliament, however. *Varia Peradilan* 1, Perdana (1 October 1985): 96; *Kompas*, 21 November 1985.

[121] Law no.15/1985 art.20(1)(e) says that, as in the case of Supreme Court judicial recruits, the Supreme Court registrar must have served at least five years as a chairman of an appellate court, or ten years as an appellate judge. The only other provision is that substitute registrars with fifteen years experience may also qualify. These substitute registrars are also recruited from the judiciary, cf.art.20(3)(4).

started out at a registrar under the first chairman, Kusumah Atmadja.[122] As a result (and though originally perhaps this position was not quite on a par with the Supreme Court judges), the registrar currently enjoys equal, if not higher, status than most of the common judges on the Supreme Court bench.[123]

The registrar's high status may have its historical roots in the judicial system, but its tremendous power has accumulated over time. As this civil servant answers only to the Supreme Court chairman (not, to the Court "leadership"), their partnership effectively constitutes the heart of the Court's institutional management.[124] Judges recount that, even during the term of the diminutive Supreme Court of the 1950s, the registrar and the chairman essentially managed judicial personnel in the lower courts, bypassing other Supreme Court judges. Insiders refer to the registrar of that era, Ranuatmadja, as "Chairman Wirjono's right-hand man."[125] One Supreme Court judge recalled Ranuatmadja's complete autonomy in granting him his first judicial appointment, testimony to the registrar's power.

> **Ranuatmadja**: Shall I place you in [X], since that's the town where you come from?
> **Judge**: Well, that may not be a good idea. I mean, I know all the little thieves and crooks there, and people might think me prejudiced.
> **Ranuatmadja**: So do you have any other preferences?
> **Judge**: Are there any vacancies in Bogor? I don't have any books, and Bogor being near Jakarta, I can pop off to Jakarta at times to check out the libraries.
> **Ranuatmadja**: Can't do that, I'm afraid. Bogor is all filled up already.
> **Judge**: How about Bandung?
> **Ranuatmadja**: Ah yes, there's still a vacancy in Bandung. So shall I put you there? All right, that's settled then.[126]

Another judge recounts how his transfer (also to Bandung) was realized by registrar Iskak in 1964, notwithstanding some objections from the minister at the time, Astrawinata.[127] Chairman Seno Adji reportedly relied heavily on his registrar Pitoyo in carrying out his financial and administrative ploys and schemes. Pitoyo

---

[122] The fact that Supreme Court registrars are recruited from the judicial corps facilitates their re-entry to the judiciary, of course. Note that all the registrars cited in the text returned to lower courts to improve their judicial skills (and seniority ranking) before being promoted to the Supreme Court bench. These promotions seem to be based not just on the former registrars' professional proximity to the Court's judges, but also on the fact that Supreme Court registrars are well placed to build up the crucial networks that further their careers.

[123] Despite this institutional reality, which clearly marks the registrar as a top civil servant, in constitutional terms, officially, the registrar ranks lower than any of the Supreme Court judges. See Law no.8/1987 art.4(2) on State Protocol. Still, as representatives of the Golkar Party pointed out during the 1985 parliamentary debates, until 1985 the law said very little about the Supreme Court registrar. A. Hasibuan MP (Golkar), *Dewan Perwakilan Rakyat Rapat Paripurna Ke-9 (1985-1986)* (Jakarta: DPR, n.d.), pp. 18-19.

[124] Presidential Decree no.75/1985 art.5(2).

[125] Personal communication, 15 July 1994.

[126] Personal communication, 15 July 1994. It appears from this account that the registrar really managed lower judicial postings, but he may have consulted with the Supreme Court chairman regarding the more senior ones.

[127] Personal communication, 3 August 1994.

had a reputation for honesty, and apparently Seno Adji was afraid to let him go lest he reveal his secrets.[128] The registrar's authority resides in his control of the administration, a position that gives him the power to oversee hiring, or dismissal, of all administrative officers of the Court. In practically all respects, whether dealing with case management and supervision or the Supreme Court's budget, housing facilities, and equipment, the Court chairman must work with, and to a large extent depend on, the registrar to both formulate and implement Supreme Court policies.

Important from the outset, the registrar became even more powerful as the judiciary and Supreme Court functions expanded under the New Order government. The bureaucracy multiplied as the Court's functions increased. The added importance of this position in the Supreme Court's bureaucracy was recognized in 1985, when the registrar came to be officially titled the "Registrar/Secretary General" of the Court.[129] This reflected in part the emerging organizational and conceptual distinction within the Supreme Court between case administration and general administration. In addition, however, the new title explicitly ranked the registrar's position as the highest function within the civil service, an implicit acknowledgement of his pivotal role within the Supreme Court administration.[130]

(ii) The Case Administration and the General Administration

These two branches, case administration and general administration, constitute the bulk of the Supreme Court's bureaucracy. Starting out with an administrative staff of merely twenty or thirty in the 1950s, these units grew to include almost two hundred persons in 1973 and three hundred in 1974; presently they incorporate approximately 1,300 personnel.[131]

---

[128] *DSL*, 30 October 1978.

[129] Presidential decree no.75/1985. Note that it already had become a habit under Chairman Mudjono prior to 1985 to refer to the Supreme Court registrar as the registrar/secretary general. See for instance *Rapat kerja Komisi III dengan Ketua Mahkamah Agung (Mudjono) no.798/Kom.III/83* dated 10 February 1983, p. 4. There are indications that under Chairman Subekti, the hierarchical system patterned on the government bureaucracy was resisted by the Court. Subekti quite emphatically states in 1973 that the Supreme Court's organization does not involve the functions of secretary general, director general, and so on, but only the rough distinction between the judicial corps and the administration under the registrar. *Catatan sementara rapat Komisi III DPR-RI dengen Ketua Mahkamah Agung (Subekti)* dated 9 February 1973, p. 2.

[130] For the (short) explanation and debates on this issue, see Government Statement (Minister Ismael Saleh) during the debates on the 1985 Supreme Court Bill in: *Dewan Perwakilan Rakyat Rapat Paripurna Ke-3 (1985-1986)*, p. 14, and his statement in Jawaban pemerintah atas pemandangan umum fraksi-fraksi di DPR-RI dated 4 October 1985 (mimeo), pp. 14-15. All parties agreed with the move, with the exception of the vocal Golkar fraction, which asked that the functions no longer be handled by the same person and that he not be allowed to act as a judge. The latter proposal was accepted by the government, but it stuck to its ideas on the former. See A. Hasibuan MP (Golkar), *Dewan Perwakilan Rakyat Rapat Paripurna Ke-9 (1985-1986)*, pp. 18-19.

[131] For figures see a.o. *Catatan sementara rapat Komisi III DPR-RI dengan Mahkamah Agung no.1119/Kom.III/1973* dated 9 February 1973, and *Varia Peradilan* 10 (January 1995): 5. In an interview (15 July 1995), a present Supreme Court judge said that he did not think the Supreme

The case administration, the registry proper, is the original administrative backbone of the Court. Its function is to manage the flow of cases to and from the judicial corps. It is the old Dutch *griffie*, originating from the French *greffe*, called the *panitera* in Indonesia, and it is currently organized in Directorates (*direktorat*), each headed by a director.

The general administrative branch emerged from the Court registry's administrative support staff. Originally, it was an integral part of the registry, consisting of a somewhat shadowy and insignificant pool of administrators, typists, accountants, managers, and the like. Nevertheless, this part of the Court administration both bore the brunt of and reaped the benefits from the Supreme Court's increased managerial functions under the New Order government. Its strength and autonomy vis-à-vis the registry proper matched this growth in functions, and by the 1970s it had evolved into a distinct part of the Court, no less important in many ways than the original registry. It is currently organized into three bureaus (*biro*)—general, budget, and personnel—all headed by bureau chiefs operating under the control of the secretary-general of the Court.

The gradual distinction between the case and the general administrations began to take shape under Subekti, as increased supervisory functions and responsibilities began to take their toll on the Supreme Court. In 1968, Chairman Subekti provided for the Court to be organized into "Sectors" and "Bureaus." The sectors were oriented toward case management along the old civil/criminal distinction, while the bureaus were meant to give general support to the administration, and were divided into General, Upgrading, Budget, and Personnel.[132] Subsequent developments essentially followed the lines set out by Subekti. The most important change came with Presidential Decree no.75/1985 and the Decision of the Registrar/Secretary General no.MA/PANSEK/02/SK of 1986. Most significantly, case administration was reorganized as a result of the Mudjono reforms, while Court Upgrading switched from general into case administration.

As a result of these changes, the case administration sector now consists of five directorates (Civil, Religious, Administrative, Criminal, and Court Upgrading), each headed by a director, who also serves as a substitute registrar. These directors can then assist Court sessions in lieu of the registrar. As we shall see shortly, they are also very influential, and some of them have risen to the Supreme Court bench.[133] The general administration largely retained its original form of three bureaus (General, Budget, and Personnel), under the secretary general, with each bureau chief also functioning as substitute secretary general. This is still its structure.

(iii) The Clerks: Expert Staff, Clerks and Senior Reporting Clerks

The third and final administrative branch of the Supreme Court consists of the law clerks and the so-called expert staff. They came last to the Court, as these

---

Court administration in the 1950s numbered more than ten persons; Professor Daniel S. Lev estimated it at about twenty.

[132] Keputusan Ketua Mahkamah Agung RI no.1/Kpts/MA/1968.

[133] Supreme Court judge Djohansjah prior to his 1993 appointment to the Court bench served as director in civil matters.

positions were created with the Mudjono reforms in 1981-82.[134] They constitute a separate entity, the so-called "Functional Group" (*Kelompok Fungsional*).[135] Even though technically part of the Court administration, they are directly involved in the decision making and, more broadly speaking, the judicial process. Their part-administrative, part-judicial position is reflected in Presidential Decree no.75/1985, which states that while the clerks are appointed and dismissed by the Supreme Court registrar, they answer not to him but to the Supreme Court chairman. In reality, this means that the clerks answer to the team of Supreme Court judges (or one Supreme Court judge) to which they are attached.[136]

These clerks are equipped to straddle the administration and the judiciary because, unlike the situation in the United States, for instance, all Supreme Court law clerks in Indonesia are former judges,[137] temporarily detached from their judicial functions in the country to serve on the Court.[138] This means that they exchange their decision-making role in the countryside for an advisory function on the Supreme Court. For this reason, Court clerks are sometimes referred to as "judges without mallets" (*hakim non-palu*).

The law distinguishes two categories of law clerks: the expert staff (*tenaga ahli*) and the clerks assisting Supreme Court judges in their decision-making capacities (*hakim yustisial*).[139] The former group is fairly small, numbering perhaps five clerks, and assists in such matters as upgrading courses and publication of Supreme Court decisions.[140] It is an interesting group, generally consisting of very bright judges, some of whom even make it to the Supreme Court bench.[141] The expert staff provides a means by which young talented judges can be

---

[134] There was some talk during the late Seno Adji years of creating clerks, but as far as could be traced nothing came of it. *Catatan sementara rapat kerja Komisi III dengan Mahkamah Agung RI (Seno Adji) no.3128/Kom.III/78* dated 7 February 1978, pp. 4-5.

[135] Presidential Decree no.75/1985 art.7(i).

[136] Presidential Decree no.75/1985 art.10(5) & art.13(2).

[137] Keputusan Penitera/Sekretaris Jenderal Mahkamah Agung RI no.MA/PANSEK/02/SK (1986), art.114 & 115. They must have served at least ten years as a judge in a lower court. Mahkamah Agung RI & LPPIS FISIP UI, "Masalah dan faktor yang mempengaruhi pelaksanaan tugas administrasi dalam proses penyelesaian perkara di Mahkamah Agung Republik Indonesia, (mimeo, Jakarta, 1992)," p. 27.

[138] For this reason, law clerks remain within the Department of Justice bureaucratic domain and do not become part of the Supreme Court's bureaucracy. This situation is reflected in their civil servants' registration code, which retains the Department of Justice prefix NIP 04 rather than the Supreme Court prefix, NIP 22. So, besides floating between the Supreme Court administration and judicial corps, they also straddle bureaucratic boundaries between the Court and the Department of Justice. Mahkamah Agung RI & LPPIS FISIP UI, "Masalah dan faktor yang mempengaruhi pelaksanaan tugas administrasi dalam proses penyelesaian perkara di Mahkamah Agung Republik Indonesia," p. 27.

[139] Presidential Decree no.75/1985 art 7(i).

[140] Presidential Decree no.75/1985 art.10(3) envisages a maximum of six expert staff clerks.

[141] Thus, before her appointment to the Court bench in 1992, Supreme Court judge Retnowulan Sutianto headed the expert staff on the Court. Another expert staff member was Setiawan, regarded by insiders as one of the most prominent legal theoreticians in the field of Indonesian private law. The Supreme Court put their considerable talents and skills to good use by bringing them in. Other recent examples are current junior chairman Paulus Lotulung Effendi, a noted expert on administrative law and a university professor, with a PhD in administrative law from France, and Eddy Djunaedi, with a PhD in the field of criminal law.

relieved of their duties in the anonymous district courts and direct their skills to serve broader interests in Jakarta.

The other group, consisting of clerks assisting Supreme Court judges, is much larger, numbering between sixty and seventy persons.[142] As a general rule, each Court judge has a single clerk, though the chairmen may have more than one.[143] These clerks also serve as substitute registrars in their judges' chambers.[144] The most important function of any clerk involves summarizing the facts and legal issues involved in cases "his" judge is handling. The summary appears on a cover sheet attached to the dossier. In addition, the clerk to the chairman of each chamber manages the administration of that chamber's cases and ensures that all judges try cases in proper order. For this reason, the chamber chairman's clerk is called the "coordinating assistant," or ASKOR (Assisten Koordinator). Sometimes clerks also write up draft decisions in accordance with the Supreme Court judge's instructions. Within these broad outlines, working routine differs from chamber to chamber and also from judge to judge.

The substantial workload that Chairman Purwoto Gandasubrata inherited brought him to expand the system of court clerks. In 1993-94, he introduced a new type of Supreme Court clerk by recruiting so-called *Hakim Tinggi Raporteur* (senior reporting clerks) from the appellate, rather than the first instance, courts (most clerks are recruited from first instance courts).[145] A total of seventeen such clerks were appointed, one for each chamber. These senior reporting clerks, who effectively act as associate justices of the Supreme Court, handle the large number of simple cases on the Court docket. These are so-called NO cases (cases that on procedural grounds can be summarily dismissed; from the Dutch *Niet Ontvankelijk*, dismissals), marriage and divorce cases, and small claims (any case with a claim not exceeding one million Rupiah). The Registry marks the files of these cases with a special stamp, indicating they are simple. After allocation to chambers, these cases are directly given over to the senior clerk, who handles them with relative autonomy, as he fully drafts the decision and only comes to the chamber chairman for final approval and signature.[146]

---

[142] Mahkamah Agung RI & LPPIS FISIP UI, "Masalah dan faktor yang mempengaruhi pelaksanaan tugas administrasi dalam proses penyelesaian perkara di Mahkamah Agung Republik Indonesia," p. 15.

[143] Some junior Supreme Court judges have no clerk at all. In Team A, clerks are not allocated to the team judges specifically, but constitute an autonomous group in their own right, serving the team judges on a rotating basis. Ibid., p. 15.

[144] Mahkamah Agung RI & LPPIS FISIP UI, "Masalah dan faktor yang mempengaruhi pelaksanaan tugas administrasi dalam proses penyelesaian perkara di Mahkamah Agung Republik Indonesia," p. 15.

[145] Decision of the Mahkamah Agung Registrar/Secretary General no. MA/PANSEK/02/SK (1986) art.114 & 115 allows for the recruitment of both first instance and appellate judges as Supreme Court clerks.

[146] I was unable to trace the decision instituting the senior clerks, and this information is based on interview material. By 1994, it seemed that Purwoto's plan to use these additional clerks in order to catch up with the backlog had misfired, in part, apparently, because many of the recruits were not of the highest caliber. Thus, one senior reporting clerk was said to be in poor health and, as a result, unable to handle the turnover of cases, while a number of other senior reporting clerks were close to retirement and reportedly took things easily. Personal communication, 3 August 1994. The issue was also raised in Parliament when MP Susanto Mangunegara in 1994 queried Supreme Court chairman Purwoto regarding the situation: "I heard that some of the senior reporting clerks have been recruited from junior judges and that

2. CASE MANAGEMENT

The 1992 Internal Audit of the Supreme Court concluded that there was no clear working order in the Court.

> To the present day, there is no clear provision concerning the specialization of functions, tasks, responsibilities and accountability of the various parties involved in deciding cases. This results in a situation in which these matters are dealt with on the basis of conventions . . . [147]

The essentially unregulated nature of the Court's method of handling cases creates considerable confusion. Nevertheless, its basic conventions and characteristics are clear.

As in so many civil courts, Indonesian Supreme Court procedure is essentially all written.[148] There is no oral argument, and parties hardly ever appear in person at the court. Indeed, since the time of Mudjono, parties are apparently no longer summoned to court to hear the verdict, and indeed are not even officially informed that their case has been decided.[149] As a senior Supreme Court judge blandly stated: "Nobody knows we are deciding their case, so nobody comes."[150] Only in exceptional high-profile cases are decisions pronounced in open court, with the date and time posted in advance. Parties only become aware of the Supreme Court decision when they receive notification from the *district court* where they originated the case.

Cases are introduced into the court at the registrar/secretary general's office. The registrar checks the dossiers, transfers the cases, then categorizes and distributes them according to jurisdictional background and, in the case of the general courts, by substance, among the directors (who are also substitute court registrars). The directors have a number of functions: they register the cases, classify them as either priority or non-priority cases,[151] and determine which cases cannot be heard because of important errors of form or procedure (these files are stamped with NO).[152] Finally, the directors distribute the cases among the

---

they sometimes are in bad health. I mean, we have had cases in the past in which a court clerk failed his exam to become a judge in the regular courts three times, yet when the administrative courts were established and they were in need of judges, he immediately became an administrative judge. Let's not make this a precedent." *Konsultasi Komisi III DPR-RI dengan Ketua MA (Purwoto)* dated 23 June 1994 (taped recording).

[147] Mahkamah Agung R.I. & LPPIS FISIP UI, "Masalah dan faktor yang mempengaruhi pelaksanaan tugas administrasi dalam proses penyelesaian perkara di Mahkamah Agung Republik Indonesia," pp. 17-18.

[148] Other sources also report that current procedure relies entirely on written testimonies and decisions, so that there are no appearances at all before the Court. Soedirjo, *Kasasi dalam perkara perdata* (Jakarta: Akademika Pressindo, 1983), p. 70.

[149] This was still regular practice during Subekti's days, but became less frequent during Seno Adji's administration.

[150] Personal communication, 4 August 1994.

[151] Mahkamah Agung RI & LPPIS FISIP UI, "Masalah dan faktor yang mempengaruhi pelaksanaan tugas administrasi dalam proses penyelesaian perkara di Mahkamah Agung Republik Indonesia," p. 21. On the criteria for prioritizing or not, see also hereafter.

[152] The principal reasons a case may be disqualified from a hearing: if the plaintiff has made a direct application to the Supreme Court without going through the lower courts; if a legal

Supreme Court teams after the Supreme Court chairman approves the decisions of the registrar.

The directors' offices figure as the Court's traffic junctions (not just for cases on the way up, but also on the way down), and while the offices of some Supreme Court judges at least look quite empty, those of the directors often resemble Picadilly Circus during rush hour. People mill about as huge stacks of cases are brought in, carted out, or just left lying about in monstrous heaps, blocking passageways and keeping out the light. I found that directors, unlike judges, often had little time to talk, for they were in a constant frenzy.

The directors draw up a register that allocates the cases to the various Supreme Court teams. The register, as a general rule, follows a first-come first-served basis: cases are assigned a registration number when received and are arranged in sequence, in batches, for assignment to chambers. As former Supreme Court chairman Purwoto S. Gandasubrata stated:

> We instruct the directors to order cases according to their registration number of entry, and then divide them up. (. . .) This batch goes to Team A, this one to team B and so on. (. . .) It is all done by the order of the registration number given to the case when it comes in.[153]

Before allocating the cases to the teams as proposed, the director passes the register to the Supreme Court chairman for approval, and the chairman makes the revisions he thinks necessary, based on the significance of the cases, his particular interest in certain cases, and so on.

> Of course, there are exceptions. For instance, a case that receives much public attention escapes the order of the registration number and is given priority because we want to settle it quickly. But otherwise, cases are usually allocated on the basis of their number . . . [154]

Chairman Seno Adji, with his background in public prosecution, is said to have rarely handled civil cases; he consistently selected the criminal ones. It is also said that Supreme Court chairmen tend to reserve politically sensitive cases for themselves. As one junior Supreme Court chairman put it:

---

representation has been put forward without mandate by notary deed; if delays have exceeded the limits; and in the absence of motivation. Ibid.

[153] *Forum Keadilan*, 6 May 1996. The system of allocating cases according to the sequence of their registration numbers is well established, as illustrated by the *Gandhi Memorial School case* (1996), where a departure from that order was one of the factors that aroused suspicion about the proceedings. As junior chairman Adi Andoyo put it at the time: " . . . people intervened to the effect that the case was assigned to the D-team. Nevertheless, as far as its registration number went, it should have been assigned to the H-team. I don't know why the D-team got it, there must have been collusion." *Gatra*, 20 April 1996. Still, the registration system, while indicative, is not conclusive. In fact, as will become apparent later, it was only after other aspects of the *Gandhi Memorial School* case raised suspicions of collusion or corruption that people bothered to look at the order of registration and discovered the irregularity. Indeed, Adi Andoyo himself had approved the assignment of the case to the H-team, though he can hardly be blamed for failing to notice a single misfit registration number in the large batches to be approved. *Forum Keadilan*, 22 April 1996.

[154] *Forum Keadilan*, 6 May 1996.

The chairman in the end determines the allocation of cases, often reserving politically sensitive ones for himself. It is a system of dictates, with the chairman saying: you take this case, he takes that one, and so on.[155]

In later years, beginning in the later stages of Supreme Court chairman Ali Said's administration, the task of approving the list was delegated to junior chairmen, though the Supreme Court chairman retained the final say.[156]

Occasionally certain cases may be side-tracked or, alternately, moved ahead of their proper place in the order. For instance, if a case has attracted a great deal of publicity or promises to be politically sensitive, the hearing may be postponed. One Supreme Court judge recalled:

> There is this difficult case involving two politically well-connected persons who oppose each other in a multi-million dollar affair, and who have already spent much money on the case. They regularly come to court, with powerful friends to pressure Supreme Court chairman Purwoto. In cases such as these, Purwoto and the Court can only lose, so what we do is delay the decision, endlessly hoping that the parties will settle out of court.[157]

In cases that undergo special review (that is, they are reopened after having been decided in a lower court), the Supreme Court prefers to wait until the judges who decided the case in cassation have retired, so as not to embarrass them. This means that special review cases sometimes are put on hold for quite a while.[158] It also is possible for certain cases to be given priority treatment and handled much faster than the regular ones. In the aftermath of the controversial *Gandhi Memorial School case* (1996), junior chairman Adi Andoyo Soetjipto indicated three grounds for accelerating the process: if a suspect is in provisional detention awaiting final judgment, if the case attracts public attention, or if it has a political angle.[159]

---

[155] Personal communication, 16 July 1994. There are examples in which this convention was breached, however, such as the *First Kedung Ombo case*, which was decided by junior chairman Asikin Kusumah Atmadja.

[156] In the *Gandhi Memorial School case* (1996), the problem acquired an extra twist because junior chairman Adi Andoyo Soetjipto, who suggested that his brethren on the bench had been corrupt and that the court administration had steered the case their way, turned out to be the person who had approved the case register as drawn up by the relevant director. *Forum Keadilan*, 22 April 1996. In the process, it became clear that he had handled case-lists from the late 1980s onwards. *Kompas*, 23 April 1996. Supreme Court chairman Purwoto S. Gandasubrata after his retirement indicated that final responsibility for the list was shared by the chairman and vice-chairman, along civil-criminal lines. *Forum Keadilan*, 6 May 1996. Nevertheless, in view of the fact that highly publicized cases generally are handled by the Supreme Court chairman, it would appear that it is he who ultimately decides.

[157] Personal communication, 3 August 1994.

[158] Personal communication, 22 August 1994.

[159] Concluding that none of these grounds applied in the *Gandhi Memorial School case* (1996), but that the case had been given priority treatment nonetheless, Adi Andoyo Soetjipto accepted it as evidence that "collusion" had taken place. A. Andoyo Soetjipto, "Uraian secara kronologis terjadinya masalah 'kolusi' di Mahkamah Agung RI," (unpublished, 1996), p. 5.

Ultimately, however, it may not be clear why the Supreme Court chairman chooses to revise the directors' register. According to one of the Supreme Court directors:

> I sometimes don't know why he makes the changes. It may be that he got a letter or a phone call from one of the parties, asking for priority treatment.[160]

But the chairmen's revisions by and large are incidental. The system is fully geared toward realizing a rapid turnover of cases, and the lists are simply too long for a single person to grasp.

> The directors are very powerful because as a general rule the Supreme Court chairman just agrees with the lists which they have drawn up. The lists simply are too long to change, so whatever changes are made, are incidental.[161]

> ... the directors manage the flow of cases to the judges ...[162]

After the list is approved, the cases are distributed among the teams once a month on a rote basis: all Court teams get eighty cases, except for the (single-chamber) A and B teams of the chairman and vice-chairman.[163] The monthly allocation in the offices of the junior chairman is marked by huge stacks of red-ribbon-bound dossiers lining the walls right up to the ceiling and spilling out into the corridor, several rows thick. It is a daunting sight, and one cannot help but wonder how judges withstand such monthly onslaughts. The various chairmen divide the cases among their chambers.

Most of the docket is a mixture of civil and criminal cases originating from the general courts. Criminal cases often get priority treatment, particularly when suspects are in detention, as noted above. The directors first allocate them to the various teams,[164] some of which receive more criminal cases than others. Cases coming up through special jurisdictions are generally allotted to the teams specializing in those jurisdictions. Thus, the C-team handles administrative cases, and the E-team consists entirely of Muslim judges and handles cases originating from the Islamic courts. This team was chaired for a long time by the respected Muslim junior chairman, Busthanul Arifin, who was succeeded by junior chairman Taufiq—the sole judge on the Supreme Court to have come from the fiercely Muslim Aceh area.[165] Similarly, most military (i.e., criminal) cases are handled by the H-team, which consists largely of military judges.

---

[160] Personal communication, 16 July 1994.

[161] Personal communication, 5 August 1994.

[162] *Forum Keadilan*, 22 April 1996.

[163] Personal communication, 22 August 1994. Traditionally, the A-team is the chairman's, and the B-team the vice-chairman's. However, when Purwoto became chairman in 1992, he remained with his B-team, so that during his administration the order was reversed. Allotment does not proceed as team's reservoirs of pending cases empty, but the cases are allocated on a monthly basis irrespective of case turnover in each team.

[164] Personal communication, 22 August 1994.

[165] Mr. Taufiq became vice chairman of the Court after *Reformasi*.

Cases are only distributed if all documents are complete, which means that sometimes the allotment fails to meet the prescribed levels. The operation of the system as regards criminal cases has been described by Supreme Court director Mrs. Sujatmi Soedarmoko in the following terms:

> (. . .) In accordance with instructions of the Court leadership on the monthly distribution of criminal cases, this is realized as follows:
>
> | | |
> |---|---|
> | Team A: 30 cases | Team E: 20 cases |
> | Team B: 20 cases | Team F: 20 cases |
> | Team C: 20 cases | Team G: 80 cases |
> | Team D: 20 cases | Team H: 80 cases |
>
> From the middle of 1994, the total number of case files ready for distribution did not reach the required 290 files, with a result that the number of cases distributed to the teams matched the number of case files that were actually ready for distribution. In February 1995 the number of criminal case files ready for distribution numbered 155 files, and they were distributed as follows:
>
> | | |
> |---|---|
> | Team A: 20 cases | Team E: 15 cases |
> | Team B: 15 cases | Team F: 15 cases |
> | Team C: 15 cases | Team G: 30 cases |
> | Team D: 15 cases | Team H: 30 cases (. . .)[166] |

While by and large constant, teams are not immutably fixed. Occasionally judges are allocated to another team on an ad hoc basis because of their special expertise.

> It is not at all uncommon for judges to "jump over" and temporarily change teams. The usual reason has to do with personal expertise. There are a number of judges with specific expertise in administrative law, such as Indroharto, Olden Bidara, Boestomi, Karlinah, Bismar Siregar, Suraputra, and Djohansjah, who even though they do not sit in Team-C, are still sometimes placed there to decide administrative cases. The same applies to Team-E, where Yahya, Bismar Siregar, Masrani, and Samsoedin sometimes jump in.[167]

Occasionally special chambers are composed by judges from different teams, assigned because of their knowledge or, perhaps, the importance of the case in question.[168] When the Court is confronted with a notably important issue, a special "heavy" panel of judges, made up of Supreme Court chairmen, is sometimes drawn up. Thus, the review case of *Kedung Ombo* was decided by the Supreme Court chairman Purwoto Gandasubrata together with two junior chairmen, and similarly a judicial review case of a Ministry of Information Regulation was decided by a panel consisting of junior chairmen only. In this way, such decisions are given extra

---

[166] Memo no.1498/Dir.Pid/X/1995 dated 25 October 1995 to Supreme Court junior chairman Adi Andoyo Soetjipto. A. Andoyo Soetjipto, "Uraian secara kronologis terjadinya masalah 'kolusi' di Mahkamah Agung RI," Attachment X.
[167] Personal communication, 22 August 1994.
[168] Personal communication, 31 August 1994.

weight, making it harder to overturn them if litigation involving a comparable issue should arise in the future.[169]

Cases enter chambers by way of the chamber chairman's law clerk, the so-called ASKOR (*Assistent Koordinator*). He transfers the simple cases, stamped with NO, directly to the senior reporting clerks, effectively bypassing regular procedure in the teams. These cases are only submitted to the team chairman for final signature. The ASKOR will give the other cases to a judge within each chamber for a first written draft outlining the facts and arguments. They are handled by this judge's clerks, who type up a summary of the facts and, if possible, of the legal issues, which is then attached to the dossier and passed on to the relevant first judge. The clerk's summary is meant to help judges go through the files and speed up the decision-making process. Its role and significance very much depend both on the clerk and the judge, and on the case in question. Some judges told me they practically ignored these summaries because the clerks missed some important issues: "You really cannot rely on the clerks' summary because they are frequently mistaken on the basic issues."[170] Other judges worried that the summary might influence decision making, stating that they preferred going through the dossier first and making up their own minds before consulting the clerk's report. Still other justices followed such reports closely and relied on them. After reviewing the dossier and, perhaps, the clerk's report, the judge writes down a brief summary of his own and his decision on a cover-sheet, still referred to sometimes with the Dutch *"adviesblad"* (advisory form), which he attaches to the file.[171] This may be very brief: one *"adviesblad"* I saw consisted of four small telegram-style sentences.

What happens after this point varies from team to team:

> Some teams have the "cans and jugs" system, in which cases are handled with the basic understanding that if one judge has looked at it, the others will defer to him and say that they will not have to review it.[172]

In such teams, cases are not all given to the most junior judge for preliminary review, but are divided among all the judges. In other teams, cases are dealt with by all the judges within one chamber, sometimes with a fixed routine, such that, for example, the judicial summaries of each case may be passed from young to old in order to minimize influence. One judge stated, for example: "In my team all judges handle all cases in order of seniority, starting out with the youngest."[173]

Most frequently, judges scrutinize the case on the basis of the *adviesblad*. Sometimes a debate ensues, whose outcome depends very much on the persons involved. Some judges tend to be passive, others just whip their brethren along, and others are hard to budge.

---

[169] In review procedures, they sometimes are also necessitated by the fact that the prior cassation decision was taken by a junior chairman. It is felt to be demeaning to have such decisions tested in review by junior Supreme Court judges.

[170] Personal communication, 23 August 1994.

[171] Personal communication, 22 August 1994.

[172] Personal communication, 11 August 1994. "Cans and jugs" refers to Dutch expression that everything is all right (*kannen en kruiken*).

[173] Personal communication, 22 August 1994.

The way in which judges in each team look at your *adviesblad* varies. Some are rather obstructive but others are pretty useless, they always say "I agree, I agree."[174]

If agreement is reached, all judges sign a special form, and the case is returned to the judge handling it so that he can draw up the final verdict. If no agreement is forthcoming—this happens infrequently—the decision is taken by vote, with the youngest called upon to vote first.[175] Although rare, it does happen that sometimes the discussion ends in stalemate. Thus, one senior Supreme Court judge told me that he had a case in which one of the other judges on the panel refused to sign, and a standoff ensued. The situation was complicated further by a third judge's frequent absences from the sessions. In the end, the senior justice reconstituted the panel with judges who were willing to sign.[176]

Cases are officially pronounced after the completion of the process. Usually the final decision has been completely drawn up before the pronouncement, but, as the 1992 Internal Audit pointed out, this is not always the case. Thus, final decisions are sometimes taken on the basis of drafts, occasionally when only the introduction and conclusion to the decision have been completed. The judges who officially pronounce the verdict need not be the same as the one who went through the dossier and drew it up. One session of an ad hoc group of judges makes the official pronouncement for a series of cases that have been decided by the various chambers. This rarely consists of the verdict explained *in extenso*; more often, the outcome is announced in a couple of words: claim denied, awarded plaintiff, and so on.

This official pronouncement is an important moment, for at this point the decision technically acquires the force of law. For this reason, the law provides that the declaration be made in public. The architectural layout of the Supreme Court building does not allow all teams to read their verdicts in an official courtroom, however, for the simple reason that there is only a single, huge hall available, which is used only for ceremonial purposes. As a result, judges are forced to pronounce the verdicts officially in their own chambers; usually this takes place in the chambers of the team chairman. The event is rendered public, as stipulated, by opening the outer doors to the corridors.[177] As a result, the pronouncement is hardly a spectacular affair. The judges do not wear robes, but just sit around a desk and go through the cases, droning out their decisions.[178] The ritualistic, rather muffled nature of the process is particularly evident from the fact that parties are not summoned to court to hear the decision. Despite the unofficial channels which the Court could use to inform lawyers about the progress of their cases, litigating

---

[174] Personal communication, 23 August 1994.

[175] Personal communication, 22 August 1994.

[176] Personal communication, 11 August 1994.

[177] Personal communications, 4 August 1994, 5 August 1994.

[178] The unceremonious and largely ritualistic character of this process was illustrated for me by a small event. I was interviewing a Supreme Court judge when he suddenly got a call from his team chairman summoning him to his office, apparently because they were one judge short of the required panel for reading decisions. So the judge bolted out the door and ran off to sit in on the reading of a list of decisions, most of which he had not been involved with himself.

parties only become aware officially that the Supreme Court has decided their case when the decision is handed down by the district court after it has been passed back down the tube from the highest court.[179]

Following the verdict, the ASKOR returns the cases with their decisions to the directors. Final reports, with the verdicts, are returned to the judges for signature. Finally, they are sent off to the litigating parties, by way of the first instance court.

3. BUDGET[180]

The Supreme Court's budget is a factor that never figures prominently in debates, yet budget restrictions do limit the Court's activities in a number of ways. Under the New Order government, the state budget was roughly divided into two sections: the routine budget, which is more or less fixed and routinely allocated on an annual basis, and the development budget, which must be reapplied for and the terms of one's application resubstantiated every year.

Figure 3
Comparative Budgetary Ranking of the Supreme Court
(x million Rupiah, standard: based on 1990/91 budget, adjusted figures)

1. Parliament (DPR): 22,126
2. President: 13,500
3. State Audit Board (BPK): 11,920
4. Supreme Court: 7,700
5. State Congress (MPR): 3,700
6. State Advisory Council (DPA): 2,900

In absolute terms, there has been a spectacular increase in the Supreme Court's budget under the New Order government, as it grew from Rp.96.3 million in 1970-71 to Rp.11,436.5 million in 1992-93. Nevertheless, the rupiah's loss of value over the years means that this adjustment is not as impressive as it seems. Moreover,

---

[179] Under Subekti's leadership, sessions were still held in public, with the judges dressed in togas and advocates allowed to attend. This practice was applied more selectively by Seno Adji, who held sessions behind closed doors. It was discontinued under Mudjono, when the large number of judges rendered it unworkable. *Catatan sementara rapat Komisi III DPR-RI dengan Ketua Mahkamah Agung (Subekti) no.1119/Kom.III/1973 dated 9 February 1973*, p.14.

[180] The Supreme Court's budget was difficult to trace, in part because, from 1970, the method for determining the budget in the *State Gazette* changed, so that it was calculated and reported by sector, rather than by institution. Thus, whereas budget Laws no.15/1968 or no.2/1969 listed the specific budgets for each state institution, from 1970 such reports only mentioned the broad category of "law" when listing amounts allotted to the judiciary, without specifying how much went to the Supreme Court, to the Department of Justice, to the Public Prosecution, and so on. As a result, the specific applications and awards had to be researched. They consist of effectively four bundles, namely the budget claimed and the budget awarded on both the routine and development basis discussed hereafter. I found the documents eventually in the parliamentary archives, which had suffered from water damage, and they were incomplete. As a result, the source for all data hereafter is the *Anggaran pendapatan dan belanja negara* (estimate of state income and expenditure), either *rutin* (routine) or *pembangunan* (concerning budgetary provision for development).

proportionally the Supreme Court's budgetary position has hardly improved at all. Over the past two decades, the Court has been consistently allocated 0.02 percent of the state budget,[181] suggesting a more or less fixed division of the state's allotments, regardless of the amount the Supreme Court claims each year for its development budget. It may be added by way of comparison that during the 1990s the Supreme Court's budget was about half that of the president's, one third that of Parliament (DPR), twice that of the State Advisory Council, double that of the State Congress (MPR), and two-thirds that of the State Audit Board.

In fact, the Supreme Court's budgetary claims are rather modest, to the point, it seems, that its accounting service on one occasion actually underestimated its budget. In 1978 the Court expressed its gratitude to Parliament for increasing its budget by 10 percent, an act which drew quite a bit of criticism:

> Indeed, compared to last year the Supreme Court budget increased by 10 percent. But inflation over the same year stood at 12 percent, so in real terms the Supreme Court budget actually dropped. And while the Court might think its budget sufficient, I myself, as a representative of the people dedicated to the rule of law, believe that the Supreme Court budget is a pittance.[182]

Despite acknowledged increases in funds allotted to the Supreme Court, the budget has constrained the Court's activities and ambitions in two important respects. Budgetary restrictions over the years were instrumental in limiting the publication and distribution of Court decisions, as well as the training of judges. This insecure and inadequate funding hampers crucial initiatives:

> One major problem with the publication of Supreme Court decisions is that it always depended on insecure funding. We always had to apply for the money to the State Planning Board, and then wait for it to come, or perhaps not. Some of the reasons for the irregular appearance of published decisions recently must have to do with this.[183]

> The Supreme Court consistently aims at secure funding, possibly with foreign aid, to set up its own institute for training judges. The Prosecution and Department of Justice already have such institutions, but the Supreme Court doesn't. Now it must apply for funding every year, which is a hassle, and what's more creates insecurity that precludes continuity and serious efforts in this direction.[184]

In fact, for twenty years now the Supreme Court has consistently pushed for secure (routine) funding on both issues, but without success. Budgetary constraints have

---

[181] With some highs and lows, of course. Thus, in 1976–77 the Supreme Court budget jumped to 0.048 percent in relative terms, but in 1979–80 it fell to 0.016 percent.

[182] *Catatan sementara rapat kerja Komisi III dengan Ketua Mahkamah Agung* (Seno Adji) no.3128/Kom.III/78 dated 7 February 1978, p. 25. The speaker is MP Ghazali Mashoeri. The Supreme Court responded lamely that it could only " . . . express its gratitude to MP Ghazali Mashoeri on the attention he gives . . . " (p. 37).

[183] Personal communication, 25 September 1995.

[184] Personal communication, 4 July 1994.

thus clearly limited the role of the institution. At least as regards training, this appears to be intentional, as the limited budget and annual reapplication process keep the Supreme Court dependent on the government, particularly on the Department of Justice. Budgetary restrictions remain instruments by which the government can curtail the Court's attempts to acquire a stronger grip over the judiciary. In conversations, Supreme Court judges often attach an almost disproportionate importance to supervision over the lower courts, and to the establishment of separate training facilities for judges. Supreme Court chairman Purwoto Gandasubrata expressed this in indirect terms in parliamentary hearings:

> If it is the wish that the administration of justice runs smoothly, the Supreme Court sincerely hopes that it will get adequate means and funding to realize its tasks of upgrading and supervising the four current jurisdictions, so that they can work properly. According to the Supreme Court, funding at present is simply inadequate, and we can do little but make the best of it. Nevertheless, we feel that it is time that the Supreme Court be provided with breathing space in terms of sufficient men, money, and means to shoulder its functions, which are becoming heavier by the day.[185]

Privately, Supreme Court judges are more blunt about the matter:

> The Dutch Legal Cooperation Program made it possible for the Supreme Court to organize its judge-training courses. This allowed it to escape the grasp of the Department of Justice. We initiated the program from within the Supreme Court, but funding remains the crucial problem. [. . .] In fact, while the program was operating, we were able to train sixty judges at a go under quite favorable circumstances. But when it collapsed, we were back where we started. Fortunately, the State Planning Board and the Asia Foundation realized the importance of judge training courses, and continued to fund it. But it was more modest and, again, in financial terms, essentially insecure. This was one reason why we had to exclude judges from outlying areas such as Kalimantan, Ambon, and Menado. I am really angry at the Department of Justice, which doesn't provide well for the interests of the judges.[186]

4. PROBLEMS

The organizational structure of the Supreme Court is the natural outcome of the extraordinary pressures under which the institution has had to operate since Guided Democracy. Its institutional response to these pressures, besides quite simply adding more personnel, was to delegate tasks and diversify the institution. As a result, the Supreme Court judicial corps and bureaucracy became more bulky, as well as much more complex.

---

[185] Just before this passage in his address, the speaker, then vice-chairman, Purwoto, had pointed out that the administrative appeal courts would become operative by the end of 1991, and the Supreme Court would acquire full supervision over that jurisdiction also. *Catatan rapat komisi III DPR-RI dengan Ketua Mahkamah Agung (Ali Said) no.2156/K.III/90 dated 10 September 1990*, pp. 5-6.

[186] Personal communication, 24 April 1995.

As we have seen, the additional personnel failed to meet the most imperative need, which was to confront and manage the increasing workload. In addition, the Court's expansion lay at the root of a number of painful problems, particularly because it made the Court singularly hard to control. As the 1992 Internal Audit stated: "There are problems with the internal coordination of the Court."[187] These problems reflect poorly both on the judicial corps and the bureaucracy. In its search to realize quantitative goals, the Supreme Court has sacrificed a good deal of quality. As one Supreme Court junior chairman stated:

> The fixation on quantity from Mudjono onwards made us forget about the quality of our decisions. The present motto is that it doesn't matter how you decide, as long as you empty your slate.[188]

And one senior Department of Justice official succinctly expressed the problem in the following, rather dismissive, terms: "Before thinking about improving the law, the Supreme Court must first think about improving its own management."[189]

(a) The Judicial Corps

(i) Strong Hierarchy and Excessive Deference

Reforms in the Supreme Court organization strengthened the position of the leadership, particularly of the Supreme Court chairman, weakening that of all other Court judges. We have already seen that this development began under chairman Wirjono Prodjodikoro in the 1950s, but it was reinforced under the New Order, particularly in the cases when the government appointed chairmen who did not have a judicial background, and whose allegiances, therefore, tended toward the executive rather than to the Court. Moreover, over time the Supreme Court chairman was given a number of prominent posts that pushed him into governmental rather than judicial circles. These included, notably, involvement in consultations with various sectoral departments concerning the management of the judiciary (particularly the Mah-Dep forum[190]), in the forum for judicial-police matters which effectively covers the entire field of criminal-judicial policy (MAHKEJAPOL[191]), and in parliamentary consultations. Within the Court, a

---

[187] Mahkamah Agung R.I. & LPPIS FISIP UI, "Masalah dan faktor yang mempengaruhi pelaksanaan tugas administrasi dalam proses penyelesaian perkara di Mahkamah Agung Republik Indonesia," p. 34.

[188] Personal communication, 10 May 1996.

[189] S. Hartono, director of the National Legal Development Agency (BPHN, Badan Pembinaan Hukum Nasional), Department of Justice, during a conversation with the Dutch director-general for courts, The Hague, 28 June 1994.

[190] The Mah-Dep forum, established in 1984, constitutes the most important commission for personnel management within the judiciary. The Department of Justice is represented by the minister and the director general for the general courts. The Supreme Court is represented by the chairman and vice-chairman. J. C. T. Simorangkir, *Sejarah Departemen Kehakiman Republik Indonesia 1945-1985* (Jakarta: n.p., 1985), p. 317. A comparable consultative forum with the Department of Religious Affairs was established in 1983, see for example joint decision MA Chairman no.1/1983 and Minister of Religious Affairs no.KMA/001/SK/I/1983.

[191] The first joint session of the MAHKEJAPOL (Mahkamah Agung, Departemen Kehakiman, Kejaksaan Agung, Polisi, Consultative Forum of Law-enforcing Offices) was held in 1984. The

number of measures have strengthened the chairman's position vis-à-vis the other judges, allowing him to determine their work assignments, whether they can go abroad, whether they may leave town for more than seven days, and so on. Supreme Court chairmen have increasingly acted without consulting the other judges, indeed sometimes consciously so in cases which ran counter to the institutional interests of the Court. Whereas, as late as the 1970s, this might have given rise to anger and opposition from within the Court (ineffective though these reactions may have been), by the 1980s the hierarchical position of the leadership was accepted as natural within the Supreme Court, and the *primus inter pares* system had been effectively abandoned. One MP described the system as follows:

> These governing constructs are increasingly structured in the so-called Javanese way. What this means is that if critical questions are asked that confront senior judges, this is considered to be not "Asian" [*ketimuran*], and hence impolite, disloyal. [. . .] It is a big-man decision-making structure in which the dominant chairman governs all, and everybody defers to him. Do you think that in the *pleno* Supreme Court meeting anyone questions Supreme Court chairman Purwoto? Don't think of it, everyone just shuts up and agrees.[192]

Observers agree that to challenge the Supreme Court chairman would inevitably weaken one's position in the Court or jeopardize one's career prospects.

> The race for the junior chair for administrative courts was between Ketut Suraputra and Boestomi, but now Boestomi definitely is out of the race because he started this discussion during a *pleno* meeting with Supreme Court chairman Purwoto.[193]

This hierarchy and deference even affect the Court leadership meetings (RAPIM), in which decisions are generally not taken by consensus, but by the Supreme Court chairman, to whom others defer. This had already become apparent before Purwoto Gandasubrata's term as chair, as one junior chairman recalled:

> When Mudjono's illness became acute, much administrative work was transferred to vice-chairman Purwoto. Purwoto effected some transfers of judges. Mudjono didn't like that and instructed Purwoto to undo the transfer, and move other judges. Purwoto just sat there quietly, without saying anything. This so infuriated Mudjono, that he picked up the phone and shouted that if Purwoto would not do as he required, he would call the president etc. Then Purwoto did as he was asked to do.[194]

The hierarchical *modus operandi* within the RAPIM continues to the present day:

---

aim was to deal with practical problems arising from the implementation of the new Code of Criminal Procedure. See for instance Mahkamah Agung Circular Letter no.MA/Pemb/1519/84 dated 17 March 1984.

[192] Personal communication, 19 July 1994.

[193] Personal communication, 24 April 1995.

[194] Personal communication, 16 July 1994. I said in reaction to the story that to me this rather created the impression of Purwoto as a courageous, diplomatic operator.

The mode of operation within the RAPIM remains very hierarchical. Even the vice-chairman has limited autonomy and essentially defers to the Supreme Court chairman. In a recent incident, I objected to a proposed nomination of a judge as vice-chairman of a district court, because I knew for a fact that he just didn't know the law. He made silly mistakes on elementary matters and so on, so I mentioned this to the chairman. "Don't worry," he replied, "we'll just appoint a strong chairman to keep him in line." "But he's old also," I objected. "Well, we'll be rid of him soon then, won't we?!" said the chairman. I mean, the entire thrust of the conversation was: shut up, I am the one who decides. The same thing occurred just a couple of weeks ago also, when a list of candidates for the Supreme Court was drawn up at the RAPIM. One of the names listed was judge S., who is popular in some circles because he has a good sense of humor and in fact sings well also, so he sort of performs during judicial outings. The point is that he is a total legal nitwit. So I said this during the RAPIM, at which point the chairman reacted by saying that this man would sit in a chamber of judges, so wouldn't do much harm anyway. It infuriated me, and I said that we should gather the legal elite here, that this is what society expects from us, and so on. But the chairman didn't say a word, and sort of stared at me.[195]

The hierarchical mode of operation makes the Supreme Court dependent on its chairman, so that changes in leadership immediately influence the institution as a whole. In the opinion of the person quoted above, this helps explain why the Supreme Court can alter so drastically when a new chairman arrives, even though all other aspects of the institution remain fairly constant.[196]

(ii) The Failure of the RAPIM to Implement Central Guidance in Supreme Court Decision Making

The major problem for the judicial corps is coordination concerning interpretation and implementation of the law, or central guidance. The diverse structure of teams and chambers makes it necessary to introduce some mechanism to coordinate the judiciary at this level, to prevent judges from following their own paths when applying the law. The original purpose of the chairmen's meeting, the RAPIM, was in fact to provide that guidance. In the words of one author:

---

[195] Personal communication, 16 July 1994.

[196] Personal communication, 16 July 1994. In my personal experience at the Court, I was often confronted with the signs of this powerful hierarchy, yet one experience in particular impressed me. This was in 1992, just before Purwoto's nomination as Supreme Court chairman. I walked the corridors of the Supreme Court building talking to a Supreme Court junior chairman and noticed how, along the way, other Supreme Court judges would push themselves against the walls and bow to him; one even saluted, with what appeared to me excessive zeal. In fact, the junior chairman walked with truly regal bearing, very upright, gently nodding left and right. Yet when he came to the offices of the vice-chairman Purwoto, he said "Just a moment," and completely changed. Popping into the office, he looked around the corner with a deep bow, saying: "Sir, I am going out to the regions now, but I wish you to become chairman, and I assure you that I will come flying back immediately should you be appointed." The complete transformation of his attitude when he stepped inside the vice-chairman's office was startling.

The eight teams pose a risk that Court decisions will vary between different teams. To overcome this problem there is a regular [RAPIM] meeting, during which legal problems arising out of cases before the Court are addressed in a general manner so as to achieve a consensus on the matter.[197]

A former Supreme Court judge put it as follows:

The function of the various chairmen is to control the chambers and ensure unified interpretation of the law by the Court.[198]

Indeed, the original idea behind the appointment of junior chairmen was that they would coordinate Supreme Court decisions for the various jurisdictions. They were not meant to get involved with other Supreme Court functions, which is why the original plan proposed their appointments extend for a limited period of time, after which they would be replaced with other judges.

In reality, things worked out altogether differently. The junior chairmen were recruited from among the most senior judges and proved hard to replace. No junior chairmen ever returned to the fold of common Supreme Court judges. Instead, together with the chair and vice-chair, they constituted a stable leadership, an influential group whose members surrendered their posts only on retirement. In the process, they merged with the Supreme Court chairman and vice-chairman, becoming involved in a much wider range of issues that faced the Court. As a result, RAPIM, the chairman's meetings, developed a management routine that was not really oriented toward addressing legal issues, let alone ensuring legal unity within the Court. "Legal issues are barely discussed at all," one Supreme Court junior chairman remarked.[199] A former associate judge closely involved in preparing the meetings commented as follows: "The RAPIM really concentrates on matters of personnel only, nothing else really."[200] This absence of central guidance concerning the law extends downwards in the organization, as the chairmen of most chambers also tend to shirk this responsibility—though there are some exceptions.[201]

The problem is, in part, that with a system fully geared toward realizing a high turnover of cases, the substance of those cases and the legal uniformity of the judicial responses to them clearly figure as secondary concerns on the RAPIM's agenda. This situation is compounded by a number of other factors, such as the

---

[197] Soedirjo, *Kasasi dalam perkara perdata*, p. 70. Soedirjo says that these are weekly *pleno* meetings, but this assuredly is a printing error and what he probably meant was weekly RAPIM meetings.

[198] Personal communication, 18 July 1994.

[199] Personal communication, 16 July 1994.

[200] Personal communication, 18 July 1994.

[201] According to sources, the forceful junior chairman for civil cases, Asikin Kusumah Atmaja, imposed considerable discipline on the cases handled by his chamber until he was disabled by a stroke in his final years in office. Others, such as Olden Bidara, junior chairman for administrative cases, is said to have had a more hands-off approach. Even so, for many years during the 1990s the Supreme Court judges who specialized in administrative law were the only group to have regular meetings in so-called POKJA (kelompok kerja—working committees), during which they discuss legal issues and provide some guidance concerning legal procedures. Personal Communication, 31 August 1994.

judges' subtle resistance to submitting to what they perceive as outside dictates—even if these originate from the Supreme Court's leadership.

> What, I sometimes wonder, is the authority of the RAPIM? . . . What I really mean is, can the RAPIM determine on the application of the law in a way that actually is binding upon Supreme Court judges? I think this cannot be done legally, but there has been little thought on the matter.[202]

Because the leadership provides so little guidance, Supreme Court teams and chambers operate in almost total autonomy.

> The chambers are actually autonomous, the reason being that there is no guidance imposed by the chairmen. Decisions go in all directions, and for each case you can find a similar one going exactly the other way. You also get totally unexpected, sometimes absurd decisions, such as the one saying the death penalty is unconstitutional, or the one where the existence of cassation is denied, or *Kedung Ombo*. Judges do not know what is decided in other chambers. Even in the highly politicized *Kedung Ombo case* Supreme Court chairman Purwoto didn't know what the case actually said after it came out, and stated publicly that he first had to study it. Isn't it extraordinary that the chairman of the Supreme Court doesn't know what his own Court decides in such important cases?![203]

These inconsistent decisions, the consequence of poor coordination and supervision, strike at the root of the Supreme Court's judicial function. The Court speaks not with a single voice but with seventeen voices. Chairman Ali Said acknowledged this when commenting on the apparent lack of coordination within the Supreme Court:

> This is a problem which in fact might very well wreck the working mechanism of the Supreme Court. It sometimes looks as though there are various tribes on the Court. Like the Ali Said tribe and Purwoto tribe. If I do not give a disposition, parties just turn to the vice-chairman.[204]

The unwillingness or inability of the RAPIM members to ensure central guidance and coordination on the law has important consequences, because the Supreme Court judges disagree on a fair number of elementary legal issues. Deep-seated disagreements on the law within the Supreme Court result partly from the legislature's failures—the laws themselves are not always clear or practical—but it is also true that the Indonesian judiciary has never been able to decide what modern Indonesian law should look like. On some issues, differences of opinion acquire ideological content, which makes central guidance all the more difficult. All in all, the absence of consensus within the Court on a broad variety of legal issues promotes a lack of uniformity in the way the law is applied.

---

[202] Personal communication, 5 August 1994.

[203] Personal communication, 16 July 1994.

[204] *Forum Keadilan,* 17 September 1992, p. 25. Ali Said was commenting on the complicated issue of executing Court decisions pending appeals (*uitvoerbaar bij voorraad, putusan serta merta*).

(iii) Absence of Uniform Supreme Court Decision Making

The absence of uniformity manifests itself generally in three principal ways. First, fundamental differences of opinion on legal interpretation are often not settled behind closed doors, but are expressed in conflicting Court decisions, a practice that creates legal uncertainty. Second, clearly erroneous or absurd decisions are sometimes allowed to pass, which of course undermines the Court's status and authority. Third, in the absence of internal legal guidance and with inadequate case management, the Court sometimes makes serious errors in case management.

Manifest Conflicts between Decisions. The absence of central guidance tends to allow each chamber, and sometimes each judge, to develop and voice its own legal views on an issue, or perhaps to act arbitrarily. After the Supreme Court's expansion under Mudjono, it began to manifest clear differences of opinion regarding what the law entails. These differences struck at the heart of the judicial apparatus in two ways. They were reflected in Court decisions, which created contradictory legal precedents, a serious matter, since a number of these inconsistencies did not merely concern peripheral issues, but elementary questions of law. "You know, we really disagree here on many important legal issues, from the age of majority, to purchase of land and inheritance," said one Supreme Court judge.[205] He proceeded to give an example of the extent to which chambers differed on basic legal issues, and described how this played out in Court proceedings.

> I fundamentally disagree with [Supreme Court judge X] on whether and when Book I of the Civil Code still applies. As a result, we have completely opposed views on such issues as the law governing Chinese estates, particularly when a Chinese person has converted to Islam. We have quite a few of these cases before the Court, sometimes involving millions of dollars. My view is that, if such a person is married under the Civil Code, his marital property is governed by that code under any circumstances, because that is what the code says. Since the code only acknowledges monogamy, well that's just too bad for any subsequent wives. Judge X argues that if that person converts to Islam, he is assimilated to the Indonesian community, which is not subjected to Book I Civil Code. In this case, Islamic rules should determine the division of marital property, and subsequent wives will in fact inherit. Should a case come up and be decided by the Judge X chamber along the lines he's indicated, I'll most certainly strike him down when the case comes up for review. Of course, should I first get the case, he'll do the same to my decision in review.[206]

While this example illustrates the profundity of legal disagreements within the Court and the way these can affect procedure, another interview underscores the fact that such disagreements sometimes cover really elementary legal issues, such as the sale of land.

---

[205] Personal communication, 22 August 1994.
[206] Ibid.

There are a lot of problems with the sale of land. Let me give you an example. The Land Law imposes a uniform regime according to which only a specially designated land official [the PPAT, Pejabat Pembuat Akta Tanah, official in charge of land acts] can effect a transfer of land ownership. This caused problems in outlying areas, where such officials may be located far away. Well, Supreme Court junior chairman Y decided that in such areas, land ownership transactions could also be effected by going through the proper steps without an official land official present. I'd go along with him there. But then, in a later case, Judge Y said that an area just to the south of Jakarta also qualified as an outlying area. And to my amazement, there was finally a case in central Jakarta where Judge Y accepted a chit, a mere receipt, as valid evidence of transfer of ownership, applying his former logic. That cannot be right.[207]

In responses to questions concerning the age of majority, members of the Supreme Court have expressed significant disagreements, and those disagreements subsequently confused the lower courts.

- In 1976 the Supreme Court stated that, pursuant to the 1974 Marriage Law, the age of majority stood at eighteen years of age (no.477K/Sip/1976 dated 13 October 1973). Still, it was not clear from the decision whether this ruling only concerned a citizen's marriage capacity, or whether it was meant to stand as a general rule of majority for all transactions by law. This uncertainty was exacerbated by the fact that, barely a year before, the Supreme Court had issued a Circular Letter stating that the age of majority still stood at twenty-one years (Circular Letter no.Pemb./0807/1975 dated 20 August 1975). Nevertheless, in 1989 the then vice-chairman Purwoto argued in a publication that the Marriage Law took precedence, and that a citizen attained majority at age eighteen (Media Notariat no.10 (1989), p.93). Lower courts could not make heads or tails of this mess, and now decisions go both ways. Thus, the North Jakarta district court determined the age of majority to be eighteen (North Jakarta District Court no.1530/Pdt/1987/PN.Jkt.Ut. dated 5 November 1987), while within the same month the Central Jakarta court put it at twenty-one (Central Jakarta District Court no.1138/Pdt.P/1987/Pn.Jkt.Pst. dated 22 December 1987). When the issue arose in a foreign court, the advice of six instances was sought, and those decisions were evenly split between the two ages (Verwaltungsgerichtshof Baden-Württemberg Case 13 S 1479/89). The matter is totally unsettled, and the Supreme Court has provided no guidance to resolve the matter.

* *Absurd Decisions*. In the absence of central guidance, even within chambers, judges have considerable leeway in deciding cases. This explains perhaps why the Supreme Court sometimes takes decisions that lie somewhere on a scale ranging from the wholly and totally unexpected to the manifestly absurd, by way of the

---
[207] Ibid.

evidently incorrect. A number of examples will serve to illustrate the range of these decisions.

Indonesia's Supreme Court excels in wholly and totally unexpected performances. Its decisions concerning arbitration are a case in point, as has been mentioned previously. Briefly summarized, the Supreme Court upheld enforcement of foreign arbitral awards, until the *Maritime Bulgare case* (1984) when it denied it, only to reinstate it with a Regulation in 1990. This did not mean that after 1990 things were back to normal with respect to the enforcement of foreign arbitral awards, for when the issue emerged again in a different context, the Supreme Court again played a totally unexpected role. This happened in the infamous *Sugar Lee case* (1991).

- The case arose out of a dispute between the English seller and Indonesian buyer of a sizeable quantity of sugar to the value of US$146 million. In the case of a dispute, the contract provided for mandatory arbitration to be conducted in London. A dispute arose, when the Indonesian buyer unilaterally broke the contract in response to falling sugar prices. The dispute was brought before the arbitrator, who awarded the case to the seller, a decision later affirmed by the English High Court and court of appeal. A settlement for damages was reached for the total amount of US$ 27 million, to be paid in three installments, the first of which was actually paid. Then, suddenly, the Indonesian party brought an action in an Indonesian court arguing that the contract was void *ab initio*. The argument was that under Indonesian law, the Logistical Supply Organization (BULOG, Badan Urusan Logistik) holds a monopoly over sugar purchases. This case eventually came up for appeal before the Supreme Court, even as the request for enforcement of the arbitral award was also being considered by the same Court. As a result, the Supreme Court suddenly found itself handling the same case twice: first as an application for an executory order of a foreign arbitration award, and second as a full-blown cassation case. The Court came up with a really curious response. First, a chamber headed by chairman Ali Said in March 1991 allowed enforcement of the arbitration award (finding for the English seller). Subsequently, in the other case, a chamber headed by junior chairman Busthanul Arifin in December 1991 voided the contract (finding for the Indonesian buyer). As a result, as the Supreme Court explicitly stated, since the underlying contract was void, the arbitration award lacked ground in law and could not be effected. It was, at best, a totally and wholly unexpected situation. "What do you want," commented the press, "our law can be shaken up really easily."[208]

From the totally unexpected to the manifestly erroneous and absurd is only a short step. Cases range across the board. Thus, in criminal law, contrary to precedent, the Supreme Court held that rape could not occur if the victim was sleeping, because the Criminal Code provided that rape had to be realized "with violence." In the same case, the Court allowed a full defense on the basis of

---

[208] *Forum Keadilan*, 6 August 1992, pp. 59-61; *Tempo*, 28 September 1991; *Tempo*, 21 March 1992, p. 28.

traditional *adat*, meaning that no action can be brought if a crime, even such a hideous one as rape or murder, has already been punished according to the *adat*. This, in my respectful opinion, is definitely erroneous.[209] The Supreme Court also declared itself no longer a court of cassation but rather a full appeals court. This may be a correct description of reality, but is in flagrant opposition with relevant legislation.[210] In a case involving the printing of false money, the Public Prosecution appealed to the Supreme Court to ask a question concerning the validity of evidence that supposedly had been improperly acquired. The Supreme Court did not decide the case until after the defendant had already served his prison sentence, but when it did take up the matter, it tried the case anew and imposed a harsher prison sentence. When everyone balked (including the prosecution), the Supreme Court reversed itself, acknowledging its mistake and apologizing all around.[211] Wholly absurd is the case in which the Court seemed to accept a defense that the death penalty violated the Pancasila doctrine[212] (absurdity may have its positive aspect also). The *First Kedung Ombo case* in which the plaintiffs were awarded seven times as much as they had claimed was equally extreme.[213]

These cases certainly reveal the Supreme Court's extraordinary leeway in decision making. Again, inconsistent, confusing legislation may be partly to blame, but I would submit that the principal cause is the organizational fragmentation of the Supreme Court and the absence of clear guidance from its leadership.

---

[209] Mahkamah Agung no.1644.K/Pid/1988 dated 15 May 1991. The relevant article is art.285 Criminal Code. In colonial times, it was established several times that the wording "with violence" includes acts committed against the will of the victim, which is deemed to be absent in such cases unless clearly indicated (*Landraad* Sambas 14 April 1913). Further, the action could have been brought under art.286, which fully covers the issue, since the meaning of "unconsciousness" used therein also applies to the state of normal sleep (*Hoog Militair Gerechtshof* 18 January 1935). See also S. Pompe, "Between Crime and Custom: Extra-Marital Sex in Modern Indonesian Law," *Bijdragen tot de Taal-, Land- en Volkenkunde* 150,1 (1994): 110.

[210] Personal communications, 18 July 1994, 21 September 1994.

[211] *Tempo*, 20 October 1990, p. 28.

[212] Mahkamah Agung no.14 K/Mil/1987 dated 20 November 1987. The first ground of cassation in this case was as follows: "... that the death penalty in our country which follows the Pancasila doctrine is felt to be misplaced, because only the Almighty has the right to bring someone to life or to kill him ... " It was followed by some references to extenuating circumstances. The verdict reads: "... that this ground must be accepted ... " The meaning of the Court was probably to refer to the extenuating circumstances, but this was not clear from the verdict's wording, which, on the contrary, rather seemed to indicate that the death penalty conflicts with the Pancasila state doctrine. At any rate, this was the way some Indonesian observers read the case, and why photocopies of it were distributed.

[213] As discussed in Chapter Four, in the *First Kedung Ombo case*, plaintiffs claimed Rp.10,000 per square meter damages but were awarded 70,000 by the Supreme Court. The fact that the plaintiffs won at all, compounded by the enormity of the award, explained why the government chose to apply for a review. This led to the *Second Kedung Ombo case*, in which damages were disallowed on the basis that there is no law enabling the Court to award more damages than claimed by parties. Adding inconsistency to absurdity (as noted above), barely one year after the *Second Kedung Ombo case*, a powerful Supreme Court panel chaired by the new Supreme Court chairman Soerjono effectively rejected that precedent when he explicitly upheld the view that more could be awarded than claimed. The *Small Credits case* (1996) Mahkamah Agung no.3714.K/Pdt/1992 dated 22 February 1994, *Varia Peradilan* 11 (March 1996): 126.

Serious Errors in Decisions. Because of the absence of central guidance and the consequent autonomy of the various chambers, the Supreme Court has made serious errors in handling cases that have resulted in extraordinary inconsistencies. This situation is best exemplified perhaps by the fact that on occasion the Supreme Court has decided the same case, or very closely related cases, twice in separate chambers, and come up with quite different results.

A recent example is the *Yatim case* (1995).

- The *Yatim case* arose in Spring 1995, when the Supreme Court handled appeals lodged by thirty-three families resisting collective eviction from a plot of land. The appeals were split, so that each case was dealt with individually. The underlying factual and legal situation was identical for all the plaintiffs because all the families had bought their plots of land out of a larger estate owned by a third party.[214] The cases were allocated to different chambers, with the astonishing result that some stays of action were awarded, while others were not.[215]

Yet the lack of coordination between teams and chambers is perhaps most clearly illustrated by the dramatic *Saputra case* (1985).

- Here, both the plaintiff and defendant applied for a special review of the same case.[216] The Supreme Court Registry did not identify their respective appeals as applying to the same case; instead they were handled as if they were completely different cases. Assigned to different chambers, the judges decided the appeals unaware of each other's involvement in this issue, and their decisions were diametrically opposed. The problem was discovered when both parties sought to realize "their" Court decision at about the same time. Note that these were review procedures, which are final, and no further procedural venues were open. As it happened, the Supreme Court chairman at the time, Ali Said, instituted a special appeal

---

[214] This original ownership was at issue in the case. The purported original owner for twenty-three years, one Aw Kim Liong, had carved up the estate into little holdings, which he then sold off. Then a certain Yatim contested Aw's original ownership. In 1988, the Supreme Court in fact awarded original ownership to Yatim, who then sought to realize his hold on the land by asserting that, since he was the original owner, the sale of the smaller holdings by Aw was legally void, and the occupants could be evicted. The occupants claimed that they had legal title to the land and resisted eviction. *Forum Keadilan* 3,22 (1995), p. 88.

[215] Ibid. As it turned out, thirty-one stays of action were awarded and two were not. It is not quite clear whether this difference was caused by differences in legal opinions between chambers, or by a typing error. Depending on what happened, the case serves either as an example of lack of central guidance for the judges or lack of central control over the Court administration.

[216] *Saputra vs. Soedjadi and others*, decided in cassation (no.625K/Sip/1977); the review decision of Soedjadi is no.114 PK/Pdt/1981 dated 7 February 1985, while the review procedure of Saputra is no.321 PK/Pdt/1984 dated 21 February 1985. The final decision of the chairman of the Supreme Court, Ali Said, closing the case (and awarding it to Soedjadi) is decision 1/KMA-RI/V/1987 dated 9 May 1987. This was a case given to me by members of the Commission III on law of the Indonesian Parliament. They assured me that there had been a number of such cases.

and settled the case which, by that time, had been decided four times already by the Supreme Court.[217]

The *Yatim* or *Saputra* cases may be viewed as aberrations, but they are by no means exceptional in the Supreme Court administration, as noted by the outspoken member of Parliament, V. B. da Costa.[218] Indeed, not long after the *Saputra case*, which the Supreme Court managed to keep quiet, a couple of identical errors in case handling were made public. In 1995 the press reported an incident in which the Court decided the same case twice in special review.[219] Incidents such as these, and their frequency, led Parliament by the mid-1990s to call for a system by which Supreme Court judges might be dismissed for dereliction of duty.[220]

In short, the Supreme Court is unpredictable, and occasionally its decisions border on absurdity. It offers no clear guidance on the application of the law, and lower courts have little to go by. This problem has an important side effect: opportunities for judicial malfeasance increase. It is difficult always to draw a clear division between an honest difference of opinion among the judges, an erroneous application of the law, and a purposeful perversion of that law's intent. This is particularly so given the fragmented condition of the Supreme Court, where one finds disagreement concerning elementary legal issues, frequent legal errors, and chambers working largely unaware of each other's decisions. This lack of clarity is made worse, of course, by the heavy workload, which ties judges to their case files and makes it difficult for them to learn what goes on elsewhere. This situation contributed to the rise of improprieties among Supreme Court judges.

(iv) Problems in Supervision

Work pressure has created conditions that make it very hard for the Supreme Court fully to realize its supervisory function, which is effectively left to the supervising Supreme Court judges, the HAWASDA. These judges are not really able to digest the massive amounts of information generated by the intensive reporting system imposed on the lower courts. The Supreme Court's desire to control an increasing number of courts and judges in ever greater detail has been self-defeating, as the Court is simply unable to manage that much information. Its supervision, as a result, has become essentially reactive: it reacts to problems, and does not monitor the system so as to adjust course before problems materialize. To make matters worse, while the judiciary's system of reporting is intensive, it is not necessarily adequate, and there is a strong urge to cover up problems, or to distort reporting in other ways.

---

[217] The chairman of the Court, Ali Said, decided the case with a "decision" (*penetapan*). A "decision" is unknown in Indonesian procedural law before the Supreme Court. But the legislature can hardly be blamed for failing to provide for a procedure to be used in those cases when the highest court errs both in cassation and review. In this situation, the Supreme Court effectively gave four final decisions: once in cassation, twice in review, and once by "*penetapan.*"

[218] *Kompas*, 7 February 1995.

[219] *Media Indonesia*, 6 July 1995; *Media Indonesia*, 7 July 1995.

[220] *Kompas*, 7 February 1995.

Unable to spend sufficient time and effort on these matters, the Supreme Court has been forced to be highly selective, and ultimately reactive, in its supervision. As one Supreme Court judge put it:

> The Supreme Court judges supervising the appeals courts don't go down to the regions very often, once a year at the most, I'd say. They correspond of course, and do something when there is a problem.[221]

Supervision of the lower courts by the Supreme Court tends to be sketchy not only because there is too much information to handle, but also because of a natural tendency, both on the part of district courts and of appeals courts, to pretend everything is fine rather than to expose problems. Reporting is slanted, and the Supreme Court often is only notified of problems after the lid blows off, frequently in public. One Supreme Court judge outlined the situation as follows:

> The supervising system has become reactive: it only moves when a problem occurs. Supervision has effectively collapsed. The appeals courts fail in their supervision over the district courts, and really are little more than post boxes. [...] To be certain, the Supreme Court's workload quite simply does not allow active supervision. Moreover, problems rarely come to the notice of the Supreme Court through judicial channels. There is a very strong tendency on the part of district court chairmen to cover up and say that everything is fine. So it is really via the press or private legal professions that problems come to the notice of the Supreme Court, but then it usually is too late. [laughs] Of course, if the Supreme Court doesn't like a judge, they will get at him no matter what, so it serves to curry Court favors.[222]

Indeed, in the absence of adequate supervision (and neutral standards governing advancement in the judicial hierarchy), the positions of the HAWASDA judges have become both important and exposed. The widespread practice of currying favors further weakens the supervisory system. One junior Supreme Court chairman recounted his experiences while on a supervisory tour in his region:

> Ever so often, the supervising Supreme Court judge will descend into his region of supervision and call a working meeting with the appeals court there. These are important contacts, but they are messy. When I last came down, straight away upon arrival, before I had said a word, I was given an envelope filled with money. The idea behind it was as simple as it was effective: accepting such gifts creates a social obligation, which will make the supervising Supreme Court judge embarrassed to take tough supervisory measures.[223]

Indeed, the pressure on supervising Supreme Court judges to accept gifts from lower court judges has become so strong that some judges have taken draconian measures to stop the flow of large and small gifts.

---

[221] Personal communication, 3 August 1994.

[222] Personal communication, 5 August 1994.

[223] Personal communication, 16 July 1994.

I know for a fact that former Supreme Court judge Sri Widoyati refused even a gift of apples from a lower judge for fear that this might prejudice her supervisory position. I actually find that very hard, and personally am not as strict, just as a matter of collegiality. But I also know that Supreme Court judge M. tries her utmost not to get into such potentially compromising situations in the first place. She rushes home after work, and when someone rings at the door, she asks the servant to check who it is first. If it is a judge, the servant is to check also whether he has any presents with him. If he has, judge M. has instructed the servant to tell the visiting judge that judge M. isn't at home.[224]

Because the pressures on supervising Supreme Court judges are tremendous and hard to resist, supervision is in a poor state generally.

(b) The Bureaucracy

The major problem besetting the Court bureaucracy is that it cannot be controlled. This chief characteristic of this problem is often referred to in Indonesia with the generic term "leaks" (*pembocoran, bocor*). Never precisely defined, this term calls to mind the image of a pipeline system, with valves and joints dripping, and the product at the end not quite the same as what was put in at the beginning. It is an adequate image, but in some ways fails fully to capture the complexity of the "leaks" in the Court administration. This complexity exists particularly in the fact that the condition involves two-way traffic: the bureaucracy is not just leaking out, but also leaking in. It is not relevant who initiates the contacts. In this sense, "leaks" broadly refer to any unauthorized contact between the Supreme Court administration and the outside world if that contact influences the outcome of a case pending before the Court. For this reason, and others that we will consider in the next chapter, the leaks are also referred to as "collusion" (*kolusi*).[225] As the 1992 Internal Audit pointed out,[226] the Supreme Court bureaucracy constitutes the prime source of such "leaks" or "collusion"—though there are indications that the bureaucracy serves, to some extent, as a front for some of the Supreme Court judges.

Leaks exist throughout the entire administrative process, from the registration of a case, through the phase when the administration must back-up the judges in decision making, until the final implementation of a decision at the lowest levels of the judicial organization and in the field.

---

[224] Personal communication, 3 August 1994.

[225] A very frequently used term in both official and unofficial documents, "collusion" was defined by one prominent Supreme Court judge, after referring to an English dictionary, as "a secret agreement or understanding for a deceitful or fraudulent purpose," to which may be added that the understanding or agreement must be between a Court outsider and insider. A. Andoyo Soetjipto, "Uraian kronologis terjadinya masalah 'kolusi' di Mahkamah Agung RI," p. 8.

[226] Mahkamah Agung RI & LPPIS FISIP UI, "Masalah dan faktor yang mempengaruhi pelaksanaan tugas administrasi dalam proses penyelesaian perkara di Mahkamah Agung Republik Indonesia," p. 19.

(i) Registration Problems

At the commencement of a proceeding before the Supreme Court, all litigants must cross one important hurdle: registration. Unfortunately, the intake of cases is so vast and the administration so bulky that there is no effective control over the actual handling of incoming cases. This creates space even within the registration phase that allows all sorts of shadowy dealings to be carried out on the side. Bureaucrats can pressure litigants in two ways, either by delaying registration or by assigning the case to a particular chamber, for that assignment can be influential in determining the outcome of a case.

The fact that registration does not follow automatically upon appeal, but constitutes a bureaucratic hurdle in its own right, creates problems. In the clear but cautious wording of the 1992 Internal Audit: "There are instances in which the processing of a case is intentionally delayed," with the evident aim of soliciting money from the parties.[227] The whole process of deciding whether or not to grant priority to certain cases thus develops its own bureaucratic momentum. In fact, some cases have remained stuck in the Supreme Court administration for lengthy periods —with the most dismal record to my knowledge standing at thirty-four years. Although some of these delays may be the result of the large turnover, it is also true that the administration repeatedly shuffles some cases to the bottom of the pile so that judges never get around to deciding them.

(ii) Problems in the Assignment of Cases

The fact that Supreme Court judges have been known to interpret the same laws differently may make it important which chamber decides any one case. Litigants and advocates try to get a case heard by a chamber that they know most favors their viewpoint, and a number of administrators have learned how to manipulate this system. One Supreme Court junior chairman told me the following story to illustrate the point:

> Chairman Ali Said was once approached by an important party who had a case before the Court and who asked Ali Said how the case could be best managed through the Court administration. Ali Said answered: "Chamber [X] really sticks closely to the law and you will not have a chance there, but chamber [Y] is more flexible . . . So which one do you want?"

The implication of this story is not just that outcomes differ depending on chamber, but, more notably in this context, that the assignment of cases can be steered, and, by extension, the outcome determined. In part, this is the natural consequence of the fragmented nature of the judicial corps, but at the same time it is intricately linked to a problem that seriously threatens judicial professionalism, and that is corruption, as will become apparent in the next chapter. The *Gandhi Memorial School case*, referred to earlier, illustrates the importance attached to steering assignments within the Supreme Court.

---

[227] Mahkamah Agung RI & LPPIS FISIP UI, "Masalah dan faktor yang mempengaruhi pelaksanaan tugas administrasi dalam proses penyelesaian perkara di Mahkamah Agung Republik Indonesia," p. 20.

- This case arose out of a dispute in which the Indian Association in Indonesia, proprietors of the Gandhi Memorial School, accused the schoolmaster, Mr. Ram, of fraud. Both the district and appeal courts found the schoolmaster guilty, but he was freed by the Supreme Court. The key to the decision was Mr. Ram's advocate DB, who also happened to be a former Supreme Court judge and obviously retained strong ties with his former colleagues. Supreme Court judge A. was reported to be his good friend and was soon due to retire. The advocate was also a long-standing colleague of the Supreme Court director for criminal cases who handled the *Gandhi Memorial School case*. He appears to have made good use of this network: he contacted the Court director and steered the case toward his friend, judge A. Hidden in the great mass of cases, the doctored registration order passed unnoticed until after news of the case broke. This occurred because the Indian Association had kept close watch on the advocate, fearing that he might use his Supreme Court contacts to steer the case; as it happened, even while serving on the Court he had established a reputation for manipulating the assignment of cases. When its sources confirmed that this had actually happened, the association reported the fact to the Supreme Court leadership. A few days later, Supreme Court junior chairman Adi Andoyo Soetjipto, wrote a secret letter to the prosecution in the case, urging it to apply for a reopening of the case on grounds of "collusion" between parties and certain Supreme Court judges. The letter became public.[228]

The assignment of cases is clearly not just an administrative affair, but can be an important factor influencing the final decision. The *Gandhi Memorial School case* also revealed that, aside from the Supreme Court chairmen and apparently some deft judges, the directors too play their part in this game. It is not surprising that there have been reports in the press about directors involved in institutional "leakages."[229]

(iii) Problems within Chambers

Even after cases are assigned to chambers, problems arise due to the fact that most judges have little control over their office staff. As pointed out by the 1992 Internal Audit, the law clerks play a crucial role in this situation.[230] In fact, for a long time the Supreme Court clerks were, and to some extent still are, a discontented crew, for as their informal designation—"judges without mallets" (*hakim non-palu*)—implies, they are relatively powerless, not unlike swordless knights or toothless tigers. They lack the decision-making power they enjoyed when they

---

[228] *Forum Keadilan*, 22 April 1996; *Gatra*, 20 April 1996; *Forum Keadilan*, 6 May 1996. See also the official account by Soetjipto, "Uraian kronologis terjadinya masalah 'kolusi' di Mahkamah Agung RI."

[229] There have in fact been rumors in the press, fiercely denied by the persons involved, of Supreme Court directors being corrupted. What matters is not whether such rumors are true or false, but that it makes sense to try and influence Supreme Court directors in their allocation of cases.

[230] Mahkamah Agung RI & LPPIS FISIP UI, "Masalah dan faktor yang mempengaruhi pelaksanaan tugas administrasi dalam proses penyelesaian perkara di Mahkamah Agung Republik Indonesia," p. 14 and ff.

were still judges in the regions. In general terms, the Supreme Court evidently wants to employ as good a clerk as the judiciary can offer, and it takes the view that appointment as a Supreme Court clerk should be perceived as career advancement for a judge.[231] Yet such "advancement" can prove costly. Aside from lacking judicial power, until recently, Supreme Court clerks were blocked from enjoying functional benefits of judges in the regions. As a result, their income dropped by 20 percent compared to their income as judges.[232] In addition, their workload on the Supreme Court is much heavier than in most district courts.[233] And there is yet another fact tarnishing such appointments: on several occasions evidently compromised judges have been "promoted" to these positions.[234] This created the impression that one method for punishing malfeasance in the lower courts was to take away the judicial gavel, i.e., make these judges *"non-palu"* by appointing them to Supreme Court clerkships. Chairman Purwoto Gandasubrata took some steps to redress this problem, notably by raising clerks' salaries to the level of appellate judges in 1993.[235] Nevertheless, the workload remained a serious problem, as did morale.

If, therefore, clerks are poorly rewarded, suffer a drop in status and power, and must also work hard, they are powerful in the sense that they can have considerable control over a chamber's case-flow, and, indeed, depending on the judge, also on a case's outcome. This combination of power and poverty makes them singularly vulnerable to "leakages." These leaks can occur at several points in the procedure. The first such point is when the case is assigned in chambers. In important cases, the parties concerned will know within hours who has been assigned the case, and contacts are established at that point. One Supreme Court judge said:

> If a sensitive case is assigned to me, I'll decide it immediately, and send on the file afterwards. You can be absolutely certain that the parties will know within a couple of hours which chamber and which judge will handle their case and will try to bring pressure to bear. If I get the case away from me as quickly as possible, I can just tell them that it's been decided and is out of my hands.[236]

This judge is convinced that the source of leaks is the law clerks:

> Within a day after Supreme Court judges have held their secret conference on a case, letters start coming in from parties involved asking why we put them in

---

[231] Ibid., p. 27.

[232] Ibid.

[233] Ibid., p. 28.

[234] Thus, in one notorious case in 1993, judge Sarwono of Surabaya was accused of significant malfeasance. His guilt was never established in a court of law. No procedures or official investigations were initiated against him, and instead the Supreme Court pulled him off the Surabaya court and made him a Supreme Court clerk. The failure of the Court to resolve the case publicly meant that Sarwono's name was never fully cleared. His appointment as a Supreme Court clerk, moreover, did little to bolster the prestige of Court clerks, nor by extension, of the Supreme Court as a whole. There are many comparable examples.

[235] Personal communication, 15 July 1995.

[236] Personal communication, n.d.

> the wrong and so on. Mark you, these meetings are secret, with access restricted to three Court judges and one or two clerks, barely anything will have been noted down on paper yet, but already they are informed, and there's lobbying going on. It must be the clerks.[237]

One Supreme Court law clerk readily acknowledged being a focus of the Court's problems:

> The law clerks play a central role in the "playing with cases" [*permainan perkara*]. I know of several advocates who have running deals, called "subscriptions," with Supreme Court law clerks. These clerks send draft decisions to the advocate, expecting a commentary from him, and indicating that if the decision is altered to favor his client, they might go along with it. This benefits all parties: the clerk because he will have less work to do and make some money on the side, the advocate because his client has a better chance of winning, while the Supreme Court judge will not know.[238]

These arrangements are called "subscriptions" because they occur with such regularity that payment by the advocate to the law clerk no longer occurs on a per item basis, but in regular monthly installments.

The selection of law clerks, as a result, is highly important for Supreme Court judges.

> I could take over the offices and staff of judge [X], whom I replaced. But I refused. You see, we all know that this law clerk is corrupt, and one cannot really control him. So I selected my own clerk. He is a very decent man, of humble origins, and of the old school, proud to be a judge. I can trust him.[239]

Note: just as a Supreme Court judge must take care in the selection of a clerk, he must also be careful about the location of his office. There is a so-called "highway" in the Supreme Court building, consisting of the central corridor at the front on the second floor. Here all the middlemen float about, trying to get access to judges' chambers, and it is hard to keep them out.

> I didn't want offices on the highway. You just can't keep everyone out. So I took one located somewhat apart. Also there is a guard post, and they stop anyone who doesn't have business around here. Still, one day two visitors slipped through. The guards were having their lunch break or something. I had a hell of a time to get them out of my chambers. It took me an hour. They tried to make me grant a case higher priority for them, but I refused. I said, I don't even want to hear what case it is.[240]

---

[237] Personal communication, 23 August 1994.

[238] Personal communication, 18 July 1994. Supreme Court vice-chairman Purwoto reported publicly in 1987 that advocates would occasionally pretend the draft decision was the final decision, thereby convincing clients or the other party that the case had been settled, collecting their fees, and hoping for the best. *Tempo*, 26 September 1987, p. 80.

[239] Personal communication, 23 August 1994.

[240] Personal communication, n.d.

(iv) Problems after Decisions Are Taken

Besides problems occurring before and during trial, evident problems arise after a decision has been made, for the large number of cases and the size of the administration prevent any effective control over what happens after the case has concluded and been shunted down the administrative conduit. For the judicial corps, the workload quite simply does not allow them to check on the progress of a case after it has been decided. The governing reality is "out of sight, out of mind," as the following interview testifies.

> **Supreme Court Judge**: We only have written procedure, we hardly ever call parties, and practically never call for additional evidence. Cases are written on the "roll," and after a decision is taken they go downstairs, to the registry. Then they are effectively out of our sight.
> **SP**: And what happens then?
> **Supreme Court Judge**: I basically don't know. It's possible that the case is shaken up quite a bit down there. There are cases all over the place. I mean, they get lost and all sorts of things happen to them. Sometimes we're asked by Registry people about case such and such, but then we only look at our "case roll" and inform them whether it's decided. If it is, it's out of our hands, and we tell them to solve their own mess.[241]

As a result, control over what happens to the case effectively rests with the bureaucracy itself. With the high turnover of cases, such control is almost impossible to realize in full. This results in petty badgering by administrators. Supreme Court junior chairman Adi Andoyo stated during a public interview that he knew for a fact that " . . . Supreme Court decisions sometimes are not sent on but held back, so that their 'price' rises.'"[242] Waiting for a Supreme Court decision to come down the pipeline is rather like "Waiting for Godot," comments the press, referring to Samuel Beckett's play, in which the character Godot never arrives.[243] Parties sometimes wait up to ten years for official confirmation after a case has been decided.[244] The mechanism behind such postponements is simple and effective, as exemplified by this instance:

> . . . a lady, taking 25,000 *rupiah* with her, wanted to get a copy of a Supreme Court decision. This is when malice sets in. "That can be done, Madam. But how do you want it done, fast or slow?" asks [the Supreme Court administrator]. When the price, running in the hundreds of thousands of course, is agreed upon he still is not forthcoming. Flapping the bills he holds in his hands, the administrator says: "Why, this is just for me. How about my friends?" Of course, he pockets all the money.[245]

---

[241] Personal communication, 4 August 1994.
[242] *Tempo*, 25 May 1991, p. 79.
[243] Ibid., p. 74.
[244] *Tempo*, 9 July 1983, p. 25.
[245] *Tempo*, 25 May 1991, p. 74.

After being caught, the junior Supreme Court administrator described here admitted that his *daily* income based on such illegal transactions sometimes was more than twice his official *monthly* salary.[246] Little wonder Supreme Court administrators sometimes refer to themselves as "having the status of Corporals but the income of Generals."[247]

(v) Falsification of Supreme Court Decisions

Even more serious instances of malfeasance result from this lack of control. The 1992 Internal Audit put it quite clearly:

> In this phase, cases run out of control. This is one of the factors causing leaks of Court decisions that are still secret, or even falsification of Court decisions.[248]

One of the most significant and damaging sorts of leak occurs after the decision is taken, because the report of the decision is never thoroughly checked by chambers after it has been typed up. In a great number of cases, this allows some administrative officers to alter the reported outcome, with little risk of discovery. Falsifications of Supreme Court decisions have come to light on a number of occasions.

- For example, in the 1989 *Goritman Smuggling case*,[249] Tony Goritman was caught trying to smuggle a sizeable quantity of rattan out of the country and was tried in the port town of Surabaya. The district court found him guilty, but upon appeal in 1990 he was freed by a Supreme Court chamber chaired by junior chairman Adi Andoyo. In November of that year, Adi Andoyo toured his area of supervision, which was East Java. In the course of his trip, he also visited Surabaya and met the chairman of the district court there. As they were talking about the ins and outs of their trade, the district court chairman mentioned the smuggling case and expressed his surprise that the Supreme Court had overturned his decision on appeal. After searching his memory for a while, Adi Andoyo replied that, as he recalled, this was not at all what he had decided. Yes you did, said the Surabaya judge, and even showed him the decision. Adi Andoyo was not so sure, and after returning to Jakarta he checked up on the case and found that he had been right: in his decision, he had actually sent Goritman to jail for three years. Clearly the Surabaya decision had been falsified. News of this fraud was a bombshell, all the more because the deception had been exposed by chance. If Adi Andoyo had not gone on tour so soon

---

[246] His official monthly salary stood at Rp.90,000, while his daily income based on illegal transactions was estimated at between Rp.150,000-250,000. Ibid.

[247] Ibid.

[248] Mahkamah Agung RI & LPPIS FISIP UI, "Masalah dan faktor yang mempengaruhi pelaksanaan tugas administrasi dalam proses penyelesaian perkara di Mahkamah Agung Republik Indonesia," pp. 19-20.

[249] See generally *Tempo*, 8 December 1992, p. 39; *Tempo*, 25 May 1991, p. 72.

after the case was decided, and if the issue had not been raised in conversation, the trick would probably never have been discovered.[250]

Apparently Goritman, eager to stay out of jail, had tried to influence the Supreme Court through a middleman, but the Court resolved the case before this intermediary had even begun his effort. At first the suspect attempted to have the decision's outcome blocked by arranging for the junior public prosecutor to instruct his underlings in Surabaya not to implement it. Apparently such an instruction was actually sent, but the Surabaya prosecutor indicated that he would ignore it if the suspect were convicted. This decision prompted the middleman to mobilize his contacts in the Supreme Court administration; subsequently, an administrator intercepted the Court's decision and falsified it.[251]

The press reports that Supreme Court decisions have regularly been falsified, as far back as 1985.[252] Indeed, another example of this practice emerged only a couple of months after the *Goritman Smuggling case*.

- This time, a Supreme Court typist concocted her own decision in a case that had not even been decided by the Court.[253] Apparently the typist was approached by an administrator in a first instance court to help speed up a decision involving a family member.[254] The case had been pending before the Supreme Court for some time, and the approach in itself reveals the way the administration works. The typist, who had ten years experience typing out Court reports, made up her own version of a Supreme Court decision in return for Rp.3.5 million. The losing party was unhappy with the result and asked for a certified copy of the decision from the Supreme Court Registry. At that point the fraud came to light.

It is strongly suspected that more falsifications occur, but never come to light. One Court judge put it as follows:

---

[250] The decision did arouse suspicions in some Surabaya circles, in part because of the long lapse in time between the decision, which was taken on 8 May 1990, and its arrival in Surabaya on 23 August. It so happened that another case from the Surabaya district was decided by the Supreme Court on 9 May 1990 and arrived in Surabaya on 22 May. It didn't make sense that one case took two weeks to get there while another took more than three months. So advocates apparently asked the Surabaya chairman to check up on the case with Adi Andoyo when he came down. Still, this was all pretty coincidental. If the fraud had been slightly better managed and more lucky, it would not have been exposed.

[251] It appears that the prominent Indonesian advocate for the suspect in this case played a shadowy role throughout. Though he denied any involvement in the falsification and was not prosecuted, he acknowledged that he had been in contact with Supreme Court administrators, and that money had passed hands. Nevertheless, the advocate claimed this money had been reimbursement for "travel expenses," and the case against him fizzled out.

[252] Press reports on falsifications of Supreme Court decisions reach back to 1985. *Tempo*, 26 September 1987, p. 78; *Tempo*, 25 May 1991, p. 78; *Tempo*, 11 January 1992, p. 82.

[253] See generally *Tempo*, 11 January 1992.

[254] There was some dispute concerning whether the administrator only asked for the case to be speeded up, or whether he requested the decision to be falsified. The minister of justice Ismael Saleh opted for the former interpretation, but he may have just been defending his own turf.

> Falsification is possible all the way down the line. It really cannot be controlled, for we sign only the last page of the verdict. The other pages are not given a paraph. Decisions are simply too thick, we cannot do that. So far only a few cases of falsification have come to the surface, by sheer coincidence, but I certainly wouldn't be surprised if there were more.[255]

Another Supreme Court judge said that, in his opinion, there was not a shade of doubt that falsifications were possible up and down the line. Taking one case file from his desk and leafing through it, he spoke almost pensively:

> Just take this case. There is a lot of money involved. It involves an application for enforcement of two mortgages. Now the district court judge awarded the enforcement at first, but the next day rescinded his decision, and similar weirdness really runs through the entire case. But there is more. All documents seem in order, but for some reason there is no mention of the plot of land involved, the name, number of the land registry office, and the size. This is not even mentioned in the official document from the land registry attached to the file. It makes me suspicious that the file has been tampered with, and my doubts are reinforced by the fact that the plea in cassation doesn't make sense. Agreed, the pages have not been numbered and sentences run on in logical sequence when turning the page. Nevertheless, the text is just meaningless. I have the strong impression that pieces are missing. In fact, I believe that documents have been taken from the case file, and the text of the claim in cassation has been tampered with. It could have been done here in court, who is to tell? Cases such as these are a real bitch.[256]

In fact, it is very possible that Supreme Court decisions are falsified outside the Court apparatus. If the examples noted above suggest that the Supreme Court is barely able to control its own administration, its control over cases is certainly even more tenuous. In fact, cases have been reported in which Supreme Court decisions were falsified by the first instance registrar.[257] Falsifications of Supreme Court decisions have reached the point, it seems, where there is no more need to go to the Supreme Court at all, or to any court for that matter. Apparently one can have false Supreme Court decisions drawn up outside the judicial apparatus altogether. The recent *Sulehani case* (1996) is a case in point, as scathing press reports testify:

> It certainly is not easy to start a court case. After much talk and costs, one may have to wait for the final decision for years. Under such conditions, it is tempting to use "the law" to trick people. This is what happened to Mr. Sulehani. Barely a month after applying for cassation to the Supreme Court, the decision "by chance" came down. And, no less important, the decision favored his side. [. . .] But his joy was brief. Within a couple of weeks after the outcome, people voiced their doubts about the authenticity of the decision. The advocate to Sulehani said: "The decision referred to Siagian as the chairman

---

[255] Personal communication, 3 August 1994.

[256] Ibid.

[257] In 1987, a middleman was caught operating in the Central Jakarta district court who admitted having falsified around twenty court decisions. *Tempo,* 26 September 1987, p. 78.

of the Supreme Court Civil Directorate, whereas by my knowledge that function is usually referred to as the director. And then even though the file number was authentic and could be found in the Supreme Court Registry, it applied to an altogether different case being conducted in Magelang . . . " There was overwhelming evidence that, in fact, the case had never gone to the Supreme Court, but had been falsified by one of the staff of the local branch of the Legal Aid Organization.[258]

Given such evidence, it appears that falsification of Supreme Court decisions, emanating from both in and outside the institution, is not uncommon. It is hard to exaggerate the corrosive effect of this practice on the standing of the Court and the authority of its decisions. It is not just that the public has begun to assume the Supreme Court is for sale (indeed Indonesian advocates are currently being sued by their clients because they fail to rig the Court system to their advantage).[259] Even when the Supreme Court hands down decisions, parties refuse to accept them, arguing that they must assuredly be false. Indeed, even Indonesian government authorities are not above casting doubt on the integrity of its Supreme Court. Central Java government leaders, surprised no doubt by the suddenly obstructionist Court, at first just bluntly refused to accept the authenticity of the Supreme Court decision in the *First Kedung Ombo case*, contending that the decision must have been falsified. They only recognized its validity after the Supreme Court registrar traveled into the region to hand over an authentic copy of the decision personally.[260] This was hardly a display of government confidence in the reliability of the state judicial apparatus.

5. CONCLUSION

This chapter argues that the increasing number of courts and the facilitated access to the Supreme Court described in earlier chapters have been factors contributing to a significant increase in the Supreme Court's workload. This development had an important impact on the Court's structure and mode of operation.

Usually the workload crisis was addressed by expanding the Supreme Court itself. Both the number of judges and the size of the administration increased significantly under the New Order, a numerical increase matched by added diversification within the bureaucracy. From 1982, the judges were organized in chambers and teams, headed by junior chairmen. While formally distinguished along jurisdictional lines, all teams and chambers had to combine in order to confront their extensive caseload. The general administration of the Court, directed toward institutional management, was distinguished from the case administration, which was concerned with regulating the traffic of cases. In addition, clerks were instituted to help Supreme Court judges increase their turnover. Hierarchical divisions within the Court were strengthened, in part as a natural response to the increased and more diversified court, but also doubtlessly

---

[258] *Forum Keadilan*, 15 January 1996.
[259] *Tempo*, 4 August 1990, p. 84.
[260] *Forum Keadilan*, 4 August 1994.

because they were favored by external (non-judicial) appointees the government selected to be Supreme Court leaders.

The burgeoning caseload and personnel contributed to the increasing complexity of the case-handling process, compared to which the actual decision-making process seems rather simple. Cases go through many hands before reaching the judges, and again go through many hands before leaving the Court after a decision has been taken.

Finally, budgetary limitations frustrate the Court's attempts to improve training facilities for lower court judges and to strengthen the Court's decision-making function through a regular and guaranteed publication of its decisions.

This situation has led to a series of problems. The principal one as regards the judges is a lack of central coordination and control, which roots decision-making inconsistencies within the Court structure. Moreover, the Court's heavy caseload prevents it from supervising the lower courts effectively. With respect to the administration, the lack of tight control has led to irregularities, which have manifested themselves from the point of entry (namely registration) to the point of egress, when decisions are sent back to the parties. This important problem remains to be resolved. We will see in the next chapter how it has indirectly contributed to lowering professional standards among individual judges.

Chapter Nine

The Judges

This chapter will consider the judges on the Supreme Court. It has essentially two goals: to define who these judges are and to give an indication of the way in which the changing composition of the Court colored their professional outlook.

The first section will look at some structural features of the Court that influenced its composition and outlook from the outset. It will consider the way judges are recruited to the Court and the conditions of their employment and dismissal. There are two basic methods of recruitment: "closed" and "open," described below, and the process of recruitment influences the outlook of the Court. This first section will also consider remuneration and the system by which judges leave the Court, whether by retirement or dismissal, factors that are also important in influencing the composition of the Court. More significantly, remuneration and dismissal are crucial elements in determining judicial independence, security of tenure being one of its cornerstones.

The second section describes the Supreme Court judges on the basis of a number of professional characteristics and their personal backgrounds, and describes important changes in the composition of the Court over the years.

The third section pays particular attention to the Supreme Court's leaders. One notable feature of the Court is the great power of its chairmen, which may help explain why recruitment of candidates for this position has been so politicized, while recruitment for other positions has not. Throughout the Court's history and with only a few exceptions, judges have been unable to counterbalance the power of the chairmen. His leadership role has been crucially important in the way the Court has performed its functions and conceived its own political format.

1. Conditions of Office

The careers of Supreme Court judges are shaped by the process they undergo when recruited to the bench and the conditions of employment under which they must perform their duties. Of these elements, recruitment in particular has attracted attention in Indonesia because it obviously influences the outlook of the Court, though not in a simple or predictable way, as we shall see.

(a) The Theory concerning Judicial Recruitment and Some Problems

(i) The Closed and the Open Recruitment Systems

The closed recruitment system, which has been defined and analyzed in a number of publications, is generally associated with the career judiciary. In this system, only members of the judiciary are considered to be candidates for the positions. A judiciary selected in this way is patterned on government bureaucracies, with an elaborate personnel hierarchy, supervisory structures, transfers, promotions, supervision, and so on. Career judiciaries typically are bulky organizations, with a comparatively high number of judges and courts, and a sizable administrative apparatus to back them up. There is also a marked differentiation of incomes, prestige, and power in judicial ranks. Judges enter the system at the bottom when they are young, often through comparative entrance exams. They then struggle their way up to the top through some demonstrated combination of seniority and ability.[1] With "closed" recruitment, senior judges are exclusively selected from the circle of lower judges: "lateral entry in the judiciary is rare."[2]

Judges spend their entire professional life in a working environment similar to that found in state bureaucracies. Scholars who have studied judiciaries of this sort argue that such judges tend to resemble ordinary civil servants, notably in their relative anonymity, the consequence of a variety of rules designed to depersonalize the justice system. Thus, decisions are usually made by a full bench of judges and rarely by a single judge (with the exception of the inferior courts). Moreover, they are taken collectively, which does not allow for individuals' concurring or dissenting judgments. Decisions typically are strictly structured in such a way that they tend to resemble administrative documents rather than personal judgments. Judges have an explicit obligation to motivate their decisions with reference to legislation, which in some jurisdictions has been interpreted to mean that the method and presentation of court reasoning must be presented in a specific format.[3] All these features conspire to foster anonymity by obscuring the personalities of the judges and the individual opinions that they hold on important issues. "The tendency is to think of the court as a faceless unit."[4]

In an open recruitment system, by contrast, judges are recruited from a broader field than the ranks of the judiciary; for instance, notably, senior members of the advocacy are considered eligible to join the bench. Lateral entry is more frequent, indeed the rule, and judges typically are appointed after a successful career in the private sector, which means that they tend to be more financially secure and less strongly motivated to rise in the judicial hierarchy. Typically therefore, open recruitment systems are less directed towards providing careers for their judges, and administrative hierarchy in terms of a marked differentiation in incomes and benefits, or even prestige, is much less pronounced than in career judiciaries. Judicial organization in these systems is comparatively small, with fewer judges

---

[1] J. H. Merryman, *The Civil Law Tradition* (Stanford: Stanford University Press, 1985), p. 35.

[2] Ibid.

[3] This condition of and the perception of their role is reinforced (and justified) by underlying constitutional ideas of the French-based civil law system. Rooted in the separation of powers doctrine, each power of government is perceived as having its own separate function, and one institution may not encroach upon the other. W. Witteveen, *Evenwicht van machten* (Zwolle: Tjeenk Willink, 1991), p. 20 *passim*. As regards judges, this rather has the effect, as the French comparativist A. Tunc put it, of "putting the judges in their place." André Tunc, "Synthese" (La court supreme. Enquete comparative), *Revue internationale de droit compare* 30,1 (1978): 25. (My own translation from the French.) As Tunc explains, judges are meant to have the essentially mechanical role, "un role mécanique," of applying the law created by Parliament. They typically lack political powers of control—such as the power of judicial review—over the democratically elected law-making institutions. Career judges are perceived as clerks, exalted perhaps, but clerks nonetheless. Merryman, *Civil Law Tradition*, p. 36.

[4] Merryman, *Civil Law Tradition*, p. 37.

and courts, and it generally requires a minimal administrative apparatus to serve its needs.

Many open recruitment systems (though by no means all, as we shall see later) tend to have greater trust in individual judges than the career judiciaries do. They emphasize the personality of judges and more easily accommodate individual decision making. Cases are decided by single judges, or by judges who offer individual opinions, concurring or dissenting, as members of a team. There is considerable leeway in the motivation of decisions, whereby one's "own conviction" may be sufficient grounds for deciding a case. The system exposes the personality of judges and the views they individually hold in ways unknown in a career judiciary. As a result, in societies that rely on open recruitment systems for the judiciary, the public is better able to discover what views judges hold, how they have decided important cases in the past, and therefore how they are likely to behave in the future.

The differences between closed and open recruitment systems are reflected in the recruitment mechanisms, particularly for the superior courts. In a career judiciary, recruitment tends to be a closed-shop affair. The control that political institutions such as government and Parliament can exert over such recruitment is, in practice, limited in essentially two ways. For a start, selection is restricted to the group of professional judges, and then only from the select group that has filtered upwards through the judicial hierarchy in ways that are largely controlled by the judiciary itself. Moreover, political institutions find it difficult to assess and select judges for superior courts because, as we have seen, the system is geared towards anonymity. So the individual opinions of the judges are harder to determine objectively.

It is to some extent inevitable, therefore, that closed recruitment systems are characterized by limited political control over promotions within the judiciary, notwithstanding constitutional guarantees. For this reason, the process of recruiting judges in such systems often heavily relies on co-optation and is frequently described as non-politicized, or bureaucratized. This relatively opaque method of recruitment to superior courts is tolerated, at least in part, because the power of the superior courts has been restricted. Closed recruitment generally prevails in career judiciaries and is typical for separation-of-power systems, in which superior courts lack the comparable political power of judicial review. To put it another way, the more powerful the courts, the more likely it becomes that political institutions will seek to ensure the loyalty of the judiciary through a more active management of recruitment. Politically powerful courts inevitably invite a politicization of the recruitment process, as the US example clearly shows.

(ii) The Relationship between Recruitment and Outlook

A number of respected scholars have argued over the years that there is an intimate connection between the method of recruitment and the political outlook of judiciaries, as closed recruitment tends to produce judges who act more like civil servants.[5] The closed recruitment system is not particularly conducive to creating assertive, independent-minded judges. Scholars such as Merryman have argued that, as a result, career judges tend to hold back from making controversial

---

[5] Ibid.

decisions and political choices. According to the legal comparativist Mauro Cappelletti:

> Career judges have less personality and, ultimately, are more inclined toward a bureaucratic mentality than judges selected from talented advocates or even elected. They don't particularly mind handling thousands of little "routine" cases, rather than take the responsibility of selecting and deciding cases of greater impact.[6]

Also, legal scholars have contended that the bureaucratic background of judges in closed recruitment systems makes them identify more closely with the state than with society or the private sector. In cases where the two conflict, judges will tend to side with the state's rather than with society's interests.

Judges selected through open recruitment are said to be different. In such cases, most judges, if not all, will have spent their formative years in the private sector. Since they generally will have been appointed after a successful private career, they will be comparably less vulnerable to the material pressures (salaries, benefits), more inclined to be politically assertive,[7] and more likely to identify with society, rather than with the government.

(iii) Some Questions

The legal analyses described above are useful as a starting point, but some questions remain that challenge some of their basic assumptions. Most troubling, not all facts support the contention that the closed recruitment system conditions the judges to side with government. One might remember here that the scholars who argue this point, such as John Henry Merryman, Cappeletti, and André Tunc, focus on France and, to a lesser extent, Italy, and consider years that predate the 1990 judicial revolution in both countries. Their publications singularly fail to explain developments in those nations over the last decade.

There are authors, such as J. A. G. Griffith, who make the opposite argument based on the same sources.[8] Griffith contends that the career judiciary allows for more radically independent judges because recruitment at the lower levels does not and cannot take account of the political sympathies and loyalties of the candidates (who are too young overall to have a pronounced political track record).[9] Recent history in France and Italy seems to support Griffith, and this fact warrants a brief detour to those countries.

---

[6] Quoted in Tunc, "Synthese," p. 25. My translation from the French.

[7] This is supported here by a constitutional system based on the doctrine of balance of powers, originating from the United States. Such a system relies on "checks and balances," in which each government power partially controls the other. As a result, the political assertiveness of judiciaries is institutionalized within the system, as it were, a condition notably exemplified by the power of judicial review. Witteveen, *Evenwicht van machten*, p. 20 passim.

[8] J. A. G. Griffith, *The Politics of the Judiciary* (London: Fontana Press, 1997).

[9] Griffith's book too has aroused some controversy. For a summary of criticisms of his views, see *inter alia* R. Cotterrell, *The Sociology of Law: An Introduction* (London: Butterworth, 1992), pp. 233-34. Nevertheless, the criticism is essentially a defense of the British system and does not challenge Griffith's arguments concerning the merits or demerits of closed recruitment

A remarkable aspect about France is that its judges have generated a sizable number of publications critical of their own condition over the past decades.[10] There is no comparable body of literature, either in volume or in critical nature, from any other western country. We can draw a number of conclusions from this fact. One is that the literature reflects chronic dissatisfaction within the ranks of the French judiciary on its position, as well as frustration about its inability to change that position. If French judges were to have greater power, authority, and responsibility, then presumably their energies would be directed towards exercising those, rather than to writing books reflecting exasperation. This literature therefore reflects political weakness and frustration at the absence of significant responsibilities. The French literature, and indeed the struggle of the Indonesian judiciary from 1945 until at least 1972, suggests that it may be too simple to say that judges adopt a civil-servant mentality merely as a result of participating in the career system, as the earlier publications contend. It suggests instead that a judiciary is willing to assert itself if political institutions give it the autonomy and independence to do so, and the closed or open recruitment system really is only secondary to that. Experience across the globe shows that if political institutions fail to honor those rules, a judiciary will be reduced to a subservient role under any structure.

This view is supported by the fact that when the political reins were loosened by the socialist government in France in the early 1990s, the judiciary manifested remarkable aggressiveness in prosecuting political leaders and major companies.[11] By the time the reforms became ensconced in constitutional amendments and new legislation in the late 1990s, close to twenty of the country's top political leaders and businessmen were under criminal investigation (which in France is conducted by independent investigatory judges) or convicted. This group included the president of the Republic, a former prime minister, and the chairman of the Constitutional Council, as well as three ministers of finance.[12] If this tells us something about French political morals, it also says something about the assertiveness and outlook of the supposedly docile, compliant judges.[13]

---

judiciaries. There are grounds to regard Lord Woolfe's reforms in the late 1990s as a response to some of Griffith's criticism and an acknowledgment of its essential merits.

[10] For reasons of space, no full inventory can be given here; let it suffice to name just a few: L. Greilsamer and D. Schneidermann, *Les juges parlent* (Paris: Fayard, 1992); D. Robert, *La justice ou le chaos* (Paris: Stock, 1996); A. Gaudino, *La mafia des tribunaux de commerce* (Paris: Albin Michel, 1998); J. P. Thierry, *Credit Lyonnais: L'enquete* (Paris: Fixot, 1997); H. Haenel and F. Arthuis, *Justice sinistrée: Démocratie en danger* (Paris: Economica, 1991); F. Gerber, *Justice indépendente: Justice sur commande* (Paris: PUF, 1990).

[11] The Mitterand government made the first break, but the changes were consolidated under the Chirac government with the Truche report and the Guigou legislative reforms. One of Chirac's specific policy instructions of January 21, 1997 was to review the system with an aim to reduce political controls.

[12] The list of political leaders under criminal investigation, or convicted by 2001, include President J. Chirac, former Prime Minister A. Juppe, R. Dumas (former foreign minister and president of the Constitution Council), Ministers of Finance D. Strauss-Kahn, E. Alphandery and M. Sapin, as well as four other ministers, two governors of the Central Bank (J.C. Trichet and J. de Larosiere), the leader of the Communist party, R. Hue, the mayor of Paris, J. Tiberi, etc. *The Economist*, 2 June 2001, 4 November 2001, 22 January 2000.

[13] In fact, political leaders in France have begun to regard the judiciary as so aggressive in its approaches that some have tried to escape conviction by asserting judicial bias.

As in France, in Italy the rise to prominence of the judiciary is directly related to changes in the political environment in the 1990s. It resulted from the collapse of the Christian Democratic Party's forty-year stranglehold on government and the bureaucracy. After this collapse, and not unlike their French counterparts, Italian judges systematically attacked problems in the most contentious political area: the area of influence controlled by political leaders and vested economic interests. More than any other force, the Italian judiciary helped mount significant challenges to the status quo, in which political power was linked with both economic corruption (*Mani Pullite*), and organized crime (*mafia*).[14]

These developments, in which the French and Italian judiciaries have passed from compliance to outright confrontation, suggest that the political outlook of judges is less conditioned by the closed recruitment system, per se, as by political interference in the affairs of the judiciary. Different recruitment systems create different entry points for political interference. It remains to be established where these differences lie, and whether open or closed recruitment systems are significant factors determining whether a judiciary will maintain its independence when political institutions seek to control them.

The second question I would like to pose regarding the theories summarized above concerns the fact that publications on judicial recruitment often roughly equate closed recruitment systems with career judiciaries and open recruitment systems with the Anglo-Saxon system. This dichotomy is an oversimplification. Most career judiciaries have opened up recruitment; this is true even of the French, which for reasons specific to that country's history is comparatively traditional in such procedures compared to its neighbors. The Dutch judiciary, for example, has for a long time allowed and encouraged lateral entry at all levels in the judiciary. This practice is grounded in the belief that the judiciary should reflect broad sections of society and a proper mix of judicial skills, and that it should be strengthened not only by the members' professional experience and discipline, but also by input from the bar, the business world, academia, and the public prosecution. As a result, approximately 50 percent of the modern Dutch judiciary is recruited from outside the career system, and the bench is composed of individuals with a variety of skills.[15] This notably also applies to the superior courts.

Dutch judicial recruitment is interesting when compared to that in Britain, which scholars traditionally categorize as an "open" system. The British judiciary is recruited from the bar. Griffith contends that this restricts the social and professional pool to such an extent as to impair the neutrality of the judiciary. It may still be impartial, he argues, but its professional, social, and political outlook make it partisan in its views on critical political and social issues.

Interestingly enough, the Dutch judiciary has been rather independent and aggressive in its decisions, and not just on such contentious issues as the right to strike, abortion, and euthanasia (which it decided long in advance of legislative

---

[14] See, for instance, V. Bufacchi and S. Burgess, *Italy since 1989: Events and Interpretations* (London: Macmillan, 1998); S. H. Burnett and L. Mantovani, *The Italian Guillotine: Operation Clean Hands and the Overthrow of Italy's First Republic* (Boston: Rowman and Littlefield, 1998); V. S. Pisano, *The Dynamics of Subversion and Violence in Contemporary Italy* (Stanford, CA: Hoover Institution Press, 1987),

[15] L. E. de Groot-van Leeuwen, *De rechterlijke macht in Nederland* (Arnhem: Gouda Quint, 1991).

changes).[16] The Dutch courts have also developed a tendency to decide cases in direct conflict with statutory wording if they feel that the statute meant to achieve something different from what it says.[17] In comparison, the British judiciary generally is viewed as more restrained. This is in part the result of constitutional restrictions, such as the doctrine of parliamentary sovereignty, a legal interpretative tradition that values wording above intent, and a public policy traditionally directed to minimize the role of British courts in the contentious domain of administrative law.[18]

The Dutch and British examples show that it is too simple to equate closed recruitment systems with career judiciaries or open recruitment systems with Anglo-Saxon judiciaries. Examination of these systems, based on such categories, is most useful when it offers information about the scope of the candidate pool from which judges are recruited, in the sense that the size and variety of the pool will help influence or determine the abilities and outlook of the judiciary that emerges from it. Bureaucracy and the private sector are not the only alternative sources for judicial candidates. Any form of judicial recruitment that relies too heavily on a limited pool is likely to inherit the strengths and weaknesses of that faction, whether it is public or private sector based. This therefore is an argument for mixing inflows and broadening the pool of candidates. After that, each country must determine what, ideally, the abilities and outlook of a judiciary should be and how the recruitment pool might be constituted to further those goals.

The final problem is that scholars often make little distinction between judicial recruitment for the judiciary, generally, and recruitment for the superior courts. There are various reasons why such distinction should be made, notably for the sake of appreciating the significance of political legitimacy to the superior courts. Whenever superior courts are invested with powers that encroach on the other political institutions, judges must be invested with the political legitimacy that allows them to perform that function. It is unacceptable in a constitutional democracy for statute that is constituted by the representatives of the electorate to be nullified by functionaries not appointed by popular mandate. The appointment of judges to powerful courts therefore requires a direct involvement of parliament and the executive.

---

[16] P. J. Koppen, "The Dutch Supreme Court and Parliament: Political Decisionmaking versus Nonpolitical Appointments," *Law and Society Review,* 24,4 (1990).

[17] Research suggests that from the 1970s onwards, the Dutch Supreme Court began to make decisions that were in direct contradiction with statutory wording. Comparable research on the previous periods does not uncover such decisions, which indicates that decision making in Dutch courts shifted from a legalistic and textual approach to one in which greater importance came to be attached to the basic principles of the law and what it proposed to achieve. G. J. Wiarda, *Drie typen van rechtsvinding,* ed. T. Koopmans (Deventer: Tjeenk Willink, 1999), pp. 38-39.

[18] "British administrative law is principally a series of doctrines that command the courts to defer to bureaucratic lawmaking and thus to render themselves incapable of providing a neutral and independent resolution of most conflicts that might arise between government and citizens." Martin Shapiro, *Courts: A Comparative and Political Analysis* (Chicago: The University of Chicago Press, 1981), p. 33 & chapter 2.

(b) Supreme Court Recruitment in Indonesia

   (i) Emerging from Obscurity: A Troubled History

In Indonesia, Supreme Court recruitment was never seriously debated until the 1985 Supreme Court Bill. We have seen elsewhere that the bill really did not challenge the status quo significantly and that on many issues the government had its way. Indeed, the extraordinarily short time (four months) it took to whip the bill through Parliament suggests that the government was in firm control throughout.[19] Nevertheless, there still was a debate, and if one issue in 1985 mobilized forces both inside and outside Parliament, it was the question of how Supreme Court judges were to be recruited. In fact, when minister of justice Ismael Saleh presented the bill to Parliament on August 28, 1985, he specifically mentioned recruitment as one of the cornerstones of the proposed new law.[20] From their first general observations, all parties in Parliament focused on the issue, at which point the first signs of political fissures appeared. Although the parliamentary debates were short, recruitment remained a stumbling block until the very last moment, and the debate over the issue soon spilled out into the streets. Everyone who cared to speak up on the bill—politicians, judges, advocates, and university professors—agreed on one thing, namely that recruitment was a "crucial" issue (the English word was used for added weight and emphasis).[21] As one MP readily acknowledged: "The *crucial* issue of the 1985 Supreme Court Bill is the way in which Supreme Court judges are to be recruited."[22]

Conferences, meetings, interviews, and public debates were organized throughout the country, involving all the prominent actors, such as the Judges' Association (IKAHI, Ikatan Hakim Indonesia), the Legal Aid Institute (LBH, Lembaga Bantuan Hukum), various universities, and important figures in the field of law.

The reasons for this public attention are obvious. For a start, it really was the first time the issue of Supreme Court recruitment had been openly debated. Important and controversial revisions of legislation and recruitment practice had been introduced in the past, as we shall see shortly, but all had been effected in an underhanded manner that precluded public debate. Previous attempts to open up a debate on the issue failed because they lacked political backing.[23] Consequently,

---

[19] The bill was presented to Parliament by the minister of justice, Ismael Saleh, on August 28, 1985. Dewan Perwakilan Rakyat RI, Persidangan I Rapat Paripurna Terbuka Ke-3 Tahun Sidang 1985-1986. See also *Varia Peradilan* 1, Perdana (October 1985). The law was enacted on December 30, 1985.

[20] Presentation by the minister of justice, Ismael Saleh, during the First Session on the 1985 Supreme Court Bill, Dewan Perwakilan Rakyat RI, Persidangan I, p. 12. See also *Varia Peradilan* 1, Perdana (October 1985): 92.

[21] See, for instance, statement by an unnamed parliamentarian in *Kompas*, 7 November 1985; see also comment of a prominent chairman of the Central Jakarta court, Amarullah Salim, in *Sinar Harapan*, 15 November 1985, and *Kompas*, 7 December 1985. In the last case, the Indonesian translation for the English word "crucial" is added between brackets: "causing problems."

[22] *Kompas*, 7 November 1985.

[23] During its 1966 and 1968 Conventions, the Judges' Association proposed making the entire personnel management of the judiciary, including that of the Supreme Court itself, subject to a High Judicial Council, patterned on the French *Conseil de la Magistrature* of the Fourth Republic (i.e. dominated by judges, not by politicians, as it is under the Fifth Republic). The council would

many viewed the 1985 bill as an opportunity to set things right. Nevertheless, the principal reason for this new public focus on Supreme Court recruitment was that it was widely viewed as the determining factor in shaping the Court's outlook. The system of recruitment came under debate: whether to continue in the old manner, with politically deferential judges, or perhaps to break new ground with new outside appointees.[24]

To understand fully the arguments and positions of all parties in the 1985 debates, it is worth looking at the system of Supreme Court recruitment before 1985. Two issues will be dealt with: who was recruited, and who did the recruiting.

Who is Recruited? From the Dutch colonial system, Indonesia inherited a career judiciary recruited through an essentially "closed" system.[25] No serious consideration was ever given to introducing another method, notably the more loosely structured Anglo-Saxon system in which candidates are recruited primarily

---

consist of five members, three of whom came from the judiciary (i.e. the Supreme Court chairman, a member of the Supreme Court, and the judge from the lower courts), the minister of justice, and a member of the advocacy. Nothing came of the proposal at first, but it was implemented in a diluted version in 1986, when a Judicial Council (Majelis Kehormatan Hakim) was established with advisory powers pertaining to the dismissal of judges: Law no.2/1986 art.20(2)(3) envisaged the establishment of a council and its powers. Government Regulation no.26/1991 distinguished between a special council for the Supreme Court and one for the other courts, and gave each council investigatory and decisive powers in the dismissal of judges. See generally A. Salim, "Majelis Kehormatan Hakim," *Varia Peradilan* 8,86 (November 1986): 139-43. A Judicial Commission was established after *Reformasi* with the Third Constitutional Amendment of August 2001 (Art.24B), which was effected with Law nr.22/2004.

[24] It is worth recalling that in the United States John Marshall was the moving force behind the seminal case of *Marbury vs. Madison,* which established the power of the US Supreme Court to declare federal laws unconstitutional. H. J. Abraham, *The Judicial Process,* 6th ed. (Oxford: Oxford University Press, 1993), p. 301. Marshall was appointed instead of George Washington's favored nominee, J. Rutledge, who was rejected by the Senate even though he was legally better qualified. L. E. H. Tribe, *God Save this Honourable Court: How the Choice of Supreme Court Justice Shapes our History* (New York: Penguin, 1986), p. 95.

[25] Unlike the judiciary in the Netherlands, the colonial judiciary was based on a closed career system. Outside recruits sometimes joined the bench, but they were rare and opposed by the judiciary. In 1914, the new chairman appointed to the colonial Supreme Court was Mr. I. A. Nederburgh. He was not a career judge, but had previously served as colonial director of justice—a function comparable to minister of justice. The appointment of Mr. Nederburgh—dubbed an "outsider" even in contemporary reports—caused an uproar, which indicates that such appointments were extremely rare. The colonial Supreme Court judges fully lived up to their reputation as a quarrelsome bunch. (Rows apparently were so frequent in the colonial Supreme Court that a favorite expression of the Indonesian Court clerks, "*tuan tuan berkelahi*" (the gentlemen are fighting), became a standard phrase. See "Bisbilles in den boezem van het Hooggerechtshof," *De Indische Gids* 1 (1915): 695). Both the vice-chairman and a judge of the colonial Supreme Court resigned in protest at this appointment, and one more colonial Supreme Court judge refused to serve on the same bench with Mr. Nederburgh, which led to all sorts of organizational problems. E. A. A. van Eekeren, "De benoeming van Mr. G. André de la Porte tot Procureur Generaal en van Mr. I. A. Nederburgh tot President van het Hooggerechtshof van Ned. Ind.," *De Indische Gids* 2 (1914): 973-77. The appointment of an outsider may have been related to the fact that the reactionary judges on the colonial Supreme Court, without exception, made it known to the liberal Governor-General Alexander Willem Frederik Idenburg that they declined promotion under his administration. This forced the hand of the minister of the colonies (Th. B. Pleyte) primarily responsible for this appointment. It must be added that Pleyte and Idenburg did not get along, and the Nederburgh appointment was probably part of a political ploy by Pleyte to counteract some of the liberal Idenburg reforms in the colony. Given the context, this was clearly a political appointment.

from the bar (advocates), despite the fact that early legislation said nothing about how recruitment to the Supreme Court was to be effected. Even though Law no.1/1950 is quite explicit on other entry requirements, such as professional qualifications, age, and family bonds, no single article states that only career judges may be considered as candidates for the Supreme Court. Closed recruitment became general policy, but external (non-judicial) recruits were not by law excluded. The subsequent Law no.13/1965 Art.31(3)(g), which stated that qualified candidates must have a minimum of ten years' experience in the field of law, was purposely directed to allow external recruitment to the Supreme Court.[26] The revolutionary Guided Democracy government wanted a clear mandate to appoint government loyalists to the Court, and Law no.13/1965 was designed with that in mind.

Nevertheless, no external appointments were made until the advent of the New Order government. This is not to say that no one had tried. In 1954, the then secretary-general of the Department of Justice, Besar Mertokusumo, proposed the prominent Semarang lawyer, Ko Tjay Sing, as a candidate for the Supreme Court. He failed to secure this appointment, it is said, not because Ko Tjay Sing was an outsider, but because of the candidate's Chinese ancestry. This is a significant nuance, because it shows that, at least in the eyes of the government, career judges had no monopoly on Supreme Court recruitment.[27]

The New Order government for some years evaded the recruitment issue. A number of developments suggested, however, that it would maintain the prevailing practice, that is, the closed recruitment system. Thus, when it sought to expand the Supreme Court in the late 1960s, all the appointees were career judges — including notably Asikin Kusumah Atmadja, Sri Widoyati Soekito, and Busthanul Arifin. The New Order government repealed Law no.13/1965,[28] allowing external candidates to be considered, and emphatically stated a number of times that the judiciary, up to the Supreme Court, would be based on a closed career system.[29]

---

[26] On the meaning of art.31(3)(g) Law no.13/1965, see for instance Minister of Justice Ismael Saleh, Jawaban pemerintah atas pemandangan umum fraksi-fraksi di DPR RI mengenai Rancangan undang-undang tantang susunan kekuasaan dan acara Mahkamah Agung pada sidang paripurna DPR RI dated 4 Oktober 1985, (mimeo), p. 7. The issue was never thoroughly debated, as Parliament had devolved into a club of yes-men by this time, and the most flagrant violations of constitutional principle were applauded in harmonious revolutionary unanimity. This was one of the skeletons in the government cupboard that toppled out when the issue was debated openly in 1985.

[27] Daniel S. Lev archives (hereafter *DSL*), 30 September 1960. (These are the personal interview notes of Daniel S. Lev; copies will be deposited in the University of Washington library [Seattle, WA], the Cornell University Kroch Collection [Ithaca, NY], and Pusat Studi Hukum dan Kebijakan [PSHK] in Jakarta.)

[28] Law no.6/1969 appendix III. The legal basis for allowing non-judicial appointments is obscure. The most evident explanation is that Law no.13/1965 may have been formally repealed, but continued to apply on a number of points in the absence of clear new legislation. Indeed, one of the psychological complications of the 1985 debate was perhaps that the law could not be dismissed as one of the many political aberrations of Guided Democracy, precisely because the New Order government seemed to have relied on its provisions regarding recruitment.

[29] For example, during parliamentary debates in 1968, the then minister of justice, Seno Adji, stated that recruitment to the Supreme Court would be based on the career principle. *Tempo*, 20 October 1973.

An important further development in this direction was the Law on the Civil Service, which came into effect in 1974 (Law no.8/1974).[30] One controversial aspect of the law was that it included the judiciary in its ambit.[31] Henceforth, judges would be civil servants, which also meant that they could be subjected to an arsenal of supervision, sanction, and rewards like any bureaucrat—a source of much dissatisfaction in the judiciary right until *Reformasi*. The law also explicitly made the judiciary a careerist organization patterned on government bureaucracies, envisaging, in fact, a system of recruitment and advancement similar to the one that had prevailed since colonial times: recruitment would exist only at the lowest rank, records would be kept noting the performance of each judge, these records would be used to generate a ranking list, and up to a certain level in the civil service hierarchy, advancement would occur automatically on the basis of that list.[32] Strengthening career structures still further within the judiciary, in later years the Supreme Court introduced a judicial seniority list (*Daftar Urut Senioritas Hakim*) to serve as standard for advancements within the judiciary.[33] As in colonial times, Supreme Court judges were excluded from this system. Law no.8/1974 stated, in fact, that Supreme Court judges were not civil servants, but state officials, like the president, cabinet ministers, and the like.[34] The defining characteristic of state officials, according to the government explanation at the time, was that these were political functions held for a limited period only. Also, they were selective (not to say elective) functions, in the sense that these are functions for which people are selected, and not functions which are more or less automatically attained with seniority.[35] Regarding the Supreme Court, however,

---

[30] See for a brief exposé Minister of Justice Ismael Saleh, Jawaban pemerintah atas pemandangan umum fraksi-fraksi di DPR RI mengenai Rancangan undang-undang tantang susunan kekuasaan dan acara Mahkamah Agung pada sidang paripurna DPR RI dated 4 Oktober 1985, pp. 5-6.

[31] Official Explanation to art.11 Law no.8/1974 specifically includes judges within the ambit of the law.

[32] Ranking list: Daftar Urut Kepangkatan—Government Regulation no.15/1979. Law no.8/1974 art.18 states that two types of advancement exist: regular and by selection. Regular advancement, being advancement by right, occurs to slot III/d PGPS (the civil service hierarchy). Advancement by selection occurs from slot IV/a PGPS upwards. Advancement by selection is no right, and even if all conditions are complied with, no advancement will occur unless a vacancy has arisen. Art.20 refers to the ranking list drawn up on the basis of personal records (*conduite*). The criteria determining the order of the list are objective, such as seniority, education, and age.

[33] This was done in 1983, cf. *Varia Peradilan* 12 (September 1986): 210. Practical implementation was another matter. Three months later, during a lecture for new judges, the director general for the courts of the Department of Justice stated that good judges were to be rewarded during their careers, a proposal that effectively broke down the prevailing fixed-rank-list system of recruitment based on seniority. *Varia Peradilan* 15 (December 1986): 106-108.

[34] Law no.8/1974 art.11.

[35] See for instance, Member of Parliament (Government Fraction Karya Pembangunan) Albert Hasibuan, Dewan Perwakilan Rakyat RI, Persidangan I Rapat Paripurna Terbuka Ke-6 Tahun Sidang 1985-1986, 17 September 1985, pp. 19-20. Hasibuan, himself a lawyer, was the main advocate for opening up recruitment along American lines during the parliamentary debates, as we shall see shortly. His clever argument was that the definition of "state official" in Law no.8/1974 should fully extend to the Supreme Court, which would mean that, just as with other state officials, Supreme Court positions should be open to all. Hasibuan did not go so far as to advocate having judicial tenures limited in time, of course.

the government added that even though Supreme Court judges were state officials and occupied selective functions, these individuals would be an integral part of the judicial career service. It stated in unequivocal terms that the career principles underlying the lower courts also extended to the superior judiciary.[36]

Against this background, the 1974 Subekti succession crisis came as a rude shock to the career judges.

When in 1974 Chairman Subekti reached the mandatory retirement age, it became known that the government considered appointing an outsider to the Supreme Court to succeed him.[37] This was a total surprise, in part because it would break a thirty-year tradition, and, moreover, it ran contrary to what was generally assumed to be government policy. Supreme Court chairman Subekti apparently went to see President Suharto to argue against outside appointments and in favor of a closed recruitment system. It was quite a step for the timorous Subekti, revealing the importance the judiciary attached to the issue. Notwithstanding his reputation as an excellent card player, the chairman was outbluffed by Suharto. Stating that he had not had much experience before becoming president, President Suharto dared Subekti:

Suharto: Are you asking for an extension as Supreme Court chairman?
Subekti: Well, no, that is not what I mean.
Suharto: In that case, Seno Adji will replace you. That's settled then.[38]

And so in 1974 the first non-judicial candidate was appointed to the Supreme Court, and the closed recruitment system seemed to have been breached. Adding insult to injury, Seno Adji did not come alone, but was joined by three other non-judicial recruits, all army generals.[39]

Perhaps the New Order government had been planning the move all along, but one important background factor was the massive 1974 rioting in Jakarta known as MALARI (Malapetaka 15 Januari, Disaster of 15 January, the anti-Japanese riots in January 1974), which shocked the government and impelled it to consolidate its support in the state apparatus, including in the judiciary. The appointment of Seno Adji and the generals to the Supreme Court in 1974 was meant to ensure the political loyalty of the institution (and through it the entire judiciary). As one contemporary Supreme Court judge put it:

The real trouble in the Supreme Court began in 1974 with the appointment of all the new judges, notably Seno Adji and the military judges. It was quite different from the way in which Asikin Kusumah Atmadja, Sri Widoyati Soekito, and Busthanul Arifin were appointed in 1968. At that time, Parliament examined everything, including the personal lives of candidates, and that is the way it should be. But the 1974 appointment came hard on the

---

[36] See reference Minister of Justice Ismael Saleh, Jawaban pemerintah atas pemandangan umum fraksi-fraksi di DPR RI mengenai Rancangan undang-undang tantang susunan kekuasaan dan acara Mahkamah Agung pada sidang paripurna DPR RI dated 4 Oktober 1985, pp. 6-7.

[37] See for instance *Tempo*, 20 October 1973.

[38] *DSL*, 21 October 1978; *DSL*, 30 October 1978.

[39] *Dewan Perwakilan Rakyat Republik Indonesia Periode 1971-1977* (Jakarta: DPR, n.d.), pp. 42-43.

heels of the MALARI incident, and everything was rushed, and government leaders were not going to listen to Parliament or anyone else. Before MALARI, there had been various rumors, but there was general agreement that enough judges would be appointed to make up a full complement of nine judges. Then came MALARI, and, stubborn, the president appointed a whole slew of judges, including Seno Adji, without anybody having anything to say about it. This was simply forced down the parliamentary throat, without examination or anything of the sort.[40]

The 1974 external appointments to the Supreme Court set a dangerous precedent that would influence policy for almost twenty years, at least, in which the chairman was appointed from the outside, along with a batch of military officers, sometimes complemented by a recruit or two from the public prosecution. Seno Adji was succeeded as chairman by General Mudjono, and when the 1985 Supreme Court Bill was submitted to Parliament, the Court chairman was General Ali Said—all of these were external appointees. Until the 1990s, the New Order government exclusively appointed senior officials from its own circles, never from the private legal professions, to the Supreme Court. In fact, no one from the private legal professions was ever appointed to the Court during the thirty years of the New Order regime.[41] These lawyers were too independent, as they had operated in relative autonomy throughout their professional careers, and most were men and women of independent means.

Under the New Order, after MALARI, the closed recruitment system was not, in fact, replaced by a system of open recruitment, but by what amounted to a system of court packing, whereby Supreme Court appointments depended less on judicial expertise than on political loyalty to the government. The regular appointment of outsiders to the influential top positions of the Court from 1974 onwards suggests that they were meant to function no less as instruments of political control than as judges. In fact, military Supreme Court judges continued to operate within the military hierarchy, benefiting from advancement in military rank even while serving on the Court, dual responsibilities meant to remind them where their ultimate political loyalty ought to lie.[42]

The New Order government's policy of appointing outsiders who were professionally weak and politically questionable gave legitimacy and force to the professional judiciary's express preference for a closed recruitment system. Still, the private legal professions, which were consistently excluded from recruitment,

---

[40] *DSL*, 14 November 1978.

[41] Apparently some advocates were approached for recruitment, but declined. Thus, it is said that the prominent Jakarta lawyer, Kartini Muljadi, who in fact started out her career as a judge, was invited to become a Supreme Court judge, but she refused. Similarly, Mochtar Kusumaatmadja, a former minister of justice and foreign affairs, and with a background both in academia and in private practice, was reportedly solicited, but he also declined. Personal communication, 5 August 1994. These incidents underscore the fact that, compared to its public sector recruitment, the government did not pursue private practice recruitment very vigorously.

[42] While serving on the Supreme Court, both General Mudjono and General Ali Said were promoted in rank. *Tempo*, 12 September 1981.

called for a broadening of the selection system to include candidates from their own circles.[43]

Who Recruits? Investigation into this matter reveals that the Indonesian government over the past decades has consistently aimed at shielding recruitment from political debate. Clinging to nineteenth-century civil law tradition, the Indonesian government has tried to depoliticize recruitment and indeed present the entire Supreme Court as a non-political institution, emphasizing the supposedly bureaucratic character of the Court and the judiciary as a whole. This meant that Parliament's role was consistently reduced, and recruitment to the Supreme Court came to be essentially decided by the Court itself and the Department of Justice in the so-called Mah-Dep forum.

According to Law no.1/1950, the president appoints a Supreme Court judge on the basis of a recommendation by Parliament (art.6). The parliamentary list had to consist of at least two candidates for each vacancy. Notwithstanding Parliament's significant role under law, in actuality it rarely influenced the recruitment process.

> Procedure in the 1950s was for the government to make proposals for a Supreme Court vacancy by way of the Department of Justice, which would then be forwarded to Parliament. For each vacancy there would be several proposals, and Parliament would choose from the list forwarded. Parliament can make its own proposals in addition to those offered to it by the Department of Justice, but custom dictated that it chose from among the top four names suggested by the Department.[44]

Recruitment was, in fact, decided by the government, to the effective exclusion of Parliament. Several examples testify to the Supreme Court's role in this recruitment process. Thus, Subekti was recruited as Court clerk principally because chairman Kusumah Atmadja liked him. He reportedly owed his later appointment as a Supreme Court judge to his family relationship with Supreme Court chairman Wirjono Prodjodikoro. Supreme Court judge Abdurrahman was recruited because the Court justices thought it important to have a university graduate on the Court—even though Abdurrahman had sided with the Dutch during the Revolution.[45] The government's role was similarly clear: we already saw that President Sukarno selected Wirjono Prodjodikoro to succeed Kusumah Atmadja as Supreme Court chairman because he wanted to install a more pliant candidate

---

[43] The government has little incentive to pursue private sector recruitment energetically, but on the other hand there seems to be little response from the private sector even when it is solicited. The reasons are not hard to guess; for prominent Jakarta lawyers, the Supreme Court is a major step back in all respects: salary, prestige, administrative environment, and independence. So external recruitment will only attract top private-sector candidates if working conditions on the Supreme Court are changed significantly. This pattern also suggests that the private sector in Indonesia, with some notable exceptions, despite its sometimes quite vocal criticism of the system, finds it difficult to meet its responsibilities. It has exposed itself to the criticism of being *fauteuil*-reformers.

[44] *DSL*, 30 September 1960.

[45] *DSL*, 9 July 1960.

after his difficulties with the assertive Kusumah Atmadja.[46] Wirjono's appointment set a dangerous precedent for a politicization of the recruitment of Supreme Court chairman.

Guided Democracy Law no.13/1965 with refreshing, revolutionary directness made explicit what had been recruiting practice up to then. The law stated that Supreme Court appointments would be effected by the president on the basis of a recommendation by Parliament. That recommendation would, however, be based on a proposal formulated by the Supreme Court chairman and the minister of justice (art.43). It is not quite clear how the law envisaged parliament would be involved in the matter, but it is obvious that input from members of parliament was not intended to be important.

This did not prevent Parliament from asserting itself on the recruitment issue to an astonishing degree in the early years of the New Order, when Law no.13/1965 was still in force. This was a politically turbulent time, when political boundaries between institutions were being redrawn, and recruitment briefly figured as a hot issue on the Indonesian political scene.

Under the leadership of General Nasution, Parliament was pitted against Sukarno from 1966 until 1968. After the resignation of Supreme Court chairman Wirjono in 1966, Parliament put his succession to the vote and selected Subekti with a clear majority, listing Soerjadi second. It was felt that this settled the matter, to the point that Subekti resigned his function as university professor with the firm expectation that he would be nominated forthwith. This appointment did not materialize, however, for, as we have seen, Sukarno selected Soerjadi.[47] By law, Sukarno, of course, was allowed to take his pick from the parliamentary list, and technically he was well within his rights. In that atmosphere, however, Parliament considered his selection a political affront. The fact that Soerjadi was an old PNI (Partai Nasional Indonesia, Indonesian National Party) stalwart and strong Sukarno loyalist, who had clearly been selected in order to support a politically embattled president, intensified dissatisfaction and brought Parliament to the barricades.

When Parliament failed in its initial attempts to force Soerjadi's resignation, it then blocked the recruitment process altogether.[48] This posed a problem for the Supreme Court. The many vacancies that had arisen under Guided Democracy made it almost impossible for the Court to perform its most elementary functions properly. Soerjadi's fall eventually resulted from his conflict with the Judges' Association, which was firmly allied with Parliament in favoring the proposed appointments of the anti-Sukarno Association leaders Asikin Kusumah Atmadja and Sri Widoyati Soekito. Soerjadi indicated that he would not tolerate these appointments. This broke the deadlock. The Judges' Association advanced these two candidates as its favorites, and Parliament accepted them. In the meantime, there had been a change of political leadership at the top, with Suharto replacing

---

[46] *DSL*, 13 January 1959; *DSL* 28 June 1960. Both respondents say that Sukarno feared Kusumah Atmadja, but that he understood Wirjono and knew how to use him for his own purposes.

[47] See above, Chapter Three; *DSL*, 20 June 1967; *DSL*, 25 June 1967.

[48] *DSL*, 20 June 1967; *DSL*, 25 June 1967.

Sukarno, and as a result the new judges were duly promoted to the Supreme Court. Soerjadi resigned.[49]

The Parliament-led quasi-dismissal of Soerjadi is the only case where Parliament was able to assert itself on the recruitment issue. This brief moment of glory was immediately undone by rapid retreat. It occurred at a time and was perhaps in part a result of Parliament itself being re-elected. Members of Parliament had so many other worries that the choice of Soerjadi's successor seemed comparatively insignificant. There was even a feeling among MPs that, since they had originally selected Subekti, now that Soerjadi was out of the way there was no reason to go through the whole circus again to select Subekti for a second time.

Both the government and Subekti himself certainly felt this way. So, once the new president, Suharto, indicated his preference for Subekti (after some hesitation), it was decided to bypass the parliamentary nomination procedure and appoint Subekti as Supreme Court chairman by executive decree. As the Judges' Association pointed out, this was unconstitutional, and it would haunt Subekti in his later conflicts with the government when he felt that the irregularity of his appointment eroded his legitimacy.[50] More important in this context, however, the Subekti appointment completely sidetracked Parliament and marked the beginning of its progressive loss of control over Supreme Court nominations. As a natural consequence of this development, for instance, the three judges who were appointed with Seno Adji in 1974 were never nominated by Parliament.[51]

The marginalization of the legislature in Supreme Court recruitment was institutionalized with the establishment of the so-called Mah-Dep forum in the early 1980s. This forum was a monthly consultation meeting between the Supreme Court (Mahkamah Agung, hence the *Mah*) and the Department of Justice (Departmen Kehakiman, hence *Dep*). One of the items on the forum's agenda was Supreme Court recruitment, and it was during these monthly meetings that the preliminary lists of Supreme Court candidates would be hashed out between the Court and the government.

The Mah-Dep forum's power in this matter was strengthened by the lack of an effective parliamentary counterweight. During the 1970s, Parliament had become fatally weakened from within,[52] as evidenced in part by the fact that, by 1974, the members could no longer reach agreement on the list of candidates for the Supreme Court. Instead of presenting the president with just two candidates for each

---

[49] Personal communications, 1 July 1994, 16 July 1994.

[50] *DSL*, 13 July 1968; *DSL*, 20 July 1968. Apparently Asikin Kusumah Atmadja pushed for direct appointment, and Sri Widoyati Soekito pushed for a parliamentary vote.

[51] Its list of recommended candidates for the vacancies arising in 1974 was partly adopted by the DPR and the president. See *Dewan Perwakilan Rakyat Republik Indonesia Periode 1971-1977*, pp. 42-43. This document points out that the Supreme Court suggested 1. Saldiman, 2. Hanindioputro, 3. Soejono, and 4. Joesran, but only the first two were included in the parliamentary list.

[52] B. Saragih, "Beberapa catatan mengenai hak *recall* di Indonesia," in *Pembangunan politik, situasi global dan hak asasi di Indonesia*, ed. M. Budiardjo (Jakarta: Gramedia, 1994). Saragih reveals how the right of recall functions as an instrument to ensure discipline within each party. Members of Parliament can be recalled at any time by their party, an event that costs them their prestige, perks, and money. Since party leadership is in many cases strongly tied to government rather than to its own program, the threat of recall developed into a prime instrument of political manipulation.

vacancy, thus restricting the government's options, Parliament introduced a practice whereby each political party added on names to the list regardless of the number of vacancies. Candidates favored by both the Supreme Court and the Department of Justice in the Mah-Dep forum could hardly fail to be appointed. Parliament would not critically assess the names sent to them on the Mah-Dep list; instead, each party simply added its own names to the list—with the government (Fraksi Karya Pembangunan) and military parties (Fraksi ABRI) nominating the Mah-Dep candidates. Thereupon the candidates would be duly selected when the list was passed on to the president. One MP described the process in the following terms:

> We all eat from the same hand, and the same goes for Supreme Court appointments. The Supreme Court and the Department of Justice draft their first list of candidates, each parliamentary party adds a couple of names, no use protesting because party leadership is completely tied to the government, that's why they're party leadership, after all. The inflated list is then sent on to the president. So in fact, the executive proposes to Parliament, and Parliament never scratches out a name, but only adds to it.[53]

This is a ludicrous practice that completely nullifies Parliament's constitutionally mandated control over selection of Supreme Court nominees. As the parliamentary lists of Supreme Court recruits became dramatically inflated, hardly a single law graduate from the main parties did not at one time or other become a candidate for nomination to the Supreme Court. In 1979, Parliament forwarded seven names for the single vacancy arising from Judge Lumbanradja's death; in 1980, a list of eighteen candidates for four vacancies was drawn up; in 1982, a list of sixty-six names was drafted for thirty vacancies; and in 1990, Parliament presented the president with a list of nine names for two vacancies.[54] One member of Parliament told me that he added to the list on a week's notice on the sole ground that, since the other parties had added names, his own PDI (Partai Demokrasi Indonesia, Indonesian Democratic Party) was eager to claim their turn (he was one of the senior law graduates in that party).[55] "Never stood a chance, of course," was his dry comment. Supreme Court judge Bismar Siregar sarcastically remarked that if in 1990 Parliament had cooked up a list of nine candidates for only two vacancies, how many did it think it would come up with the next year, when eight Supreme Court judges were due to retire? The parliamentary practice of inflating candidate lists undermines the "credibility" of the recruits, he said.[56]

---

[53] Personal communication, 19 July 1994.

[54] *Dewan Perwakilan Rakyat Republik Indonesia Periode 1977-1982* (Jakarta: DPR, n.d.), p. 42; *Hukum dan Pembangunan* 9,4 (1979): 448; *Kompas*, 8 December 1990.

[55] Personal communication, 19 July 1994.

[56] Bismar Siregar, "Pencalonan Hakim Agung," *Varia Peradilan* 6,67 (April 1991): 123-25. In this article, Bismar also notes that the Supreme Court itself is much better placed to select candidates than Parliament. So instead of adding names to the list drawn up by the Supreme Court and the Department of Justice, Parliament should shut up and agree with the Court's proposals. It is a characteristic point for a career judge to make, and indeed only has validity in the context of a career judiciary. The question is whether that is the kind of judiciary Indonesia and Parliament ultimately want.

Bismar's point is valid. If Parliament wants to uphold the authority of judicial office, it must not use its power to select candidates so sloppily. In fact, the role of Parliament in Supreme Court recruitment since the 1970s has been essentially passive. It has not subjected the Mah-Dep list to serious scrutiny and has selected its own candidates on the basis of party affiliation rather than professional appraisal. The inflated lists erode parliamentary control over government appointments to the Supreme Court and deplete the authority of the Court judges who go through the charade. The 1985 debates revealed broadly shared frustrations in Parliament regarding its own political impotence. They also showed that the parliamentary struggle for a different Court was an institutional struggle between Parliament and the government in the Indonesian political and constitutional order.

(ii) The 1985 Debates and Their Outcome: Law no.14/1985

The Bill. The 1985 Bill[57] was essentially aimed at maintaining the status quo. The government was obviously quite happy with the ad hoc procedures that enabled it to steer the recruitment process. Its prime concern was, therefore, to limit the role of Parliament. This meant that recruitment had to remain closed and, almost by implication, be based on the career system. The added benefit of the career system as it operated in Indonesia was that it made for a politically deferential and "clerkish" Supreme Court both in theory and in practice. The 1985 bill was oriented toward realizing these goals.

The bill proposed to select recruits exclusively from the career judiciary. A candidate had to have served for at least five years as chairman of an appellate court, or alternately for ten years as an appellate judge [art.6(c)]. The Official Elucidation of the law allowed for a small escape clause, however, whose portents were not immediately clear.[58] Moreover, the definition of the judges' professional qualifications in the bill, namely "with university or equivalent degrees in the field of civil law, criminal law, or constitutional law" [art.6(a)], made clear that recruitment was oriented toward the general courts. The definition notably excluded the religious courts (whose judges have professional expertise in Islamic law) and military courts (whose judges are expert in military law).[59] Art.7(1) again emphasized the closed character of recruitment, with a final restriction in art.7(2) stipulating that the chairman and vice-chairman of the Supreme Court henceforth would be recruited only from among sitting Court judges. This stipulation would end the tradition exemplified by the appointments of chairman Seno Adji through Mudjono to Ali Said, as these men had all been parachuted into the top job from outside the judiciary.

---

[57] The bill is published in the *Varia Peradilan* 1, Perdana (October 1985): 95-106.

[58] The elucidation says that, "if specific expertise is needed, persons who have not graduated in the field of law may be recruited, such as for instance judges in the sphere of administrative courts." The ambiguity rests in the fact that one might interpret this article as requiring only that a nominee to the courts hold a university degree, which would open up recruitment entirely, or, by virtue of the example given, as still requiring the candidate to have served as a professional judge.

[59] The Official Elucidation to art.7(1) allows the possibility of recruitment from the religious and military courts, which shows that framers of the 1985 bill intended such recruitment to be exceptional.

The law stated that Supreme Court judges were to be selected by the president on the basis of a list drafted by the Supreme Court chairman and the minister of justice and forwarded to Parliament "to be passed on to the president" [art.7(1)]. Under the bill, each new chairman would be appointed on the basis of a proposal by the residing Supreme Court chairman himself [art.7(2)].

Politically, it was a clumsy bill that trampled vested interests both in Parliament and even in the judiciary itself. By making it almost impossible for religious or military judges to get on the Court, it antagonized the religious PPP (Partai Persatuan Pembangunan, United Development Party) and military fractions in Parliament and also was in conflict with vested interests within the judiciary itself, which had its own special religious and military jurisdictions. The bill placed the Mah-Dep forum in the center of the recruitment process, reducing Parliament to a letter box. It was hard to escape the impression that the government did not think anything had changed since Guided Democracy.

Two causes, in particular, underlie the problems evident in a close examination of the 1985 Supreme Court Bill. First, the Bill, in fact, was not an original piece of work, but was a reworked version of an earlier piece of legislation. This prior version had been presented to Parliament in 1968, but had gotten buried during that turbulent period.[60] Coming soon after the 1965 law, the 1968 bill retained some vestiges of Guided Democracy thinking, such as its emphasis on the role in recruitment played by the precursors to the Mah-Dep forum. The second reason was that, while a number of Supreme Court judges had been asked to help draft the bill,[61] no members from other professional groups—notably, for instance, the advocacy or members of Parliament—had been asked to do so. As a result, the bill was almost entirely oriented toward the interests of the government and the Supreme Court (not including religious or military courts), and barely reflected other professional perspectives.

The Debates. Minister of Justice Ismael Saleh presented the bill with enthusiasm. He argued that the professional and political integrity of the Supreme Court could only be safeguarded by a closed career system, and in that argument referred to the quality (*mutu*), professional capacity (*kemampuan profesional*), intellectual maturity (*kematangan intellektual*), and moral integrity (*integritas moral*) of the Supreme Court.[62] What's more, said the minister, a closed career system fit with the way the entire government bureaucracy was organized.[63]

---

[60] Minister of Justice Ismael Saleh, Jawaban pemerintah atas pemandangan umum Fraksi-fraksi di DPR RI pada sidang Pari Purna DPR RI dated 4 Oktober 1985, p. 7.

[61] Direktorat Djenderal Pembinaan Hukum, *Undang-undang tentang ketentuan-ketentuan pokok kekuasaan kehakiman* (Jakarta: Departemen Kehakiman, n.d.).

[62] Minister of Justice, "Dewan Perwakilan Rakyat RI, Persidangan I Rapat Paripurna Terbuka Ke-3 Tahun Sidang 1985-1986," dated 28 August 1985, pp. 12-13; also *Varia Peradilan* 1, Perdana (October 1985): 92.

[63] There are some aspects of the episode that merit more attention than can be given here, particularly the relationship between the minister of justice, Ismael Saleh, the Supreme Court chairman, Ali Said, and the vice-president, Sudharmono. All three were graduates of the Military Law Academy, with Sudharmono the senior graduate, followed by Ali Said and finally Ismael Saleh. Sudharmono established his power base when serving at the State Secretariat, which at the time controlled the lucrative and politically important government contracts. Ali Said and Ismael Saleh joined him there. After the fall of Ali Murtopo in the 1970s, Sudharmono was the principal political "operator," which is the usual way of referring to the

When the bill was first presented, the minister said no word about the method of recruitment. Apparently he felt that explicit reference to the guiding role of the Supreme Court and the Department of Justice in drafting the proposal, and the resulting marginalization of Parliament, were so natural as to merit no specific mention.

Parliament rallied to oppose the bill and the minister. It was motivated partly by its desire to strengthen its own institutional role, partly by some of the parties' professional interests, and partly by a desire to curtail the wide ambit of executive power in Indonesia. It concluded that breaking down the system of career recruitment and opening up the Supreme Court would answer all these points, for that reform would politicize recruitment, facilitating partisan appointments of the sort many party representatives desired, and potentially broaden the Court's political outlook. All this would in the end benefit Parliament. As a result, the political parties without exception opposed the government proposals on recruitment during the 1985 debates on the Supreme Court Bill.[64]

Legislative representatives did not appreciate the government's proposed scenario, according to which Parliament would function as a kind of "dispatch service" (*kurir*), as one party put it,[65] for passing on lists of recruits drawn up by the Supreme Court and the Departments of Justice. "It should be we who do the proposing," one MP said.[66] "We do not want to be only a post office," exclaimed another MP (but because by that time the atmosphere was becoming so tense, it was decided to strike his exclamation from the parliamentary records).[67] There was serious and justified concern that the Supreme Court and government would just "wrap up Supreme Court candidates in a tidy package, which it would pass on directly to the president," as the government party put it.[68] During a conference in Bandung concerning the issue, Albert Hasibuan said that parliamentary input was required precisely because it constituted the democratic legitimation for judicial

---

principal political power brokers acting on behalf of President Suharto. As he was not a field officer, Sudharmono was traditionally opposed by the army, a conflict that resulted in a political crisis when his candidacy for vice-president was announced. During his heyday from the late 1970s to the late 1980s, Sudharmono took on legal institutions as his bailiwick, which explains the consecutive appointments of Ali Said and Ismael Saleh to top legal jobs. By extension, access to these institutions for army loyalists was hard. Sudharmono's control was only broken with the appointment of General Djaelani as Supreme Court vice-chairman in 1992, as Djaelani did not belong to the Sudharmono group. Ali Said, a wily and independent political agent, looked down somewhat on Ismael Saleh, and was widely perceived as his intellectual superior. Ismael Saleh's awkward operation generated quite a bit of opposition in legal circles, as discussed in earlier chapters. However, Ismael Saleh may be given too little credit, in view of the fact that much of the new legislation on the judiciary was realized under his administration at the Department of Justice, not that of Ali Said. The fact that the 1985 bill so expressly undercut Ali Said's position at the Supreme Court (since Ali Said was a non-judicial recruit) may be a result, in part, of the petty infighting between the two.

[64] Parliament received support from unexpected circles. Thus, former Supreme Court chairman Seno Adji, with his unbeatable knack for sensing the way the wind was blowing, argued in the press that the role of Parliament should not be that of a mere rubber stamp. *Kompas*, 13 September 1985.

[65] *Sinar Harapan*, 8 October 1985.

[66] *Kompas*, 7 November 1985.

[67] *Kompas*, 20 November 1985.

[68] *Sinar Harapan*, 20 November 1985.

recruitment.[69] During the debates, Parliament, with the government Golkar party at point position, asserted that constitutional principle required that Parliament participate actively in this process.[70]

This issue provided the springboard for questioning the recruitment system in its entirety. In fact, none of the parliamentary parties liked the idea of closed recruitment as it was proposed in the bill. Some of the opposition was motivated by parochial reasons; for example, the religious and military parties felt that the bill excluded access to the Supreme Court for religious and military judges.[71] But there was a more fundamental challenge to the very system of closed recruitment. Unexpectedly, it was the government KP (Karya Pembangunan, or Fraction Golongan Karya, Golkar) party that voiced this fundamental point and proved unwilling to accept the government's contention that career recruitment would guarantee the professional and political integrity of the judiciary. From its perspective, the closed recruitment system might have precisely the opposite effect, that is, it might condition judges to political subservience and professional sterility. "Might it not be," the first party spokesman Albert Hasibuan said, "that career judges have a narrow outlook that comes from working in one environment only?" The party stated that it was not prepared to accept recruitment to the Supreme Court on the basis of the career system only.[72] "Recruitment must be opened

---

[69] *Sinar Harapan*, 18 November 1985; *Sinar Harapan*, 20 November 1985.

[70] *Kompas*, 18 November 1985; *Sinar Harapan*, 20 November 1985.

[71] Drs. Hanefa for the Fraksi ABRI, *Varia Peradilan* 1, Perdana (October 1985): 89. Harahap for the Fraksi PPP, ibid., p. 78.

[72] *Varia Peradilan* 1, Perdana (October 1985): 52. Hasibuan's role in the 1985 debates belies the simplistic picture of the government KP party as entirely subservient to Suharto. Hasibuan has a subtle mind. His professional background was that of an advocate, initially as a vocal critic of the government in legal aid circles. At one point he decided to work inside the system, without relinquishing his ideals of changing it, I would argue. Though opponents to the government never fully forgave him for this shift, Hasibuan did try to reform the system from within. He was the one who saved the newspaper *Sinar Harapan* from complete dissolution when it was banned in the 1980s. He was also the person to open the debate on recruitment in Parliament as a spokesman for the government party, but contrary to expectations he voiced the most serious and fundamental criticism of the bill to date. He did not reappear after the opening statement. The reason lies outside Parliament and had little to do with the views he expressed, which were admirably defended later on by another KP spokesman, Baramuli. What happened was that in the course of 1985, the government had been putting into effect a plan engineered by Ali Said aimed at bringing all Indonesian advocates into one organization. Until then, the advocates were by and large members of two professional organizations, one of which (IKADIN, Ikatan Advokat Indonesia, Association of Indonesian Lawyers) was rather critical of the government. By bringing them under one roof, the government aimed at controlling the critical advocates more effectively. By fall 1985, the plan was succeeding, and the new organization (PERADIN, Persatuan Advokat Indonesia, Indonesian Advocates' Association) was established. Nevertheless, and contrary to all plans and expectations, the opposition advocates won elections to the board, and the new organization misfired badly. Hasibuan was a member of the critical IKADIN group and played an important role in frustrating government plans. In fact, this led to his election as secretary-general of the organization in 1985. His role in the advocates' affair, and particularly his confrontation of Supreme Court chairman, Ali Said, evidently complicated his position in the parliamentary debates on the 1985 Supreme Court Bill. This may have been a factor in his withdrawal as spokesman of the government party on the bill. This withdrawal did not prevent him from speaking up, however. Thus, Hasibuan figured prominently in a conference on the 1985 Supreme Court Bill organized in Bandung, and he stated his views clearly in a series of newspaper articles that appeared during the debates. See *Sinar Harapan*, 25 & 26 October 1985; *Kompas*, 11 November 1985; *Angkatan Bersenjata*, 11

up."[73] The notoriously opposition-minded PDI supported this proposition, emphasizing that the closed career system was no guarantee at all for professional integrity. "How good it would be if the career system were to be matched with a system based on achievement," the party spokesman exclaimed provocatively, making it clear that he did not believe the system currently worked by rewarding merit. Might it not be advisable in this context, the party wondered, to open up the Court to politicians, lawyers, and professors with proven expertise and integrity?[74]

The recruitment issue was, then, evolving into an institutional struggle between Parliament and government. In its assault on the bill, Parliament was joined by the private sector, notably the advocacy, which had argued for a long time that lawyers ought to be considered for judicial posts. It held to the view that the Supreme Court's political conservatism was rooted in the system of closed recruitment. Outside recruits from advocacy circles would enhance the Court by providing both the professional skill and political personality required to turn it around and develop it into a truly powerful institution.[75] The most determined expression of these ideas (aside from Albert Hasibuan's in Parliament, of course) perhaps came from prominent lawyer and human rights activist Mulya Lubis, who fully agreed with the KP parliamentary party. He too argued that government was mistaken in its judgment that the professional and political integrity of the judiciary would benefit from closed recruitment; according to him, in such a system advancement was too much determined by seniority, rather than ability. Outside recruitment would have the effect of strengthening quality, he argued, because it would bring in fresh blood and competition, and in that way constitute a form of

---

November 1985; *Pelita*, 13 November 1985; *Kompas*, 18 November 1985; *Sinar Harapan*, 20 November 1985. On Ali Said's disappointment at the outcome of the advocates organization and his opposition to the new board, see also *Kompas*, 4 December 1985.

[73] Albert Hasibuan quoted in *Suara Karya*, 18 November 1985. Parliament argued that precisely because the Supreme Court was one of the superior organs of state, as reflected in the fact that Court judges were state officials, recruitment should be opened up, just as it was for the other institutions. *Kompas*, 19, 20 November 1985.

[74] *Varia Peradilan* 1, Perdana (October 1985): 67.

[75] The Indonesian advocacy has a tendency to oversimplify the issue, perhaps as a result of tactical considerations, for it actually does function as a lobby. Even so, judges should be given more credit than many advocates are prepared to grant. Simply put, the advocates assert that they should be recruited to the Supreme Court and that this action would substantially improve the judiciary. In the process, they conveniently forget that many advocates who were invited to become Supreme Court judges in past years declined, as noted above. This was understandable in view of the dramatic drop in income (and status in the commercial world of Jakarta) that such a "promotion" would involve. In addition, Supreme Court work is in large part stifling by the standards of "jet-setting" advocates. Lawyers can select their cases, control their offices and firms, and have a sense of power, control, and freedom that Supreme Court judges do not share. The Supreme Court judges, in large part, follow a dreary and thankless routine in an environment marked by all sorts of bureaucratic constraints and unrewarded by social respect. It is not so clear how many of the most active, promising, and successful advocates who are most vocal on the issue would themselves be prepared to submit to current Supreme Court working conditions, routines, and environment. But even if they were, it is unclear whether the appointment of a greater number of advocates would have sufficient impact on the bulk of the Supreme Court and the judiciary to change much of anything. Maybe the professional background of advocates inclines them to overstate their case and have excessive confidence in their ability to overhaul the judiciary. This does not deny that their impact on the Court would change it to some degree.

internal quality control.[76] But the fundamental problem, he stated, rested with the political outlook of career judges: "The career service and the cooptation of the judiciary in the civil service only serves to tie judges to the political system and erodes their personal value."[77]

During a parliamentary hearing, university professor Satjipto Rahardjo also argued in favor of opening up recruitment. He argued that sound professional criteria warranted such a step.[78] More important, perhaps, in a separate newspaper article Satjipto indicated that much depended on the distribution of power between Parliament and the government. The way in which Parliament realized its role in shaping the judiciary was central to this issue and would have a significant impact on the courts, he said.[79]

For their part, the judges quite liked the bill, which they had helped draft in the first place. They wanted to maintain the career judiciary's monopoly over Supreme Court recruitment and keep a firm grip on the recruitment process through the Mah-Dep forum. Institutional interests partially motivated the response; judges contended that open recruitment would harm their career prospects and thus lower morale. "If the Supreme Court is opened up for outside recruitment," commented a lower judge, "this will kill off the entire career system and the expectations and professional ambition of career judges."[80] Bismar Siregar, later a Supreme Court judge, claimed that the competitive nature of the career system, with a Supreme Court appointment as possible reward, induced judges to do their best.[81] Judicial resistance in this case was also based on experience, which showed that external appointments were primarily directed toward increasing government leverage on the Court, not to enhancing the judiciary's professional expertise. Over the previous ten years, the government had appointed generals and public prosecutors to the bench who had little understanding of the judiciary's place, felt little allegiance to the institution, and were generally unskilled in court work or the intricacies of civil law, in particular. Thus career judges concluded that open recruitment tended to weaken the Court, both professionally and politically. As a result, they took the view that the best guarantee for increasing the Court's professional quality and political strength was to screen it off from the political sphere entirely. During a conference on the bill, organized at the Legal Polytechnic in Bandung in October 1985, former Supreme Court chairman Subekti voiced what was on many judges' minds:

> I am positively delighted with the bill. Restricting recruitment to professional judges will best ensure the professionalism and integrity of the judiciary. It

---

[76] *Sinar Harapan*, 18 November 1985.

[77] Forum diskusi Human Rights Organization LBH Yogyakarta, *Kedaulatan Rakyat* 5 (October 1985).

[78] *Suara Karya*, 2 November 1985; *Kompas*, 2 November 1985. He argued that the closed career system had the effect of isolating judges from their environment and subjecting them to the bureaucratic rules of their service—increasingly so as they reached the top. From his perspective, if Supreme Court judges wanted their institution to match the professional quality that society expected from them, members would have to be recruited directly from that society.

[79] *Kompas*, 6 November 1985.

[80] Amarullah Salim, chairman of the court for the Central Jakarta district, *Sinar Harapan*, 15 November 1985.

[81] *Kompas*, 20 November 1985.

will finally put an end to the practice in which persons who never did any judging before are appointed to the Supreme Court.[82]

The reactions from Parliament and the private sector shook the Judges' Association members. They might manage a handful of religious and military judges, but the idea of completely overhauling the recruitment system and opening it up to outsiders, as a response to perceived failings of the judiciary, cut at the roots of their professional self-esteem and their political program. The Judges' Association decided to join forces with the government and take a stand.

The Association's leadership organized a meeting with all regional representatives, who issued a statement asserting that, in order to have an "able and strong court, with intellectual maturity and moral integrity," it was essential that "the function of Supreme Court judge not be political, but based on a closed career system." The wording is almost literally the same as that of the minister of justice in his opening statement in Parliament two weeks before. This was presumably no coincidence, but designed to give the stance of the Judges' Association extra political clout. The Association's leadership added that it had been constitutional *practice* over the years to place the Supreme Court and the Department of Justice at the center of the recruitment process.[83] It hastened to add, however, that this did not, of course, exclude Parliament, but meant only that the former institutions would make the first pass, with Parliament heading in the ball.[84] The Association's leadership then went to Parliament and presented this statement to its chairman.[85]

Also taken aback by the parliamentary reaction, minister of justice Ismael Saleh dug in his heels.[86] He tried to ease the atmosphere with some banter and

---

[82] *Sinar Harapan*, 12 October 1985. Note that Subekti on later occasions did not exclude the possibility of recruiting outsiders, notably university professors and advocates. *Berita Buana*, 15 October 1985.

[83] *Kompas*, 21 November 1985.

[84] *Terbit*, 21 November 1985.

[85] For good measure, the letter was published in the judges' law journal, *Varia Peradilan* 1,3 (December 1985): 14-16. This was a courageous decision, not in the least because the Supreme Court chairman, Ali Said, was likely to disapprove. In fact, Ali Said, a former general who had just moved into the judiciary from government, did not like the Judges' Association or what it stood for; it has even been said that he did not like the judiciary as a whole. The chairman had come into conflict with the Association some months before, in June 1985, after the Judges' Association made another presentation to Parliament, reiterating its contention that the administration of the judiciary should be transferred from the Department of Justice to the Supreme Court. This stance had been supported both quietly and overtly by previous Supreme Court chairmen, notably Subekti and even Mudjono, but Ali Said was different. He dissociated himself completely from it, reportedly stating, "There is no use in harking back to old songs." He indicated that he would summon the Association's leadership to his office to call them to order. The June affair was bad for the judiciary, as it exposed divisions within the institution. As had happened so many times before, the Supreme Court leadership failed to support rank-and-file ambitions and claims. For members of the Association, the June affair underscored its point that outside recruits to the Supreme Court had no appreciation of what the judiciary needed, and that they were essentially appointed as instruments of political control who ultimately weakened the institution. As a result, the incident stiffened the Association's resolve to try and exclude outside recruits from the judiciary.

[86] *Kompas*, 18 November 1985, describes him as being "stubborn." Continuous lack of agreement forced repeated suspensions of sessions. The minister reverted to the tactic of having "special committees" work out the problems. He used this tactic so frequently that he developed a special

joking,[87] but Parliament was not in a mood for small talk. At one point, the session developed into a full-fledged swearing match.[88] The minister was fully aware of what was at stake here. Denying that Parliament would only function as a "bus stop,"[89] he also said that if recruitment were to be opened up along the lines proposed by Parliament, the Supreme Court would become politicized (*mempolitisir*),[90] an unfortunate development. This viewpoint was reiterated by the Judges' Association, which published its resolution under a heading that identified Supreme Court functions as "non-political."[91] This terminology and approach originated in the nineteenth-century civil law perception of judges as clerks, administrators of the law who had no political role.

This perspective on the role of the Court differed fundamentally from that prevailing in Parliament, particularly in the KP and PD (Partai Demokrat, Democrat Party) parties. "Why, it is evident that the Supreme Court is not just a legal institution or a common court, it is very much a political institution. How can one distinguish between law and politics?" was the parliamentary reaction.[92]

Given such divergent views on recruitment and, more generally, on the role of the Supreme Court in the modern Indonesian state, the debate was clearly deadlocked. As late as December 3, 1985 and while the rest of the bill had been agreed upon, the recruitment issue remained unresolved.[93] In response to this crisis, Parliament simply put a stop to debate on the issue.[94] The parliamentary KP party, with backing of the PD party, held firm, stating that it would not give way on the issue unless ordered to do so by the leadership of the government's overarching GOLKAR party.[95] There were in fact rumors that the impasse would be addressed at the highest—presumably presidential—levels for resolution.[96]

Law no.14/1985. In the end, the new Supreme Court Law no.14/1985 was presented as a compromise. In its hotly debated art.7(1), the law provided that Supreme Court judges would have to (a) be of Indonesian nationality, (b) be true to the Almighty, (c) be faithful to the state ideology Pancasila, (d) not be associated

---

word for it: "*dipanjakan*" (based on the root *Panitia Kerja*, becoming *Panja*, which is here made into the verb).

[87] The minister said at one point that "if we open the door [of recruitment], we'll let the wind in; now, we don't want the wind to enter, do we?!" The Indonesian term for "wind entering" (*masuk angin*) is commonly used to describe catching the flu. *Pelita*, 19 November 1985.

[88] *Sinar Harapan*, 20 November 1985. The minister, in fact, demonstrated a knack for rubbing Parliament the wrong way. He refused to describe the situation as "confrontational," stating that "usually, after a day or two, parties will find their way out of this." This suggested that Parliament was to blame in the matter, so that the statement failed to calm and instead complicated the situation. *Kompas*, 20 November 1985.

[89] *Sinar Harapan*, 20 November 1985.

[90] *Pelita*, 19 November 1985.

[91] *Varia Peradilan* 1,3 (December 1985): 14-16.

[92] See for instance MP (Member of Parliament) Sastrosehardjo for the KP (Karya Pembangunan) in Dewan Perwakilan Rakyat RI, Persidangan II Rapat Paripurna Terbuka Ke-18 1985-1986, p. 44.

[93] *Suara Karya*, 3 December 1983; *Kompas*, 3 December 1983.

[94] *Suara Karya*, 9 December 1985.

[95] *Kompas*, 4 December 1985.

[96] *Suara Karya*, 3 December 1985.

with the former Communist party or 1965 uprising, (e) have a university law degree, or a university degree with legal expertise, (f) be no younger than fifty years of age, and (g) demonstrate honest and good behavior. There were compromise elements in this final draft of the article, particularly in the way it added mention of religious and military law to the original section requiring judicial candidates to have expertise in criminal, civil, and administrative law; this was done to accommodate the religious and military parliamentary parties, no doubt, as well as the special courts.[97]

Provision 7(1)(g) made it clear that the prime recruits for the Supreme Court would, in the first place, come from the professional judiciary. It stated that a Supreme Court recruit would have to have had at least five years' experience as a chairman of an appellate court or ten years as a judge in an appellate court. There were some compromises here as well; thus, art.7(2) stated that outside recruitment would be allowed on the condition that the recruit had had at least fifteen years' experience in the field of law. This provision opened the door for recruitment from the private legal professions. Nevertheless, the Official Elucidation clearly established that such outside recruitment would be the exception rather than the norm: "In principle Supreme Court judges are recruited on the basis of the closed career system. Nevertheless, in specific cases, Supreme Court judges can also be appointed from outside this system."

As regards procedure, the terminology of the Bill was watered down, but not completely dissolved. Art.8(1) said that judges would be appointed by the president on the basis of a list drawn up by Parliament. Art.8(2) stated, however, that the parliamentary list would be drawn up in consultation with the Supreme Court and the government. Thus, the initiating and guiding role of the Mah-Dep forum was ensconced in law notwithstanding parliamentary protests. Here another compromise was introduced to help satisfy all parties: in making recruitment decisions, the government would be expected to consult not only with the minister of justice (a process that which would naturally favor Supreme Court recruits coming from the General and Administrative Courts), but with the minister concerned, a provision meant to accommodate the ministers of religion and of defense.

The compromise formulae could hardly disguise the fact that the law was a victory for the government and the judges. It firmly entrenched the Supreme Court in nineteenth-century civil law thinking. The pro forma drafting of the list of recruits by Parliament and selection by the president did not fundamentally affect the Mah-Dep forum's decisive, supervisory role in the recruitment process. Supreme Court recruitment would be essentially non-political and closed. Notwithstanding its resistance, Parliament had again been marginalized.

(iii) Some Realities of Supreme Court Recruitment

The 1985 Law, then, confirmed the key position of the Mah-Dep forum in the Supreme Court recruitment process, enabling the government and the Court to maintain tight control over the system, which would be essentially "closed," with some rare exceptions.

The Supreme Court chairman and the minister of justice preside over the Mah-Dep forum. Sometimes they call other representatives to the meeting, notably the

---

[97] Official Elucidation art.7.

Supreme Court vice-chairman and the director general of Courts Upgrading. Typically, the Court begins by offering a proposed list of candidates drawn up by the Supreme Court chairman, usually after consultation with the Court leadership, i.e., the vice-chairman and junior chairmen. Junior chairman Olden Bidara, for instance, was said to have been highly influential in decisions concerning recruitment from the administrative jurisdiction.[98] Nevertheless, the junior chairmen ultimately have no control, only some influence. As noted previously, a Supreme Court junior chairman told me that when he objected to the proposed recruitment of one particular judge, the chairman just stared him down: ". . . the entire thrust of the conversation was: shut up, I am the one who decides."[99]

Compiling the list of recruits is a complicated process involving various methods and criteria. The first criterion concerns outright or presumed quality. Thus, when the Supreme Court was expanded in 1982, Mudjono recruited all the appeals court chairmen and junior chairmen. His actions were based on the military view that the higher the officers (or in this case, judges), the better they must be. In fact, however, many of the Outer Island appeals court judges had never dealt with complicated cases of the sort that originate in the big cities and were at a complete loss after arriving at the Supreme Court. Mudjono's recruitment program, as a result, had a negative effect on the quality of the Court, the more so because many of the judges recruited were comparatively young. As one Supreme Court judge recounted:

> Mudjono just had no idea about how the judiciary functioned, and quite simply had the appeals court chairmen and vice-chairmen appointed because these were the senior judges—even if they came from Aceh or Samarinda. In reality, these judges were much less well versed in the law than simple appeals court judges in Jakarta or Bandung, and the quality of the Supreme Court collapsed like a pudding.[100]

Another interview revealed the impact of Mudjono's reforms:

> The Mudjono recruits remain a problem to the present day. It is not just that these candidates revealed themselves to be mostly poor judges, but they were also young when they were appointed, so they have stuck with us a long time.[101]

The point is that Mudjono apparently had sufficient grip on the appointment process to implement his method of assessment, regardless of how mistaken he may have been.

Names may also be added to the recruitment list as a result of strategic name dropping and networking. One judge told me that, since it was impossible for the Supreme Court chairman to keep track of everyone in the extended judicial system, Court judges would often mention names offhandedly, favorably, to draw the chair's attention to certain junior judges, hoping that the chairman would then

---

[98] Personal communication, 22 January 1995.
[99] Personal communication, 16 July 1994.
[100] Personal communication, 11 July 1994.
[101] Personal communication, 28 June 1994.

"discover" this potential recruit, as it were, and in due time propose his or her name.[102] Candidates may also be considered thanks to their networks. As we shall discover in the next section, an astonishing number of judges have some kind of relationship with one another, sharing social or family backgrounds or being professionally linked in various ways. Such relationships can be influential in determining who gets added to the list. One Court junior chairman said of one of his (prominent) brethren on the Court:

> I was his senior. I was on the Supreme Court, and he was still an appeals court judge when he came to visit me with his wife to ask me to put him on the list of candidates. And I did, so he really owes his job to me.[103]

Candidates may also further their cause by currying favors, and, ultimately by paying up. Various sources confirmed that the way to advancement can be smoothed by giving presents or just paying money. As a member of Parliament put it to me:

> **MP:** I heard from various sides that sometimes judges pay to get their names on the list of candidates to the Supreme Court.
> **SP:** Who must they pay?
> **MP:** The Supreme Court chairman.[104]

In fact, as we shall see, certain judges who were put on the list and appointed to the Supreme Court had previously been found guilty of corruption and suffered disciplinary punishment.

The Supreme Court chairman's list is not entirely decisive, but it is very important in the Mah-Dep forum. It constitutes the opening bid in what one judge described to me as a "cow trade."[105] The list of candidates is presented to the Department of Justice, which will propose some changes, in part out of institutional pride and in part because it will have its own candidates to recommend, many of them channeled from wider government circles. Thus, recruits from the military and public prosecution are often added to the list at this juncture. There will some to-ing and fro-ing, during which both parties have to give a little, leading to final agreement.

> There is an ongoing tension between the Supreme Court and the Department of Justice regarding judicial recruitment. The general rule is that the Supreme Court comes with a list to the Mah-Dep, and the Department messes about in it. It's a real *tawar* [bartering] situation.[106]

How much each party gives away, and more importantly, what names they strike off, depend on their respective strengths and on the candidates involved. Sometimes, it appears, the Supreme Court leadership tends to overstate its case, i.e., add some names to the list with the sole aim of sacrificing them in the Mah-

---

[102] Personal communication, 4 July 1994.
[103] Personal communication, 10 May 1996.
[104] Personal communication, 19 July 1994; Personal communication, 9 May 1996.
[105] Personal communication, 4 July 1994.
[106] Ibid.

Dep forum. This "sacrifice" would then be presented as a concession, leaving the shorter list of core candidates intact. Personal chemistry is also important, of course. Thus, the fact that the pivotal figure at the Department of Justice, the director general for the judiciary, Mrs. S. Sugondo, was the niece of her judicial counterpart, Supreme Court chairman Purwoto Gandasubrata, in the early 1990s may have strengthened the Court's hand at the Mah-Dep bargaining table—particularly as Mrs. Sugondo reportedly respects Mr. Gandasubrata.[107]

As a result, the selection system is essentially one of qualified internal co-optation. The absence of public scrutiny is evidenced by the fact that sometimes Supreme Court judges with tarnished reputations are nominated. Describing the recruitment process as "fundamentally corrupt," one Supreme Court junior chairman went on as follows:

> A number of judges were actually convicted of corruption, but even so secured their appointment to the Supreme Court afterwards. There is this Supreme Court judge N., who in all three appeals courts where he served before coming here was involved in corruption affairs and actually was exposed. Even Supreme Court chairman Ali Said said at the time that it could not go on like this with judge N. So I expected that he would be fired, but what happens: he is appointed to the Supreme Court. Here he is not allowed to decide cases, but may only do administrative work. There are others like this. It's crazy.[108]

A number of examples confirm this bleak assessment. For instance, Supreme Court judge I. was actually punished for corruption before being appointed to the Court. Judge I had served on the controversial Jakarta appeals court targeted by the anti-corruption OPSTIB (Operasi Tertib, Anti-Corruption Operation) program in the early 1980s. Four judges from that court were removed as a result of that investigation, and some received prison terms. I. was one of the judges removed and advised to leave the judiciary. Subsequently he worked for two years at the Department of Justice, then in 1982 he reentered the judiciary and was assigned regular judicial duty as chairman of the Tanjung Karang appeal court. He was appointed to the Supreme Court in 1984.[109] Similar conditions prevailed in the Central Jakarta district court, and were exposed in May 1987, after judge M. had been accused of malfeasance. Following official investigations, almost all judges of that court were transferred in what the press clearly defined as a punitive action. Practically all disappeared into the wilderness, with the exception of judge M., who was promoted to the Supreme Court.[110]

---

[107] Personal communication, 23 August 1994.

[108] Personal communciation, 11 August 1994.

[109] Judge I. denies that his two years at the Department were a punishment, pointing out that he was not excluded from the normal rules of advancement and that he received regular salary increases. Still, this forced exile from the judiciary lowers one's status and is an instrument often used to reprimand judges. It is hard to define in other terms than punishment, however mild and symbolic an action it may be. *Tempo*, 16 June 1984, p. 59.

[110] *Merdeka*, 25 May 1987; *Prioritas*, 2 June 1987; *Bisnis*, 4 June 1987; *Suara Karya*, 6 June 1987; *Kompas*, 6 June 1987; transfer list in *Varia Peradilan* (October 1987); Personal communication, 13 June 1991.

(c) Conditions of Service and Tenure

Conditions of service and tenure of Supreme Court judges have never received much attention in Indonesian political and legal discourse, with the possible exception of the issue of salaries. The reason lies in the fact that, but for the brief and largely ineffectual Guided Democracy period, the Court's service and tenure conditions were never directly challenged by the Indonesian government. Even publications critical of the Indonesian legal system and judiciary have difficulty outlining precisely how the political loyalty of Supreme Court judges is ensured, for legal provisions seem solid and the government to date has never twisted the Court's arm to realize its goals—at least not openly.[111]

In fact, such tactics aren't necessary since the Supreme Court's political loyalty is ensured by other more discreet and effective methods. As we have already seen, these notably include the recruitment system, through which the judiciary is kept away altogether from politics. Unlike the situation in other developing countries, therefore, the government in Indonesia has never confronted or threatened Supreme Court judges directly. No Supreme Court judge was ever dismissed prematurely or had his pension rights revoked or was forced to resign on grounds of injudicious behavior.

Indeed, we will find that, with respect to the Supreme Court, Indonesian law essentially complies with and indeed respects international standards on judicial service and tenure, such as those inscribed in the "1985 UN Declaration on the Basic Principles on the Independence of the Judiciary." The Declaration requires that the conditions of office for judges, including their independence, security, adequate remuneration, conditions of service, pension, and age of retirement, be secured by law. Moreover, their tenure must be guaranteed until retirement. The Declaration further states that judges shall only be removed for reasons of incapacity or behavior that render them unfit to discharge their duties, a condition to be determined in independent review.[112] This section will briefly consider Indonesian law and practice in the context of two core issues: remuneration and retirement/dismissal.

---

[111] Publications critical of the system typically concentrate on the dual management of the lower courts, which are supervised by the Department of Justice and the Supreme Court, and claim that this system invites interference. They rarely speak about how the government ensures the political loyalty of the Supreme Court, since that Court is not subjected to dual management. Alternately, these publications focus on the *Mahmillub*, the extraordinary military courts instituted to decide the political cases resulting from the 1965 coup d'état, but these analyses do not tell us anything about political interference in the regular judiciary. International Commission of Jurists, *Indonesia and the Rule of Law* (London: Frances Printer, 1987), p. 61; J. Southwood and P. Flanagan, *Indonesia: Law, Propaganda, and Terror* (London: Zed Press, 1983), p. 151; T. Mulya Lubis, *In Search of Human Rights: Legal-political Dilemmas of Indonesia's New Order 1966-1990* (Jakarta: Gramedia, 1993), p. 96.

[112] The relevant articles run as follows: 11. The terms of office of judges, their independence, security, adequate remuneration, conditions of service, pensions, and the age of retirement shall be adequately secured by law. 12. Judges, whether appointed or elected, shall have guaranteed tenure until a mandatory retirement age or the expiry of their term of office, where such exists. [. . .] 18. Judges shall be subject to suspension or removal only for reasons of incapacity or behavior that renders them unfit to discharge their duties. [. . .] 20. Decisions in disciplinary, suspension or removal proceedings should be subject to an independent review. This principle may not apply to the decisions of the highest court and those of the legislature in impeachment or similar proceedings.

(i) Adequate Remuneration

As we have seen, the political struggle of the judiciary to a large extent consisted of a struggle for better salaries. Nevertheless, this effort was very much restricted to the lower courts and, but for a few flare-ups, never really touched the Supreme Court to the same degree.[113] Indeed, it is said that when in the early 1970s the government proposed supplementing Supreme Court salaries with so-called "tactical funds," Subekti rejected the offer "because we don't need them."[114] He may have had other reasons as well, for the incidental nature of tactical funds almost inevitably would have increased the judges' dependence on the government, but at any rate he did not think conditions sufficiently dire to motivate him to compromise on this point. Indeed, in 1986 a Supreme Court judge stated: "Supreme Court judges are financially okay. They earn about 1.2 million a month,"[115] and in 1994 another Court judge described his salary as "very good."[116]

Yet despite the fact that some Supreme Court judges may be satisfied with their salaries, there is a general feeling that the Court's judges earn too little. They are not very vocal about it, in part, no doubt, because in the context of the judiciary, generally, Supreme Court incomes are indeed excellent. In fact, even after the 1994 pay hike for lower court judges, the average Supreme Court income was four times as high as that of the most senior appeals court judge.[117] The problem is that many Supreme Court judges don't compare their situation with that of lower court judges, but instead look to their study mates from university who entered legal practice and made a fortune. As elsewhere, state salaries, even in the highest ranks, never match the incomes enjoyed by top lawyers, but in Indonesia the gap is so formidable that it fuels professional jealousy and dissatisfaction in the judicial ranks. In 1994 the average official income of a Supreme Court judge equaled that of a secretary in a Jakarta law firm (albeit a top secretary in a prestigious law firm).[118]

This dissatisfaction was probably a factor that helped convince members of the Supreme Court to accept "tactical funds" in recent years, and, in addition, to initiate an incentive system based on case turnover. Under the late New Order, the State Secretariat provided all Supreme Court judges with a supplement from "tactical funds." In addition, they received Rp.5,000 per case decided, part of

---

[113] See Chapter Three.

[114] In 1978, the Supreme Court judges made about Rp.300,000 a month and the chairman Rp.500,000. During Subekti's term, the government proposed increasing salaries to Rp.750,000, but the chairman rejected the proposal. *DSL,* 30 October 1978.

[115] *DSL,* 27 November 1987.

[116] Personal communication, 23 August 1994.

[117] Even after the 1994 pay hike, the most senior judge (with thirty-two years of service) in the lower courts only earned Rp.1,075,200 without supplements, i.e. a quarter of the average income received by Supreme Court judges. Government Regulation no.33/1994. According to a prominent member of the Judges' Association, Ali Boediarto, the ideal judicial salary would be around Rp.2-3 million. *Kompas,* 5 July 1995.

[118] Personal communication, 2 September 1994. The secretary netted US$30,000 a year, which more or less equals the average income of a Supreme Court judge, including various supplements. See hereafter.

which they were expected pass on to their staff.[119] The remuneration packages for different Supreme Court judges varied as a result. The average monthly compensation for 1992 can be summarized roughly as follows:[120]

Salary plus benefits:	Rp. 4,500,000
Special Allowance State Secretariat:	Rp. 500,000
Incentive for cases decided (minus typing pool costs)	Rp. 130,000
Total:	Rp. 5,130,000

In addition to this income, there were material benefits. Thus, on appointment, a Supreme Court judge received a one-time special allowance for the purchase of an official car. All Court judges got an official residence, for which a sum was deducted from their salaries. The house often was of rather poor quality, but because the amount deducted was also small (Rp.12,500 a month), most judges took it anyway.[121]

While these salaries were enough to live on, they could only support a modest lifestyle. Supreme Court judges who relied on their official income had to forswear the luxuries of Jakarta if they wanted to stay solvent, fueling dissatisfaction with their compensation packages.[122]

(ii) Retirement and Dismissal

According to the law, Supreme Court judges leave office in either of two ways. They may be honorably discharged, an action that follows automatically upon the realization of certain conditions, or dishonorably discharged in cases where an individual has been accused of behaving in a manner unbefitting a judge.

Honorable discharge occurs when a judge reaches the mandatory retirement age, or requests retirement, or if he has developed an incurable physical or mental disability, or, finally, if he reveals himself to be unfit to discharge his

---

[119] I was unable to trace how the system came into being, largely because Supreme Court judges viewed it as a fixture and did not wonder much about its origins. Personal communication, 23 August 1994.

[120] Personal communication, 23 August 1994.

[121] Personal communication, 23 August 1994. The judges can make a profit if they rent out the house, which many of them do.

[122] One academically inclined Supreme Court judge with a strong reputation for honesty wondered about the chic shopping complexes that are mushrooming in Jakarta and about who might shop there: "Why do they build these expensive shopping malls such as Pondok Indah if no one goes shopping there? And what persons, I wonder, do go shopping there?" Personal communication, 3 August 1994. In fact, the Pondok Indah Mall is often crowded, and not just with tourists and foreigners. This comment indicated to me that this Court judge, in all his honesty and naiveté, and on the basis of his lifestyle, found it hard to imagine shopping in the chic, expensive Jakarta malls.

duties—which the official description refers to as a "blunder" (art.11[1] law no.14/1985).

It is most common for judges to be honorably discharged upon retirement. Judges may retire from the judiciary of their own volition at any point, or upon reaching a certain age. The age limit was established at sixty for Supreme Court judges in 1950 (art.9[1]) and 1965 (art.43[2][d]). The 1950 law created an exemption "in the interests of the state," which was discontinued in 1965, however. Law no.14/1985 raised mandatory retirement age for all Supreme Court judges to sixty-five years (art.11[1][c]), without exceptions, although in fact there have been and still are some exceptions to the rule. For instance, Supreme Court judge Bismar Siregar was still in office in 1994, even though he had reached sixty-seven years of age, because of a simple error on his identification card: "He should have retired two years ago, but for this error on his identification card."[123] More problematic was the case of Seno Adji, who was appointed in 1974 at the age of fifty-eight and should have retired in 1976, but did not.

> Seno Adji was appointed slightly more than a year before his mandatory retirement age. But he just stayed in office when he reached it, with presidential benediction of course. Mind you, after his retirement from the Court he became a university professor until his death, even though the same retirement rules apply there also. It helps being family to Suharto.[124]

Seno Adji remained in office at the discretion of the president, an arrangement which, it may be pointed out, was unconstitutional.

Judges may also be dishonorably discharged or "dismissed." According to the latest legislation, Supreme Court judges can be dismissed if they commit a serious offence, offend public decency, are guilty of gross neglect in the realization of their functions, violate their oath of office, or violate restrictions associated with their function, as would happen if they served conjunctly as an advocate or an entrepreneur (Law no.14/1985 art.12[1] jo. Government Regulation no.13/1993). Prior to any dismissal, an impeachment procedure must be brought before a disciplinary council composed of Supreme Court judges (Law no.14/1985 art.12(2)).

As far as I could determine, there has never been an official impeachment procedure leading to the dismissal of a judge in Supreme Court history. This is not to say that Supreme Court judges were never investigated or that they were never forced to resign prematurely under pressure. The Supreme Court in fact had at least one near-miss impeachment and several premature resignations resulting from allegations of malfeasance.

The Court came nearest to impeaching one of its members in the early 1950s, when there were strong suspicions that Supreme Court judge Sutan Malikul Adil was involved in corruption. A committee was established to investigate the allegations, but in the end the case fizzled out, essentially because Supreme Court chairman Kusumah Atmadja, who had pursued the matter with vigor, died prematurely. Suspicions had been aroused by a smuggling case that Malikul Adil handled, in which he was expected to give advice to the president concerning

---

[123] Personal communication, 9 September 1994. As noted in *Forum Keadilan*, 3 September 1992, such errors are not infrequent in Indonesia.

[124] Personal communication, 29 June 1994.

amnesty. Adil gave his advice three times, sending it out, then taking it back, sending it out again, taking it back again, and so on, altering his recommendation each time. At first he advised the sentence be lightened, then proposed a bigger reduction, and finally he advised freeing the gold smuggler altogether. The final document sent to the Department of Justice showed these vacillations, as sections were marked out here and written over there in a way that caught the attention of a senior Department of Justice official, who mentioned it to the Supreme Court chairman, Kusumah Atmadja. Kusumah Atmadja was very strict and tough in dealing with corruption and insisted that every judge on the Supreme Court be absolutely clean. He forbade Malikul Adil from entering the Supreme Court building or working as a judge until the matter was resolved, so Adil stayed at home, with wages and car, and did no work. A committee was established to examine the evidence, but the members could not reach consensus. One member said that Adil was wrong, one said he was innocent and should return to court, and one took the middle road, concluding that Adil's actions were fishy, but that there was no firm evidence to show he had been corrupted. No action could be taken on the committee's findings as a result. Then Kusumah Atmadja died, and Wirjono replaced him. When the Department of Justice raised the matter with Wirjono, he cut short the discussion, saying that if officials were convinced Adil had done something wrong, he should be brought to trial, and never mind everything else. The judges on the Supreme Court did not want to take Adil back and threatened to resign if he returned, but in the end Adil did return and no one resigned.[125] (As we have seen, Supreme Court chairmen Wirjono Prodjodikoro and Soerjadi subsequently resigned prematurely from the Court, but these resignations arose out of conflicts within the judiciary and were voluntary.)

Even though no Supreme Court judge has been officially impeached, some judges have been forced to retire prematurely. Voluntary resignation is sometimes used as a cover to conceal the fact that a judge has been pressured to vacate his seat. A Supreme Court junior chairman described such a situation in 1994:

> ... last month a case came to light in which Supreme Court judges M.B., S. and S. all were bribed to the amount of 10 million. When the matter was exposed, the judges returned the money and that basically was it. Nothing really happened to them. S. died soon afterwards, S. was a month away from his retirement, and M.B. was gently nudged into early retirement. The chairman said, let's not make a fuss about this, the matter is resolved ...[126]

So early retirement may be a form of quasi-dismissal. I asked about how judges are "nudged" out of office:

> **SP:** How is pressure exerted on Supreme Court judges to get out prematurely? I mean, do they withhold salary and so on?
> **Supreme Court judge:** Oh no, such direct measures are not required. There are other effective means, such as creating an unpleasant working environment, whisper campaigns, and press actions.[127]

---

[125] DSL, 7 October 1960.

[126] Personal communication, 16 July 1994.

[127] Personal communication, 11 July 1994.

In short, whereas solid guarantees do exist to protect Supreme Court judges in Indonesia against arbitrary dismissal, there are underhanded ways by which they may be imposed upon to vacate office. These seem to be exceptional and rare occurrences.

2. THE ANATOMY OF THE SUPREME COURT

"I don't think anybody on the bus knows that I'm a Supreme Court judge," said one of the justices who takes a city bus to work. Indonesian judges keep a relatively low public profile, in a manner that typifies the brotherhood of civil judiciaries. In contrast to Anglo-Saxon courts, the Indonesian system abhors displays of judicial individuality. Like their brethren on the Dutch Supreme Court, the French *Cour de Cassation*, or the German *Bundesverfassungsgericht*, Supreme Court judges in Indonesia walk the streets unrecognized, spending their lives in relative anonymity.

In this section, I intend to pierce this veil of anonymity and find out who the judges on the Supreme Court are and how the composition of the Court has changed over the years. This is a pragmatic study of traits, rather than of dispositions.[128] It distinguishes between two sets of characteristics, the first relating to the professional background of the judges, namely their career patterns and education, and the second to their social background, namely their social class, family, place of origin, ethnicity, religion, and gender.

The second aim of this review is to clarify further Supreme Court recruitment methods. We have seen in the previous section that recruitment is largely managed by the Supreme Court chairman in conjunction with the Department of Justice in the Mah-Dep forum. Little was said, however, concerning how this was effected in practice. This chapter will investigate the ways in which the Supreme Court chairman helps shape the Court's composition and inclinations.

(a) Judicial Anonymity

The conceptual reasons underlying the judges' deliberate adoption of anonymity were dealt with in the previous chapter. They are based on the concept of the judge as an administrator of the law, a concept inherent in the civil system involving a *separation*, rather than *balance*, of powers; in this model, the clerkish judge performs an essentially passive, "mechanical" function. It is worth briefly reviewing some of the elements of this system and their manifestation in the Indonesian context, which will help reveal the complex anatomy of the Indonesian Supreme Court.

Judicial anonymity starts with the selection procedure, which, as we have seen, is highly bureaucratized. While Parliament nominally selects candidates, they do so on the basis of lists forwarded by the Supreme Court and the Department of Justice. Prior to *Reformasi*, there was no critical parliamentary hearing, as in

---

[128] J. Ten Kate and P. J. van Koppen, *Determinanten van privaatrechtelijke beslissingen* (Arnhem: Gouda Quint, 1984), p. 16, referring to J. P. Guildford, *Personality* (New York: McGraw-Hill, 1959).

the United States, to discover what candidates think about certain issues, what they presumably would do when faced by them, or what skeletons they might be hiding in their closets. Thus, when a judge retires and is replaced in Indonesia, the process is not as exciting as it is in the United States, and, what's more, the general public is given very little information about the new appointee and what he stands for.

As we have already seen, a career judge's work, whether carried out before or after his recruitment to the Supreme Court, does not reveal much about his thinking either. The civil system of collegiate decision making, which also found its way to Indonesia, allows little space for individual views to shine through in decisions, either in support or in dissent (certainly not in dissent). It is exceptional for judges to express themselves publicly on certain issues, in part, perhaps, because their bureaucratic experience does not incline them to assert opinions in public. Also, the consensual professional culture resists such manifestations of individuality: in one characteristic recent case, in which a Supreme Court judge dared to express his disagreement with a decision reached by his own Court, his behavior attracted obvious disapproval.[129] Decision making is reached by consensus (a process that should appeal to the supposedly consensual Indonesian society), or by vote in the exceedingly rare cases when views cannot be reconciled. This typically Continental judicial system, which has been imported to the archipelago, leaves no room for individual dissent and also fails to clarify who represents the majority.[130]

Court decisions are couched in a language and with traditional formulae that are purposely designed to conceal the judges' identities. The language of even the most forceful and important opinions is aimed at depersonalizing their presentation and neutralizing the contents (hence they make for dreary reading). This depersonalized quality is enhanced by the explicit legal obligation to

---

[129] Bismar Siregar, "Benarkah perkawinan beda agama rechtvacuum?" *Varia Peradilan* 4,50 (November 1989): 150-51. In his article, Bismar criticized a Supreme Court decision on interreligious marriage. In this decision, the Supreme Court had taken an important step toward creating its own law to allow interreligious marriage. It quashed a colonial regulation making such marriages possible on the grounds of its "secular" character. Finding that there was no statute to provide for the matter (*rechtsvacuum*, legal vacuum), it created a special procedure to enable such marriages to take place. Bismar argued in his article that the Supreme Court had erred on the point that, having quashed the colonial regulation, a legal vacuum had arisen. In his view, the Marriage Law no.1/1974 art.2(1), which provides for a marriage to be concluded in accordance with the religion of both parties, covered the issue of interreligious marriage. The natural consequence of this line of reasoning is that religious marriage prohibitions also apply, which would exclude marriage between Muslims and Hindus, for instance, or between Muslim women and non-Muslim men. This consequence was wholly unsatisfactory to the Indonesian government, and, presumably, to many judges on the Supreme Court, leading to the decision at issue. Many Supreme Court judges were angered by Bismar's article and felt that, particularly on so sensitive an issue, it was important to stick together. Bismar was soiling his own nest. As another Supreme Court judge put it to me: "Bismar went completely overboard. He is carried away by his ideas and his oratory. Criticizing the Court the way he did in the interreligious marriage case is beyond the pale." Personal communication, 21 September 1994.

[130] Dissents were introduced for select after *Reformasi*, starting with the Commercial Court, then the Constitutional Court and the Supreme Court itself. The first formal dissent issued by the Supreme Court was in the Akbar Tandjung corruption case in 2004. The career system prevents a wholesale introduction of the dissent system throughout the Indonesian judiciary. The reason is that dissents will generally involve junior judges disagreeing with superior judges. Since it is the senior judges who help determine the careers of the junior ones, the dissent system doesn't harmonize with a career system.

motivate decisions with reference to the law, which means that decisions must cite legislation, a practice that restricts the method and presentation of the Court's arguments. Unlike English or American court decisions, court decisions in civil law countries will probably never be regarded worthy for inclusion in literary compilations.

Supreme Courts in civil law countries, including Indonesia, tend to be large, a characteristic that serves to further obscure the distinct opinions of individual judges. Legislation in civil law countries often does not specify the number of Supreme Court judges to be appointed, establishing merely the minimum, but not the maximum, number, so that such courts tend to increase in size, with their composition in constant flux. In general sociological terms, the composition and outlook of such huge courts are nearly impossible to define, whether as a sum of their individual components or with respect to their overarching philosophy. The Indonesian Supreme Court is a prime example of the typically anonymous civil judiciary, and it functions in a way characterized by all the factors cited above, the most significant being its enormous size.

With the exception of Law no.1/1950, which set a minimum standard of six judges,[131] Indonesian legislation does not determine the size of the Court. Unfettered by legislation, the Court experienced a number of sudden and unexpected increases in its statutory size under the New Order in response to increasing workloads and changes in the judicial organization.[132] It must be noted that these increases were engineered by presidential intervention and were not expressed in legislation. Given this precedent, the president could presumably also reduce the size of the Supreme Court to levels authorized by law.

A further complication regarding size is that the Indonesian government has not always been consistent or prompt in filling vacancies as they arise. As a result, the statutory size and actual occupancy of the Court sometimes diverge considerably. The Guided Democracy government neglected to fill vacancies, so that by 1965 the number of Supreme Court judges had fallen to three, well below the statutory minimum of six judges mandated by Law no.1/1950. After the Court was brought up to statutory strength under the New Order, Seno Adji inherited a court of six judges in 1974. That same year the size of the Court was increased to nineteen, but by the time Seno Adji retired (1981), a number of Court vacancies had been left open and actual occupancy was back to twelve.[133] Similarly, when Mudjono succeeded Seno Adji, existing vacancies were filled, but within two months there were two vacancies that were not filled for the rest of the year.[134] It was only from 1982 onwards that the government proved more consistent in filling vacancies as they occurred.

This brings us to the third complication, common to all sizeable organizations, namely the large turnover of personnel. The large number of judges ensures constant shifts in court composition: judges come and go, usually due to retirements,

---

[131] Law no.1/1965 art.2.

[132] For the official correspondence, a variety of views on the issue of Court expansion, and the unexpected expansion by presidential intervention in 1974, see *Dewan Perwakilan Rakyat Republik Indonesia Periode 1971-1977*, pp. 41-44.

[133] *Tempo*, 2 February 1974, p. 8; *Tempo*, 20 September 1980, p. 44.

[134] *Catatan rapat Komisi III dengan Ketua Mahkamah Agung no.682/Kom.III/1982* dated 8 November 1982, p. 5.

occasionally to resignations. Thus, during Ali Said's eight-year administration (1984-1992), insofar as could be traced, fourteen judges resigned and were replaced. Unlike the US Supreme Court, with its judges who sit on the bench for years, Indonesia's Supreme Court is of a more fluid composition, with old names disappearing and new faces coming in all the time. While the Court evidently retains some important features and steering mechanisms over time, which qualify it generally as an entity, it is difficult for this group of judges to be regarded as a constant. The name lists occasionally published are often outdated by the time they come off the press.

When talking about the Court's anatomy, it is necessary to be specific regarding the constant shifts in Supreme Court composition that have resulted from changing statutory size, actual occupancy, and judicial turnover. For the purposes of this review, I will address this problem in two ways, first, by discussing the Court at those junctures when the statutory minimum was altered by the government. For practical purposes there were essentially two such expansions: one in 1974 when the Court was increased from six to nineteen judges, and the other in 1981-1982 when it was increased in two phases, initially from nineteen to twenty-four judges in 1981, and subsequently to fifty-one within a couple of months into the next year. Second, I will also discuss the specific administrations of its various chairmen. In the history of the Supreme Court over the past fifty years, there have been nine Supreme Court chairmen, namely Kusumah Atmadja (1945-1952), Wirjono Prodjodikoro (1952-1966), Soerjadi (1966-1968), Subekti (1968-1974), Seno Adji (1974-1981), Mudjono (1981-1984), Ali Said (1984-1992), Purwoto Gandasubrata (1992-1994); Soerjono (1994-1996), and finally Sarwata (1996-*Reformasi*).

(b) Professional Background

(i) Career Judges vs. Outsiders

The most important professional distinction among Supreme Court judges is their professional background, particularly whether they are career judges or recruits from outside the judiciary. The first outside recruits were appointed to the Court in 1974, most of them coming from the armed forces, complemented with a regular number from the public prosecution. No practicing lawyers were ever appointed to the Supreme Court. The breakdown can be briefly presented as follows.

Figure 1
Supreme Court Judges' Professional Background (Actual Occupation)

	1950	1954	1965	1968	1974	1982	1992	1994
Career	6	5	4	8	6	40	43	44
Military	-	-	-	-	3	8	5	5
Public pros.	-	-	-	-	1(+)	2	2	2
Other	-	-	-	-	-	1(*)	1(*)	-

(+) O. Seno Adji previously served as minister of justice and public prosecutor
(*) I Gde Jaksa previously served in Parliament

The major professional distinctions between the three groups of judges can be briefly described as follows.

The *career judges* all graduated from university and entered the judiciary at a young age, usually immediately after leaving law school.[135] They tend to closely identify with the judiciary and its interests, and, moreover, having served in the lower courts, are generally aware of the problems there. Finally, they have had varied professional experience, having dealt with both criminal and civil cases, the latter of which constitute the bulk of Supreme Court work.

The *former prosecutors* are also university graduates, but they enrolled in the prosecution. They moved up the prosecution hierarchy, and, upon reaching the top, switched to the Supreme Court. To date, prosecutors have only shifted into the courts after attaining the top job of *jaksa agung muda* (associate prosecutor general).[136] Having worked all their lives as prosecutors, their expertise is in criminal law. They may be familiar with some problems of the lower courts, if only because they interacted with those courts as prosecutors, but they often do not identify closely with the authority of judicial office at those levels because they always operated on the government side of the bench.

The *military judges*, unlike the former two groups, are not university graduates, as these candidates graduated from the law branch of the military academy — the Perguruan Tinggi Hukum Militer (PTHM, Military High School in Law) and the Akademi Hukum Militer (AHM, Academy of Military Law). As the certificate of graduation from AHM is equated with a university law degree, it was possible for graduates from these military academies to be recruited to the judiciary. Nevertheless, unlike the other two groups, military judges rarely have a professional background in actual legal practice. Their careers (epitomized

---

[135] There are, however, numerous exceptions to this standard. A number of judges first served a year or two in some other professional capacity. Thus, Supreme Court chairmen Purwoto and Soerjono started out as prosecutors, though very briefly. Chairman Soerjadi started out as a judge, but switched to the Public Prosecution during the early years of Guided Democracy, only to return to the judiciary in 1963. Bismar Siregar was a prosecutor during the first three years of his professional career (1957-1960). In all cases noted here, however, career judges invested from fifteen years upwards in the judiciary before promotion to the Supreme Court.

[136] Examples are Ismail Rahardjo and Kohar Hari Sumarno in the Mudjono and Ali Said Courts.

perhaps by general-judges Mudjono, who came over from Parliament, Ali Said, who switched from being minister of justice and chief public prosecutor, and Djaelani who had previously served as head of the military legal department) were more concerned with general administration and management, and only incidentally with adjudication.[137] Of the batch of military judges appointed to the Court in 1974, General Purwosunu had been chief of staff of the central coordinating office of intelligence (BAKIN, Badan Koordinasi Intelijen), General Hendrotomo previously served as head of the military legal section, and only General Kabul Arifin had ever performed as a judge (in military tribunals). Even if military appointees had experience as judges, this was invariably limited to the field of military criminal law. They have no expertise in the complicated civil cases that make up the Court's main burden.

Career judges in general, consequently, identify closely with the professional judiciary and are better prepared for the complicated cases brought before the Supreme Court. Former prosecutors may help out on criminal cases, but they are generally not well equipped to handle the civil cases, and they do not tend to identify as closely with the judiciary. The military judges lack both professional expertise and any sense of identification with the interests of the judiciary. As one civilian Supreme Court judge bluntly described one of his brethren: "He's from the military, so he's useless."[138]

Numerically the size of these groups has been uneven and subject to constant shifts. Three general observations can be made here.

First, outsiders were always a distinct minority, and career judges, in numerical terms, have dominated the Court throughout. From the time the first batch of non-judicial appointees arrived with Seno Adji in 1974, the proportion of outsiders has never exceeded 25 percent. Military and public prosecution judges remained at a steady 20 percent of the Court complement during the Mudjono and Ali Said years. In the 1992 Purwoto Court, there were five military judges (including admiral Suwardi Martowirono and Air Marshal [and later Chairman] Sarwata), as well as two public prosecutors, making the total number of outsiders around 17 percent.[139]

Second, particularly under the New Order government, outsiders, and notably military judges, are strongly represented in the leadership of the Supreme Court, and, as a result, wield power in excess of their numbers. When the New Order government got its hands on the Supreme Court after the retirement of chairman Subekti in 1974, for two decades it made certain that the Court was chaired by outsiders, with only a brief (four year) and fragmented interregnum during which

---

[137] Here again, this is the general rule. Note that both Mudjono and Ali Said did do some judging in the early days of their careers. Nevertheless, the emphasis of their careers was on general administration. Mudjono for instance, worked for a year or two in the Jakarta and Medan military courts, but soon switched to general administration where he worked for almost twenty-five years amongst other things as secretary-general of the Department of Agriculture, secretary-general of Parliament and minister of justice, before coming to the Supreme Court. *Varia Peradilan* 2,17 (February 1987).

[138] Personal communication, 16 July 1994.

[139] The first military judges were appointed in 1974, when they numbered three out of a total of sixteen judges (6.5 percent). There were no recruits from the public prosecution, unless, of course, one wishes to count the chairman, Seno Adji, as one. In the enlarged Mudjono Court of 1981, there were eight military judges (15 percent) and three judges from the public prosecution (barely 5 percent). This composition changed little until 1993.

Purwoto and Soerjono, professional judges, headed the Court. In that period, the Supreme Court was chaired by generals (Mudjono, Ali Said, and Sarwata), for a total of fourteen years, and military officers were active participants in the broader Court leadership even when it was in civilian hands. Thus, when the career judge Purwoto was chairman, General Djaelani was vice chairman, and the later chairman, Air Marshal Sarwata, was junior chairman. In the prevailing hierarchical Court organization, power thus is disproportionately weighted in favor of the non-career judges, particularly from the military branch. This trend is complemented by the fact that a number of these highly placed military judges are said to have strong connections with political leaders, such as President Suharto.[140]

Third, the professional background of outside recruits renders them ill prepared to deal with the bulk of the Supreme Court's workload, namely civil cases. This is probably the main reason why many outside recruits are concentrated in certain chambers; for example, the H team handles all cases originating from military courts. While this indicates that military judges specialize in certain kinds of cases, by the same token it means that they are minimally involved in other cases. At the same time, the role of civil judges in deciding military cases seems to be a thing of the past.[141] Even though the Supreme Court is a civilian state institution, military cases are handled exclusively by military personnel.[142]

---

[140] General Djaelani, who is widely regarded as a presidential favorite, has considerable political clout. He headed the National Commission investigating the 1991 Dili massacre. He was generally expected to replace Purwoto as Supreme Court chairman in 1994, but was dropped at the last moment in favor of the surprise appointee, Soerjono. A number of reasons can be advanced for his failure to secure the top job. One factor may have been that Djaelani lost backing from the armed forces as a result of the Dili Report. (Personal communication, 15 November 1994.) Another factor was that the appointment coincided with the discussion in the United States concerning whether to renew GSP trade conditions for Indonesia. This discussion was highlighted in the US media as a result of the APEC (Asian Petroleum Exporting Countries) conference in Jakarta, when President Clinton visited Indonesia. Former Supreme Court chairman Ali Said, who was consulted by President Suharto regarding the succession, obliquely referred to the fact that it might be politically inopportune to appoint a military man to the top judicial function at that particular juncture. In reaction, the government, through State Secretary Moerdiono, played down the military-civilian controversy. Note finally that the succession issue coincided with two other important developments that were possibly connected. The first was the internationally politicized case *Kedung Ombo*, which was decided by Purwoto on October 29, 1994, two days before his retirement, and in which he found in favor of the government. The second was a separate regulation by law of judicial salaries, in the course of which judges won a 100 percent pay raise. This regulation was officially announced two days after *Kedung Ombo*, on the day of Purwoto's retirement (1 November 1994). As we have seen, there are strong indications that this pay raise was the direct result of constant Purwoto lobbying with the president. The many lines and conflicting interests in all this suggest a trade-off in which *Kedung Ombo* was sacrificed by the Supreme Court in return for a pay raise, and Djaelani was sacrificed for Soerjono, to the benefit of both the Supreme Court/judiciary and the government. See generally *Forum Keadilan*, 24 November 1994.

[141] In Indonesian history, civil judges originally served conjunctly on the military supreme court, which effectively imposed civilian control over the military in judicial affairs. Even though the Supreme Court pretends to be the preeminent judicial body of the nation and civilian institution, the role distribution between former military personnel and civilian judges effectively means that the military now controls its own legal process.

[142] There is a problem with "former." As indicated before, there are strong indications that military Supreme Court personnel continue to be part of the military apparatus, as evidenced by the fact that general-judges can rise in rank in the military hierarchy even after their appointment to the Supreme Court.

(ii) Universities

The career judges, who constitute the majority of the Court are all university graduates,[143] and analysis shows a remarkable consistency in their university backgrounds over the past fifty years. They can be roughly divided into three groups, which coincide with periods of recruitment.

The Generation of the Old Guard: The Colonials. The first group consists of judges trained in the colony, sometimes with ongoing education in the Netherlands. They usually served in the colonial administration or judiciary. They enjoyed remarkable professional longevity and retained control over the Supreme Court for more than a quarter century after independence. In fact, until 1968 all Supreme Court judges were colony educated, and the last colonial graduates, Subekti and Abdurrachman, continued to lead the Court for an additional six years after that, retiring only in 1974.[144]

The Generation of the 50s: The Mohicans. The second group consists of the judges trained in the early years after independence, with many of them (though certainly not all) entering the judiciary before the collapse of Parliamentary Democracy in 1957. The first Supreme Court judges who were part of this wave, Asikin Kusumah Atmadja, Sri Widoyati Soekito, and Busthanul Arifin, were appointed in 1968. The group came almost entirely from one of two universities, namely the Jakarta-based Universitas Indonesia or Gadjah Mada University in Yogyakarta.[145] They have dominated the Supreme Court until the present day, but their power is currently fading. In fact they have started calling themselves "the last of the Mohicans," reflecting the fact that a new group of judges is progressively taking over.[146]

The New Generation. The third group of judges yet has to break through, as the last of the Mohicans are still holding out. Still, the members of the younger group have sufficient seniority to qualify for nomination and are eagerly waiting in the wings of the appellate courts to make their entry on the Supreme Court's center stage. This group is distinguished from the second in that it was not educated in the 1950s, is more diversified in its university backgrounds, and did not enter the

---

[143] In the history of the Supreme Court, only a single judge never acquired full academic honors. This was Sutan Abdul Hakim, who was a graduate of the colonial *rechtsschool*. What constitutes academic honors, of course, is a relative concept. The first two generations of Supreme Court judges argue that the requirements for a modern Indonesian law degree are far below old standards, while the professional judges tend to regard a law degree from the military academy (AHM) as having little value.

[144] There was a clear preference on the part of the old Court to recruit good judges, regardless of their political antecedents. The fact that Supreme Court judge Abdurrahman had apparently sided with the Dutch during the revolution caused some tensions within the judiciary, since when promoted he bypassed other judges who had been politically loyal to the Republic but lacked a law degree. DSL, 9 July 1960. Abdurrahman's son in the 1990s became personal assistant to the Supreme Court chairman.

[145] Though not exclusively. Thus, junior chairman Olden Bidara came from Universitas Hasanuddin in Ujung Pandang. Personal communication, 31 August 1994.

[146] Personal communication, 28 June 1994. Sometimes this is stated in Dutch, a language still mastered by this generation but lost in the next, a fact that reinforces the distinction.

judiciary until well after the collapse of Parliamentary Democracy, generally in the New Order. The first of these new recruits are now entering the Court.[147]

Figure 2
University Background (Actual Occupation)[148]

	1950	1954	1965	1968	1974	1982	1992	1994
UI	-	-	-	2	4	17	18	-
Gadjah Mada	-	-	-	3	9	18	15	-
Mil. Academy (AHM)	-	-	-	3	8	6	5	-
Colonial	6	5	3	2	-	-	-	-
Other	-	-	-	-	-	2	3	4

Universitas Indonesia and Universitas Gadjah Mada dominate Supreme Court recruitment in part because until the late 1950s these were the only two universities in Indonesia. With many more universities established under Guided Democracy and the New Order, the academic background of the third wave of judges (will) show greater diversity. Already now, it is increasingly difficult to pin down the relevance of the judges' academic background in recruitment or social bonding. Figure 2 gives an impression of the judges' university backgrounds.

A notable aspect of university backgrounds not reflected in Figure 2 is that, at least regarding the second wave of appointees (the Mohicans), Supreme Court judges don't come only from the same university, they even seem to be bunched together into classes. Thus, in the Mudjono and Ali Said Courts, a total of seven Supreme Court judges studied together in Universitas Indonesia and graduated in the same year (1955). Chairman Purwoto Gandasubrata belonged to that group, and under his administration an additional recruit from that august graduation year

---

[147] The seven principal state universities in Indonesia, referred to sometimes as the "seven samurai," are Universitas Indonesia (Jakarta), Universitas Gadjah Mada (Yogyakarta), Universitas Diponegoro (Semarang), Universitas Padjadjaran (Bandung), Universitas Airlangga (Surabaya), Universitas Hasanuddin (Ujung Pandang), and Universitas Sumatra Utara (Medan). While until the 1980s these were the most prestigious state universities and through that time they received preferential treatment from the government, currently funding is more diversified, and other universities, notably Andalas (Padang), are emerging. Moreover, challenging academic programs and excellent scholarship can be found at various private universities, such as Parahyangan (Bandung) and Satya Wacana (Salatiga). In the 1950s, the picture was much simpler. It may be noted that Padjadjaran was effectively established as a subsidiary to Universitas Indonesia, and even today sticks closely to its outward-looking orbit, with a strong tradition in comparative research, particularly oriented towards commercial and Anglo-American law. Similarly, Airlangga was established as a subsidiary to Gadjah Mada.

[148] No data could be found on one judge in 1968; eight judges in 1982; and nine judges in 1992. Note also that Seno Adji completed most of his studies at Gadjah Mada, but graduated from UI in 1949. Because he received most of his education at Gadjah Mada, I listed him as a Yogyakarta man.

joined the Court (Mrs. Retnowulan Sutianto).[149] Similarly, in the Mudjono court, four judges of the 1961 Gadjah Mada class served together.[150]

These collective appointments can in part be explained with reference to the specific conditions in the 1950s, when the individuals who would make up the "second wave" of judges graduated, as well as in 1982, when many of them were recruited to the Supreme Court. In the 1950s, very few law graduates entered the judiciary, and career opportunities for law graduates were good; it should be recalled that many judges at the time did not hold law degrees, which placed university graduates at an advantage. Relatively well-qualified judges could move speedily up the ladder and land top jobs.

The career of Supreme Court judge Purbowati is a case in point. Purbowati graduated in 1955, and, after a first brief posting in Sukabumi, was transferred in 1957 to the then established Special Court (PN Istimewah) for State Enterprise in Jakarta, where she became chairman in 1967-69. She then moved to the Jakarta appeals court in 1969 and was appointed to the Supreme Court in 1982. She served almost exclusively in Jakarta, which placed her at the political center and greatly increased her chances for nomination to the Supreme Court.

Few judges nowadays would be posted in a single city for so long.[151] The other judges in the 1955 Universitas Indonesia classes, or for that matter the 1961 Gadjah Mada classes, have comparable careers, one common denominator being that by the 1980s all had reached positions in the appellate tribunals. It was at this time that Supreme Court chairman Mudjono pushed through his plans for the drastic enlargement of the Supreme Court, and appellate chairmen were skimmed off to fill the newly created vacancies on the Court. It was as a result of these developments that cohorts of judges who had graduated together entered the Court.

---

[149] The complete list of 1955 graduates who became Supreme Court judges reads as follows: Purwoto S. Gandasubrata, Ismail Rahardjo, Poerbowati Djokosoedomo, Martina Notowidagdo, Siti Rosma, Karlinah Palmini, Retnowulan Sutianto. Note that Sri Widoyati Soekito, who preceded them on the Court, also belonged to this class.

[150] Siti Tanadjoel Tarki Soejardjono, Soebijantono, Soekamto Poerwopoetranto, and Soenarto.

[151] Formerly judges could spend their entire career on Java, a situation very unlikely nowadays. The judiciary at that time was not very geographically integrated. Advancement within the system was based on a case-by-case approach, in which personal connections were important, and general provisions outlining how transfers and advancements should be effected were lacking. The Java-centered career patterns of university graduates in those years were supported by the system of vocational judge schools (Sekolah Hakim Djaksa, SHD). These were situated in Medan and Ujung Pandang and primarly served the Outer Islands' judiciary. The SHD judges were non-university graduates, and as a result were handicapped when contending for the attractive postings on Java. Under the New Order, their lack of a degree effectively excluded them from rising beyond appellate level. All this does not deny that some university-educated elite judges did at times spend some time on the Outer Islands, but only in certain coveted postings. One of these was Tanjung Pinang, which at the time was the capital of Riau province. The post was attractive for a variety of reasons, such as the proximity to Singapore and the fact that salaries there were paid in dollars (for reasons that are not entirely clear, but may be related to the fact that this was a busy and challenging circuit). In any case, Asikin Kusumah Atmadja, Rusli, Kurdi, and later Pengadilan Istimewah chairman Azan Nasution, all of whom would eventually join the Supreme Court, also served at some time in Tanjung Pinang in the 1950s and 1960s. As recounted to me, these appointments were made in response to personal requests. This system was discontinued under the New Order. Personal communication, 3 August 1994.

Nevertheless, the personal connections of a shared university background provide an important bond for career development. Strong ties of loyalty and respect clearly exist within university classes and between classes.

> You must realize that for our generation, Asikin Kusumah Atmadja was the elder. A 1954 graduate, he was the first from Universitas Indonesia to become a judge. We all came after him, first Sri Widoyati Soekito and then the whole bunch from late 1955, Poerbowati, Karlinah, Martina, and Rosma. Purwoto, Gunawan, Aslamiah, Bismar Siregar, Retnowulan, and Soerjono came the year after. In 1957 came Dora Sasongko and Tomy Boestomi, and then, in 1958, people like Adi Andoyo [Soetjipto] and Moersiyah.[152]

In the administrative culture prevailing in Indonesia, such personal connections are a vital ingredient for career development. As one Supreme Court judge put it: "I was lucky, I knew Purwoto from university, and it helped me a lot."[153] What's more, alumni associations may facilitate networking. The Gadjah Mada alumni organization in particular is said to be well organized and purposeful in supporting "GaMa graduates," as they are generally referred to. As a result, there is talk of fairly cohesive blocks based on university ties and loyalites that aim "to take control" of government departments and state institutions. So these university and notably class loyalties may reflect both personal and institutional preferences in recruitment.

(iii) Secular/Nationalistic vs. Religious

The final characteristic of the career judges on the Supreme Court is that practically all came up through the general courts and graduated from non-religious universities. Judges with a religious orientation in their professional background hardly figure at all. Even though the Supreme Court serves as the final court of appeal to the Islamic courts, and Islamic courts are in fact staffed with graduates from religious universities, this has yet to be reflected in the Court composition. Only in 1993 was the monopoly of secularly trained judges broken with the appointment of a Supreme Court judge from the religious courts, Judge H. Taufik.[154] In 1995, this was followed with another appointment from the religious courts: Judge M. Muhaimin.[155]

While these appointments breached the wall, the Supreme Court judges who served on the general courts—who constitute a substantial majority of the Court—by and large seem to maintain a bias against religious judges. In fact, the religious judges recruited to the Supreme Court, besides being trained in religious law, are also graduates from regular law schools, as was specifically pointed out to me by a former Supreme Court chairman:

---

[152] Personal communication, 3 August 1994

[153] Personal communication, 7 August 1994.

[154] Interview, 9 September 1994. Mr. Taufik became vice chairman in 2000.

[155] Mr. M. Muhaimin came from the Semarang religious court of appeal. Personal communication, 19 October 1995

> **SP:** Is it correct that there is now a single judge from the religious courts on the Supreme Court?
>
> **Judge:** Yes, there is one. But note that he is a SH [Sarjana Hukum, Master of Law] also [i.e. graduated from regular law school]. It is not enough that religious judges graduate from religious universities [IAIN, Institut Agama Islam Negeri, State Institutes for the Study of Islam] only, they must have a law degree from the regular law schools. In fact, it is for this reason that many religious judges now do an additional law course of two years to get their SH degree.
>
> **SP:** So there is no direct access for judges who graduated from religious universities to the Supreme Court?
>
> **Judge:** No.
>
> **Judges' wife:** [looking at her husband] But that's not something you object to, isn't that so?
>
> **Judge:** [smiles][156]

The subtle bias against religious judges that this interview suggests was more forcefully expressed by other Supreme Court judges. As one of them said of his colleague: "He plays the Muslim card very heavily. That is dangerous."[157]

This attitude is characteristic throughout the Supreme Court's institutional history, being apparent, for example, in the 1985 Supreme Court bill, which purposely aimed to exclude religious judges from nomination to the Supreme Court. The bill stated that candidates had to have proven expertise in "civil law, criminal law and/or constitutional law" (art.6 para A), making no reference to religious law (or military law), and it cannot be interpreted other than as a conscious attempt to exclude religious judges. The law was eventually amended as a result of parliamentary pressures, but it retained an emphasis on the general courts as the main recruiting ground for the Supreme Court.[158] Further evidence of the problems facing religiously trained judges is that, unlike the military law academy, the law sections (*syariah*) of religious universities (IAIN) are not yet fully acknowledged law schools—one indication being that law graduates from state universities and the AHM are titled SH, and those from the IAIN are still Drs. (*doctorandus*). As a result, they do not legally have access to the Supreme Court, and it is not surprising that the PPP faction in Parliament pushed for these law degrees to be recognized equally.[159] Recall in this context that recruitment for the Supreme Court is largely orchestrated by the Supreme Court and the Department of Justice, with only a residual role for Parliament.[160] This excludes

---

[156] Personal communication, 21 April 1995.

[157] Personal communication, 7 August 1994.

[158] Official elucidation to art.7 Law no.14/1985. The way this article is drafted suggests that religious and military law are thrown in for good measure. They are counterbalanced by three references to subjects of the general courts (i.e. criminal, civil, and constitutional law). The Fraksi Karya Pembangunan wanted to have the list extended to military law and the religious Fraksi PPP to religious law cf. *DPR-RI Persidangan I Rapat paripurna terbuka ke-6 tahun sidang 1985-1986* dated 17 September 1985, pp. 24 and 90.

[159] *DPR-RI Persidangan I Rapat paripurna terbuka ke-6 tahun sidang 1985-1986* dated 17 September 1985, p. 90.

[160] In the presentation of the 1985 Supreme Court Bill, the minister of justice said in so many words that "the role of the Supreme Court chairman and the minister of justice, with the ultimate

the Department of Religious Affairs, a situation that reduces the chances of religious (or military) judges to be promoted to the Supreme Court.[161]

(c) Social Background

(i) Social Class, Family, and Geography

Throughout the Court's history, intense class, family, and geographical ties have bound the judges who serve together. These ties, though different in essence, in practice interact in complex ways that do not always allow for clear distinctions.

The Javanese Old Boy Network. Not all Supreme Court judges can be distinguished on the basis of their class background. Still, the traditional Javanese administrative elite, the *pangreh praja*, enjoys an advantage in Supreme Court recruitment. The principal reason is that the limited reservoir of judicial candidates in the early years and the predominance of the Javanese elite in the colonial bureaucracy provided this group with a background and a social network that facilitated their access and upward mobility in the bureaucracy, including the judiciary. Moreover, members of this group have a strong tradition of involvement in administration, which orients them toward public service even now. Finally, and as will be apparent in the next chapter, these elite Javanese share an outlook in tune with that of the government, an agreement that enhances their chances for a successful career. As a result, out of a total of nine Supreme Court chairmen, at least six were from this Javanese bureaucratic elite,[162] while those who were not had a vice-chairman from that group. Thus, Supreme Court chairman Mudjono, son of a stationmaster in a small East Javanese town, had Purwoto Gandasubrata as vice-chairman. It is barely an exaggeration to say that the Supreme Court leadership has always had a strong complement from the traditional Javanese elite.

This class background is important,[163] and is often referred to in conversation. One Court judge described Supreme Court chairman Purwoto in the following terms: "You know, he is the son to the *regent* of Purwokerto, and still has the family *kris* in his house."[164]

---

final decision of the president, are the decisive factors." See *Statement of the Minister of Justice I. Saleh on presenting the bill to the DPR, DPR-RI, Persidangan I rapat paripurna terbuka ke-9 tahun sidang 1985-1986* dated 4 October 1985, p. 7. Note the law does not explicitly reiterate this viewpoint.

[161] *DPR-RI Persidangan I Rapat paripurna terbuka ke-6 tahun sidang 1985-1986* dated 17 September 1985, p. 90.

[162] Wirjono Prodjodikoro, Soerjadi, Subekti, Seno Adji, Ali Said, Purwoto Gandasubrata.

[163] Indonesian society is image conscious, marked by considerable emphasis on tidy outward appearances and on observing proper forms. Image is an important factor in advancement in and outside of government. One of the problems facing the expert jurist Nusantara when he was being considered as new chairman of the most prominent Indonesian Legal Aid Institute, LBH, in the late 1980s was that, in the view of kingmaker Adnan Buyung Nasution, he was a bit of a peasant, coarse in speech and behavior.

[164] Family heirlooms such as *kris* (daggers), spears, and so on function to legitimize the authority and descent of the owner. In addition, they are said to have magic qualities. During a 1993 fire in Purwoto's house, the blade of the *kris* was apparently recovered, but the carved wooden hilt was lost. Personal communication, 27 June 1994.

Class and family are closely intertwined, for the traditional Javanese elite has a strong tradition of intermarriage that can be traced back for generations. In the Supreme Court, too, class and family bonds closely overlap. For example, both Wirjono Prodjodikoro and Subekti, chairmen of the Court from, respectively, 1954-1966 and 1968-1974, were part of the Central Javanese elite. They also were related to the second degree through their wives, who were sisters, and they were descended from one of the central Javanese princedoms. In fact, their family relationship was so close that, according to Law no.1/1950, the two judges were prohibited from serving together on the same court, as they did from the late 1950s until 1966.[165] The fact that the brother of Wirjono's and Subekti's wives also became a Supreme Court judge in the 1970s (Hanindyoputro) confirms the significance of class and family in promotions. Another sister was married to the well-known chairman of the Semarang appeal court, Hapsoro, who was asked in the 1960s to become a Supreme Court judge, but declined because he felt he was too old to relocate.[166]

The case of Supreme Court chairman Purwoto S. Gandasubrata exemplifies the ways in which class, family, and shared geographical origins together may influence career advancement. As one of his brethren on the bench told me: "Purwoto was meant to be a judge from childhood onwards. Not me. I had to fight for it all the way."[167] This comment was not meant to suggest that Purwoto was a born judge, in the sense of being a judicious and wise man (which in fact he may also be). What was meant rather is that the public service tradition of Purwoto's family is oriented toward the legal profession and provided him with an extensive network, so that Purwoto's professional orientation and career path were set out from his youth.[168] Purwoto was born into the regent family of Purwokerto, with a most auspicious judicious ancestry. A whole battery of uncles, serving in the judiciary or closely related functions, smoothed his way in the judiciary. They include former public prosecutor Gatot; Sudirman, who at one time was chairman of the Cilacap and Purbolinggo court (and refused to become appeals court judge in Semarang because he enjoyed archery, which was not possible there); Sudarman, who used to be director of prisons; Sukana, an appeals court judge; and Budiman Bintoro, head of the training center of the Department of Justice. Last but not least, Purwoto counts

---

[165] Personal communication, July 1992.

[166] Interview, July 1994.

[167] Personal communication, 23 August 1994.

[168] Another source points out that Purwoto briefly considered becoming a public prosecutor after finishing his law degree. He moved over to the judiciary because the prosecution "didn't feel right." Letter, Supreme Court judge Bismar Siregar to Chief Justice Soerjono, dated 1 November 1994, pp. 3-4. The judge interviewed here contrasted Purwoto's background with his own, in which peasant origins, parental obstruction, lack of family relations, and ethnicity all conspired to block a career in the judiciary. These drawbacks would normally have doomed him to remain stuck in a first instance court throughout his entire career, but he overcame these obstacles as a result of a number of fortuitous circumstances, "sheer luck," as he calls it himself. He has a most acute legal mind, was born in the same region as a number of *pangreh pradja* judges (though of different ethnicity), and managed to link up with these better connected judges. And so this peasant judge could fit into the social elite as regards language and culture, and the elite found him useful thanks to his extraordinary legal expertise. At the same time, he was never really a political or social contender, as he lacked the social network and necessary clout. This left him dependent on the judges with higher status, so that he always had to work in their shadow.

among his numerous uncles two prominent members of the first generation of Supreme Court judges: Wirjono Kusuma and Satochid Kartanegara.

Satochid is an important link for Purwoto. Satochid's son (who died of cancer at a young age) was married to S. Soegondo, who had been director of Court Upgrading at the Supreme Court itself, but was appointed in November 1992 to become director general for Court Upgrading at the Department of Justice. During Purwoto's tenure, therefore, the administration of the judges was quite literally managed within the family.[169]

Throwing the net somewhat further, we discover a fair number of judges related to Mr. Purwoto in terms of family, class, or geographical origins were appointed to the Supreme Court after Mr. Purwoto became vice-chairman under Mudjono in the early 1980s. For example, Supreme Court judge M. Iman is Purwoto's cousin. Supreme Court judge I. Rahardjo's father was the *patih* (vizier) to Purwoto's father, and hence shares *pangreh pradja* and regional roots. Similarly, the father of Supreme Court junior chairman Adi Andoyo Soetjipto was a law clerk in Purwokerto, where Purwoto's father was regent, which makes him a part of the bureaucratic family, as it were. Finally, Supreme Court judge Retnowulan comes from Purwokerto also, went to school and university with Purwoto, and served on many of the courts where Purwoto also served. As a Chinese, she is not related to Purwoto, but the shared geographical background, language, and traditions, and the basic affinity that these entail, are no less significant as links. So during Purwoto's tenure as chairman and vice-chairman, four Supreme Court judges were appointed to the Court who were related to him in terms of family, class, or geography.

Bonds of the sort described here act as a strong social glue within the Court, as indeed one Supreme Court judge commented: "These Supreme Court judges all come from the same area, they speak the same language. Why, they're all related."[170]

---

[169] Note that the appointment of Mrs. Soegondo as director general came only two months after Purwoto's appointment as Supreme Court chairman in August 1992, which may be a coincidence, or then it may be not. *Varia Peradilan* 8,87 (December 1992). The appointment is remarkable because Mrs. Soegondo had a career in the decentralized services of the Department of Justice (KAKANWIL, Kepala Kantor Wilayah, Head Regional Office of the department of Justice) rather than the judiciary and the Supreme Court itself, from which circles the director general has traditionally been selected ever since the position was instituted in 1969. In fact, it was part of the political compromise formula in 1969 that the director general would be a judge. On the surface, the appointment of Mrs. Soegondo bears the markings of a political trade-off between the judiciary and the Department of Justice, as she had family connections in the judiciary and was an employee of the justice department. (The Soegondo appointment set a dangerous precedent, as her successors as director general for courts all came from the Department of Justice rather than the judiciary, as the 1974 compromise between the Department and the judiciary fell into disuse.) The idea of a trade-off is contested by the parties involved, as in fact Mr. Purwoto apparently opposed the Soegondo appointment precisely on the grounds that the director general had always been, and should be, a judge—and that the government had promised in 1974 to honor this precedent. The principal point remains that key figures in the judiciary and the department that manages its personnel come from a very small, closely-knit group of people who, notwithstanding some differences, share interests and outlook.

[170] Personal communication, 23 August 1994. This is not to say that professionals from similar backgrounds necessarily get along well with each other. Indeed, relations between Supreme Court figures Purwoto S. Gandasubrata and Adi Andoyo Soetjipto, for instance, are difficult despite their shared antecedents. As with old marriages, this tension is partly generated by intimate knowledge of each other's histories. Nonetheless, these professionals do share some basic assumptions and operating styles that, for all their differences, set them apart from outsiders.

New Emerging Networks. Aside from the old Javanese elite, there are a number of relatively new family-based networks in the Supreme Court that branch out into the judiciary and the entire legal apparatus. A modern example of such a network is the Nasution family. The central role in the family was played by Az. Nasution, a prominent judge who chaired the Jakarta *istimewah* (Special) court in the late 1950s and early 1960s. All the senior judges at one point or other served under Az. Nasution, a shared experience that apparently acted as a social lubricant. As a result, Az. Nasution's two children did quite well in the judiciary. Mangatas Nasution was appointed senior reporting judge to the Supreme Court in 1991, and in 1994 became Supreme Court vice secretary general—one of the most influential functions in the Court administration.[171] In 1995, he became a Supreme Court justice. Mangatas's sister, Marianne Sutadi-Nasution, subsequently served on a Jakarta court, as clerk on the Supreme Court, and as vice-chairman to the Tanjungkarang district court.[172] Tanjungkarang is a coveted post because, while it qualifies as a outlying function—and all judges must serve their stint in such places before being allowed to move up the judicial hierarchy—it is within easy reach of Jakarta. As this candidate was clearly a favored judge, her appointment to the Supreme Court in 1995 was almost inevitable.[173] Marianne Sutadi is married to Mr. Sutadi Djajakusuma, who was special assistant to the minister at the National Development Planning Board (BAPPENAS, Badan Perencanaan Pembangunan Nasional) on Legal Matters. This position was created in 1993 to bolster legal development in the country.

This case connects with and exemplifies a whole new web of family connections within the judiciary, a web centered in the Supreme Court. As far as could be traced, these personal connections are generally limited to the nuclear family and are very much bound to a specific Supreme Court judge. The 1992 Purwoto Court may serve as an example. In this Court, junior chairman Asikin Kusumah Atmadja (himself the son of a Supreme Court chairman, of course) and Olden Bidara both have a son who is a judge. Supreme Court judge Moersiah's daughter is a judge, as is the son-in-law of Supreme Court judge Mohammad Djanis. The wives of Ketut Suraputra and Olden Bidara are judges—Olden thus has both a son and a wife in the judiciary. The son of junior chairman Soegiri is a judge temporarily detached as an assistant on the Supreme Court, while the son of former vice-chairman Abdurrahman is the assistant to former chairman Purwoto. Asikin Kusumah Atmadja's daughter, two of Busthanul Arifin's sons, Amiruddin Noer's daughter, and Kabul Arifin's son all work as staff members on the Supreme Court. More than ten judges, i.e., almost 20 percent of the sitting judges, have immediate relatives within the judiciary or the administrative staff of the Supreme Court.

---

[171] Personal communication, 12 May 1995.

[172] Transfer List of Judges, *Varia Peradilan* 9,108 (Sept. 1994): 157.

[173] Personal communication, 19 October 1995. After *Reformasi* Marianne Sutadi was appointed as Vice Chief Justice.

Figure 3
Second-Degree Family Relations in the Supreme Court
(Purwoto Administration)

* Junior Chairman Asikin Kusumah Atmadja: father, Supreme Court chairman; daughter, Supreme Court staff; son, judge
* Junior Chairman Busthanul Arifin: two sons on Supreme Court staff
* Junior Chairman Olden Bidara: wife, judge; son, judge
* Junior Chairman Soegiri: son, judge (detached to Supreme Court)
* Judge Moersiah: daughter, judge
* Judge Moh. Djanis: son-in-law, judge
* Judge Ketut Suraputra: wife, judge
* Judge Amiroeddin Noer: daughter, Supreme Court staff
* Judge Kabul Arifin: son, Supreme Court staff

If family and class generally go together, so do family and geographical origins. The Batak judges on the Supreme Court are an example of a new emerging network that is partly geographically based and seems to rely also on family connections, as the following interview testifies.

SP: Are you the only Batak judge on the Court?
Judge: Oh no, there are five of us. In fact, four of them are Siregars: Aslamiyah, Palti Radja, Bismar, and Chaeruddin.
SP: But isn't Siregar just a clan name, I mean, clan names do not denote a family relationship.
Judge: But in the Supreme Court they do! We're all related. In fact, the Siregar judges even come from the same small town: Sipirok.
SP: And who is the fifth Batak Judge?
Judge: Yahya Harahap.
SP: And where's he from?
Judge: *[laughing and sticking up his thumb]* Sipirok also. Sipirok is a great place.[174]

There are several reasons why Sipirok is doing comparatively well in the Batak region, but the fact that it is outperforming almost all other Indonesian towns as a source of Supreme Court justices is little less than remarkable.[175]

---

[174] Personal communication, 29 August 1994. Interview adapted by adding a name in the first answer to hide the identity of the respondent.

[175] Sipirok is, in fact, a great place. It is a small district in the border area of the Batak and Minangkabau regions in central Sumatra, a socially challenging place, where ethnicities and religions mingle. Most Batak are Protestant, and the Minangkabau are Muslim. The southern Batak clans generally are Muslim, but in some cases both religions can be found in a single clan. Thanks in part to the strong schooling tradition brought to the Batak area by the German missionary organization, the Rheinländische Missionsgesellschaft, the southern Muslim parts of the Batak region have brought forth a number of skilled and vocal professionals. The same Sipirok is not just the home town of five Supreme Court judges, but is even better known perhaps as the home town of the politicians Amir Sjarifuddin, prominent socialist leader during the revolution; Burhanuddin Harahap, prime minister 1955-1956; and D. Siregar, prime minister of the federal member state of East Indonesia during the brief federal period 1949-1950.

(ii) Ethnicity

There is no official policy directed toward giving individuals from minority ethnic groups seats on the Court alongside members of the Javanese majority. Still, in the past recruitment seems to have been directed, at least in part, to granting minority ethnic groups adequate representation on the Court. Thus, the appointment of Sutan Malikul Adil in the first Supreme Court is likely to have been influenced by his Sumatran origins. Particularly in those early days, when the hold of the Java-based republic on the Outer Islands was often tenuous, leaders evidently believed that broadening the ethnic base of the Supreme Court would reinforce its legitimacy in the country as a whole.[176] Judging from a breakdown of the ethnic affiliations of Court personnel, this unofficial policy has continued to the present day, although there is no system of fixed quotas or reserved seats for certain ethnic minorities. The ethnic breakdown can be presented as follows:

Figure 4
Ethnic Backgrounds of Supreme Court Justices

	1950	1954	1965	1968	1974	1982*	1992	1994
Java		2	3	3	4	11	28	20
Sunda		2	1	-	1	1	3	1
Minangkabau		1	1	-	1	1	9	5
Batak		-	-	-	1	2	2	6
Aceh		-	-	-	-	1	1	1
Bali		-	-	-	-	-	2	3
Minahasa		-	-	-	-	-	2	1
Kalimantan		-	-	-	-	-	1(+)	2
Chinese		-	-	-	-	-	1	3

(*) 1982: one judge with mixed Javanese-Batak ancestry (not listed)
(+) Ethnic origins of Judge Henoch Tesan Binti from Kalimantan are not clear, probably coastal Malay rather than inland Dayak.

Three general observations can be made on the basis of Figure 4. First, throughout its history the Supreme Court has been dominated by the Javanese. With the exception of the evenly balanced Kusumah Atmadja Court, Javanese presence on the Court barely ever dropped below 60 percent.[177]

Second, minority ethnicities are represented on the Court with ever increasing diversity. Traditionally, and some say because of their culturally argumentative temperament, some ethnicities have a strong representation on the Court. These

---

[176] Conversely, when Sutan Malikul Adil became enmeshed in a corruption scandal, as we saw earlier, the situation was interpreted in some newspapers at the time as an essentially ethnic conflict.

[177] Javanese constituted 66.6 percent under Wirjono, 57 percent under Subekti, 62 percent under Subekti, 68 percent under Seno Adji, 62 percent under Mudjono, 55 percent under Ali Said, and 39 percent under Purwoto.

notably include the Sumatran Batak and Minangkabau (but also the Sundanese), as representatives of these groups have been on the Court from the early days of independence. Nevertheless, from the 1980s this representation was strengthened and diversified, to include judges from Bali, Kalimantan and even some of Chinese descent. This diversification seems to be increasing with time.

The third general observation is that representatives of certain ethnic groups are notably absent from the Supreme Court. The Court is heavily oriented to the islands of Java and Sumatra. Some minority ethnic groups from Sumatra are weakly represented, however, such as the Acehnese and those from Bengkulu, Lampung, or Jambi. The same goes for the various ethnic groups of Kalimantan[178] and Sulawesi,[179] which have been largely ignored in Court recruitment. Most remarkable, however, is that no judge from east of the Wallace line was ever appointed to the Supreme Court. Thus, all the ethnic groups from the provinces of Nusa Tenggara Timor, East Timor, the Moluccas, and Irian have been excluded. Supreme Court recruitment seems to stop at Bali in the south and the Minahasa in the north.

An additional note with respect to ethnic breakdown is that, aside from the Kusumah Atmadja years, the Court leadership from 1954 onwards has consistently been Javanese. This includes the chairman and the vice-chairman, as well as the great majority of junior chairman, only three of whom hailed from other regions of the country (Asikin Kusumah Atmadja was Sundanese, Olden Bidara was Minahasan, and Sjamsoedin, appointed in 1993, was Acehnese). Thus, despite increasingly diversified ethnic recruitment, the Javanese remain dominant both numerically and organizationally.

Finally, even though there has been a fair representation of Chinese judges on the Court over time, those who remain on the bench are the last remnant of the large group of Chinese judges from the 1950s generation, all but a few of whom have left the judiciary. Three Chinese judges have recently served on the Supreme Court, namely Dora Sasongko, Retnowulan Sutantio, and Djohansjah, the first two of whom retired in 1993-1994.[180] Nevertheless, they have few successors and, unlike judges from most other ethnic groups, none of the senior Chinese Supreme Court judges have family members in the judiciary.[181]

---

[178] Until *Reformasi*, which is the period covered by this study, there was no representative from the inland Dayak on the island of Kalimantan. Supreme Court judges Henoch Tesan Binti and Masrani Basran originated from Kalimantan, but were both coastal Malays.

[179] Until *Reformasi*, which is the period covered by this study, there were only two judges from Sulawesi, both from the predominantly Protestant north (the Minahasa), which differs considerably from the heavily Islamicized south. Junior chairman Olden Bidara retired in 1995, but Sulawesi retained its prominent positions with the emerging new star Paulus Effendi Lotulung, who soon after *Reformasi* shot up through the ranks to become junior chairman in administrative cases. Paulus Lotulung claims part Sulawesi ancestry, and in fact has been traditionally installed as a Minahasa nobleman

[180] Personal Communication, 23 August 1994. Until *Reformasi*, which is the period covered by this study, the number of Chinese judges in the Indonesian judiciary was estimated at thirty. Some Chinese judges traditionally were situated in very strong posts within the Supreme Court administration. Their number seems to have declined a bit in the early twenty-first century, as some reached retirement age, but others remain in positions of considerable influence.

[181] Personal communication, 23 August 1994. This is not to say that there are no alliances of Chinese judges and administrators in the judiciary at all, but they are small in number and much less prominent than was the case in the 1950s. The Chinese clearly have a harder time breaking

No evidence could be found of a system whereby cases are allotted to judges on the basis of a shared ethnicity with the parties involved, or on the basis of shared experience with the regional (customary *adat*) law governing a case.

(iii) *Religion*

As with ethnicity, there is no explicit policy of quotas or reserved seats for judges representing minority religions. The Supreme Court reflects the clear Muslim majority of the country, which in fact fully controlled the Court in the first thirty-odd years and has progressively colored some of its traditions and customs. Thus, for their official dress, Supreme Court judges dropped the original ermine-ringed beret and opted instead for the black *peci* headdress for men. While this *peci* is associated with Islam, the dress code applies to all male judges, irrespective of religious denomination. On Fridays, the central hall of the Court is reserved for Muslim prayers—though the Court is closed on Sundays, as are all government institutions.

Figure 5
Religious Breakdown[182]

	1950	1954	1965	1968	1974	1982	1992	1994
Islam	6	5	3	7	16	45	46	41
Catholic	-	-	-	-	-	2	1	3
Protestant	-	-	-	-	-	2	2	3
Hindu	-	-	-	-	-	2	2	3

As is apparent from the above figure, religious diversification in Court recruitment began in the 1980s. Although religious denominations are not always easy to trace, as far as I could gather the first non-Muslims were appointed to the Supreme Court in 1981, during the initial stage of the Court's expansion under Mudjono. They included the Catholic Soedjadi and the Protestant Olden Bidara. When the expansion was completed a couple of months later, representatives of these minority religions were increased with a few additional appointments, such as the Catholic Soenarta, as well as the Hindus Gde Djaksa and Ketut Suraputra. Since then, important minority religions have consistently been represented on the Court. Though no system is spelled out, it seems that an informal system does exist whereby seats are reserved for judges from the minority religions, so the Hindu, Catholic, and Protestant minorities in the country have steady representation on the Court.

Judges who belong to these minority religions, it may be noted, are not restricted to the lower regions of the Court, although they have never secured the top functions of chairman or vice-chairman. Thus, Olden Bidara became junior chairman for the administrative jurisdiction and Ketut Suraputra was nominated to succeed him as junior chairman in 1994. Still, it is evident that the Court, in both

---

through the administrative crust now than was the case forty years ago. Personal communication, 15 July 1994, 16 July 1994, 11 August 1994.

[182] In June 1994 nine new judges were appointed, of whom four were Muslim, three Catholic, one Protestant, and one Hindu.

numerical terms and as regards leadership is dominated by Muslims. This majority religious group is not homogeneous, however.

The 1950s Supreme Court was religiously neutral, one might even say secular. With the arrival of the second group, distinctions began to develop between, on the one hand, the religiously neutral judges and, on the other, those oriented toward advocating a more active role for their religion. Most Javanese judges, notably those such as Purwoto Gandasubrata, belong to the first group of men and women who have their roots in the traditional Javanese elite.[183] Other judges, particularly those from Sumatra, are definitely more ambitious on behalf of Islam. These include people like Bismar Siregar or Busthanul Arifin, who seemed to grow increasingly Muslim the older he got.[184] To date, control of the Court has been steadily retained in the hands of the first group of judges, with the second marginalized as much as possible in Court affairs. Nevertheless, as the role of Islam in the world and the country has grown, this second group has been gaining power, so that competition is emerging.

Not all cases involving religious affairs are assigned to the judges on the basis of their own religious background. Thus, typical Hindu cases are not necessarily dealt with by Balinese judges.[185] This does not apply to Islam, however, and cases involving questions of Islamic law that have come up through the Islamic courts are invariably decided by Muslim Supreme Court judges.[186] This is partly ensconced in Court organization, where Chamber J is specifically assigned to handle Islamic appeals; non-Muslims are not appointed to that chamber, presumably to avoid accusations of ignorance or, worse, religious bias.

---

[183] Though not only those: Sri Widoyati Soekito was a strong Muslim in her private life (even slightly anti-Christian because of what she perceived as that religion's historical arrogance), but was absolutely neutral and even secular in the way she performed her professional functions. She even gave a lecture once at Universitas Indonesia in which she warned against Islam encroaching in the sphere of family law. Many of the group of judges from the 1950s demonstrated attitudes similar to hers.

[184] As one senior government official (of Muslim Arab descent) told me, Busthanul Arifin, while starting out on the secular side, in his later years became a prominent actor on behalf of Muslim parties. In the field of law, advocacy of this sort peaked in the early 1990s with a movement to restate the Islamic laws that would be binding on all Indonesian Muslims. While the restatement was effected, it was not enacted into law as a result of opposition from the senior state official interviewed here:

> Busthanul Arifin and I were among those most closely involved in the discussions surrounding the large "restatement of Islam" project two years ago. Busthanul was one of the foremen in Muslim circles. They wanted the restatement to be like a law, with headings, sections and sub-sections, ideally even enacted in the form of a Presidential Decree. We [i.e. the government. SP] wanted this restatement to be a guideline, in textbook form, and we managed to convince the president of this. Muslim circles were livid, Busthanul even publicly called into question my religious belief, which I felt was a bit personal. Of course, we're good friends now.

Personal communication, 6 July 1994.

[185] As an example, two recent Balinese inheritance cases were decided by an all-Islamic chamber.

[186] Mahkamah Agung no.402.K/Pdt/1988 dated 29 June 1992, *Varia Peradilan* 8,89 (February 1993).

(iv) Women

In June 1986, a conference was organized in Bangkok on the "ASEAN women judges." (ASEAN, Association for Southeast Asian Nations) The Indonesian delegation to the conference, headed by Supreme Court judge Mrs. Siti Tanadjoel Tarki Soejardono, delivered a paper that stated emphatically the "women and men judges are treated equally and have equal opportunities in all fields."[187] According to the paper, there was also "no discrimination in the appointment of women or men judges into specific positions," including those of Court chairmen. Indeed, the statistics attached to the paper testified to the strong female representation in the Indonesian judiciary. From a certain perspective, the self-confidence of women judges is understandable.[188] At the same time and notwithstanding the protestations of the Indonesian delegation at the Bangkok conference, the troubling reality also apparent from these statistics was that, at least in 1986, no Indonesian woman held a position as court chairman at any level of the judiciary.[189] Indeed, early interviews conducted by Prof. Daniel Lev reveal the male respondents' mixture of pride and embarrassment at the fairly large component of women in the Indonesian judiciary. The prevailing view of many men is that if the profession attracts too many women, then this will reflect negatively on its status.

This relative success of women in the judiciary is reflected in the Supreme Court. The first female judge took her place on the Court in 1968, long before most Western supreme courts accepted female justices.[190] This was Sri Widoyati Soekito, by all accounts an extraordinary lady, who in the 1970s maintained her moral integrity at a time when the entire Court was run to ground, and other Supreme Court judges succumbed to the temptations posed by financial handouts. Her reputation for integrity was so strong, that when she died prematurely of cancer in 1982, her office apparently was not occupied for an entire year, remaining a sort of hallowed ground. In her last days, Sri Widoyati apparently called some of her women colleagues in the lower courts and told them that she would leave the Supreme Court in their care.[191]

These women would soon be called to join the Supreme Court. Since the 1980s, the Court, by Western standards, has included a strong component of women judges, as the following figures testify.

---

[187] "ASEAN network of Women Judges," *Varia Peradilan* 15 (December 1986): 193-94.

[188] According to these 1986 statistics, the figures are as follows: Appeal Courts 182 male and 55 female (31 percent); district courts 1,877 male and 312 female (16.5 percent). These are figures from the general jurisdiction (*peradilan umum*), of course. There are hardly any female judges in the military courts and no female judges at all in the religious courts.

[189] That condition has since been remedied.

[190] The first woman justice on the US Supreme Court was Sandra Day O'Connor, appointed in 1981 by Ronald Reagan.

[191] There is some female solidarity, but it is low-key. Apparently there was a women's lawyers club in Jakarta in the 1950s. Sometimes pictures of all the Supreme Court's women judges are published in the journal *Varia Peradilan*. Nevertheless, I found no evidence that the women judges stick together and act as advocates for each other.

Figure 6
Number of Women on the Court

	1950	1954	1965	1968	1974	1982	1992	1994
Women	-	-	-	1	1	9	8	8
Men	6	5	3	6	15	42	43	43

Interestingly, many (though not all) of the women judges on the Supreme Court have a reputation for honesty and legal correctness that few of the men can match. Thus, Supreme Court judge Poerbowati was said to keep the door closed to all visitors, fearing that they would pamper her with gifts that would incur social liabilities. She is the supervising Supreme Court judge of the vitally important Jakarta province, and performs her task with almost draconian severity and an uncompromising attitude. Similarly, Supreme Court judge Retnowulan refused to have a large office in Court, as was her due, and instead opted for a little office in one of the outer wings of the Court building with the aim of keeping visitors and their potentially compromising gifts far away.

This gender-related honesty is due at least, in part, it would appear, to the fact that many women judges have wealthy husbands. In fact, Poerbowati's husband was twice director of the Bank Indonesia and Retnowulan's husband also had a senior position there. As one male judge put it somewhat spitefully: "They can afford to be strong and independent."

Nevertheless, despite their reputation for integrity and intellectual honesty, and even though quite a few of them head chambers, none of the women judges ever made it to the Court leadership. Apparently, Sri Widoyati was mentioned as a successor to Subekti, and she reportedly liked the idea, but her candidacy was killed when the military got wind of it and started a whisper campaign.[192] Since then—and even though in the Purwoto Court, for instance, two of the three most senior judges were female—no woman has never become junior chairman of the Supreme Court, let alone achieved one of the top two functions.[193]

3. THE ROLE OF SUPREME COURT CHAIRMEN

We already noted on several occasions that the Supreme Court chairmen have become increasingly important in the Court over the past decades. Their importance derived, in part, from changes in the internal organization of the institution that strengthened the powers of the chairman vis-à-vis the other

---

[192] Personal communication, 30 June 1994. According to the story as it was recounted to me, a safe way to kill off a candidate's chances for a top job in Indonesia is by spreading the rumor that he wants the position. This reportedly is what happened to Sri Widoyati. Of course, Asikin Kusumah Atmadja desperately wanted the top job as well at the time, which explains perhaps why the military intelligence, with which Asikin was closely associated, started the campaign.

[193] The fact that S. Soegondo became director general at the Department of Justice shows that such high-level jobs are accessible to women, however.

judges.[194] It also resulted from a tendency on the part of Supreme Court judges to defer to the chairman, as we have noted elsewhere.[195] The resultant dominant role played by the Supreme Court chairman has contributed to the tendency of some commentators to define the Court's institutional history in terms of its leaders, rather than according to changes in the political environment or the law.[196]

The chairman's enhanced power should not be confused with improved leadership. Whereas our picture of the individual performances of the various Supreme Court chairmen as leaders remains blurred, it is possible to discern some of the dominant features. These reflect both on their external leadership (i.e., the way in which Supreme Court chairmen imposed the institutional interests of the Court upon its environment), and on their internal leadership (the way in which they motivated and enhanced institutional solidarity and achievement).[197]

With regard to external leadership, Supreme Court chairmen, instead of being trendsetters, have largely been trend-followers. With a few exceptions, Supreme Court chairmen did not defend the Court against encroachment or propagate its values and interests among other state institutions. Nor did they generally mount a strong defense against external interference in the Court or its erosion of power and status.

Notable examples of this trend have been evident throughout this study; recall, for instance, the unwillingness of Supreme Court chairmen after Kusumah Atmadja to insist on treatment befitting their position with respect to proper protocol during state banquets,[198] delays in reception by state officials,[199] or summonses regarding important before the Court.[200] The authority and interests of the institution he represents require the Supreme Court chairman to resist, publicly, if need be, treatment that generates the impression, however unintended, that the Court or its officers are not on a par with other high institutions of state.

With respect to internal leadership, the impact of Supreme Court chairmen, by and large, has resulted in more fission than fusion. While the limited backlog issue was addressed with some consistency, most Court chairmen failed to develop consistent policies or practices to stimulate internal loyalty, integrity, and productivity among their fellow Supreme Court justices. On the contrary, particularly under the New Order government, the Court's chairmen have contributed to the erosion of these internal institutional values and tended to defend external—notably executive—interests within the Court.

One example among many of this tendency is the way Supreme Court chairmen handled accusations of corruption on the Court. As we saw in the *Malikul Adil case*, Kusumah Atmadja would come down hard on judges if he felt they had not lived up

---

[194] See above, Chapter 8, section 1.

[195] See above, Chapter 8, section 4.

[196] Daniel S. Lev tends to view the history of the Court in these terms. This approach, of course, flows naturally from traditional political science, which defines power relationships in terms of actors rather than institutions or laws.

[197] For a theoretical definition of leadership abilities cf. J. M. Otto, *Aan de voet van de piramide* (Leiden: DSWO Press, 1987), p. 14; P. Szelnick, *Leadership in Administration: A Sociological Interpretation* (New York: Harper & Row, 1957).

[198] See above, Chapter 2, section 2.

[199] See above, Chapter 4, section 4.

[200] As happened to Chairman Purwoto in the *Kedung Ombo case*, Chapter 4, section 4.

to the professional standards of the judiciary.²⁰¹ The mere accusation of corruption prompted him to establish a team, which included outsiders to the Court, to investigate the matter. This showed that, in his view, institutional integrity was so important that it had to be reinforced by public scrutiny. Admirable and courageous, he figures as proof of the famous adage that in matters of institutional integrity, justice must not only be done, but also be seen to be done. His attitude stands in stark contrast to the attitudes of chairmen who came after him, as evidenced, for instance, by Chairman Soerjono's handling of the *Gandhi Memorial School case*, where very strong accusations of improprieties were dealt with internally by the Supreme Court. Outsiders were deliberately excluded from the investigation, which was handled in such a way that the Court leadership was accused of trying to silence the whole affair.²⁰² The Court was definitely harmed by the fact that it did not try to resolve the issue in a public and transparent manner.

Examples of this sort indicate a tendency on the part of a number of chairmen to protect government interests within the Court, or at least to behave in a manner that suggests such an inclination. The behavior of Supreme Court chairman Seno Adji might be a case in point. "Seno is very responsive to the will of the government," said one Supreme Court judge. He continued:

> To take just one example, there was a change in the relationship between the Supreme Court and the military courts. The 1950 law was still in effect and said that civilian judges also served as military judges. But in 1974 Seno Adji sheared off the military high courts at the request of the Department of Defense, so now there is no doubling up of functions at all. I object to this because it violates the law, of course, but the important point is that Seno Adji allowed it to be done, indeed he did it, in response to military will.²⁰³

This was one of the numerous incidents demonstrating that Seno Adji consistently opted for the government line whenever such sensitive issues arose, and at no point did he try to impose the judiciary's institutional ideals on its political environment. As another Supreme Court judge relates:

> The Department of Defense sent a letter to Seno Adji, not to pressure him actually, but just a simple question concerning whether in political trials the time of detention could not be excluded when imposing sentence. Seno Adji could have easily refused. Instead, he set Indroharto on working out a formula to distinguish between judicial and non-judicial detention.²⁰⁴

This willingness of the Court chairmen to serve as conduits for government interests contributed to serious tensions between the Court's leadership and the

---

[201] See above, section 1:b of this chapter.

[202] Thus, Supreme Court junior chairman Adi Andoyo Soetjipto obliquely stated that he feared the delays in the investigation might give rise to "speculations and intrigues." *Forum Keadilan*, 20 May 1986.

[203] *DSL*, 14 November 1978.

[204] *DSL*, 21 October 1978. As it happened, the plan caused an uproar, and apparently Seno Adji was forced to retract his proposal.

other judges, eroding cohesion within the institution. The tenure of chairman Seno Adji had a destructive effect on court solidarity, as Supreme Court insiders have testified:

> The Court barely works as a pleno court anymore, therefore there is no way to know what Seno Adji is doing, or what kind of pressure he is under, and for what reasons he decides cases. Seno Adji divided the judges up into teams to work on cases, and the Court seldom meets in pleno. At the same time, Seno Adji interfered quite a lot in the teams, in that judges are constantly being asked to do all sorts of things, seminars and the like, which are not really their concern, and so the backlogs keep building up.[205]

Witnesses have also commented on chairman Wirjono Prodjodikoro's inability to hold his Court together. At last, Wirjono ceased consulting his fellow judges about various important issues, or if he did choose to speak with his colleagues, he would just bluntly confront them with his ideas, concluding "do you agree or not?"—more as a statement than a question.[206] He did not merely exclude his fellow judges from the political discourse, but promoted internal conflicts and disagreements, according to a justice who served in that court:

> Contacts between the Supreme Court and the government are strictly Wirjono Prodjodikoro's job. The other Supreme Court judges are not in and don't know about his relations with government, or what is said by Wirjono Prodjodikoro to other ministers on the Court . . . [207]

Another Supreme Court judge fiercely criticized Wirjono Prodjodikoro and expressed his opinion that internal communications were clearly at a low ebb: "I utterly condemn Wirjono Prodjodikoro for what he has done to the Supreme Court. [. . .] There is no close cooperation at all within the Court . . . "[208]

As relations between the judges became governed by suspicion and distrust, the Court grew more fragmented.

> There may be some solidarity among Supreme Court judges, but there is no real communication within the Court. The problem here again is the leadership. The Court is totally fragmented because nothing holds the edifice together, as an institution.[209]

---

[205] DSL, 14 November 1978.

[206] DSL, 5 January 1960. Prof. Daniel Lev recounts that he asked Wirjono whether he consulted the other judges on the bench. Wirjono replied in the affirmative, adding that he was quite open to ideas, criticism, and so on. When Lev asked if he could recall when he had last been criticized, Wirjono thought for a long while and said he could not recall. This suggests that, while Wirjono may have neglected to consult his brethren frequently, they also failed to confront him directly concerning this lack of communication.

[207] DSL, 28 July 1960.

[208] DSL, 11 September 1960.

[209] DSL, 14 November 1978.

Later administrations were described in comparable terms.[210]

It is not unjustifiable, therefore, to talk of a leadership problem on the Supreme Court, a problem that is at least in part deliberately generated. The chairman's pivotal position makes him the lever through which the Supreme Court, and by extension the lower courts, can be controlled. Successive Indonesian governments have employed two basic methods to ensure that chairmen have not manifested themselves as overly forceful leaders. Most Supreme Court chairmen fit within one of these two molds.

The first type may be termed the "strong government chairman." Notable examples are Seno Adji, Mudjono, and Ali Said. These are Supreme Court chairmen appointed from outside the institution, men with a proven track record of political loyalty to the government. Though in some cases forceful characters, their long-standing careers with the government ensure that their primary political loyalties reside there. This is particularly evident from the fact that all three Supreme Court chairmen referred to above functioned as ministers of justice before their appointment to the Court. As a number of observers put it: "Because Seno was appointed to the Supreme Court from the Department of Justice, he is tied to positions he took earlier as minister of justice."[211]

As a result, strong government chairmen are generally unwilling to confront the government when internal or external Court interests so require, but are inclined rather to conform to government preferences and policies. Their restricted interpretation of institutional interests imposes a cap on leadership and weakens it. These chairmen are weak Supreme Court leaders by professional disposition.

The second type may be called the "accommodating judicial chairman." Notable examples are Wirjono Prodjodikoro, Purwoto S. Gandasubrata, and, most dramatically, Soerjono. These Supreme Court chairmen were appointed from within the institution and had a professional background in the judiciary, which weakened their bonds of loyalty to the government and, indeed, potentially pitted them against the executive. Nevertheless, the government ensured their loyalty by selecting chairmen of an accommodating and compromising disposition, who had no track record of being outspoken and confrontational. Insiders describe them as "following a tacking course,"[212] "balancing interests,"[213] or *"plin-plan"* (from *plintat-plantut*—bending with the wind).[214]

Some Supreme Court chairmen do not fall into either of the above categories. Sarwata, for instance, was neither a strong government man nor an accommodating judge, but was instead, unfortunately, a combination of the weakest elements of both categories: a weak-willed government appointee. On the upside, the first and fourth chairmen, Kusumah Atmadja and Subekti, combined the strong elements of both categories. Both (the former in particular) were forceful judges, who tried to impose the judiciary's institutional values on other state institutions and did the

---

[210] "Other judges distance themselves from him because they hold him in contempt. People like Asikin and Busthanul Arifin don't even bother to listen to him." *DSL,* 27 November 1987.

[211] *DSL,* 18 October, 21 October 1978.

[212] Personal communication, 16 August 1994.

[213] Personal communication, 5 August 1994.

[214] Personal communication, 11 August 1994.

best they could to uphold internal discipline and morale. Both also were willing to challenge the government when they felt institutional interests were at stake.

4. CHANGES IN PROFESSIONAL CULTURE

Hard data quite simply do not exist with respect to the professional culture of the Supreme Court, and the picture must be painted in broad brush strokes based on secondary material, such as personal impressions of persons intimately acquainted with how the institution has evolved over the years. These sources strongly suggest, however, that the changing composition of the Supreme Court led to a lowering of professional standards, as knowledge and agreement on the law (including foreign law), as well as strict standards of behavior, steadily declined. They were replaced by new cultural qualities. Supreme Court judges have become more aware politically, more status conscious and, as a result, perhaps more open to corruption, while at the same time mystical belief systems have come to play a more important role in Court work. These points will be considered next.

(a) Lowering of Professional Standards

(i) Declining Knowledge of and Agreement on the Law

Over the past fifty years, the Indonesian judiciary has suffered from an erosion of professional standards. As one prominent Jakarta advocate noted as early as 1959:

> Many judges lack understanding of legal concepts and problems. This is not just true of judges on district courts in the outback, but applies right here in Jakarta. I just handled the case of a traffic accident, in which a child was killed by a truck. A case was brought, but the driver, aware of the social requirements of the situation, gave some money to the parents of the child. Now, this is a common practice here, and the parents evidently felt that satisfaction had been given. They felt that the driver was not really at fault and that his gift of money showed his heart to be at the right place. So in court they showed the judge a receipt which they themselves had written for the money, and which said that the money had been received so the case could be stopped. But when the judge saw this, he accused the driver of bribery and sentenced him accordingly. My point is that the judge simply didn't understand the elements of the case and what had happened. No bribery was involved at all. No money was given to the prosecutor, who alone could actually have stopped the case. Nor was any money given to the judge. But the judge could not see this logic. He could not logically reason the matter out.[215]

The apparent inability of judges to reason their way through the legal maze was a condition that hardly improved as time passed. In fact, as the prestige of the judiciary declined and the gap between judicial and private-practice salaries grew

---

[215] *DSL*, 9 July 1959.

wider, the better law graduates tended to go into private practice and the judiciary suffered as a result.[216]

> There is a complete turn-about in the focus of law students. Whereas under the Old Order they were oriented toward government service, from the 1970s they have directed their attention predominantly to the advocacy and selected subjects that are useful there.[217]

Indeed, one Supreme Court junior chairman said that he had specifically instructed his children who were studying law not to become judges, "because I know how the judiciary works, you're doomed to penury here."[218] In short, unattractive working conditions have cost the judiciary, even compared to other legal professions. One senior Surabaya judge in 1964 commented that "some young judges know the law to some extent, but generally they are deficient."[219] Three years later another described his experiences in court in 1967 in the following unequivocal terms:

> Judges know little about the law now and care less. I must be one of the only advocates who still writes full briefs, citing books and relevant court decisions. But when I recently presented such a brief to court, the judge, a younger man, complainingly asked me why I had to submit all that crap and why didn't I write a short brief to make everything easy.[220]

Yap Thiam Hien, the famous human rights' lawyer, in 1986 said he had "very little respect for judges, who know little and do not want to take advice."[221]

> The initial presentation of a case is followed by a statement called the *conclusie* [*kesimpulan*]. The judge saw this and said, no, not yet, the *conclusie* will be later. I explained to the judge that no, the *conclusie* must be taken at this point as a simple statement of position before indicating whether witnesses be called and who and so on. This is usual. Then the judge refused to accept a summing up. So in the end both sides decided to write a letter to the judge explaining their position and entering it into the case file in the hope that the appeals court will read the document later. Judges of little experience are brought to Jakarta, and they know very little indeed. A few are willing to learn from advocates or others and will ask advice, but many will not.[222]

This condition persists—perhaps it is even growing worse—to the present day. In 1993, prominent administrative judge Benyamin Mangkoedilaga stated during a public lecture that, "the quality of judges is, with increasing frequency, minimal."[223] In 1994, a Supreme Court junior chairman commented: "I am pretty

---

[216] Personal communication, 2 September 1994.
[217] Personal communication, 10 September 1994.
[218] Personal communication, 31 August 1994.
[219] *DSL*, 7 December 1964.
[220] *DSL*, 20 July 1967.
[221] *DSL*, 12 July 1986.
[222] *DSL*, 12 July 1986.
[223] *Forum Keadilan*, 24 June 1993.

desperate about the quality of the judges in the lower courts. They make such basic mistakes . . ."[224]

A poor knowledge of the law among lower court judges inevitably worked its way up the hierarchy, as the judges themselves rose within the court system. From the 1970s, the Supreme Court was apparently increasingly affected. According to one Supreme Court junior chairman in 1987: " . . . many of the Supreme Court judges really do not know the law now and don't know how to handle cases."[225] This decline has been exacerbated by some additional factors. The increase in the number of Supreme Court judges implemented under Chairman Mudjono led to the recruitment of many new justices who were notoriously underskilled, and, as a result, this expansion significantly weakened the Court for many years to come.[226] Moreover, the recruitment of military judges diluted the competence of the Supreme Court even further. "None of the military judges on the Supreme Court knows the law,"[227] one Court judge commented. But this criticism extends to other Supreme Court justices as well, and professional expertise, or rather the lack of it, became one of the methods for determining the internal pecking order. One Supreme Court junior chairman said:

> Supreme Court judges nowadays in essence no longer understand the law. Why, even Supreme Court chairman [. . .]. He said in a newspaper interview that judges are essentially passive, which quite simply is not true. How about Law no.14/1970 art.26, which must be read conjunctly with art.27 that actually summons the judges to delve for unwritten law?[228]

A notable law scholar told of another prominent Supreme Court judge:

> His book on civil procedure is stupid, there is no other word for it. In fact, I was told that the Supreme Court chairman [. . .] said to the judge, I don't care what sort of nonsense you write, but please don't put on the cover that you're a Supreme Court judge also, because it reflects badly on the entire Court.[229]

Their lack of security with respect to the law motivates some Supreme Court judges to consult with other senior judges, though this practice seems to be the exception rather than the rule.

> As I was interviewing Supreme Court judge A. who has a reputation for great knowledge, Supreme Court judge B. barged in. He had been asked to go off to a national judicial workshop to talk about arbitration. He twice asked judge A. if he wouldn't go, but he said he had too much work. Then, somewhat embarrassed, he said, well if you won't go, I'll have to ask you some questions for I haven't quite caught one or two things. He then pointed out one or two passages out of a book he had with him. Judge A. gave a response of only four

---

[224] Personal communication, 7 July 1994.
[225] *DSL*, 13 July 1987.
[226] Personal communication, 28 June 1994.
[227] *DSL*, 27 November 1987.
[228] Personal communication, 11 August 1994.
[229] Personal communication, 16 August 1994.

words, almost dictatorial, at which judge B. got up, thanked him, and walked out. In the doorway he turned to me and said with a shy smile, "Now judge A. is really smart, don't you think."[230]

In this incident, a justice was not only given a brief lesson in the law, but his ignorance was exposed in front of an outsider.[231]

Within the Supreme Court there is a tendency to define judges as "good" or "useless." As one Supreme Court judge put it: "Judge A., judge B., judge C. are so-called 'good judges,' others, such as judge E., are useless."[232] Based on comments of this sort, which are so widespread, we can conclude that the declining quality of Supreme Court judges has become a serious problem for modern Indonesia.

(ii) Declining Knowledge of Foreign Law and Languages

One important element that has contributed to the decline of legal understanding is that currently the Indonesian judiciary in general finds it difficult to assess their own legal system by comparing it with systems in other countries because of the significant decline in knowledge of foreign languages and cultures over the years. As a result, the Indonesian judiciary, including the Supreme Court, has become more strongly focused on national law.

The most significant result of this development is the disappearance of Dutch as the legal vernacular. This has been an important development in two respects. For a start, the loss of Dutch has severed modern Indonesia from the legal system existing in the country at the time of independence. The great bulk of legal sources then were written in Dutch, and no systematic translation has been undertaken of court decisions or textbooks essential to a better comprehension of the law and its evolution. Although selected translations of legislation have been made available, the loss of Dutch has effectively meant that the Indonesian judiciary's understanding of its own legal system has declined. Knowledge of indigenous *adat* norms has also declined, since *adat* laws and customs were systematically recorded in Dutch before the war, but research in that area essentially collapsed after independence. Consequently, the present generation of Indonesian judges at all levels tends to be disoriented with respect to legal discipline. One Jakarta lawyer put the point as follows:

> I don't think modern lawyers in any of the legal professions nowadays fully grasp such basic legal concepts as good faith in the Continental legal tradition, and the way it differs from the Anglo-Saxon concept. And the method of legal analysis has not been taught for many decades, with a result that statutory interpretation, such as analogy or teleology, the entire branch of law which you call legal refinement [*rechtsverfijning*], has been replaced by the blunt instrument of literal interpretation.[233]

---

[230] Personal communication, 22 August 1994.

[231] Though judge B. later informed me that these were unstructured meetings that didn't occur often. Personal communication, 9 September 1994.

[232] Personal communication, n.d.

[233] Personal communication, 20 May 1996.

There is, in fact, an enormous library of Dutch materials on law that remains in whole or part relevant to modern Indonesia, but it is inaccessible to all but a few who can read Dutch or, in the Netherlands, those who are interested in Indonesia. It includes several hundred doctoral dissertations (not a few of them written by Indonesians), extensive card indexes and published registers to jurisprudence (court decisions), as well as sophisticated legal journals and treatises.

The collapse of the supporting body of Dutch-language legal sources and the Indonesian judiciary's consequent alienation from a prime source of their own laws has had a notable impact on legislative interpretation in two ways. First, the established method of statutory interpretation is lost. The established civil law method of statutory interpretation by the courts (literal, analogical, historical, and teleological) is broader than the literal approach prevailing in Anglo-Saxon systems. This has an immediate impact on the statutory drafting style. Much Indonesian legislation is drafted in the broad terms characteristic of the civil law system, which relies on the court to use the statutory interpretation method when necessary to refine the law in its application. Similarly, the logic (and status) of documents such as the Official Elucidation to legislation derives directly from its role as a support instrument to statutory interpretation by the courts. Nowadays, barely anyone in Indonesia remembers the established method of statutory interpretation and, as a result, no one can really explain the role of the Official Elucidation; the legislative institutions themselves, which offer scant information in the Elucidation, are befuddled by the process. Since the accepted method of statutory interpretation has been lost, court decisions tend to be unstructured, creating more legal uncertainty.[234]

Second, the vast body of Dutch-language court decisions is ignored as a source of law, to the point that some scholars in Indonesia (and occasionally abroad) have argued that these decisions do not constitute a source of law at all. This interpretation reveals an astounding misconception of how legal systems work generally, the status of court decisions in the Dutch system, and the body of literature available in libraries. The results of this neglect, in practice, are even more disturbing, as Indonesian courts of legal scholars ignore the major body of structured interpretation and application of statute compiled by the courts and instead reach back to the barebones statutory wording of nineteenth-century laws. As a result, the substantive colonial law—including the major codes (Civil Code,

---

[234] Indonesia's New Order government never protested against this erosion of knowledge of the broad interpretative method because in fact such tools tend to make courts harder to handle. Dutch courts in a number of cases have decided in direct opposition to statutory wording on grounds that the legislator evidently meant to achieve something different from what he said (teleological interpretation). The Indonesian New Order government surely would not have welcomed such a show of independence. In fact, one of the instruments by which the New Order government sought to tie down the courts was to legislate through administrative instructions, excluding discretion and allowing for little substantive law development. The extent to which this method permeated the judiciary became apparent after *Reformasi*, when judges were at a loss concerning how to handle the broadly drafted provisions of new commercial legislation. The New Order legacy—defined by the absence of an established method of statutory interpretation and an atmosphere that discouraged judicial assertiveness—effectively immobilized them. There is some merit in the prevailing view within the Indonesian judiciary that more specific legislative instructions would help them work their way out of this dilemma, but an interpretative method must be established and accepted, and statute must be drafted to accord with it. Given a major body of statute drafted in broad terms, the judiciary must seriously consider reviving the civil law interpretive method.

Civil Procedure, Criminal Code, etc.)—that is still applied in modern Indonesian courts differs significantly from the law that was in force in these areas during the late-colonial period.

Perhaps the more insidious aspect of the loss of the Dutch language by Indonesia's judiciary is that Dutch education also constituted a window to the outside world. Judges who learned Dutch also generally received extensive schooling in other foreign languages, such as English, French, and German. Indonesian Supreme Court judges of the first generation, whatever their shortcomings, were definitely more comparatively oriented than the generations that followed or than many judges abroad. They possessed an understanding of foreign legal systems that placed Indonesian law and its institutions in a broader context, which allowed their worth to be measured. In this broader perspective, therefore, the loss of Dutch and the failure to replace it with another foreign language closed the shutters to the outside world. It made Indonesian judges, and the entire legal profession perhaps, more inward looking. The Indonesian legal professions tend nowadays to see the Indonesian condition as exclusive and unique, and are hesitant to look seriously at foreign legal systems and the solutions they have devised. Since these informative alternatives are largely ignored, a good deal of energy must be expended on reinventing legal wheels and correcting old errors.

Unlike other colonial services, the legal profession was very much a Dutch-language service, for that was the only way to realize full access to the law and its subtleties. The colonial generation of judges, as a result, was fluent in Dutch to the point that the justices used it to communicate in private and felt uncomfortable at times when speaking in Indonesian, since their delivery was sometimes "badly structured and hesitant."[235]

During the 1950s, some universities, notably Universitas Indonesia, retained Dutch as an important subject for law studies, but others, such as Gadjah Mada University, abolished it almost from the start. The result was that the generation educated in the 1950s at UI—"the last of the Mohicans"—still speak Dutch well enough, though often not with the ease and intimate familiarity of their predecessors. Others from that generation do not speak it at all if they came from other universities. This split has resulted in quite different approaches to the law, as one Supreme Court judge noted:

> The relationship between Universitas Indonesia and Gadjah Mada graduates at the Supreme Court is not always fluent and on the contrary sometimes quite strained. I find my Gadjah Mada brethren on the bench poor at debating. They tend to hold to pre-set positions and do not allow open discussion. It may have something to do with the Javanese influence on Gadjah Mada. The entire philosophy of Universitas Indonesia is more outward looking and focused on foreign law, while Gadjah Mada is more inward looking and nationalist.[236]

The additional requirement that law students study Dutch made education at Universitas Indonesia comparatively tougher, and in time students began to escape

---

[235] *DSL*, 8 July 1960 describing Wirjono Prodjodikoro's address at the Pasir Putih East Java conference.

[236] Personal communication, 3 August 1994.

the university to go elsewhere. As a result, by the end of the 1950s, even Universitas Indonesia had abolished Dutch as a mandatory subject.[237] The resultant loss of competence in Dutch among law students severed their bonds with the generations educated in colonial times and in the 1950s at Universitas Indonesia. When interviewed on the subject, Supreme Court judges Abdurrahman, Malikul Adil, Tirtaamidjaja, and Wirjono Kusuma " . . . all lamented the fact that students no longer read Dutch. They were all of the opinion that for this reason law students were not as well equipped to practice law."[238]

Clearly, the importance of Dutch in upholding the legal edifice was little appreciated by Indonesia's politicians, as indeed the legal edifice itself was declining in importance. When queried on the matter, Guided Democracy Minister of Justice Sahardjo was "surprised" that students no longer read Dutch and said that then assuredly they studied it in informal classes. Anyway, he said, they can use Indonesian translations of the old laws.[239] The reality was that students did not go to private classes and only used translations if and when they were available. The few translations there were did not cover the law by any means and, as a result, only generated piecemeal knowledge of the underlying legal system. When members of the Dutch-educated generations retired or died, as so many have, loss of the language was no longer lamented for the simple reason that no one could remember what purposes it had served.

Loss of Dutch has generated a condition that one Supreme Court insider termed, somewhat dismissively, "slogan-thinking," where the judiciary hides behind "an abstract, formalistic, and ultimately meaningless professional jargon." This jargon is characterized by its "repetitive character and the use of [Dutch] slogans such as *beslag* [seizure] which at first may be understood within a small circle but in the end are used without any understanding at all."[240]

(iii) Declining Personal Discipline

Though hard data are impossible to come by, it appears generally that judges have become less self-disciplined over the past fifty years. A solid stream of press reports nowadays deals with the questionable behavior of judges within the courts, behavior far worse than anything that went on in the 1950s and 1960s. Reports have described judges in the lower courts knifing each other,[241] falling asleep in court,[242] staging a walkout during the reading of a verdict because they disagreed with it,[243] and simply failing to show up for the job. Indeed, the Supreme Court on a number of occasions has been forced to remind lower court judges of official working

---

[237] As one graduate recalled, the requirement was scrapped in 1959. Personal communication, 11 August 1994. Currently it is being taught again—together with such languages as English—but as a wholly subsidiary subject. One recent graduate described Dutch language classes to me as "not serious at all" and "a time to have fun." Personal communication, 27 November 1995.

[238] *DSL*, 13 December 1959.

[239] *DSL*, 5 September 1960.

[240] Personal communication, 18 July 1994.

[241] *Forum Keadilan*, 11 November 1993.

[242] *Forum Keadilan*, February 1989.

[243] *Forum Keadilan*, 4 December 1995.

hours because these justices were simply failing to show up for work. The rise of such incidents has generated increasing calls for stronger "professional ethics" among the judges.[244]

As regards the Supreme Court, the times when a strict judge like Wirjono Kusuma might be seen trailing his finger over the surfaces of judges' desks to check for dust have long since passed. Apparently, things began to unravel under Seno Adji, who paid little attention to his official attire and, as indicated before, brought in food to eat even while hearing cases—a grievous breach of etiquette at the time.[245] Though this may have been frowned on in the 1970s, now anything goes on the Court, to the point that some Supreme Court judges take their girlfriends to Court in their official cars and are so flagrant about their affairs that the chairman has felt called upon to give instructions in manners.[246] Many Supreme Court judges are not particularly discriminating or self-disciplined in their behavior, and their subordinates even less so,[247] a situation that threatens the prestige of the Court, as well as the judiciary's sense of duty and self-respect.

(b) Emerging New Standards

(i) The Increasing Importance of Status and Rise of Corruption

Status: On Bicycles, Limousines, and City Buses. As we have already seen, the political struggle of the judiciary in the 1950s contributed to a growing political awareness within the profession, as the judges changed from a politically atomized group of individuals to one that was much more cohesive. In addition, they moved from political innocence to a kind of maturity marked by broad agreement on the fundamental political goals to be achieved. This transformation appears to have made members of the judiciary more aware of themselves as part of a group, and more aware of that group's public image. One of the more subtle yet significant changes among Supreme Court judges is that over the past decades status has become much more important to them than before. As they have become acutely aware of a general increase in outward displays of wealth and the impressions of power such displays communicate in modern Indonesian society, Supreme Court judges have become caught up in a consumerist whirlwind, in which it seems less important to do something than to be somebody. A quick study of judges' typical modes of transportation illustrates the distance between the 1950s and the 1990s.

> Wirjono Kusuma was a superb judge. Straight backed, he'd walk past our desk with a finger on the top to check it for dust. And he would come and go to the

---

[244] See for instance the 1993 call issued by Supreme Court chairman Purwoto S. Gandasubrata in *Forum Keadilan*, 11 November 1993.

[245] *DSL*, 15 November 1978

[246] Personal communication, 4 July 1994.

[247] During my research, I often witnessed incidents one would not have expected to encounter in offices associated with a Supreme Court. Once when I was waiting to interview a Supreme Court junior chairman, one of the judge's staff brought out several shoeboxes and quite openly began to sell Nike sport shoes, even within the judge's office (she didn't have my size), which couldn't have been done without the judge knowing. One of the clerks commented laughingly when he saw me: "Yes, well there's no harm in a little trade, is there?" Personal communication, 31 August 1994.

office on his bike, and give you a fatherly wave with his hand from the other side of the street.[248]

The idea of Supreme Court judges riding bicycles is wholly inconceivable in modern Indonesia. The reason is not because of the traffic conditions, but because riding a bicycle nowadays is seen as demeaning. This attitude derives from an official and professional culture in which outward manifestations of wealth and status are perceived as indispensable trappings of power and influence.

And so, as bikes left the scene (a natural result of the decolonization process, some might argue), they were replaced with more dignified modes of transportation that reflected the status of the judges. Today's Supreme Court judges typically insist on having an official car, for which they get a special allowance upon appointment, and on using it when going to court.[249] The occasional Supreme Court judge still commutes by city bus, but tellingly is loath to reveal this to his brethren on the bench, or even to fellow bus travelers.

This rising emphasis on outward appearances poses certain dangers, which certain judges in the past have recognized. A person close to the prominent and scrupulously honest Supreme Court judge Sri Widoyati Notoprodjo recounted:

> Sri was tempted by corruption, but just didn't dare. The point was that she saw what money did to status in modern Indonesia, and that the low salaries of Supreme Court judges eroded their status. So she wanted to be rich and suffered poverty not for her own sake, but for the place and role of the Court.[250]

It is possible that money appeared to some judges as a necessary evil, a means of reinforcing the dignity to their office in modern Indonesia. But the dividing line between this attitude and simple greed is a slim one. The pervasive emphasis of official and professional culture on outward appearances undoubtedly adds to the job frustrations of the Supreme Court judges, who view themselves as underpaid, and it certainly generates constant temptations to make some money on the side. Press reports indicate that many judges are not satisfied with just any car as their official mode of transport, but covet a Mercedes Benz.[251] Or, as former Supreme Court chairman Ali Said put it:

> The corruption problem used to be simple: in the 1970s judges were corrupt because they were underpaid. Their salary was too low [...] The situation now is more difficult. It no longer is a matter of material goods, but a mental affair. [...] The roots of modern corruption must be found in the mental makeup of Indonesian society.[252]

Collusion and Corruption. Assuredly the rise of corruption within the Indonesian judiciary cannot be attributed to changes in professional culture alone. Other factors must be sought in the Supreme Court's internal structure. As we have

---

[248] Personal communication, 15 July 1994.

[249] Personal communication, 23 August 1994.

[250] Personal communication, 30 June 1994.

[251] *Forum Keadilan*, 17 September 1992.

[252] Ibid.

seen, the large size of the Court, the severe lack of internal coordination and guidance, and the almost total autonomy of the various Supreme Court chambers, contribute significantly to potential opportunities and temptations that invite judicial malfeasance. The dividing line that would discriminate between an honest difference of opinion between judges, an erroneous application of the law, or a purposeful perversion of the law's intent cannot be clearly drawn under all circumstances. This is particularly so given the fragmented condition of the Supreme Court, where one chamber is totally unaware of what the other is doing, and where so often justices disagree on a wide range of elementary legal issues. The situation is made worse, of course, by the heavy workload, which ties judges to their dossiers and makes it almost physically impossible for them to know what goes on elsewhere. The emergence and structure of judicial corruption in Indonesia or even on the Supreme Court would require a study of its own. Suffice it here to indicate the way it emerged over time and some of its basic features.[253]

The first rumors of corruption in the lower courts emerged in the late 1950s. In 1960, statesman Mohamad Rum gave an interview that, with the benefit of hindsight, can be viewed as prophetic: "Corruption in the courts has begun. It is only a little so far, one or two judges. But it has begun and that is what is important. This beginning may well develop into something deeper and more widespread."[254] This deeper and more widespread corruption, predicted by Mohamad Rum, did not materialize until much later, however.[255] The large-scale corruption that marks the Indonesian judiciary is really a New Order phenomenon. As one respected legal observer commented: "Such things never occurred under the Old Order. It is under the New Order that the mentality of the people began to change."[256]

Indeed, from the 1970s onwards, as the judiciary was being strengthened through the addition of new courts and justices, that upward trend was matched by a steep decline in professional morale among judges. By the early 1980s, and coinciding with Seno Adji's retirement as Supreme Court chairman, the problem had become so great that the government started a special anti-graft operation specifically directed at the judiciary. This so-called OPSTIB campaign uncovered such massive networks of judicial corruption that around this time the term "judicial mafia" first emerged.[257] The campaign led to the first highly publicized

---

[253] I define corruption as "behavior which deviates from the formal duties of a public role because of private-regarding (personal, close family, private clique), pecuniary or status-gains; or violates rules against the exercise of certain types of private-regarding behavior." cf. R. Klitgaard, *Controlling Corruption* (Berkeley: University of California Press, 1988), p. 23. Inevitably, the emphasis rests on deviating behavior induced by pecuniary and status-gains. .

[254] *DSL*, 10 February 1960.

[255] According to some observers, corruption in the lower courts "was rife by 1959," but I maintain that conditions under the New Order were substantially worse. *DSL*, 8 July 1959.

[256] *Forum Keadilan*, 17 September 1992.

[257] *Tempo*, 17 March 1979. According to prominent advocate M. Assegaf, it emerged when he was discussing a case with the OPSTIB leaders Sudomo and Kanter. The term remains controversial to the present day, principally because some circles deny the structured nature of corruption it implies. Nevertheless, others argue that the term is appropriate, because, in fact, judicial corruption is not just pervasive but also organized, with active involvement of outside parties such as advocates and government officials. In any case, the term has taken root in the press lore and is generally accepted.

dismissals (and in some cases subsequent imprisonments) of a number of prominent lower court judges such as Soemadijono, Heru Gunawan, Hanky Azhar, Loudoe, and Staa.[258] From that point the pressure increased, until by 1992 a grand total of 666 general court judges (30 percent of the entire judicial corps) had suffered a variety of disciplinary sanctions for corruption; four hundred of them were either dismissed from the service or so drastically demoted as to make resignation their only option.[259] And the pace intensified, as in May 1992 alone, fifty-seven judges were dismissed and seventy others were punished on corruption charges.[260] By the 1990s, corruption in the lower courts had become endemic, to the point that Supreme Court chairman Purwoto opened a special PO Box for anonymous complaints concerning judicial malfeasance.[261] The Supreme Court chairman had to allow for the possibility that up to half of the entire Indonesian judiciary was involved in corruption—"I don't think the number of corrupt judges exceeds 50 percent," said Supreme Court chairman Soerjono somewhat tentatively in 1995.[262] Former Supreme Court junior chairman Asikin Kusumah Atmadja confirmed this figure in less unequivocal terms, saying, "about 50 percent of the judges are corrupt,"[263] but knowledgeable observers considered even this to be a conservative estimate.[264]

The corruption hemorrhage in the lower courts inevitably affected the Supreme Court, but at least until 1974 it remained essentially clean.[265] This purity is remarkable because during the 1950s and 60s Supreme Court judges were comparatively much poorer than Court judges nowadays, when corruption has clearly infected the Court. Thus, as we saw, Supreme Court chairman Wirjono Prodjodikoro only managed to survive by renting out his official car as a taxi, and practically all Supreme Court judges had to write books on the side to make a living. This disciplined morale collapsed when Seno Adji became chairman. "Subekti was squeaky clean. Corruption on the Supreme Court started with Seno Adji."[266]

The principal cause of the problem was Seno Adji himself, who is said to have begun fiddling with funds almost from the start. Insiders allege that when one of his children took a honeymoon trip to Surabaya, Seno Adji forced the Surabaya court chairman to stamp the bills as office expenses, thus enabling him to cover these personal expenses with funds from the Supreme Court budget. (This story is

---

[258] See for instance *Tempo,* 6 December 1980; *Tempo,* 25 July, 1981; *Tempo,* 21 January 1981; *Tempo* 7, 14 February 1981.

[259] *Kompas,* 15 August 1992; *Pelita,* 11 January 1994.

[260] *Forum Keadilan,* 17 September 1992. Sixty other judges were punished on other grounds.

[261] *Forum Keadilan,* 1 October 1992; 21 January 1993. The PO Box was numbered 1992. The effectiveness of the measure is hard to gauge. Nevertheless, PO Boxes in which the public was asked to deposit anonymous complaints had been opened by the government before with mixed success. In fact, in one recent case a person who lodged a complaint was prosecuted, which surely must have reduced the effectiveness of this system. *Forum Keadilan,* 28 May, 1992; *Forum Keadilan,* 9 July 1992.

[262] *Far Eastern Economic Review,* 20 April 1995, p. 20 quoting the Jakarta Post.

[263] *Forum Keadilan,* 19 January 1995.

[264] Advocate and human rights activist T. Mulya Lubis stated that the percentage assuredly was higher. *Forum Keadilan,* 19 January 1995.

[265] The one exception perhaps was the Malikul Adil incident, which never was clearly decided one way or the other. See above, Chapter 9, section 1.

[266] Personal communication, 19 July 1994.

contested by the Seno Adji family.) As report of this scam was widespread, other judges soon felt little held them back from charging their own families' travel expenses—perhaps initially for trips to places like Bandung, but then farther afield—as business expenses. Seno Adji could not really restrain this practice because he had compromised himself with his own behavior, and apparently, as his former colleagues and those intimately aware would later recount, was continuing to do so.[267] A Supreme Court junior chairman reported that a holiday trip that Seno Adji took with his family to Japan was entirely funded from kickbacks.[268] Seno Adji allegedly established networks within the judiciary, "with lines running through the appeal courts."[269] As one of his close associates in the Court related:

> Seno Adji is deeply involved with money, as are several other judges on the Supreme Court. There are only two or three honest ones, the rest are all on the take. Money comes in sometimes directly from litigants or their counsel, and also from the district court, which has a line to Seno Adji through which part of their take is submitted. Thus there are several district court chairman who are Seno men, and they send in the dough.[270]

With the Supreme Court chairman operating in this manner, many other judges on the Court found it hard to resist the temptations and were drawn into the corruption net. Sometimes they were actively compromised by Seno Adji himself. As one Supreme Court judge recounted:

> At one time, after I had another falling-out with Seno Adji, he sent his registrar along with some "household" money. I rejected it, but the registrar then said that all the other Supreme Court judges got it. This is not right.[271]

As a result, from the late 1970s onwards it became increasingly hard for a Supreme Court judge to maintain their integrity. The numbers of good and honest judges decreased, and such justices came to be threatened with isolation. As one Court judge commented: "If before one had to search for a corrupt judge with a lantern, now one must use the lantern to find an honest one."[272]

Corruption on the Supreme Court became as pervasive as in the lower courts, and while some chairmen tried to address the dilemma, it proved to be uncontrollable. Prominent lawyers would recount that no one "can get anything done on the Supreme Court without kickbacks."[273] One Supreme Court judge admitted to the press in the 1990s: "Yes, I often get gifts from litigants. If you call that corrupt, well indeed, then I must be corrupt. If I wasn't, how do you think I could have a car and a house?"[274] Advocates said they didn't "remember a single case in my nearly

---

[267] Personal communication, 30 June 1994.
[268] Personal communication, 16 July 1994.
[269] *DSL*, 18 October, 1978.
[270] *DSL*, 30 October 1978.
[271] *DSL* 21 October 1978.
[272] Personal communication, 12 July 1994.
[273] Personal communication, 4 July 1994.
[274] *Forum Keadilan,* 17 September 1992.

twenty years of practice, in which I didn't have to pay. And it goes all the way to the top, including the Supreme Court leadership."[275] One junior chairman on the Court emphatically stated: "The entire Supreme Court fabric is permeated by corruption and it is rooted in the very top of the institution. Everyone, from the leadership to the new recruits, is involved."[276]

It is currently common knowledge that the Supreme Court is affected by corruption, and judges in private conversation have referred to it for many years as a routine matter. Nevertheless, for a long time the press was hesitant to expose this reality. This only changed in 1980, when, in a famous incident, parliamentarian V. B. da Costa stated publicly that middlemen were operating within the Supreme Court, which amounted to accusing Court judges of corruption.[277] His castigation of the Court as the "rotten Supreme Court" was an important turning point in the Court's history, as it initiated a loss of public respect for the institution and signaled the failure of Supreme Court judges to maintain the moral high ground.[278]

Since then, reports of the Court's improprieties have multiplied, particularly since the early 1990s, when the press began to cover the Court quite intensively.[279] Da Costa's public accusation apparently breached the taboo, as afterwards more cases came to be reported in which Supreme Court judges were accused of corruption.[280] In fact, Supreme Court history in the past five years amounts to an ongoing litany of allegations of smaller and larger crimes. In 1996, one of the individuals who had campaigned against graft, Supreme Court junior chairman Adi Andoyo Soetjipto, openly stated in the press that he had a "barn full of material on corruption in the Supreme Court."[281] Unfortunately evidence of wrongdoing was often made up of strong allegations and suspicions, hard to prove in legal terms. This nearly impossible burden of proof helped spawn a new concept and term, namely *kolusi*, or collusion.

The term *kolusi*, as it has come to be used in this context, indicates the cooperation between Supreme Court insiders and outsiders to steer a case in such a way as to realize a favorable outcome.[282] This practice is much easier to establish, because all one needs to show is that the regular procedure in case handling was violated without reason, and that the relevant Court staff was instrumental in realizing this violation. As one Supreme Court judge put it:

> I have always been careful in my official documents to distinguish between collusion and corruption. Corruption is almost impossible to prove; not so with collusion. Of course, the charge of collusion will only lead to an internal

---

[275] Personal communication, 8 July 1994.

[276] Personal communication, 7 July 1994.

[277] *Tempo*, 17 May 1980.

[278] His statement was that "in the history of the Court never has the picture been as rotten as it is now." *Tempo*, 20 September 1980.

[279] *Pelita*, 3 November 1992; *Tempo*, 7 November 1992.

[280] *Forum Keadilan*, 21 July 1994, p. 21.

[281] *Kompas*, 9 May 1996.

[282] See for instance Adi Andoyo Soetjipto, "Uraian secara kronologis terjadinya masalah 'kolusi' di Mahkamah Agung RI" (unpublished paper, 1996), p. 7.

administrative sanction at best, but at least something will have been achieved.[283]

For the public, however, the distinction between collusion and corruption is slim at best. As Adi Andoyo Soetjipto himself pointed out: " . . . isn't it fair to assume that behind collusion, money plays its part also?"[284]

Supreme Court collusion and corruption significantly weaken the authority of the Court, both within the judiciary itself and in society. It fuels widespread suspicion and cynicism concerning the Court's role and actions, and is at the root of the apparent inability of both the judiciary and the government to eradicate graft in the courts. Finally, collusion and corruption contribute to the unpredictability in the outcome of cases and to inconsistent decision making, so that ultimately they obstruct the lawmaking authority of Supreme Court decisions.

(ii) Rationality and Mysticism

Mysticism broadly refers to the belief that there are intangible and unseen forces that can influence the course of events and can be manipulated, for better or for worse. In the Indonesian and, notably, Javanese contexts, believers rely on mediums when they wish to influence such forces. These are persons who are deemed susceptible to supernatural powers and skilled in such matters, and who can summon mystical forces to manifest themselves. Sometimes they can also direct them. Rituals, such as meditation or appropriately timed visits to holy spots, are often performed for these purposes. Sometimes objects are used, such as the Javanese dagger (*kris*). Believers also accept that forces can also be unleashed from objects themselves without intervention by mediums. Such mystical objects are perceived to have soul and will and to exercise power.

The extent to which Supreme Court judges follow this belief system is difficult to quantify precisely. It seems that a number of key judges in the Court leadership over the past decades have to some degree or the other attached credence to these beliefs. One shaman of reported integrity said that he was consulted by five Supreme Court judges,[285] but he certainly was not the only one consulted.[286]

Judges who follow this belief system share a number of characteristics. The first is that most of them are from the island of Java, more specifically from the Javanese population group, and notably the Hinduized Javanese social elite. This is not to say that Supreme Court judges from the other islands are not open to mysticism, however, as indeed I found a number of them quite receptive to its ideas. The second characteristic is that judges who are more orthodox as Muslims tend to be less susceptible to mysticism, as if the two faiths were, to some degree, mutually exclusive. This does not necessarily mean that a more orthodox (*santri*) Muslim judge would reject the claims of mysticism entirely, but merely that he is convinced

---

[283] Personal communication, 10 May 1996.

[284] Soetjipto, "Uraian secara kronologis terjadinya masalah 'kolusi' di Mahkamah Agung RI," p. 7.

[285] Personal communication, 16 August 1994.

[286] Personal communications, 4, 7 July 1994.

it has no grip on him. One Outer Island Supreme Court judge, a firm Muslim, put it as follows:

> **Supreme Court judge**: I am not susceptible to mysticism because I am a good Muslim. It is only when one is empty that these forces can enter.
> **SP**: And when is one empty?
> **Supreme Court judge**: Well during times of personal difficulties, for instance. Such as when you have love trouble, or start losing your faith.[287]

Another Supreme Court judge, non-Javanese and non-Muslim, put it as follows:

> I am too strong for mysticism. But I was brought up with it. When I was born, my lips were painted red with my mother's blood so that they would remain so always. My head would be squeezed every morning to elongate it and make it beautiful, and my ears would be massaged to take away the ugly little wrinkles and curls that you have. And then, in the Javanese tradition my mother for years put little offerings in the four corners of the room to ward off evil spirits.[288]

People resort to mystic intervention most often to resolve personal problems. Judges resort to it when other, more rational, methods fail, or quite simply are inadequate. Health problems are a typical reason for turning to mysticism.

> Already in 1965 Supreme Court junior chairman X began practicing *jalangkung* within the Court—one of these things [rituals] in which a sort of metal pyramid stands on a table with a pencil hanging from the center on a string. Someone goes into a trance and begins to write, in circles and twirls, and everyone crowds around, trying to figure out what it means. I think he started with this because his brother and sister had problems, and he was seeking guidance.[289]

The line between the personal and professional is easily breached, and mysticism inevitably came to influence the justices' professional behavior in the Supreme Court. For instance, one of the reasons for the specific shape of the Court reorganization under Chairman Mudjono was to give the number of judges, chambers and teams "mystical quality." There were of course substantive arguments for increasing the number of judges, but the precise number of new judges and their division into teams and chambers also involved some "mystical arithmetic." Adding these new judges would bring the total number of chambers to seventeen, which Supreme Court chairman Mudjono deemed a "holy" figure, in part because it is the date of Indonesia's Declaration of Independence. The chambers would be grouped into eight teams, again a "holy" number because Indonesia's Declaration of

---

[287] Personal communication, 16 August 1994.

[288] Personal communication, 4 July 1994.

[289] Personal communication, 3 August 1994. Based on an additional interview, I believe Supreme Court judge X turned to mysticism because he had a son with serious health problems, who ultimately died young, which made the judge despair and seek solutions in mysticism. Personal communication, 24 April 1995. [shifted this comment to footnote]

Independence was delivered in August (the eighth month). Moreover, some projected the number of Supreme Court justices minus the chairmen and came up with the number forty-five, again a holy figure because 1945 is the Year of Indonesian Independence. What's more, as a prominent member of Parliament stated, the numbers four and five, if added together, make nine, which coincides with the number of letters in INDONESIA; nine is also a purportedly mystical figure because the sum of the numerals for any of its multiples is always nine (18, 27, 36, and so forth). These numerical mystical concepts were frequently mentioned during the parliamentary debates.[290]

Supreme Court chairman Mudjono was very much involved in this mystic mathematical exercise, as evidenced by his somewhat baffling statement in Parliament on February 11, 1982:

> The figure seventeen also is a holy figure—currently we only have eight chambers, so we still need an additional nine chambers, a holy figure again. So *in concreto* we are still short of 9 x 3, which equals twenty-seven judges—note that two plus seven equals nine. Functionally speaking 24 + 27 = 51, the composite figures of which make six, which is a reversed nine.[291]

Supreme Court judges would later acknowledge that the figure seventeen has significance beyond the fact that it marks the date of Indonesian independence, though what significance precisely they couldn't tell: "Those seventeen chambers instituted under Mudjono have something to do with his Javanese mysticism, but I don't know what precisely. I just associate it with our date of independence."[292]

Aside from influencing the judiciary's organization, mysticism also plays a role for individual judges in their professional capacity. Supreme Court chairman X first established contact with a spiritual leader in Central Java for personal reasons, namely that his daughter had inexplicably developed difficulties in walking. Medical doctors were at a loss how to handle the problem, and she had been bedridden for two years. The spiritual leader managed to cure the woman.

---

[290] See for instance MP Professor Soenarjo in *Catatan Komisi III DPR-RI dengan Ketua Mahkamah Agung (Mudjono) no.2115/Kom.III/82* dated 11 February 1982, p. 10; Supreme Court chairman Seno Adji *Catatan sementara rapat Komisi III PR-RI dengan Ketua Mahkamah Agung (Seno Adji) no.02/Kom.III/78* dated 3 November 1977, p. 3, who calls the increase to seventeen Supreme Court judges under his administration a "holy" figure. Mudjono would later point out that this increase to seventeen judges coincided with the number plate of the official car of the chairman at the time (B 17) *Catatan rapat kerja Komisi III dengan Ketua Mahkamah Agung no.798/Kom.III/83* dated 10 February 1983, p. 6. Similarly, he said, the subsequent increase to twenty-four judges coincided with the license plate number on the official car of the minister of justice.

> The figure twenty-four is a telling one [...], if only because art.24 of the 1945 Constitution is the article that states the administration of justice will be realized by a Mahkamah Agung and other courts as established by law. Also, President Suharto once said that a day consists of twenty-four hours, [...] and when I received this message from him when still minister of justice, my official car had the figure B 24 on its license plate.

Rapat kerja Komisi III dengan Ketua Mahkamah Agung (Mudjono) no.650/ Kom.III/82 dated 1 December 1982, p. 46.

[291] *Catatan rapat kerja Komisi III DPR-RI dengan Ketua Mahkamah Agung (Mudjono) no.2115/Kom.III/82* dated 11 February 1982, p. 17.

[292] Personal communication, 4 August 1994.

Some years later, the chairman's daughter developed other health problems, and again the spiritual leader was called in and managed to remedy the situation for which, apparently, Chairman X was so grateful that he gave him an expensive Swiss watch. The connection became more intense still when the spiritual leader was called in for the most difficult task. Chairman X's mother had been in a coma, with no signs of brain activity, for a few years, but had hung onto life; the shaman was called in to help her die. Through exercising his power, he allegedly removed the shadows from around her, and she died shortly after his visit.

Some years later, the government put out feelers to enquire whether this same judge might consider becoming minister of justice. Using his brother as an intermediary, the judge asked the advice of the spiritual leader, who at first refused to answer because he felt the issue was not in his realm. But the judge insisted. Ultimately the leader conceded, and after some introspection suggested that the judge remain on the Supreme Court.[293]

There was a gradual shift from the personal to the professional. Judges who gave credence to mysticism "began to take their clerks to graves and volcanoes, meditating and doing magical stuff there," as one clerk put it.[294] But then, rather than simply serving as a guide under difficult conditions, mysticism actually came to be used as a weapon for fighting internal power struggles within the Court. "Junior Chairman X began to have these trances, sometimes even during RAPIM (Rapat Pimpinan, leadership meetings), in which he would directly accuse other Supreme Court judges, even the chairman, of malfeasance."[295] "It happened so frequently, we got rather used to it."[296] With time, according to several current Supreme Court judges, mysticism evolved into an instrument by which the Court's staff can be and are personally threatened. Following the retirement of a prominent junior chairman recently, one of his four senior clerks suddenly died, another developed cancer, a third had a serious stroke forcing him to retire, the fourth, while in good health, has family members who are very ill, and a number of the judge's administrative staff met with misfortune. Mysticism was blamed for this pattern of events. As two Supreme Court judges put it:

> There are so many ill and dead on the Supreme Court recently that I do not doubt that this is the work of Junior Chairman X. In our offices, the newly born son of one employee suddenly died for no apparent reason whatsoever, and another employee had a child who suffocated from having the umbilical cord twisted around his neck, and then so many others are seriously ill or have died.[297]

> I think that somehow Junior Chairman X has had a hand in using mysticism to make some of his close associates ill. He cannot touch me, I am too strong, but family members of mine have fallen seriously ill recently.[298]

---

[293] Personal communication, 16 August 1994.

[294] Personal communication, 28 June 1994.

[295] Personal communication, 4 July 1994.

[296] Personal communication, 4 August 1994.

[297] Personal communication, 22 August 1994.

[298] Personal communication, 3 August 1994.

Such interpretations fueled distrust of this judge and people closely associated with him.

> After the retirement of this highly mystical judge, one of his clerks was attached to another judge. She scared the wits out of him, he wouldn't even take a glass of water from her, and within a week he had her moved out of his offices.[299]

I have not heard of cases in which mysticism determined decision making, although there have been instances of litigating parties trying to contact and influence key Supreme Court judges through their spiritual leaders.[300]

These reports regarding mysticism tell us something about the characters of some Supreme Court judges and the way in which they define their place and role in the world. The impact of mysticism on their professional behavior, however, is difficult to assess precisely.

5. CONCLUSION

This chapter began by looking at the conditions of employment for Supreme Court judges. Apart from discussing the issues of remuneration and dismissal, it has concentrated on the method of recruiting Supreme Court judges, particularly the issue of whether or not to recruit "outsiders"—those who have no professional experience in the judiciary—and the transparency of the recruitment process. Notwithstanding the constitutional role of Parliament, the prevailing system of recruitment is predominantly and effectively controlled by the bureaucracy, is not at all transparent, and is open to many improprieties. This lack of transparency is an important factor in obscuring the personalities of the judges who are recruited and the views which they hold.

Despite the obscurity shielding judges from examination, an obscurity exacerbated by the Court's constantly changing composition, some basic data on the judges can be provided. First, and in terms of professional background, career judges remain the overwhelming majority on the Court and constitute its professional backbone. The large majority of judges still come from either Universitas Indonesia or Gadjah Mada University, though there has been increasing diversity in recent years. While most of the judges are Muslim, almost all quite deliberately restrict the role of religion in their professional performance. The Court, in fact, has a history of mild resistance against Islam, though that may be declining at present. Second, as regards social background, the old Javanese bureaucratic elite still dominates the Court, to the extent that a number of judges who share this background are in fact closely related. This influence, however, seems to be receding and is being replaced by new, somewhat ad hoc networks, based in part on the leverage which powerful judges wield during recruitment, and in part on new emerging power groups. At least half of the judges are Javanese, but lately an increasing number of justices from different ethnicities have found their way to the

---

[299] Personal communication, 4 July 1994.

[300] Apparently NGOs involved in the *First Kedung Ombo case* attempted to recruit a spiritual leader who had served a number of key Supreme Court judges to act as an intermediary for them, but he refused. Personal communications, 9 September 1994; 23 November 1994.

Court, including a sizeable representation of Bataks. It should be noted, however, that there are no judges at all from the eastern half of the archipelago. Finally, female judges have consistently been strongly represented on the Court. They are respected for their integrity, but they have not yet achieved leadership positions on the Court.

In looking at the judges, it is apparent that the Court's leaders play an important role. The leadership standards of many Supreme Court chairmen have fallen far short of the ideal, however, as a number of chairmen have failed to impose institutional values on the Court's environment and have also failed to enhance internal cohesion and morale. This condition, characterized by weak leadership, sprang naturally from the nature of the recruitment process, which has been largely directed toward recruiting leaders who have either strong ties to the executive branch of the government or accommodating dispositions.

Finally, we find that over the past decades the judges' professional disposition seems to have changed in a number of significant ways. Professional standards have declined in three important fields: first, in terms of a decreasing knowledge of and agreement on the standing law; second, in terms of declining comparative legal knowledge; and third, in terms of declining personal strictness. We find, at the same time, that new standards have emerged, including increased political awareness on the part of the justices, the increased importance they attach to status, a related tendency toward corruption, and finally, a more pronounced inclination to put their faith in mysticism, which has been reflected in both the work and personal relations on the Court.

Prior to *Reformasi*, there was already widespread agreement in Indonesia that the Supreme Court was weak on independence and professional skills. Yet at the same time a fundamental difference of opinion existed concerning how this should influence the recruitment of Supreme Court judges. This theme has dominated debates before and after *Reformasi* in equal measure.

The judiciary by and large saw (and continues to see) government interference as the principal cause for its weakened performance, particularly in the recruitment mechanism. Its response to society's increased demand for strengthening court performance has been to argue that outside interference in the recruitment process be minimized. This means both exclusion of outsiders in deciding who is appointed to the (Supreme) court, and exclusion of outside recruits. The judiciary in essence proposed to restrict the recruitment pool for the superior courts to the sitting judges only. On the other hand, broad sections of people outside the courts took the view that poor court performance is, at least in part, the result of the existing closed recruitment mechanism that prevails in Indonesia, in which judicial recruitment amounts to a process of qualified co-optation.

Responses to the problems, as a result, are diametrically opposed: the judiciary fundamentally believes that the problems cannot be overcome unless its own grip on recruitment is strengthened to the exclusion of outside agencies. Also, it believes that the system cannot work properly unless it is staffed with professional judges. The other view holds that problems will not be overcome unless both the recruitment mechanism and the candidates come from outside the system.

Both approaches share a distrust of Indonesian political institutions and the political process. The outside view is that a system of closed recruitment in the end inevitably generates a self-serving professional elite, and reduces transparency and accountability. There can be no denying that resistance among many judges against opening up recruitment is motivated in part by self-serving reasons. But at the same time, a review of historical reality shows that judges have lived through two or three generations of systemic neglect and interference at the hands of government and parliament. Those who ignore this legacy fail to do justice either to history or to the judges.

The judges, in reality, are a mixed bag. Some only try to preserve the present, but other serious and reform-minded judges try to recover from the past and are looking to save the future. One of the striking features of judicial opposition against opening up recruitment is that it cuts across the political spectrum, and notably includes serious and reform-minded judges. The principal motive of this group is distrust of institutional stability and the political process. Drawing on bitter experience spanning several decades, these reform-minded judges oppose opening up recruitment not because they think there are no outside people who would do well on the bench. Instead, they do not trust political institutions to perform their tasks over the long run in a manner that would insure qualified candidates are recruited. Basically, history teaches them only to trust themselves. This outlook may not generate much enthusiasm with observers, but there is a brute realism informing this view that is hard to dismiss. The highly mercurial, unprofessional, and ineffective performance record of political institutions over the past four decade makes the judiciary understandably reluctant to grant those institutions more power over its affairs and gives the open recruitment system a somewhat speculative character.

At issue is the relation between institutional empowerment and performance. Basically, reformers must ask what the response should be to poor institutional performance; this question is just as relevant for the political institutions as it is for the judiciary. Is it best to restrict or to expand authority, and how can one enhance mechanisms by which these institutions can be made to account for the exercise of their authority? However understandable the position of the reform-minded judges may be, it also is flawed. For reasons of democratic legitimacy and political-power dynamics, it will not be possible for the judiciary to secure the more powerful political function it aspires to gain (in terms of greater control over its internal affairs and the exercise of its functions, such as judicial review) unless political institutions take part in determining the way the judiciary is constituted. Also, in the end, there is no way for parliament and the executive to step back from their responsibilities in positioning the judiciary in the democratic system. The current weaknesses of the judiciary, in the end, are rooted in a poorly developed commitment of the political institutions to the rule of law. For structural change to take place, political institutions must increase, rather than decrease, their engagement. The Indonesian judiciary's conviction that it can fix its problems all by itself—however understandable this attitude may be in a historical context—is basically ill conceived. It is wrong on constitutional principle, it fails to acknowledge the dynamic of politics and the way politics has an impact on institutional power relationships, and, in the end, it reflects a limited understanding of the judiciary's own place and role.

Independence was delivered in August (the eighth month). Moreover, some projected the number of Supreme Court justices minus the chairmen and came up with the number forty-five, again a holy figure because 1945 is the Year of Indonesian Independence. What's more, as a prominent member of Parliament stated, the numbers four and five, if added together, make nine, which coincides with the number of letters in INDONESIA; nine is also a purportedly mystical figure because the sum of the numerals for any of its multiples is always nine (18, 27, 36, and so forth). These numerical mystical concepts were frequently mentioned during the parliamentary debates.[290]

Supreme Court chairman Mudjono was very much involved in this mystic mathematical exercise, as evidenced by his somewhat baffling statement in Parliament on February 11, 1982:

> The figure seventeen also is a holy figure—currently we only have eight chambers, so we still need an additional nine chambers, a holy figure again. So *in concreto* we are still short of 9 x 3, which equals twenty-seven judges—note that two plus seven equals nine. Functionally speaking 24 + 27 = 51, the composite figures of which make six, which is a reversed nine.[291]

Supreme Court judges would later acknowledge that the figure seventeen has significance beyond the fact that it marks the date of Indonesian independence, though what significance precisely they couldn't tell: "Those seventeen chambers instituted under Mudjono have something to do with his Javanese mysticism, but I don't know what precisely. I just associate it with our date of independence."[292]

Aside from influencing the judiciary's organization, mysticism also plays a role for individual judges in their professional capacity. Supreme Court chairman X first established contact with a spiritual leader in Central Java for personal reasons, namely that his daughter had inexplicably developed difficulties in walking. Medical doctors were at a loss how to handle the problem, and she had been bedridden for two years. The spiritual leader managed to cure the woman.

---

[290] See for instance MP Professor Soenarjo in *Catatan Komisi III DPR-RI dengan Ketua Mahkamah Agung (Mudjono) no.2115/Kom.III/82* dated 11 February 1982, p. 10; Supreme Court chairman Seno Adji *Catatan sementara rapat Komisi III PR-RI dengan Ketua Mahkamah Agung (Seno Adji) no.02/Kom.III/78* dated 3 November 1977, p. 3, who calls the increase to seventeen Supreme Court judges under his administration a "holy" figure. Mudjono would later point out that this increase to seventeen judges coincided with the number plate of the official car of the chairman at the time (B 17) *Catatan rapat kerja Komisi III dengan Ketua Mahkamah Agung no.798/Kom.III/83* dated 10 February 1983, p. 6. Similarly, he said, the subsequent increase to twenty-four judges coincided with the license plate number on the official car of the minister of justice.

> The figure twenty-four is a telling one [. . .], if only because art.24 of the 1945 Constitution is the article that states the administration of justice will be realized by a Mahkamah Agung and other courts as established by law. Also, President Suharto once said that a day consists of twenty-four hours, [. . .] and when I received this message from him when still minister of justice, my official car had the figure B 24 on its license plate.

Rapat kerja Komisi III dengan Ketua Mahkamah Agung (Mudjono) no.650/ Kom.III/82 dated 1 December 1982, p. 46.

[291] *Catatan rapat kerja Komisi III DPR-RI dengan Ketua Mahkamah Agung (Mudjono) no.2115/Kom.III/82* dated 11 February 1982, p. 17.

[292] Personal communication, 4 August 1994.

Chapter Ten

The Impact of Supreme Court Decisions (Jurisprudence)

Preceding chapters have been directed toward describing the way the Supreme Court performs its functions, notably its core decision-making function. This chapter proposes to consider the implementation of Court decisions. It will argue that the degree of authority of Court decisions can be traced back, in part, to the doctrinal roots of the civil law system, but can be linked more specifically to the way in which this system has been interpreted and applied in Indonesia over the past fifty years. In addition, however, this chapter will show that there are real and basic problems with the authority of Supreme Court decisions, deriving from access difficulties, the inconsistent and inadequate method of selecting decisions for publication, and the like. Finally, this chapter will try to explain how, in some areas of the law, the Supreme Court is, in fact, quite consistent. By the early 1990s, it was plain that the Supreme Court was in a profound crisis. Its lawmaking capacity, weakened by political interference and organizational obstacles, was floundering completely as a result of the massive backlogs. As we shall see shortly, in its frantic attempts to overcome the increasing workload, by 1990 the Supreme Court seemed to have abandoned all hope of keeping the lower courts in line or contributing to legal development through its Court decisions, the publication of which had ceased altogether.

It is against this background that the 1993 Five Year Development Plan was unveiled. One of the most notable changes in this document compared with preceding plans was in the field of law, as the section on law improvement was upgraded from a mere paragraph to a full chapter—a change in status that inevitably would involve budgetary increases and organizational reinforcement.[1] More significant from the perspective of the judiciary was that this important policy document acknowledged, for the first time, the necessity of strengthening the role of the courts in the development of substantive law. Earlier plans, insofar

---

[1] Law is one of seven fields requiring specific attention, as defined in the 1993 Five-Year Development Plan, which is an integral part of the Guidelines of State Policy, which are defined every five years by the Indonesian People's Congress (MPR, Majelis Permusyawaratan Rakyat). The field is specified as follows:

> The establishment of the national law by implanting a pattern of ideas conducive to the arrangement of a national legal system based on Pancasila and the 1945 Constitution; the arrangement of the framework for a national legal system; and the inventorying and adjustment of elements of law codes in the framework of national legal renewal; the improvement of law enforcement and promotion of the legal apparatus; and the improvement of legal facilities and infrastructure.

The 1993 Guidelines of State Policy (Jakarta: Department of Information, 1993), p. 45.

as they dealt with the courts at all, had focused only on court infrastructure and had seemed little concerned about what went on inside. Now, policy makers emphasized that court decisions must play their part in the development of Indonesian law. Substantive law must be developed, the document stated,

> by strengthening the lawmaking function of the judiciary; and improving the position and role of jurisprudence as a source of law, as well as broadening the publication of jurisprudence so that it will not just be limited to the courts, but be extended also to the other legal professions, higher education and the public at large.[2]

As usual, the plan generated a flutter of activities. The July 1994 National Law Seminar was a new high point, with one of its principal themes the role of the courts in legal development. In fact, attention was entirely focused on the role of court decisions outside the courtroom; in other words, how jurisprudence might serve as an instrument shaping the law, not just for litigating parties, but for society at large. Minister of Justice Oesman put it in somewhat plastic terms during the opening address:

> In the formation of our substantive National Law, we must pay attention to the development and upgrading of firm jurisprudence. Starting with the VI Five-Year Development Plan, it has become imperative now to determine what really constitutes jurisprudence, while the compilation of and computer access to court decisions now has first priority, so as to ensure rapid and easy public access.[3]

The seminar's exclusive emphasis on the lawmaking effect of court decisions was also made unequivocally clear in the concluding statement of the seminar, which concisely summarized the legal agenda in a handful of points:

2. On jurisprudence
2.1. Jurisprudence constitutes a source of law in our legal system, and as a result is a fundamental requirement to complement legislation in law enforcement;
2.2. Without jurisprudence, the function and authority of courts as instruments of the administration of justice will stagnate and become sterile;
2.3. Jurisprudence is needed to keep statutes up to date and effective, in addition to upholding the dignity of the courts, because it ensures legal certainty, social justice, and protection;
2.4. Systematic measures must be taken to improve jurisprudence as a source of national law;
2.5. The principle of judicial independence does not conflict with firm jurisprudence as a source of national law. The principle of judicial independence is directed towards the freedom of the judges from executive interference.[4]

---

[2] *Rencana Pembangunan Lima Tahun Keenam 1994/95–1998/99* (Buku IV) (Jakarta: Government Publications), pp. 474-75.

[3] "Address of the Minister of Justice of the Indonesian Republic, Mr. Oetoyo Oesman, to the VI National Law Seminar," *Varia Peradilan* 108 (September 1994): 123.

[4] "Hasil Seminar Hukum Nasional VI," *Varia Peradilan* 115 (April 1995): 149-50.

As a result of the upgrading of substantive legal development in the 1993 Five-Year Development Plan, a new position of Assistant Secretary for Law Upgrading was created at the Central Planning Board, BAPPENAS (Badan Perencanaan Pembangunan Nasional). Immediately after taking office, the newly appointed assistant secretary, Mr. Sutadi Djajakusuma, formulated the new government commitment toward enhancing the lawmaking capacity of the courts in unequivocal terms:

> In order to further the creation and effectiveness of a stable national legal system . . . the organization of national law shall be realized by . . . improving the upgrading and strengthening the position and role of jurisprudence as a source of law, as well as broadening the scope of the distribution of jurisprudence so that it will not just be restricted to the judiciary itself, but will also extend to other legal professions, higher education, as well as society at large.[5]

The 1993 Five-Year Development Plan and subsequent responses to this issue officially brought to light the widening gap between what the courts were expected to do and what they were actually accomplishing. They revealed a rising concern within government and broad sections of society about the failure of the courts, notably the Supreme Court, to contribute significantly to Indonesian legal development. As the plan stated, in so many words, "the quality and ability of the legal apparatus is as yet insufficient."[6]

The plan called for the judiciary to accept a greater role in explicating and defining ambiguities unresolved by statute in an increasingly complex society, a call echoed at the National Law Seminar, where a Supreme Court judge, in unambiguous terms, demanded that the courts cut a clear path through the messy thicket of statute and generate their own law.[7] The plan also revealed its concern about the inability of the courts to be consistent in their own decision making. This, too, was reflected at the seminar, where a senior government official advised the courts to be more consistent in their decision making:

> The most important thing is that the principle be recognized in Indonesian procedural law that lower judges must follow decisions of senior judges in cases of a more or less identical fact and law setting. If this principle is fully grasped, then firm jurisprudence will speedily develop by itself, so that it no

---

[5] S. Djajakusuma, *Perencanaan pembangunan hukum nasional dalam Pembangunan Jangka Panjang Kedua* (Jakarta: Badan Pembinaan Hukum Nasional, June 1995), pp. 11-12. Mr. Djajakusuma's interest in the role of the courts may have been stimulated by his wife, Mrs. M. Sutadi, who is a prominent and well-connected Supreme Court judge.

[6] *Rencana Pembangunan Lima Tahun Keenam 1994/95–1998/99*, pp. 474-75.

[7] The paper commenced with an extensive review of new legal developments that the Indonesian legislature had been slow to recognize or address (such as leasing, franchise, and negotiable instruments) and the complete failure of lower legislation to respond adequately to such social requirements. Inevitably, therefore, as the paper put it, "in order to realize legal certainty in Indonesia, jurisprudence as shaped by court decisions is absolutely required . . . " Prof. Dr. C. F. G. Sunaryati Hartono, "Pengembangan yurisprudensi tetap," Paper presented at the VI National Law Seminar, July 1994, p. 11.

longer becomes necessary to wonder how many times a judge must make an identical decision?[8]

This reference to senior judges made it clear that the Supreme Court was not exempted from the developments that were unfolding, since lawmaking was to be initiated by this august judicial body. From a political perspective, there is little doubt, in fact, that the 1993 Five-Year Development Plan was essentially a call for the Supreme Court to clean up its act and tighten control over the lower courts in order to improve their reliability and predictability.[9]

The particular value of the 1993 Five-Year Development Plan was that it raised a number of fundamental questions upon which the legal communities were then able to focus. These questions were essentially twofold. The first was the more conceptual issue of the precise meaning and function of court decisions in the Indonesian legal system; in other words, the plan instigated a serious reconsideration of the role of jurisprudence as a "source of law," an issue raised at the 1994 National Law Seminar, and of the purported principle in Indonesian procedural law "that lower judges must follow decisions of senior judges in cases of a more or less identical fact and law setting." The second issue involved the more practical matter of the function and realization of access to court decisions, as indicated by references to the importance of "the compilation and computer access to court decisions to ensure rapid and easy public access" and of "the distribution of jurisprudence." Both issues touch upon fundamental conceptual and real problems relating to court decisions and their application in the Indonesian context over the years. In this chapter, it will become apparent that the lawmaking powers of the Supreme Court are thwarted, at least partially, by the conceptual origins and development of the meaning of court decisions in the civil law system inherited from the Dutch and by the formidable access problems that plague the judiciary. Yet it would be an exaggeration to say that the Supreme Court has not been able to realize any role whatsoever in legal development. The final section, then, will briefly illustrate some of the areas in which the Court has been able to exercise its lawmaking powers and will offer some explanations as to why this is so.

1. COURT DECISIONS IN THE INDONESIAN CIVIL LAW CONTEXT (JURISPRUDENCE)

The primary question raised by the 1993 Five-Year Development Plan concerns the precise meaning and effect of court decisions in the Indonesian legal system. What is it, to repeat the words of minister of justice Oetoyo Oesman, that constitutes jurisprudence? The point at issue is whether the legal effect of court decisions is limited to litigating parties or reaches beyond the courtroom and actually contributes to legal development. This question generated the frequent references to jurisprudence as a "source of law" and to the purported principle in

---

[8] Ibid., p. 6.

[9] It must be noted that one of the most crucial questions in any legal system—namely, what purposes court decisions actually serve—is still the subject of debate in Indonesia fifty years after the national legal framework was established. This suggests that the Indonesian legal system is still, in many respects, engaged in defining its anchorage.

Indonesian law that lower courts are bound by higher court decisions. In reality, things are much less clear.[10] Even if policy makers and members of the legal professions are oriented toward strengthening the lawmaking effect of court decisions, this merely reaffirms existing uncertainties with regard to the meaning and role of jurisprudence in Indonesia.

The constant references to "jurisprudence" in the Indonesian policy documents and legal texts are a prime indication that the Indonesian legal system is still solidly embedded in the civil law system inherited from the Dutch. The term "jurisprudence," in fact, refers to the civil law court decisions following the French, not the Anglo-American, meaning of legal philosophy. This civil law tradition arguably granted court decisions relatively weak authority from the start, as shall become apparent.

The differences between *stare decisis* and jurisprudence lost their sharp edges during the twentieth century.[11] Just as the formidable impact of statutes increasingly pushed the Anglo-American system in the direction of civil law,[12] civil law courts, for their part, began to look more and more like their Anglo-American brethren. In fact, the courts' role in the civil law system has changed rapidly over the past fifty years, as traditional fears of and objections against judicial tyranny subsided and were replaced by concerns about ever-increasing government power. In the process, the authority of jurisprudence increased far beyond its historic and dogmatic constraints and has come to approximate the authority of judicial precedent in the Anglo-American system. If Anglo-American court decisions have "binding authority," civil court decisions acquired a "persuasive authority" that in some ways was no less strong. Admittedly, in the diverse and hierarchical civil law system, this authority attaches particularly to Supreme Court decisions rather than to decisions of lower courts, but this is only a minor point.

The authority of civil law decisions most closely approaches Anglo-American binding precedent when the Supreme Court gives an identical decision in a series of cases—the so-called "firm jurisprudence." So, whereas the decision in an incidental case (jurisprudence) in the civil law system can have great persuasive authority, a series of consistent decisions on a legal issue (firm jurisprudence) is actually seen as binding.[13] This consistency is enhanced by the fact that, contrary to early civil law doctrine and practice, supreme judicatures in various civil law systems have, in the past decades, actually begun to refer to their own cases as laying down "a firm rule," or "firm jurisprudence." As a result, court decisions in most civil law countries

---

[10] Indeed, whatever may have been intended by the qualification of court decisions as a "source of law," this by itself does not resolve the issue, as it remains unclear whether a court decision only serves as source of law between litigating parties or also for the general public.

[11] In his authoritative political analysis of judicial systems, Shapiro goes as far as to state that the qualification of Anglo-American law as case law and civil law systems as codified now is "fundamentally incorrect." Martin Shapiro, *Courts: A Comparative and Political Analysis* (Chicago: University of Chicago Press, 1981), p. 126.

[12] This has reached the point, in fact, that recently US Supreme Court justice Anthony Scalia qualified the US legal system as "civil" in its own right. See the 1995 Tanner lecture: "Common Law Courts in a Civil Law System: The Role of Federal Courts in Interpreting Statutes and the Constitution" and the comment of Professor M. A. Glendon (mimeo, 1995).

[13] The issue of how such a firm line of cases is recognized has never been fully resolved, though recently civil law courts have begun to define such firm jurisprudence themselves.

have lawmaking relevance that quite definitely reaches beyond the litigating parties. The distinctions between the Anglo-American *stare decisis* and civil law jurisprudence, then, should be viewed with attention to subtle nuances, in shades of grey, not black and white.[14]

Nevertheless, as John Merryman has put it, "folklore persists,"[15] and although the body of jurisprudence may have crossed the Rubicon to become equivalent to Anglo-American binding precedent, most civil law theory still remains on the shores of that river. Many legal scholars continue to assert that court decisions effectuate statute, but by themselves lack lawmaking capacity. In fact, civil law doctrine has sometimes been able to accommodate the increasing authority of jurisprudence in practice, if not in theory, even if only by bending over backwards. Thus, while civil law doctrine, by definition, would not acknowledge the overwhelming authority of "firm jurisprudence" as a source of law in its own right, it does give it binding authority through the backdoor of custom. Thus, it holds that it is not the series of court decisions, as such, that is binding, but the fact that the consistent line generates "custom," which that system acknowledges as a source of law.[16]

Yet in other cases, the gap between doctrine and reality quite simply could not be bridged. This is most apparent, perhaps, when one attempts to reconcile lawmaking by precedent with prevailing civil law notions of judicial independence—a point explicitly raised during the 1994 National Law Seminar. In the Anglo-American system, the doctrine of binding precedent is not perceived as something that affects judicial independence at all. This does not deny the reality that binding precedent, like statute, is an instrument by which the compliance of judges is ensured. Its doctrinal quality, however, prevents debate on what effectively is a restriction, however justifiable, of the freedom of judges to decide according to their own consciences. The civil law tradition lacks that doctrine, however. Civil law jurists are trained that judges may be restricted and directed by statute and custom, but not by any other instrument. The civil law concept of judicial independence, as a result, quite notably precludes the possibility of lower judges being directed by senior judges. As a result, the legal professions and the judges must make a mental leap to accommodate the idea of binding precedent, and this generates quite a bit of resistance. What's more, the civil law system does not really need binding precedent to realize compliance within the judiciary. The bureaucratic judicial organization ensures that judges who do not follow Supreme Court decisions will be unlikely candidates for advancement, and, as a result, will

---

[14] C. A. Uniken Venema, *Van common law en civil law: Inleiding tot het Anglo-Amerikaanse recht in vergelijking met het Nederlandse* (Zwolle: Tjeenk Willink, 1971), p. 28. I might add that the concept of "binding precedent" is generally oversimplified. It notably denies prevailing practices by which judges manage to evade precedent that might force them to undesirable outcomes. As John Merryman put it, "Everybody knows that civil law courts do use precedents. Everybody knows that common law courts distinguish cases they do not want to follow, and sometimes overrule their own decisions." John H. Merryman, *The Civil Law Tradition* (Stanford: Stanford University Press, 1985), p. 47.

[15] Ibid., p. 47.

[16] See, for instance, Van Apeldoorn (bew. Langemeijer), *Inleiding tot de studie van het Nederlandsche Recht* (Zwolle: Tjeenk Willink, 1946), p. 89; Van Apeldoorn, *Inleiding tot de studie van het Nederlandsche Recht* (Zwolle: Tjeenk Willink, 1985), p. 142.

be harmed in their career prospects. One Indonesian commentator quoted a Dutch Supreme Court judge as follows on the workings of the system:

> Even though the rule of binding precedent is not written down in black and white, if a lower judge in his decision were to differ or conflict with a decision of a higher court, his decision will of course be overturned on appeal, and this will reflect on the *conduite* of the judge.[17]

This approach has the theoretical attraction of, on the one hand, upholding the principle of judicial independence, yet, on the other, creating a strong incentive for judges to follow superior court decisions.[18]

Therefore, in the civil law system to the present day, doctrine has prevented court decisions from being acknowledged as binding authority, despite their influence in practice. This may not seem very important in the Western context, but in Indonesia it hobbled the courts in their struggle to assert their role in shaping law. This inheritance, without doubt, constituted the setting for developments in the 1990s. Yet even though doctrine may have been important as a background factor in undermining the authority of court decisions in Indonesia, post-independence changes in the system were no less important. The civil law system inherited by Indonesia at independence was, in fact, marked by an exceptionally strong jurisprudential tradition, and it is worth considering why that tradition subsequently plummeted.

Indonesia inherited the Dutch, rather than the French, civil law traditions, and, as previously established, the Dutch were not burdened by historical French fears of judicial tyranny; on the contrary, they had a long-standing history of quite effective and respected jurisprudence.[19] Though charmed by the logic of the separation of powers, the Dutch never pushed the system to its doctrinal extremes, and their legal system remained more open to judicial lawmaking. Indeed, the cassation system was never transplanted in its entirety to Holland; unlike the French *Cour de Cassation*, the Dutch Supreme Court, on various occasions, could actually decide a case on final appeal without obligation to remand.[20] This gave much greater lawmaking potential to Supreme Court decisions from the start, which the Court was not slow to use.

This lawmaking tradition was enhanced in the colonial context, in which a sprawling and understaffed judicial apparatus called for much tighter Supreme Court control than was necessary under European conditions. As we have seen, dogmatic restrictions of cassation were watered down even further, so that in

---

[17] Sunaryati Hartono, "Pengembangan yurisprudensi tetap," p. 8. As we saw in previous chapters, the *conduite* is the career record of a judge that determines his advancement in the judicial apparatus.

[18] Of course, and as I have indicated before, this approach will inevitably be more effective in the civil law system, in which closed recruitment and a diverse organization significantly affect whether a candidate is able to rise in the hierarchy, rather than in the Anglo-American system, where judges are, to a large extent, recruited from the pool of successful advocates and need not continue to prove themselves once they have been appointed to the bench.

[19] The low countries had been familiar with a Supreme Court system from the fourteenth century (the *Grote Raad* in Mechelen), which had worked to general satisfaction and had lawmaking powers. J. Th. de Smidt, "Een vergeten jubileum?" *Nederland Juristenblad* (1982): 492.

[20] D. J. Veegens, *Cassatie in Burgerlijke Zaken* (Zwolle: Tjeenk Willink, 1989), pp. 20-27.

practice Indonesian courts nearly claimed for themselves the power to revise or challenge legislation, preparing the ground for enhanced judicial lawmaking. As it happened, the authority of colonial Supreme Court decisions was also stimulated by a number of outside developments, including the fact that the colonial legislature was sometimes slow to keep track of legislative developments in the mother country. As a result, it was left to the judges to fill the gaps between lagging colonial legislation and legal practice that was governed by new insights and developments emanating from Europe. Colonial company law can serve as an example here. The colonial legislature failed to respond to the important 1928 amendment of the company code, and, as a result, relevant legislation was still firmly anchored in the 1848 Commercial Code. It was the courts that kept company law in touch with modern conditions and concepts; indeed they were sometimes so innovative that they forged ahead of developments in Europe.[21] Another factor that reinforced the authority of court decisions was the fact that the Indonesian judiciary was partly responsible for administering unwritten Indonesian *adat* law, regarding which court decisions were the principal, if not the only, source of legal consistency. This situation naturally pushed colonial courts toward a system that, in many ways, resembled the Anglo-American *modus operandi* even more closely than the one in Holland itself. In fact, a debate erupted in the colony concerning whether, with regard to *adat* law, the precedent system should actually be officially instituted, as the prominent *adat* law scholar Ter Haar argued.

A number of closely connected factors contributed to a decline in the role of jurisprudence after independence. Perhaps most importantly, civil law doctrine never acknowledged or spelled out the position of jurisprudence as a source of law. The authority of court decisions, as a result, was not one of the unquestioned pillars of the legal edifice, but instead depended essentially on what the legal actors were prepared and able to make of it. The political marginalization and organizational problems of the judiciary certainly weakened the authority of court decisions after 1950, so that legal precedent during subsequent decades had little effect on the evolution of Indonesian law. This situation was enhanced by an increasing government reliance on statute for shaping the country's laws. The government's social engineering policies called for directive and interventionist lawmaking, rather than the essentially passive and reactive judicial intervention that, because of the judiciary's diffuse organization, was likewise not always easy to steer. The erosion of the courts' authority and decisions was facilitated by the executive, which considered judges to be inadequate instruments for realizing the government's goals of rapid reform.

This erosion was, of course, further enhanced by a variety of technical factors. The rapid disappearance of the Dutch language definitely hit jurisprudence harder than statute, in part because jurisprudential analysis calls for more reading than does drafting a law, and the *ratio decidendi* of court decisions must be deduced by close reading and careful analysis. Statute, by way of contrast, is formulated in straightforward one-sentence instructions. In addition, as shall be apparent in the

---

[21] Thus, the colonial Supreme Court held in 1931 that the company was no longer based on contract, but instead should be viewed as an institution, and, as a result, the General Meeting of Shareholders lacked a general power of instruction toward the Board of Directors. Colonial Supreme Court HGH 12, February 1931, *Indisch Tijdschrift van het Recht* 133 (1931): 447. This decision preceded developments in the Netherlands by at least fifteen years. See J. W. Winter, "De pendule in het Nederlands vennootschapsrecht," *Advokatenblad* 68 (March 4, 1988): 110.

next section, haphazard and inadequate publication of court decisions quite clearly became an element that undermined the courts' authority.

The result was that jurisprudence all but lost its lawmaking authority after independence and was actually reduced to having legal effect only on both litigating parties, as required by strict civil law doctrine—a restriction that had never been actually followed either in Holland or in the colony. Neither colonial nor post-independence court decisions were consulted any longer in modern Indonesia, and the law was thrown back to its statutory basis. As a result, Indonesia, rather than building on the law as it stood at independence, turned back the clock on various issues.

As legislation came to be viewed as the sole and final statement of Indonesia's law, when the judiciary dealt with matters guided by colonial law it was sometimes forced to resurrect ossified pieces of nineteenth-century legislation that, even in colonial times, had been profoundly altered by jurisprudential interpretation. Moreover, after independence, the courts revealed themselves to be unable adequately to address this problem. To return to company law as an example, the Supreme Court case reporting series, *Yurisprudensi Indonesia*, lists a paltry nine Court decisions in this absolutely pivotal field of law in modern Indonesia.[22] These cases, moreover, do not address a whole batch of fundamental legal questions that demand an answer and that had, at least in part, been resolved by jurisprudential reform in colonial times or in the 1950s. These involve such important matters as the precise role and relationship of central company organs, such as the General Meeting of Shareholders and the Board of Directors. In fact, fundamental questions such as these inevitably came before Indonesian courts, but decisions never hit the books or took root in the legal system.[23]

As a result, this neglect of the role of jurisprudence in statutory interpretation contributed significantly to legal uncertainty in Indonesia. Examples abound, but for good order two may be given here. First, there is a massive body of clear and

---

[22] See S. Pompe and F. J. de Vries, "Preconstitutieve rechtshandelingen in Indonesië," *Tijdschrift voor Vennootschap, Vereniging en Stichting* 86 (July 1986): 171.

[23] Both examples were, in fact, subjects of legal dispute after independence, but remained essentially unresolved. The first concerned a dispute about whether the Board of Directors is bound in all matters to follow instructions of the General Meeting of Shareholders (GMS) or if it retains some autonomy. The former contractual view of the company equates the company interest with that of the shareholders, a very Anglo-American view, whereas the latter approach takes the view that the directors must protect other interests, such as those of employees and creditors. This view has come to prevail in countries such as Holland, Germany, and Japan (and explains, in part, the existence of a Board of Supervisors in company structures in those countries). In the latter case, the directors need not follow GMS instructions on all matters. The GMS can, of course, dismiss the directors, but members will be liable for breach of contract if they do. In Indonesia, the matter seems to be going in this direction.

The second case involved the question as to whether company management is joint, as held in the Dutch legal tradition, or individual, as in the Anglo-American tradition. The case arose out of an American investment company's decision to exclude an Indonesian company director from decision making on the grounds that he was not part of management—an impossible construct by Dutch law. It was held in Indonesia that directors could not be excluded and that, presumably, company management is jointly held. While both cases are known in the Indonesian advocacy, they are unreported and, as a result, these important issues remain fundamentally unsettled. See F. Tumbuan, "The Two-Tier System—Management and Supervision," (unpublished, 1987), pp. 6-8; and R. Prasetya, *Kedudukan mandiri dan pertanggungjawaban terbatas dari Perseroan Terbatas* (Surabaya: Universitas Airlangga, 1983), p. 122.

unequivocal jurisprudence—thirteen cases involving six Supreme Court decisions—regarding the precise moment at which legal personality attaches to a company in the establishment procedure and regarding the pre-incorporation liability of directors. Nevertheless, for no apparent reason, the Indonesian legislature turned the system upside down in 1958,[24] creating quite a bit of confusion,[25] and was forced to backtrack some years later.[26] Second, and has already been noted, in a recent case the Supreme Court held that sexual intercourse with a victim in a state of sleep did not constitute rape. The argument was that, since legislation defined rape as sexual intercourse "with violence" (art.285 Criminal Code), sexual intercourse with a victim in a motionless state, such as sleep, cannot qualify as rape because there is no violence involved. Unwilling to let the suspect off the hook (the logical outcome of this line of reasoning), the Supreme Court was forced to twist and turn to find grounds on which to convict. Yet its task would certainly have been made much simpler if it had looked up published colonial jurisprudence, which states in unequivocal terms that the meaning of the term "violence" includes acts committed against the will of the subject, which will must be declared in acts as intimate as sexual intercourse.[27] Further, according to colonial jurisprudence, the next article (art.286 Criminal Code) fully covers the case, as the meaning of "unconsciousness" used therein also applies to the state of normal sleep.[28]

It is evidently too early to tell what will result from the current debate on the role of lawmaking through court decisions, and the basic issues clearly need serious reconsideration. Yet the 1993 Five-Year Development Plan and subsequent reactions to the state of Indonesian jurisprudence seem to be essentially geared toward restoring the lawmaking function of court decisions to their former state within the civil law context, rather than breaking with the system and experimenting with the Anglo-American binding precedent. Thus, the 1994 National Law Conference firmly opted for the civil law system, as revealed by both the wording and reasoning of a prominent contributor to the seminar:

> Considering the characteristics of both systems of precedent, it is better to opt for the system of persuasive rather than coercive [i.e. binding] effect for Indonesia. This system is more in accordance with the development of the autonomy and independence of judges in the centralized judicial system in Indonesia.[29]

---

[24] Decisions of the Minister of Justice no.J. A. 5/84/24 dated 16 September 1958, *Indonesian State Gazette* 752 (1959).

[25] The effect of the regulation was to extend directors' pre-incorporation liability to include potentially any act before registration, which rendered part of the Company Code meaningless; moreover, in view of the fact that many companies in Indonesia dispensed with registration requirements, it undercut legal certainty, as their distinct legal personality was incomplete.

[26] See Pompe and de Vries, "Preconstitutieve rechtshandelingen," p. 169. Limping behind, the Supreme Court confirmed this return in its decision Mahkamah Agung no.297K/Sip/1974 dated 12 January 1977.

[27] Landraad Sambas 14 April 1913.

[28] Hoog Militair Gerechtshof 18 January 1935, *Indisch Tijdschrift van het Recht* 141 (1935): 529. See generally: S. Pompe, "Between Crime and Custom: Extra-Marital Sex in Modern Indonesia," *Bijdragen tot de Taal-, Land- en Volkenkunde* 150,1 (1994).

[29] Sunaryati Hartono, "Pengembangan yurisprudensi tetap," p. 28.

References to jurisprudence as a source of law were quite specifically not oriented toward jurisprudence generally, but rather toward "firm jurisprudence" (*yurisprudensi tetap*).³⁰ As the government spokesman stated in unequivocal terms during the 1994 National Law Seminar: "Firm jurisprudence . . . constitutes an integral part of our system of national law."³¹

The distinction between jurisprudence and firm jurisprudence was strongly emphasized at the 1994 National Law Seminar. Participants noted the problem that, while it is clear not all Supreme Court decisions should be regarded as authoritative, nothing really distinguishes authoritative from non-authoritative decisions. In this context, the distinction between jurisprudence and *firm* jurisprudence becomes a useful instrument for separating the wheat from the chaff in Supreme Court decision making. Ideally, it will weed out the handful of decisions that are actually meant to make law from the mass of Supreme Court particularistic decisions with no intended legal effect beyond the courtroom. In this sense, seminar participants showed an awareness that political and infrastructural problems prevented the Supreme Court from getting its affairs in order overnight, yet at the same time they pressed the Court to start firming up its jurisprudence.

2. ACCESS TO COURT DECISIONS AND THE PROBLEM OF LAWMAKING

The second issue that dominated the debates on jurisprudence in the 1990s dealt with the ostensibly mundane matter of access to court decisions. As stated during the 1994 National Law Seminar:

> What needs to be done at any cost at this point is the following:
> a. the selection and compilation of good court decisions that can function as *firm* jurisprudence;
> b. the publication of decisions that qualify as firm jurisprudence in great numbers, so as to allow
> c. the broad distribution of firm jurisprudence, particularly toward all judges in our country, but also to the general public, who will get to buy these books in any bookshop . . .³²

In fact, access is a complicated problem in Indonesia, which touches directly on the entire issue of legal certainty in that country. The poor access to legal information is, in part, a general problem of the legal infrastructure. In the words of one of the most knowledgeable commentators in the field:

> There are significant limitations on the public's access to legal information in Indonesia. This lack of access to legal information constitutes an obstacle to development efforts in all fields of activity and a detriment to the substantial

---

³⁰ Ibid. In this perspective, the qualification of "firm jurisprudence" as part of substantive Indonesian law is not as radical as it may appear at first sight, but rather now resembles "firm jurisprudence" as it has functioned all along in most civil law countries.

³¹ Sunaryati Hartono, "Pengembangan yurisprudensi tetap," p. 5.

³² Ibid., p. 7.

efforts which are being expended on law reform. The primary limitation is the lack of availability of legal material to the interested public. Many laws and regulations, court decisions, regulatory procedures, and other useful information about the application of legal rules are often unavailable or very difficult to obtain on a timely basis, due to inadequate publication and dissemination.[33]

In the case of the Supreme Court, this access problem is most strikingly apparent, perhaps, in the inordinately small number of published Court decisions. To give just one example: in 1990 the Supreme Court decided close to eight thousand cases, of which only fifty-eight were published in its jurisprudence series, *Yurisprudensi Indonesia*—about 0.6 percent. Furthermore, in the early 1990s (1991-1995), no jurisprudence was published at all by the Court. Lack of access to and inadequate publication of court decisions fundamentally undermines the lawmaking effect of Supreme Court decisions in two respects.

First, it reduces the impact of Court decisions on legal development. Access makes it possible for Court decisions to have an effect beyond the litigating parties, which is what lawmaking is all about. It is a simple reality: without access and publication, there can be no judicial lawmaking, and the more restricted the access, the smaller the impact of lawmaking will be.[34]

Second, the access problem reduces the precedent or predictive value of even the small number of decisions that are actually accessible and published.[35] Restricted access effectively prevents public scrutiny of court work, as more than 99 percent of the cases are swept under the carpet after being settled and their outcomes in this way completely obscured. Without public scrutiny, no one can tell whether unequivocal published precedent is actually followed in subsequent inaccessible cases, and, as a result, such precedent has poor predictive value. The absence of public scrutiny generally impedes a proper assessment of court performance and creates room for all sorts of shady deals on the side. Admittedly, not all members of the Supreme Court staff are dissatisfied with this situation, which makes it very difficult to resolve the problem, as will become apparent hereafter. It may well be that some Supreme Court elements deliberately limit access to decisions, with the aim of preventing public scrutiny of the Court's work.

---

[33] Gregory Churchill, *The Development of Legal Information Systems in Indonesia: Problems and Progress to Date*, Van Vollenhoven Institute for Law and Administration in Non-Western Countries Research Reports 2 (Leiden: Van Vollenhoven Institute, 1992), p. 1.

[34] See for instance, Setiawan, "Publikasi putusan hakim," *Varia Peradilan* (August 1993): 112.

[35] What I mean to say here is that, even if the Supreme Court consistently publishes its decisions on a certain issue, one can never be certain that this is what the Court will decide in any future case because one doesn't know what the Court decided in comparable unpublished cases.

(a) The Access Problem: Public Scrutiny and Predictability[36]

Under the New Order, access to Court decisions by the general public or legal professions in Indonesia was very restricted, despite the supposedly "public character" of these decisions and clear legal provisions regarding access.[37]

> Court decisions, including decisions of the Supreme Court, are treated as private decisions available only to those persons or officials having an interest in a particular case and are not regarded as public documents which can be studied by legal scholars and other interested members of the public.[38]

Throughout the 1950s, courts were much more open about what they were doing, even if relatively few cases were published. The self-confidence, and perhaps also the integrity, of the judges allowed early pioneers in the field to roam the corridors of court buildings with a freedom and ease of access that would later come to be unimaginable. Under Guided Democracy and, particularly, under the New Order, courts increasingly began to display an "oyster" mentality. Generally speaking, two obstacles stand in the way of a smooth access to court archives.

The first is that court archives generally have rapidly declined in quality and are currently in a poor state. It must be acknowledged that archival rules, which require that records be maintained for thirty years, are exceedingly hard to comply with.[39] For the bulky Supreme Court docket, in any case, the rule simply would not work, even under ideal conditions: at its present turnover rate of about eight thousand cases per year, a rough assessment is that the Supreme Court would require forty-eight square kilometers of storage to meet the specified requirements.[40] In fact, of course, circumstances are anything but ideal. The damp climate makes paper simply dissolve within a couple of years, while swarms of red ants have been known to consume entire archives—indeed they seem to quite like legal material.[41] In addition, archives do not seem to be of great interest to

---

[36] As will be apparent in this section, access and publication are not the same. Publication is only one method by which access can be realized; access is much broader and might involve public scrutiny of unpublished decisions. Although publication by definition involves access, the reverse is not true.

[37] This also flows from the fact that Court decisions must be pronounced in public, cf. art.17(1) Law no.14/1970. Of course, and as we have seen, for the Supreme Court at least, this has become an essentially empty letter. Parties are rarely summoned to Court to hear decisions, which, moreover, are not pronounced in the courtroom, but in judges' chambers, with a token opening of doors to satisfy the law, which requires decision making be public.

[38] Churchill, *Development of Legal Information Systems*, p. 12.

[39] A prominent Indonesian archival expert told me that this thirty-year rule was exceedingly burdensome on government institutions and, in practice, was impossible to implement. Personal communication, 24 April 1996.

[40] This is calculated on the basis of an average thickness of Supreme Court case files of twenty cm, by my own estimate.

[41] The archives of the colonial Prosecutor General were partially lost in the revolutionary mayhem, and were only found in the early 1990s in the attic of the old Supreme Court building. Part of the archives had decomposed, while other parts had been colonized by ants, who transformed the documents into a substance closely resembling concrete. The ants were smoked out, and the archive was hacked out with pneumatic drills and burned. It is a historical tragedy for Indonesia, as the archive contained interesting and important material on modern Indonesian history, notably on revolutionary activity in the immediate prewar period. Indeed,

Indonesian policy makers. Little valued and respected, archives and their proper maintenance are not given a high priority anywhere in Indonesia.[42] One district court judge described the judiciary's chaotic archival system in terms of total anarchy:

> Decisions are impossible to find. Cases are generally just dropped into the lap of the court clerk, who does with them much as he pleases. If a judge asks for a particular decision, the clerk may or may not remember it, and if he remembers he will have to search for it, and perhaps he will find it, but then he may not, and when he does, the file may be incomplete. And this does not count the reality that cases sometimes do not get to the archive at all, but drop off the trolley somewhere along the route . . . .[43]

This 1959 tale of the Bandung court archive is a pretty accurate description of the Supreme Court archive in the 1990s. Jakarta lawyers recount how Supreme Court decisions are just thrown on a big pile in the old court building on Banteng Square, and that there really is no system by which they can be traced and recovered. As in the case described above, persons seeking particular documents must rely on the unfathomable methods of the archival staff, who, through some mystical process, sometimes do manage to trace and unearth a record. Indeed, this chaotic condition of the Supreme Court archive might be gently cultivated by the Court's archival staff, which is said to supplement its meager income by selling off documents to law firms looking for cases to satisfy their demanding clients. In fact, material leaves the Supreme Court archive with the same facility as it goes in. One Jakarta lawyer recounted how she wheedled cases out from the Supreme Court haystack.

> I went into the Supreme Court archives, it's disallowed of course, but I talked my way in. The archives are in disorder, I mean, total chaos. Actually there were attempts to reduce the chaos, in which cases were allotted to members of the archival staff for filing. But at the time, there really was no system to speak of. So I went to them and said: I need a case on shipping [etc. etc. giving the specificities of the case she was looking for] and anyone who brings one to

---

it is believed that some of Sukarno's political correspondence, which he is said to have written from the Sukamiskin prison and which has never been traced, was to be found in these archives. Personal communication, 24 April 1996.

[42] This helps explain why the nation's archives have a record of losing important material. Thus, the original document of the declaration of Indonesian independence is apparently lost, as are the original notes on the 1944-1945 constitutional debates. M. Simandjuntak, *Pandangan negara integralistik* (Jakarta: Grafiti, 1994), postscript. Although the Yamin records of the debates on the 1945 Constitution are still accepted as authoritative, this is rather *faute de mieux*. Prominent archival insiders have stated that the records were incomplete, but that there was authentic material in private collections that conflicted with Yamin's account. They claimed that because of political pressure publication was withheld. Personal communication, 24 April 1996. Poor archival maintenance seems an altogether too literal application of the famous adage that blessed nations have no history, based on the fallacious assumption, perhaps, that nations with a history can return to the blessed state of collective amnesia.

[43] Daniel S. Lev archives (hereafter *DSL*), 13 August 1959. (These are the personal interview notes of Daniel S. Lev; copies will be deposited in the University of Washington library [Seattle, WA], the Cornell University Kroch Collection [Ithaca, NY], and Pusat Studi Hukum dan Kebijakan [PSHK] in Jakarta.)

me will get Rp.20,000. So they looked through their batches to see whether any of the cases fitted the description, and that's how I got the case.[44]

Similarly, a Supreme Court judge with an interest in the Court's institutional history said he simply walked in and out of the Court archives with important historical material, which he said was falling to pieces anyway. No one batted an eye as he carted off file after file, which he collated at home in several large albums. He showed them to me, and they included fascinating material, such as official Supreme Court correspondence on political matters from the first Court chairman Kusumah Atmadja, as well as his passport (numbered 10). The judge said that he also showed the albums to the Supreme Court chairman and other Court leaders at the time and suggested that the Supreme Court do something with them: "[But] they were perfectly uninterested and didn't care where it came from or where it went. So I just kept them."[45]

The second obstacle to access is the judges themselves. Although the disordered and neglected state of most court archives might lead one to expect that no one is interested in them, Indonesian judges typically guard their own records as jealously as if they held the crown jewels. The general rule is that access is denied to any member of the general public or legal professions. The reason for this attitude is not difficult to divine: the archives contain figurative skeletons, and logic dictates that the more skeletons there are, the more the judges will try to keep the doors locked. This helps explain why Indonesian courts were pretty open and accessible during the 1950s, but closed up increasingly under the New Order. Assuredly there are variations, as some courts are more likely to harbor unpleasant secrets than others. Thus, it is easier to gain access to the documents of outlying district courts that generally deal with "horse-theft cases only," as one judge put it, or to the papers of newly established courts than to the archives of a district court with a long-standing record in a large commercial city where money flows easily, such as Surabaya or Semarang, or those of a military court, which handles sensitive political cases. But in the prevailing political and institutional climate, it is hard to be a judge anywhere without dirtying one's hands, and, as a result, access to court archives is almost invariably a difficult business. This applies even to people with excellent personal connections, as I heard from perhaps the most renowned private collector of court decisions in Indonesia, Chidir Ali. Calling himself "an excellent case thief," his account of the circumspect and necessarily somewhat devious ways of getting hold of important court decisions is revelatory:

> I really am an excellent case thief. Oh yes, yes. Let me tell you how I get my court decisions. I track down important decisions from hearsay, or newspaper reports, sometimes I am tipped off. I have some support from certain Supreme Court judges, who will tell me about cases, and even occasionally send me verdicts themselves. But most often it is me who has to get hold of court decisions. This is difficult business, and the thieving comes in here. Sometimes

---

[44] Personal communication, 9 October 1995. This lawyer added: "We needed such authority for our clients in Hong Kong. We knew they were wrong, of course, and told them what they wanted to hear." The way she talked about the use of Supreme Court cases was that they came close to serving just as a sop for foreign clients, though she did not say so explicitly.

[45] Personal communication, 16 July 1994.

I go to court myself. I don't tell them my name, and since I look like a country bumpkin and in fact play the idiot pretty well, judges or court clerks will not think much of me and just give me access to some of the stuff I am looking for. But sometimes they are tipped off or know me, and I have to resort to other ruses. Recently there was an interesting land case in Ujung Pandang I read about in the newspapers. I sent off two of my students to try and get hold of it. The routine is as follows. The students, a boy and a girl, pretend to be a couple very much in love, and they present themselves to the court with a bored expression on their faces complaining about some university paper they must to write on land law. Often the court clerk will think them harmless, so he will give them access to the cases—under his supervision of course. They'll behave as lovers would, pretend to be more interested in each other than in the cases, mind you they actually might be, and leaf through them rather listlessly. They will take every opportunity to get away, walk out quite frequently to have a drink and a bite or some such thing, taking odd bits and paper such as their notes with them. So after a while the court clerk will sort of get used to the scene and turn to his own affairs. At that point they'll walk out with the case I want, photocopy it at one of those copyshops, and surreptitiously return the case. Then they bring the case to me, since after all I'm the one who pays for the trip. So I'm quite a thief, you see.[46]

Chidir Ali's story demonstrates the ways courts attempt to control the archives and generally forbid public access. There are a few exceptions to this general rule. Decisions are, of course, sent to litigating parties, who may decide to publish them. But then, it is not clear whether parties have either the interest or the proper channels for publication, and such precedents cannot be traced by the general public because no one knows which cases were handled in the first place. It may also be that some cases attract public attention and cannot be withheld from publication. Yet all this does not detract from the reality, which is that, essentially, the courts decide which cases will be made available to the general public through publication, and more importantly, which ones will not be. There is no public scrutiny of court work.

This condition undermines Supreme Court lawmaking. For one thing, it means that even court decisions that are accessible through publication or otherwise are hard to verify. Given the poor state of court archives and the reluctance of judges to grant access to them, there really is no way to check decisions against the original document. In a world in which court decisions, by the Supreme Court's own admission, are known to be fabricated, doctored, and falsified, even at the highest level, such cross checking becomes a necessity, not a luxury. The more insidious point

---

[46] Interview, Chidir Ali, Summer 1989. When I interviewed him, Chidir Ali lived in an old, collapsing shack in the back of somebody's yard, and this shack was filled to the ceiling with unpublished court decisions. He suffered a stroke and died soon after I met him for the second time in 1991. I tried to track down his collection of unpublished court decisions after his death, but fear it is lost. I only met Chidir Ali a couple of times, and he remained a bit of a mystery to me. Yet based on what little I knew of him, given his living conditions and the mild contempt in which he was held at his university, my impression is that his contribution to Indonesian legal development may be as significant as it is undervalued. With dogged determination and without seeking credit, he singlehandedly saved many important cases from the historical dustbin of court archives. His probably is the most comprehensive series of court decisions in Indonesia to date. If Chidir Ali was a thief, this worked to benefit Indonesian legal development.

is, however, that impediments preventing access to these archives effectively hide what the Court really does. With more than 99 percent of the cases hidden from the public eye and without any real possibilities of finding out what happened in them, there simply is no way to tell whether the Supreme Court sticks to the law (including its own published precedents) or simply just does as it pleases.

> Aside from functioning as a source of law, the publication of court decisions also is important in the framework of public control over court decisions, both with regard to their legal motivation as well as their reflections of prevailing notions of justice in society, for courts in the end derive their legitimacy from public trust. As a result the publication of court decisions in the end also serves to insure some sort of "accountability" of jurisprudence in relation to the general public...[47]

In the absence of public scrutiny of court work, even a clear, unequivocal, and firm line of published jurisprudence is no guarantee that the cases will not disappear into the great void. The Supreme Court becomes essentially unpredictable as a result.

> Lack of ready access to new legislation and regulations and uncertainty about the status and applicability of the major law codes used in Indonesia have resulted in much confusion about the legal system and have in turn fostered distrust and cynicism about the courts...[48]

(b) The Selection Problem: Unrepresentative Cases

In the face of the huge volume of cases generated by the Supreme Court and its near-total control over access, the crucial question then is how, and on what basis, are the small batch of published cases selected. In order to have lawmaking effect, cases selected for publication must be firm rulings on the law as the Supreme Court perceives it. They must be "exemplary," as one author put it,[49] which essentially means that they should have predictive quality: they should inform the general public how the Supreme Court would apply the law in any comparable case it might encounter in the future. It is this exemplary or predictive quality that gives the Court lawmaking power.

The selection mechanism, as a result, is highly important for lawmaking, but unfortunately, in the case of the Indonesian Supreme Court, it is fraught with difficulties.[50] As shall become apparent, far from being a balanced, objective procedure oriented toward generating only cases with predictive quality, the

---

[47] P. Effendie Lotulung, *Yurisprudensi dalam perspektif pengembangan hukum administrasi negara di Indonesia* [Inaugural lecture] (Bogor: Universitas Pakuan, 1994), p. 20.

[48] Churchill, *Development of Legal Information Systems*, p. 2.

[49] Ibid., p. 12.

[50] Little attention is paid to the selection issue in Indonesia. The only publication that discusses this matter, to my knowledge, is by Setiawan, "Publikasi putusan hakim," p. 112. Setiawan, a former judge and prominent Supreme Court clerk, probably is one of the most scholarly, erudite, and original legal minds in Indonesia at present.

mechanism is personalized and arbitrary, with the result that cases selected for publication are not exemplary at all and essentially lack predictive quality. The selection procedure is arbitrary in two ways: first, it deliberately excludes whole swathes of the law; and second, it is capricious.

As regards the first point, the series of publications is notable, in part, for excluding most or all cases in quite a number of fields of the law. The reason is that these are considered "sensitive" areas of the law in which the Supreme Court has really no role to play. As Supreme Court chairman Subekti described this restriction:

> In realizing legal unification, we can say as a rule of the thumb that there are fields of law that may be qualified as "neutral" and other sectors that should be called "sensitive."[51]

Only in the "neutral" fields, Subekti continued, could the Supreme Court hope to shape the law. In a later interview, he added that the Court's hands were pretty well tied in all other fields of law.[52]

This distinction between sensitive and neutral areas of the law slants the selection procedure in the run-up to publication. Thus, in its more than two decades of publication (from 1969 to 1990), the Supreme Court-controlled series, *Yurisprudensi Indonesia*, partly or completely ignored many fields of law that are clearly crucial in Indonesian society. By way of example, very few or no cases are reported on a broad range of politically sensitive criminal acts, such as criminal acts against the state (no cases), narcotics (no cases), inciting religious hatred (no cases), political subversion (two cases), corruption (four cases), or economic crimes generally (five cases). Similarly, private law matters of considerable practical relevance and legal complexity remain essentially uncovered, such as labor contracts (no cases), agency (no cases), or mortgage and securities (four cases). This dearth of cases stands in stark contrast to the intensive coverage of other issues, which are granted attention disproportionate to their marginal significance in Indonesian legal development. Thus, fifty-three *adat* cases are reported (of which twenty-five are inheritance cases), which is three times as many as the number of published cases concerning the broad field of commercial law (sixteen cases). Also, selection very much favors subjects dealing with innocuous legal technicalities rather than the substantive legal issues. Even in absolute terms, many more cases are selected in the fields of criminal and civil procedure, which are in many ways subsidiary, than in the broad categories of substantive law.[53] It is clear that the selection mechanism discriminates between "neutral" and "sensitive" fields of law and practically excludes the latter.

---

[51] R. Subekti, *Kumpulan karangan hukum perikatan, arbitrase dan peradilan* (Bandung: Alumni, 1980), p. 39.

[52] Conversation between R. Subekti, Dr. J. M. Otto, and myself, Bandung, November 1989.

[53] There were seventy-nine cases in criminal procedure against seventy-five cases in substantive criminal law. The number of cases selected for publication in some other areas are as follows: civil procedure 118 cases, which constitutes the largest paragraph in private law; personal and contract law seventy-two cases; *adat* law fifty-three cases; civil law fourteen cases; commercial law sixteen cases.

The second point refers to the arbitrariness of the way cases from even "neutral" fields of law are actually selected for publication.[54] The organization of the selection process exacerbates this condition. For approximately twenty years, from 1975-1995, selection was carried out basically by two respected senior Supreme Court judges (hereafter called "the selecting judges") whose primary qualification was that they had long been interested in the matter. They were not specifically chosen for the job on substantive grounds, such as background, relevant legal expertise, or geographic area of supervision (which might make them more responsive to specific legal problems in the regions). What's more, they did not seem to be representative of the Supreme Court in the 1980s and 1990s, as they differed from their colleagues in a number of ways: for example, they belonged to the 1950s generation, spoke fluent Dutch, were non-military and secular in orientation, were oriented toward civil law, and were strongly focused on Java because they originated from the island and barely ever served outside it. This arbitrary composition of the selection "committee," together with the strong affinity between the two judges and their long-term management of this process, promoted professional bias in the way the selection was effected. Nobody else on the Court was really involved, and administrative support was minimal.

To make matters worse, selection of the cases by these judges was completely unsystematic and unstructured. When the deadline for publication came up, the selecting judges would go through the building and make some internal phone calls asking their colleagues to bring in cases for publication. They did not approach all their brethren, but only a small number, usually their friends or judges they respected. Nor did they go through all Supreme Court decisions, which admittedly would be an arduous task. There was no considered, balanced, and objective system to insure that the selection of cases reflects what actually goes on in all the chambers.[55]

Facing a pile of cases haphazardly gathered, the selecting judges would then leaf through the stacks very rapidly, often in about a single afternoon, and pick out a handful of cases on some undefined basis. Criteria for selection were not spelled out and, in fact, seemed to amount to little more than that the cases coincided with the views of the selecting judges. In the words of two Supreme Court insiders at the time:

> People keep on talking about the backlog of cases . . . pending before the Supreme Court. But they generally forget that ever more cases are being decided . . . It is impossible to publish all decisions. Precisely for that reason it is absolutely necessary to develop criteria for selection and systemization.[56]

> Two Supreme Court judges browse through a huge stack of about a thousand cases and select a handful for publication. It is a wholly arbitrary selection, based essentially on some unspecified gut feeling that these are "good cases."

---

[54] Setiawan, "Publikasi putusan hakim," p. 112.

[55] As with the original "examination" system of the lower courts, this might conceivably be based on an obligation for all Supreme Court chambers to send in three civil and three criminal cases on a monthly basis. This system could be oriented, instead, towards the various fields of law, a reform that would do away with the now largely defunct civil-criminal distinction.

[56] Setiawan, "Publikasi putusan hakim," p. 119.

No criteria have ever been developed to determine what cases are to be selected for publication.[57]

The problem in the selection of cases is not just its arbitrariness. The selecting judges, to be certain, were firmly committed to strengthening the Supreme Court's lawmaking ability, which is why they took on the job in the first place. Yet their attachment to selecting "good cases"—their commitment to legal correctness, in other words—sometimes led them to indulge in fabrications, as they were known to *edit* some of these decisions before publication to make them accord with their own views of legal correctness.[58] This editing did not consist of correcting spelling mistakes and changing a comma or two, but extended to blatant revisions of legal considerations, the *ratio decidendi*. As one of the selecting judges put it:

> The reason why we haven't published any jurisprudence since 1990 is that copy remains to be corrected. Many of the newly appointed Supreme Court judges are not very good, they mess up their decisions, and therefore we sometimes have to "rework" their legal considerations for publication.[59]

As a result of all these conditions, the selection of cases for publication failed to represent what actually went on in Court and instead only indicated what two judges *thought* Supreme Court decisions *should* be.

This evident arbitrariness in the selection system has generated subdued but nonetheless deep-rooted differences of opinion within the Supreme Court concerning what the selection and publication of cases is actually meant to achieve. There may be general agreement on the need to strengthen the Court's lawmaking powers, yet when it comes time to consider the method by which this is to be realized—which necessarily involves the role of case selection and publication and the ways in which this reflects on the Court's work—views diverge considerably.

Some progressive and committed Supreme Court judges are convinced the selection system is part of the problem, rather than a step toward the solution. Briefly summarized, their view is that cases should be selected and published for the benefit of the general public and, as a result, should have predictive quality. The present system doesn't add an iota to the Supreme Court's lawmaking capabilities. What's more, professional discipline in court, legal consistency in decision making, and a true return to lawmaking will be realized only by opening up court work to public scrutiny, which means expanding publication. "All the colors of the rainbow must show through," as a Supreme Court clerk put it.[60]

> I am an advocate of widening publication, because it is only by exposing our mistakes that internal discipline will eventually be realized. In fact, I once

---

[57] Personal communication, 18 July 1994.

[58] The practice of editing decisions is potentially harmful in the context of lawmaking, i.e., as it affects the predictive quality of Supreme Court decisions. Another dimension to this practice, which may help explain the behavior of the selecting judges, is that, given the problems in legal discipline within the Supreme Court and the judiciary at large, decisions are selected and published to help guide and educate judges, not to lay down a firm ruling on the law for the benefit of the general public.

[59] Personal communication, 20 September 1995, 16 April 1994.

[60] Personal communication, 18 July 1994.

suggested that a blatantly erroneous Supreme Court decision be published, but this was not approved: "You will embarrass the judge," the argument was. Which, I suppose, was the whole point.[61]

During a meeting of court leaders the idea was voiced that a much broader selection of cases should be published, showing what we really do here, warts and all. The suggestion was that only by publishing our mistakes and problems will people see what really goes on here and will we be forced to do something about it. But Ali Said looked at [the person making the suggestion] as if he was mad and said: "Of course, we will only publish good cases." This means that selection is in fact wholly arbitrary.[62]

These progressive judges are opposed by the Supreme Court leadership and others on the Court who want to stick to publishing "good cases" only. This selection mechanism is directed more toward the judicial profession itself than toward the general public. Cases are selected on grounds of their educative quality for the judicial corps, rather than because they constitute firm rulings on the law on which the general public can rely. "Legal correctness," the way cases really ought to be decided, is more important than reality, a state which judges certainly recognize. From this perspective, the editing of Court decisions, rather than being an act of deliberate falsification, is actually almost required: judges will not learn from their errors unless they are confronted with correct models. As a result, the jurisprudence books are not meant to be sources of law at all, but rather reference works for the judges, authoritative but not necessarily binding. The restricted function of the published case books, as they are constituted now, is explicitly acknowledged in the recent 1993 Five-Year Development Plan, which states that in order to promote reform, jurisprudence must be made a source of law by:

> broadening the publication of jurisprudence so that it will not just be limited to the courts, but be extended also to the other legal professions, higher education and the public at large.[63]

The ultimate result of the arbitrary and sometimes purposely distorted selection mechanism is, of course, that cases have no predictive quality whatsoever.

The motive behind this emphasis on "good cases" is to hide aspects of Supreme Court decision making that are better kept under wraps. It is an approach oriented toward safeguarding Supreme Court institutional interests and prestige, intentionally concealing the reality of what goes on in the Court. The huge store of unpublished cases, which make up more than 99 percent of the whole, certainly include a number of correct decisions, yet in that pile one would also find evidence of ad hoc decision making and shadowy side-deals by some Supreme Court judges, demonstrating some of the problems that plague the institution. In the absence of public scrutiny and a more balanced selection system, hardly a single outsider is in a position to gauge fully the extent to which the Supreme Court decides cases on their legal merits or on their factual specificity. By the same token, only insiders

---

[61] Personal communication, 5 August 1994.
[62] Personal communication, 18 July 1994.
[63] *Rencana Pembangunan Lima Tahun Keenam 1994/95–1998/99* (Buku IV), pp. 474-75.

can adequately measure judicial performance and be aware of the fact that some Supreme Court judges can be bribed and others are simply not up to their task,[64] indeed, that apparently some judges never decided a single case during their whole career on the Court.[65]

These conflicting views of what selection and publication of Supreme Court decisions are meant to achieve help explain why, even though the Court may strive to strengthen lawmaking powers in general terms, when it comes to nuts-and-bolts issues many Supreme Court judges are strongly opposed to broadening case selection and making it reflect what actually goes on in Court. Thus, on the one hand, the Court's judges tend to agree that strengthening lawmaking through publication ought to be a long-term goal, and they have expressed this commitment, for instance, through the Court's consistent application for supplementary funding to strengthen jurisprudential facilities[66] and by making this need a top priority in contacts with international aid organizations.[67] Yet on the other hand, in terms of concrete actions, this Supreme Court commitment reveals itself to be heavily qualified. Thus, over the years, the Court leadership was generally not prepared to allocate sufficient facilities for expanding publication of jurisprudence. Presumably, it felt that two selecting judges were quite enough to handle the small number of "good cases" required for their educative value. Worse, since 1990, work pressure has prevented the selecting judges from keeping up with publication, but nothing has been done about this. Other matters were deemed more important, such as the hopeless mopping up of the backlog. One of the selecting judges explained the failure to publish jurisprudence between 1991-1995: "We get so many cases to decide if we wish to catch up with the backlog that we simply don't have time for jurisprudence now."[68]

And when the two selecting judges finally retired in 1994-95, nobody was appointed to replace them, and the selection and publication mechanism, dormant for five years, collapsed altogether. One commentator dryly commented: "What is needed is not just an adequate selection mechanism, but also sufficient personnel

---

[64] According to the older judges, nearly the entire batch of thirty-one new Supreme Court judges appointed under Mudjono in 1982 were not up to standard. Personal communications, 16 April 1994; 11 July 1994; 20 September 1995.

[65] Supreme Court judge G. failed his entrance exam to become a professional judge, but nevertheless landed his job as a Supreme Court justice on account of his service to Mudjono when the latter was still in Parliament. It is said that G. did not decide a single case in his thirteen years' service on the Court. Personal communication, 11 July 1994.

[66] With the exception of the budget years 1990/1991 and 1991/1992, when Supreme Court case selection and publication were largely funded by the Indonesian-Dutch legal cooperation program, the Supreme Court applied every year for special "development funding" to finance selection and publication of its decisions. With barely an exception, in all these years this item had top priority, followed by such items as resolving backlogs, upgrading the court building, and computerization. See generally *Mahkamah Agung: Anggaran pendapatan dan belanja negara* (State income and expenditures budget) (1970-1994) (Jakarta: Government Printing Office, n.d.).

[67] See discussion of the Indonesian-Dutch legal cooperation program referred to hereafter. In 1993, the Supreme Court applied for a grant to the Asia Foundation for a reprint of its 1977 compilation of jurisprudence. *Rangkuman Yurisprudensi Mahkamah Agung Republik Indonesia* (Jakarta: Mahkamah Agung, 1993), p. 1. In its recent contact and applications for supplementary funding to the World Bank, publication of its decisions, again, figured as a top item. Personal communication, 25 September 1995.

[68] Personal communication, 20 September 1995.

allocations to make the system work in a reliable manner."[69] Indeed, for a more balanced and objective selection and publication mechanism oriented toward actual lawmaking, much larger allocations of funds and personnel than have ever been invested in the history of the Court and a much firmer commitment on the part of the Supreme Court leadership would be required.

This ambivalence within the Supreme Court about case selection and publication is clearly demonstrated in the rise and fall of the Indonesian-Dutch cooperation program from 1986 until 1992. This program was, in part, directed toward improving the mechanism for the selection procedure and involved computer storage and indexing of all Supreme Court decisions and subsequent publication of cases selected on the basis of their legal merits. It also involved analyzing and excerpting Court decisions, so as to standardize procedure and allow for computer retrieval. Some prominent Supreme Court judges who had called for the program in the first place aggressively supported it. Yet as it inevitably exposed Supreme Court failings, it also generated a good deal of internal Court opposition. As one Dutch participant recounts:

> In preparation for central logging and eventual publication, courses were given to administrative staff in the Supreme Court on how to analyze Court decisions, make excerpts, and attach defining key-words for the computer. It involved close reading and some debate of Supreme Court decisions. Sometimes decisions were quite strongly criticized. In fact, in not a few instances the administrative staff was directly confronted with outright errors in Supreme Court decisions. This would generate an embarrassed and sometimes frosty silence.[70]

Thus, despite the support for the project from some committed judges, as well as the public, opposition within the Supreme Court eventually prevailed. In fact, it is said that even while Dutch and Indonesian experts were entering cases into the computer, elsewhere in the Court building judges were hiding case files to prevent them from being logged in. When the program was terminated in 1992, following the rupture in Indonesian-Dutch relations resulting from the Santa Cruz massacre in East Timor, the computer system was operative, and a first selection of cases based on their legal merits had been made and was waiting to be published. At this point the Supreme Court revealed how limited its commitment to the project was. This first selection, based on qualitative criteria, was never published. Instead, some old cases selected with the familiar arbitrary mechanism appeared.[71] The personnel team established to maintain the computers was disbanded. The computer infrastructure was discarded to the point, it seems, that rats were actually gnawing their way through the hardware—a condition that the Supreme Court cats evidently were unable to prevent.[72] The massive investments in this

---

[69] Setiawan, "Publikasi putusan hakim," p. 120.

[70] Personal communication, 25 August 1995.

[71] Personal communication, 25 August 1995.

[72] One day, in the large entrance hall of the Supreme Court building, my way was blocked by a well-fed cat reclining at full stretch and suckling her six young with great ceremony. After observing the situation for a while, I asked some nearby guards whether this was normal. "Oh yes," answered one of them, "that's where she lives in fact," pointing at the cavity under the large ceremonial stairwell in the center hall. It was one of series of similar incidents in my experience during which officers of the state accepted nature's encroachment on prestigious

program, as a result, were unable to reform the arbitrary selection system and address its formidable weaknesses.

(c) The Publication Problem: Too Little and Too Late[73]

Following the 1993 Five-Year Development Plan, central importance was attached to compiling and disseminating Court decisions to the general public through publication. Calls were made for massive jurisprudence dissemination through cheap and widely marketed books, as well as more ambitious (and prestigious) computerization projects:

> Firm jurisprudence also must be recorded on CD-ROM so as to be easily available and used by all judges. So in order to upgrade the communication between courts in the entire national territory, the time has come to train judges and court clerks to use the computer and CD-ROM system, including the on-line systems between the courts.[74]

These plans remain to be realized, of course, and it is worth looking at what has happened in the field of publication so far. Aside from the problems of access and selection, practically all publication series of jurisprudence over the past fifty years have suffered from three handicaps: irregularity of publication; lack of timeliness; and restricted distribution.

Hukum (1950-1959). During much of the 1950s, the Indonesian Law Association published court decisions in its journal *Hukum*. Almost from the start, the journal perpetuated some of the access problems we have just discussed, notably because the percentage of cases published was so small. In fact, even by civil law standards, only a very limited selection of Supreme Court cases ever appeared in the journal. Thus, throughout 1952, only thirty-seven cases were reported, and by 1957 this figure had declined to twenty-five.[75] In addition, there were rapidly emerging problems in timeliness and distribution. While *Hukum* started out as a quarterly, by the mid-1950s publication was six months late and issues were combined as a result (though the journal recovered some of its élan in the last year of its publication).

These problems cut at the roots of the authority of Supreme Court decisions, as two judges in the 1950s and 1960s related:

---

state buildings with astounding ease. I would not want to push this point too far, but it gives rise to the thought that institutions of state are viewed in less permanent and more transient terms by Indonesians than in the West, and that the interests and ideologies they represent are perceived in the same manner—a not altogether unpleasant thought.

[73] See, for instance, Setiawan, "Publikasi putusan hakim," p. 112.

[74] Sunaryati Hartono, "Pengembangan yurisprudensi tetap," p. 7.

[75] This approximated 10 percent of the Supreme Court docket at the time, which stood at 250–400 cases. The journal succeeded the colonial *Indisch Tijdschrift van het Recht* which, by way of comparison, reported 161 cases (1936 figures) on an annual basis.

The journal *Hukum* is generally deficient in its reporting of cases, aside from its wholly irregular appearance.[76]

We have no jurisprudence anymore. It causes us all sorts of problems . . . Now there is only the journal *Hukum,* and it falls far short of what is required. Many important cases are unknown. I never read past decisions anymore, that is cases decided after 1950, quite simply because they are hard to find.[77]

In fact, although in the larger cities judges were still able to uphold some consistency by keeping contact amongst themselves, the shortcomings of the journal *Hukum* effectively severed the ties between the Supreme Court and the geographically more isolated courts, as District Court judge Soeparto observed:

> There is no jurisprudence nowadays. Before the war, judges received the *Tijdschrift* every month and so knew what new decisions there were and which they had to decide themselves—so there actually was overall guidance in forming the law. But the journal *Hukum* is wholly deficient, it appears irregularly and does not have enough decisions in it. District judges receive little guidance, and their decisions may deviate considerably from new judge-made law and legal principles of great importance. This particularly applies in out-of-the-way districts, of course. In Gresik or Sidoardjo, judges are close to Surabaya, and so difficulties are not as great. They can talk over decisions with fellow judges. But in many other districts the solitary judge, or maybe two of them, have no contact at all with what goes on in the world of the law. Thus, in Banyuwangi judges are far removed from the larger courts.[78]

Note that judge Soeparto was talking about Banyuwangi, which in the late 1950s may have been a remote court, but was still located on the central island of Java. The fact that courts on the Outer Islands go unmentioned is probably because they had dropped off the judicial map altogether by that time.

While this is to some extent a chicken-and-egg situation, these developments also suggest that court decisions were becoming less and less relevant in shaping legal development. Perhaps it was not just that the judiciary, with the Supreme Court at its head, marginalized itself in this context as a result of its poor publication record, but also that its political marginalization in the 1950s obviated the need for regular and broadly based publication. Subtle changes in the composition of cases reported in *Hukum* provide evidence for this latter theory. The first is the gradual near-total exclusion of lower court decisions from publication. This indicates that the lower courts, at least, were losing their role in shaping legal development as they floundered in their particular problems. They never really recovered from this condition, as the later revival of case publication concentrated almost exclusively on decisions reached by the Supreme Court. The second is that publication was increasingly restricted to certain fields of law, to the

---

[76] Supreme Court judge Abdurrahman, *DSL,* 13 December 1959.
[77] District Court judge Siem, *DSL,* 13 August 1959.
[78] *DSL,* 5 November 1959.

practical exclusion of many others. Fields selected for recognition, such as *adat* inheritance law, were hardly of central concern to most district courts; the Court gave little or no guidance in its published court decisions regarding all other areas of the law. Thus, the political marginalization of the Court meant that its lawmaking was henceforth also restricted to the legal periphery. Although there was a fair bit of subsequent breast beating by the judiciary in the 1950s about its role in shaping *adat* inheritance law, the fact that the Court's impact on jurisprudence was restricted to such a relatively isolated and peripheral field of law demonstrated the dramatic erosion of Supreme Court standing.

The collapse of the journal *Hukum* in 1959, as a result, resembled the demise of a terminally ill, rather than a healthy, patient. Indeed, the fact that the Supreme Court did not even seriously try to resuscitate case reporting for a full decade after that collapse indicates the depth of the crisis of confidence in its own decisions—though assuredly a variety of Guided Democracy factors also contributed to the absence of case reporting.

Yurisprudensi Indonesia and the Rangkuman (1969-1990). The collapse of *Hukum* in the late 1950s was a disastrous development for Supreme Court lawmaking. It cut the umbilical cord between Court decisions and legal development: the Supreme Court, quite simply, was no longer able to inform the legal community or society at large even of those decisions that it wanted to be known.[79] As a result, after 1959 nothing remained to rescue Supreme Court decisions from the obscurity that already blanketed activities of the district courts. If the Court wanted to regain any grip on the process, it would have to face up to the fact that case publication must be restarted.

It would have been difficult to establish a new journal with the same format as *Hukum*. For a start, the district courts were struggling to keep their heads above water, and their decisions were barely worth reporting. In addition, Supreme Court decision making was becoming increasingly particularistic, so that not all of its decisions merited publication. With publication dependent on Supreme Court acquiescence, case reporting would have to be heavily weighted in favor of the Court. All this called for a publication series controlled by the Supreme Court, rather than some outside third party, as had been the case with the *Hukum* journal.

These pressures coalesced and resulted in action in the late 1960s, when the early New Order government was committed to restoring the law and its institutions, and the judiciary, in response, sought to recoup some of the ground it had lost during Guided Democracy. It was a period of great activity, during which the Supreme Court deliberately tried to move back to the political center. One of the ways to do this was to reclaim authority over the law through its court decisions, which would require the Court to reinstitute case publication. In 1969, therefore, Supreme Court chairman Subekti resumed official publication of Supreme Court decisions in the so-called *Yurisprudensi Indonesia*. This journal was under the control of and published by the Court and limited to publishing cases

---

[79] This does not deny that the Supreme Court had, and indeed used, other instruments to shape legal development in this period, such as, notably, its Circular Letters. Nevertheless, these letters lacked forced because they were viewed as somehow irregular or, at the very least, not a formal source of law.

more broadly relevant for Indonesian legal development.[80] The series remains the principal officially sanctioned source for court decisions in the country to the present day. While it evidently restored some of the Supreme Court's lawmaking power, in many ways its weaknesses were even greater than those of its predecessor, *Hukum*.

Yurisprudensi Indonesia was even more selective than *Hukum*. Thus, in 1970 only thirty-five cases were reported in the series, and in 1990 the number had barely risen to fifty-eight cases. The latter figure, it may be recalled, approximates only about 0.6 percent of all cases decided by the Supreme Court in that year. It is little less than extraordinary that the Court found so few of its decisions worthy of publication and accorded lawmaking authority to such a minute portion of its activities. Moreover, many cases reported from the late 1970s onwards have had no lawmaking effect at all.[81] They are not characterized by legal incisiveness or innovation, but instead tend to be bland rehashes of issues that already command wide agreement or are simply unimportant. Moreover, not a few among the reported cases are particularistic, notably those dealing with *adat* law, and therefore completely ineffective as implements to help ensure legal consistency for the judiciary and society. In addition, as noted above, the series has been singularly inactive on issues where there is a general demand for more clarity from the courts. Thus, in the field of company law, assuredly a highly important and active area of Indonesian law, only sixteen cases were published in the series over the past twenty-five years.

Aside from these fundamental difficulties, the *Yurisprudensi Indonesia* series has also suffered from the same problems of timeliness and distribution that had handicapped *Hukum*. Unlike its quarterly predecessor, the series appears only annually, sometimes after a considerable delay, and can, as a result, hardly be called timely. Moreover, by 1995 it was running four years late and seemed close to collapsing altogether. Under such circumstances, it hardly is the appropriate instrument by which to inform the legal professions and the general public of new developments in Supreme Court decision making.[82]

The fundamental problem here is funding. To the present day, the *Yurisprudensi Indonesia* series cannot rely on secure funding, despite the fact that in its funding applications the Supreme Court has steadfastly made publication of its decisions a top priority for more than twenty years. The refusal of the central government to guarantee funding for the publication of Supreme Court decisions suggests a much deeper-rooted ambivalence about these decisions.

Seeking further ways by which to strengthen its lawmaking function, in 1976-77 the Court commenced the so-called jurisprudence project. Placed under the authority of the judge Purwoto S. Gandasubrata, who would later become Supreme

---

[80] The 1989 and 1990 issues were published by the printing house Ichtiar Baru/Van Hoeve with help from the Dutch-Indonesian cooperation program, but the Supreme Court retained effective control of the substance of the journal.

[81] The Subekti years (until 1974) are an exception to this, as the old-school Subekti was determined to make this a serious effort. As a result, the cases in "sensitive" areas referred to earlier, such as cases on political subversion and corruption, were all published during his tenure as chairman, but not afterwards.

[82] Distribution is excessively poor also. There are regular complaints that judges quite simply do not receive their copies of the series because of shortages or that courthouses lack the series because the chairmen took the volumes home.

Court chairman, this was an ambitious project, aimed at systematically collating, indexing, and summarizing important Supreme Court decisions from 1950 onwards.[83] Projected to appear twice a year,[84] it was not just oriented towards judges, but was also meant to benefit "public prosecutors, advocates, notaries public and legal scholars."[85] In fact, in 1977 the first index, the so-called *Rangkuman*, was published.[86]

Nevertheless, this new series failed to live up to expectations. Despite its initially ambitious publication schedule, over the past eighteen years only four issues have, in fact, been published, and the last issue (1993) was a reprint of the first. As a result, it was even less timely than the *Yurisprudensi Indonesia* series. In addition, the *Rangkuman* series did not fundamentally resolve the selection problem. It only summarized cases very briefly, and access problems and poor indexing made it increasingly difficult to consult the integral texts of the decisions. The sometimes cryptic summaries were not always comprehensible.

The result is that both the *Yurisprudensi Indonesia* and the *Rangkuman* series have largely been ignored by the legal professions and have thus failed to have a solid impact on legal development:

> These collections suffer from ... problems of insufficient copies, ineffective distribution, and lack of timeliness ... with the effect that such collections are known to and used by only very few Indonesians ...[87]

Varia Peradilan (1985–). One of the factors that may have contributed to the weakness of the case collections published and controlled by the Supreme Court is that from 1985 another case-reporting series emerged which quite clearly does not suffer from some of the major drawbacks of the *Yurisprudensi Indonesia* and *Rangkuman*. This is the journal *Varia Peradilan*, published by the Judges' Association (IKAHI, Ikatan Hakim Indonesia).[88]

Varia Peradilan publishes about sixty cases a year and, in that respect, does not fundamentally resolve the problem of selectiveness marking the other series. Yet it has distinguished itself positively in two ways, and so has begun to serve as the principal reference work for jurisprudence in the country. First, it is a timely series, appearing as it does on a monthly basis. Second, unlike the rather bland *Yurisprudensi Indonesia*, *Varia Peradilan* publishes cases that have "news-value," as one member of the editorial board put it.[89] This refers to the fact that the journal

---

[83] See the introduction by Purwoto S. Gandasubrata in *Rangkuman Yurisprudensi Mahkamah Agung Indonesia II (Perdata dan Acara Perdata)*, p. 3.

[84] Ibid.

[85] Ibid.

[86] Purwoto S. Gandasubrata related in Parliament that the model for the index came from the indexing system prevailing in the Netherlands, where it is generally referred to as the "*Klapper*" (the index-card system). He added humorously that because the Dutch word so closely resembles the typically colonial term for coconut tree (*klapperboom*), the series was renamed the *Rangkuman*.

[87] Churchill, *Development of Legal Information Systems*, p. 12.

[88] In fact, the journal has roots reaching back to the 1960s, but after a long hiatus it resumed publication in its present form only in 1985.

[89] Personal communication, 25 September 1995.

publishes cases that have attracted public attention or that the editors believe should attract public attention. This doesn't mean that the cases always have great legal relevance, but it often happens that cases with great news value also settle important legal issues. Thus it is this series, rather than *Yurisprudensi Indonesia*, that publishes controversial decisions, such as those in *Kedung Ombo I and II* on compensation for expropriation,[90] the *Prioritas* judicial review case,[91] and the *Ohee* case, in which the Supreme Court denied execution of its own decision.[92] As a result of these advantages, *Varia Peradilan* has rapidly supplanted the Supreme Court-controlled series as the principal reference work for Court decisions in the legal professions in Indonesia.

It may seem surprising that the *Varia Peradilan* series should contain more interesting Supreme Court cases than *Yurisprudensi Indonesia*, which after all is published by the Court itself. Perhaps, this fact can be explained partially by the difference in the compilers: the Association judges are trying to run a journal, whereas the selecting judges on the Supreme Court rather are oriented toward legal correctness and doctrine. Moreover, as we have seen, the Judges' Association is traditionally more assertive than the Supreme Court, as one member of the *Varia Peradilan* editorial board obliquely indicated in an interview with me:

SEBASTIAAN POMPE (SP): What is it that allows *Varia Peradilan* to be so different from the *Yurisprudensi Indonesia* series?
VARIA PERADILAN (VP): The reason is that we are more free than the selecting judges on the Supreme Court. The Supreme Court judges are held back by their institutional bonds and ties of loyalty, collegiality, and pressure, of course.
SP: Who is "we"?
VP: Basically it is the non-Supreme Court group of judges, the Judges' Association really.
SP: But the Association nowadays is led by Supreme Court judges; how can it be more free?
VP: The Court leadership of the Association doesn't amount to much. They just sit back and wait for things to happen. All initiatives and action are generated by the lower judges; they are the real engine of the Association, and it is they who effectively control *Varia Peradilan* . . .
SP: So if pressures of various sorts prevent publication in *Yurisprudensi Indonesia*, why should it be allowed in *Varia Peradilan*?
VP: We have direct access to the Supreme Court directors, and it is through them that we get cases. The Court doesn't really check on this.[93]

In the complex and not wholly transparent relationship between the Supreme Court and the Judges' Association (the so-called MA-IKAHI relationship), the Court may have its own purposes for allowing a publication forum not formally associated with it to exist. This raises some delicate questions about what, in the eyes of the Court, publication is actually meant to achieve.

---

[90] *Varia Peradilan* 108 (September 1994): 5; *Varia Peradilan* 112 (January 1995): 8.
[91] *Varia Peradilan* 95 (August 1993): 27.
[92] *Varia Peradilan* 117 (June 1995): 5.
[93] Personal communication, 25 September 1995.

(d) Publication and Authority

As suggested by Gregory Churchill, published court decisions are generally viewed as "selected, and presumably exemplary decisions,"[94] i.e., such decisions are often published because of their supposed precedential quality. That may, in fact, be one of the primary criteria guiding selection of cases for the Supreme Court-controlled series, but it need not be so under all circumstances. As noted before, the blandness and lack of innovation that characterize several issues of *Yurisprudensi Indonesia* suggest that the Supreme Court often selects cases merely to realize publication targets. Publication can serve other functions also; for instance, it can be used to sound out society on difficult and sensitive legal issues, a practice already apparent in the 1950s, when the Supreme Court tried to reform the law of inheritance. As one Court judge recounted in the late 1950s:

> Not long ago, the Supreme Court decided an *adat* inheritance case from East Java, in which it held that a man and woman each had a right to equal portions of the estate, rather than upholding the prevailing disparity in favor of the man. The intention of the Supreme Court in so ruling was to provide for a more just settlement. The Court laid down the rule and then awaited reactions from society to gauge the extent and intensity of opposition. In this case, there hardly was any reaction whatsoever, which indicates that the ruling was acceptable.[95]

Thus, Supreme Court decisions are sometimes published to see whether a new rule is socially acceptable. If it is, the case will constitute a basis on which to proceed and for that reason will be regarded as an authoritative case. But if it is not, the case will be ignored as bad law. Authority, as a result, does not flow directly from publication as such, but from the reactions of society to such published decisions. This presumably applies particularly in cases concerning controversial issues. In this context, it is useful to recall briefly the conversation I had with a senior Supreme Court judge and a Supreme Court chairman on the distinction between legal and factual questions, so important in cassation:

> **SP:** I was told that you decided a case that actually said that the distinction between law and fact could no longer be maintained.
> **Judge** [after searching his memory a bit]: That may be so, I do not quite remember. In any case, it is plainly unfair to stick too closely to the fact-law rule in cases in which the district court judge plainly erred on the facts. We must deal with these cases also.
> **Chairman:** [who overheard the conversation as he walked past] That was just one case. It doesn't mean that it is jurisprudence.
> **SP:** But wasn't it published, in *Varia Peradilan*, as I recall?
> **Judge:** Maybe so. But publication doesn't say all that much about the legal authority of a case. Case publication in such journals as *Varia Peradilan* is sometimes used as a means by which we can solicit reactions from the legal

---

[94] Churchill, *Development of Legal Information Systems*, p. 12.
[95] *DSL*, 13 December 1959.

community on a case, critical commentaries and such, to check whether we are on the right track. If cases are published, this doesn't say much really about the authority of a case.[96]

In certain cases, publication may also be intended to put an end to debate. Thus, in a controversial murder case where press reports interpreted a Supreme Court decision as asserting that the death penalty conflicted with the state ideology, *Varia Peradilan* published the relevant decision with the express intent of refuting that idea, not to make law. As the commentary to the case put it:

> That it must be pointed out in this context that it is clear from this Supreme Court decision that the transformation of the death penalty into a life-long prison sentence is not based on the argument that the death penalty conflicts with the Pancasila State ideology, as has been suggested in society recently, but, on the contrary, on the argument that the decision of the lower court was improperly motivated in imposing the death penalty.[97]

Similarly, controversial cases such as the *Kedung Ombo I and II cases*[98] or the falsified Supreme Court decision on rattan smuggling[99] were published, it would appear, to end speculative public commentaries rather than generate debate or create law. The journal explained its reason for publishing the rattan smuggling case by stating summarily that, because the decision had been falsified, this would put things right.[100] We can surmise that the Supreme Court might wish to keep the journal *Varia Peradilan* at arm's length so it can be used to test public opinion without sullying the Court itself, should things turn out to its disadvantage. Publication therefore does not, by itself, establish the authority of any particular case or mark it as "exemplary."

Of course publication series that are not under some sort of official sanction have even less power to establish useful legal precedents than do more official series. In this sense, *Varia Peradilan* straddles the divide somewhat, being the journal of the state-sanctioned Judges' Association. The authority problem is particularly evident with private compilations of jurisprudence. For the greater part, these private compilations are quite simply selected reprints of the (quasi-) official *Hukum, Yurisprudensi Indonesia,* and *Rangkuman* series and, in that sense, have an equivalent influence as sources of jurisprudence.[101] By and large, this even applies to private compilations published by the redoubtable "case thief," Chidir Ali. Thus, his interesting compilation of tort cases against government (for a long time, the only legal recourse against government action) contains only six cases that

---

[96] Personal communication, 21 September 1995.

[97] Decision Mahkamah Agung no.14/K/Mil/1987 dated 20 November 1987.

[98] Publication of the *Kedung Ombo cases* may also have been directed toward putting local government in its place for suggesting that the first decision, which allowed the claim for adequate compensation and damages against the local government, must surely have been falsified.

[99] Mahkamah Agung no.1805K/Pid/1989 dated 21 March 1990, *Varia Peradilan* 64 (January 1991): 57.

[100] *Varia Peradilan* 64 (1991): 60.

[101] Churchill, *Development of Legal Information Systems*, p. 12.

had never been published elsewhere, but which Ali managed to wriggle out of the archives,[102] while his other books, such as his compilation of corruption cases, are entirely based on the series mentioned above.[103] Yet even if his compilations had been entirely based on cases stolen out of Court archives, their influence in shaping the law would probably be minimal. The access problem ensures that such cases are hard to verify against original records, and this fact fundamentally undercuts their authority. In an oblique way, this was made obvious to Chidir Ali himself, who encountered remarkable problems in getting his compilations published. He complained that, as a result of a widespread feeling that jurisprudence carried no authority, his books were not even used in university courses, and he could not find any publishers as a result.[104]

There are, in sum, a number of serious problems with the access and publication of Supreme Court decisions. There is no public scrutiny of the Court's work because the general public has no access to Court archives. With more than 99 percent of the cases going unreported, there is no way to tell what the Supreme Court decided in those cases and to assess objectively the Court's performance. This in itself undermines the predictive (and hence lawmaking) quality of cases that are actually published. Moreover, this predictive quality is further undermined by the highly discriminatory mechanism for selecting cases to publish. This mechanism not only ignores broad fields of law that are highly relevant in practice but, in addition, disguises what goes on in the Court by giving a very idealized picture of its reasoning; certain Court decisions have actually been revised to make them more fit for publication. These problems are compounded by tardy, inadequate, and poorly distributed publications of cases; the officially sanctioned jurisprudence series are annual at best and, in addition, are difficult for many judges and lawyers to acquire because of inadequate funding. While the Judges' Association has made efforts to bolster the authority of Supreme Court decisions through more regular publication and better distribution of cases, there are strong indications that cases published in its journal need not be regarded as authoritative by the Supreme Court itself. They are published not to shape the law, but "to sound out society" or to put an end to controversy. Ultimately we must conclude that even published Supreme Court decisions lack any predictive value whatsoever, a situation that weakens the lawmaking power of the institution even further.

3. THE ROLE OF JURISPRUDENCE

The whole thrust of this chapter, and indeed of the entire book, is directed toward proving that Supreme Court decisions have all but lost their lawmaking power. And yet the Court has carved out some niches in the legal edifice where, it

---

[102] Of the total of forty cases listed in the book, thirteen had previously been reported in *Hukum*, eight in *Yurisprudensi Indonesia*, and twelve in a smattering of legal journals. Only six cases come from what Ali euphemistically called the "archives" (*Arsip*). C. Ali, *Yurisprudensi Indonesia tentang perbuatan melanggar hukum oleh penguasa (onrechtmatige overheidsdaad)* (Bandung: Binacipta, 1978).

[103] C. Ali, *Yurisprudensi Indonesia tentang hukum pidana korupsi* (Bandung: Binacipta, 1979).

[104] Chidir Ali, Interview, Summer 1992. This is one of the reasons, Chidir Ali told me, why he had to shop around for publishers, and various volumes of his series were published in different places.

would appear, its decisions are reasonably predictable and where it has retained some control over the evolution of the law. Some of these areas, such as procedural law (chapter 6), were obliquely referred to in previous chapters. These areas where Court decisions have maintained some consistency are interesting in their own right, however far apart and isolated they may be, yet their existence raises a more fundamental question. How, in the face of so many adverse factors and in this jungle of particularistic Supreme Court decisions, can the existence of little clearings of effective lawmaking be explained at all? By offering some general explanations, however tentative, of Court behavior in this respect, we can also make similarly tentative predictions about how long this consistency will hold and in what new areas responsible lawmaking might take root.

It must be understood from the start that the Supreme Court confronts a number of factors in attempting to achieve complete consistency on any one issue, however basic it might seem. The determining variables have been defined in the previous chapters, but the effects of these variables in their actual operation cannot be wholly predicted. Any case might generate environmental reactions from the political establishment or the court system itself,[105] might lead to internal Supreme Court malfunctionings of various sorts that cannot possibly be foreseen, and at last might simply disappear in the great mass of unreported cases. So consistency, if accepted as a desirable goal, must not be seen as an absolute, but rather as a relative concept with changing boundaries.

Nevertheless, it would seem that basically three factors help explain why Supreme Court decisions are more consistent (and more effective in shaping the law) in some areas of the law than in others. The first factor is that the Court's close ties with the political and institutional environment not only generate particularism, but can also impose consistent decision making. This may be termed the *"political factor."* Second, some areas in the law command such strong consensus in Indonesian society that they do not allow for much deviance in legal interpretation or Supreme Court lawmaking. These areas usually relate to matters of preeminent importance to the national state and, for that reason, are termed the *"public policy factor."* Conversely, the overarching importance of the political and institutional environment in which it operates may lead the Supreme Court to exercise its lawmaking function on issues that are furthest removed from that environment, namely highly technical legal matters. This I will define as the *"technical factor."*

(a) The Political Factor: Twisting the Supreme Court's Arms

In 1995, the renowned Indonesian lawyer, Gautama, published an article in which he referred to trademark law as a specific area of Indonesian law in which Supreme Court jurisprudence was highly influential.[106] While the Supreme Court's jurisprudence has had a considerable impact on Indonesian intellectual property

---

[105] It is important to note that it is not just reactions from outside of the Court that determine the way cases are handled, but that internal reactions can be just as important.

[106] S. Gautama, "Law Reform in Indonesia through the Courts with Special Reference to Trademark Cases," *Indonesia Law and Administration Review* 1,1 (1995): 17.

law broadly speaking,[107] Gautama singled out what perhaps is the first and most important area in which the Court made its influence felt, namely the principle of "good faith" in the registration of a trademark. It is worth briefly considering this point, for it constitutes an excellent illustration of the way in which external pressures can bring the Supreme Court to consistent decision making.

The original Trademark Law no.21/1961 had the somewhat complicated provision that the first party to use his trademark in Indonesia would be the owner, with registration constituting the presumption of first use (art.2). Needless to say, this article gave rise to considerable litigation. One of those cases was the highly important *Tancho case* (1972), which evolved into a seminal case in Indonesian trademark law.[108] The basic point addressed in this case was how to qualify registration of a trademark in bad faith, a situation about which statute said nothing at all. Insofar as relevant, the facts of the case are simple. An Indonesian party registered the Japanese firm name "Tancho" before the Japanese owner did, and the owner then started an action before the Indonesian courts. It was evident that the Indonesian party was not acting in good faith: he had made a general practice of registering famous foreign brands with the aim of marketing local products under those names. In addition, he added the words "Trade Marks Tokyo Osaka Co." to the trademark, suggesting that the products he offered were, in fact, produced by the well-known Japanese firm. Still, there was nothing in the law that prohibited such practices, and the case was dismissed on those grounds in the lower courts. Not so in the Supreme Court, however, which was led at the time by the professional and strict chairman, Subekti. The Supreme Court upheld the claim and stated that only registration "in good faith" would create the presumption of first use and ownership. Its reasoning was as follows:

1. It is the purpose of the Indonesian Trademark Law to protect the general public from falsified brands, of which the original is known to be of good quality.

2. Traditionally there is a tendency in Indonesian society to regard imported goods as being of better quality. There is a tendency in this society to make use of this attitude, resulting in attempts to copy foreign well-known brands which are as yet unregistered in Indonesia. Indonesian judges should take a stern attitude to counter this acting in bad faith.

This was, by any account, an important case, but if the proof of the pudding is in the eating, the question here was whether the ruling would hold when similar cases came before the Supreme Court later. In fact, it took a while for the *Tancho* rule to take root. As was to be expected, the district courts hardly took note of it, and trademark law in the lower courts remained pretty much in shambles, with cases going off in all directions.[109] The Supreme Court was also evidently still in search of its own bearings, as it upheld the *Tancho* rule in some cases while denying it in

---

[107] See, for instance, C. B. Kaehlig and G. J. Churchill, *Indonesian Intellectual Property Law* (Jakarta: Tatanusa, 1993), ch. 1; C. Antons, "Urheberrecht und gewerblicher Rechtsschutz in Indonesien" (PhD dissertation, University of Amsterdam, 1995), pp. 311-23.

[108] Mahkamah Agung no.677K/Pdt/1972 dated 13 December 1972 (*Tancho*).

[109] Antons, "Urheberrecht und gewerblicher Rechtsschutz," p. 316, n. 199.

others, even when there was evidence of bad faith.[110] Indeed, in 1985, the Supreme Court decided a case involving the famous US sportswear manufacturer Nike that, in many respects, was identical to the *Tancho case*. Yet in this instance, it refused to apply the "good faith" rule and denied the foreign action (*Nike I* 1985).[111] In the mid-1980s, however, something happened that would change this situation drastically.

The unlikely spark that ignited reform of Indonesian intellectual property law was an English pop singer, Bob Geldof.[112] Geldof, originally lead singer for the group "Boomtown Rats," had a St. Paul-on-the-way-to-Damascus experience during a visit to Africa in 1984–85, during which he was confronted by the human misery resulting from a massive famine. This brought Geldof to organize the so-called Live Aid pop concert in the summer of 1985. The revenues from this concert and sale of its recordings would be dedicated to fight the famine in Africa. In December 1985, however, large numbers of pirated tapes (the first batch estimated at 1.5 million) originating from Indonesia began to flood the markets. News of the piracy was broadly publicized and caused an international outcry, fanned by Geldof. Indonesia took steps to contain the damage by (among other things) withdrawing all tapes from the market, but the incident quite clearly tarnished its international image. Then in December 1985 the FBI caught an Indonesian businessman trying to sell several hundreds of thousands of tapes to a US company. It transpired that the tapes had entered the United States by diplomatic pouch, which did little to diminish the embarrassment for Indonesia.[113]

The effect of both incidents was to place the issue of intellectual property rights high on the agenda of Indonesian political leaders, including President Suharto. The incidents also allowed foreign states to increase their pressure on Indonesia to do something about its poor intellectual property rights conditions. The US, in particular, put on the thumbscrews, threatening to withhold GSP (Generalized System of Preferences) status in June 1986.

What perhaps made the greatest impact, however, was the visit of US president Reagan to the ASEAN (Association of Southeast Asian Nations) summit in Bali in the spring of 1986. During this visit, Reagan specifically raised the issue of intellectual property rights with President Suharto[114] and mentioned the *Nike case*. As a result, when Suharto returned to Jakarta from the Bali summit, he was highly focused on the intellectual property rights issue generally and the *Nike case* in particular. The result was acceleration of the lumbering legislative process, and within a year a new Copyright Law was enacted, with the Patent and Trademark Laws following soon afterwards (in 1989 and 1992 respectively).

---

[110] The *Tancho* rule was followed in the *Bata* (1982) and *Snoopy and Woodstock* (1985) *cases* but, in the *Seven Up case* (1983), the first registration rule was purposely upheld, even though there evidently was bad faith. Mahkamah Agung 3042K.Sip/1981 dated 25 March 1982 (Bata); Mahkamah Agung 1272K/Pdt/1984 dated 30 November 1985 (Snoopy and Woodstock); Mahkamah Agung 2858K/Sip/1981 dated 17 February 1982. See also Antons, "Urheberrecht und gewerblicher Rechtsschutz," p. 316, n. 199.

[111] Mahkamah Agung no.294K/Pdt/1984 dated 20 July 1985.

[112] Concerning the subject of the next paragraphs, see Elisabeth Uphoff, *Intellectual Property and US Relations with Indonesia, Malaysia, Singapore, and Thailand* (Ithaca: Cornell Southeast Asia Program Publications, 1991), p. 29.

[113] Ibid.

[114] Ibid., p. 30.

Suharto also instructed the Supreme Court to rethink the *Nike case*.[115] Consequently, when the case was reopened for review in December 1985 (*Nike II*),[116] the outcome was altogether different from *Nike I*, in which the *Tancho* rule had been denied. Instead, in *Nike II*, the Supreme Court applied the "good faith" principle, and *Tancho* was affirmed. This decision set a firm precedent in a highly publicized case, and, following *Nike II*, "good faith" became firmly entrenched in Indonesian trademark law. In subsequent cases, the Supreme Court consistently upheld the principle,[117] and when the new Trademark Law was enacted in 1992, the "good faith" principle laid down in the *Tancho case* acquired statutory basis (art.4[1]).

The Supreme Court's decisions in the *Tancho* and *Nike II cases* are generally viewed as significant contributions to legal development. As we have seen, however, the Court initially was not at all inclined to follow precedent. It was only after the government twisted its arm that the Court revised its decision and used the *Tancho* ruling as a precedent.

The impact of political arm-twisting on Supreme Court lawmaking is all the more apparent in the *Nike II case*, because in that situation the government forced the Court to violate the law on another no less important point. The Court's decision in that case did leave its mark on the field of trademark law, but in procedural terms the Court made an ass of the law—not to speak of itself, since it knew full well what it was doing. For while the decision in *Nike II* dutifully applied precedent and thus strengthened Supreme Court jurisprudence, it also violated procedural rules of review. It is worth considering this angle because it illustrates how limited is the scope of the Supreme Court when political pressure is on. Review before the Supreme Court is allowed only in a few specified cases, essentially when new facts directly relevant to the outcome of the case have been brought to light or in cases of gross judicial error.[118] New legal interpretation is deliberately excluded as a ground for review, lest each change in the law lead to a flood of old cases being reopened. The Supreme Court has affirmed this rule in a number of cases.[119] Yet it was precisely on the basis of new legal interpretation that the Court felt compelled to decide *Nike II*.

The case focused on the issue of whether an action for annulment of a trademark could be commenced after registration of the trademark or only after its subsequent publication in the State Reports Supplement. The 1961 law clearly opted for the latter, stipulating that annulment must be applied for within nine months of *publication* (art.10[1] law no.21/1961). According to firm Supreme Court jurisprudence, it was not possible to start an action of annulment either before or

---

[115] Personal communication, 5 August, 5 September 1994.

[116] Mahkamah Agung no.220PK/Pdt/1986 dated 16 December 1986.

[117] See, for instance, Mahkamah Agung no.3394K/Pdt/1985 dated 9 September 1987 (*Lily Ball Bagus*).

[118] See Law no.14/1985, art.67 which refers to the following cases: deceit, new evidence, condemning a defendant to a sentence longer than requested by the plaintiff, indictment not fully decided without grounds, conflicting court decisions or judgments, gross judicial error on the law by the judge. These conditions are identical to the conditions prior to 1985, based on Mahkamah Agung Regulation no.2/1982, on which the *Nike case* was based.

[119] Mahkamah Agung no.109PK/Pdt/1984 dated 15 August 1985.

after this period.[120] The legal consistency imposed by the Supreme Court posed an important practical problem with this rule, as the claimant in *Nike II* did not fail to point out. This was that publication of the State Report Supplement was seriously delayed—by 1986 it was more than six years late. This delay allowed an Indonesian party to register a well-known foreign trademark and benefit from its use for a full six years before an action for annulment could even be begun.

In *Nike I*, this was the stumbling block for the foreign claimant, with the Supreme Court holding firm to its earlier line of cases and to the law that publication was the crucial point. In *Nike II*, the Court allowed the review action, however, and decided in favor of the foreign claimant. It stated that a *male fide* Indonesian registration of a well-known foreign trademark should not benefit from the delayed publication of the State Reports Supplement. In such a case, the Court said, an action for annulment may be commenced after registration but before publication.

The review case was based on a new, extended interpretation of the "good faith rule" laid down in the *Tancho case*. Review was not granted, therefore, in response to a discovery of new facts or gross judicial error, but was based on new legal interpretation—a ground for review specifically excluded by law and by the Supreme Court itself. In procedural terms, therefore, the *Nike II* decision seems to have been incorrect and probably should have been thrown out.[121]

The Supreme Court could hardly have missed the fact that it was violating basic rules of review procedure in *Nike II*, but still opted to ignore the point deliberately. In fact, the defendant raised the issue explicitly during the trial:

> I.2. We submit to the attention of the Supreme Court that the request for review submitted by the claimant is not based on any of the grounds for review mentioned in art.2 sub a to f, whereas the law clearly states that the grounds for review are exhaustively listed therein and are binding for any such action to be allowed by the Supreme Court.
> (. . .)
> II.7. . . . that a change of legal opinion by the Supreme Court cannot serve as sufficient ground to start an action in review before that court.

This led to a brief internal debate within the Court, which was, however, cut short. A Supreme Court law clerk closely involved in the handling of the *Nike II case* related events as follows:

> I was very surprised when I saw the drafts of *Nike II*. They indicated that the review of *Nike I* was to be allowed on a wholly novel extensive interpretation of the good faith principle. So I went to the presiding judge and said: "Sir, this decision really allows review on the basis of new law instead of new facts. This

---

[120] Interestingly enough, the two important cases often mentioned in this context were decided on the same day. Mahkamah Agung no.3293K/Pdt/1983 dated 30 March 1983 (*Bos*); Mahkamah Agung no.2674K/Pdt/1983 dated 30 March 1985. In *Nike I*, the Supreme Court upheld this rule also, with extensive argumentation. See generally Kaehlig and Churchill, *Indonesian Intellectual Property Law*, ch. 1, pp. 55-56.

[121] See also Kaehlig and Churchill, *Indonesian Intellectual Property Law*, ch. 1, p. 62.

violates basic procedural rules on review, and assuredly should not be allowed."[122]

The presiding judge had also decided the *Tancho case* and was generally perceived to be one of the sharpest legal minds on the Court at the time, so there can be little doubt that he was aware of what was at issue here. Yet when confronted by his clerk, he cut off discussion immediately. Just bobbing his head, he made a chopping movement with his hand and said, "Hush." The clerk had no doubt what this meant: that he was correct, but had to keep his mouth shut. In the decision, the Supreme Court merely qualified the extension of the "good faith" principle as a "gross judicial error" that allowed for review.

The senior Supreme Court clerk said that this outcome of the *Nike II case* could be explained only in light of the political arm twisting that was going on.[123] In fact, this extra dimension just shows the extent to which political pressure can be brought to bear on the Supreme Court to apply the law despite all procedural hurdles.

(b) The Public Policy Factor: Nation Building and Fighting Competing Norms

If the above case exemplifies the effect that external pressure can have on Supreme Court jurisprudence, this is not to say that the Court makes law only when external pressures are imposed. In fact, there are clear examples in which the Supreme Court maintained jurisprudential consistency despite strong external pressures to break with it and return to particularism. The best-known illustration of this, no doubt, is the Supreme Court-initiated reform in inheritance law, in which the equal rights of parties irrespective of gender were established. This decision was made despite vociferous opposition in the regions, as Supreme Court chairman Wirjono Prodjodikoro recounted in later years:

> The Supreme Court inheritance cases inevitably became known in the Batak region... and I was invited over for a public debate on Batak inheritance law. It surprised me a bit, but I accepted anyway and went. There was very little debate, but instead a public critique of the Supreme Court and myself on the grounds that our decisions on *adat* inheritance simply were wrong because they violated Batak *adat* and were intended to change Batak social structure. The argument also was that the Supreme Court was actually taking the place of the legislator and had no right to do so... There really was considerable pressure during the meeting, until, much to my relief, finally a *woman* got up to argue in my support. She said that Batak women actually were grateful for the Supreme Court decision. When I heard her speak, I was happy that at least Batak women actually supported the Supreme Court decisions. But she was the only one to argue in its favor. I reacted to the criticism by saying that the Supreme Court had not intended to change Batak social structure. Also, if it was clear that all of Batak society actually opposed the Supreme Court decisions on inheritance, I promised that the Court would rescind the decisions

---

[122] Personal communications, 5 August and 5 September 1995.
[123] Ibid.

by declaring itself incompetent on the matter. But only on the condition that the women also agree that the decisions were wrong.

As Wirjono Prodjodikoro was returning home from the meeting, a *man* secretly slipped a note that supported the Supreme Court line of decisions into his hand. The man clearly was not willing to do this publicly, but his action suggested that at least some of the men must have supported the Supreme Court in private.[124]

What made Wirjono Prodjodikoro dig in his heels in the face of so much external pressure? It would appear that a number of elements played a role here. The first concerns the substance of the case at issue: these cases involve basic tenets of state law, in this instance the equality of persons before the law, irrespective of gender. In truth, it is not always clear what these basic principles are, and sometimes they only become apparent when the Court runs into them. Yet, it appears that basic tenets must comply with at least two elements. First, they must touch directly upon the two ideological pillars of the Indonesian state, namely nation building and economic development. Second, they generally involve state rules that conflict with non-state norms and values. When such a conflict arises, judges will naturally be inclined to let national law prevail over competing normative systems since Supreme Court judges are members of the national elite and in that capacity "are subject to the same ideological pressures as the rest of the [political] elite and usually share the same psychology."[125]

This inclination has brought the Supreme Court to reform various bits and pieces of the law, with consistent decision making that flies directly in the face of *adat* and religious normative values. Perhaps the most notable example, extensively commented upon by Daniel Lev, is *adat* inheritance law, which was completely overhauled by the Court to the effect that a surviving widow and children have equal rights to an estate, irrespective of gender.[126] Yet there are other examples, one of which—interreligious marriage—I consider briefly here.[127]

Over the past decades, marriage between people of different religions has emerged as one of the more sensitive issues in modern Indonesian law, for religions generally are very restrictive about allowing their followers to marry outside the faith.[128] Islam, in particular, is specific on the issue, stating that Muslim men may marry "women of the Book" (Jews and Christians, but not Buddhists or Hindus) and Muslim women may not marry a non-Muslim at all. Nevertheless, in a multi-religious country such as Indonesia, strict enforcement of such restrictions would prevent various population groups from intermarrying, which is in outright opposition to the nation-building ideology of the Indonesian state. As a result,

---

[124] *DSL*, 10 July 1967.

[125] Daniel S. Lev, "The Supreme Court and Adat Inheritance Law in Indonesia," *The American Journal of Comparative Law* 1,1 (1962): 205.

[126] Ibid.

[127] See generally: Sebastiaan Pompe, "Mixed Marriages in Indonesia: Some Comments on the Law and the Literature," *Bijdragen tot de Taal-, Land- en Volkenkunde* 144 (1988): 259; Sebastiaan Pompe, "A Short Note on Some Recent Developments with Regard to Mixed Marriages in Indonesia," *Bijdragen tot de Taal-, Land- en Volkenkunde* 147 (1991): 261 and the sources cited therein.

[128] For a review of various marriage restrictions in various religions prevailing in Indonesia, see R. S. Prawirohamidjojo, *Pluralisme dalam perundang-undangan perkawinan di Indonesia* (Surabaya: Airlangga University Press, 1986).

there has been a consistent drive on the part of central state institutions to allow interreligious marriages, notwithstanding evident social pressures to restrict and even to forbid them. Thus, from the early 1950s, the Supreme Court consistently decided that colonial law upholding the validity of interreligious marriages still applied.[129] The volatility of the issue was perhaps inadvertently fueled by Marriage Law no.1/1974, which stated in so many words that a marriage must be concluded in accordance with the religions of both parties (art.2[1]). The intention of this article quite clearly was to restrict the role of religion to the *conclusion* of marriage, and then it was still subordinate to statute law. Nevertheless, the idea took root in some sections of the religious communities that this reference to religion meant that all religious prescripts were incorporated into state law, including marriage prohibitions. This placed the government in a quandary. To deny this view would place it in outright opposition to the religious communities, which had acquired considerable political clout over the years. Yet to accept the view that religious prescripts applied would institutionalize religious discrimination in the country, reducing the government's own authority in this matter—a wholly unacceptable proposition. The Indonesian government, facing a highly volatile political issue, adopted a wait-and-see attitude, hoping perhaps that the problem would go away if ignored long enough. Yet the judiciary could not enjoy such leisure as cases were being brought on the issue. For a while, the Supreme Court stuck to the line that these marriages should be allowed on the basis of colonial statute.[130] Yet in a spectacular 1989 decision, it turned to new logic altogether. In this decision, it stated that the essentially secular colonial statute was no longer in line with the non-secular modern Indonesian state and nullified the statute on that basis. Yet in the same decision, the Court provided an alternative procedure for Indonesians of different faiths who wished to marry, as it held that interreligious marriage should be allowed by special court order.[131] There are many problematic aspects to the decision, not least that the woman is assumed to have given up her religion in such marriages, but in substance it shows that, despite evident public pressure to disallow interreligious marriages, the Supreme Court firmly upheld them.

---

[129] Mahkamah Agung dated 16 February 1955, *Hukum* 3 (1955): 44.

[130] See for instance: Mahkamah Agung no.1650K/Sip/1974 dated 13 November 1979, *Yurisprudensi Indonesia* 1980 (I): 111; Mahkamah Agung no.32K/AG/1983 dated 22 August 1983 in Z. D. Basuki, "Perkawinan antar agama dewasa ini di Indonesia, ditinjau dari segi hukum antar tata hukum," *Hukum dan Pembangunan* 17,3 (1987): 235. See also Circular Letter no. MA/Pemb.0807 dated 20 August 1975. The colonial statute was the *Regeling op de Gemengde Huwelijken* S.1898-158 (Mixed marriage ordinance).

[131] Mahkamah Agung no.1400K/Pdt/1986 dated 20 January 1989, *Varia Peradilan* 45 (June 1989): 73; see also *Tempo*, 24 June 1989. It is a noteworthy case in another respect also. By voiding colonial statute, the Supreme Court created a "legal vacuum," as it called this itself. Yet in the same case, it provided an alternative procedure by which the marriage might be saved. In another famous case involving arbitration, the so-called *Maritime Bulgare* [Mahkamah Agung no.2944K/Pdt/1983 dated 29 November 1984, *Varia Peradilan* 2 (March 1987): 103], the Supreme Court declared various treaties and colonial statutes inapplicable, thus again creating a legal vacuum. But here it simply dismissed the action rather than offering an alternative procedure in its decision. It provided for that procedure some time later with a separate regulation. Nevertheless, it is not wholly clear why the two cases were treated differently—with such obvious and immediate impacts for the litigating parties.

(c) The Technical Factor: The Splendid Isolation of Legal Technique

> Nothing we did excited people as much as the *adat* inheritance cases in the 1950s, but to me there was another problem which takes second place among the difficult Supreme Court cases. This relates to the establishment of currency value. It started out with the problem of *gadai* (land serving as collateral to a loan). The increasing disparity in currency value between the Dutch Indies Guilder and the Indonesian Rupiah caused injustice as people tried to recover their land by repaying after the war with exactly the same amount as they had loaned before the war. Yamin gave the problem an edge by suggesting that land which had served as collateral for seven years should be returned to the owner without obligation of repayment. He thought that the owner of land who transfers his land as collateral must be poor. I wholly disagreed with this ... and felt that the one who gives land in collateral must repay to recover his land. The reason is that it quite simply is incorrect to hold that only the poor give their land in collateral for a loan. I know for a fact that in Bali just the opposite is true—that it is the rich who give their land in collateral.[132]

In this interview, Wirjono Prodjodikoro is referring to a 1955 case, in which a pair of landowners tried to redeem their land by repaying a 1943 loan originally contracted in high-value guilders with the same amount in low-value postwar rupiahs. The Supreme Court held that this was manifestly unjust and allowed the stated amount of such loans to be corrected with reference to the gold standard. As it happened, this decision did not take root in the field of land law, as Wirjono had hoped, but with respect to contract law it did set an important precedent.[133]

This case is interesting because it appears that strong external pressures or public policy were not actually the determining factors in the decision. There was no external pressure to speak of. The only thing that really pushed the Supreme Court was the land case itself and the Court's perception that the rapid devaluation of the rupiah was sure to provoke more litigation, which meant they would need to resolve the point. Neither was accommodation of the rupiah's devaluation an issue of public policy. Indeed, the Indonesian government does not appear to have developed any policy whatsoever concerning the rupiah's loss of value, or if it did, it was certainly not public. As a result, market forces were left to respond to the challenges generated by the falling rupiah. Astonishingly, the government did not even attempt to mitigate the devaluation's effects on criminal law, although the currency's loss of value emasculated most, if not all, sanctions in regulations of some age, a dilemma which the government has done little to redress. Apparently, law enforcers must use their own system of scales and equity in apportioning fines and penalties.

The motive that might have spurred the Court to adjust sums of money contractually agreed upon does not clearly fit into the categories discussed above,

---

[132] *DSL*, 10 July 1967.

[133] Contrary to Wirjono's hopes, it was Yamin's views that would find their way into the Land Reform Act. Nevertheless, in the 1950s, Wirjono's perception concerning how to deal equitably with growing disparities in currency value drove a wedge into the body of Indonesian contract law, which up until that time had been iron solid and unyielding. If not in the field of land law, then at least with regard to contract law, Wirjono's ideas generated important consequences.

which suggests that some other factor was in play. It shows that sometimes the Supreme Court can be quite constructive in the little corners of the law. In fact, the distinguishing character of this example seems to be precisely that the relevant issue was tucked away in the legal recesses. It is only when questions arise concerning arcane constructs that few outside the legal professions understand and which deal with "neutral" niches of reality that the Supreme Court dares to experiment effectively with jurisprudence.

The Supreme Court's influence on contract law to accommodate the steady loss of value of the Indonesian currency is a typical example of this "no-risk" factor.[134] In law, this is a pretty complex subject, marked by a number of legislative provisions primarily directed at shoring up currencies under pressure. Indonesia inherited a legislative system from the Dutch marked since the 1930s Depression by attempts to prevent a value loss of the Netherlands-Indies guilder. This was effected in essentially two ways. The first was to include a new article in the colonial Civil Code that explicitly stated that currency terms in loan agreements must be taken at their nominal value, regardless of the possible depreciation in the value of that currency (art.1756 colonial Civil Code). The second was to forbid securing contractual liabilities defined in currency terms against the gold standard, which was the predominant stable standard at the time.[135] These provisions were upheld during colonial times and even shortly after independence.[136]

The colonial measures were meant to bolster public confidence in a currency by enforcing its nominal rather than its "real" value. As the Dutch succinctly summarize the seminal Dutch Supreme Court case on the issue: a Mark is a Mark.[137] By themselves, these measures were unable, of course, to prevent value loss once economic rot set in, as the Indonesian case quite clearly illustrated.[138] Colonial statute was completely ineffective at slowing the precipitous devaluation of the rupiah and consequent inflation in Indonesia during the 1950s and 1960s. In inflationary terms, the rupiah's drop in value came close to a free fall. To take just

---

[134] See generally Sebastiaan Pompe, "Some Comments on the Depreciation of Currency Value in Indonesian Law," *Varia Peradilan* 70 (July 1991): 102.

[135] Ordinance on the Gold Clause S.1937-585 dated 28 October 1937.

[136] See, for instance, colonial Supreme Court dated 25 May 1939, *Indisch Tijdschrift van het Recht* 150 (1939): 359; and Magelang District Court no.139/1951 dated 15 October 1951, *Hukum* 4-5 (1952): 107, where the judge said, "The function of currency is to serve as a value standard of other economic goods. As a result, it generally cannot be accepted that the value of such currency is determined by any other standard, however this is realized."

[137] This refers to a case in which the Dutch Supreme Court held that, notwithstanding rampant inflation in Germany, a loan in German marks should be repaid nominally, i.e. in the amount of marks originally agreed upon. The loan was made before inflation in the amount of one-hundred thousand marks (roughly equal to one-hundred thousand Dutch guilders), and repayment was due after inflation had set in and the amount was valued at less that a single Dutch cent. F. J. Ballendux, "Geldlening, inflatie en goede trouw" (PhD dissertation, Tilburg University, 1980). Frederick Mann points out that the exclusion of gold clauses to secure contractual liabilities is a typical measure of governments seeking to bolster public confidence in their currencies by adopting nominalist policies. Frederick A. Mann, *The Legal Aspect of Money* (Oxford: Clarendon Press, 1982), p. 167 passim.

[138] Indeed, when currency value deteriorates rapidly, legislation imposing currency nominalism quite clearly has an adverse effect on its recovery. The market inevitably flees an unstable national currency in its contractual arrangements, which obstructs rather than supports recovery of public confidence.

a few examples, inflation rates stood at triple-digit levels between 1961-66 (when it averaged 330 percent) and only came down to double digits in the 1970s. Moreover, during 1971-86 the rupiah was devalued four times, with a loss of value of 9 percent (10 percent relative to the US dollar) in 1971, 34 percent (51 percent relative to the US dollar) in 1978, 28 percent (38 percent relative to the US dollar) in 1983, and 31 percent (45 percent relative to the US dollar) in 1986.[139]

As a result, it was very possible, and it no doubt happened, that contractual liabilities stated in terms of rupiahs halved in value overnight. Indeed, in Wirjono's land case, cited at the start of this section, the original loan after five years was worth one-thirtieth of its original value—and this was before the economic devastation of Guided Democracy. It is not surprising that courts were confronted with increasing frequency by cases involving the rupiah's loss of value. Sooner or later these reached the Supreme Court, which acted not just because of the obvious inequity involved in sticking to nominalism, as statute required, but because this was the sort of issue that the Supreme Court could effectively address and even influence. A good deal of legal technique was involved, and while broadly relevant, the rupiah's loss of value was essentially accepted as a fact of life in Indonesian society and hardly stirred the masses.

As Wirjono indicated in the interview, he rejected the strictly nominalist approach in interpreting contractual obligations expressed in monetary terms and imposed by colonial statute.[140] Instead, he applied the gold standard. This abandonment of nominalism in favor of equity was justified in later years with reference to art.1339 Civil Code. As stated by former Supreme Court chairman Subekti:

> In case a question does not find its answer in the Civil Code nor in any living custom, the judge has to give a decision according to equity. For example: A had a claim on B for a thousand rupiahs in 1954, he claims twenty thousand rupiahs because the price of gold is now twenty times the price in 1954. The court approves A's claim to the amount of ten thousand rupiahs, deciding that the risk of inflation of currency be borne by both parties equally.[141]

Subekti refers to firm jurisprudence developed by the Supreme Court following Wirjono's land case in which contractual liabilities defined in rupiahs can, in fact, be modified by the judge to take account of depreciation. All types of contracts are

---

[139] A. Abimanyu, "The Declining Exchange Rate, its Influence on the Indonesian Foreign Debt," *Prisma* 44 (1987): 52, as corrected by W. A. I. M. Segers, *Indonesië van olie- tot industrieland* (Leiden, 1989), p. 168.

[140] On early developments, see Oey Peck Hong, *Peranan kodifikasi, jurisprudensi dan ilmu pengetahuan dalam perkembangan hukum perdata* (Surabaya: Slamet Muda, 1959), p. 15; Gouw Giok Siong, "De rechtsontwikkeling van Indonesië na de souvereiniteitsoverdracht," *Weekblad voor Privaatrecht, Notariaat en Rechtsvergelijking*, nos.4982-4984 at no.4982 (1968), p. 104, n. 71; M. B. Hooker, *Adat Law in Modern Indonesia* (Kuala Lumpur: Oxford University Press, 1978), p. 133. On recent developments, see Pompe, "Some Comments on the Depreciation of Currency Value in Indonesian Law"; D. Widjaja, "Dampak devaluasi terhadap hutang piutang," *Varia Peradilan* 15 (1986): 142.

[141] R. Subekti, *The Law of Contracts in Indonesia: Remedies of Breach* (Jakarta: C.V. Haji Masagung, 1989), p. 9. See also Setiawan, "Several Notes Concerning the Indonesian Legal System: Role of Judges in Civil Court Proceedings," *BW-Krant Jaarboek 1989: Een internationale code* (Arnhem: Gouda Quint, 1989), p. 137.

involved, including real property,[142] loan agreements,[143] and straightforward purchase agreements.[144] The only exceptions to this approach seem to be default cases[145] or cases in which the risk of value depreciation is explicitly allocated.[146]

The appropriate amount is determined by a fixed calculation, in which the monetary amounts are related to the gold standard. Contracted debts are converted into their gold value according to the rate prevailing at the time of contracting, which in turn is then converted back into present currency value. The resultant figure is halved to account for changes in the gold standard, which are considered to be a risk equally shared by both contracting parties.

In its decisions, the Supreme Court itself refers to a "firm line of jurisprudence" on this point, and, in fact, no published legislation could be traced in which the Supreme Court deviated from this line. Clearly, then, the Court effectively voided art.1759 Civil Code as well as the Ordinance on the Gold Clause, and replaced these with great lawmaking. Nobody even seems to notice these drastic moves, as indeed this is a pretty obscure area of the law in which the Supreme Court can do whatever it wants with relative impunity. There are no political risks involved.

4. CONCLUSION

The limited role of Supreme Court decisions in shaping the law has been clearly defined as one of the major problems of national legal development in recent years. Whereas the whole thrust of this study has been to indicate the factors that caused this condition to arise in the first place, some characteristics proper to the theory regarding Court decisions and their actual operation merit attention.

This chapter has indicated that for a number of reasons there has been a tendency in the Indonesian legal professions over the past half century to deny court decisions any law-shaping authority. This effectively led to a return to the doctrinal roots of the civil law system, which had been applied neither in France nor in the Netherlands or her colony, and which ignored the very real contributions of both the colonial and independent judiciaries to Indonesian legal development. A number of reasons underlie this restrictive interpretation of Court decisions, such as legal doctrine itself, the progressive loss of the Dutch language (as regards colonial law), and the increasingly errant and unpredictable courts after independence.

---

[142] For examples, see: Mahkamah Agung dated 11 May 1955, *Hukum* 3 (1955); Mahkamah Agung dated 27 April 1955, *Hukum* 1,2 (1959); Mahkamah Agung 22 May 1957, *Hukum* 1,2 (1958); Mahkamah Agung no.74K/Sip/1969 dated 14 June 1969, *Yurisprudensi Indonesia* (1971): 259; Mahkamah Agung no.380K/Sip/1975 dated 15 April 1976, *Yurisprudensi Indonesia* (1976): 90; Mahkamah Agung no.3703K/Pdt/1986 dated 10 December 1988, *Varia Peradilan* 5,51 (Dec. 1989): 36.

[143] Mahkamah Agung no.410K/Pdt/1959 dated 25 November 1959, *Persahi* (1964): 64; Mahkamah Agung no.547K/Sip/1969 dated 6 June 1970, *Yurisprudensi Indonesia* (1970): 381; Mahkamah Agung 224K/Sip/1973 dated 24 September 1974, *Rangkuman Yurisprudensi Mahkamah Agung Indonesia* (1977), p. 50.

[144] Mahkamah Agung no.610K/Sip/1968 dated 23 May 1970, *Yurisprudensi Indonesia* (1970): 487.

[145] Mahkamah Agung no.208K/Sip/1971 dated 17 July 1971.

[146] Mahkamah Agung 960K/Sip/1973 dated 16 March 1976, *Yurisprudensi Indonesia* (1976): 107.

This chapter has also considered obstacles to redressing this situation as regards Supreme Court decisions. It indicates that Court decisions are currently hard to obtain, selection of cases for publication is arbitrary and does not represent what goes on in Court, and cases are published in too small numbers and too late. As a result, it is not at all clear what goes on in the Court, which makes its actions unpredictable.

All this does not deny that on some issues the Supreme Court is fairly consistent, which, in view of the foregoing, calls for an explanation. This chapter has offered essentially three reasons for this consistency. The first is that consistency itself may be imposed by the very same outside elements that normally impose particularism on Court decision making. The second is that on a number of basic issues, fundamental agreement may exist in Indonesian society or at least the body politic, disallowing deviance by the Court. The third is that there may be areas of the law that are relatively untouched by the environmental or institutional factors that influence Court performance, and, as a result, permit consistent decision making. These areas are most likely to relate to subjects involving legal technique, subjects little understood and appreciated beyond the select circle of the legal profession.

Conclusion

One of the best known photographs from Indonesia in recent years captures the ceremony of President Suharto's resignation in May 1998. It was shown on the front pages of most international newspapers and broadcast on television stations across the globe. The picture freezes in history the fall of the leader of one of the world's largest countries and the collapse of its political order.

In the photograph, Mr. Suharto stands before the microphone reading his statement, with his successor, Mr. Habibie, at his left, two steps back. The two men are flanked by various officials. To the right stand members of the Cabinet, most prominently the ministers of defense and justice. But it is the left flank that draws the most attention: there is represented the Supreme Court. There is not just one justice, but the entire leadership of the Court, eight in all, so many that they run off the page. They have shown up, moreover, in full dress. In Indonesia, the robes of Supreme Court justices sport not only a couple of modest Rehnquist stripes, but full gold fronts. Reflecting the many camera flashes, they even managed to attract attention away from center stage. "Who are these guys?" wondered a member of the foreign press. One respected newspaper speculated that, as they wore such magnificent robes and stared sternly into the distance, "these must be the priests." "And what do they do?" asked another. Indeed; what did they do? The judges trooped onto the stage at the beginning of the ceremony and trooped off again after it was done without performing any function at all of which anyone was aware. The justices were, in a manner of speaking, just holding their horses.

"Holding the horses" in gold robes undeniably suggests a powerful political symbolism. Indonesia is little used to an orderly and constitutional transfer of power, and the battery of justices clad impressively on the front row represented state legitimacy. The intended message evidently was that if the supreme guardians of the law were there to witness the occasion, then this must be a legitimate process, even if they actually had no function to perform. To the extent that politics relies on symbols and images, the metaphysics of "holding the horses" of state was meant to convey a very real message.

Yet the symbolism belied a reality that was the exact opposite. For the gowns and plumage were unmatched by any real power or meaningful role during the ceremony. Presented in this light, the picture and indeed the entire ceremony made the judges actually appear somewhat absurd and ridiculous. Having a battery of judges turn up solely to be there conveys a sense of vacuous banality. It made the judges seem little more than decoration, an image reinforced by their colorful dress; it rather reduced them to a servant role. It is telling that Habibie was not sworn in by a justice, presumably because that would have leant a prominence to courts and the law that was inimical to New Order thinking. In this light, the entire imagery, instead of implying judicial prominence, demeaned the judges and confirmed the role of the judiciary under the Suharto regime as little more than that of servants of the executive, maintaining and affirming the political status quo.

To be sure, the judges fit that role snugly. The emphasis on appearance above substance matched the role that the judiciary had been shaped to play since the collapse of Parliamentary Democracy. That collapse triggered forty years of political marginalization and battering, marked by a radical decline in status, restrictions on jurisdiction, debilitating funding constraints, and more. In the background lumbered a manipulative and unscrupulous state, unprepared to give any power or respect to the judges or legal institutions generally. These conditions had a debilitating effect on the judicial profession, which over time, by and large, lost an understanding of its professional trade and its place and role in the state. The collapse of educational standards and the abandonment of performance assessment and its replacement with arbitrary decision making—not least in the process of professional placement and promotion—all conspired to create judges who were, by natural disposition and professional outlook, comfortable in a subordinate role. The career process, from recruitment through (notably) advancement, ensured that senior judges particularly served the executive, not so much in response to explicit instruction, but by conditioning and personal disposition, increasingly so with the passage of time. That the government didn't lose a single major case before the Supreme Court in the forty years of Guided Democracy and New Order is testimony enough.

This level of snug judicial comfort, reinforced by the judiciary's generally obedient disposition, after years of evolution would soon be put to the test. *Reformasi* was not only about changing presidents or rotating various other officials, but about the failure of state institutions. *Reformasi*, in its initial years at least, was very much a matter of social engagement, which banged on the doors of institutions, sometimes quite literally. It challenged the political and institutional status quo with which the judiciary was most familiar. Despite the evident fluidity of the substance of Reformasi, it undeniably sloshed and swirled around some core concepts of justice, a wide gamut that included strengthening democratic process; combating state abuse, fraud, and corruption; protecting human rights; reinforcing local authority; and more. *Reformasi* meant to replace the executive-heavy, centralized state with something more just. Whatever that was, courts clearly ought to stand at its core, both as symbols of justice and as counterweights to the executive. And so, to its intense discomfort and much against its basic instincts, the Supreme Court suddenly found itself pulled from the easy, essentially decorous and irrelevant political periphery to the center of the maelstrom of political and institutional change.

It was, inevitably, wholly unprepared. What is most astounding is not the inevitability of that unpreparedness, but the full extent of it, which surprised even experienced Indonesia observers. The Supreme Court after all stood to benefit most from political change and should have grasped at the plentiful opportunities that suddenly appeared. Instead, it turned out to be a striking laggard in the reform process. All court reforms undertaken in the turbulent early *Reformasi* period of 1998-2000 were initiated and pushed by Parliament or the Government, often in the face of Supreme Court opposition and obstruction. *Reformasi* plainly exposed the weaknesses of legal institutions, which in previous decades had been obscured by evidence of political stability and economic growth. We are, in reality, only beginning to appreciate the full impact of more than four decades of patrimonial government on the courts and legal institutions generally. That impact—why the Court could not recognize a golden opportunity in *Reformasi*—has been the central concern of this book.

The dramatic failure of the Supreme Court leadership in the critical first years of *Reformasi* made the decline of the institution graphically apparent. Over previous decades, the government had ensured court compliance by strengthening hierarchy along military lines and securing the loyalty of the chief justice. This was done by putting in place either an assertive outsider with a track record of loyalty to the government (with chief justice Ali Said as a role model), or a weak and pliable professional (exemplified by Guided Democracy's chief justice Wirjono Prodjodikoro or by Soerjono). Sarwata combined the worst of both categories. Being neither competent nor assertive, his vacuity in so many ways embodied the condition of the agency that he headed.

All this became painfully obvious when initiatives were called for. Supreme Court insiders recall of that critical period, 1998-2000, that "nothing happened, nothing at all." Part of this institutional inaction was caused by chief justice Sarwata, who was singularly inept. But the problems ran much deeper. The weakness was pervasive in the top echelons of the Supreme Court. Even in 2000, with *Reformasi* in full swing and the media boiling over to an unprecedented degree in its reports of court problems, hardly any of the senior judges would admit to such problems or make a beginning, however modest, to analyze them, even in private discussions. The Judges' Association, IKAHI (Ikatan Hakim Indonesia), which had been at the vanguard of institutional reform in the 1950s and 1960s, by the 1990s had been co-opted by the judicial elite. It was chaired by senior judges and had developed into a reactionary and self-serving organization from which nothing emerged at all by way of reform initiatives. Well into *Reformasi*, as the country simmered with ideas about institutional change and newfound freedoms, there was nothing to show that the Supreme Court was even thinking about the condition of the judiciary or about reform.

This baffling lethargy was, to a considerable extent, endogenous to the servant mentality that the New Order had instilled in the Supreme Court, and on which almost four generations of professional judges had been weaned. But it ran deeper than that. It was not just a mentality at issue, but also capabilities, faculties, and facilities. The consistent political marginalization was reflected in reduced status, reduced budget and pay, reduced power, declining educational standards, skewed recruitment policies, and the collapse of internal management and performance monitoring, all of which contributed to a dramatic weakening of professional standards. *Reformasi* exposed a judiciary hobbled by political oppression, but also by the reduced and now mostly very limited capacities of the judges, along with the clipped support available to them. Their problems were manifold, as they still are, rooted not only in government treatment of the institution, but also in how government helped shape judicial outlook and limited their ability to think differently. The reality is that the 1998 career judiciary would not have been able to come up with a good reform plan even if it wanted to; and if such a plan had miraculously emerged, it could not have been implemented for lack of institutional and budgetary support. The New Order robbed courts of their place and role, and it also ensured that the judges lost their memory and, in a manner of speaking, their minds.

Hence, during the early years of *Reformasi*, the institutional culture of the Supreme Court was characterized by extreme defensiveness. Publicly, the judiciary took the position that whatever ills their institution had suffered (and most judges were loath to admit even those) could all be blamed on external conditions. If only the world would leave the judiciary to do its work, then things would turn out fine; such was the essence of judicial thinking. It was a position that nicely absolved the judiciary from any responsibility or from doing anything at all. In fact, privately, inside the judiciary, the truth was the judges could not agree on anything, even on whether there were problems, let alone on how they might be resolved. Institutional defensiveness was not actually based on protecting some core institutional values, whose very existence or meaning few judges could recall. Instead it was based on hiding professional incapacity. The calls to restore judicial independence or the like sounded increasingly hollow, and in the end served to conceal the fact that the judges really did not know what it all meant.

What survived was ordinary self-servingness. Judges blindly clung to their old agenda, which sought status, independence, and power, not because of some deep understanding that this approach best served the public good, but for reasons that were fundamentally self-interested and, to a large extent, corrupt. Thus, the one-roof system was finally achieved under *Reformasi*, though typically prompted by Parliament rather than the Supreme Court itself. But while in the 1960s the public had perceived a similar reform to reflect a justified concern about judicial independence, to many in 1998 this action seemed to be little more than an ordinary money grab by the courts. The fact that judges called for a constitutionally secured, fixed percentage of the budget to be relegated to the judiciary (which would have effectively absolved the judiciary from submitting reasoned budgets and further reduced budget accountability) did little to improve this impression. The proposal was rejected.

The reactionary attitude of the Supreme Court lasted for almost four years after Suharto's fall. Short of dismissing the entire Supreme Court (which was an option discussed at some point), potential remedies seemed hopeless. All the deep-seated conservatism and ineptitude of the court could only be expected to improve as the current generation of judges was replaced by a new generation that understood the problems and might put in place structural changes.

The first opportunity for change came in 2000, with the recruitment of a relatively large number of new Supreme Court justices. This was the first recruitment of Supreme Court justices under *Reformasi*, and it turned out to be an unprecedented affair that was to have a major impact on the court for a few reasons. First, Supreme Court vacancies had gone unfilled over the extended crisis period, and an extraordinary number of twenty vacancies were on offer now—close to half the full complement. Also, this was the first time Supreme Court recruitment would not be conducted as a largely back-room government affair, rubber-stamped by a demure Parliament; this time a newly elected and more assertive Parliament took the driver's seat, thus initiating a public and appropriate test of the candidates.

The result was noteworthy. A large number of the candidates from the career judiciary, many of whom would have been shoo-in's under the old regime, were rejected; and a large complement of outside recruits who would not have stood a chance two years before did make the cut. It was the first time that private sector recruits had made it to the bench in such numbers, with a broad range of senior academicians, prominent human rights activists, and notaries public being represented. A good number of them had secured their position on the basis of an established track record of courage and integrity. Never before was there a justice on the Supreme Court who at one point in his career had had the police stick a gun to his head; never before had a justice scored so high on probity and integrity; never before had so many justices been recruited to the Court who knew how the legal system worked at ground level; never had minorities or societal marginals stood a chance. The Parliamentary "fit and proper" process has been criticized and may not have been perfect in a number of ways, but we should not ignore the historical role it played in breaking the governmental and judicial grip on Supreme Court recruitment and creating the opportunity for a new Court to emerge.

That new Supreme Court after 2000 was a complex entity. Major tensions emerged between the outside recruits, many of whom disliked much if not all they found upon taking office, and an old guard of largely career judges who were loath to change and disliked having people they regarded as upstarts challenge institutional conventions. And in between there was a floating mass of undecideds, fence-sitters, the simply confused, or those who agreed with each side on different issues. These institutional tensions are not an easy thing to overcome, and they still have to play out in full. But by and large they created a court that is more open-minded, more capable, and in places more honest and courageous than it has ever been since 1972.

Of critical importance was the appointment of an outside recruit, professor Bagir Manan, as the new chief justice in 2002. His appointment turned the Supreme Court into a reform agency, indeed perhaps the leading agency of reform in the legal sector. Under Bagir Manan's direction, the Supreme Court accepted and engaged in an incisive reform plan, cast in five "Blueprints," which were remarkable in several ways. This was the first time that the Supreme Court began to think about comprehensive reform and put together major policy papers on all issues regarded as critical. Moreover, these documents were conceived with extensive outside participation, most notably from the NGO community. The contrast with the situation under the career judiciary in previous years is striking, and it emphasizes how ineffective, inward looking, and weak the career judiciary had become by 1998.

By the time these reforms got underway, however, the political spring of *Reformasi* was petering out, and the Supreme Court leadership faced an uphill battle to carry out its plans. If the "Blueprints" charted the course, now the institution had to travel that course, and the implementation process from the onset posed challenges that only increased with time. This not only involved confronting vested interests within the judiciary itself, reaching down to the district courts and encompassing the management structures, but also securing the necessary support from other state institutions. Some felt that history had repeated itself, and that much like the situations in 1945, 1956-57, 1965, and again in 1972, the Supreme Court, through its own ineptitude, had once again missed its chance to make fundamental changes in constitutional and political structure. That in the early *Reformasi* period the Court was inept and missed out on great opportunities there can be no doubt, but the situation after 2002 is too unsettled for any definite conclusions yet to be reached. For the Supreme Court, the legacy of *Reformasi* and Bagir Manan will be judged by the success or failure of the "Blueprint" implementation.

It is tempting to describe the history of the Indonesian Supreme Court as one in which courage turned to cowardice, capability to incompetence, integrity to structural corruption, and respect to contempt. Perhaps history can sometimes be captured in such simple opposites, and the image is compelling for many reasons. Indeed, for all its simplicity, such a portrayal may not be far from reality, if we are to trust historical sources and testimonies. It serves to remind the vast majority of us who did not live through the 1950s that there was a time in Indonesia when the courts worked well. It also raises awareness that the current destitute condition of the court (or the legal system) is not a given, but that institutional courage, professional skills, and integrity were lost and destroyed by a deliberate process. The Court did not wither of its own accord, but contempt was generated, integrity was eroded, incompetence was bred, and cowardice was rewarded. It is through identifying, describing, and analyzing the causes of decline that the strategy for recovery can be defined.

By 2004, with an economy that is picking back up, political stability improving, the military restored to most of its former privileges, and the old political elite firmly in place once again, one may be forgiven for thinking that the genie of judicial reform might be put back in its bottle. This is indeed a possibility, notably in a state that, judging by its history, is accustomed to and does not shirk from unconstitutional action or the use of unlawful force. At the same time, conditions have changed significantly over the past decade, and an argument may be made that the price for ramming the courts back into the bottle would be high and could not be sustained. Three elements deserve consideration, if we wish to make predictions about the likely future of the Court and judicial reform.

First: security. As people turn away from the courts in increasing numbers, they need other ways by which to resolve their disputes. If these are not available or are inadequate, then disputes are resolved through violence. The less effective courts are in defusing disputes, the greater the incidence of low-level societal violence. Courts are a way through which the state can defuse disputes and control force; courts help control violence levels in society and make society more secure. Logically therefore, there is a correspondence between the rise of structural low-level violence in this country and court ineffectiveness. Bad courts promote societal violence. Courts are a security issue.

Second: economics. Economists routinely point to legal certainty and reliable and predictable judiciaries as factors that help instill and support investor confidence, which is necessary for sustainable growth, improved employment, and poverty reduction. In the global economy, Indonesia must compete with other transitional economies to attract investments, and the security of property rights is one of the most important reasons for investing in this country. Good courts are therefore necessary to fill rice bowls and enhance employment. Also, recent studies have shown that court ineffectiveness leads to an increase in late payments and defaults. It's not rocket science: the absence of effective sanctions reduces the incentives to perform on a contract. It is not just that bad courts stand in the way of growth; they actually foster economic decline. Bad courts are an economic issue because they directly contribute to poverty and unemployment.

Third: legitimacy. Effective and independent courts are critical to secure government effectiveness and state legitimacy. If society turns away from courts, this doesn't just tell you something about its perception of the judiciary. Distrust of the judiciary affects attitudes to government broadly. If courts are not viewed as reliable, independent arbiters of disputes—not least disputes involving the government itself as a party—then the authority and legitimacy of that government is undermined. That government will be viewed less as the legitimate caretaker of the common good and increasingly as just a caretaker of its own particular interests. Its policies will be seen as fundamentally lacking in legitimacy, which is the key to effective implementation of policies and the survival of the government, and ultimately of the state itself. The government needs effective courts in order to be legitimate and effective, and in the end it needs them to survive. And that, after all, was what *Reformasi* was all about.

To return to the 1998 photograph of Mr. Suharto's resignation, these dimensions should therefore be added. What weakened and undermined the credibility and effectiveness of the New Order administration in the end was the Supreme Court's subservient role. The justices in the photograph were meant to symbolize legitimacy, but instead illustrated marginality and subservience. Consequently, the photograph not only portrays regime failure, but it captures one of its root causes.

Abbreviations and Acronyms

ABRI	(Angkatan Bersenjata Republik Indonesia), Indonesian Armed Forces
ASKOR	(Assisten Koordinator), Coordinating Supreme Court clerk
BAPPENAS	(Badan Perencanaan Nasional), State Planning Board
DPR	(Dewan Perwakilan Rakyat), Parliament
GESTAPU	(Gerakan September Tiga Puluh), Purported coup d'état in 1965
HAWASDA	(Hakim Pengawas Daerah), Supreme Court judges supervising Appeal Courts
IKAHI	(Ikatan Hakim Indonesia), Judges' Association
Kadarkum	(Keluarga Sadar Hukum), social legal awareness program
KAMI	(Kelompok Aksi Mahasiswa Indonesia), High School Students' Activist Group (1960s)
Kanwil	(Kantor Wilayah), Departmental District Offices
KASI	(Kelompok Aksi Sardjana Indonesia), University Students' Activist Group (1960s)
KORPRI	(Korporasi Pegawai Republik Indonesia), Civil Servants Corporation
MA	(Mahkamah Agung), Supreme Court
Mah-Dep forum	Consultative forum on lower court administration between the Supreme Court and the Department of Justice
MAHKEJAPOL	(Mahkamah Agung, Departmen Kehakiman, Kejaksaan Agung, Polisi), Consultative forum of law-enforcing offices
Mahmillub	(Mahkamah Militer Luar Biasa), Extra-ordinary military tribunals
MALARI	(Malapetaka), 1974 rioting on the occasion of Japanese Prime Minister Tanaka's visit to Indonesia
MPPH	(Majelis Pertimbangan Penelitian Hakim), Judicial Council
MPR	(Majelis Pemusyawaratan Rakyat), People's Assembly
OPSKIS	(Operasi Kikis), Operation to clean up of backlogs under Mudjono administration (1981-1983)
OPSTIB	(Operasi Tertib), anti-corruption operation during the early 1980s
OPSUS	(Operasi Khusus), Special Operations (intelligence)
PKI	(Partai Komunis Indonesia), Indonesian Communist Party
PNI	(Partai Nasional Indonesia), Indonesian Nationalist Party
PP	(Peraturan Pemerintah), Government Regulation
RAPIM	(Rapat Pimpinan), Supreme Court leadership meeting

APPENDIX ONE

SCHEMATIC HISTORICAL OVERVIEW

(President Sukarno 1945-1968)   **NEW ORDER**

                                        (President Suharto 1968-present)

	1950	1959	1965	1985	present

Political periodization

	Parliamentary Democracy (1950-1957)	Guided Democracy (1959-1965)	New Order government (1965-present)		

Constitutions

1949: Fed. Const.	1950: Provisional Const.	1959: 1945 Constitution reintroduced			

law nr.1/1950		law nr.19/1964	law nr.14/1970	law nr.14/1985	

| W. Prodjodikoro (1952-66) [judge] | | Soerjadi (1966-68) [judge] | Seno Adji (1974-81) [govt.] | Ali Said (1983-92) [General] | Soerjono (1994-) [judge] |
| | | | Subekti (1968-74) [judge] | Mudjono (1981-83) [General] | Purwoto (1992-94) [judge] |

Appendix Two

Court Dockets in Indonesia, 1969-1993[*]

	MA Total Docket	MA % Settled	PT[*] Total Docket	PT % Settled	PN[*] Total Docket	PN % Settled
1969	2,026.	63.00	16,434.	11.00	95,470.	64.00
1970	1,024.	66.00	10,575.	22.00	124,944.	70.00
1971	2,433.	57.00	12,122.	26.00	162,323.	74.00
1972	2,677.	63.00	12,075.	30.00	202,537.	61.00
1973	2,914.	50.00	12,368.	42.00		
1974	2,914.	60.00	15,574.	95.80	314,884.	97.00
1975	3,541.	21.00	6,115.	98.30	385,736.	96.90
1976	4,976.	20.50	9,197.	72.50	319,611.	97.50
1977	6,174.	24.60	7,023.	89.30	319,645.	97.50
1978	7,447.	22.90	9,105.	90.00	324,645.	98.00
1979	8,030.	16.75	9,176.	76.42	320,995.	97.26
1980	10,425.	28.75	9,228.	92.64	322,429.	97.10
1981	11,729.	20.50	9,818.	76.88	299,979.	98.27
1982	14,559.	46.17	9,225.	82.03	557,144.	93.05
1983	12,956.	35.44	6,941.	69.27	660.110.	97.04
1984	14,746.	52.41	7,297.	71.04	766,880.	97.50
1985	14,307.	47.26	10,617.	71.01	1,482,624.	97.92
1986	14,599.	38.57	10,315.	75.55	1,931,338.	99.15
1987	17,121.	34.96	13,002.	76.51	1,998,399.	99.42
1988	18,720.	32.98	11,092.	79.80	1,570,983.	99.88
1989	22,952.	28.79	11,360.	80.29	1,705,917.	96.64
1990	22,305.	24.93	10,341.	78.88	1,245,365.	95.46
1991	24,381.	23.80	11,350.	83.00	1,545,467.	96.70
1992	26,325.	22.20	8,477.	82.50	1,690,990.	99.00
1993	27,950.	31.00	8,104.	67.80	1,393,277.	98.80

[*] MA, Mahkamah Agung, Supreme Court; PT, Pengadilan Tinggi, Appellate Court; PN, Pengadilan Negeri, First Instance Court.

APPENDIX THREE

HIGH-PROFILE CASES IN THE 1990s

Kedungombo case (1992)

Judges	Issue
Purwoto Gandasubrata Soerjono Sarwata Olden Bidara Samsudin Abubakar	Nationalization and compensation. Hydroelectric dam and individual rights. In an earlier decision the Supreme Court upheld the claim of the farmers and granted them compensation in excess of their claims. In the review case under Gandasubrata, the claim was denied on grounds that the court cannot award more than is claimed.

Prioritas case (1993)

Judges	Issue
Purwoto Gandasubrata	Judicial Review. Freedom of the Press. Journal closed by the government; owner challenges legal basis of government action. Supreme Court denies claim on grounds that there are no rules of procedure.

Ohee case (1995)

Judges	Issue
Soerjono	Chairman Soerjono stops enforcement of a court decision with a simple letter. While Supreme Court in its decision upholds validity damages to Papua tribe for unlawful occupation land by the state, the letter nullifies enforcement.

Gandhi Memorial School case (1996)

Judges	Issue
Soerjono Adi Andoyo Soetjipto	Suspicion of corruption; attempt to reopen case frustrated by the Supreme Court; Soerjono seeks dismissal of Supreme Court Junior Chairman Adi Andoyo Soetjipto who issued letter stating that there were indications of corruption.

Tempo case (1996)

Judges	Issue
Soerjono Sarwata Ketut Suraputra	Freedom of the Press. Closure of well-known journal is upheld by the Supreme Court. Decisions of the lower courts overturned.

Pakpahan case (1996)

Judges	Issue
Soerjono Sarwata Palty Radja Siregar	Well-known labor activist condemned to prison. In prior Supreme Court procedure the activist was freed from all charges, but the government re-filed the case in apparent violation of criminal procedure.

Megawati PDI case (1997)

Judges	Issue
Soeharto Sudario I Gusti Bagus Mahardika	Political interference in the political process, political freedom. Claim by Megawati challenging the legitimacy of her ouster rejected by the Supreme Court.

Appendix Four

Photographs

The first Supreme Court Chairman Kusumah Atmadja (1945–1951) taking the oath of office, administered by Sukarno and the president of the Indonesian Federated States in the palace of the Yogyakarta Sultanate, December 17, 1949. (reprinted with permission, personal collection)

A rare informal picture of Chairman Kusumah Atmadja (second from right) at marriage of his daughter, November 11, 1950. (reprinted with permission, personal collection)

Chairman Wirjono Prodjodikoro (1951–1966) appointed as Supreme Court Chairman by President Sukarno, October 24, 1951. Compare the sober judicial gowns with the military-style uniform of the 1960s and brighter attire of the 1990s.
(reprinted with permission, personal collection)

A more informal picture of the same occasion, with President Sukarno congratulating Satochid Kartanegara upon his appointment as Vice Chief Justice.
(reprinted with permission, personal collection)

A low point. July 10, 1959. Supreme Court Chairman Wirjono Prodjodikoro justifies the dissolution of the Constituent Assembly by presidential order and the return to the 1945 Constitution without parliamentary backing. (reprinted with permission, personal collection)

Supreme Court Chairman Soerjadi (1966–1968) installed by President Sukarno on June 21, 1966. Note how unifoms have replaced judicial robes, part of the process of identifying judges as allies of the revolution. (reprinted with permission, personal collection)

Installation of Soerjadi (1966–1968) as Supreme Court Chairman by President Sukarno, June 21, 1966. This was one of President Sukarno's last official acts.
(reprinted with permission, personal collection)

Supreme Court Chairman Subekti not long before his retirement.
(reprinted with permission, *TEMPO*/Syahrir Wahab)

Subekti attending graduation ceremony at Universitas Indonesia. After retiring, he chaired the Indonesian National Arbitration Board. (reprinted with permission, *TEMPO*/Herry Komar)

Supreme Court Chairman Mudjono (1980–1982), the first Chairman with a military background. He was hard working, disciplined, and honest, yet had a limited understanding of judicial independence. (reprinted with permission, *TEMPO*/Karni Ilyas, 1981)

488 *The Indonesian Supreme Court*

Supreme Court Chairman Ali Said (1982–1992). A military man, he opposed the judiciary's drive to greater independence. (reprinted with permission, *TEMPO*/Donny Metri, 1991)

Ali Said made his name as an aggressive judge in the anti-communist military tribunals (*Mahmillub*), 1966–1968. (reprinted with permission, personal collection)

Supreme Court Chairman Purwoto S. Gandasubrata (1992–1994). Dignified and perceptive, he was the first career judge to regain the chairmanship in two decades.
(reprinted with permission, *TEMPO*/Robin Ong, 1992)

Supreme Court Chairman Soerjono (1994–1996), a comprehensive disappointment both as a judge and a manager. (reprinted with permission, *DR*/Rully Kesuma)

Soerjono (Chairman), Sarwata, and Ketut Suraputra reading the decision in *The TEMPO Case*, by which the Supreme Court upheld a government order closing the Indonesian weekly. (reprinted with permission, *Forum Keadilan*/Gatot Sriwidodo)

Supreme Court Chairman Sarwata (middle; 1996–2001) sharing tea with President Suharto. Deputy Chief Justice Ketut Suraputra stands to his right. A former military man, Sarwata was the first Chairman to be publicly accused in the media and Parliament of corruption. (reprinted with permission, *DR*/Rully Kesuma)

Subject and Name Index

Note: This index includes only references to the text and does not list citations in footnotes.

SUBJECT INDEX

1945 Constitution, 12, 14, 38, 52, 71, 75, 175, 180, 182-84, 201, 214
Adat, 29, 210, 213, 229-31, 432, 442, 462-63
Appeal on verdict freeing suspect, 238, 242-44
Arbitration, 247, 253-55
Balance-of-powers doctrine, 13-14, 33
BAPPENAS, 427
Cassation, 207-9, 211-237, 250
Colonial Indonesian courts, 29-33, 209
Colonial Supreme Court, 33, 209-10
Department of Justice, 53, 60, 64, 70-73, 87, 106
Directorate General for Court Upgrading, 106-7, 113, 116-18, 124
Enforcement pending appeal, 237-40
Exorbitante rechten, 23-24
Expedited enforcement (*grosse akte*), 238, 240-42
Governor General, 17, 21, 23, 31
Guided Democracy, 36, 50, 52-53, 57, 59, 61-64
Hakim masuk desa, 201-02
HAWASDA (supervising judges), 299, 330-31
IKAHI (Judges' Association), 36, 47, 49-51, 62-70, 74-76, 79-87, 94-95, 104-8, 112, 123, 130-31; Tretes meeting (1961), 59; Tugu meeting (1964), 63-66; Semarang meeting (1968), 86-87; Medan meeting (1971), 112-15
Indigenous courts, 28, 30, 33
Judges' strike, 49-50, 67-68
Judicial recruitment, 12, 24-27, 33, 343-71, 377, 388
Judicial independence, 49, 56, 60-62, 101-2
Judicial organization, 175; Japanese influence on, 176-78; position of Mahkamah Agung in, 181-86; role of lower courts in, 186-97; unification of court structure, 175-181
Judicial review, 88-91, 107, 110, 132-33, 136-37, 144, 146-48, 172, 247
Judicial status, 36, 43-44, 51, 60, 88, 101, 128-29; and salaries, 45-50, 61, 101-2, 110, 114, 148-49; and integration into the civil service, 128-29
Judicial supervision, 255-58; and the black book, 271; via circular letters, 255-56, 259-70, 274; via *conduite*, 272-72; via *eksaminasi*, 119, 272
Kadarkum, 202
Landraad, 28-33, 209-11
Law no.14/1970 on the Judiciary, 107-10
MALARI riots, 354-55
National Law Seminar (1968), 79, 101-5
Nederburgh Report, 18-22, 31
OPSUS, 79, 92-97, 105
Parliament, 51-52, 73-74, 117
Parliamentary Democracy, 35, 43, 50
Prosecutors (*jaksas*), 46-50
Raad van Justitie, 29, 31, 209-11
RAPIM, 136, 296, 321-24
Separation-of-powers doctrine, 13-18, 21-23, 31, 33
Soerjadi testament, 88
Special review, 150, 159, 164-65, 208, 244-46, 284
Supreme Court administration, 277-81; and 1992 Internal Audit, 278-80; and backlogs, 257, 260-61, 278, 282-85, 294-95, 299-303; and the budget, 307, 317-19, 342; and clerks, 307-9, 315, 334-36; and corruption, 332-37; and falsified decisions, 278, 337-41; and Mah-Dep forum, 320, 356; and OPSKIS, 278, 294-95, 299-301; and pleno, 281, 287, 292, 297-98; and teams & chambers, 286, 295-99, 313-17
Supreme Court appointments, 350-71
Supreme Court case reporting, 436, 453-56; and access to cases, 435-41; journals used for, 442, 448-453; and selection of cases, 441-448
Supreme Court cases;
 Adnan Kopli case (1995), 246; Cosmas case (1962), 61-62; Dharsono case (1986), 139-40; Gandhi Memorial School case (1996), 160-63, 312, 333-34; Goritman Smuggling case (1989), 338-39; Haris Murtopo case (1977), 126-27; Jasin case (1980), 122, 127-28; Kandaga Shopping Centre case (1986), 241; Kedung Ombo I & II cases (1992/1994),

149-53, 155-56, 170, 341; Kipas case (incident) (1993), 203; Lingah-Pacah-Sumir case (1994), 246; Maumere nationalization case (1990), 140-41; Megawati PDI case (1997), 155, 169-70; Monitor case (1990), 139; Navigation Maritime Bulgare case (1984), 247, 254; Nichimen case (1986), 242; Nike I & II cases (1985/1986), 459-62; Nuku Suleiman case (1994), 203; Ohee case (1995), 156, 158-60, 163, 168, 248; Pakpahan case (1996), 164-65; Pedicab case (1990), 137-39, 145; Prioritas case (1993), 144-46, 254; Saputra case (1985), 329-30; Schmidt case (1959), 54-55; Sengkon-Karta case (1980), 245-46; Sudarsono case (1948), 41; Sugar Lee case (1991), 327; Sutomo case (1984), 243; Tancho case (1972), 458-62; Tempo case (1996), 155, 165-66; Unlawful dismissals case (1993), 146-47; Yap case (1970), 126; Yatim case (1995), 329-30

Supreme Court judges, 344ff.; anonymity of, 344-45, 377-79; and the civil service, 45, 128-31; corruption of, 371, 376, 400-401, 411-417; numbers of, 278, 280-82, 286, 289, 295-96, 341; professional background of, 380-87, 421; salaries of, 45-50, 61, 101-2, 373-74; social background of, 370, 389-93; terms of office, 372

Supreme Court regulatory authority, 251-55

Yogyakarta compromise, 79, 106-8

NAME INDEX

Abdurrahman (MA judge)   83, 356, 392, 410, 449
Adil, Sutan M. (MA judge)   375-76, 394, 400
Ali, Chidir   439-40, 455-56
Arifin, Busthanul   85-86, 93, 95, 98-99, 108, 114, 125, 313, 327, 352, 354, 384, 392-93, 397
Arifin, Kabul (MA Junior Chairman)   382, 393
Astrawinata (Minister of Justice)   59, 305
Bagir, Manan   v-vii, 475
Baud (Minister of the Colonies)   31
Benda-Beckmann, C. E.   202
Bidara, Olden (MA Junior Chairman)   314, 369, 392-93, 395-96
Bintoro, Budiman   390
Boestomi, Tomy (MA judge)   314, 321, 387
Cappelletti, Mauro   25, 346
Costa, V. B. da (member of Parliament)   249, 330
Daendels, H. (Governor-General)   21, 31
Djaelani, M. (MA Vice-Chairman)   158, 382-83
Djaksa, G. (MA judge)   396
Djohansjah (MA judge)   314, 395
Eisenhower, Dwight   44
Gandasubrata, Purwoto S. (MA Chairman)   70, 86, 98-99, 132, 141-158, 172, 221, 239, 249, 254, 261, 272, 293, 302, 309, 311-12, 314, 319, 321, 324, 326, 335, 371, 380, 382-83, 385, 387, 389-93, 397, 399, 403, 414, 451
Gani, A. (politician)   44
Gatot   390
Gautama   457-58
Geldof, B.   459
Gondokoesoemo, Djody (Minister of Justice)   49, 57, 71
Gunawan   387
Gunawan, Heru   414
Haar, B. Ter   432
Habibie   371
Hadipurnomo (Director General Court Upgrading)   107, 115, 117-18, 172, 195
Hakim, Sutan A. (MA judge)   83, 86
Hapsoro (lower court judge)   86, 98-99, 390
Harahap, Y. (MA judge)   393
Hasibuan, Albert (member of Parliament)   162, 283, 362-64
Iman, M. (MA judge)   304, 391
Indroharto (MA Junior Chairman)   314
Jasin, M. (General)   122, 127-128
Juanda (Prime Minister)   55
Karlinah (MA judge)   300, 314, 387
Kartanegara, S. (MA judge)   391
Ko, Tjay Sing (Semerang advocate)   352
Kusuma, Wirjono (MA judge)   391, 410-11
Kusumah Atmadja, R. Z. (MA Chairman)   37-38, 41-44, 81, 305, 356-57, 375-76, 380, 394-95, 400, 403

Kusumah Atmadja, Asikin (MA Junior Chairman)   65-66, 81, 84-86, 90-91, 93-99, 101-03, 105, 108, 125, 130, 144, 150, 153, 188, 193, 249, 265, 352, 354, 357, 384, 387, 392-93, 395, 414,
Kusumaatmadja, Mochtar (Minister of Justice)   120-21, 127, 160, 189, 195-97, 199-201
Lev, Daniel S.   3-5, 7, 30, 41, 49, 57, 104, 187, 230, 398, 463
Lie Oen Hok (lower court judge)   55
Lubis, T. Mulya   364
Lumbanradja (MA judge)   85, 91, 359
Mahadi (lower court judge)   68
Mahendra, Oka (MP)   294
Mangkudilaga, Benyamin   166
Martina (MA judge)   387
Martowirono, Suwardi   382
Masrani   314
Mertokusumo, Besar (Secretary General Dept. of Justice)   42, 82, 352
Moeliono, Ciel Suparni (lower court judge, IKAHI secretary)   85, 93, 95
Moerdiono (State Secretary)   142
Moersiyah (MA judge)   387
Mudjono (minister of justice; MA Chairman)   122, 124, 127-28, 142, 265, 278, 293-302, 307-8, 310, 320-21, 325, 355, 360, 369, 379-80, 382-83, 385-86, 389, 391, 396, 403, 406, 418-19
Muhaimin, M. (MA judge)   387
Murtopo, Ali (General)   92, 94-95, 113-14, 126
Nainggolan, Bob   129
Nasution, A. Buyung   95, 99
Nasution, A. H. (General)   42, 54, 357
Nasution, Az. (lower court judge)   392
Nederburgh, I.A. (colonial judge)   25
Njono   81
Noer, A.   392-93
Oesman, Oetoyo (Minister of Justice)   426, 428
Paloh, S.   138-139, 144
Pitoyo (MA judge)   304-6
Prodjodikoro, Wirjono (MA Chairman)   44, 51-52, 54-55, 57-58, 61-62, 68-69, 81-82, 123, 154, 158, 286-87, 305, 320, 356-57, 376, 380, 390, 402-3, 414, 462-63, 465, 467
Purbowati (MA judge)   108, 386, 473
Raffles, Sir Th. (Lt. Governor General)   22
Rahardjo, I. (MA judge)   391
Rahardjo, Satjipto   249, 365
Ranuatmadja (MA clerk)   305
Reagan, Ronald   459
Retnowulan Sutianto (MA judge)   386-87, 391, 395, 399
Rosma, Siti (MA judge)   387
Rum, Mohamad   413
Rusli (MA judge)   85
Sahardjo (Minister of Justice)   71, 184, 410
Said, Ali (MA Chairman)   70, 93, 111, 123-124, 130-31, 138-39, 141, 143-44, 146,

153, 166, 254, 265, 278-79, 297, 301-2, 312, 324, 327, 329, 333, 355, 360, 371, 380, 382-83, 385, 403, 412, 445
Saleh, Ismael (Minister of Justice) 123-4, 128, 133, 140, 142-43, 165, 350, 361, 366
Samsoedin (MA judge) 314
Santoso, Amir 73
Sartono (Parliament Speaker) 81
Sarwata (MA Chairman) 153, 158, 166-171 173, 380, 382-83, 403, 473
Sasongko, Dora (MA judge) 387, 395
Semadikoen (lower court judge) 55
Seno Adji (Minister of Justice and MA Chairman) 75, 85, 98-99, 103, 112, 114-117, 119-22, 125-27, 141, 153, 172, 184, 186, 195, 202, 272, 289-95, 298, 300, 305-6, 311, 354-55, 360, 375, 379-80, 382, 401-3, 411, 413-15
Shapiro, Martin 251
Siregar, Aslamiyah (MA judge) 393
Siregar, Bismar (MA judge) 359-60, 365, 375, 387, 393, 397
Siregar, Chaeruddin (MA judge) 393
Siregar, Palti Radja (MA judge) 393
Sjahrir, Sutan (Prime Minister) 41
Soedarmoko, Sujatmi 314
Soedjadi 396
Soegiri (MA judge) 392-3
Soegondo, S. (Director General Court Upgrading) 113, 391
Soekito, Sri Widoyati (MA judge) 61-62, 65, 81, 84-86, 89-91, 93, 95-99, 332, 352, 354, 357, 384, 387, 398-99
Soenarta, F. X. 396
Soeparto 449
Soeprapto (Prosecutor General) 55
Soerjadi (MA Chairman) 55-6, 59, 65, 69, 79, 81-8, 95, 103, 271, 287, 357-8, 376, 380
Soerjono (MA Chairman) 75, 152-53, 158-166, 168, 173, 473
Soetjipto, Adi Andoyo (MA Junior Chairman) 160-62, 164, 167, 312, 334, 337-38, 387, 391, 416-17
Subekti, R. (MA Chairman) 72, 81-83, 86, 91, 96, 98, 106-7, 112, 116, 125-27, 131, 134-35, 141, 154, 156, 172, 232, 244, 265-66, 270, 272, 287-91, 294, 304, 307, 354, 356-58, 365, 373, 380, 382, 384, 390, 399, 403, 414, 442, 450, 458, 467
Sudarman 390
Sudirman 390
Soejardono, Siti T. T. (MA judge) 398
Suharto (President RI) 66-67, 77, 81-82, 85, 92-93, 98, 100, 114, 120, 126-28, 149-41, 155, 157-58, 166, 170, 354, 357-58, 375, 383, 459-60, 471, 477
Sukana 390
Sukarno (President RI) 37, 41, 44, 52-53, 56-62, 64, 71, 77, 81-83, 85-86, 88, 91-92, 184, 188, 259, 265, 356-58
Suleiman, Nuku 203
Sunaryati Hartono, C. F. G. (Director General, Department of Justice) 162
Suparni Moeliono, Ciel (judge) *see* Moeliono, Ciel Suparni

Supomo (law scholar, politician) 14-16
Suraputra, I. Ketut (MA judge) 314, 321, 392-93, 396
Sutadi-Nasution, Marianne (MA judge) 392
Sutadi Djajakusuma 392, 427
Taufik (MA judge) 387
Tirtaamidjaja (MA judge) 89-90, 410
Waal, de (Minister of the Colonies) 32
Widoyati Soekito, S., *see* Soekito, Sri Widoyati
Wiriadinata, Lukman (Minister of Justice) 71
Yahya (MA judge) 314, 393
Yamin, M. (law scholar, politician) 14-15, 41
Yap Thiam Hien 126, 405

SOUTHEAST ASIA PROGRAM PUBLICATIONS
Cornell University

Studies on Southeast Asia

Number 39 *The Indonesian Supreme Court: A Study of Institutional Collapse,* Sebastiaan Pompe. 2005. 494 pp. ISBN 0-877277-38-9 (pb).

Number 38 *Spirited Politics: Religion and Public Life in Contemporary Southeast Asia,* ed. Andrew C. Willford and Kenneth M. George. 2005. 210 pp. ISBN 0-87727-737-0.

Number 37 *Sumatran Sultanate and Colonial State: Jambi and the Rise of Dutch Imperialism, 1830-1907,* Elsbeth Locher-Scholten, trans. Beverley Jackson. 2004. 332 pp. ISBN 0-87727-736-2.

Number 36 *Southeast Asia over Three Generations: Essays Presented to Benedict R. O'G. Anderson,* ed. James T. Siegel and Audrey R. Kahin. 2003. 398 pp. ISBN 0-87727-735-4.

Number 35 *Nationalism and Revolution in Indonesia,* George McTurnan Kahin, intro. Benedict R. O'G. Anderson (reprinted from 1952 edition, Cornell University Press, with permission). 2003. 530 pp. ISBN 0-87727-734-6.

Number 34 *Golddiggers, Farmers, and Traders in the "Chinese Districts" of West Kalimantan, Indonesia,* Mary Somers Heidhues. 2003. 316 pp. ISBN 0-87727-733-8.

Number 33 *Opusculum de Sectis apud Sinenses et Tunkinenses (A Small Treatise on the Sects among the Chinese and Tonkinese): A Study of Religion in China and North Vietnam in the Eighteenth Century,* Father Adriano de St. Thecla, trans. Olga Dror, with Mariya Berezovska. 2002. 363 pp. ISBN 0-87727-732-X.

Number 32 *Fear and Sanctuary: Burmese Refugees in Thailand,* Hazel J. Lang. 2002. 204 pp. ISBN 0-87727-731-1.

Number 31 *Modern Dreams: An Inquiry into Power, Cultural Production, and the Cityscape in Contemporary Urban Penang, Malaysia,* Beng-Lan Goh. 2002. 225 pp. ISBN 0-87727-730-3.

Number 30 *Violence and the State in Suharto's Indonesia,* ed. Benedict R. O'G. Anderson. 2001. Second printing, 2002. 247 pp. ISBN 0-87727-729-X.

Number 29 *Studies in Southeast Asian Art: Essays in Honor of Stanley J. O'Connor,* ed. Nora A. Taylor. 2000. 243 pp. Illustrations. ISBN 0-87727-728-1.

Number 28 *The Hadrami Awakening: Community and Identity in the Netherlands East Indies, 1900-1942,* Natalie Mobini-Kesheh. 1999. 174 pp. ISBN 0-87727-727-3.

Number 27 *Tales from Djakarta: Caricatures of Circumstances and their Human Beings,* Pramoedya Ananta Toer. 1999. 145 pp. ISBN 0-87727-726-5.

Number 26 *History, Culture, and Region in Southeast Asian Perspectives,* rev. ed., O. W. Wolters. 1999. Second printing, 2004. 275 pp. ISBN 0-87727-725-7.

Number 25 *Figures of Criminality in Indonesia, the Philippines, and Colonial Vietnam,* ed. Vicente L. Rafael. 1999. 259 pp. ISBN 0-87727-724-9.

Number 24 *Paths to Conflagration: Fifty Years of Diplomacy and Warfare in Laos, Thailand, and Vietnam, 1778-1828,* Mayoury Ngaosyvathn and Pheuiphanh Ngaosyvathn. 1998. 268 pp. ISBN 0-87727-723-0.

Number 23   *Nguyễn Cochinchina: Southern Vietnam in the Seventeenth and Eighteenth Centuries*, Li Tana. 1998. Second printing, 2002. 194 pp. ISBN 0-87727-722-2.

Number 22   *Young Heroes: The Indonesian Family in Politics*, Saya S. Shiraishi. 1997. 183 pp. ISBN 0-87727-721-4.

Number 21   *Interpreting Development: Capitalism, Democracy, and the Middle Class in Thailand*, John Girling. 1996. 95 pp. ISBN 0-87727-720-6.

Number 20   *Making Indonesia*, ed. Daniel S. Lev, Ruth McVey. 1996. 201 pp. ISBN 0-87727-719-2.

Number 19   *Essays into Vietnamese Pasts*, ed. K. W. Taylor, John K. Whitmore. 1995. 288 pp. ISBN 0-87727-718-4.

Number 18   *In the Land of Lady White Blood: Southern Thailand and the Meaning of History*, Lorraine M. Gesick. 1995. 106 pp. ISBN 0-87727-717-6.

Number 17   *The Vernacular Press and the Emergence of Modern Indonesian Consciousness*, Ahmat Adam. 1995. 220 pp. ISBN 0-87727-716-8.

Number 16   *The Nan Chronicle*, trans., ed. David K. Wyatt. 1994. 158 pp. ISBN 0-87727-715-X.

Number 15   *Selective Judicial Competence: The Cirebon-Priangan Legal Administration, 1680–1792*, Mason C. Hoadley. 1994. 185 pp. ISBN 0-87727-714-1.

Number 14   *Sjahrir: Politics and Exile in Indonesia*, Rudolf Mrázek. 1994. 536 pp. ISBN 0-87727-713-3.

Number 13   *Fair Land Sarawak: Some Recollections of an Expatriate Officer*, Alastair Morrison. 1993. 196 pp. ISBN 0-87727-712-5.

Number 12   *Fields from the Sea: Chinese Junk Trade with Siam during the Late Eighteenth and Early Nineteenth Centuries*, Jennifer Cushman. 1993. 206 pp. ISBN 0-87727-711-7.

Number 11   *Money, Markets, and Trade in Early Southeast Asia: The Development of Indigenous Monetary Systems to AD 1400*, Robert S. Wicks. 1992. 2nd printing 1996. 354 pp., 78 tables, illus., maps. ISBN 0-87727-710-9.

Number 10   *Tai Ahoms and the Stars: Three Ritual Texts to Ward Off Danger*, trans., ed. B. J. Terwiel, Ranoo Wichasin. 1992. 170 pp. ISBN 0-87727-709-5.

Number 9   *Southeast Asian Capitalists*, ed. Ruth McVey. 1992. 2nd printing 1993. 220 pp. ISBN 0-87727-708-7.

Number 8   *The Politics of Colonial Exploitation: Java, the Dutch, and the Cultivation System*, Cornelis Fasseur, ed. R. E. Elson, trans. R. E. Elson, Ary Kraal. 1992. 2nd printing 1994. 266 pp. ISBN 0-87727-707-9.

Number 7   *A Malay Frontier: Unity and Duality in a Sumatran Kingdom*, Jane Drakard. 1990. 2nd printing 2003. 215 pp. ISBN 0-87727-706-0.

Number 6   *Trends in Khmer Art*, Jean Boisselier, ed. Natasha Eilenberg, trans. Natasha Eilenberg, Melvin Elliott. 1989. 124 pp., 24 plates. ISBN 0-87727-705-2.

Number 5   *Southeast Asian Ephemeris: Solar and Planetary Positions, A.D. 638–2000*, J. C. Eade. 1989. 175 pp. ISBN 0-87727-704-4.

Number 3   *Thai Radical Discourse: The Real Face of Thai Feudalism Today*, Craig J. Reynolds. 1987. 2nd printing 1994. 186 pp. ISBN 0-87727-702-8.

Number 1	*The Symbolism of the Stupa*, Adrian Snodgrass. 1985. Revised with index, 1988. 3rd printing 1998. 469 pp. ISBN 0-87727-700-1.

SEAP Series

Number 21	*Securing a Place: Small-Scale Artisans in Modern Indonesia*, Elizabeth Morrell. 2005. 220 pp. ISBN 0-877271-39-9.
Number 20	*Southern Vietnam under the Reign of Minh Mạng (1820-1841): Central Policies and Local Response*, Choi Byung Wook. 2004. 226pp. ISBN 0-87727-138-0.
Number 19	*Gender, Household, State: Đổi Mới in Việt Nam*, ed. Jayne Werner and Danièle Bélanger. 2002. 151 pp. ISBN 0-87727-137-2.
Number 18	*Culture and Power in Traditional Siamese Government*, Neil A. Englehart. 2001. 130 pp. ISBN 0-87727-135-6.
Number 17	*Gangsters, Democracy, and the State*, ed. Carl A. Trocki. 1998. Second printing, 2002. 94 pp. ISBN 0-87727-134-8.
Number 16	*Cutting across the Lands: An Annotated Bibliography on Natural Resource Management and Community Development in Indonesia, the Philippines, and Malaysia*, ed. Eveline Ferretti. 1997. 329 pp. ISBN 0-87727-133-X.
Number 15	*The Revolution Falters: The Left in Philippine Politics after 1986*, ed. Patricio N. Abinales. 1996. Second printing, 2002. 182 pp. ISBN 0-87727-132-1.
Number 14	*Being Kammu: My Village, My Life*, Damrong Tayanin. 1994. 138 pp., 22 tables, illus., maps. ISBN 0-87727-130-5.
Number 13	*The American War in Vietnam*, ed. Jayne Werner, David Hunt. 1993. 132 pp. ISBN 0-87727-131-3.
Number 12	*The Voice of Young Burma*, Aye Kyaw. 1993. 92 pp. ISBN 0-87727-129-1.
Number 11	*The Political Legacy of Aung San*, ed. Josef Silverstein. Revised edition 1993. 169 pp. ISBN 0-87727-128-3.
Number 10	*Studies on Vietnamese Language and Literature: A Preliminary Bibliography*, Nguyen Dinh Tham. 1992. 227 pp. ISBN 0-87727-127-5.
Number 8	*From PKI to the Comintern, 1924–1941: The Apprenticeship of the Malayan Communist Party*, Cheah Boon Kheng. 1992. 147 pp. ISBN 0-87727-125-9.
Number 7	*Intellectual Property and US Relations with Indonesia, Malaysia, Singapore, and Thailand*, Elisabeth Uphoff. 1991. 67 pp. ISBN 0-87727-124-0.
Number 6	*The Rise and Fall of the Communist Party of Burma (CPB)*, Bertil Lintner. 1990. 124 pp. 26 illus., 14 maps. ISBN 0-87727-123-2.
Number 5	*Japanese Relations with Vietnam: 1951–1987*, Masaya Shiraishi. 1990. 174 pp. ISBN 0-87727-122-4.
Number 3	*Postwar Vietnam: Dilemmas in Socialist Development*, ed. Christine White, David Marr. 1988. 2nd printing 1993. 260 pp. ISBN 0-87727-120-8.
Number 2	*The Dobama Movement in Burma (1930–1938)*, Khin Yi. 1988. 160 pp. ISBN 0-87727-118-6.

Cornell Modern Indonesia Project Publications

Number 75 *A Tour of Duty: Changing Patterns of Military Politics in Indonesia in the 1990s.* Douglas Kammen and Siddharth Chandra. 1999. 99 pp. ISBN 0-87763-049-6.

Number 74 *The Roots of Acehnese Rebellion 1989–1992*, Tim Kell. 1995. 103 pp. ISBN 0-87763-040-2.

Number 73 *"White Book" on the 1992 General Election in Indonesia,* trans. Dwight King. 1994. 72 pp. ISBN 0-87763-039-9.

Number 72 *Popular Indonesian Literature of the Qur'an,* Howard M. Federspiel. 1994. 170 pp. ISBN 0-87763-038-0.

Number 71 *A Javanese Memoir of Sumatra, 1945–1946: Love and Hatred in the Liberation War,* Takao Fusayama. 1993. 150 pp. ISBN 0-87763-037-2.

Number 70 *East Kalimantan: The Decline of a Commercial Aristocracy,* Burhan Magenda. 1991. 120 pp. ISBN 0-87763-036-4.

Number 69 *The Road to Madiun: The Indonesian Communist Uprising of 1948,* Elizabeth Ann Swift. 1989. 120 pp. ISBN 0-87763-035-6.

Number 68 *Intellectuals and Nationalism in Indonesia: A Study of the Following Recruited by Sutan Sjahrir in Occupation Jakarta,* J. D. Legge. 1988. 159 pp. ISBN 0-87763-034-8.

Number 67 *Indonesia Free: A Biography of Mohammad Hatta,* Mavis Rose. 1987. 252 pp. ISBN 0-87763-033-X.

Number 66 *Prisoners at Kota Cane,* Leon Salim, trans. Audrey Kahin. 1986. 112 pp. ISBN 0-87763-032-1.

Number 65 *The Kenpeitai in Java and Sumatra,* trans. Barbara G. Shimer, Guy Hobbs, intro. Theodore Friend. 1986. 80 pp. ISBN 0-87763-031-3.

Number 64 *Suharto and His Generals: Indonesia's Military Politics, 1975–1983,* David Jenkins. 1984. 4th printing 1997. 300 pp. ISBN 0-87763-030-5.

Number 62 *Interpreting Indonesian Politics: Thirteen Contributions to the Debate, 1964–1981,* ed. Benedict Anderson, Audrey Kahin, intro. Daniel S. Lev. 1982. 3rd printing 1991. 172 pp. ISBN 0-87763-028-3.

Number 60 *The Minangkabau Response to Dutch Colonial Rule in the Nineteenth Century,* Elizabeth E. Graves. 1981. 157 pp. ISBN 0-87763-000-3.

Number 59 *Breaking the Chains of Oppression of the Indonesian People: Defense Statement at His Trial on Charges of Insulting the Head of State, Bandung, June 7–10, 1979,* Heri Akhmadi. 1981. 201 pp. ISBN 0-87763-001-1.

Number 57 *Permesta: Half a Rebellion,* Barbara S. Harvey. 1977. 174 pp. ISBN 0-87763-003-8.

Number 55 *Report from Banaran: The Story of the Experiences of a Soldier during the War of Independence,* Maj. Gen. T. B. Simatupang. 1972. 186 pp. ISBN 0-87763-005-4.

Number 52	*A Preliminary Analysis of the October 1 1965, Coup in Indonesia (Prepared in January 1966)*, Benedict R. Anderson, Ruth T. McVey, assist. Frederick P. Bunnell. 1971. 3rd printing 1990. 174 pp. ISBN 0-87763-008-9.
Number 51	*The Putera Reports: Problems in Indonesian-Japanese War-Time Cooperation*, Mohammad Hatta, trans., intro. William H. Frederick. 1971. 114 pp. ISBN 0-87763-009-7.
Number 50	*Schools and Politics: The Kaum Muda Movement in West Sumatra (1927–1933)*, Taufik Abdullah. 1971. 257 pp. ISBN 0-87763-010-0.
Number 49	*The Foundation of the Partai Muslimin Indonesia*, K. E. Ward. 1970. 75 pp. ISBN 0-87763-011-9.
Number 48	*Nationalism, Islam and Marxism*, Soekarno, intro. Ruth T. McVey. 1970. 2nd printing 1984. 62 pp. ISBN 0-87763-012-7.
Number 43	*State and Statecraft in Old Java: A Study of the Later Mataram Period, 16th to 19th Century*, Soemarsaid Moertono. Revised edition 1981. 180 pp. ISBN 0-87763-017-8.
Number 39	Preliminary Checklist of Indonesian Imprints (1945-1949), John M. Echols. 186 pp. ISBN 0-87763-025-9.
Number 37	*Mythology and the Tolerance of the Javanese*, Benedict R. O'G. Anderson. 2nd edition, 1996. Reprinted 2004. 104 pp., 65 illus. ISBN 0-87763-041-0.
Number 25	*The Communist Uprisings of 1926–1927 in Indonesia: Key Documents*, ed., intro. Harry J. Benda, Ruth T. McVey. 1960. 2nd printing 1969. 177 pp. ISBN 0-87763-024-0.
Number 7	*The Soviet View of the Indonesian Revolution*, Ruth T. McVey. 1957. 3rd printing 1969. 90 pp. ISBN 0-87763-018-6.
Number 6	*The Indonesian Elections of 1955*, Herbert Feith. 1957. 2nd printing 1971. 91 pp. ISBN 0-87763-020-8.

Translation Series

Volume 4	*Approaching Suharto's Indonesia from the Margins*, ed. Takashi Shiraishi. 1994. 153 pp. ISBN 0-87727-403-7.
Volume 3	*The Japanese in Colonial Southeast Asia*, ed. Saya Shiraishi, Takashi Shiraishi. 1993. 172 pp. ISBN 0-87727-402-9.
Volume 2	*Indochina in the 1940s and 1950s*, ed. Takashi Shiraishi, Motoo Furuta. 1992. 196 pp. ISBN 0-87727-401-0.
Volume 1	*Reading Southeast Asia*, ed. Takashi Shiraishi. 1990. 188 pp. ISBN 0-87727-400-2.

Language Texts

INDONESIAN

Beginning Indonesian through Self-Instruction, John U. Wolff, Dédé Oetomo, Daniel Fietkiewicz. 3rd revised edition 1992. Vol. 1. 115 pp. ISBN 0-87727-529-7. Vol. 2. 434 pp. ISBN 0-87727-530-0. Vol. 3. 473 pp. ISBN 0-87727-531-9.

Indonesian Readings, John U. Wolff. 1978. 4th printing 1992. 480 pp. ISBN 0-87727-517-3

Indonesian Conversations, John U. Wolff. 1978. 3rd printing 1991. 297 pp. ISBN 0-87727-516-5

Formal Indonesian, John U. Wolff. 2nd revised edition 1986. 446 pp. ISBN 0-87727-515-7

TAGALOG

Pilipino through Self-Instruction, John U. Wolff, Maria Theresa C. Centeno, Der-Hwa V. Rau. 1991. Vol. 1. 342 pp. ISBN 0-87727—525-4. Vol. 2. 378 pp. ISBN 0-87727-526-2. Vol 3. 431 pp. ISBN 0-87727-527-0. Vol. 4. 306 pp. ISBN 0-87727-528-9.

THAI

A. U. A. Language Center Thai Course, J. Marvin Brown. Originally published by the American University Alumni Association Language Center, 1974. Reissued by Cornell Southeast Asia Program, 1991, 1992. Book 1. 267 pp. ISBN 0-87727-506-8. Book 2. 288 pp. ISBN 0-87727-507-6. Book 3. 247 pp. ISBN 0-87727-508-4.

A. U. A. Language Center Thai Course, Reading and Writing Text (mostly reading), 1979. Reissued 1997. 164 pp. ISBN 0-87727-511-4.

A. U. A. Language Center Thai Course, Reading and Writing Workbook (mostly writing), 1979. Reissued 1997. 99 pp. ISBN 0-87727-512-2.

KHMER

Cambodian System of Writing and Beginning Reader, Franklin E. Huffman. Originally published by Yale University Press, 1970. Reissued by Cornell Southeast Asia Program, 4th printing 2002. 365 pp. ISBN 0-300-01314-0.

Modern Spoken Cambodian, Franklin E. Huffman, assist. Charan Promchan, Chhom-Rak Thong Lambert. Originally published by Yale University Press, 1970. Reissued by Cornell Southeast Asia Program, 3rd printing 1991. 451 pp. ISBN 0-300-01316-7.

Intermediate Cambodian Reader, ed. Franklin E. Huffman, assist. Im Proum. Originally published by Yale University Press, 1972. Reissued by Cornell Southeast Asia Program, 1988. 499 pp. ISBN 0-300-01552-6.

Cambodian Literary Reader and Glossary, Franklin E. Huffman, Im Proum. Originally published by Yale University Press, 1977. Reissued by Cornell Southeast Asia Program, 1988. 494 pp. ISBN 0-300-02069-4.

HMONG

White Hmong-English Dictionary, Ernest E. Heimbach. 1969. 8th printing, 2002. 523 pp. ISBN 0-87727-075-9.

VIETNAMESE

Intermediate Spoken Vietnamese, Franklin E. Huffman, Tran Trong Hai. 1980. 3rd printing 1994. ISBN 0-87727-500-9.

* * *

Southeast Asian Studies: Reorientations. Craig J. Reynolds and Ruth McVey. Frank H. Golay Lectures 2 & 3. 70 pp. ISBN 0-87727-301-4.

Javanese Literature in Surakarta Manuscripts, Nancy K. Florida. Vol. 1, *Introduction and Manuscripts of the Karaton Surakarta.* 1993. 410 pp. Frontispiece, illustrations.

Hard cover, ISBN 0-87727-602-1, Paperback, ISBN 0-87727-603-X. Vol. 2, *Manuscripts of the Mangkunagaran Palace.* 2000. 576 pp. Frontispiece, illustrations. Paperback, ISBN 0-87727-604-8.

Sbek Thom: Khmer Shadow Theater. Pech Tum Kravel, trans. Sos Kem, ed. Thavro Phim, Sos Kem, Martin Hatch. 1996. 363 pp., 153 photographs. ISBN 0-87727-620-X.

In the Mirror: Literature and Politics in Siam in the American Era, ed. Benedict R. O'G. Anderson, trans. Benedict R. O'G. Anderson, Ruchira Mendiones. 1985. 2nd printing 1991. 303 pp. Paperback. ISBN 974-210-380-1.

To order, please contact:

Cornell University
Southeast Asia Program Publications
95 Brown Road
Box 1004
Ithaca NY 14850

Online: http://www.einaudi.cornell.edu/southeastasia/publications/
Tel: 1-877-865-2432 (Toll free – U.S.)
Fax: (607) 255-7534

E-mail: SEAP-Pubs@cornell.edu
Orders must be prepaid by check or credit card (VISA, MasterCard, Discover).

www.ingramcontent.com/pod-product-compliance
Lightning Source LLC
Chambersburg PA
CBHW080922300426
44115CB00018B/2915